THE BLUE GUIDES

The Double Cube Room at Wilton House, Wiltshire, after the fire of 1647, showing the Van Dyck paintings

BLUE GUIDE

Country Houses
of England

Geo  indle

A&C Black
London

WW Norton
New York

First edition 1994

Published by A & C Black (Publishers) Limited
35 Bedford Row, London WC1R 4JH

© Geoffrey Tyack and Steven Brindle

ISBN 0–7136–3780–3

A CIP catalogue record for this book
is available from the British Library

Published in the United States of America by
W W Norton & Company, Inc
500 Fifth Avenue, New York, NY 10110

Published simultaniously in Canada by
Penguin Books Canada Limited,
10 Alcorn Avenue, Toronto, Ontario M4V 3B2

ISBN 0–393–31057–4   USA

The publishers and the authors have done their best to ensure the accuracy of all the
information in Blue Guide Country Houses of England; however, they can accept no
responsibility for any loss, injury or inconvenience sustained by any traveller as a result
of information or advice contained in the guide.

Geoffrey Tyack was educated at St John's College, Oxford, and received his PhD in
architectural history from the University of London. Having taught for Stanford University at Cliveden, Buckinghamshire, he subsequently taught in the History Department
at Stanford University, California and is now Director of the Stanford University
programme in Oxford. He is also a fellow of Rewley House. Geoffrey Tyack has written
several articles and papers on the history of the English country house and has lectured
widely on the subject. His latest book, *Warwickshire Country Houses*, will be published
by Phillimore and Co. in 1994.

Steven Brindle was eductaed at Keble College, Oxford, and gained a D.Phil in history,
also at Oxford. He joined the London Division of English Heritage as an historian. He
was recently appointed an Inspector of Ancient Monuments and Historic Buildings in
the Central Government and Palaces Branch. This is his first book.

Please write in with your comments, suggestions and corrections. Writers of
the best letters will be awarded a free Blue Guide of their choice.

Printed and bound in Great Britain by
Butler & Tanner Ltd, Frome and London

Preface

This book describes the majority of the 400 or so English country houses which are regularly open to the public without prior appointment. The term country house, though preferable to the unctuous 'stately home', is an imprecise one. Country houses are best defined as the non-fortified rural residences of England's social élite—a continually changing group of people. They are not the same as castles, although some castles have become country houses, nor are they merely houses in the country. Country houses are inseparable from the landed estates which once supported, and in some cases still do support, them. Until at least the last quarter of the 19C, the possession of such estates guaranteed power and social prestige in England, and, even after land lost its value with the onset of agricultural depression, the idea of the country house retained an allure which cannot be explained in purely rationalistic or utilitarian terms. It is a paradox that so many of the inhabitants of one of the world's most urbanised countries should still identify not only with the countryside which their ancestors fled often many generations ago, but also with buildings which are the relics of a largely vanished social order. This deeply felt identification helps explain the current passion for conservation and for 'doing up' old houses in the country; it also underlies the enthusiasm for country-house visiting which prompted the writing of this book.

There are several criteria for the inclusion of a house here. One is its current condition. Except for some ruins which are of special architectural interest, the houses described are all roofed, and most contain some interior decoration or furnishings of historic or artistic interest. Ruined castles are not included, nor, with a few exceptions, are houses which have been so completely turned over to museum use that no original interiors are visible. Though all the houses were once in the country, or on the edges of towns, several have now been engulfed by urban growth. Most of these have lost their original contents, but many are excellently maintained by local authorities, and, as a bonus, they tend to be open more frequently than houses in rural areas.

The houses included here were all open to the public for more than 20 days a year in 1993, irrespective of whether those days were scattered through the summer, or bunched together in one month. The opening times cited at the head of each section are those which applied in 1993, but some will almost certainly change in the future. The annual publication *Historic Houses, Castles and Gardens* (Reed Information Services) contains opening details for most, but not all of the houses in the book, and should be consulted by any serious country house visitor. Especially before setting out on a long journey, it is also wise to telephone in case a house in unexpectedly shut; telephone numbers are given for each house, unless the owner prefers otherwise (please note that dialling codes sometimes change). There is a growing and understandable tendency for private owners to open their houses only to pre-arranged groups, or by appointment to individuals. Houses which fell into this category in 1993 have been excluded from the book, but some of those described here may well eventually be open 'by appointment only'. Others may be sold, and still more may change their opening times, so a degree of vigilance is advisable.

Minimal directions have been given for each house. Some houses are not well signposted, and in these cases the relevant map from the Ordnance Survey 'Landranger' series can be invaluable. The opening times for each house refer to the hours when the building is accessible to the public. Visitors should not try to gain admission early, and should take care to arrive at least three quarters of an hour before the closing time to be sure of admission. Months of opening should be treated with some caution, especially at the beginning and end of the 'season'; some houses, for instance, open their doors at the beginning of April, others at Easter, and this sometimes changes from year to year, as does the last date of opening (often the first or last weekend in October). Spring and summer bank holiday weekends are particularly popular times for country-house visiting, and most houses are open then, although some get very crowded.

The word 'refreshments' can cover anything from a cup of tea to a three-course meal, and no attempt has been made to distinguish between different kinds of catering. Admission charges have not been given, since they change so often. Those planning to visit many country houses should consider becoming members of the National Trust, or Friends of the Historic Houses Association (the body which safeguards the interests of private country-house owners); this not only gains free entry to many houses, but helps preserves them for future visitors.

The description of each house summarises the history of the family or families which have lived there, the architectural evolution of the building, and the history of the collection. The main decorative features and contents are pointed out, usually in the order in which the visitor sees them; please note that routes through houses change from time to time, and also that rooms are sometimes closed for restoration. Country house collections are usually of a very heterogeneous nature, and lack of space makes it essential to be highly selective. The main criterion for mentioning a picture or object is its artistic and historical interest; items of mainly associational value, fascinating though they often are, are usually left out. Works of art are often moved, lent to exhibitions and sometimes, alas, sold; it should not therefore be assumed that a picture or object mentioned here will be on show all the time, or in the same place. Many houses have excellent guidebooks, on which we have relied heavily for factual information, and readers wishing to find out more should consult them. Gardens are not described in detail; for these, *Blue Guide to the Gardens of England* is recommended.

We have visited all but a few of the houses in the book over the six years or so in which it was in preparation, and have incurred several debts of gratitude in the course of the research. Edward Chaney kindly handed over the material he collected after being obliged to withdraw from co-authorship. A.F. Kersting supplied the photographs. Judy Tither has been a cheerful and highly efficient editor. Above all, we are grateful to the many owners, administrators, and National Trust Historic Buildings representatives throughout the country who have generously responded to our enquiries, and read and commented on sections of the text. We owe it to them to say than any inaccuracies which remain are our own responsibility, and we would be grateful for their being pointed out by readers so that they can be corrected in future editions. We would particularly like to thank the owners and administrators of Alnwick Castle, Belvoir Castle, Blenheim Palace, Hampton Court Palace, Harewood House, Hatfield House, Holkham Hall, Warwick Castle and Wilton House for permission to draw ground plans of these properties.

Geoffrey Tyack and Steven Brindle

CONTENTS

Ground Plans

INTRODUCTION

The Middle Ages

The story of the English country house starts with the castles built after the Norman Conquest of 1066. Military and utilitarian considerations played an obvious part in the design and construction of these formidable structures, but from the beginning many Norman castles served not only as fortresses but also as palatial residences for the King, or for the tenants-in-chief who received the lion's share of the lands confiscated from the defeated Anglo-Saxon nobility. Like the country houses of later generations, they were the largest and most impressive residential buildings of their time.

Norman castles were not single buildings, but rather collections of buildings arranged around defensible enclosures. The layout and indeed the very idea of the castle was brought from Normandy by William I's conquering army, and so too was the nomenclature of the different parts: the 'bailey', referring to the fortified enclosure around which the 'houses in the castle' were arranged, and the 'motte' or artificial mound to which the defenders could retreat in times of trouble. The motte was usually topped at first by a wooden palisade, but in the 12C this was often replaced by a stone shell-keep; a surviving—though much rebuilt—example is the round tower at Windsor Castle (Berkshire). At the same time the outer curtain walls of many castles were rebuilt in stone. Many early motte-and-bailey castles have been abandoned, but some, like those at Warwick (Warwickshire) and Berkeley (Gloucestershire) survived to be rebuilt in later generations and to serve as the homes of important landed families down to modern times.

Sometimes, in place of a motte, or even in addition to it, a stone tower keep—the equivalent of the Norman-French *donjon*—was built both as a fortifiable strong-point and to house a set of state rooms at upper-floor level for the lord and superior members of his household; one of the first examples is the White Tower at the Tower of London. The upstairs rooms were usually heated by wall-fireplaces, and were reached by spiral staircases at the corners, where *garderobes* or privies could also be found. Most early tower-keeps have been abandoned—some were blown up in the Civil War of the 1640s—but a few (eg, Bamburgh, Northumberland) still survive as parts of country houses. The idea of the tower house as a desirable mode of residence lingered on in the turbulent districts near the Scottish border, where stone tower houses, known locally as peles, continued to be built in large numbers down to the 16C (eg, Levens Hall and Sizergh Castle, Cumbria; Belsay, Northumberland).

Another adjunct to the standard Anglo-Norman castle was the hall, a large structure open to the wooden roof in which the whole of the household could congregate and dine. Aisled halls of timber were an important feature of the greater Anglo-Saxon houses, though none survive today, and many of the sub-tenants of the Anglo-Norman nobility lived in similar structures. Aisled halls of stone still survive at Oakham Castle, Leicestershire (late 12C) and Winchester Castle, Hampshire (early 13C), but not in any of the castles which survived as country houses. By the mid 13C it had become customary to dispense with aisles by roofing the hall in a single wooden span, often with arched braces placed at regular intervals to strengthen the structure; an early example is the late 13C hall at Stokesay Castle (Shropshire).

The hall was the ceremonial centre of the medieval castle, and was correspondingly more spacious than the other rooms. At the 'upper' end there was a dais for a high table at which the lord and his most important guests would sit on grand occasions. The rest of the household dined in the body of the room, their seating determined according to rank. The centre of the floor was occupied by an open hearth, and above it in the roof was a louvre covering the opening through which the smoke could escape. The entrance was at the 'lower' end, opposite the high table, and from at least the 14C it became customary to close off the entrance passage with a wooden screen. The kitchen was invariably detached from the hall, often in a tower, as can still be seen at Raby Castle (County Durham). Serving rooms were placed between kitchen and hall, the most important of which were the buttery—the domain of the butler or 'bottler'—for drink, and the pantry, for serving food (from the French word *pain*, meaning bread). The doorways to these rooms were often placed on either side of another door leading to a passage to the kitchen, as can be seen at Warwick Castle, where the doors were uncovered (and restored) after a fire in 1871.

The private apartments of the lord of a castle were usually to be found next to the 'upper' end of the hall. At Stokesay—more a fortified manor house than a full-scale castle—there is a great chamber, used for private dining, above a storage undercroft, with more rooms, which contained beds, in a polygonal tower beyond; the great chamber is reached by an external staircase. By the late 13C, when Stokesay was built, lords were already deserting the hall in favour of their private apartments; the author of the 14C poem *Piers Plowman* saw this as a sign of the collapse of the social values which underlay feudal society.

Medieval castles could play host to very large numbers of people: not only the lord's own family and armed retinue, but also estate officials and, on occasion, visiting potentates with their own hangers-on. In 1420 the Earl of Warwick had 125 people in his household, and Warwick Castle was capable of accommodating another 60 guests. Guests and members of aristocratic households occupied 'lodgings', or temporary dwellings within a house (the term is still used for the residence of the head of an Oxford or Cambridge college); they consisted of a bedroom, a closet and often a garderobe. The external defences of many castles were strengthened in the 13C and 14C, with square, rounded or polygonal towers arranged around a high curtain wall to create an impression of awesome strength, and the more important lodgings were often placed in these towers. The increasing emphasis on the external defences also meant that the gateway into a castle assumed a new strategic importance, proclaimed by a proliferation of turrets and battlements, and sometimes by the building of an outer gateway or barbican in front of the main one, as at Warwick or Alnwick (Northumberland), the latter dating from c 1310.

The country house, as distinct from a castle, does not begin to emerge as a sophisticated type of building until the 13C, when wealthy country gentlemen began to build non- fortified, or lightly fortified, houses which were large enough and substantial enough to have survived in their original use down to modern times. This development coincided with an increase in the buying and selling of land, sometimes to rich merchants like Lawrence Ludlow, the builder of Stokesay Castle, who traded in wool.

Meanwhile there was a decline in feudal obligations, a process which accelerated rapidly after the Black Death in the 1340s.

The earliest surviving country houses of the gentry all contain at the very least a hall block and one or more 'cross wings' for the great chamber, bedrooms and storage rooms. The hall could be placed at first-floor level, as at Markenfield Hall (North Yorkshire), but was more commonly on the ground floor, as in the mid 14C Penshurst Place (Kent), where it is entered through a projecting porch at the 'lower' end. When two cross-wings were built, as in the mid 15C Great Chalfield Manor (Wiltshire), a balanced, though not strictly symmetrical, elevation could ensue, with the high-roofed hall, lit by large windows, in the centre, flanked by two-storeyed wings on either side. By the end of the 15C it was becoming common to place a parlour (an everyday living and reception room) under the great chamber at the 'upper' end of the hall; the surviving early 16C parlour at Haddon Hall (Derbyshire)—one of the first rooms of its kind to survive in anything like its original form—shows a growing concern for comfort, with its wood- panelled walls, glazed windows and painted ceiling. The kitchen was usually in a detached structure (an impressive example survives at Stanton Harcourt Manor, Oxfordshire), and in many houses ancillary buildings of various kinds were loosely arranged around an enclosure or courtyard in front of the hall; the enclosure was often entered through a detached gatehouse, like the one which still survives at Broughton Castle (Oxfordshire). Many gentlemen's houses were built within moats, which served both to deter raiders and to keep the household supplied with fish. Provisions were stored in farm buildings, often grouped outside the moat, as at Markenfield and also at Lower Brockhampton (Hereford and Worcester).

In several of the larger late-medieval gentlemens' houses, like Haddon, Cotehele (Cornwall) and Igtham Mote (Kent), the hall is placed on one side of a square or rectangular courtyard, with chambers, lodgings, service rooms, and often a domestic chapel occupying the other ranges. A tall gatehouse tower, like those in the late 15C Oxburgh Hall (Norfolk) and the early 16C Coughton Court (Warwickshire), often imparts a note of quasi-feudal splendour. The larger courtyard houses, like the mid 15C Knole (Kent), had two or more courtyards, the outer one or 'base court' being given over to lodgings and the hall and main reception rooms occupying an inner courtyard reached through a second gatehouse. Ranks of tall chimneystacks, often incorporating garderobes, can sometimes be seen against the outer walls of former lodgings, as in the mid 15C Gainsborough Old Hall (Lincolnshire).

Late medieval country houses were built of a wide range of materials. England contains many good building stones, but where no stone was readily available, as in much of the West Midlands, north-west England, the south-east and East Anglia, timber was widely used, often to lavish external effect (eg, in the early 16C Rufford Old Hall, Lancashire). Brick first began to be employed on a large scale in the 15C, especially in the more prosperous eastern and south-eastern parts of the country, either on its own, as at Oxburgh Hall, or in conjunction with timber.

Tudor and Jacobean Houses

Castle building declined dramatically with the development of artillery in the 15C and the imposition of a greater degree of internal order by Henry VII and Henry VIII after the bloodletting of the Wars of the Roses. The early Tudor kings did not look kindly on castle building by their subjects, and, with the exception of some coastal fortresses built by Henry VIII (eg, Walmer Castle, Kent), they concentrated their own efforts on building large courtyard houses. Hampton Court (Greater London), begun by Cardinal Wolsey in 1515 and completed by Henry VIII in 1532–34, contained not only a magnificent hall and chapel but also a lavish series of state apartments, with elaborate plaster ceilings decorated with Renaissance motifs and tapestry-hung walls. These rooms were linked by covered passageways or galleries to the other parts of the palace. Some of the innovations of the early Tudor royal palaces were adopted by Henry VIII's courtiers, like Lord Sandys, who introduced a wood-panelled gallery into his house at the Vyne (Hampshire) in the 1520s, and Lord Marney, who made copious use of Italian Renaissance detailing on the outside of his gargantuan gatehouse, containing no fewer than 39 chambers, at Layer Marney (Essex). Like Hampton Court, these houses are built of brick.

The most important of Henry VIII's legacies to the English country house was the release of vast quantities of ecclesiastical land onto the market after the Dissolution of the Monasteries in the 1530s. This enabled existing gentry families to enlarge or consolidate their holdings, lawyers and merchants to become country gentlemen, and courtiers and royal officials—most of them drawn from the gentry—to build up vast landed estates. They, and even more their descendants, could now live in a splendour recalling that of the medieval aristocracy, albeit without any military ramifications. The families who thus came to prominence—the Cecils, Russells, Cavendishes and others—have played a dominant part in English landed society ever since.

A surprising number of the houses of the 'new' gentry and aristocracy were built on the sites of abandoned monasteries, and many incorporate parts of the former monastic buildings. At Buckland Abbey (Devon) the bulk of the accommodation was incorporated within the walls of the church, but more often, as at Lacock (Wiltshire) and Newstead (Nottinghamshire), the church was demolished and the house created out of the residential buildings around the cloister. At Newstead and Lacock the cloisters survived, along with some of the medieval rooms at ground level, the main reception rooms being placed above, with galleries to facilitate internal communications. However, elsewhere, as at Woburn Abbey (Bedfordshire), Longleat (Wiltshire) and Wilton (Wiltshire), later rebuildings have removed virtually all traces of the medieval origins of the house.

The second half of the 16C saw a great increase in country-house building. It was fuelled by an active land market following the Dissolution of the Monasteries, by price inflation—which benefited landowners so long as they increased their rents—and by a growing taste for greater domestic comfort and display. More and more rooms were now heated, windows became larger, and furnishings more lavish. It became increasingly common to place one or more floors over the hall, as can be seen at Broughton Castle, a medieval house drastically remodelled in the 1550s. Houses thus became appreciably taller than their medieval counterparts, sometimes reaching to three full storeys with attics above, as at Montacute (Somerset), finished in 1603. Here a spacious stone staircase leads up from the hall to the main reception rooms, with a long gallery—an essential feature of any late 16C house of any size—on the top floor.

The halls, parlours, galleries and great chambers of late 16C and early 17C gentry houses were often sumptuously decorated with carved wood panelling on the walls and intricate plasterwork on its ceilings. Contemporary inventories reveal the growing amount of carved wooden furniture, some of which can still occasionally be seen *in situ* along with other items of more dubious (usually 19C) provenance. Chimneypieces of stone, wood or plaster are usually elaborately embellished with heraldry or with carvings of an allegorical nature (cf. Levens Hall, Cumbria and Burton Agnes Hall, Humberside), and they are commonly adorned with the classical orders. Some rooms were still hung with tapestries or painted cloths, as in medieval houses, but it was at this time that the first panel pictures, almost invariably portraits, were introduced.

Except for timber-framed buildings like Little Moreton Hall (Cheshire) and Speke Hall (Merseyside), Elizabethan and Jacobean gentry houses were usually much less elaborate outside than inside. Four main plan-forms were employed: a simple rectangular block, often with projections for the porch and a bay window or windows lighting the hall and parlours (eg, Loseley, Surrey); the so-called E-plan with a main block containing the hall, entered through a centrally-placed porch, and two long wings projecting to create an open-ended courtyard (eg, Melford and Kentwell Halls, Suffolk); the H-plan, with wings projecting on both sides of the hall block (eg, Mapledurham, Oxfordshire); and a reduced version of the courtyard plan, with the hall on the entrance side and a light-well behind around which the main rooms were disposed (eg, Chastleton, Oxfordshire). A few early 17C houses like Gawthorpe Hall (Lancashire) were built on a compact rectangular or near-rectangular plan, with the service rooms in a basement. Others still, like Levens Hall and Sizergh Castle (Cumbria), were rebuildings and extensions of medieval houses. Elevations were, as far as possible, symmetrical, and the wall surfaces were broken up by large mullioned and transomed windows reflecting the sunlight, with the skyline enlivened by tall chimneys and gables, sometimes elaborately embellished in the Flemish or German manner (eg, Trerice, Cornwall).

Some Elizabethan and Jacobean houses were altogether more curious and romantic than those just described. Some country-house owners built lodges, like Lyveden New Bield (Northamptonshire) and Sherborne Castle (Dorset) for occasional use, and they are sometimes like visual poems, full of arcane meaning. Lyveden alludes to its Catholic owner's deeply-felt religious beliefs; other houses of the same kind, like the 'Little Castle' on the site of the keep at Bolsover (Derbyshire), or Lulworth Castle (Dorset), deliberately evoked the medieval past, while containing, as at Bolsover, complex and elaborate Renaissance-style decorative schemes inside.

Something of the same complexity and ambiguity can be found in the great houses of the Elizabethan and Jacobean nobility and courtiers. Some noblemen still lived in medieval castles and refurbished them. Others, like Queen Elizabeth's chief minister William Cecil, Lord Burghley, built vast new houses which, especially from a distance, were intended to evoke the glamour and prestige of the medieval aristocracy to which men like Burghley were in a sense the heirs. But these medievalising elements were often juxtaposed with classical features derived from the printed treatises and pattern-books those same men owned, read and communicated to the building craftsmen. The classical orders were extensively used externally as decoration at Burghley House (Cambridgeshire), as well as at Kirby (Northamptonshire) and Longleat (Wiltshire), all of them under construction during the 1570s; at Longleat the roof is even hidden behind an Italianate balustrade. The orders also appear prominently at Wollaton Hall (Nottinghamshire), begun in 1580, and later at Hatfield House (Hertfordshire), built by Burghley's son Robert Cecil, Earl of Salisbury, and begun in 1607. Yet in all these houses the complex skyline and the use of mullioned and transomed windows place the architecture firmly in the native tradition which stretched back to the early Tudor royal places, while the use of towers and shaped gables in several of them adds to the eclectic effect.

Some of the most important Elizabethan houses, like Burghley and Longleat, were built around courtyards, and the courtyard plan remained in use until the early 17C, when it was employed at Audley End (Essex), in its heyday the most magnificent of all Jacobean houses, and at Blickling Hall (Norfolk). Now, though, the rooms were designed mainly to look out onto the gardens, which henceforth became an important feature of the country house ensemble; gardens could also be observed from the roof of a house, and at Longleat 'banqueting houses' were built on the roof, from which elaborate confections could be served. In two of the largest and most ostentatious Elizabethan houses, Wollaton and Hardwick Hall (Derbyshire), the latter begun in 1591, the courtyard plan is abandoned and the hall is placed centrally: an important innovation. Both houses are placed on hilltops to 'command the prospect', and in both tall towers cluster around the central block in the manner of medieval castles.

Most of the great houses of the period have been extensively remodelled inside, but Hardwick retains much of its original interior decoration and some of the contents, including porcelain and carpets, as well as pictures, plate and tapestries. The house is conceived in 'layers', with the kitchens and service rooms at ground level, everyday living rooms and lodgings above, and state rooms—a great chamber (or dining room), withdrawing chamber and bedchamber—on the top, flanked by a long gallery. The upstairs rooms are reached by a stone staircase, but at the more conventionally planned Hatfield, and also at Knole, extensively remodelled in the early 17C, the main staircase is of wood. Here, as in most of the larger Jacobean houses there was a proliferation of Renaissance woodwork and plasterwork inside, sometimes of a rather indigestible Mannerist kind, as in the hall screen at Audley End.

Renaissance and Baroque

The first English house to be both planned and decorated throughout in the style of the Italian Renaissance was the Queen's House at Greenwich (Greater London), begun in 1617. It was designed as a lodge or villa for James I's Queen by the Court architect, Inigo Jones. Unlike the master masons and carpenters who had designed earlier country houses, Jones had travelled in Italy, and in its uncompromising use of the classical idiom the house set a new standard of somewhat frigid perfection.

Somewhat later, in the reign of Charles I, the greatest of all royal patrons of the arts in England, Jones was consulted by the 4th Earl of Pembroke over the remodelling of Wilton House. In its external elevations and internal decoration—both remodelled under the direction of Jones's pupil John Webb after a fire in 1647—Wilton represents the first thoroughgoing adaptation of the High Renaissance idiom to the English nobleman's country house. The state rooms are on the first floor or piano nobile, and are richly decorated with wood panelling and painted ceilings to convey a mood of classical splendour and abundance. The beauty of the exterior, like that of the Queen's House, derives not so much from ornament, which is conspicuous largely by its absence, as from the meticulous proportions, following Jones's own dictum that buildings should be 'solid, proportional according to the rules, masculine and unaffected'. This contrast between external reticence and internal splendour was to characterise many English country houses down to the end of the 18C.

Meanwhile, important changes were taking place in the design and layout of smaller country houses. In remoter parts of the country, the gentry continued to build in a traditional style well into the 17C (eg, Eyam Hall, Derbyshire, and East Riddlesden Hall, West Yorkshire), but in the south-east, and especially in the out-of-town residences of London merchants, the 'double pile' plan came increasingly into vogue during the reign of Charles I, with the rooms placed in a compact rectangular block two rooms deep. Many of these houses were built of brick, and some, like Kew Palace (Greater London), have 'Dutch' gables with pediments resting on scrolls, but at Forty Hall (Greater London, 1629), gables are replaced by a hipped roof over a projecting wooden cornice: an arrangement which was very popular in contemporary Holland, and which derived ultimately from France.

The Civil War, which broke out in 1642, caused a temporary hiatus in house-building, and led to the final destruction of some of the medieval castles which were still inhabited. Building resumed in the time of the Interregnum, but it was not until after the Restoration of Charles II in 1660 that country houses were built once again in large numbers. The classical ideal now penetrated beyond the courtiers and nobility to the gentry. They were gradually shedding their provincial idiosyncrasies and succumbing to the allure of a more metropolitan, cosmopolitan culture which could hardly fail to influence the layout of their houses, down to the smallest minutiae of daily life.

In late 17C houses like Belton (Lincolnshire), the camaraderie of the great hall vanished as the servants were banished 'below stairs', leaving the main floors solely to the use of the owner, his family and guests. It now became fashionable for houses to have two main floors of equal height, with the centre occupied by an entrance hall, and another large reception room often called the saloon (from the French *salon*), both of them reached by external flights of stairs, and two other reception rooms above. On either side of the centre were bedrooms, closets, ante-rooms and staircases, including back stairs used only by the servants; in some houses the main staircase was placed on the main axis, behind the hall, where the saloon might otherwise go. The internal walls were panelled in wood, with large panels over a dado moulding, and the ceilings were often elaborately adorned with plaster-work, sometimes of extraordinary virtuosity, as in Sudbury Hall, Derby-shire. Chairs and tables, often elaborately carved, inlaid or lacquered, were placed against the walls, but the most elaborate pieces of furniture were the richly upholstered state beds. Oriental and Dutch porcelain began to be collected in large quantities and was often placed over chimneypieces, especially in closets, the most intimate of the rooms in a suite or 'apartment'.

Above the two main floors were the servants' bedrooms, lit by dormer windows in the hipped roof, and there was often a platform at roof level from which the owner and his guests could survey the gardens and parkland beyond: an experience which can still be savoured by visitors to Ashdown House (Oxfordshire). The growth of travel and the increasing popularity of hunting on horseback meant that extensive stabling now had to be provided, usually to one side of the house, but sometimes as part of a formal French-inspired forecourt with lower outbuildings on either side of the central *corps de logis*, as at Antony (Cornwall).

Post-Restoration houses were sometimes designed by gentleman amateurs like Sir Roger Pratt, the architect of Kingston Lacy (Dorset) a friend of Sir Christopher Wren. But the new style was also taken up by London and provincial craftsmen and builders, like the Smith brothers of Warwick (cf. Stanford Hall, Leicestershire). Craftsmen were also responsible for the design, as well as the execution, of the internal features, and many of these men established reputations which spread well beyond a particular locality. Equal care was taken over the gardens, which now began to expand beyond the immediate vicinity of the house, as owners sought to impose their presences on the rural landscape. Late 17C gardens were formally planned, like those of Louis XIV's France (and to a lesser extent contemporary Holland), with ornamental parterres, as at Cliveden (Buckinghamshire), canals, and avenues of trees aligned on the house: an arrangement which still survives at Hampton Court.

French influences were also paramount in the planning of the royal palaces and noblemens' houses of Charles II's reign. Here it became fashionable to provide a splendidly decorated 'great apartment' made up of an ante-room, dining room, withdrawing room, state bedroom and closet with the doors aligned in *enfilade*, as can still be seen at Warwick Castle and, on a smaller scale, at the Duke of Lauderdale's remodelled Ham House (Greater London), dating from the 1670s; here the original furniture of both the state and 'private' rooms is still largely *in situ*. A note of Baroque exuberance was introduced in the new set of state apartments designed at Windsor Castle in the 1670s by Hugh May, Comptroller of the King's Works, and lavishly decorated with allegorical frescoes by the Italian Antonio Verrio. Verrio went on to decorate the interior of Burghley House in an even more extravagant manner for the 5th Earl of Exeter, a great traveller and collector; here, from the beginning, the state rooms, and especially the closets, had something of the character of a museum for the display of precious and beautiful pictures and objects.

The architect at Burghley was William Talman, May's successor as Comptroller of the King's Works, and he was also employed by the 1st Duke of Devonshire in 1687 to replace the south range of Chatsworth (Derbyshire) with a new range containing a full-scale 'great apartment' on the second floor. The façade is adorned with giant Ionic pilasters to impart a Baroque sense of scale and majesty, and the roof-line is hidden behind a balustrade, as it is at Talman's slightly later Dyrham Park (Avon). These features were to be much imitated in early 18C country houses.

The Glorious Revolution of 1688 enhanced the political power of the English nobility at the expense of the monarchy. The new king, William III, employed Sir Christopher Wren to build extensively at Hampton Court, but plans for a totally new palace in imitation of Versailles were abandoned, and the internal decoration, fine though much of it is, is no more lavish than that which can still be seen in the houses rebuilt by noblemen soon after 1688; these include the strikingly Francophile Petworth (West Sussex) and Boughton (Northants). The prestige of the post-1688 nobility is even more eloquently displayed at Castle Howard (North Yorkshire), the vast palace built for the 3rd Earl of Carlisle to the designs of the dilettante soldier and playwright Sir John Vanbrugh. Here, to an extent rarely matched in England, the Baroque ideals of scale, rhetoric, drama and movement find compelling expression, above all in the richly ornamental garden front and in the lofty domed hall. Vanbrugh adapted the main features of the design of Castle Howard to the even larger Blenheim Palace (Oxfordshire), begun in 1705, notably the provision of two 'great apartments', one on either side of the saloon on the garden front. At Blenheim, however, the dome is replaced by a pedimented attic, and low towers are placed at the four corners of the house, imparting an almost medieval effect which recalls that of some of the great Elizabethan and Jacobean houses. Towers were also used by Vanbrugh with powerful effect at Seaton Delaval (Northumberland) and Grimsthorpe (Lincolnshire).

The great houses of the early 18C can only be properly understood in the context of their landscapes. Bramham Park (West Yorkshire), Melbourne Hall (Derbyshire) and Wrest Park (Bedfordshire) are relatively little-changed examples of early 18C landscaping on the grand scale, with formal vistas aligned on the house and rectangular canals. Ornamental buildings now begin to play an important part in the total effect, and some, like Thomas Archer's cascade house at Chatsworth and domed pavilion at Wrest, and Nicholas Hawksmoor's brooding mausoleum at Castle Howard, vie in grandeur with the house itself. Many of the gentry, by contrast, remained content with more modest walled gardens laid out as a series of 'outdoor rooms'. Most were later obliterated, but some, like those at Canons Ashby (Northamptonshire), remain substantially intact.

Canons Ashby is a good example of a largely 16C house which was modestly adapted, both internally and externally, to the more comfortable—if to later generations somewhat starchy—life-style of the early 18C. Other gentry of the period preferred to replace their old houses with new ones, especially after the return of economic confidence which marked the end of the War of the Spanish Succession in 1713. Houses like Beningborough Hall (North Yorkshire) were still formally planned on the 'apartment' system, and their internal craftsmanship and, to a lesser extent, their external design, often shows the influence of the Baroque. The Baroque spirit was kept alive by emigré Italian painters like Pellegrini and Amigoni who came to England after 1713, and the Swiss-Italian plasterers who were associated with the widely employed (and Italian-trained) architect James Gibbs (cf. Orleans House, Greater London; Ragley Hall, Warwickshire).

Palladian, Rococo and Neo-Classical

While Baroque decoration remained popular among some sections of the gentry and nobility until the middle of the 18C, changing tastes among the *cognoscenti* soon began to dictate a return to a more strictly classical approach. Andrea Palladio's *Four Books of Architecture* were published in an accessible English edition in 1715 by Giacomo Leoni, the architect of Clandon Park (Surrey) and Lyme Park (Cheshire), and in the same year the Scottish architect Colen Campbell brought out the first volume of his *Vitruvius Britannicus*, with a preface denouncing the Baroque and praising the architecture of Palladio and Inigo Jones (and, *a fortiori*, their disciple Colen Campbell). These masters, it was argued, had understood the true principles of good architecture as they first evolved in classical antiquity, and those who wanted to build well should follow their example. The torch was later taken up by the 3rd Earl of Burlington and his protégé William Kent, a man of extraordinary virtuosity who left his mark not only on the architecture of the early Georgian period, but also on gardening and internal decoration. Thus the Palladian movement came into being.

Palladian ideas were applied both to the design of great houses and to villas, which came into their own in England in the 18C. Palladian great houses were in many respects like public buildings, designed for large-scale entertaining by men who controlled politics at both local and, after the Hanoverian Succession of 1714, national level. They were often entered through a classical portico, and the main rooms were usually placed upstairs in a piano nobile, allowing for the provision of a suite of everyday living rooms in the 'rustic' below. The rooms were commonly grouped around two top-lit staircases, allowing for easy circulation; ample provision was also made for the display of works of art, both Old Master paintings and classical statuary, which began to flood into the country in ever-increasing quantities as the Grand Tour grew in popularity. As in the houses of Inigo Jones, external plainness gives way internally to great lavishness of decoration, much of it taken directly from classical antiquity, like the painted ceilings at Houghton (Norfolk), the magnificent palace of George I's and II's Prime Minister Sir Robert Walpole, and the majestic basilica-like entrance hall at Holkham, also in Norfolk, begun in 1734. Heavy upholstered furniture, doorways framed by columns supporting pediments, and richly-carved chimneypieces all combine to impart a feeling of monumental unity evoking the Roman magnificence with which the Georgian nobility and gentry liked to identify.

Villas were altogether less ponderous buildings. The word villa can be applied both to the quasi-suburban residences of noblemen and merchants which proliferated along the banks of the Thames to the west of London in the early 18C, and to those smaller country houses which were designed along Palladian principles. These principles dictated a compact, square plan, with the main rooms on a piano nobile and a portico, or at least pedimented feature, in the centre of the main façade, as at Colen Campbell's Stourhead (Wiltshire) and Sir Thomas Robinson's Rokeby Park (County Durham). At Lord Burlington's famous villa at Chiswick, Greater London (begun 1727), the rooms were grouped around a central domed rotunda, and the layout and details allude with great subtlety both to the buildings of Palladio, Scamozzi and other Italian Renaissance masters, and to the monuments of ancient Rome.

The rise of the villa was parallelled by that of the landscape garden, an innovation destined to sweep not only England but also the whole of Great Britain, the American colonies and much of Western Europe. Lord Burlington's garden at Chiswick was intended to conjure up the 'genius of the place' and to evoke the gardens of antiquity by means of calculated irregularity, careful management of woodland and water, and a judicious placing of buildings and statuary. William Kent carried the style to a new degree of refinement at Stowe (Buckinghamshire) and Rousham (Oxfordshire), both of them dating from the 1730s, and it reached its apogee in the exquisite Virgilian garden at Stourhead (Wiltshire), created by the owner, Henry Hoare, with the advice of Lord Burlington's pupil Henry Flitcroft, starting in 1744. Thereafter, in the masterly hands of Lancelot ('Capability') Brown—also a highly competent architect in the Palladian idiom (cf, Broadlands, Hampshire)—and his imitators, it swept all before it, leaving few country-house landscapes untouched. Walls, gates, avenues and parterres were cleared away, clumps of trees planted, irregular lakes created and lawns taken up to the house. Thus the idyllic landscapes of Petworth, Bowood (Wiltshire), Blenheim Palace and many other houses came into being.

By the middle of the 18C Palladian architectural ideas had triumphed over the Baroque. Internally, though, there was an increasing tendency to experiment with non-Palladian styles. In the 1740s and 50s there was a vogue for Rococo decoration, inspired by France and reflecting a growing reaction against what was perceived as the rigidity of early Georgian decorative art. The Rococo style, with its deliberate cultivation of asymmetry, originality and whimsical invention, left its exuberant mark on houses as diverse as Wallington (Northumberland), Farnborough Hall (Warwickshire) and Saltram (Devon). But the wildest flights of extravagance were reserved for Claydon (Buckinghamshire), where all the decorative styles of the second half of the 18C can be seen juxtaposed in different rooms: an early sign of the stylistic relativism which was eventually to shatter the classical cultural consensus and usher in the individualistic chaos of the modern world.

Part of the appeal of the Rococo lay in its sense of the exotic, and this quest for the novel and the *recherché* led some adventurous spirits in the mid 18C to experiment with medieval or even non-European architecture and decoration. There are neo-medieval elements in the houses of Sir John Vanburgh, and Gothic garden buildings first appear in the 1730s (eg, Fawley Court, and Stowe, but in Buckinghamshire). By the 1750s some owners of ancient houses, like Lacock Abbey and Arbury Hall (Warwickshire), were using Gothic in a deliberate attempt to evoke the distant English past, as opposed to the idealised world of classical antiquity. Meanwhile, at Claydon and elsewhere, orientalism, and in particular Chinoiserie, began to have an effect on interior decoration. Finally, at Sezincote (Gloucestershire) at the beginning of the 19C, a returned Indian nabob took the final step of having his house designed in a style which would not have looked out of place in Delhi.

The mid 18C saw an important change in the layout of rooms, with less space being devoted to formal 'apartments' on the main floor and more to large rooms in which growing numbers of guests—their visits made possible by improvements in the road system—could meet and be entertained together. The resulting way of life was memorably described by contemporary chroniclers like Mrs. Lybbe Powis, and later in the novels of Jane Austen. By the 1750s it was becoming increasingly common for the main floor of a country house to contain three large reception rooms—the dining room, drawing room and library—and some smaller rooms for the family alone, with all the bedrooms upstairs. Thus the Baroque 'apartment' system finally went out of use.

In the 1760s the Rococo gave way throughout Europe to a more sparse and disciplined neo-classical style. Neo-classicism was profoundly influenced by new discoveries of the remains of classical antiquity, not only in Italy but also in the eastern Mediterranean and the Middle East. These served not only to deepen knowledge about Roman architecture and decoration, but also in time to widen awareness of the merits of the art of the Greeks, and publications illustrating the new discoveries soon began to find their way into country-house libraries. The man most responsible for introducing the neo-classical idiom into the English country house was Robert Adam. On returning from a Grand Tour in the 1750s, he developed a personal style of decoration in which elements taken from the art of the classical antiquity were mingled with others derived from the English and French Rococo, and even from Palladianism, to produce a synthesis acceptable both on the grounds of classical propriety and of domestic comfort. His success derived to a large degree from his understanding—anticipated by Kent—that a room could be treated as an integrated work of art, and a sequence of rooms as a sequence of contrasting aesthetic pleasures, comparable to those experienced in the circuit of a landscape garden. These qualities can be seen not only in great aristocratic houses like Syon (Greater London), Kedleston (Derbyshire) and Harewood (West Yorkshire), but also in the smaller but no less exquisite houses of art-loving country gentlemen like Newby Hall (North Yorkshire) and Saltram (Devon), or of wealthy bankers like Osterley Park (Greater London). The pleasures of these houses are enhanced by the quality of their furniture, often, as at Nostell Priory (West Yorkshire), made by cabinet-makers of the calibre of Thomas Chippendale.

Adam's fame should not blind us to the merits of his contemporaries and rivals. Some form of neo-classical decoration would have prevailed in England even if Adam had never practised as an architect. James Wyatt, the most famous member of a dynasty of late 18C and 19C architects and decorators, was in many ways as successful an exponent of the neo-classical decorative idiom as Adam, and the garden front of his Heaton Hall (Greater Manchester, 1772), is as effective and original a composition as Adam's better-known garden front at Kedleston. Henry Holland, the son-in-law of 'Capability' Brown, evolved a refined and understated version of neo-classical decoration which owed much to late 18C France, and can be seen to good effect in new houses like Berrington Hall (Hereford & Worcester), as well as in the internal remodelling of the older seats of the Whig aristocracy who employed him extensively, like Woburn Abbey (Bedfordshire) and Althorp (Northamptonshire). Some of the finest late 18C houses, like Attingham (Shropshire), were conceived and executed by men who have remained virtually unknown.

Many smaller late 18C country houses, like Berrington and Basildon Park (Berkshire), were planned with the reception rooms wrapped around a central top-lit staircase: an arrangement which made it easier for guests to circulate through the house, and also allowed for the provision of a dramatic internal space. Rooms in late 18C houses were increasingly designed to command views over the newly landscaped grounds, and by the end of the 18C it had become normal to dispense with a basement and put the reception rooms on the ground floor, as at Killerton (Devon), with the kitchen and service rooms placed discreetly in a wing to the side of the house or behind it. The service wing was often hidden behind a shrubbery, and was joined to the house by a corridor, as can be seen at Tatton Park (Cheshire), where it is flanked by a private wing for the family.

The new arrangements were advocated by Humphry Repton, the leading landscape gardener of the period, and in his copious and fascinating writings Repton also celebrated the growing fashion for scattering comfortable furniture around the main reception rooms of country houses, in contrast to the earlier practice of arranging it along the walls when the room was not in use. The drawing rooms and libraries of houses like Tatton still contain their heavy, upholstered furniture by firms like Gillow of Lancaster, matching the draped curtains which were also becoming fashionable in the early 19C. In dining rooms, the table was now increasingly no longer removed at the end of each meal, but remained *in situ* all the time. Thus a style of country-house decoration came into being which, with some inevitable alterations, has survived until modern times.

The 19th and 20th Centuries

The early 19C saw an often bewildering proliferation of architectural and decorative styles. Under the influence of Romanticism, the dominant cultural movement of the era, the idea of a single standard of taste collapsed, the individual became the sole judge of beauty, and the effect on the emotions became the most important criterion for the success of a work of art. This pluralism was reflected in the character of country house collections, which now began to include armour, unusual furniture, natural history specimens and other items which appealed to the growing taste for the strange and exotic.

For those who continued to employ the classical style of architecture, the delicacy of the Adam and Holland era gave way to a starker, more assertive and more monumental style, seen in a particularly overpowering form at Ickworth (Suffolk), begun in 1795; here the body of the house takes the form of a giant rotunda joined by curved wings to two pavilions, each as large in itself as a moderately sized country house. The same quest for simplicity can be seen at the Grange (Hampshire), where an older house was encased in the form of a Grecian temple, and at Belsay (Northumberland), England's most impressive Greek Revival house; here external decoration is virtually banished, except for the giant Doric columns at the entrance. A different kind of reinterpretation of classical architecture can be found in the houses of Sir John Soane, a pupil of Henry Holland who went to Italy and returned to build up a substantial country-house practice before embarking on a career as an architect of public buildings. He was at his best in creating mysteriously lit interiors with vaulted or domed roofs, and examples of his imaginative and idiosyncratic style can be seen at Wimpole Hall (Cambridgeshire), Chillington (Staffordshire) and Aynhoe Park (Northamptonshire).

The cult of romantic medievalism, so wittily sent up by Jane Austen in *Northanger Abbey*, led to a proliferation of country houses in the form of baronial castles, pinnacled abbeys and lovingly recreated Elizabethan or Jacobean manor houses. These buildings not only appealed to the growing cult of the 'olden time', which was seen as a welcome refuge from the problems of an increasingly urban and industrial society; they also satisfied the characteristically 19C yearning for the 'sublime' and the 'picturesque', qualities expounded at length by aesthetic theorists at the end of the 18C. Although the castle style had been occasionally employed by Vanbrugh and by architects in 18C Scotland, notably Robert Adam, its popularity in England dates from the 1790s to the 1820s, a period which significantly encompasses both the Napoleonic Wars and the years of social unrest which followed. Notable examples include Belvoir Castle (Leicestershire), begun to the designs of James Wyatt in 1801, Eastnor Castle (Hereford & Worcester), and, most famous of all, Windsor Castle, lavishly remodelled for George IV by Wyatt's son Sir Jeffrey Wyatville in the 1820s. The interiors of these ponderous behemoths were decorated in a surprising variety of often contrasting styles, ranging at both Belvoir and Windsor from neo-Gothic to a luxurious version of French Rococo, a style cultivated by another of the Wyatt clan, Benjamin Dean Wyatt. Accessible examples of what Humphry Repton called Abbey or Church Gothic are less common, but the style can be savoured at Conishead Priory (Cumbria), begun to the design of yet another Wyatt, Philip, in 1821.

More influential in the long run was the revival of early Tudor, Elizabethan and Jacobean architecture, something which can be traced back to the second half of the 18C (there are examples at Warwick Castle, Audley End, and at Burton Constable, Humberside). The 16C and early 17C evoked warm feelings among patriotic Englishmen in the early 19C, not least by virtue of the novels of Sir Walter Scott. Not long after the publication of his best-selling *Kenilworth* in 1821, many 16C country houses began to be purged of Georgian woodwork and sash windows and restored to something approaching their original character, a process which usually involved introducing stained glass and new furniture (or furniture made up from old fragments) and dusting down the portraits of beruffed ancestors; examples include Browsholme Hall, (Lancashire) and Charlecote (Warwickshire). Meanwhile, various forms of Tudor-Gothic and 'Jacobethan' architecture were used in new houses, or in recasting Georgian houses like Highclere (Hampshire) in an 'Old English' style intended to evoke and encourage family pride and paternalistic values rooted in the past. The architects of these houses revelled in picturesque irregularity. Ground-plans sprawled, with service wings often taking up as much floor space as the main house, and dramatic, broken skylines came once more into vogue, as they had been in the 16C and early 17C.

The 'Old English' style in its various manifestations—Tudor, Elizabethan, Jacobean, neo-vernacular—was more popular than any other in the country-house architecture of Queen Victoria's reign. Examples open to the public include Somerleyton Hall (Suffolk) and Sandringham (Norfolk), although many similar houses have gone into institutional use, or have become hotels. But the cultural diversity of the period was such that no one style prevailed. Some Victorian houses are Gothic, like Allerton Park (North Yorkshire) and Knightshayes Court (Devon), others Italian Renaissance, like Cliveden and Queen Victoria's own seaside villa, Osborne (Isle of Wight), while Peckforton Castle (Cheshire) is a 19C reproduction of a 13C fortress. Genuine medieval castles were also expensively modernised. Alnwick Castle was restored by Antony Salvin, the architect of Peckforton, and transformed internally in the richest Italian Renaissance style as a setting for the 4th Duke of Northumberland's outstanding collection of Old Master paintings. Arundel Castle (West Sussex) was remodelled in a neo-Gothic manner deemed appropriate for one of England's oldest families, the Howards, Dukes of Norfolk, and Raby Castle was given a new and sumptuous set of reception rooms designed by William Burn, one of the most prolific domestic architects of the period. Other older houses transformed internally in the mid 19C included Kingston Lacy and Longleat, both of them after their respective owners had amassed important art collections, and to a lesser extent Calke Abbey (Derbyshire), a house which has remained extraordinarily immune to changes of taste over the last 130 years.

Many houses acquired new carriage porches, billiard rooms and conservatories in the Victorian era, and in many cases the service quarters were also enlarged and modernised. The formal garden returned to favour, and in many houses, like Harewood and Bowood, the lawns were driven further and further away from the house, to be replaced by parterres, balustrades, terraces, with bedding plants grown in the huge hothouses which were an adjunct to any large country house of the time, and planted out by squads of gardeners. The rebuilding or redecoration of many 19C country houses was accompanied by the building of the estate church and sometimes of the entire estate village, as can be seen at Edensor, the Chatsworth estate village, laid out by the 6th Duke of Devonshire in 1838–42 after he had enlarged the house and carried out major alterations to the grounds.

The wealth which sustained the early and mid Victorian country house derived from booming agriculture, buttressed in some instances by the profits of urban development, coal mining or banking. The agricultural depression, which started in the 1870s and continued until the Second World War, had a greater effect on English landed society than anything since the Dissolution of the Monasteries. The price of agricultural products dropped as grain was imported in vast quantities from North America, and large-scale country-house building by the old landed gentry and aristocracy declined dramatically. The Settled Estates Act of 1882 made it easier to sell off parts of estates—hitherto preserved from fragmentation by strict legal settlements often imposed in the 17C—and the introduction of death duties in 1894 marked the beginning of high, and eventually penal, levels of taxation of large land holdings. The social structure of the countryside changed irrevocably. Many great houses were sold, some were demolished, and others which survived did so with an ever-shrinking basis of land to support them.

The depression did not bring country-house building to an end. Successful bankers and businessmen had always managed to find a niche in the English landed elite, and now, as land became more easily available, they took the lead in new building. Waddesden Manor (Buckinghamshire), one of the most magnificent of all 19C country houses, was built in 1874–89 by Baron Ferdinand de Rothschild, heir to a great banking fortune, on land sold by the Dukes of Marlborough, and both Cliveden and Hever Castle (Kent) were lavishly remodelled internally after being bought by the prodigiously wealthy American William Waldorf Astor (he made an even more lavish transformation of Hever Castle, Kent). The armaments manufacturer Lord Armstrong bought and planted vast quantities of bare moorland around his new house—originally a shooting lodge—at Cragside (Northumberland), and Henry Mildmay, a partner in Baring's Bank, bought a substantial estate around Flete (Devon). But many of the new late 19C country houses were villas or 'houses in the country' rather than country seats of the traditional kind, and lacked large estates of agricultural land. Such houses were especially common in the Home Counties (eg, Polesden Lacey, Surrey, and Standen, East Sussex), and near the great industrial conurbations (eg, Wightwick Manor, Staffordshire).

Two main stylistic trends are discernible in the country houses of the late 19C and early 20C. The first appealed especially to the plutocratic bankers and financiers who played such a large part in late Victorian and Edwardian society. It was cosmopolitan and fundamentally classical, even if, as at Waddesden Manor, the underlying classicism of the plan was overlaid externally by a profusion of turrets and projections which derived from the architecture of the early French Renaissance. The interiors of Waddesden are mostly in a French 18C style, and the same style can be seen at Polesden Lacey, and at Luton Hoo (Bedfordshire), expensively rebuilt by a French-trained architectural firm; all these houses were designed with a view to displaying their outstanding collections of pictures, furniture and porcelain.

The other, and far more common style, was 'Old English'. The houses of Norman Shaw, like Cragside, Flete, and Adcote (Shropshire), and those of Philip Webb (eg, Standen 1892–94) are calculatedly picturesque, carefully detailed, and, to an extent rarely matched in the earlier part of the 19C, sensitive in their choice of materials appropriate to the locality. This approach also influenced younger architects like Edward Ould at Wightwick Manor, Guy Dawber at Hamptworth Lodge (Wiltshire) and, most famous of all, Edwin Lutyens, whose stylistic repertoire ranged from the castle style (eg, Lindisfarne Castle, Northumberland and Castle Drogo,

Devon) to the neo-Georgian of Great Maytham (Kent). In some late 19C houses, like Wightwick, there was a return to the medieval ideal of the great hall, but in general the rooms were designed with comfort in mind, often demonstrated by the presence of vast chimneypieces with inglenooks. The choice of furniture tended to be eclectic. William Morris textiles and chintzes jostled with reproduction Georgian furniture, comfortable sofas, oriental rugs and Chinese porcelain. Further amenity came with the introduction of electric lighting (Cragside was one of the first houses to be so lit), and, as wages rose, servants' quarters began to shrink.

Meanwhile many old manor houses, especially in newly 'discovered' areas like the Cotswolds and the Weald of Kent and Sussex, were bought up and lovingly restored by new owners, usually with the profits of manufacturing or commerce and often after years of neglect; examples include Lytes Cary (Somerset), Owlpen Manor (Gloucestershire), Sheldon Manor (Wiltshire), Packwood House (Warwickshire), and Great Dixter and Bateman's (East Sussex). These restorations were often carried out with great sensitivity to texture, under the influence of the doctrines of William Morris, whose own Kelmscott Manor (Oxfordshire) is in itself an excellent example of 'conservative restoration'. The restoration of old manor houses was usually accompanied, as at Barrington Court (Somerset) by the creation of new gardens with 'outdoor rooms' bounded by walls with herbaceous borders. This method of gardening, championed by William Robinson and Gertrude Jekyll, has always been celebrated in the pages of journals like *Country Life* (founded in 1897), and is still regarded by many as quintessentially English.

The renovation of old houses continued through the 1920s and 30s; some of the most notable examples are Upton House (Warwickshire), Snowshill Manor (Gloucestershire) and Anglesey Abbey (Cambridgeshire), all of them now accessible largely because of their excellent collections and gardens. But the Second World War and its aftermath dealt what many believed at the time would be a mortal blow to the way of life, and even the very survival, of the English country house. Many houses were requisitioned and severely damaged, and some disappeared permanently under the onslaught of post-war taxation and the virtual impossibility of finding domestic servants. Many houses that survived were turned over to new uses—schools, hotels, local government offices, flats, old peoples' homes—and in the process lost their collections and sometimes their surrounding landscapes.

It was at this time that the National Trust began to acquire houses in large numbers and to open them to the public, often for the first time in their history (though some of the larger houses had been open to visitors since the 18C). Other houses were acquired by public authorities and opened as museums, a process which had begun in the 19C (cf, Aston Hall, West Midlands), and still more were opened to the public by private owners as a condition of receiving maintenance grants from the public purse. Today, with some 400 houses in England regularly accessible to the public, interest in the country house both as a repository of the arts and as a way of life is probably greater than in any previous period in English history. For all the forebodings of those who have for a long time predicted the imminent end of country-house civilisation, this most resilient of English institutions still seems likely to retain its place in national life and culture, and in the curiosity and affections of native and overseas visitors, for a long time to come.

GCT

Further Reading

M. Girouard, *Life in the English Country House* (Yale 1978); G. Beard, *The National Trust Book of the English House Interior* (Viking/Penguin 1990); G. Jackson-Stops, *The Country House in Perspective* (Pavilion Books 1990); G. Jackson-Stops (ed), *The Treasure Houses of Britain* (Yale 1985); M. W. Thompson, *The Rise of the Castle* (Cambridge 1991); M. W. Thompson, *The Decline of the Castle* (Cambridge 1888); M. Wood, *The English Medieval House* (Phoenix Books 1965); J. Summerson, *Architecture in Britain 1530–1830* (Penguin 1991); M. Howard, *The Early Tudor Country House* (George Philip 1987); M. Girouard, *Robert Smythson and the Elizabethan Country House* (Yale 1983); P. Thornton, *Seventeenth Century Interior Decoration in England, France and Holland* (Yale 1978); O. Hill & J. Cornforth, *English Country Houses: Caroline* (1966, repr. Antique Collectors' Club 1985); G. Beard, *Craftsmen and Interior Decoration in Britain 1660–1820* (Bartholomew & Son 1981); J. Lees-Milne, *English Country Houses: Baroque* (Country Life 1970); J. Fowler & J. Cornforth, *English Decoration in the 18th Century* (Barrie & Jenkins 1974); C. Hussey, *English Country Houses: Early, Mid and Late Georgian* (3 vols 1955, repr. Antique Collectors' Club 1986); M. Girouard, *The Victorian Country House* (Oxford 1971); J. Franklin, *The Gentleman's Country House and its Plan* (Routledge 1981); C. Aslet, *The Last Country Houses* (Yale 1982).

Reference books: A. Foss, *Country House Treasures* (Weidenfeld & Nicholson 1980); A. Tinniswood, *The Country Houses of the National Trust* (1992); H. M. Colvin, *Biographical Dictionary of British Architects 1600–1840* (John Murray 1978); N. Pevsner and others, *The Buildings of England* series (Penguin Books)—volumes for each of the old (pre-1974) English counties.

A NOTE ON BLUE GUIDES

The Blue Guide series began in 1918 when Muirhead Guide-Books Limited published Blue Guide London and its Environs. Finlay and James Muirhead already had extensive experience of guide-book publishing: before the First World War they had been the editors of the English editions of the German Baedekers, and by 1915 they had acquired the copyright of most of the famous 'Red' Handbooks from John Murray.

An agreement made with the French publishing house Hachette et Cie in 1917 led to the translation of Muirhead's London guide, which became the first 'Guide Bleu', Hachette had previously published the blue-covered 'Guides Joanne'. Subsequently, Hachette's Guide Bleu Paris et ses Environs was adapted and published in London by Muirhead.

In 1931 Ernest Benn Limited took over the Blue Guides, appointing Russell Muirhead, Finlay Muirhead's son, editor in 1934. The Muirheads' connection with the Blue Guides ended in 1963, when Stuart Rossiter, who had been working on the Guides since 1954, became house editor, revising and compiling several of the books himself.

The Blue Guides are now published by A & C Black, who acquired Ernest Benn in 1984, so continuing the tradition of guide-book publishing which began in 1826 with 'Black's Economical Tourist of Scotland'. The series continues to grow: there are now more than 50 titles in print, with revised editions appearing regularly, and new titles in preparation.

AVON

Clevedon Court

1½m east of Clevedon on B3130 Bristol–Clevedon, M5 exit 20: National Trust, tel. 0275 872257. Open Apr–Sept Wed, Thur, Sun, BH Mon 2.30–5.30. Refreshments.

This venerable house, built of the red-tinged local stone, dates from the early 14C, when the lord of the manor was Sir John de Clevedon (d 1336). He chose a sheltered site on a hill slope not far from the Bristol Channel, but facing inland towards the Mendip Hills. A 13C stone tower already existed here, and the new house was built adjacent to it. In the 15C the estate passed by inheritance to a branch of the Wake family from Northamptonshire, and some alterations were made in the 16C, notably c 1570, when John Wake added a wing to the west of the medieval parlour wing. Sir John Digby, 1st Earl of Bristol (cf. Sherborne Castle, Dorset), bought the estate in 1630, but in 1709 it was sold again to Abraham Elton, a successful Bristol merchant with interests in shipping and copper manufacturing, who became mayor of the city in 1710 and subsequently a Baronet and Member of Parliament. Improvements to the house and grounds were made by the 2nd and 4th Baronets in the 18C, and in the 19C the family did much to develop the town of Clevedon as a fashionable seaside resort—a character which it still to some extent retains.

Meanwhile, the formerly bare hillside around the house was planted with woods, and the house itself underwent several changes with a view to enhancing its appeal as a mansion of the 'olden time'; some of these have since been reversed. The property was conveyed to the National Trust after the Second World War, and the much-altered 16C west wing was demolished in 1960, thus returning the house to its original dimensions. It still remains the home of the Elton family, and it retains the satisfyingly timeless atmosphere of a long-established family home, marred only by the disturbing proximity of the M5 motorway.

As seen from the south or entrance front, the medieval origins of the house are very clear. In the centre is the early-14C hall, with a two-storeyed porch to the right and another two-storeyed projection to the left, the upper floor of which is occupied by the domestic chapel mentioned in the will of Sir John de Clevedon. This is lit by square-headed early-14C windows filled with flowing ogee tracery—something not found in any other English country house. To the left is the medieval parlour wing, refronted c 1570 with a gabled top and mullioned and transomed windows; the west wall, facing the lawn, was reconstructed in 1960 after the demolition of the Elizabethan west wing. There is another Elizabethan façade to the former service wing at the east ('lower') end of the hall, and to the right of it is the medieval kitchen, built onto the 13C tower. The tower, a stark defensive-looking structure with a gabled roof and tiny windows, is best seen from the attractive 18C terraces which climb up the hillside to the north, and at the end of the widest of the terraces—known as the Pretty Terrace—there is an octagonal temple of the mid 18C.

The house is entered through a screens passage, to the right of which is the usual row of three pointed-arched medieval doorways, one of which leads into the Justice Room (formerly the buttery or pantry), with a good collection of the locally-made Nailsea glass. The Hall has been much altered since it was first built in the early 14C, but it still retains its open, spacious dimensions, and it now contains a good collection of late-17C high-backed chairs, along with ranks of Elton portraits gazing down from the walls, many of them by West Country artists, including Thomas Hudson. The chimneypiece and windows are early 16C in form (the front window is a 20C replacement), the screen and flat plaster ceiling date from the time of the 2nd Baronet in the 18C, and the elaborate Elizabethan west doorway was introduced from elsewhere in the 19C. The upstairs rooms are reached by an early-18C staircase hung with prints of railways and other 19C civil engineering works collected by a recent Baronet. At the top is a portrait by Edgar Boehm of the writer William Makepeace Thackeray, who often stayed at the Court as a guest of the 6th Baronet, a serious classical scholar and *litterateur*, and wrote part of his novel *Henry Esmond* here. A bedroom contains more Thackeray memorabilia, including a sketch by him of the house, and also items relating to the 6th Baronet's nephew Arthur Hallam, whose early death prompted Tennyson to write his poem, 'In Memoriam'.

A 14C arch leads to a landing, on which is hung a bird's-eye view of the house in the early 18C (it is still quite recognisable today, but note the bareness of the surrounding hills). Beyond is the State Bedroom, the former great chamber. This contains some good Regency furniture, and there are more Elton portraits, including one dated 1584 (over the fireplace) and several of the children of the 6th Baronet, painted by Thomas Barker of Bath in 1823; another group portrait (by the Bristol artist Edward Rippingille) shows the 6th Baronet with Wordsworth, Coleridge, and other contributors to the *London Magazine* in 1823. Beyond is the tiny Chapel with its original 14C wooden roof and windows filled with stained glass by Clayton & Bell (1883); an internal window looks down from here into the Hall. The last room to be seen is the former kitchen, reached through a triangular service courtyard on the other side of the screens passage. It is now used as a museum and tea room, and contains specimens of the strikingly original 'Elton ware' made in the late 19C and early 20C by Sir Edmund Elton, 8th Baronet, and an assistant, in a kiln in the stable courtyard; there are influences from oriental and 'primitive' sources, and the exotic effect has much in common with Art Nouveau—a taste rarely encountered in English country houses.

GCT

Dyrham Park

8m north of Bath on A46 Bath–Stroud, M4 exit 18: National Trust, tel. 0272 327501. Open Apr–Oct Sat–Wed 12–5.30. Refreshments

Beautifully situated on the precipitous western edge of the Cotswolds, Dyrham was created in its present form between 1692 and 1704 by William Blathwayt, a civil servant and politician who, in the words of John Evelyn, 'raised himself by his industry from very moderate circumstances' to become one of William III's Secretaries of State and one of his closest advisers. Blathwayt married Mary Wynter, the heiress to the estate, in 1686, and six years later he called in the otherwise unknown French architect S. Hauduroy to add a new range of buildings to the west of the hall of the existing house. This was followed in 1698 by a new east range, on the other side of the hall, designed by William Talman, Comptroller of the King's Works and perhaps the most influential country-house architect of his generation. At the same time the surrounding landscape was laid out, under the direction of George London, with a canal and terraced gardens focused on the house. Blathwayt's garden survived until the 1790s, but it fell victim in the end to the landscaping enthusiasm of the Bath surveyor Charles Harcourt-Masters and Humphry Repton, and it can now only be appreciated in Kip's engraving of 1712, which can be seen in the house.

The house itself, however, survived remarkably unaltered, with much of its original furniture, in the hands of Blathwayt's descendants, who eschewed politics and settled down as ordinary country squires. The house, gardens and the most important contents were acquired for the nation with the help of the National Land Fund in 1956, and were transferred to the National Trust, which now manages the property in an exemplary way.

In William Blathwayt's time, visitors would have approached the house from the west, but since the rerouting of what is now the A46 road in the late 18C, the entrance has been from the east, so that the house is first seen from above, nestled in a hollow of the steep hills with the landscape spreading out to Bristol and the River Severn beyond. There is a particularly good view from Neptune's Fountain, to the north of the main drive, placed at the top of the former cascade and one of the few pieces of sculpture to survive from the original garden. The house is built of Bath stone, and is now entered through Talman's **east range**, a restrained but accomplished design which owes something to contemporary French architecture, and also to engravings in Rubens' *Palazzi di Genova* (1622); the roof is hidden behind a balustrade, a fashion which Talman did much to popularise at Chatsworth, Derbyshire (qv.), a few years earlier, and there is abundant sculptural detail, some of it by John Harvey of Bath. To the south (left) is a single-storeyed Orangery (now the tea room), also by Talman, partly inspired by the orangery at Versailles. The west or **garden front** is reached by walking through the house, and before exploring the interior in detail it is worth going outside to see Hauduroy's west elevation, plainer than Talman's, and the medieval parish church on the hillside to the north, with monuments to the Wynter family and their predecessors at Dyrham inside. The attractive garden is only a shadow of what it once was, but the terrace walls can still be seen, as can a pair of rectangular ponds illustrated by Kip; they are overlooked by the strangely primitive-looking front to the stable block (1698–99), articulated by Tuscan columns without an entablature.

Since its rebuilding by Blathwayt, the house has consisted of the remodelled hall of the former house sandwiched between the Hauduroy and Talman ranges, each of them one room deep. At first the entrance was through the **West, or Ante, Hall**, a room which has changed little since the 1690s and still retains its original stone floor and plain oak panelling. Blathwayt embraced the fashionable taste of the 1690s for things Dutch, and landscapes by minor Dutch masters hang on the walls. To the south (right on entering from the garden) is the original family parlour, redecorated as a Print Room, and ahead is the **Great Hall** which retains the tall and spacious dimensions of its pre-17C predecessor. There are portraits by Michael Dahl of a bewigged William Blathwayt and his wife, and lacquer cabinets and late-17C high-backed chairs are placed against the walls. Bird paintings by Melchior Hondecoeter, a Dutch artist much represented at Dyrham, hang on the wall of the **Walnut Staircase**, to the north of the West Hall, but the space is dominated by a huge perspective view by another Dutchman, Samuel van Hoogstraten, of the classical courtyard of a house; this hung originally in the London house of Thomas Povey, Blathwayt's uncle and fellow civil servant, where it was admired by Samuel Pepys and John Evelyn. The stairs lead up to Blathwayt's 'apartment', more lavishly decorated than the ground-floor rooms, with Ionic pilasters adorning the wood-panelled walls of the ante-room or **Balcony Room** at the centre of the west front (the present dark graining dates from the 19C), and 17C Flemish verdure tapestries showing the gardens at Enghien, near Brussels, in the adjacent bedroom; the bed, with its hangings, has been at Dyrham since Blathwayt's time.

Returning to the ground floor, the **Drawing Room**, to the north of the Walnut Staircase, now has a largely mid- to late-18C appearance, partly due to 20C alterations undertaken by Lady Islington, who tenanted the house from 1938 to 1946. There are two Rococo looking-glasses of c 1760 by John Linnell, and a set of chairs and tables by the Gillow firm (one of them dated 1797), a striking view of 'Antwerp from across the Scheldt' by the 17C Dutch artist Hendrik van Minderhout (there is another picture by him in the Great Hall) and a 'Peasant Woman and a Boy' by Murillo, with a copy of the same picture possibly painted by Thomas Gainsborough in Bath in 1760. The Dining Room was created out of two smaller rooms in the 19C, and now contains portraits of Thomas Povey (by John Michael Wright) and the playwright Thomas Killigrew, by William Shepherd, which originally hung in Povey's house.

From here a small door leads into the east (Talman) range. This contained 'apartments' for important visitors, as well as a grand new vestibule (the East Hall) and a 'great room above stairs' (not shown to the public). The upstairs apartments were reached by the **Cedar Staircase**, *from the foot of which is an enfilade* through the ground-floor rooms. At the north end, visible through the open door of the Library (called the Plod—or plaid—Room in a 1710 inventory), is another trompe l'oeil perspective view by Hoogstraten (1662), also from Povey's London house. The East or **Entrance Hall** was hung, in 1702, with leather bought by Blathwayt in The Hague, and contains late-17C walnut armchairs, pictures by Hondecoeter and some good examples of the blue and white Delftware popularised by Queen Mary. Finally, to the south, there is a complete 'apartment', turned into drawing rooms in the 19C but since reconstituted with late-17C furniture from different parts of the house. Mortlake tapestries of 'Alexander visiting Diogenes' and 'The School of Plato' after Salvator Rosa hang on the walnut-panelled walls of the ante-room known as the **Diogenes Room**, and there is a seaweed marquetry table flanked by torchères and an excellent pair of pyramid Delftware tulip vases by Adrien Kocks. Beyond lies the bedchamber (the **Queen Anne Room**), with a richly hung state bed of 1704–5 in the style of Daniel Marot (originally in the best bedchamber on the first floor), a marquetry table, and chairs arranged en suite with the bed. At the end of this suite of rooms is the more private closet, containing a 17C view of a Brazilian coffee plantation to serve as a reminder of the colonial wealth which helped buttress the fortunes of Blathwayt and his contempories.

GCT

Horton Court

1m west of A46 Bath–Stroud to north of the village of Horton:
National Trust. Hall and 'ambulatory' open April–Oct Wed, Sat 2–6.

There is not a great deal for visitors to see at Horton, but what there is to
see is of considerable interest. The main part of the house, a stone-built
early-16C structure much remodelled in the late 19C and 20C, is not open
to the public, but there are two highly unusual appendages which justify a
visit to this attractive place on the western Cotswold escarpment: a late 12C
stone hall next to the house and an early-16C loggia (the word ambulatory
is a misnomer) in the garden.

The hall was built by Robert de Beaufeu, Rector of Horton and Prebendary
of Salisbury Cathedral from c 1150, or by his successor. It is a single-storeyed aisleless building with enriched Norman (Romanesque) doorways,
small round-arched windows on the north side, next to the church (the south
windows are later), and a 14C arch-braced wooden roof: a remarkable
survival which may well be the oldest rectory in England. This well-built
though unpretentious dwelling sufficed for the Rectors of Horton until the
1520s, when William Knight, a chaplain to Henry VIII and Apostolic
Protonotary (and later Bishop of Bath and Wells), built the core of the
present house at right angles to the older building. He had studied law at
Ferrara and subsequently spent some time in Rome, and the main doorway
of the house is enriched with Renaissance motifs of the kind which were
currently becoming fashionable at court. More surprising is the garden
loggia, to the south. Structures of this kind were used for outdoor dining in
Italy, and, while it is hard to see Knight or his successors spending much
time doing this at Horton, the building nevertheless speaks of a cosmopolitan outlook on life which must have appeared strange to the Gloucestershire gentry of the time. There are six arches of a somewhat late-Gothic
shape under a roof tiled with stone slates, and inside there are four stucco
busts of classical figures, including Hannibal, recalling the terracotta
medallions which adorn the gateways of Cardinal Wolsey's Hampton Court.

The Horton estate was secularised under Edward VI and the land went
to the Paston family, from Norfolk, who sold it in the 19C, after which it
passed through several ownerships before being given to the National Trust
in 1946; the house is now looked after by a tenant.

GCT

BEDFORDSHIRE

Chicksands Priory

About 10m south east of Bedford, in Chicksands RAF base; entered by the main gates on the A507 or the A600. The Ministry of Defence and the Friends of Chicksands Priory; tel. 023482 4195. Open Apr–Oct 1st and 3rd Sun of each month 2–5, last tour 4.30. Refreshments.

Chicksands Priory is a low square house around a courtyard; it is based on part of a 13C Gilbertine priory, much of which remains under later alterations, the most important of these being the work of James Wyatt of c 1813. It is an unusual place to visit, as historic houses go, as it is now entirely surrounded by an enormous RAF base, occupied by the United States Air Force; the house is maintained and run by a group of Friends, with the blessing of the RAF and the USAF. The house is nearly empty, and is in the early stages of redecoration and presentation.

In 1150 Payne de Beauchamp gave the manor of Chicksands to the Gilbertine Order, for the foundation of a priory. A notable feature of the Order was that their houses all comprised twin communities, for monks and nuns. Chicksands was thus built with two cloisters surrounded by monastic buildings, with the church standing in between. At the Dissolution in 1539 the estate was seized by the Crown, and in 1553 it was bought by the Osborne (later Osborn) family, and they remained its owners until 1936. In the 16C, the church and half of the conventual buildings were demolished and the Osbornes converted the remaining cloister with its surrounding buildings into a house; this is essentially what remains today, although much altered. It had a picturesque, irregular appearance with many gables and mullioned windows until 1740, when Sir Danvers Osborn commissioned Isaac Ware to remodel some of the main interiors and the south and east fronts in correct Palladian style. His son, General Sir George Osborn, beautified the grounds, planting the great cedar trees and bringing in James Wyatt to carry out more alterations in 1813. Wyatt remodelled the east and south fronts again in his Gothic style, added the north wing and contributed the vaulted Gothic revival interiors. In 1936 the estate was sold to the Crown, and in 1939 leased to the Air Ministry, which has remained here ever since. After the War and until 1971 the house was used as an officers' mess and as officers' quarters. By 1975 it was empty and in poor condition; the MoD paid for structural repairs, and a group of volunteers, the Friends of Chicksands Priory, was formed to look after the house, open it to the public, and carry out redecoration.

Chicksands' large park has been covered with the enormous airforce base; the surroundings are much marred, but the lake and some of the 18C planting remain. The house is an irregular oblong around a courtyard; much of the structure is still basically medieval. The main (south and east) fronts owe their present appearance to Wyatt, with their cement rendering, buttresses and Gothic windows. To the north there are later wings in red brick. The house is entered on the south front. Left of the Hall is a former Library, really part of the medieval undercroft with pillars and vaulting. The pillars and vaulting continue in the two rooms to the north. On the north side of the cloister or courtyard runs a passageway with Tudor beams and windows; the courtyard has been laid out as a herb-garden. Below there are vaults, of 16C and 18C date.

On the east side of the house are Wyatt's Entrance Hall and staircase, with vaulting and decoration in his brand of the Gothic style. Off this at first floor level is a long room with Palladian decoration by Isaac Ware, overlaid with mid-Victorian painted decoration, in a melancholy state. Ware was also responsible for the line of rooms along the south side at first floor level, with 18C panelling, again with an overlay of Victorian ornament. The tour continues through empty bedrooms on the west side. A wing was added to the north by Wyatt, and here on the first floor there is an octagonal bedchamber with a Gothic vault and a bed alcove. Finally, the tour ascends to the attic storey, where the impressive 15C roof structure over the south range is visible. The tour ends up on the first floor of the east side, and thus back down Wyatt's staircase. A wide passageway with Coade stone reliefs leads back to the entrance.

Chicksands has begun a long journey back from dereliction; there is much for the brave group of Friends to do, and they deserve every support and encouragement in this daunting task.

SB

Luton Hoo

2m south east of Luton off A6129, M1 exit 10: the Wernher Family, tel. 0582 22955. Open Easter–mid Oct daily except Mon (but open BH Mon) 1.30–5. Refreshments.

The word Hoo means the spur of a hill, and Luton Hoo stands high on the edge of the Chilterns, in an extensive 'Capability' Brown park just outside the suburban sprawl of Luton. The stately ashlar-faced house owes its basic shape and proportions to Robert Adam, who transformed and greatly enlarged an earlier house on the site for the 3rd Earl of Bute, George III's former mentor and first Prime Minister, in 1769–74. Adam's grandiose plans were never carried out in full, and c 1825 Bute's great-grandson engaged Sir Robert Smirke, the architect of the British Museum, to finish off the house and add the giant Grecian portico of the Ionic order. This now dominates the west or **entrance front**, which is made up of an elongated main block with wings at each end. Smirke's and Adam's interiors were all consumed by fire in 1843, and the house was sold five years later to John Leigh, a Liverpool solicitor, who made it habitable again and in 1873 employed G.E. Street to create a chapel in the north wing.

Further extensive changes occurred in 1903–7 after the sale of the estate to Sir Julius Wernher, possessor of a South African gold and diamond mining fortune, and epitome of the new plutocracy of the Edwardian era. He spared no expense in remodelling the interior once again, also adding a Mansard-roofed attic storey and altering Adam's south front, which now overlooks an attractive **formal garden** with terraces by W.H. Romaine-Walker. The architect for the house was the Frenchman Charles Mewès, partner in the firm which designed the Ritz in London, and his beautifully proportioned rooms still exude a sense of the rather claustrophobic opulence of the years before the First World War. Wernher was a serious and discriminating art collector, and soon after the Second World War his son, who had married the great-granddaughter of Tsar Nicholas I of Russia, adapted the former chapel and some of the service rooms for the display of pictures and objects formerly kept in the family's London house. They were then opened to the public, along with some of the Edwardian rooms, the family retreating to the southern half of the house (not open to the public, and now used for meetings and conferences). Since 1981 the house has been managed by a charitable foundation, and a substantial rearrangement of the interior has recently taken place.

Luton Hoo has the atmosphere of a well-endowed private art gallery of a type more common in the United States than in England. The mood of Edwardian opulence is immediately established in the Entrance Hall, designed in the ultra-elegant manner of the Ritz, and appropriately furnished with a set of Louis XV and XVI chairs covered in Beauvais tapestry; four Gobelin tapestries of the Months (1699) hang on the walls, along with a sumptuous *chancellerie* tapestry of c 1700 from the same factory. To the left is a room with photographs illustrating the history of the house and the Wernher family, and beyond are two rooms containing Dutch, Flemish and Italian paintings collected by Sir Julius Wernher, including works by Gabriel Metsu ('Gentleman and Lady at a Harpsichord'), Rubens, van de Velde and Filippino Lippi ('Rest on the Flight into Egypt'). There are superb examples of 15C and 16C maiolica and Turkish ceramics to be seen in the Lower Corridor, which leads to the **Chapel**, built in the Early Christian style, with windows by Clayton & Bell and paintings on the ceiling and in the apse by the same firm. It was restored and rededicated as a Russian Orthodox chapel in 1991, having been used for 40 years as a picture gallery, and a collection of Russian heirlooms from the late Lady Wernher is displayed in the ante-chapel. The Russian theme is maintained in the adjacent rooms, now used to display costumes and Fabergé ornaments.

The **Dining Room**, with its bow window on the site of Adam's semicircular portico overlooking a valley to the east, is an overwhelming mass of colour, with sumptuous marble enrichments framing a splendidly extravagant and beautifully preserved set of Beauvais tapestries of 'L'Histoire du Roi de Chine', designed in 1690 and made in 1708. But the most memorable interior is the oval-shaped **Marble Hall**. Here the mood is set by F. Bergonzoni's erotic marble sculpture of 'Cupid and Psyche', which stands at the foot of the sinuous main staircase with its wrought-iron balustrade. Renaissance bronzes, including a 'St John the Baptist' by Sansovino, are displayed here, as is a portrait by Sargent of the first Lady Wernher. She was responsible for amassing the collection of 18C English porcelain now shown in three former bedrooms at the top of the stairs; this includes particularly fine items from the Chelsea and Worcester factories, and also some chinoiserie pieces. Another room contains 18C and early-19C English pictures and furniture, and from here a corridor with cases of Limoges enamels leads to the **gallery of the Chapel**, where there is an excellent collection of German and Spanish 16C and 17C plate. An adjoining room is full of ivories, mostly Byzantine and French of the 10C to the 14C, many of them of exquisite quality. Finally, in **St Michael's Gallery**, there are late-medieval and Renaissance paintings, with a small Virgin and Child by Memling and a spectacular altarpiece of c 1470–71 by the Spanish artist Bartolmé Bermèjo showing St Michael smiting an improbable-looking Devil, with a donor in attendance; there are also excellent examples of 16C and 17C Italian, Spanish and German jewellery and wood carving.

GCT

Woburn Abbey

1m east of Woburn on A4012/A418, M1 exit 13: the Marquess of Tavistock and Trustees of the Bedford Settled Estates, tel. 0525 290666. Open Jan–March Sat, Sun; April–Oct daily 11–6. Refreshments.

The site of the Cistercian abbey of Woburn was granted to Henry VIII's Lord Privy Seal, John Russell, 1st Earl of Bedford, in 1548, but it was his great-grandson Francis, the 4th Earl, who fixed the family's main country residence at Woburn, in preference to Chenies, Buckinghamshire (qv.), in 1619. The 4th Earl was also responsible for commissioning Inigo Jones to lay out Covent Garden in London a few years later, and in time the rents of the family's London estate, which eventually encompassed all of Bloomsbury, rose to prodigious levels. The 5th Earl, whose son Lord William Russell was executed in 1683 on a charge of complicity in the Rye House Plot, was given a dukedom by William III in recognition of the family's support of the Protestant interest, and throughout the 18C and 19C the family were staunch Whigs, producing several politicians and one Prime Minister, Lord John Russell, younger son of the 6th Duke.

The 4th Duke greatly enlarged the park, later improved by Repton, and in 1747–61 employed Henry Flitcroft to build what was in effect a new house on the old low-lying site of the medieval monastery, incorporating part of the 17C north range and the monastic east range. The new state rooms were on the first floor of the new west range, which has a suitably monumental neo-Palladian **façade** of local Totternhoe stone—best seen from the circuitous drive through the park—with a pedimented centrepiece and end pavilions lit by Venetian and 'Diocletian' windows. Flitcroft also designed the massive quadrangular **stable blocks** which still stand on either side of the main axis of the east of the house. The 5th Duke, an agricultural improver and friend of the Prince of Wales, added to the already notable art collection and employed Henry Holland to remodel the south range in 1788–89; Holland also designed an entrance portico to the now-demolished east range, built a riding school and tennis court connecting the two stable blocks, and also a conservatory which was converted by Wyatville into a Sculpture Gallery for the 6th Duke in 1816–18. There were few changes in the rest of the 19C, but in 1950 the 12th Duke pulled down the east range and riding school, employing Sir Albert Richardson to design discreet façades to the truncated north and south ranges. Three years later the present Duke inherited and subsequently pioneered the 'stately home business' by opening Woburn on a more regular basis and vigorously marketing its attractions. His son, the Marquess of Tavistock, now lives here.

After the magnificent approach through the park, visitors sidle up to the obscure public **entrance** in the north range, which gives access to the Book Room, lined with glass-fronted bookcases in which smartly-bound folios are displayed. The next room, formerly the 4th Duke's bedroom, is hung with Mortlake tapestries of 1661–64 after the Raphael Cartoons, and leads into a corridor, supposedly on the site of the medieval cloister, in which there are family mementoes including a cane given to the 4th Earl by Charles I in 1647. At the end is a **staircase**, by Flitcroft, with a portrait of Admiral Pareja, attributed to Velasquez, at the foot, and a superb, chrono-logically displayed, set of Tudor and Stuart family portraits on the upper walls, of which the most striking is that of Lucy Harrington (d 1627), wife of the 3rd Earl, in masque costume, probably by John de Critz. At first-floor level there is a good copy of Van Dyck's portrait of Anne Carr, wife of the 5th Earl, and the series of family portraits is continued into the 18C and 19C along what is aptly known as the Dukes' Corridor, with works by Reynolds, Hoppner, Richmond and others, and also a view by Richard Wilson of Houghton Conquest, another Bedfordshire house, now in ruins, bought by the 4th Duke.

A series of family rooms in the north range were remodelled by Flitcroft and his craftsmen in the mid 18C, and still contain excellent wood carving, plasterwork and furniture of the period. First comes the **Chinese Room**, one of the best ensembles of its kind in any country house, with its precious porcelain (first collected by the 2nd and 3rd Dukes in the early 18C), lacquered chests and beautifully preserved mid-18C wallpaper imported from China. A different taste is evident in the **Yellow Drawing Room**, approached through a room commemorating the exploits of the 'Flying Duchess', grandmother of the present Duke. Here the gilded plasterwork is in the spirit of the French Rococo, and there is some splendid French furniture, including commodes attributed to Antoine Gaudreau and by Pierre Langlois (1760). The walls are hung with more of the 17C family portraits for which Woburn is unrivalled among English houses. The next room, the Racing Room, with similar plasterwork and more 18C furniture, contains equestrian pictures by Sartorius and others, brought from other parts of the house by the present Marchioness, who runs a stud farm at Woburn.

The grandest rooms are arranged in *enfilade* on the first floor of the west front, starting with **Queen Victoria's Bedroom**, its name deriving from a royal visit in 1841. The doorcases and chimneypiece, as in the succeeding rooms, are of the usual English neo-Palladian type, but the richly gilded ceiling is modelled on that of the Roman Temple of the Sun at Palmyra in Syria, published in 1753. The pictures include several acquired by the art-loving 6th Duke, notably a sensitive 'View on the Coast of Normandy' (1825–26) by Bonington, a friend of the family. Pictures by Dutch and Flemish masters collected by the 5th and 6th Dukes can be found in the adjacent Dressing Room, among them Van Dyck's early portrait of Jan Snellinck (over the fireplace), Jan Steen's 'Twelfth Night Feast', and two Cuyps, including a beautifully luminescent view of Nijmegen (c 1655); there is also a roll-top desk by Riesener (1774). There are more Old Masters in the **Blue Drawing Room**, notably Poussin's 'Moses trampling on Pharaoh's Crown' (c 1643), in his severest manner, and the much softer 'Landscape with Peasants Dancing' by Claude, while an exquisite 'Ruined Roman Bridge' by Jan Asselyn hangs over the fireplace; note also the French-style furniture and wall-sconces. The **State Saloon**, at the centre of the west front, with its coved ceiling, commands a magnificent view over to the lake; the Mortlake tapestries now in the north range originally hung here, but in 1973 the walls were adorned with a series of murals by Roland Pym which do not harmonise with the stately architectural enrichments, including chimneypieces by Rysbrack. The splendid Palladian decoration of the **State Dining Room**, on the other hand, provides an appropriate setting for a series of full-length copies by Lely and Knapton of portraits by Van Dyck; there is a genuine Van Dyck, of Albert Lemire, Dean of Antwerp (c 1630), over the fireplace and also a portrait of a nobleman acquired in the Orleans sale of 1794.

The next rooms are sometimes used by the family, and are not always open to the public (and then only on payment of a small extra fee). The Reynolds Room is named after a series of portraits by Sir Joshua Reynolds, the finest of which are a small self-portrait and the magnificent 'Lady Elizabeth Keppel Adorning a Bust of Hymen', painted in 1761, three years before she married the Marquess of Tavistock, whose more conventional portrait is next to hers (she died 'of grief and decline' only a year after his untimely death in 1767, having borne the future 5th and 6th Dukes). It was Tavistock who acquired the series of bronzes made by Giacomo Zoffoli 'after the antique' c 1762–63 during his Grand Tour. The Grand Tour also looms large in the adjacent dining room, known as the **Canaletto Room**, the first of a series of rooms in the south range remodelled by Holland, who also raised the terrace outside to allow the family and their guests to wander straight from the house through French windows into the gardens. The decorations and furnishings are in Holland's characteristically restrained, ultra-elegant style, but the room is dominated by a series of 21 views of Venice (including some of buildings which no longer exist) acquired by the 4th Duke soon after inheriting in 1732, probably through the British Consul, Joseph Smith, and hung until 1800 in Bedford House, Bloomsbury. The finest of Holland's rooms is the **Library**, divided into three by Corinthian columns; each section contains fine paintings, including two Rembrandts (a self-portrait—possibly a copy after a lost original—and the 'Old Rabbi' 1643), a double portrait by Van Dyck and a portrait by Cuyp.

Earlier portraits hang in the **Long Gallery**, which flanks the state rooms in the west range. Though it occupies the site of the gallery of the 17C house, this is now a mid-18C room, designed by Flitcroft. The main interest lies in the 16C and 17C portraits, of which the most famous is George Gower's 'Armada Portrait' of Elizabeth I, showing the bejewelled Queen with her hand on a globe, to signify England's colonial ambitions, with the ships of the Spanish Armada behind; there are also magnificent full-lengths by Gheeraerts of Elizabeth's favourite, the Earl of Essex, and James I's queen, Anne of Denmark, and smaller pictures of the notorious Frances Howard, in a low-cut dress (by William Larkin), and of Lucy Countess of Bedford, in a melancholy posture (attributed to Johann Priwitzer). A **staircase** close to this picture leads down, via a showcase containing Greek vases of the 5C and 4C BC and a corridor with two Vernet seascapes, to the basement, in which the best of the family's **porcelain collection** is shown. This includes late-17C Japanese items, several mid-18C Chelsea pieces, and a Sèvres dinner service presented to the 4th Duke by Louis XV of France (whose portrait is here) in appreciation of his role in negotiating the Treaty of Paris, which brought to an end the Seven Years War, in 1763. Even more spectacular are the **silver and gold vaults**, containing a silver-gilt standing salt (c 1610), some items of solid gold by Peter Boy of Frankfurt c 1700, and exquisite items by Willaume, Lamerie (eg, a pair of table baskets, 1737) and Storr, as well as a salver of 1837, designed by Sir Edwin Landseer to celebrate the family's agricultural achievements; miniatures by Hilliard, Oliver and others are displayed close by.

The last two rooms to be seen are on the ground floor of the north range: the Parlour, with a mid-17C chimneypiece and more Old Masters, including Murillo's 'Cherubs Scattering Flowers', and finally the strange and fanciful **Grotto**, inspired by similar structures in Renaissance Italy but almost certainly designed c 1630 by the Frenchman Isaac de Caus (cf. Wilton House, Wiltshire), who built a similar grotto (since destroyed) underneath Inigo Jones' Banqueting House in Whitehall. Always no doubt a damp and chilly place, this bizarre room with its curious 18C furniture based on shell motifs has recently been glazed and adapted to house some of the sculptures collected by the 6th Duke in the early 19C and formerly shown in the Sculpture Gallery; these include a Greek relief carving of a girl dated to the 1C BC or AD, and works by Chantrey and Westmacott ('Cupid and Psyche'). Before leaving Woburn it is worth exploring the **gardens** to the east of the house, where Holland's charming Chinese Dairy survives intact in its picturesque lakeside setting.

GCT

Wrest Park

10m south of Bedford on A6 Bedford–Luton at Silsoe: English Heritage, tel. 0525 60718. Open April–Sept Sat, Sun, BH Mon 10–6. Refreshments.

Wrest Park is an unexpected sight in the flat countryside of mid Bedfordshire: a house in the style of an 18C French château, set among well-preserved formal gardens containing one of the finest and least-known monuments of the short-lived English Baroque. The gardens were laid out in the early 18C by Henry Grey, 12th Earl (and subsequently Duke) of Kent, whose family had held the estate since the 13C. He also intended to replace the largely Elizabethan house of his ancestors, but the project languished until 1834–39, when the present impressive pile was erected by his great-great grandson, the 2nd Lord de Grey, first President of the Royal Institute of British Architects. He had spent much of his youth at Newby Hall, North Yorkshire (qv.), which he inherited from a distant cousin, and he subsequently travelled extensively on the Continent, where he developed a marked—and for the time unusual—enthusiasm for 18C French architecture. This can be clearly seen at Wrest Park, which he designed himself with practical assistance from his clerk of works, James Clephan. The restrained Bath stone façades are based on designs of executed and unexecuted buildings from 18C French pattern-books, and the interior decoration is equally Francophile. The most impressive room is the top-lit Staircase Hall, with the stairs and their curly wrought-iron balustrades rising gracefully to the landing, and portraits of Queen Anne by Kneller and Queen Caroline by Amigoni on the walls; there is also good plasterwork by an unknown craftsman (note especially the doorway on the south side, with figures representing Art and Architecture resting on French architectural books). The remaining ground-floor rooms (the only ones to be shown) stretch out in an *enfilade* along the garden front, but were divested of their original furniture and most of the pictures when the family moved away in 1917 (the family portraits are now at Newby); the house then became an agricultural college, and the atmosphere is now somewhat institutional.

The main architectural interest of Wrest lies in the gardens. The house overlooks a formal 19C layout on the site of the previous house, with an Orangery designed by Lord de Grey to the west. Beyond, a tree-lined early-18C canal (the Long Water) stretches south to a magnificent domed pavilion designed by Thomas Archer in 1709–11. This monumental building was intended for 'hunting parties and occasional suppers', and contained kitchens and a cold bath in the basement as well as a main room decorated with frescoes by Louis Hauduroy, but architecturally it has much in common with the Baroque churches seen by both Archer and his patron, the Duke of Kent, on their Italian travels. Nearer the house, to the west of the Long Water, is the less ambitious Bowling Green House of 1735, attributed to Batty Langley, with a Tuscan portico and an accomplished neo-Palladian interior. Not far from this, by way of contrast, is an absurd thatched-roofed Bath House, built to the designs of Edward Stevens, a pupil of William Chambers, in 1770, but possibly remodelled later.

GCT

BERKSHIRE

Basildon Park

2m north of Pangbourne on A329 Reading–Wallingford: National Trust, tel. 0734 843040. Open April–Oct Wed–Sun and BH Mon 2–6 (Sun and BHs 12–6). Refreshments.

Basildon Park was built out of the profits of colonial trade. The builder, Sir Francis Sykes, came from Yorkshire, but made his fortune in India—he was imprisoned in the Black Hole of Calcutta—and later purchased the Basildon estate and built a new house to the designs of John Carr of York in 1776; he then became MP for the nearby borough of Wallingford. The Thames Valley was popular with the 'moneyed interest' in the 18C (Warren Hastings rented the neighbouring Purley estate), and Sykes's house was sited so as to 'command the prospect' of the river—hence the uphill walk to the house from the car park. Like several of Carr's houses, it follows the form of a Palladian villa, with the main rooms in a compact central block and lower pavilions on either side, originally housing the kitchens, dairy and laundry. The west-facing entrance is marked by an Ionic portico *in antis* over a rusticated ground floor, and there is a canted bay window on the east front, overlooking the Thames, but there is little in the way of decoration to disturb the well-proportioned façades of meticulously cut Bath stone, transported here by sea and river.

The interior has been much altered since the time of Sir Francis Sykes, and is now in effect a successful recreation of a late 18C house, skilfully adapted to 20C needs and sensibilities. Sir Francis's grandson ran into debt and sold the estate in 1838 to James Morrison, a London haberdasher and Liberal MP, who employed John Buonarotti Papworth to complete the interior decoration, held up by the endemic extravagance of the Sykes family, and to heighten the distinctive pepperpot-shaped lodges which flank the main entrance. The Morrisons moved out in 1910, and the house remained empty for 40 years, with some of its internal detailing removed to the USA, parts of which still adorn a room in the Waldorf Astoria Hotel in New York. It was rescued by the 2nd Lord Iliffe, heir to a newspaper fortune, whose father had already purchased much of the estate. He and his wife refurnished the house, introducing doorcases and chimneypieces from another derelict Carr house, Panton Hall (Lincs), and in 1978 it was conveyed to the National Trust, along with an excellent collection of furniture and pictures.

The house is entered by a staircase ingeniously contrived by Carr underneath the portico. It leads into the Adamesque Entrance Hall, the walls articulated by paired Corinthian pilasters, with details derived from the *Book of Ceilings* published in 1776 by Adam's former draughtsman, George Richardson. To the left is the Library, with a mirror after a design by Adam, and 17C and 18C landscape paintings by minor masters collected by Lord Iliffe, whose portrait by Graham Sutherland (1976) presides over the room he recreated. The main reception rooms are reached through the dramatically lit Staircase Hall; the neo-classical urns on pedestals at the foot of the cantilevered stone staircase were originally at Fawley Court, Bucks (qv.). The pure neo-classical taste of the late 18C is strikingly evident in the Dining Room, recently repainted in its original colours by Alec Cobbe; it is entered through a Corinthian colonnade screening off the serving table.

The Drawing Room, by contrast, was decorated by Papworth in 1840 to house James Morrison's excellent collection of Old Masters, and now appropriately provides a rich setting for a set of paintings of God the Father and seven of the Apostles by Pompeo Batoni, and three canvases of classical subjects by the 18C Venetian artist Giovanni Pitoni (over the doors). The superb Grecian mirrors of c 1773 and their matching pier-tables supported by caryatids were originally at Brockenhurst Park (Hants), and the Gothic armchairs were designed by William Porden for Eaton Hall (Cheshire), c 1810. The adjacent Green Drawing Room (originally the breakfast room), with its late-18C ceiling, probably in the original colours, is more intimate in character and contains more 17C and 18C landscapes, including two Venetian views by William Marlow.

The bedrooms at the top of the house were all lavishly redecorated by Lord and Lady Iliffe in the 1950s, with luxurious bathrooms, and furnishings bought from sales at several well-known houses, including Ashburnham Place, Sussex (in the Crimson Bedroom, including the heavily upholstered bed of 1829), Stoneleigh Abbey, Warwickshire (in the Bamboo Room) and Ditchley Park, Oxon (in the Green Chintz Room, where the portraits are on loan from the Dillon family, formerly of Ditchley). But the rooms which linger longest in the memory are the claustrophobic Shell Room behind the portico, and Lady Iliffe's Bedroom, its walls hung with studies by Graham Sutherland for the Crucifixion tapestry in Coventry Cathedral. From here visitors descend by the back stairs to the ground floor, where the tea room now occupies the former servants' hall and ground-floor hall.

GCT

Frogmore House

1m south east of Windsor, off the Datchet road, just north from the A308: Her Majesty the Queen, tel. 0753 831118. Open late Aug–Sept Fri, Sat, Sun 11–5.

Frogmore is one of the hidden jewels of the great royal domain around Windsor Castle. In the 16C the Frogmore estate was a 300-acre enclave in between the Great and Home Parks. In 1680 Thomas May built a handsome seven-bay house of brick with a hipped roof, almost certainly designed by his uncle, Hugh May, who was at the time working at the Castle for Charles II. Although now unrecognisable from outside, this is the nucleus of the present house. In 1709 the house was leased to the Duke of Northumberland, a natural son of Charles II and the Duchess of Cleveland, who probably commissioned the murals in the staircase-hall by Louis Laguerre. After passing through several hands, it was bought in 1792 by Charlotte, wife of George III as a more private retreat from the Castle. In 1793 she wrote, 'I mean this place to furnish me with fresh amusements every day'. This involved landscaping the grounds, and commissioning James Wyatt to carry out a general remodelling of the house, giving it its present appearance. Here she and her daughters devoted themselves to painting, drawing, music, needlework, and above all to her interest in botany and gardening.

At the Queen's death in 1818 she bequeathed Frogmore to her eldest unmarried daughter, Princess Augusta, who lived here until her death in 1841. Queen Victoria then gave it to her widowed mother, the Duchess of

Kent, who carried out some redecoration. On her death in 1861 she was buried in the round, domed mausoleum on a little hill next to the lake. Queen Victoria was doubly bereaved, for Prince Albert died in the same year; the Queen built the famous Italianate mausoleum in the grounds, where they are both buried. Frogmore meant a great deal to Queen Victoria, and she visited it regularly during the rest of her reign. During the present century, various members of the royal family have resided here. In the recent restoration, the rooms have been returned to their arrangement in the early to mid 19C.

Cars are left just off the A308, and a shuttle bus takes visitors through the park, past immense walled gardens. The house appears behind trees, undemonstrative and clad in white stucco. The high seven-bay centre represents the 1680 house; Wyatt added an extra storey, the low wings on either side, the carriage porch, and the colonnade on the garden front. From the Hall, the visitor turns left into the Oak Room, with 17C panelling. The staircase owes its present form and decoration to Wyatt, but during repairs in 1983, the Baroque wall paintings by Laguerre of scenes from the Aeneid were discovered, fully intact behind Wyatt's plasterwork. They were uncovered, and form a spectacular, unexpected addition to the house. At the top of the stairs, the Cross Gallery, running across the breadth of the house, has Etruscan-style decorations painted on paper by Princess Elizabeth (1770–1840), third daughter to George III and a gifted artist.

The first floor rooms are not open, so the visitor descends the stairs again. The next two rooms have early Victorian furniture, and decorative objects collected by Queen Mary, wife of George V. Queen Mary's Flower Room houses wax and silk flowers under glass domes. The Black Museum has a great array of mid 19C black lacquer and papier-mâché; this kind of Victorian taste was at the depth of its unpopularity early this century, and Queen Mary, with great prescience, was able to form very fine collections. The Duchess of Kent's Sitting Room, the first on the garden front, is furnished as it was in her day. The carpets and the bright yellow silk curtains are rewoven from the decayed originals. The portraits are mostly of her time, of her many relations among the European royal families. The Green Pavilion has been returned to its appearance in Queen Charlotte's time. The brilliant green of the walls and the amazingly lavish curtains and pelmets will surprise many visitors; there is a variety of fine late Georgian furniture, and portraits of the Queen's German relations. The Charlotte Closet houses 45 drawings by Princess Charlotte, eldest daughter of George III, who is shown to have been as talented as Princess Elizabeth.

From here the Colonnade leads along the centre of the garden front, its French windows looking towards the lake. The statues and busts of Queen Victoria's children are plaster casts of originals at Osborne House, by Mary Thornycroft. The Victoria Closet is a little ante-room, symmetrical with the Charlotte Closet. This houses watercolour paintings by three generations of royal ladies, including Victoria, the Princess Royal, later the Empress of Germany (1840–1901). The Mary Moser Room commemorates a renowned flower painter, who was commissioned by Queen Charlotte to decorate this room with the panels of flower-garlands. The next room is the grandest in the house, the Duchess of Kent's Drawing Room, with bow-shaped ends. The French-style grey, gold and silver decorations was carried out c 1860 for the Duchess of Kent. The striking and strongly coloured curtains and upholstery have been re-woven, reminding one how colourful mid-Victorian taste was. Finally, the Duchess of Kent's Dining Room has rich

Rococo decoration, completed c 1862 by Queen Victoria; it is in temporary use as the bookshop.

The gardens at Frogmore are a striking example of the Picturesque movement, in the generation after 'Capability' Brown, with their dense and mixed planting. The two mausolea form striking features of the grounds, but are not normally open; the Royal Mausoleum is open on a couple of days each year.

SB

Swallowfield Park

In Swallowfield village 6m south of Reading, just east of the B3349:
Country Houses Association. Open May–Sept Wed, Thur 2–4.30.

Swallowfield Park is a big H-shaped house of 1690, built by the 2nd Earl of Clarendon, son of Charles II's Lord Chancellor, to the designs of William Talman. In 1719 the 3rd Earl sold Swallowfield to Thomas Pitt, one of the first nabobs to retire from India with a great fortune. The estate passed through many hands, until its purchase in 1820 by Sir Henry Russell, Baronet, formerly Chief Justice of Bengal, on his retirement from India. He commissioned WIlliam Atkinson to remodel and redecorate the house c 1820, living here until his death in 1852. The last Russell baronet died in 1964, and the following year his widow sold the house to the Mutual Households Association, now the Country Houses Association. It is now divided into flats.

The house stands amidst flat water-meadows; the visitor approaches it past farm buildings, including a huge dovecote dating from 1842. When new the main house was of brick with stone dressings and a hipped roof, and a wide pediment over the centre. Atkinson raised the parapet, covered it in cement rendering and altered the windows, adding the Doric porch. The stable block and service wings to the left are closer to their original (1690) appearance, the warm red brickwork left uncovered. The Hall's simple decoration dates from c 1820, although the iron fireback retains the arms of the Clarendon family. There are 18C paintings, portraits and landscapes. At the far end is the Drawing Room, with cornice and fireplace by Atkinson, and some attractive portraits. The Library has early 19C bookcases and decor, and in the middle of the garden front is an oval Vestibule, the only one of Talman's interiors to remain intact, with fine Baroque plasterwork; the arms of Clarendon appear in the middle of the domed ceiling. Opening out of this is the main staircase; the big doorcase is Talman's, but the stairs are a modern renovation.

Talman's service courtyard is less altered, with its arcades and Tuscan pilasters flanking the entrance arch. The most interesting feature of the grounds is the Walled Garden. Its entrance is a massive Baroque gateway of stone, probably the original front door of Talman's house.

SB

Windsor Castle

3m from Junction 6 of the M4. Her Majesty the Queen, Enquiries: Castle, 0753 831118; St George's Chapel, 0753 86538. Precincts open all year, daily from 10–sunset or 6.15 whichever is earlier. The State Apartments, Queen Mary's Dolls' House, the Exhibition Gallery and the Royal Mews Carriage Exhibition are also open daily 10.30–5 (last admission 4.30) June–Sept closing earlier (either 2.30 or 3.30) in other months. The State Apartments may be subject to closure and the times may be changed at short notice when the Queen is in official residence. St George's Chapel has separate opening times.

Windsor is a building which exhausts superlatives. It is the largest castle in Britain—arguably in Europe—and certainly the largest occupied castle in the world. It is the oldest and probably the grandest of Britain's royal residences, and stands in the greatest of British parks. It contains important architectural elements from every century from the 11C to the 19C. It has given its name to the royal house, and is one of the buildings which can be truly said to stand at the heart of British national identity.

William the Conqueror took over a Saxon hunting lodge and park nearby. He built a motte-and-bailey fortress on the long chalk ridge, the origin of the present castle. The mound on which the Round Tower stands is the one element of his work to remain visible; remains of the wooden palisade which once stood on top were recently found during excavations. Henry I made the castle a royal residence, and Henry II defined the present shape of the castle, with great walls of Heath stone. He rebuilt the Round Tower as a stone shell-keep, built a new palace of stone, on the north side of the Upper Ward, where the State Apartments now are, and around the Upper Ward he built square towers. A good deal of his work remains, albeit much altered. Henry III, an enthusiastic builder, carried out a great deal of work, remodelling the royal apartments on the north and east sides of the Upper Wards. He built the great stone walls around the Lower Ward—with rounded towers, in contrast to the square towers of the Upper Ward.

Edward III, another great builder, spent immense sums on the Castle. He found the Order of the Garter in 1348, and also the priestly College of St George, both based in the Castle. He built the misleadingly-named 'Norman Gateway' to the Upper Ward, and remodelled the royal apartments again, creating a Chapel and St George's Hall along the north side of the Upper Ward. The next great builder at Windsor was Edward IV, who c 1472 began a new Chapel in the Lower Ward, dedicated to St George, one of the greatest masterpieces of English Perpendicular architecture and the spiritual home of the Order of the Garter. He also founded the Horseshoe Cloister, a range of lodgings for the clergy who served the Chapel.

The Tudors often resided at Windsor, but carried out relatively little work here. Henry VIII rebuilt the main gateway with its five-sided towers. The picturesque lodgings of the Military Knights, formerly known as the 'Poor Knights of Windsor', along the Lower Ward, were built in the 1550s, and in the 1550s Elizabeth I added the Gallery range to the State Apartments overlooking the north terrace, which now houses the Royal Library. Charles II took a great liking to the Castle. He ordered the gentleman-architect Hugh May to redesign the whole of the State Apartments, executed in two stages, from 1675–83. May removed much of the picturesque irregularity of the medieval castle, driving large arched sash windows through the ancient masonry, and replacing the battlements with plain, straight parapets. The result was plain, massive and severe-looking. Inside, though, were new apartments of great richness, with murals by Verrio and carvings by Grinling Gibbons. Just three of these Baroque state rooms remain recognisable today. In the park, Charles II laid out the tremendous Long Walk, running south from the Upper Ward, 240ft wide and three miles long.

Queen Anne thought of Windsor as her home, but George I and George II neglected the place, and the castle filled up with grace-and-favour apartments. George III liked the castle, but it was in too poor a state for him to move in without enormous expense, especially given the size of his family. Instead, he remodelled and extended the Queen's Lodge—a relatively plain and domestic building, which stood immediately in front of the south side, looking down the Long Walk. Eventually, c 1800–5, he employed James Wyatt to remodel a large part of the state apartments, clothing May's plain buildings in 14C Gothic dress, and installing plaster Gothic vaulting and decoration in a number of rooms. In 1804, the royal family moved back into the castle proper. Work came abruptly to an end when, in 1811, the king lapsed into madness for the last time, never recovering before his death in 1820.

His son and successor, George IV, found May's work unacceptably old-fashioned and plain, and Wyatt's alterations insufficiently complete or convincing. He therefore employed Jeffrey Wyatville, nephew of James Wyatt, to transform the whole of the central area and the Upper Ward, at stupendous expense, starting in 1824—well over 800,000 had been spent by George IV's death in 1830, and work was still going on when Wyatville himself died in 1840. As the rebuilding went on, it became steadily more magnificent. Wyatville raised towers where none had been before, created the great George IV Gate looking down the Long Walk, and doubled the height of the 12C shell keep, because he did not think it sufficiently imposing. He destroyed May's magnificent chapel and St George's Hall, creating the present St George's Hall, 160ft long. After George IV's death, he designed the Waterloo Chamber, made by roofing over a substantial inner courtyard. His work continues to arouse controversy, but he unified the Castle stylistically, gave it the superb skyline it has today, and made of the state apartments one of the most sumptuous palaces in the world.

After Wyatville's death, Edward Blore carried out some relatively modest alterations for Queen Victoria, and Salvin then worked here in the 1860s, designing the splendid main staircase (replacing one by Wyatville) and renovating various buildings around the Lower Ward. In the present century, every monarch has resided regularly at Windsor, and in 1916 King George V assumed the name of the place, to dissociate the royal house from it Germanic origins. The present Queen spent much of her childhood at the Castle and at Royal Lodge, Windsor, and twice during the year, the castle ceases to be a museum and the royal standard flies over the Round Tower; at these times, public access is restricted. A severe fire destroyed some of the State Apartments in 1992, and restoration is expected to last until at least 1996.

The west end of the castle looms spectacularly over the pretty streets of the town. The walls here are largely of the mid 13C, though the steep pointed roof of the **Curfew Tower** is Salvin's work, of 1863. Visitors enter the **Lower Ward** through the Henry VIII Gate; it slopes upwards towards the Round Tower, but the Ward is really dominated by **St George's Chapel**, with its rows of great traceried windows, and rich architectural sculpture. The Chapel remains a 'royal peculiar', that is, a self-governing corporation answerable directly to the Queen. Behind the Chapel is what amounts to a village, where its Dean and Chapter have apartments—the Horseshoe Cloister, Canon's Cloister and other buildings, embodying elements from the 13C to the 19C. The Chapel itself is one of the great masterpieces of English Gothic architecture, and contains a wealth of magnificent fittings and tomb-monuments, rivalling most cathedrals. No fewer than ten British sovereigns are buried here, with many other members of the royal family from the last five hundred years. The superb stalls of the Garter knights dominate the chancel. To the north east is the beautiful 13C Dean's Cloister, and immediately east of St George's Chapel is the early 16C **Albert Memorial Chapel**. Built by Cardinal Wolsey on the site of an earlier chapel, this was redecorated very richly in the 1860s, as a memorial to the Prince Consort. It is dominated by the tremendous and astonishing Art Nouveau monument to Edward VII's elder son, the Duke of Clarence (d 1892), by Alfred Gilbert, the sculptor of 'Eros' in Piccadilly Circus.

Along the south side of the Lower Ward are the 17C Military Knights' Lodgings, still in the use for which they were built by Edward VI and Mary Tudor. Visitors move east, up the hill, and skirt the Norman motte on which the **Round Tower** stands, heightened by Wyatville and now housing the Royal Archives. Skirting the Round Tower to the north, you pass under the 'Norman Gate' (1359), with fine lion's masks on the vaulting and reach the Upper Ward. Wyatville's style is almost overpowering here. The south and east sides contain the royal family's private apartments, linked by the very prominent Grand Corridor. The **State Apartments** are in the north range, buildings which have developed continuously since the time of Henry II. The fire of November 1992 destroyed most of the north east corner, damaging some of the state and some of the private apartments. The undamaged State Apartments, though, remain open.

The normal entrance to the State Apartments is from the North Terrace. This great feature is the creation of Elizabeth I, Charles II and George IV, and commands views over the Thames valley, with Eton College a prominent feature in the landscape. The visitors' entrance takes you to the Gothic staircase built by Salvin, bedecked with arms and armour, and overlooked by Chantrey's statue of George IV. South of here, the **Grand Vestibule** has a high plaster vault by Wyatville. The display cases house a considerable museum of arms and armour. From here you enter the **Waterloo Chamber**. This tremendous room was the brainchild of George IV, although built after his death. The King commissioned Sir Thomas Lawrence to paint the magnificent series of portraits of the monarchs and leaders who had united to overthrow Napoleon. The chamber was designed to house these, and also the annual Waterloo Banquets, held on 18 June. Wyatville designed the room to fill the former Horn Court, with an immense top-lit roof. The huge carpet, woven in Agra and given to Queen Victoria, is the largest ever to have been made in one piece. To the north again, and looking over the Thames valley, is the **Garter Throne Room**, used for the ceremonies of investiture of new knights, decorated with panelling and carvings by Grinling Gibbons, re-used from the 17C Chapel. From these rooms, visitors can look through temporarily glazed doorways to two fire damaged areas— the **Grand Reception Rooms** and **St George's Hall**—and see the rebuilding work in progress.

Returning to the Grand Vestibule and the vaulted Queen's Guard Chamber, visitors see a circuit of state rooms, beginning with two of the surviving Baroque interiors, designed by Hugh May for Catherine of

Braganza, consort of Charles II. The **Queen's Presence Chamber** and **Audience Chamber** present an abrupt transition in tone from the Regency rooms, with their superb ceilings painted with mythological scenes by Verrio, and elaborate 17C woodwork. They are hung with great Gobelin tapestries, with the story of Esther and Ahasuerus, and have a wealth of fine late 17C French and English furniture. The **Queen's Ballroom**, remodelled by George IV and hung with blue silk, has silver 17C furniture, 18C French furniture, and paintings by Canaletto, Gainsborough, Copley and Benjamin West. The remaining State Apartments were mostly remodelled for George IV in a rich French-inspired style. They house superb furniture, and Old Master paintings from the royal collection which are the equal of anything in the world; the arrangement of these may change. The **Queen's Drawing Room** has a wealth of portraits by Van Dyck. The **King's Closet** has paintings by Canaletto and Claude, and the **King's Dressing Room** portraits by Holbein, Dürer, Rembrandt and Rubens, as well as the famous triple portrait of Charles I by Van Dyck. The **King's State Bed Chamber** has superb Louis XVI furniture. The **King's Drawing Room** has an array of great paintings by Van Dyck and Rubens, including the latter's landscapes 'Winter' and 'Summer'. Finally, the **King's Dining Room** is another survivor of the Baroque rebuilding for Charles II, with panelling, carved festoons by Grinling Gibbons, and a ceiling-painting by Verrio, depicting a Feast of the Gods. Visitors leave from here, back down Salvin's Grand Staircase and out onto the Terrace. Close by is the entrance to the rooms housing the famous Queen Mary's Dolls' House, and exhibitions of Old Master drawings from the royal collection.

SB

BUCKINGHAMSHIRE

Ascott

2m south west of Leighton Buzzard on the A418 (Leighton Buzzard–
Aylesbury) road: National Trust, tel. 0296 688242. Open mid Apr–mid May
and Sept Tues–Sun 2–6. The gardens are also open every Wed and the last
Sun in the month, Apr–Sept 2–6.

Ascott is one of the great group of Rothschild houses built in the Vale of
Aylesbury in the 1870s and 80s. Of the others, Waddesdon Manor (qv.) now
belongs to the National Trust and is regularly open; Mentmore Towers
belongs to an Eastern religious group; Halton is an RAF officers' mess. If
Ascott is architecturally the least spectacular of them, it makes up for this
in the quality of its contents. There was a small farmhouse here when
Leopold de Rothschild bought the estate, but it has been engulfed in the
additions made by George Devey from 1874, and the further additions of
the late 1930s. The 1930s saw also a major redecoration of the interior for
Anthony de Rothschild, as a setting for his collections of fine furniture and
paintings, and oriental china. He bequeathed the house and the bulk of its
contents to the National Trust in 1950.

George Devey was one of the first English architects to devote himself to
reviving vernacular styles, in particular timber-framing. Ascott looks like
the world's largest 'stockbroker Tudor' villa; it is long, low, and contrivedly
picturesque, with a superb view over the Vale of Aylesbury. Devey was also
a pioneer of a more flexible approach to planning, hence the varied shapes
of the rooms and the informal way in which they flow out of one another.

The Hall, with its wooden pillars and stencilled decoration, was redecorated in the 1980s. It contains superb pieces of early Georgian furniture,
and important paintings, such as Stubbs' 'Five Mares' over the mantelpiece,
together with portraits by Hogarth, Romney and Reynolds. On the left is
the Dining Room, with more stencilled decoration, this time simulating
Dutch tile-work. The room is lined with major Dutch paintings of the 17C,
including fine works by Ostade, Steen, van der Heyden, Hobbema,
Berchem and Wouwermans.

Visitors retrace their steps through the Hall, along the Lobby, which has
fine pieces of 18C French furniture, and Francis Grant's paintings of four
of the Rothschild family hunting, of the 1850s. At the end is the Common
Room, which alone of the main rooms retains something of its Victorian
character; the heavy cornice is labelled with reminders of the Virtues most
popular then. Over the fireplace is a Tiepolo, 'The Ascent of the Virgin'.
There is more French furniture, and important Chinese porcelain in the
large niche to the right of the fireplace. Opening off this, at the far end of
the house, is the Drawing Room. Display cases contain superb Chinese
porcelain, in particular of the Ming dynasty, and the paintings include a
portrait by Lorenzo Lotto and a superb Madonna and Child by Andrea del
Sarto. The finest of the French furniture is here, notably the black lacquer
writing table by Baumhauer and Bernard van Risenburgh.

Back through the Common Room is the Library. Decorated in sober
English 17C style, with Doric pilasters on the oak bookcases, this has more
fine furniture, with chairs upholstered in gros point and petit point needlework. It is dominated by two superb paintings. Over the fireplace is Turner's
imaginary view of Cicero's villa at Tusculum; at the other end of the room

is Gainsborough's full-length portrait of the red-headed Mary, Duchess of Richmond. The Lobby has more French furniture and oriental porcelain. The collection of fine ceramics includes early pieces from the Han, T'ang and Sung dynasties, and a great many K'ang Hsi pieces of the *famille jaune, famille verte* and *famille noire*. The Ming dynasty pieces are outstanding, in particular the late san ts'ai (three colour) pieces.

The gardens at Ascott are spacious and provide a now rare example of Victorian gardening taste. The wide lawns are shaded by a great variety of specimen trees, and there are areas of formal gardening, with beds densely planted with annuals against backgrounds of topiary and dark-leaved shrubs in the style very popular in the mid 19C; among the topiary shapes is a sundial of box and yew with the words 'Light and shade by day but love always' in box. There are also fine sculptured fountains by the American Ralph Waldo Storey.

SB

Chenies Manor

4m east of Amersham to the north of A404 Amersham–Rickmansworth, M25 exit 18: Lt Col MacLeod Matthews, tel. 0494 762888. Open April–Oct Wed, Thur, Spring and Aug BH Mon 2–5. Refreshments.

Situated in the prosperous outer reaches of 'Metroland' to the north-west of London, Chenies is a substantial portion of a 15C and early-16C brick house which served for more than a century as the main country seat of the Russell family, Earls (and later Dukes) of Bedford. The name Chenies derives from the Cheyne family, who were lords of the manor until the mid 15C, and part of their house survives within the truncated west range of the present L-shaped building. But in 1526 the estate came by marriage to John, Lord Russell, later to become Lord Privy Seal to Henry VIII and 1st Earl of Bedford, and soon afterwards he added a range of lodgings to the south, which constitutes the larger part of the present house. He also remodelled the rest of the building, and the traveller John Leland remarked c 1540 that 'the old house of the Cheynes is so translated by my Lord Russell that little or nothing of it...remaineth untranslated', going on to say that 'the house is within diverse places richly painted with antique works of white and black'. Russell died in 1555 and in the following year his widow added a mortuary chapel close to his place of burial on the north side of the adjacent parish church; this has remained in the hands of the family, and now contains one of the finest collections of funerary sculpture in the country (the chapel, which was rebuilt in 1906, is rarely open to the public, but most of the monuments can be seen through a glazed screen).

The Russells continued to use Chenies as their main country seat until the time of the 4th Earl, who inherited in 1627 and subsequently enlarged Woburn Abbey, Bedfordshire (qv.) as his principal residence. Chenies was later reduced in size, and by the mid 18C it had become a farmhouse, with the north range demolished and the south range divided into five labourers' cottages. The house was restored by the 6th Duke of Bedford c 1802–15 and also in 1829, and in the 1840s the Duke improved the village, which survives largely intact as one of the most attractive and best-preserved estate villages in south-east England. The estate was finally sold by the present Duke in 1954, and the house was then bought by the present owners, who have embellished the interior with items from their own collection.

The original layout is uncertain. The Hall of the 15C house seems to have been divided into three storeys at some stage, and the west range now contains a low crenellated staircase tower between two blocks of different heights crowned with stepped gables of East Anglian appearance, creating a picturesque ensemble when seen from the east side; there is a vaulted medieval cellar nearby. To the south is the long lodgings range, with a splendid row of elaborately patterned chimneys on the south or garden side rising from a series of six gabled projections which housed closets and garderobes. Much of the original brickwork survives, with its characteristically early-16C criss-cross patterning of blue on red, but many of the windows, especially in the south range, have been replaced. Inside, most of the original decoration has disappeared. There is some white-painted early-17C panelling in one of the downstairs rooms, and in the room upstairs, known as Queen Elizabeth's Room (she stayed at Chenies on at least three occasions), there is a good collection of largely 17C tapestries and furniture, together with some oriental carpets. Early-16C stone fireplaces survive here and in an adjoining room, and some of the garderobes can also be seen. More memorable in many ways is the beautiful garden created by the present owner's wife; within it there is a ruined early-16C brick building, possibly originally a 'banqueting house' or the 'fair lodgings' mentioned by Leland, and there are also some 18C farm buildings including a wheel-house covering a medieval well.

GCT

Claydon House

Near Middle Claydon, $3\frac{1}{2}$m south west of Winslow: National Trust, tel. 0296 730349 or 730693. Open Apr–Oct Sat–Wed 1–5. Refreshments.

Grand though it is, the present house at Claydon is a mere fragment of a much larger building constructed by Ralph, Lord Verney, between 1759 and 1771. The Verneys owned land in Middle Claydon in the 15C, and in 1620 Sir Edmund Verney moved into a house which, though much reconstructed, still survives in part as the south or family wing. He was killed fighting on the Royalist side at the Battle of Edge Hill in the Civil War, but his son Ralph recovered the estate after the Restoration and was made a baronet by Charles II; the letters and papers of the two men were published by Lady Verney in 1892. Sir Ralph's grandson was made an earl (in the Irish peerage) in 1743, and it was his son who, fortified by the fortune of his wife, the daughter of a London merchant, began constructing a mammoth west-facing extension soon after inheriting the estate ten years later. He was motivated at least in part by political rivalry with the Temples of Stowe (qv.), not far away, but he did not possess their vast territorial resources, and a combination of extravagance and misguided investments forced him to flee the country to escape his creditors in 1784. Two-thirds of his new house was demolished by his daughter and heiress in 1792, a year after his death, and when she died in 1810 the estate passed to her half-sister and subsequently to a cousin, Sir Harry Calvert, who took the name Verney, and from whom the present Verneys of Claydon are descended. The house and grounds were given to the National Trust in 1956, but the family continue to live in the south wing (not open to the public).

The house stands isolated in the quiet countryside of mid Buckinghamshire, amid parkland fashioned by James Sanderson of Caversham (Oxon) in 1763–76 out of the fields of the former village. To the south is the medieval parish church, containing a superb monument of 1653 to Sir Edmund Verney, by the London statuary, Edward Marshall (cf. Aynhoe Park, Northants). The **west front** of the house, facing a lake and the usual number of sheep or cows, represents the south part of Lord Verney's new wing, the central part of which was a domed rotunda, as can be seen in a drawing displayed inside. But even without this the ashlar-faced façade is an acceptable composition in its own right, with two floors of roughly equal height and a pedimented centrepiece with a Venetian window on the round floor, its architraves enriched with blocks of stone in the manner of James Gibbs. The design was worked out by Lord Verney with the help of a London carpenter and builder, Luke Lightfoot, but in 1768, infuriated by Lightfoot's dilatory habits, he turned to the neo-Palladian amateur architect Sir Thomas Robinson of Rokeby, Durham (qv.), with whom he was on the board of the Ranelagh pleasure gardens at Chelsea. Lightfoot was dismissed, having been damned by Robinson as 'an ignorant knave, with no small spice of madness in his composition', and Robinson was given responsibility for completing the building. But by this time Lightfoot had already created one of the most extraordinary sequences of rooms to survive in any country house of the period, and it is these interiors which make a visit to Claydon especially rewarding.

The house is approached through the stable yard and entered through an inconspicuous doorway on the north side of the 18C wing. From here visitors proceed directly into the three spacious rooms which take up the whole of the ground floor: the North Hall (originally the eating room), the Saloon, and the Library (originally the drawing room). These admirably illustrate the contrasts between the Palladian, Rococo and neo-classical tastes. Lightfoot said that the Rococo decoration of the **North Hall** was 'such a Work as the World never saw', and this is a judgment from which it is difficult to dissent. Mirrors, doorcases, and overmantel are all adorned with bizarre and exuberant concoctions of classical cherubs, Chinese ho-ho birds and naturalistic garlands, carved in wood (not plaster, contrary to first appearances). The **Saloon** is equally richly embellished, with a particularly fine plaster ceiling by Joseph Rose, a marble chimneypiece by Thomas Carter and 'tabernacle frames' to the doors, but here the decoration is fundamentally Palladian in character; the 17C family portraits include works by, or attributed to, Mytens (Sir Francis Verney, a pirate), Van Dyck (Sir Edmund Verney in military costume, and Lady Verney) and Lely. The Library is more sparsely decorated, with a neo-classical ceiling by Rose (the bookcases were introduced in the 1860s; note the steps made out of pieces of left-over Rococo carving), and there is more plasterwork by Rose in a similar vein in the top-lit **Staircase Hall**. Here the real pièce de résistance is the exquisitely beautiful staircase of inlaid wood, with its swirly iron balustrade containing representations, in iron, of husks and ears of corn: a triumph both of craftsmanship and of creative stylisation. Next to this is the Pink Parlour, with more Rococo decoration by Lightfoot.

Because of the delicate condition of the main stairs, visitors ascend by a modern staircase to the first floor. Here again the hand of Lightfoot is much in evidence, especially in the Batty Langley-ish Gothic Room and, above all, in the **Chinese Room**, perhaps the most engagingly frivolous example of 18C chinoiserie interior decoration to survive in an English country house; the bamboo furniture was made in Canton c 1800. A very different mood is conjured up in two adjoining rooms devoted to the memory of the great Victorian nursing reformer Florence Nightingale, sister of Parthenope, Lady Verney, and a frequent visitor to the house. Her bedroom survives largely as she left it, and mememtoes of her life and work are displayed in a room next door.

GCT

Cliveden House

3m north of Maidenhead on B476 Taplow–Bourne End: National Trust, tel. 0268 605069. Open Apr–Oct Thur, Sun 3–6. Refreshments.

Ever since the late 17C, Cliveden has been a comfortable out-of-town residence or villa rather than the centre of a great landed estate. The house stands on an eminence overlooking the River Thames, commanding a spectacular vista which reminded John Evelyn of Frascati in Italy when he to Cliveden in 1679. The owner at that time was the notorious 2nd Duke of Buckingham, a former member of Charles II's CABAL ministry, and it was he who built the first house on the site to the designs of William Winde and laid out the 'platform' or parterre to the south. In 1696 the estate was bought by the 1st Earl of Orkney, a close associate of William III and subsequently a general in the Duke of Marlborough's army. He lowered the height of the house and in 1706 employed Thomas Archer to add wings enclosing a French-style open courtyard on the north or entrance side—an arrangement which still exists, despite later rebuildings. He also extended the pleasure grounds with the advice of Charles Bridgeman and brought in Giacomo Leoni in the 1720s to design two still-extant garden buildings, the Octagon Temple and the Blenheim Pavilion.

The house was subsequently leased to Frederick, Prince of Wales, in whose honour the patriotic song 'Rule, Britannia' was performed for the first time on the parterre in 1740. In 1795 the main block was burnt down and remained derelict until 1824, when the estate was sold to Sir George Warrender, a notorious gourmand who employed William Burn to build a new house on the site. This was also destroyed by fire just after being sold in 1849 to the Whig grandee, the 2nd Duke of Sutherland, whose wife was one of Queen Victoria's closest friends. He lost no time in replacing it with the present house designed in 1850–51 by Charles Barry, the architect par excellence to the Whig aristocracy, and in 1861 he called in Henry Clutton to build a new stable block, crowned by a prominent clock tower, to the west of the entrance Courtyard. The house was later bought by Sutherland's son-in-law, the 1st Duke of Westminster, and he carried out further internal alterations (not visible to visitors) in the neo-Tudor style currently in vogue in his Mayfair estate in London, as well as building some of the picturesque estate cottages, designed by George Devey, which are dotted around the grounds.

The man who was most responsible for creating Cliveden in its present guise was the American-born millionaire, William Waldorf Astor (cf. Hever Castle, Kent). He bought the estate in 1893 and immediately set about remodelling the main interiors, sweeping away Barry's rooms and also

The south front of Cliveden, designed by Charles Barry (1850–51) showing a fragment of balustrade from the Villa Borghese, Rome, installed by W.W. Astor

embellishing the gardens in the Italianate style of which he had become enamoured while serving as US minister in Rome. He became the 1st Lord Astor in 1917, having handed over the house as a wedding present in 1906 to his son and his American wife, Nancy; she later became the first female Member of Parliament, and in the 1920s and 1930s the house was one of the best-known venues for political hospitality. The house and grounds were given to the National Trust in 1942, but the Astors continued to live here until 1966. The house was subsequently used by Stanford University as an overseas study centre, but in 1984 the lease was acquired by Blakeney Hotels, who have turned it into one of England's most luxurious country-house hotels—a singularly appropriate use for a building whose main function has always been to entertain the rich and famous. With the help of the decorator Rupert Lord the rooms have been rescued from their former shabbiness, and they now successfully recreate the glamour of Cliveden in its early-20C heyday.

Most visitors come to Cliveden to see the spectacular gardens, in which every style of gardening from the French-influenced formality of the late 17C to the eclecticism of the 20C can be enjoyed. The house, of brick rendered with cement, is first seen at the end of a formal avenue laid out in the early 18C, and closer inspection reveals that it is a beautifully proportioned essay in the revived Italian Renaissance style of which Barry was a master, the closest models being the villas of 16C Genoa. The Italian inspiration is most evident on the south or garden side, where the late-17C brick terrace still survives, overlooking the parterre, with a low wall of 1618–89 punctuated by balustrades and statues in front, brought by the 1st Lord Astor from the Villa Borghese in Rome.

After such a prelude the interior may at first seem something of a disappointment, especially since only an handful of rooms on the ground floor are shown. The dark wood-panelled Hall, created by F.L. Pearson (son of the famous Victorian church architect) for the 1st Lord Astor out of three former rooms, was and still is used as a living room, and opens out to the main staircase with wooden figures of personages in the history of Cliveden (by W.S. Frith) on the newel posts; there are also portraits of several past owners on the walls, notably Sargent's striking portrait of Nancy Astor which hangs next to the heavy early-16C Burgundian stone chimneypiece bought for the room. The Brussels tapestries of the 'Blenheim' series (cf. Blenheim Palace, Oxon) were made for the house c 1715. Next comes the Library, also by Pearson and panelled with South African wood (Nancy Astor compared it to being inside a cigar box), and the main hotel Dining Room, formerly a drawing room. The last and most impressive room to be seen is the original Dining Room, created by the Parisian decorator Allard for the 1st Lord Astor, using Rococo boiseries of c 1750 by Nicholas Pineau from the Château d'Asnières, near Paris, once the home of Madame de Pompadour.

GCT

Dorney Court

2m west of Eton on B3026 Eton–Maidenhead, M4 exit 7: Mr & Mrs Peregrine Palmer, tel. 0628 604638. Open Easter weekend, May, Sun and BH Mon; June–Sept Sun–Tues 2–5.30. Refreshments.

Though close to Windsor and the M4, Dorney Court stands in an unspoiled landscape of flat Thames-side meadows. Along with the neighbouring parish church, it forms part of an almost undisturbed manorial complex, and, most unusually in the Home Counties, it has been the residence of the same family since the early 17C. But the oldest parts of the house date back to the 15C, when the manor belonged to the Scott and Kestwold families; and the Hall and east cross-wing which form the core of the present building already existed when the estate was sold in 1537 to a London grocer and former Lord Mayor, Sir William Gerrard, whose family is commemorated by a monument of 1607 in the church. His daughter married Sir James Palmer, a Gentleman of the Bedchamber to James I (and also a talented miniature painter), and the Palmers have been owners of Dorney since 1629. The family were devoted adherents of the Stuarts in the 17C, which led to the house being pillaged by Parliamentary troops during the Civil War and possibly reduced in size. There were further alterations in the early 18C and again, after a long period of neglect, in the 1840s. The gardens were laid out by Charles Palmer, the present owner's grandfather, who inherited in 1895; he also modified the façades, using materials brought in from demolished 16C houses elsewhere, and introduced 16C panelling and fireplaces into some of the rooms. They now make an attractive setting for the collections of furniture and pictures accumulated by the family over the last 400 years.

The original entrance to the house seems to have been from the south, but the main front now faces east and displays an abundance of old red brick and weathered timbers. These features were revealed in the early 20C after being hidden for nearly 200 years by a classical façade; the carved bargeboards may well be original 15C or early-16C work, but the porch, window frames and moulded chimneystacks (on the original bases) are early-20C reconstructions. Around the corner to the left is the much-rebuilt front of the early-16C hall, while on the north side, to the right of the present entrance, there are two gables with 15C or early-16C close studding. Further west there is a 17C brewhouse and granary, and, on the other side of a narrow lane, the attractively unrestored brick-towered parish church with its box pews and family monuments.

The first rooms to be seen are the comfortably furnished Parlour and the bedroom or Great Chamber above, with its barrel ceiling, neither of them significantly altered since the late 16C or early 17C, when the panelling was introduced. A passage from the Great Chamber leads to the gallery over the Hall screen, hung with portraits of Sir James Palmer—the first of the family to live at Dorney—and also of seven Turks whose pictures were brought back from Constantinople in the late 17C by a younger son, Sir Roger Palmer, Lord Castlemaine, husband of one of Charles II's most notorious mistresses. The Hall itself, reached by a back staircase, is by far the most impressive room in the house; it still retains its original arch-braced 15C roof, but the 15C stone chimneypiece and early-16C linenfold panelling (originally in Faversham Abbey, Kent), were installed in the early 20C. They contribute to the atmosphere of mellow age, as do the portraits, including representations of the Earl and Countess of Castlemaine, attributed to Lely, over the fireplace; the stone pineapple commemorates the growing of the first pineapple in England at Dorney. The tour ends in the early-20C neo-Georgian Dining Room, created within an early-16C cross-wing.

GCT

Fawley Court

1m north of Henley-on-Thames on A4155 Henley–Marlow: the Marian Fathers. Open Mar–Oct Wed, Thur, Sun 2–5 (not Easter or Whit weeks). Refreshments July–Aug.

Fawley Court is a substantial and well-proportioned red-brick house built in 1684–90 on the banks of the River Thames by William Freeman, a London merchant with interests in the sugar plantations of the West Indies; despite persistent attempts to attribute it to Sir Christopher Wren, the architect is in fact unknown. The grounds were laid out in the 1720s by William Freeman's nephew and successor John Freeman, an East Indian merchant who became an enthusiastic virtuoso and amateur architect. They have since been completely refashioned, but a sham ruin of flint, designed by Freeman to house some of the celebrated Arundel Marbles (since dispersed), still survives among the later shrubberies to the south of the house; it was erected before 1732, and thus ranks as one of the first Gothic follies in England. In 1750 Freeman also designed a formidable neo-classical mausoleum next to the parish church of Fawley, a mile or so away to the north west.

The interior of the house remained largely untouched until 1770–71, when John Freeman's son, Sambrooke, employed James Wyatt and others to redecorate the main downstairs rooms in the fashionable neo-classical style; he also employed 'Capability' Brown to landscape the gardens and as part of the project Wyatt designed the pretty stuccoed temple on an island in the Thames (not open to the public, but visible from the towpath); it now marks the starting point of the Henley Regatta course and contains the first Etruscan-style interior in England. Freeman's son, Strickland, made further alterations, and drastic changes were made again in the late 19C by William Mackenzie, a railway director and son of a Scottish banker who bought the estate in 1853. These changes included refacing the formerly stucco-clad walls in a peculiarly harsh red brick, inserting plate-glass windows, adding a wing to the north side of the house and cutting the tree-lined canal which leads from the garden front to the river. In 1953 the house was sold to the Marian Fathers from Poland, who installed an interesting collection of historical memorabilia from their native country and built a Roman Catholic church in the grounds. Having been a boarding school for some time, the house is now run as a guest-house.

Despite all these changes, the house is still structurally the one built by William Freeman in the 1680s. The recessed central portion, entered through an Ionic colonnade of c 1799, contains the Hall and Saloon, the latter containing a superb plaster ceiling dated 1690—the only part of the original interior decoration to survive—and Luca Giordano's 'Delivery of St Peter from Gaol'. The other reception rooms, created out of the original 'apartments' in 1770–71, were placed on either side of this central axis, with the more 'public' rooms to the south. The Library was designed by Wyatt as the 'eating room', but the Ionic colonnade marking the sideboard recess was not introduced until 1804, when Joseph Alcott was paid for the scagliola shafts; the inlaid work in the bookcases, brought from elsewhere in the house, was carried out by Anne Seymour Damer, a friend of Horace Walpole. The former drawing room, next door, still retains its excellent plaster ceiling by Wyatt, but the space is now largely given over to cases containing Polish documents, including a legal code of 1506. Downstairs, in the former cellars, there is a collection of Polish armour and objects connected with the Polish forces who fought on the side of the Allies in the Second World War.

GCT

Hughenden Manor

1½m north of High Wycombe on A4128 Wycombe–Great Missenden: National Trust, tel. 0494 532580. Open March Sat, Sun 2–6; Apr–Oct Wed–Sat 2–6, Sun 12–6.

Hughenden is unusual among country houses in being associated almost exclusively with one man: the 19C statesman Benjamin Disraeli, 1st (and only) Earl of Beaconsfield, whose career was aptly described by Queen Victoria as 'one of the most remarkable in the annals of the Empire'. Disraeli's forbears were Sephardic Jews but his father, a successful writer, ceased to practise Judaism and settled down as a country squire at Braden-ham, a few miles away from Hughenden. Benjamin, a successful novelist but also an ambitious Tory politician, bought Hughenden from the antiquary John Norris with the help of loans from his political crony Lord George Bentinck in 1848. Two years earlier he had led the opposition in Parliament to the repeal of the Corn Laws and thereby engineered the downfall of Sir Robert Peel, in whose footsteps he eventually followed as leader of the Conservative Party and Prime Minister. Beautifully situated among the Chiltern beechwoods, but not far from London, Hughenden remained Disraeli's favourite residence, embodying his romantic ideal of an England in which a benevolent squirearchy still held sway. When he died in 1881 the house and estate went to his nephew, and in 1937 they were acquired by Mr Abbey, the founder of the Disraeli Society which transferred them to the National Trust in 1947.

When Disraeli bought it in 1848, the house was a plain stuccoed Georgian building of no great historical or architectural interest, to which the owner had made internal alterations in an unpretentious Tudor-Gothic style. More internal alterations were carried out in the same spirit in 1852, and in 1862 Disraeli employed Edward Buckton Lamb, one of the more eccentric of Victorian architects, to add red brick embellishments in an eclectic style which does not fit into any obvious category, though it was apparently intended to convey an 'Old English' message in accordance with Disraeli's political beliefs. Lamb also advised on the layout of the attractive formal gardens to the south of the house, but he hardly touched the interior, which still has an early-Victorian air. In 1874 Arthur Blomfield carried out a thorough remodelling of the parish church in the park, and it is there, against the east wall, that Disraeli is buried.

The main interest of Hughenden lies in its collection of Disraeli memorabilia, but the house can also be enjoyed as a relatively unpretentious country gentleman's residence of the mid 19C. Though close to High Wycombe, the setting remains unspoiled, and it is easy for the visitor to recapture the allure of Disraeli's rural idyll. Inside, there is little obvious logic in the arrangement of the low ceilinged rooms on the ground floor, some of which were altered after Disraeli's death by his nephew; this was clearly a house designed for comfort and not for show. The most attractive rooms are the Library, with a portrait of the statesman by Sir Francis Grant over the late-18C fireplace, and the Drawing Room, entered through a screen of Gothic arches and presided over by a portrait of Disraeli's statuesque wife (over the fireplace—to the left is the philosopher Thomas Hobbes); both these rooms were altered and refurnished after Disraeli's death. His fascinating political career can be followed through the exhibits in the Disraeli Room (note especially the drawings of him as a young man, in dandyish attire), and there are portraits of him as Prime Minister and of a rather sour-looking Queen Victoria (a copy of one by H. von Angeli at Windsor Castle) in the dark, north-facing Dining Room. The first floor is reached by a staircase hung with portraits of his political associates, and contains his Study, largely untouched since his death, along with a series of former bedrooms which are gradually being restored to their late-19C state; in one of these, drawings of the house before and after its remodelling by E.B. Lamb are displayed.

GCT

Nether Winchendon House

6m south west of Aylesbury, at Lower Winchendon, to north of A418 Aylesbury–Thame: R.V. Spencer Bernard, Esq, tel. 0353 290101. Open May–Aug Thur, BH weekends 2.30–5.30. Guided tours.

In the Middle Ages Nether Winchendon was part of the holdings of Notley Abbey, an obscure Augustinian house on the borders of Buckinghamshire and Oxfordshire. Here the monks built a house or grange of timber and stone, which was leased out in 1527 to one of Henry VIII's civil servants, Sir John Daunce. He carried out major alterations, which can still be seen, but the property was sold after the Reformation and in 1559 it was bought by a London merchant, William Goodwin, who probably built the west, or office, wing. The house later passed by marriage to the Tyringham family, and in 1771 it was inherited by a cousin, Sir Francis Bernard, the last British Governor of Massachusetts in North America. He instructed his heirs to sell the estate, but these plans were thwarted by his younger son, Scrope Bernard, a politician who had attached his fortunes to those of the Temples of Stowe (qv.) and their extensive Buckinghamshire connection. He bought out the interests of his elder brothers and, starting in 1790, refaced the house in the Gothic style to his own designs, with the help of competent local craftsmen; he then perversely went off to live at Little Kimble, a few miles away. His son returned to Nether Winchendon, and his descendants still live here today, the present owner having recently carried out major restoration work.

From the outside the low, rambling building looks much as Jane Austen's Catherine Morland first imagined Northanger Abbey in the novel of the same name, written in 1803 while Scrope Bernard was in the throes of the rebuilding. An avenue leads from the attractive village with its pleasantly unrestored church to a screen of Gothic arches in front of the entrance courtyard, with a forest of mainly neo-Tudor chimneys visible over the L-shaped house behind. Closer inspection reveals that most of the detail dates from Scrope Bernard's time, but there is some original work, including some early-16C timber-framing, to be seen on the east (parlour) side of the hall range; a second Gothic screen, linking this to the detached north-east tower (1810–12), was demolished in 1956. The highly picturesque garden front also dates mainly from Scrope Bernard's rebuilding, but the presence of the original hall is indicated by the two large pointed windows in the centre.

The interior conveys a sense of comfortable and unpretentious continuity. The elongated passage-like Entrance Hall, built by Scrope Bernard in front of the original hall range, contains portraits of the Tyringhams and Bernards, and leads into the Drawing Room (originally Sir John Daunce's parlour). This is notable above all for its linenfold panelling, whitened c 1660, and for the precocious Renaissance decoration of the carved oak frieze, clearly influenced by the work of Henry VIII's Italian-inspired craftsmen; the chimneypiece dates from the mid to late 17C, and there is also a notable upholstered settee and day-bed of about the same date. The Hall has been much altered since the 16C, and the plaster 'vault' was put in by Scrope Bernard in 1805; the 16C panelling and chimneypiece may have been brought in from Eythrope, a Buckinghamshire house demolished in 1810–11, and there are early-16C manorial records on display, along with 18C portraits, including one by Romney of Scrope Bernard's elder brother, Sir Thomas Bernard. But the most interesting work of art in the room, and indeed in the house, is a remarkable tapestry of c 1545 showing Henry VIII seated in majesty and exhorting a group of clergy and courtiers (including Lord Russell of Chenies, qv.) to 'preach the Gospel to all creatures'; this is surrounded by a border of Renaissance-inspired flowers, arabesques and cherubs.

GCT

Stowe

4m north of Buckingham: Stowe School, tel. 0280 813650 (gardens: National Trust, tel. 0280 822850). House usually open daily in Easter holidays and early July–early Sept 2–5; gardens also Mon, Wed, Fri mid Apr–late June and early Sept–late Oct and daily during school holidays (not Christmas or Good Fri) 10–6 (10–5 winter). Refreshments.

This magnificent house, one of the largest in England, presides over what is historically the most important of all English landscape gardens. The estate was acquired in the 16C by the Temple family, whose wealth, like that of many landed families in the south Midlands, derived mainly from sheep farming, and a new house was constructed in 1678–83 by Sir Richard Temple, the 3rd Baronet. His son, a soldier and Whig politician, was made Viscount Cobham in 1718, but was deprived of his regiment by Sir Robert Walpole in 1733 and became a leader of the 'Patriot' opposition, whose luminaries also included the elder Pitt and the Lytteltons of Hagley, West Midlands (qv.). Helped by his marriage to the heiress of a rich London brewer in 1715, Cobham began expanding the gardens to the designs of Charles Bridgeman, and he also called in his fellow-Whig, Sir John Vanbrugh, to make additions to the house and to design some of the garden buildings c 1719–26. Between 1733 and 1750, the house was further enlarged on the garden side; meanwhile, William Kent master-minded an eastward extension of the gardens in the 1730s, creating in the process an arcadian landscape (the Elysian Fields), dotted with ornamental buildings which made punning allusion to the family's name and motto ('Templa Quam Dilecta'—'How lovely are thy temples'), while at the same time conveying arcane political and patriotic messages. A further expansion (the Grecian Valley) was undertaken by Lord Cobham himself shortly before his death in 1749, probably with the help of the head gardener Lancelot 'Capability' Brown, then at the threshold of his career.

Lord Cobham's successor was his nephew, Sir Richard Grenville of Wotton Underwood, who, as Lord Temple, 'naturalised' Bridgeman's layout of the west part of the gardens and, soon afterwards, remodelled the interior and exterior of the house, work finishing in 1777. The designer of the new south front, and possibly also of the north, was his kinsman and political crony Thomas Pitt, Lord Camelford, an enthusiast for neo-classical architecture. However, the design of the south front, which took 20 years to finalise, owed much to an earlier scheme by Robert Adam. Temple was succeeded by his nephew, who became Marquess of Buckingham in 1784. He completed the decoration of the interior, and also started to build up a famous collection of pictures and manuscripts. The family's prestige and its notorious pride reached their apogee in his time and in that of his son, who was made Duke of Buckingham and Chandos, but nemesis struck when the 2nd Duke fell massively into debt in 1848. This led to the dispersal of the collection, but it ensured that house and gardens remained virtually unaltered. The agricultural depression of the late 19C wreaked further havoc upon the family finances, and in 1921 Lady Kinloss, daughter of the 3rd and last Duke, sold the house and gardens as the site for a public school, established two years later. The school still owns and occupies the house, but in 1989 the grounds were given to the National Trust, which is currently (1993) engaged on a major restoration programme.

The approach to Stowe reflects the overweening self-confidence of the Temples and Grenvilles in their 18C heyday, when half of Buckinghamshire revolved in their orbit. A grand approach from Buckingham was laid out in the 1770s or 1780s, culminating in a triumphal arch (designed by Pitt in 1765) which closes the southern vista from the house, but the present approach is from the west, and brings visitors past a pair of pavilions designed by James Gibbs c 1728 (but remodelled by Giambattista Borra, one of Temple's favourite architects, in 1758) to the north or **entrance front**. This consists of a massive main block, basically the house of the 1720s, with a portico, probably by Vanbrugh facing an equestrian statue of George I (by Van Nost 1727), whose succession in 1714 did so much for the Whigs; curved colonnades of the early 1770s stretch forward to enfold guests and, more prosaically, hide the service courtyards.

Visitors can choose to explore either the house or the gardens first. If they opt for the house, they enter through the north portico. The interiors are now bereft of their lavish furnishings, but they are well kept by the school, and all the main reception rooms are shown to visitors. The tour starts in the **North Hall**, a neo-Palladian room of the 1730s with a coved ceiling adorned with 'grotesques' by Kent, and two excellent relief sculptures including Christopher Veyrier's 'Family of Darius before Alexander' c 1680: on the east wall). From here visitors proceed to the state rooms on the south or garden front. These huge, largely empty rooms were decorated in the time of the 1st Marquess of Buckingham and reflect the neo-classical tastes he imbued on his Grand Tour in 1774. Most striking are the Library of 1801, still used for its original purpose; the Music Room, decorated in the Pompeian-style by the Italian-born Vincenzo Valdré, an architect much employed by the family; the magnificent elliptical **Saloon**—one of the finest (and least-known) neo-classical rooms in England—with its domed roof, scagliola columns and frieze of a Roman triumph, probably by Valdré; and the Temple Room (the original drawing room), with exquisite plasterwork of 1776 on the ceiling. The last room to be seen is the State Dining Room, built as a gallery in the 1740s and still retaining some of its neo-Palladian decoration. A broad flight of steps (by Borra1754) leads down from the massive Corinthian south portico to the gardens, and from here it is possible to see the noble **south front**, its long expanse of ashlar walling broken up into three main units drawn together by the Ionic order running along the façade at first-floor level; a composition which is hard to match in England for monumental dignity and classical poise.

There are more superb 18C buildings in the **gardens**. From the south portico, Pitt's Corinthian Arch can be seen on the horizon, on the opposite side of the lake formed by Bridgeman, but 'naturalised' by Lord Temple in the 1750s; Vanbrugh's Rotondo stands alone on a lawn to the west of the vista, the least altered garden building to survive from the Bridgeman phase, and on the south side of the lake, just inside the ha-ha, are Kent's Temple of Venus (1732) and Gibbs's ruined Temple of Friendship (1739), dedicated to Lord Cobham's political associates. To the east of the central axis are the **Elysian Fields**, formed by Kent in a valley overlooked by the medieval church, which was allowed to survive after the former village had vanished. Visitors from the house can approach this secret landscape via the circular Temple of Ancient Virtue (c 1734), both a celebration of the glory of ancient Rome, with which Whigs like Cobham liked to identify, and a political jibe against the Walpole administration whose 'modern virtue' was represented by a ruined arch (now vanished). From here there is a vista across the valley to the Temple of British Worthies (1735), containing the busts of Whig heroes like John Hampden and John Locke in a semicircular exedra, while further south is a Palladian bridge, built in

The south (garden) front of Stowe

1738 in imitation of that at Wilton, Wiltshire (qv.). The ground to the east of the Elysian Fields was originally laid out as a *ferme ornée* with more temples, including a triangular one in the Gothic style, originally called the Temple of Liberty, by James Gibbs; to the north of this, beyond the Queen's Temple, is the **Grecian Valley** with its magnificent Temple of Concord and Victory (currently being restored) which serves as a suitably splendid finale to a tour of the gardens.

GCT

Waddesdon Manor

Waddesdon village, 6m from Aylesbury on the A41: National Trust, tel. 0296 651211. Opening times not available at time of writing. Refreshments.

Waddesdon is extraordinary; a huge mock-château on a hilltop, with sumptuous interiors and one of the best collections of French furniture and decorative arts in the world. For those with a taste for the opulent it is a tremendous experience.

It was created by Baron Ferdinand de Rothschild (1839–98). He was born into the Austrian branch of the great banking family, but never worked seriously in the business. At the age of 21 he went to visit his English cousins, fell in love with the country, and settled here. He married his English cousin Evelina in 1865, but she died 18 months later in childbirth. Baron Ferdinand was desolate, and turned to collecting works of art to assuage his loss. In 1874 he bought the Waddesdon and Winchendon estates from the Duke of Marlborough. There was a sharp, bare hill, rising above Waddesdon village. The whole top of it was levelled to provide a site for the house, and a steam tramway was built to carry materials; the main building campaign went on until c 1880. Baron Ferdinand chose a French architect, Gabriel-Hippolyte Destailleur, to build him a house in the French style, doubtless to complement his collections, which from the first had a strong bias towards 17C and 18C France. He also hired a French landscape gardener, Lainé, and had hundreds of fully-grown trees planted.

Baron Ferdinand went on collecting all his life. He never married again; his sister Miss Alice acted as hostess and housekeeper for him, and she succeeded him here on his death in 1898. She added the arms and armour, and most of the present Renaissance collections. On her death in 1922, she left Waddesdon to her great-nephew, James de Rothschild, one of the French branch of the family. James inherited fine pictures and furniture from his father, and brought them here also. On his death in 1957, he left the house, grounds and collections to the National Trust.

The drive leads from Waddesdon village, curving up the steep wooded hillside. The house only appears at the last moment, in a tremendous *coup de théâtre*; one rounds a corner by a marble fountain, and there are 200 yards of straight drive, lawns on either side, and the great yellow stone château, with its intricate skyline, immense dormers and chimneys jostling with conical tower roofs: a compendium of French domestic architecture from c 1500 to 1700. There are fairly direct architectural quotations from Blois, Chambord, and Azay-le-Rideau, and doubtless others besides. The main block is broadly symmetrical, but by 1889 Baron Ferdinand found that he needed more space for his friends and his collections, and the Morning Room wing on the right was added, in a rather more Gothic manner.

Although the style of the exterior is eclectically French, the interior relates much more specifically to the 18C, in particular the reign of Louis XV (1715–74). The visitor goes under the generous *porte-cochère*, into a fairly modest oval hall. To the left is the **East Gallery**. It is dominated by two immense views of Venice by Guardi (c 1755), the largest works he ever painted. The chimney and panelling, like much else in the house, are of c 1740 and came from Paris. The seating furniture is Louis XV, and the small hearth-rug is the first of many in the house from the Royal Savonnerie factory. Next is the **Breakfast Room**; the beautifully carved panelling here and in another two rooms came from the house of the Marèchal-Duc de Richelieu (great-nephew to the Cardinal).

From here the visitor turns right into the **Conservatory**, on the garden front. This opens into an ante-room; an orchestra used to play here during dinners, and the marble fountains were used as wine-coolers. A wide arch opens into the **Dining Room**. The huge mirror-frames of 1731 come from the Hôtel de Villars in Paris, and the Beauvais tapestries are from the 'Noble Pastorale' series designed by Boucher. The carpet is Aubusson, and there is more Meissen and Viennese china on the table and side-tables.

The **Red Drawing Room** is grander still; the ceiling painting of Hercules arriving at Olympus is of 1725, by Jacob de Wit. Here as in other rooms, Baron Ferdinand combined two of his particular enthusiasms, French furniture and English portraits, to great effect; the room boasts a Reynolds and three Gainsboroughs. The chairs are covered in Beauvais tapestry, and the magnificent chests-of-drawers by Riesener were made for Versailles. The great carpet is Savonnerie, woven in 1683 for Louis XIV, with his personal emblem, the head of Apollo, in the middle. The Grey Drawing Room, next, has more the mood of the private apartments at Versailles, with beautiful Rococo panelling from c 1740. Three great full-length portraits by Reynolds look splendid against it, and there are major pieces of furniture by great ébénistes like Baumhauer, Cressent, and Carlin, and Sèvres porcelain.

The visitor then passes into the **West Gallery** (on the entrance side, symmetrical with the East Gallery). This has more 18C panelling, with French tapestries set into it, and another array of furniture including pieces by Cressent, Riesener, Dubois, and small French paintings including two by Watteau. The **Small Library** has more French panelling, and paintings by Lancret, Pater and Guardi, and a collection of Meissen figures. The visitor passes the foot of one of the spiral staircases (inspired by the one at Blois), to reach the Baron's Room. Baron Ferdinand surrounded himself here with portraits of English beauties by Romney, Reynolds and Gainsborough. The furniture here is of amazing quality, with five royal pieces by Riesener, but the room is dominated by the great desk (maker unknown) presented to Beaumarchais by a group of his friends. There is also Sèvres, Meissen and Chinese celadon porcelain. This room leads into the **Tower Drawing Room**, octagonal to fit inside a round tower. This has Louis XVI panelling, two more pieces made for the French royal family by Riesener and a carpet made for the royal gallery in the chapel at Versailles. The cabinets contain an array of Sèvres porcelain, jewelled boxes and objets d'art, made in France and Germany in the 18C. The tour returns via the Baron's Room to the West Hall.

By this point, the dazed visitor may be thinking that Waddesdon could not possibly get any more magnificent, but here is the **Morning Room**, the largest and most richly furnished room in the house. There are great paintings by Rubens, de Hooch, Cuyp, Ter Borch, Metsu, Gainsborough, Reynolds and others. The best pieces of furniture are the desk made by Riesener for the future Louis XVIII, the writing table made for Louis XVI and the gigantic drop-front desk made by Dubois and Goyer, perhaps for Catherine the Great, and there are four 18C Savonnerie carpets. There is more Sèvres and oriental porcelain, and a large collection of fine-bound books, of the 17C and 18C.

The first floor rooms will not re-open until 1995, and some of the contents may have been re-arranged by then. The tour will proceed up the West Stairs; the **West Wing** rooms contain various collections, testifying to the immense range of Baron Ferdinand and Miss Alice's interests. The Blue Room has collections of prints, lace, buttons, prints and Sèvres biscuit (unglazed china) figures. The Long Room has collections of pottery, silver toys, glassware, costumes and embroideries from Europe, Russia and the Middle East. The Drawings Room has Aubusson tapestries and French, German and Italian drawings. The Rothschild Corner contains family memorabilia. The Music Room has Louis XV furniture, English 18C portraits, and various early musical instruments. The Blue Sèvres Room is round (over the Tower Drawing Room); the display cases house a great Sèvres dessert service of over 100 pieces made in 1767 for the Razumovski family. The Fans Corridor has fans and jewelled boxes.

There is a good deal more yet; the Pastime Room has collections of toys and hunting pictures. The State Bedroom has more 18C panelling and furniture, and a great deal more Sèvres and Meissen porcelain, and another Savonnerie carpet made in 1681 for the Louvre. The Green Boudoir, over the corridor, has perhaps the finest of the 18C French panelling in the house and a very early Savonnerie carpet (1650). The Bedroom Corridor runs along the centre of the first floor, and has Dutch and French paintings, and great Brussels tapestries representing the seasons. The Central Lobby, the

Fountain Bathroom, the Fountain Bedroom, and the Portico Bedroom have more fine paintings, furniture, and china.

East of the main block is the **Bachelor's Wing**. The Low White Room has Louis XVI panelling and furniture, and paintings by Boucher and Guardi. Thereafter, this wing houses late Gothic and Renaissance objects. Waddesdon used to have an even richer collection in this area, but Baron Ferdinand left most of it to the British Museum, which is today housed in the Waddesdon Room there. The collections here today were accumulated by Miss Alice and Baron Edmond de Rothschild. The Armoury has swords, armour, firearms, embroideries and pottery. The Smoking Room has very large collections of 15C and 16C paintings, jewellery, objets d'art, miniatures, maiolica, silverware, glassware and enamels. The Billiard Room is the only one at Waddesdon to be decorated in 16C style. There is a varied collection of furniture, illuminated manuscripts, 16C walnut panelling, and another of the Savonnerie carpets woven for the Grande Galerie of the Louvre.

Outside, there are formal **gardens** below the house, and a short walk leads to the Louis XV-style aviary, still well-populated with birds of various species. The lush, wooded grounds with their fine statuary continue the tone set inside the house, of serene splendour resting on bottomless wealth.

SB

West Wycombe Park

2½m west of High Wycombe on A40 High Wycombe–Oxford: National Trust, tel. 0494 524411. Open June–Aug Sun–Thur 2–6. Gardens also Sun, Wed, BH Mon Apr–May 2–6. Guided tours.

This large and fascinating house is a monument to one man's life-long obsession with the art and architecture of classical antiquity. Sir Francis Dashwood inherited the West Wycombe estate in 1724, at the age of 16, from his father, a rich merchant who had invested some of his fortune made out of trade with Asia in building a new house of brick; this is the nucleus of the present building. Encouraged by his uncle and guardian John Fane (later Earl of Westmorland), the builder of the neo-Palladian Mereworth Castle (Kent), Sir Francis travelled extensively on the Continent, and in 1733 became one of the founders of the Society of Dilettante, in which scholarship and conviviality were mixed in equal measure. He began to create a new garden setting in the 1730s, possibly to the designs of a Frenchman, Morise Lewes Jolivet; this was largely completed by 1739, but the remodelling of the house did not begin until 1748, continuing in a piecemeal fashion until 1771. The gardens were further improved in 1770–82 by Thomas Cook, a pupil of 'Capability' Brown, and Nicholas Revett, who had been involved in the latter stages of the remodelling of the house, and since then both the house and its setting have remained largely unchanged. In 1762 Dashwood, who was currently serving as a not very successful Chancellor of the Exchequer, inherited the title of Lord le Despencer from his uncle. When he died in 1781 the estates, but not the title, went to his half-brother, and in 1944 the house and park were given to the National Trust by his descendant, Sir John Dashwood, the 10th Baronet, whose son Sir Francis Dashwood lives here now as tenant of the Trust.

In addition to the house and grounds, Sir Francis Dashwood left his imprint on the surroundings. He was responsible for realigning the main road (the present A40) and, in 1761–63, for rebuilding the parish church on the hill to the north, with its strange golden ball at the top of the tower in which he and his associates in the disreputable 'Hell Fire Club' are said to have caroused. Next to the church is a remarkable flint-built mausoleum open to the sky (by John Bastard, 1765), and further down the hill the gloomy Gothic portal (1750–52) to a series of caves formed by extracting chalk for the new road, and consecrated by legend (alas without any factual foundation) to the orgies of the Hell Fire Club.

The house is approached from the west, and the first part to be seen is the monumental Grecian **Ionic portico** or 'Temple of Bacchus', designed in 1770 by Revett, co-author of the *Antiquities of Athens* (sponsored by the Society of Dilettante) and 'consecrated' in 1771 with the help of 'paeans and libations'. This was in fact the last part of the exterior to be built, and to trace the evolution of the house it is necessary to walk round to the north front, where the rebuilding began. This is a conventional neo-Palladian façade of ochre-coloured stucco over the original brick, dating from c 1749–51 and possibly designed by Isaac Ware. It overlooks an irregular lake, with Revett's Music Temple of 1771 on an island, and a belt of trees behind it to screen the road. The east portico was added to the house before 1754, and in 1755–58 a two storeyed loggia of stuccoed wooden columns was built across the whole of the long **south front** (the original entrance), based on Palladio's Palazzo Chiericati in Vicenza and ultimately on his reconstruction of a Roman house in his *Books of Architecture*. To the left is a monumental arch known as the Temple of Apollo and, at the end of the woods facing the east front, is the Temple of the Winds, based loosely on the Tower of the Winds, illustrated by Stuart and Revett and one of the first buildings in England to follow a Greek prototype. The architect for these impressive buildings and faades appears to have been the same Jolivet who was involved in the layout of the grounds, but he left West Wycombe in 1753, leaving John Donowell, one of Lord Burlington's draughtsmen, to complete the work, guided no doubt by Sir Francis Dashwood himself.

The visitors' entrance, under the south loggia, leads into the **Hall**, one of the most thorough-going attempts of the mid 18C to reconstruct a Roman interior (it was finished c 1770); the ceiling is taken from Robert Wood's book of illustrations of the temples at Palmyra in Syria, and underneath the floor, based on Roman mosaic pavements, is a heating system copied from a Roman hypocaust found in Lincoln by William Stukeley in 1740. Though similar in inspiration to Robert Adam's much better-known interiors, the effect—partly because of the different colour scheme—is quite different, yet equally convincing. The mythological paintings on the walls of the **Staircase**, through the colonnade to the left, are also inspired by classical precedent, this time Vitruvius's description of Roman interiors; they are by Giuseppe Borgnis, an Italian protégé of Sir Francis, who with his son Giovanni and the little-known William Hannan was responsible for the decorative painting which gives West Wycombe much of its particular character. Beyond this is the **Palmyra Room**, or great dining room, with another 'Palmyra' ceiling and several portraits of Sir Francis Dashwood, including one of him in a turban (he had visited Turkey) and another dressed as the Pope; behind the Ionic colonnade on the west side is one of several splendid Rococo mirrors in the house.

The rooms on the north front are now furnished as a series of comfortable living rooms in which some of the furniture and works of art collected by Sir Francis Dashwood are displayed. The **Tapestry Room**, with a ceiling of 'grotesques' painted by Hannan from drawings of Hadrian's Villa at Tivoli, is named after a set of Brussels tapestries by de Vos after Teniers. Next comes the Saloon, with a ceiling by the elder Borgnis copied from those by Raphael's assistants in the Villa Farnesina and Palazzo Colonna in Rome, and paintings by 17C and 18C Dutch and Italian masters, including two fine views of Rome by Orizonte and a self-portrait by Artemisia Gentileschi; over the doorcase into the Hall, by Henry Cheere, is a bust of Sir Francis's uncle, the Earl of Westmorland, in Roman garb (by Thomas Adey, 1739). The **Red Drawing Room** has another ceiling by Hannan, and contains paintings by him showing the house and park c 1754, along with a 17C Florentine cabinet inlaid with precious stones, and two excellent Louis XV-style commodes of c 1765–70 by Pierre Langlois. A door in the Study gives access to the original dining room (now the **Blue Drawing Room**), with a ceiling by the elder Borgnis taken from Annibale Carracci's 'Triumph of Bacchus' in the Palazzo Farnese in Rome, and a copy of the Medici Venus in a niche at the east end (thus celebrating Dashwood's enjoyment of at least two of the Seven Deadly Sins). The last, and grandest, of the rooms is the **Music Room**, with another superb ceiling by Borgnis, based on one in the Farnesina, good furniture of the 1750s, and excellent chimneypiece by Cheere and more Old Master paintings, including Ribera's 'Pythagoras'. From here visitors proceed through the east portico past Scheemakers's splendid lions into the gardens which so effectively complement the house.

GCT

Winslow Hall

On the south edge of Winslow on A413 Aylesbury–Buckingham: Sir Edward & Lady Tomkins, tel. 0296 712323. Open July–Aug Wed, Thur 2.30–5.30, all BH weekends 2–5. Guided tours.

This handsome red-brick house of 1698–1702 stands by the side of the road at the southern entrance to the small town of Winslow. It was built for William Lowndes, Secretary to the Treasury under William III, and its historical importance lies in the fact that it is one of the handful of houses almost certainly designed by Sir Christopher Wren. Although no drawings by Wren survive, an account book kept in the house shows that he checked the bills (which came to 6585), and also that many of the craftsmen came from the Office of the King's Works, of which he was Surveyor General, and through which he came into frequent contact with Lowndes. Lowndes himself came from Winslow, and the house remained in the family until 1898, when it was sold. Since then it has been sold twice more, most recently in 1959 to the present owner, a former diplomat.

Both outside and inside, the house retains its original character to a remarkable degree. The tall three-storeyed elevation and compact plan (there are only four main rooms and four corner rooms on each floor) make it in many ways more like a town house than a country house, there are particularly close resemblances to the Governor's House at Chelsea Hospital. The most striking external feature is the hipped roof, surmounted by four prodigiously tall chimneystacks; the hearths are all placed against an internal spine wall, leaving the ends of the house free for well-lit staircases—an ingenious and effective plan. The two main faades are identical, with the three central bays brought slightly forward and surmounted by pediments, and the windows (which have always been sashed) regularly spaced across the wall surfaces. It is also worth noting the high quality of the locally-made brickwork, dark red for the walls and lighter for the window surrounds.

Inside, the main rooms were plainly panelled in oak by the carpenter Matthew Bankes, one of Wren's regular collaborators, and have remained virtually unaltered, even down to the locks and door-handles. They have been appropriately but not ostentatiously furnished by the present owners, with pieces contemporary with the house, and there is a good collection of Chinese ceramics and 17C, 18C and 19C paintings. On the first floor, reached by a simple balustraded staircase of 'dog-leg' pattern, there is a surprise in the form of a room decorated with painted canvases in the manner of Daniel Marot, possibly inspired by a set of tapestries of 'Le Chteau de Roi' by Le Brun; they bring a taste of the Baroque to an otherwise restrained house. From here William Lowndes could have looked out onto formal gardens designed by the well-known partnership of London & Wise; these have alas long disappeared, except for the red brick walls of the kitchen gardens and one oak tree 300 years old.

GCT

CAMBRIDGESHIRE

Anglesey Abbey

6m north east of Cambridge at Lode on B1102: National Trust, tel. 0223 811200. Open Apr–mid Oct Wed–Sun, BH Mon 1–5.30 (gardens open 11–5.30). Refreshments.

The Augustinian priory of Anglesey was founded in 1135, and a relatively modest L-shaped house built on the site after the Reformation, incorporating mid-13C fragments of the monastic buildings. After an uneventful history the house was bought in 1926 by the wealthy art collector Huttleston Broughton, 1st Lord Fairhaven, who inherited a mining and railway fortune made in the USA. He proceeded to transform the unpromising fenland site by creating a garden on the grandest scale, filling the house meanwhile with a rich and varied collection of pictures, furniture, tapestries, clocks, Chinese and European porcelain and much else. Both house and grounds were left to the National Trust on Lord Fairhaven's death in 1966, and today they survive intact as a valuable example of 20C country-house taste.

The main façades of the stone-built house are still much as they were before Lord Fairhaven's time. Some medieval work survives on the picturesque east front, the first to be seen by visitors, but the gabled south front—the entrance before the 19C—is largely of the early 17C, with gables added in the 20C. The house is now entered from the north, through one of the many discreet additions made by Lord Fairhaven, next to a two-storeyed picture gallery built to the designs of Sir Albert Richardson in 1955–56.

The interiors are filled with objects of many different dates and countries of origin brought together to create an ambience of luxurious connoisseurship. The Tapestry Hall (named after a 17C Flemish tapestry of 'Rebecca at the Well') gives access to the Dining Room—the parlour of the medieval monastery—whose restored stone vault rests on octagonal columns of Purbeck marble. Notable objects include a 15C German limewood statue of St Christopher (1509) with carvings of the Tree of Jesse—a most unusual example of this motif being used in a piece of furniture. A passage leads to the Living Room in the 17C part of the house, with 17C and 18C English and Continental furniture and a seascape by Gainsborough (c 1781). The adjacent Oak Room, panelled by Lord Fairhaven in a conventional neo-Jacobean style, contains landscapes by Claude and John Wootton (a view of the nearby Newmarket Heath), and a luminous coastal scene in Normandy by Bonington. A collection of nudes by William Etty hangs on one of the upstairs landings, and in the richly furnished bedrooms there are landscapes by Richard Wilson and Thomas Sandby and marine pictures by Dominic and J.T. Serres.

The spacious barrel-vaulted Library—another of Lord Fairhaven's additions—houses a good collection of colour-plate books and also a large view of the Thames in London, with the opening of Waterloo Bridge, by Constable (1817), one of whose cloud studies hangs in a corridor outside; the library chandeliers were made by William Kent for George II's palace at Herrenhausen in Hanover. On a landing at the top of the main staircase there is a superb late-18C inlaid bureau made by David Roentgen for Tsar Paul I. From here a passage leads to the Picture Gallery, the upper floor of which is devoted largely to Lord Fairhaven's collection of views of Windsor by many artists of varying degrees of talent; a spectacular silver-gilt 'Shield of Achilles' designed by Flaxman (1822) is also displayed, along with items of silver from the collection and a Garter given by Henry VII to the Emperor Maximilian in 1489. But the highlight of the whole collection comes in the Lower Gallery at the end of the tour: a pair of Claude landscapes ('The Sacrifice to Apollo' and 'The Landing of Aeneas'), painted for Prince Altieri in 1663 and 1675 and later part of William Beckford's collection. They rank among the artist's finest works, and in themselves justify a visit to Anglesey.

GCT

Burghley House

1m south of Stamford, east of A1: Burghley House Trustees, tel. 0780 52451. Open Apr–early Oct daily 11–5. Guided tours (not Sun). Refreshments.

Three people were primarily responsible for the creation of this magnificent house: William Cecil, Lord Burghley, Queen Elizabeth I's chief minister, who first built it in 1556–87; his descendant, the 5th Earl of Exeter, one of the leading collectors of his generation, who went to Italy three times and spent vast sums of money transforming the interiors in the 1680s and 90s; and the 9th Earl, who went on four Italian tours, added to the already outstanding collection of porcelain, pictures and furniture and employed 'Capability' Brown from 1756 to create the present landscape setting.

The Cecils originally came from Wales, but Lord Burghley's father married a Lincolnshire heiress and bought the Burghley estate, which had formerly belonged to Peterborough Abbey, after the Dissolution of the Monasteries. His son, the statesman, used his great wealth to build three houses, but this, 'the mansion of his barony', was the most important, and it ranks as one of the finest of all Elizabethan buildings. Like most great Elizabethan houses, it is a fascinating mixture of old and new ideas. The rooms are arranged in medieval fashion around an elongated courtyard, with a high-roofed hall (1556) at one end and a tall gatehouse (1577) at the other. They are lit by large mullioned and transomed windows symmetrically disposed across the outer façades of Barnack stone, and the roof-line bristles with cupolas, obelisks and chimneys in the form of Tuscan columns grouped together under entablatures. Lord Burghley was well-acquainted with the architectural literature of his time and with the innovations of the Duke of Somerset's circle (he had been the Duke's secretary), and his interest in classical architecture is clearly evident in the courtyard elevations with their round-arched loggias (subsequently glazed) and an astonishing, French-inspired 'frontispiece' at the east end (1585)—unfortunately invisible to visitors—consisting of three layers of columns and arches surmounted by a tower and a huge obelisk.

Little is known about how the rooms were disposed in Lord Burghley's time, and they were almost all remodelled by the 5th Earl of Exeter, starting on the ground floor c 1682 and proceeding to the grander rooms upstairs six years later; the latter comprise bedrooms and closets, a large state dining room (now called the Bow Room) over the porch at the centre of the north range, and an extravagantly decorated 'great apartment' in the south range, one of the most lavish suites of Baroque rooms to survive in England. The architect was William Talman, who had just built the revolutionary new west range at Chatsworth, Derbyshire (qv.), for Exeter's brother-in-law, the 1st Duke of Devonshire. The final appearance, though, owes much to the individual craftsmen, including the plasterer Edward Martin, the wood carvers Grinling Gibbons and Jonathan Maine, and the painters Antonio Verrio and Louis Laguerre, the first of whom lived here in great style from 1687 to 1697 at the expense of Lord Exeter, who called him an 'impudent dogg' during a dispute over payment. Much of the work was left unfinished when the 5th Earl died in 1700, and from c 1767 onwards the 9th Earl introduced neo-classical chimneypieces and wood carving in the style of the late 17C as a setting for the art collection, which has recently been rearranged.

The house is approached from the north through one of Brown's most satisfying landscapes, the creation of which swept away all traces of the earlier gardens. The original entrance was from the west, and before embarking on the long tour it makes sense to look at the **west façade**, a conscious Elizabethan recreation of medieval splendour, which originally had a gallery running along the whole of the first floor. Lord Burghley began building the house at the east end, near the present visitors' entrance, and the tour starts in the cavernous **Kitchen**, continuing up a stone **staircase** of c 1560—one of the most important pieces of early Renaissance design to survive in England—to the first floor. From here the west courtyard front can be glimpsed.

Visitors proceed around the state rooms in a clockwise direction, starting in the private **Chapel**, where there is an altarpiece by Veronese and, in the Ante-Chapel, Mattia Preti's 'Triumph of Time' and an 'Agony in the Garden' by Francesco Bassano. The panelled **Billiard Room** (originally a small dining room) is hung with family portraits, including Robert Walker's 4th Earl of Exeter (d 1669) and Kneller's 5th Earl, along with his own lively self-portrait and his portrait of Verrio; there is also a Lawrence group of the 10th Earl and his wife and daughter. The **Bow Room**, the first of the grand late-17C interiors, was painted with rather wooden representations of the stories of Scipio and Anthony and Cleopatra by Laguerre, after Verrio had been dismissed in 1697. The next two rooms contain good plaster ceilings and wood panelling with delicate naturalistic carvings over the fireplaces, by Jonathan Maine and Thomas Young; there are pictures by Gaspard Dughet, Luca Giordano and Gainsborough in the **Brown Drawing Room**, and by Guido Reni (a Sibyl) and Pietro Liberi ('Pygmalion and Venus') in the **Black and Yellow Bedroom**, the most striking features of which are the early-18C state bed with its strikingly coloured original hangings and the pair of Soho tapestries with 'grotesque' patterns made by John Vanderbank.

The **Marquetry Room** derives its name from the large quantity of late-17C inlaid furniture, but is also notable for its 16C Flemish pictures, including Bernard van Orley's 'Christ Disputing with the Doctors' and Pieter Breughel's 'Rent Day'; on the typically late-17C corner fireplace there is an outstanding collection of late-17C Japanese porcelain (including the famous 'Wrestling Boys'), mentioned in an inventory of 1688 and the oldest such collection to survive in the West. **Queen Elizabeth's Bedroom**, next door, still contains the sumptuous state bed and gilded chairs and stools mentioned in the 1688 inventory, as well as a set of contemporary Gobelin tapestries of Aesop's fables. The adjacent **Pagoda Room**, over the west gateway (named after a model pagoda in the window bay), is hung with portraits, including Joos van Cleve's Henry VIII, two by Marcus Gheeraerts (the 1st Lord Burghley and Queen Elizabeth in old age), and Nathaniel Dance's portrait of 'Capability' Brown, whose expansive landscaping can be seen from the windows. Two smaller rooms, the **Blue Silk Bedroom** and its dressing room, take up the remainder of the west front. The first is hung with Mortlake 'Bacchanals' tapestries already here in 1688 and two canvases by Luca Giordano (out of 15 by this artist bought by the 5th Earl), and the second has an excellent collection of smaller pictures including a sensitive 'Virgin and Child' by Orazio Gentileschi, Carlo Dolci's 'Flight into Egypt' and a 'Rocky Landscape' by Jacob van Ruisdael.

The 'great apartment' in the south range was originally approached from the staircase at its east end, but the rooms are now visited in the opposite order, starting with the smallest and most intimate of the set, the **First George Room**. This is hung, in the approved Baroque fashion, with small paintings, including Joos van Cleve's 'Virgin and Child' and a characteristically sentimental 'Christ Blessing the Bread and Wine' by Carlo Dolci (in the adjacent closet), one of the 5th Earl's favourite artists; the ceiling, like all the others in the suite, is by Verrio, but the neo-classical chimneypiece, like those in the adjoining rooms, was introduced by the 9th Earl. The **Second George Room**, next door, has a chimneypiece taken from Piranesi's *Camini* (dedicated to the 9th Earl) surmounted by a group of late-17C Italian boxwood figures of classical personages bought by the 5th Earl, along with beautifully preserved tapestries of the Elements by Vanderbank. The two rooms beyond, both of them furnished in the 18C, contain some of the finest of the larger pictures in the house, including Giordano's 'Rape of Europa' and 'Death of Seneca' (in the **Third George Room**) and Guercino's 'Jacob Receiving the Coat of Joseph' and 'Triumph of David' (in the **Fourth George Room**). But the most spectacular room in the house is the ante-room, always known as the Heaven Room from its painted decoration by Verrio, showing assorted deities disporting themselves in an architectural setting, with the artist himself in a supporting role on the east wall. Baroque absurdity cannot go further.

The adjoining **'Hell Staircase'** is what Horace Walpole in another context called 'a profound tumble into the Bathos', with a ceiling by Verrio but walls painted in 1801 by Thomas Stothard, and it is with something approaching relief that the visitor enters the **Hall**. This was built by Lord Burghley and still contains its original chimneypiece after Serlio and unusually high hammerbeam roof; the screen and panelling were brought in from the Abbey of Tongerloo, Belgium, c 1830, and the huge silver wine cooler is by Philip Rollos c 1710. Refreshments are now served in 'Capability' Brown's Gothic Revival **orangery** to the north of the house, and changing exhibitions of works of art from the collection are held in a room in the service courtyard near the exit over the shop called the Goody Rudkin Room after a 17C housekeeper.

GCT

Elton Hall

5m south west of Peterborough on A605: William Proby, tel. 0832 280468. Open July, Aug Wed, Sun; Thur in Aug and May, Aug BH Sun, Mon 2–5. Guided tours. Refreshments.

The deliberately picturesque exterior of this large stone-built house conceals a building with a long and complex history. The oldest visible part is the late-15C gate tower of a courtyard house built by the Sapcote family, which was bought in the 17C by Sir Thomas Proby, grandson of a Lord Mayor of London and ancestor of the present owner. He married an heiress and carried out major alterations in 1663–65, including the demolition of the ruinous north and east wings of the courtyard and the replacement of the west wing by a double-pile block of the sort which became popular after the Restoration. The present drive is aligned on this block, and to the left are the much-remodelled remnants of the medieval south range, including the gatehouse and chapel undercroft.

Further changes came after Thomas Proby's grandson married an Irish heiress in 1750 and was raised to the Irish peerage as Lord Carysfort. In 1789 his son, who had been ambassador to France and Prussia and had married the sister of the future Prime Minister, Lord Grenville, employed the Gothic enthusiast John Carter—a man better known for his books than his buildings—to build a new library (now a drawing room) in place of the medieval chapel. This faces on to what is now a formal garden, and over the next few years this side of the house was completely transformed, by Carter and latterly the 1st Earl of Carysfort himself, into an irregular neo-Gothic pile with the genuinely Gothic gatehouse at the south end (the crenellated tower dates from 1868–78). The west range was also remodelled in an outrageously castellated style in 1812–14, but in 1856–60 the 3rd Earl of Carysfort employed Henry Ashton, the designer of London's first blocks of middle-class flats, in Victoria Street, to rebuild it in its present more sober neo-17C manner; the main reception rooms in the south range were also embellished in a heavy but not unattractive classical style at about the same time. Because of these changes of plan and taste the house now has a jumbled, though undeniably romantic, appearance. The main interest, though, lies in the excellent collection of books and pictures acquired at the end of the 19C by the 5th and last Earl, partly out of compensation paid for the 'nationalisation' of the family's Irish estates under the Wyndham Acts in the 1890s; they were fortunately transferred to Elton before the Irish house was burnt down in the Troubles, and are now shown in the main rooms in the south range.

The tour begins in the rib-vaulted undercroft of the medieval Chapel and moves into an octagon room in which a number of 19C paintings collected by the 5th Earl of Carysfort are displayed, including Henry O'Neil's Eastward Ho! (1857) and Alma-Tadema's 'Dedication to Bacchus' (1889)—his most expensive purchase. The main staircase, by Henry Ashton, leads up to the Yellow Drawing Room in the west range, also remodelled in the mid 19C and containing some late-17C Japanese lacquer furniture which once belonged to William Beckford; from here there is a view through to the main Entrance Hall, with panelling brought from the family's Irish house.

The grandest rooms are on the first floor of the south range. The first is the Octagon Room, which looks out on to the late-19C formal garden through Carter's Gothick windows with stained glass dated 1783; there is a good collection of Sèvres porcelain. The Large Drawing Room, next door, occupies the site of the former chapel and contains a ceiling and frieze of the late 18C, although the overall effect was transformed by a redecoration in 1860. The room has remained unchanged since then, with gilded plasterwork, yellow wall coverings and 18C French furniture, including a set of Louis XVI chairs covered with scenes from La Fontaine in Beauvais tapestry; there are also several good portraits by Reynolds, a friend of the family, including one of the courtesan Kitty Fisher. There are more English paintings in the Small Dining Room, including excellent landscapes by Gainsborough and Constable ('Dedham Vale: Morning', 1811). Most of the Old Masters in the collection are displayed against a pleasing Pompeian red background in the Large Dining Room, which dates in its present form from 1860; they include works by Girolamo Genga ('The Virgin of Mercy'), Luini, Gaspard Dughet, Hobbema, van Mieris ('The Declaration') and Gerard Dou ('The Flute Player'). The last rooms to be seen are the main Library, next to the Drawing Room, its mullioned window brought from another house in 1807 and its decoration probably dating from after a fire in 1894, and the Small Library in the 15C tower. The books here, many of them bought by the 5th Earl of Carysfort, include Henry VIII's psalter with his handwritten annotations and a large number of 16C theological works, several of them with fine bindings.

GCT

Wimpole Hall

8m south west of Cambridge on A603 near junction with A14 Royston–Huntingdon: National Trust, tel. 0223 207257. Open Apr–Oct daily except Mon, Fri (open Fri late July–Aug) 1–5, BH Sun, Mon 11–5. Refreshments.

Wimpole Hall stands near the side of the manor house of an abandoned medieval village in the empty countryside to the south west of Cambridge. The estate has been bought and sold several times since the core of the present house was built in the mid 17C, and the changes are reflected in the architecture of the large and sprawling red-brick building. The original builder was Sir Thomas Chicheley, but his relatively modest house was enlarged by Charles Robartes, 2nd Earl of Radnor c 1693–1705, and again in 1713–30 by Edward, Lord Harley (later the 2nd Earl of Oxford), a well-known literary patron and bibliophile whose collections now form one of the nuclei of the British Library. Harley's father was one of the leading Tory politicians at the end of Queen Anne's reign, and the alterations at Wimpole (which gave its name to a street on the family's building estate in the expanding West End of London) were designed by the favourite Tory architect, James Gibbs; at the same time Charles Bridgeman was employed to lay out the grounds, the most spectacular feature of which—an immense avenue stretching far to the south of the entrance front—survived into the 1970s, when it fell victim to Dutch elm disease.

The next owner was Philip Yorke, Lord Chancellor and 1st Earl of Hardwicke, and he too carried out alterations, which he placed in the hands of 'Burlington Harry' Flitcroft (cf. Woburn Abbey, Bedfordshire) in 1742–45. They left the main façades and some of the main rooms much as they are today, but the 2nd Earl called in 'Capability' Brown to soften the formalities of the gardens, and the 3rd Earl employed John Soane, perhaps the most gifted architect of this date in Europe, to make further changes to the interior in 1791–1806, and to design the self-consciously rustic buildings of Park Farm, north east of the house. Yet more additions and alterations were made by the 4th Earl and his architect H.E. Kendall, starting in the 1840s, but his son sold the estate in 1894, and by 1938 the house had lost most of its original contents and furnishings. It was then sold for the last time to George Bambridge, son-in-law of Rudyard Kipling, and over the next 30 years he and latterly his wife sympathetically refurnished it and demolished some of the Victorian additions. It came to the National Trust on the death of Mrs Bambridge in 1976.

The approach is from the east, through Kendall's stable block of 1851. To the right, almost adjoining the house, is the parish church, an unassuming building designed by Flitcroft in 1749, but incorporating the north aisle of the previous medieval church which serves as an impressive mortuary chapel for the Earls of Hardwicke and some of their predecessors. The house itself is, for its size, a relatively unassuming building, with a central three-storeyed block of seven bays and crisply carved neo-Palladian details by Flitcroft (eg, the Venetian window over the entrance) and Kendall (the balustrade and central chimneystack), and lower wings on either side; the central block incorporates the basic structure of the original 17C house, but the wings were added in the early 18C. The garden front is plainer but more extensive, with buildings projecting at each end of the wings, that on the right (west) containing Gibbs's library for Lord Harley. It looks out on to a landscape largely created by Brown, with a **sham ruined castle**, designed by Sanderson Miller but not built until c 1768–70, serving as an eye-catcher (and, according to a print displayed in the house, a reminder of paternalistic feudal virtues) in the distance.

The house is entered through a **Hall**, enlarged in the 1840s to incorporate the former ante-chapel, and now mainly notable for a series of paintings by John Wootton of horses and animals kept by Lord Harley in his menagerie at Wimpole (eg, 'The Countess of Oxford's Dun Mare', 1715); to the right there is a view into the Chapel created by Gibbs for Harley—a magnificent extravagance in view of the proximity of the parish church only a few yards away—with its outstanding painted decorations by James Thornhill. The tour proceeds clockwise through an Ante-Room and Drawing Room (originally a dining room), both largely by Flitcroft, with good Palladian wood carving by a little-known craftsman Sefferin Alken and surprisingly unobtrusive plaster ceilings added a century later by Kendall; the pictures (works by Devis, Philip Mercier, Tilly Kettle and others, including an absurd 'Apotheosis of the Royal Family' dated 1829) and furnishings were introduced by the Bambridges. The west end of the main block is taken up by the **Gallery**, created out of three smaller rooms by Flitcroft to house the 1st Lord Hardwicke's now-dispersed picture collection. Ionic columns mark the sites of the former room partitions, and there are more excellent examples of Palladian craftsmanship, including a marble chimneypiece which may be by Scheemakers (who carved Lord Hardwicke's monument in the church) and heavy-looking side tables made for the house and probably carved by Matthias Lock to Flitcroft's design. The portraits, introduced by Mrs Bambridge, include works by Allan Ramsay and a picture of the poet Matthew Prior—who died in the house as a guest of Lord Harley—by Jonathan Richardson.

Harley's Library is reached through an ante-room (the **Book Room**) which owes its present form largely to Soane, who was responsible for the ingenious arrangement of arches spanning the space between the bookcases projecting from the walls. The **Library** is a noble and spacious room which, despite the transference of Harley's books to the British Museum, still exudes an air of serious scholarly endeavour; the splendid plaster ceiling is by Isaac Mansfield, who worked under Gibbs at the nearly contemporary Senate House at Cambridge, and the pulpit-like oak steps of 1754 were designed by Henry Keene. A room on the garden front, now containing designs for the house and grounds, leads into the **Yellow**

Drawing Room, formed by Soane in 1790–94 out of an earlier ante-room and back staircase. This splendid room was designed for fashionable socialising, but the effect is strangely solemn, almost ecclesiastical, due in great part to the clever manipulation of domed shapes and top lighting; much of the furniture is original, and there are portraits by Romney on the walls. After these flights of fancy the **Saloon**, by Flitcroft, seems somewhat staid, but there is more spatial excitement in the main **Staircase**, dating mainly from the Gibbs period, with contemporary plasterwork by Bagutti, later plasterwork by his former partner Artari and a domed skylight by Soane.

Some of Flitcroft's and Soane's interior decoration survives in the bedroom, but here the presiding spirits are those of Mr and Mrs Bambridge, who introduced the furniture and pictures, including works by Tissot and other 19C artists, both English and foreign. From here visitors descend to the **Bath House**, created by Soane out of a former courtyard in 1792 and displaying his individual architectural genius in its most severely abstract form. Finally comes the surprisingly Baroque **Chapel**, with trompe-l'oeil figures of saints in niches and an exuberant representation of the Adoration of the Magi, by Thornhill, on the east wall; there have been few changes since Lord Harley worshipped here with the help of his private orchestra in the 1720s. The last rooms to be seen are the former dining room, by Kendall, and the adjoining Breakfast Room, which now provide a majestic setting for the National Trust's tea rooms.

GCT

CHESHIRE

Adlington Hall

5m north of Macclesfield on A523 Macclesfield–Stockport: Charles Legh,
tel. 0625 829206. Open Good Fri–Sept Sun, BH Mon 2–5.30. Refreshments.

The oldest part of this attractive courtyard house is the timber-framed north
range, which carries the date 1505 inside the Hall—one of the finest of its
date to survive in an English country house. It was built by Thomas Legh,
whose ancestors had been at Adlington since the early 14C, and the house
has remained in the family ever since. In 1581 Thomas Legh's grandson
added the porch on the courtyard side and probably also built or rebuilt the
east (service) range, which has similar framing of a herring-bone pattern,
painted black and white and resting on a sandstone base with a lichen-
covered sandstone roof and red-brick chimneystacks. The family was
Royalist and suffered financially during the Interregnum, but soon after the
Restoration the hall range was widened and the Hall itself encased in brick.
Timber-framed architecture became increasingly unfashionable, even in
conservative Cheshire, in the early 18C, and in the early 1740s Charles
Legh replaced the west (parlour) range with a brick structure containing
new reception rooms. A new south (entrance) range, also of brick, followed
in 1757, the date inscribed on the giant Ionic portico, and Legh also built a
new stable block and laid out the gardens, where a rustic shell-house still
survives; the architect may have been John Norris, who worked at Dunham
Massey (qv.), not far away. The Leghs of Adlington never became as grand
as their namesakes and distant cousins at Lyme Park (qv.), and the fabric
remained virtually unchanged until 1929, when some of the 18C additions
were removed under the supervision of Sir Hubert Worthington, an architect best-known for his extensive work in inter-war Oxford.

The 18C entrance range is now the private wing, and visitors enter the
house from the north. The older parts fortunately escaped the 19C
homogenisation which affected some local houses like Bramall Hall,
Greater Manchester (qv.), and it is still possible to enjoy the contrast
between the 16C timber-framing of the east range and the 17C and 18C
brickwork and sash windows on the irregular north side of the house. An
insignificant-looking doorway leads into the screens passage, but before
embarking on a tour of the interior it is worth going into the courtyard,
where the complex architectural evolution of the house can be clearly seen.
A late-17C staircase leads up from the screens passage to a group of rooms
in the north range, in one of which there is a set of paintings of the house
in c 1760 attributed to Thomas Bardwell. The Hall is glimpsed from a
gallery, but visitors proceed first to the wood-panelled mid-18C Drawing
Room, occupying the site of an earlier great chamber, with Corinthian
pilasters lining the walls and delicate carvings of fruit and flowers over the
marble chimneypiece by the Manchester statuary Daniel Sephton; an
early-16C Limoges enamel figure displayed here is traditionally said to
have been given to the family by Cardinal Wolsey and to represent the
Papal legate Cardinal Campeggio. The ground-floor Dining Room, reached
by a mid-18C staircase, has plainer wood panelling, and the walls are hung
with family portraits, including works by Cornelius Johnson and Thomas
Hudson.

The last room to be seen is the Hall, still open to its original late-medieval carved hammerbeam roof and largely empty of furniture, the stillness only disturbed by the ticking of clocks. The original carved canopy over the high table end remains intact, and is still adorned with the coasts of arms of leading Cheshire gentry—a unique survival—but substantial alterations were made soon after the Restoration; they include the frescoes of scenes from the Trojan War by an unknown artist over the high table and along the north wall, and the building of an organ by the celebrated 'Father' Smith on a gallery at the 'lower' end between two carved early-16C spere trusses; the organ case, with its trumpeting angels, is a splendid example of wood carving of c 1670, as is the delicate gallery front. This splendid instrument was played by George Frederick Handel, who left a manuscript of a hunting song as a memento of a visit to the house in 1751, and it is still in playing order.

GCT

Arley Hall

5m north of Northwich, north east of A559, M6 exit 19, M56 exit 10: the Hon. M.L.W. Flower, tel. 0565 777353. Open late Mar–early Oct daily except Mon (open BH Mon) 12–5. Refreshments.

This large, red-brick, neo-Jacobean house was built in 1832–45 to the designs of a local architect, George Latham of Nantwich, for Rowland Egerton-Warburton, representative of a family which had held the estate since the 15C and had been in Cheshire since the Norman Conquest. Described as 'a good churchman, a good landlord, a good sportsman and a man of literary tastes', Egerton-Warburton played a large part in the evolution of the design, and the choice of style reflects his conservative tastes. The house has remained in the hands of his descendants, and despite the demolition of the service wing in 1968 it remains a good example of an early-Victorian squire's residence.

The approach is through a gatehouse in a long set of outbuildings, part of which is made up of a 15C cruck-framed barn. The layout and proportions of the house reflect those of the 18C building it replaced, which was itself an encasing of an earlier timber-framed structure. Despite the Jacobean detailing, some of it taken from other Cheshire houses, the main façade is symmetrical, and the rooms are tall and spacious; an octagonal tower over the porch was unfortunately removed in 1968. The interior, entered through the West Hall, contains the usual Victorian Library, and Hall (which now serves as the main dining room, the original dining room having been demolished in 1968) and a Drawing Room, together with comfortable bedrooms upstairs. There is ample craftsmanship in wood and plaster (note especially the Library bookcases and the barrel-vaulted ceiling of the Drawing Room), and the walls are hung with portraits of the Warburtons going back to the 16C, along with later portraits by Romney, Beechey, Hoppner and others. Although the house is not especially old, and contains few 'important' works of art, the overriding impression is of a calm and understated confidence based on ancient possession.

Rowland Egerton-Warburton was an enthusiastic supporter of the Oxford movement, and in 1845 he called in Anthony Salvin to build a domestic Chapel north of the house in the then fashionable 'middle pointed' or

Decorated Gothic style; here Matins was sung daily until the First World War by a choral establishment made up of six boys and six lay-clerks. The Chapel still survives as a virtually unchanged Tractarian ensemble (the north aisle was added by G.E. Street in 1856–57), but today Arley is best-known for its very beautiful gardens. They were laid out by Rowland Egerton-Warburton in the 1830s and 1840s, but owe most of their present appearance to Lady Ashbrook, the present owner's mother. The influence of the estate spread to several of the nearby villages, where schools, churches and houses built and restored by Rowland Egerton-Warburton can still be seen.

GCT

Capesthorne

7m south of Wilmslow, 5m west of Macclesfield, on the A34: Mr William Bromley-Davenport, tel. 0625 861221. Open Apr Sun only; May Wed, Sun; June, July, Tues, Wed, Thurs, Sun; Aug and Sept Wed, Sun 2–4. Gardens and Chapel 12–6. Refreshments.

Capesthorne, home of the Bromley-Davenport family for over 250 years, is a mid-Victorian colossus of a house, but both site and family go back a good deal further. The present owner is the direct descendant in the 28th generation of Orme de Davenport, a Saxon of the late 11C. Orme's descendant, Richard, bought Marton in Cheshire in 1176, and the Davenports slowly amassed further estates in Cheshire and Staffordshire; their hereditary office of Sheriffs of Macclesfield Forest carried with it the power of life and death over felons in their jurisdiction, and in commemoration of this, the family crest is a felon's head with a noose around the neck. Meanwhile, Capesthorne was acquired by marriage by John le Warde in 1386, and the Ward family had a manor house here. John Ward, MP (1667–1748), commissioned a big new brick house c 1719, built by William Smith, probably to designs by his brother, Francis. On Ward's death, estate and house passed to his daughter, Penelope, and her husband Davies Davenport II. The Davenports changed their name to Davenport Bromley, later Bromley-Davenport.

Edward Davies Davenport (1778–1847), inheriting in 1837, immediately set about rebuilding the solid, plain Georgian house. He employed Edward Blore to enlarge it and encase it in ornate Jacobean style, a transformation which became all the more dramatic with the addition in 1845 of an immense Conservatory 125ft long. His nephew William Davenport Bromley was the owner when, in 1861, a great fire destroyed the main block. Anthony Salvin, rebuilding the house, more or less retained Blore's design for the entrance front, but substituted his own on the garden side. The interiors are now mostly Salvin's, in his rich Jacobean style.

Although never titled, the Bromley-Davenport family has produced distinguished MPs, collectors and soldiers. With the loss of other estates to capital taxation, Capesthorne has become their principal residence; the present owner, who inherited in 1989, has carried out a major scheme of renovation and redecoration.

The house, in red brick and dark sandstone, is symmetrical and very tall, with Jacobean-style shaped gables and turrets; it has been compared to a Victorian railway station, and certainly makes quite an impact in the quiet

Cheshire countryside. The entrance is rather surprisingly placed off-centre, under an arch to the stable-court. The Entrance Hall is grandly Jacobean; the big bay window has heraldic stained glass by Willement. The furniture is mostly older, 16C and 17C pieces. There are full-length 17C portraits, and a remarkable picture of the Electors of Cleves over the chimneypiece. At the end, the visitor goes left into the Sculpture Gallery, then right into the Saloon, a great room overlooking the garden. This, like all the other main rooms, has recently been redecorated in just the strong colours which the rich decoration demands. The unusual-looking black settees and chairs are of ebony, and were made for the house in Ceylon c 1830. The right-hand wall is covered with portraits of the Bromley-Davenport family, up to the present day. Next is the long Drawing Room, lined in a deep pink silk, with ceiling and features in white and gold, and much 18C and 19C French furniture. The room is dominated by landscape paintings, including views of Italy by Canaletto's studio, Joli, Zocchi and others, brought back from the Grand Tour. From here, the main staircase hall is reached, now brilliantly decorated in yellow and white, with crimson carpeting. It is hung with several 18C portraits.

From the landing, the visitor sees several bedrooms, all furnished with a mixture of 16C to 19C pieces, but with a strongly mid-Victorian tone. The Dorothy Davenport Room has 16C panel portraits, and a great oak bed with early 17C needlework hangings by Dorothy Davenport. The passage outside has views of the family's houses and other memorabilia. The State Bedroom and State Dressing Room have a mixture of 18C French furniture, and the most opulent furniture of the 1860s. At the other end of the landing, the American Room commemorates the family's recent close links (by marriage) with the United States, and is furnished with American 18C pieces and paintings. The Bow Bedroom, next door, has a Portuguese bed of c 1830, and more early 18C family portraits. Going back down the stairs, there is evidence of the family's profoundly Tory politics; the family crest of the felon's head appears on the iron balustrade—the head is that of Gladstone. The Dining Room has a massive Salvin chimneypiece, 18C English furniture, and French and Flemish paintings. The visitor now descends to the cellars, where a number of rooms have displays, of armour, household and gardening utensils, and relating to the long history of the family.

Outside, the gardens have fine herbaceous borders, leading down to the lake. To one side is the Chapel. Although externally it retains its early 18C form, as designed by the Smith brothers, the interior was redecorated in the 1880s, when the stunning mosaic reredos, representing the Dormition of the Virgin, was installed.

SB

Dorfold Hall

1m west of Nantwich on the A534 Wrexham road: Mr R.C. Roundell; tel. 0270 625425. Open Apr–Oct Tues, BH Mon 2–5.

Dorfold is a most attractive Jacobean manor house built of brick with stone dressings, in the quiet well-wooded countryside of south Cheshire. The site is an ancient one, but the present house was built by Ralph Wilbraham in 1616; the Wilbrahams were an eminent Cheshire family with several branches. Ralph's son, Richard, was a Parliamentarian, and the house was plundered by Royalist forces in 1643. In 1754, it was bought by a Nantwich lawyer, James Tomkinson, who employed Samuel Wyatt to redecorate the ground floor. Dorfold in the late 18C was an important centre of hunting, and extra stables were added by the Tomkinson family. Ann Tomkinson married Wilbraham Spencer Tollemache, a younger son of the family who built Peckforton Castle (qv.), and in 1862 he made additions to the house, and employed W.A. Nesfield to redesign the park and gardens, planting the fine avenue of lime trees. It is said that this was carried out by Tollemache while his wife was away travelling, to be a surprise for her, but she was so disagreeably surprised on her return that she refused to speak to her husband for three months. From the Tollemaches the house descended to the Roundell family from Yorkshire; the present owner is the third generation of the family to own it.

Dorfold is entered from the main road just to the west of Nantwich. There is a picturesque lodge and the beautiful avenue of limes, with the house visible at the far end. It is symmetrical and compact. In the middle is the Hall with the Great Chamber over it. To either side are gabled wings breaking forward a little. In the angles are smaller projections—the porch and the hall bay window. Ralph Wilbraham built the house with a forecourt and little stone lodges at its corners. These remain, but in the 1860s they were linked up to the main house by service wings. Lodges and wings are low and picturesque, with shaped gables.

Through the porch, the original screens passage was rebuilt as a vaulted corridor in the 18C, to designs by Samuel Wyatt. On the right is the hall, now the Dining Room. This too was remodelled by Wyatt, with a fine decorated ceiling. To the right of the chimneypiece is a portrait of the builder, Ralph Wilbraham. At either end of the room are full-length portraits, a copy of a Gainsborough of two boys of the Tomkinson family, and a delightful one of Henry and Julia Tollemache as children, with a pet donkey. There is fine Georgian furniture here, including particularly good lacquer cabinets, Empire-style chairs and a superb inlaid longcase clock. The visitor returns through the vaulted corridor, which is hung with 19C portraits of the Roundell family, and enters the Library. Although its shape is of the 17C, it too was redecorated in the 18C. There are fine seascapes and English furniture here. Ascending the stairs, you are back in the Jacobean period, with the original elaborate oak balustrading.

On the left at the top of the stairs, the Oak Room is a small bedroom, with its original panelling all around, and arms of Cheshire families over the mantelpiece. Ahead is the Great Chamber, the undoubted highlight of the house. It is a magnificent room, with a great barrel-vaulted ceiling, with broad bands of decoration in complicated geometrical patterns. Pendants hang from the apex of the ceiling, and there are royal emblems such as the rose, fleur-de-lys and thistle. It is one of the grandest ceilings of its date in England, and a great masterpiece of provincial art. The big original chimneypiece has Doric columns, and the coats of arms prominently displayed over. The richly decorated panelling is all intact, also. There are splendid pieces of 16C and 17C furniture here, including some very fine ebony and tortoiseshell inlaid cabinets, which do justice to the grand setting.

SB

Dunham Massey

3m south west of Altrincham off A56, M56 exit 7: National Trust, tel. 061
941 1025. Open Apr–Oct (garden daily) Sat–Wed 12–5. Refreshments.

Dunham Massey is a large and unusually plain brick house, protected by
its large deer park from the encroaching suburbs of Manchester. The 18C
walls hide what is structurally a Jacobean building begun c 1616 by
Sir George Booth, a Puritan sympathiser ('free, brave, godly Booth, the
flower of Cheshire'). His grandson, a Presbyterian who led 'Booth's rebellion' of 1659, one of the events which led up to the Restoration, was created
Baron Delamer by Charles II and celebrated his new-found dignity by
adding an entrance range which turned the house into a courtyard
structure. The present austere appearance derives from a thorough internal
and external remodelling carried out in 1732–40 to the designs of the
virtually unknown John Norris for Delamer's grandson, the 2nd Earl of
Warrington, who married the daughter of a rich London merchant and was
unflatteringly described by a contemporary as 'the stiffest of all stiff things'
(after siring an heiress he refused to speak to his wife and in 1739 published
a pamphlet advocating divorce). He also embarked on a vast programme
of planting which left the park as one of the best surviving examples of an
early-18C landscape, with long avenues of trees radiating from the front of
the house. When he died in 1758 the estate passed to his son-in-law, the
4th Earl of Stamford, and for the next 150 years the house remained
relatively little altered. Its present appearance owes much to the 9th Earl
and even more to his wife, who remodelled and refurnished many of the
interiors in 1905–9 with the help of her cousin, the furniture historian Percy
Macquoid and the firm of Morant & Co.; the architect was J. Compton Hall.
Their restrained, conservative and unpretentious taste pervades much of
the house today. The 9th Earl's bachelor son left the house to the National
Trust in 1976, having enriched it with items from Enville (Staffordshire), the
family's main residence in the 18C and 19C.

The interest of Dunham Massey derives not so much from the architecture—which is plain almost to a fault—but from the carefully arranged and
beautifully preserved interiors. The rooms are still arranged around a
courtyard, with the two storeyed Great Hall occupying its Jacobean position
on the side opposite the south (entrance) front; this was much remodelled
in 1905–7, and the rooms now contain a series of early family portraits
displayed against dark polished wood panelling. The most important room
in the east range—originally the Jacobean parlour wing—is the bow-
fronted Saloon, created as a dining room by the London architect John
Shaw in 1822 and now hung with portraits of 18C and 19C Earls of Stamford
and their families by Romney and others. Early photographs show the
adjacent Great Hall to have been an empty, cheerless room, but though it
still retains its 18C proportions and its heavy stone chimneypiece by the
Huguenot, M. Boujet, the effect was greatly improved in the early 20C by
the enrichment of the upper parts of the walls and the introduction of more
furniture, including some late-17C walnut chairs and an early-18C close
stool. The religious sympathies of the Booths are clearly shown in the
Chapel, next to the Hall, first formed in 1655 but panelled with woodwork
of the utmost simplicity in the early 18C and virtually unaltered since then.

The equally plain Gallery on the first floor contains the most important
picture in the house, Guercino's 'Venus, Mars, Cupid and Saturn as Time'

(c 1625), together with a set of four views of the house and grounds painted in 1751 by John Harris for the 2nd Earl of Warrington, who is shown with his daughter and heiress in a portrait by Michael Dahl. The 2nd Earl was an avid collector of silver and some of the best items from his collection of a thousand pieces (including 14 chamber pots, one of which is still in the collection), mostly by Huguenot craftsmen (Peter Archambo, Philip Rollos and others), are shown in an adjoining room. The Tea Room (an 18C name), next door, contains pictures and objects brought back from Italy by the 5th and 6th Earls of Stamford, the first of whom was a Fellow of the Society of Antiquaries; they include two of Thomas Patch's grotesque group portraits of travellers and a portrait of the 5th Earl by Anton Raphael Mengs (1760). From here a corridor leads to the 2nd Earl of Warrington's Library, one of the least altered rooms in the house, with what is probably Grinling Gibbons's first documented piece of carving—a version of Tintoretto's 'Crucifixion' recorded by John Evelyn in 1671—occupying pride of place over the fireplace; there is also an orrery and an armillary sphere of c 1730, each in its original oak-framed case. Having regained the ground floor it is possible to see the vast Kitchen and several other service rooms arranged around a subsidiary courtyard, recalling the scale of life at this quietly impressive house in its heyday.

GCT

Gawsworth Hall

3m south of Macclesfield on A536 Macclesfield–Congleton: Timothy Richards, tel. 0260 223456. Open Apr–Sept daily 2–5.30.

Gawsworth Hall is a timber-framed house standing in an attractive village setting close to a late-15C church and one of the ponds or meres which are characteristic of Cheshire. It was built by the Fitton family in the 15C and 16C and subsequently passed to the Gerards, who later became Earls of Macclesfield. In 1693 the 2nd Earl was complaining that 'the old house at Gawsworth is ready to fall upon his head', and in 1701 his brother pulled down a large part of it. After more than two centuries in the hands of tenants of the Earls of Harrington, who purchased the estate in 1725, the house was sold and remodelled in 1961–78 by a local antiquary, Raymond Richards, whose family still lives here.

Despite certain alterations, the house is a good example of the timber-framed architecture for which Cheshire is justly famous, and the exterior is made all the more attractive by the use of local sandstone slabs to cover the low-pitched roofs. The oldest part is the north wing, where the present entrance is situated; this has been encased in brick and subsequently overlaid with fake timber-framing, but a 15C arch-braced roof can be seen in an upstairs room and there is a stone armorial tablet of 1570 on the outer wall with the arms of Sir Edward Fitton, Queen Elizabeth's Treasurer in Ireland. The core of the house is the east or hall range, with 16C framing in the outside; internally, though, it has been so divided up that it is difficult to recapture the original uses of the rooms. The taller south range was probably built by another Sir Edward Fitton, Lord President of Munster, in the late 16C or early 17C; it is architecturally the most ambitious part of the house, with its three-storeyed bay window and walls of continuous glass, but was truncated at the west end in the early 18C, when the west or gatehouse range was also demolished. To the west is a terraced walkway which seems to represent a survival from the Elizabethan gardens. Lovers of exposed oak beams will find many in the interior of the house, which is furnished as a family home and contains some early portraits and chimneypieces; there are also several items of Victorian furniture collected by Raymond Richards, including bookcases from A.W.N. Pugin's Scarisbrick Hall (Lancashire) in the Library, and furnishings and stained glass rescued from demolished Cheshire churches in the Chapel.

GCT

Little Moreton Hall

4m south of Congleton on the A34: National Trust, tel. 0260 272018. Open Apr–Sept Wed–Sun; Oct Sat, Sun 12–5.30, BH Mon 11–5.30, last admission 5. Refreshments.

Little Moreton Hall is the most famous of all the black and white timber-framed houses of England. The jumbled skyline, the varied patterns in its timber framing and the crazy irregularities of parts of the building, combine to give it an endearing kind of picturesqueness.

The Moreton family held land here from early in the 13C. They owned the place continuously, the property and name passing through the female line only once, up until 1912. On the death of Elizabeth Moreton in that year, it passed to a distant cousin, Charles Abraham, Bishop of Derby. In 1938 he and his son gave it to the National Trust.

The house stands inside a well-preserved rectangular moat; it is a prominent landmark in the flat countryside. The moat encloses a sizeable plot; the house occupies the southern half of this, and to the north there is a garden. What we now see is a courtyard house, although the yard was never fully enclosed. It has a complicated architectural history, but the earliest part is the Hall on the north side of the courtyard, probably built in the mid 15C by Richard de Moreton. William Moreton built (or rebuilt) the west, or Kitchen end of this c 1480. By the reign of Elizabeth, the Moretons were a prosperous family, with 1360 acres. William Moreton II (d 1563) and his son John (d 1598) extended and modernised the house. The former rebuilt the east wing and extended it south, with a new Withdrawing Room and Chapel. The Withdrawing Room and Hall received new five-sided bay windows, and the builder-carpenter, Richard Dale, 'signed' these on the frieze. In the 1560s, John Moreton built the south wing, closing the third side of the courtyard, housing a gatehouse and guests' accommodation above, with a 68ft Long Gallery added on top. This is what gives Little Moreton its extraordinary appearance; the immense weight of the gallery has made the south wing lean and tilt in the most drunken and picturesque way. It used to be thought that the gallery was added as an afterthought, but recent repair work turned up evidence to suggest that it was an original part of the wing. Structurally speaking, it was bold to the point of recklessness, but English architecture would be the poorer without it.

Finally, in the early 1600s the 'domestic block' was added, filling a part of the gap on the west side of the courtyard. The Moreton family suffered heavily by backing the Royalist cause in the Civil War, and they never again had the means to carry out much work on their house. In the 18C, they ceased living here, abandoning Little Moreton to a succession of tenant farmers. Many Tudor houses succumbed to neglect and destruction by this kind of process, but it turned out to be Little Moreton's salvation. Just enough was spent on the house to keep it standing without altering its character, until at the end of the last century, Miss Elizabeth Moreton took an interest in the house (though she does not seem to have lived in it) and carried out careful and timely restoration.

Approaching from the car park the south wing with the entrance is seen first, with the Long Gallery perched on top, reflected in its moat; this is one of the most famous views of any English house. Through the gateway, the courtyard is reached, dominated by the great bay windows, with elaborate patterns in the framing, and with vigorous, primitive carvings. The inscription reads:

> God is Al in Al Thing: This windous whire made by William Moreton in the year of our Lorde M D LIX
> Richard Dale Carpeder made thies windows by the grac of God

The **Hall** has an open roof, with a single truss. It is basically of c 1450, but a floor was later inserted, since removed, hence the blocked doorways at the upper level. It never had a conventional screens passage; instead there was a spere-arch at the west end, and there would have been a movable screen under it, an arrangement which still survives at Rufford Old Hall in Lancashire (qv.). The arch is now partly blocked. Only three items of original furniture remain at Little Moreton, one being the long refectory table here, with primitive Renaissance ornament.

From here, you enter the **Parlour** in the north-east corner of the house. This is in part of the 1450s building, but was redecorated in Elizabethan times, and again in Georgian times. In 1976, painted wall-decoration was discovered behind the Georgian panelling, dating from c 1580, and this is partly displayed. The walls are plastered and painted to represent panelling. Above there is a frieze with panels depicting the tale of Susanna and the Elders; Gothic lettering in scrolls gives the story in words. Next is the **Withdrawing Room**, also within the 15C building, but redecorated c 1559, when the great bay window was added, the ceiling with its heavily moulded beams put in, and the heavily framed panelling introduced. The overmantel bears the arms of Queen Elizabeth. There is very little furniture in Little Moreton now, but the octagonal table in the bay window is probably the one listed in an inventory of 1601, and valued at ten shillings. South of the Withdrawing Room is the **Chapel**. This was probably added in the 1560s. The nave is a low-ceilinged room, opening into the higher chancel, which has a pointed east window, decorated with Biblical texts framed in arabesque patterns.

Now you enter the **south wing**, built by John Moreton in the 1560s. The rooms are all empty, but the Tudor craftsmanship is everywhere visible. On the first floor are the Guests' Hall and Parlour. The massive carved console-brackets in the former were inserted in the 17C to help support the load of the Long Gallery above. The flooring here is of lime-ash, a form of concrete once much used in northern houses (qv. Hardwick Hall, Derbyshire), as a protection against fire. Opening from these rooms are the privies, with their original wooden seats, the drains letting out into the moat. On the top floor is the **Gallery**. It is very light, with near-continuous bands of windows on either side. The roof has arched and cusped braces, still firmly in the Gothic carpenter's tradition. At either end over the windows are plaster panels with symbolic figures deriving from 'The Castle of Knowledge' a treatise

The entrance to Little Moreton Hall showing the ornamental timber framing and the windows of the Long Gallery on the top floor

on geometry by Robert Recorde, 'The Speare of Destinye whose Rule is Knowledge' and 'The Wheel of Fortune whose Rule is Ignorance'.

Outside, the façades give great pleasure from their variety of form and pattern. To the north of the house, the National Trust has laid out a **knot garden**, with hedges of box and yew, a most appropriate complement to the house.

SB

Lyme Park

6½m south east of Stockport on A6, Stockport–Buxton: National Trust/
Metropolitan Borough of Stockport, tel. 0663 762023. Open Easter–Sept
daily except Mon, Fri (but open BH Mon) 2–5. Guided tours except Sun.
Garden open daily all year 11–5 (11–4 winter). Refreshments.

This large and rather forbidding house is spectacularly sited in an extensive
park, complete with red deer, on the western slopes of the Peak District
moors, far in spirit, if not in physical distance, from the Manchester
conurbation which spreads to the gates. In its present form it is an ambitious
late-17C and early-18C remodelling and expansion of a house built c 1570
by Sir Piers Legh, representative of a younger branch of the Leghs of
Adlington (qv.) who had settled at Lyme in the 14C. The 'cage' or hunting
tower which can be seen on the left of the drive up to the house seems to
date from this time (there is a similar one at Chatsworth, Derbyshire, qv.),
as does the rather crude frontispiece at the centre of the **north (entrance)
front**. Most of the rest of this façade was rebuilt by Richard Legh in 1676,
and he also made additions to the east or hall range, employing a local
mason, John Platt. But the most important contribution was made by his
son, Peter, a Jacobite sympathiser, who finished off the north range and
added two more ranges, to the west and south, thus giving the house its
present courtyard shape. The **south range**, built in 1729–35, was designed
by Giacomo Leoni, the Venetian architect responsible for bringing out an
influential English translation of Palladio in 1715, and his work at Lyme,
carried out in the pinky-brown local gritstone, is an accomplished exercise
in the style of the Italian High Renaissance, with none of the prissy thinness
which sometimes mars English neo-Palladian architecture. Thomas Legh,
a soldier and amateur archaeologist, one of the first westerners to survey
Petra, employed Lewis Wyatt to remodel the east range and add the attic
over the Ionic portico on the south front in 1814–17. Since then there have
been relatively few structural changes. The family prospered through the
development of coalfields on their Lancashire estates during the 19C and
finally acquired the peerage which their palatial house would appear to
have demanded, in 1892. But they left Lyme in 1947, when the 3rd Lord
Newton gave it unendowed to the National Trust.

The house is entered through the **courtyard**, where Leoni redesigned the
elevations with great subtlety to hide the outmoded remnants of the
Elizabethan house and to allow access between different parts of the
building at first-floor level along corridors raised on rusticated arches. The
interiors do not quite live up to the promise of this sophisticated and
beautifully executed exterior. Peter Legh spent much less on the inside than
on the outside of his house, and there have been many later alterations, not
all of them for the better. The **Entrance Hall** in the east range, approached
by an outside staircase, dates from the 1720s, but it was altered by the
French decorators Philippe and Amadée Joubert in 1903, when the original
fireplace was removed and three Mortlake tapestries of Hero and Leander
(1623) introduced. To the north is the **Chapel**, created by Richard Legh in
the late 17C but with woodwork of the 1730s by a local craftsman, John
Moore. The most important room in Leoni's south range is the wood-
panelled **Saloon**, behind the portico, which contains good Rococo plasterwork and a series of delicate late-17C wood carvings of the Fine Arts and
the Four Seasons, attributed to Grinling Gibbons and removed here in the
1730s or 1740s from a room on the site of the present Dining Room.

The adjacent main **staircase**, with a swirly plaster ceiling of 1734 by Francesco Consiglio—presumably a protégé of Leoni—leads to the top floor of the east range, where a much-altered Elizabethan **Long Gallery** runs the whole length above the Hall; it was narrowed by Lewis Wyatt when he created a corridor leading to a series of early-18C bedrooms along the west side. More of Wyatt's work can be seen in the Library, Dining Room and Drawing Room, which enfold the Entrance Hall on three of its four sides and vividly illustrate the stylistic eclecticism of the Regency period. The **Library**, in a heavy, indeterminate style, contains some of the antiquities brought back from Greece and the Middle East in 1813 by Thomas Legh, who is depicted in Turkish dress in a portrait over a doorway; they include three Greek tombstones of c 350 BC. Next to the Library is the **Dining Room**; it is an unusual exercise for its date in the decorative manner of the late 17C. Beyond, as a deliberate contrast, is the Drawing Room, approached through the **Stag Parlour**, with Elizabethan or pseudo-Elizabethan plasterwork showing a hunting scene. There is some genuinely Elizabethan work in the **Drawing Room**, including the heavy stone chimneypiece, but the overall impression is of an ornate recreation of an Elizabethan interior, with elaborately wood-panelled walls and a ceiling encrusted with plasterwork.

From here the route passes through the north range of 1676, where some of the rooms still retain their original upholstered furniture, to the west range. A plaster copy of the frieze from the Temple of Apollo at Bassae adorns Leoni's corridor, and at the end a large collection of late-17C and 18C English clocks, brought together by a younger son of the 3rd Lord Newton, is displayed in a pair of darkened rooms. Outside there are formal gardens of the 19C and 20C with an Orangery by Wyatt, overlooked by the bare moors of the Peak.

GCT

Peckforton Castle

About 10m south east of Chester near Tarporley, off A49: Mrs E. Graybill, tel. 0829 260930. Open daily late Mar–early Oct 10–6. Refreshments.

Peckforton is a most extraordinary place. Many Georgian and Victorian landowners built houses in a medieval style with battlements and turrets, to which they attached the name 'castle' but nowhere else did the builder go quite so far in the pursuit of medieval authenticity. It is an immense fortress in 13C style, on top of a thickly wooded hill which rises sharply out of the Cheshire plain. On the neighbouring hill is the real, ruined 13C Beeston Castle (owned by English Heritage and also open to the public). Peckforton is considerably the larger and more ambitious of the two. Although it has no historic contents, it remains a dramatic architectural experience. It still speaks powerfully of the complex and dynamic culture of early-Victorian Britain, with its unique mixture of faiths: passionate Christian faith, faith in science and material progress, and a romantic faith in chivalry and the Gothic past.

Peckforton is entirely the creation of John, 1st Lord Tollemache. He had huge estates in Cheshire and Suffolk, and he was widely praised as an enlightened and improving landlord. In Cheshire he built 55 new farmhouses and numerous estate buildings, becoming famous for providing all his estate workers with a cottage and three acres. At the centre of this 35,000 acre domain, in keeping with his semi-feudal High Tory image of himself, he built the castle at a cost of £60,000 to the designs of Anthony Salvin, c 1844–50. The *Illustrated London News* remarked that it 'seems to exhibit the peculiar beauties of Carnarvon Castle without its inconveniences'. Peckforton was the apogee of the 'romantic' phase of the Gothic Revival. The Tollemache family lived here until the Second World War, and photographs show their rather desperate attempts to make the rooms feel domestic. Thereafter it was abandoned, until its sale in 1988 to the present owner. It is used for banquets and receptions, and has been featured in a number of television programmes.

Peckforton Hill is covered in thick trees, and only the Castle's towers show above these. A drive winds up for a long way through the woods, and then the immense red sandstone walls loom ahead between the trees. The Castle surrounds a large irregular courtyard, entered through a convincing-looking gatehouse with a drawbridge and portcullis. On the right is the Chapel—like a small parish church. One side of the courtyard is left open as a terrace, looking down through the surrounding woods. On the left are large stable and service buildings, lining the very high curtain walls. Opposite are the huge main ranges, with great towers rising from them, on three sides of the courtyard.

Visitors enter the porch and are in the Great Hall. Here and elsewhere there are animated figures dressed as a verger, a minstrel, as Lord Tollemache and a ghost, who repeat words of wisdom to the visitor. The Hall is a sombre place, with a great vaulted roof and walls all of unplastered stone. Behind this is a complicated staircase around a light-well, again of severe plain stonework. To one side are the Gallery and Drawing Room; they are somewhat lighter, with heavily beamed ceilings and dado-height panelling. Downstairs you see some of the vaults, with a great wine cellar in the basement of the highest tower. Part-way up the stairs, above the wine cellar, is the Dining Room, again vaulted, octagonal, with deep window-embrasures. Upstairs, you see some of the former bedrooms; they are fairly well-lit, but here, as everywhere, the decoration is severe and plain; Lord Tollemache preferred to spend his money on massive masonry, rather than on frills. It can never have been an easy place in which to live. A spiral stair takes you up onto the flat roof and battlements over part of the main building, with spectacular views of the Castle's skyline, and of the Cheshire plain below.

It is hard to convey the strange quality of the interiors. The scale is enormous, and everywhere there is massive and precisely-cut masonry and woodwork. The marvellous Victorian workmanship is probably sharper and better than it would have been in an authentic medieval building. The present owner has made a bold bid to give Peckforton a new lease of life.

SB

Peover Hall

4m south of Knutsford. Turn off the A50 at the Whipping Stocks Inn, turn south at Parkgate; the gates are on the east side of the grounds: Mr Randle Brooks; enquiries to Mr J. Stocks, tel. 0565 722656. Open May–Sept Mon only (not BH Mon) 2.30–4.30.

Peover Hall (pronounced 'peever') is a brick-built manor house of the 1580s, difficult to find in the winding lanes south of Knutsford. Its history is an interesting illustration of changing architectural taste, chiefly concerning the 16C, 18C and 20C, and it boasts some very fine contents, collected by the present owner.

The house was begun in 1585 by Sir Randle Mainwaring; the family had already been here for some centuries, and St Lawrence's church, next to the Hall, has several of their tomb monuments. They added the North Chapel to the church in 1648, and Ellen Mainwaring built the architecturally very important stables in 1654 as a present for her son, Thomas. In the 1760s, Sir Henry Mainwaring made major alterations. He added a large new coach-house and stable yard. To the 16C house he added a wing at right-angles, making a T-shape. The strange thing about this was that the new wing represented two-thirds of a symmetrical façade; where the completing third should have been was the 16C building. This suggests that Sir Henry intended, in due course, to demolish the old house, and complete the newer façade. The architect of this work is unknown, though Thomas Pritchard of Shrewsbury has been named as a likely candidate.

The Mainwaring family died out in 1934; Peover had already been sold, in 1919, to John Graham Peel, a cotton magnate. The estate was sold again, c 1940, to Harry Brooks; his son, Randle Brooks, is the present owner. During the Second World War the house was requisitioned for use by General George Patton of the US Army; it was not released to the family until 1950. The Georgian wing was found to be in poor condition, so in 1964 it was demolished and the Elizabethan house renovated. Where the 1760s wing had abutted onto it, a new entrance-front was made in a simplified version of the 16C work. Mr Brooks has embellished the interior with panelling and other fittings from many other houses in Cheshire and the Midlands.

The house now is very roughly rectangular; the Entrance Hall is a passageway running across its depth; the small Sitting Room to the left has the first of the house's interesting 16C woodwork and furniture. Behind this, in the centre of the ground floor, is the panelled Dining Room, with wooden pilasters brought from Horsley Hall in Clwyd and 18C furniture and paintings. At the end of the house, the Morning Room has elaborate panelling, and the first of a set of very elaborate bookcases brought from Oteley in Shropshire, a Victorian seat of the Mainwaring family. Ascending a staircase, the visitor sees several bedrooms on the first floor, and the Drawing Room, occupying the centre of the house. This has early-18C panelling, and more of the bookcases from Oteley. There is good 17C and early-18C furniture; the paintings include a version of Van Dyck's double portrait of Strafford with his Secretary, Sir Philip Mainwaring.

Steps lead down to the landing, above the Entrance Hall, with portraits of English monarchs. Various bedrooms are shown, with a notable collection of four-post beds and other English furniture. Ascending the staircase (an oak dog-leg stair, original to the house), you reach the Long Gallery on the top floor, where the roof structure is visible, and where a lot more of Mr Brooks' collections of antique furniture and toys are displayed. Returning to the ground floor, steps lead down to the original Kitchen. This has two huge fireplaces, and a most unusual ceiling, where the massive oak beams are laid diagonally—for no apparent reason other than decoration. Mr Brooks has filled the room with arms and armour and fine 16C and 17C furniture, giving it the character of a Great Hall. As well as the earlier furniture, there are two massive and elaborate mid-19C pieces, representing the taste for historicist furniture of the time of the Great Exhibition.

The gardens, largely the present owner's work, form a most attractive setting. The 1654 stable block is architecturally more important than the house; from the outside it is a relatively simple piece of vernacular work, but inside the stalls are elaborately carved, with Tuscan columns and strapwork. Next to it is the very handsome coach house, added c 1764. The grand Rococo-style iron gates just down the drive were brought by Mr Brooks from Alderley Park.

SB

Rode Hall

5m south west of Congleton, 5m north west of Stoke-on-Trent, at Scholar Green, between the A34 and A50: Sir Richard Baker-Wilbraham, Bart, tel. 0270 873237. Open Apr–Sept Wed and BH 2–5.

Rode Hall, deep within wooded grounds, is a very attractive red-brick house of the mid 18C; the interiors and contents are chiefly of the Regency period. Happily it remains the seat of the family who built it. The Wilbraham family are recorded in Cheshire as early as 1259. Roger Wilbraham bought the manor of Rode for 2400 in 1669. There was probably an old timber-framed manor house, but the family do not seem to have settled until Roger's son Randle Wilbraham built a new house, around 1700. This is a fairly modest two-storey building, and survives as the servants' wing of the present Hall. His son, Randle Wilbraham, inherited in 1732; he was a lawyer and MP for Oxford University, and in the 1750s he added a new, square block, with bow windows on the east and west fronts, and an entrance on the north front. It is three storeys high, of brick, severe and dignified. Randle Wilbraham's son, Richard, married the heiress of Robert Bootle, of Lathom House (Lancashire) and his younger son, Randle, who inherited Rode, began carrying out improvements to the house soon after his marriage in 1798. His architect, John Hope, is best-known as designer of the Piece Hall at Halifax. At Rode, he rebuilt the big bow windows, making them deeper. He covered the brickwork with stucco and transformed the interiors in fashionable Regency style, switching the entrance to the west side. After Hope's death in 1808, further alterations were made by Lewis Wyatt, on the strength of his work for the Egerton family at Tatton Park (qv.). Randle Wilbraham's grand-daughter married Sir George Baker, Baronet, who assumed the name Wilbraham. His son Sir Philip had careful alterations made in the 1920s by the architect Darcy Braddell.

The house is approached by a long drive, appearing almost at the last minute. The entrance was switched to the west front in the 1920s, and the Ionic porch dates from then. Braddell also removed the Regency stucco work, so it is once more a red brick house; the big bow windows on either side are as rebuilt c 1800. Just to the right is the early-18C house, looking very modest by comparison. Further to the right is the handsome stable block. The Entrance Hall—previously a Billiard Room—has Regency furniture, and portraits of the last four generations of the Baker Wilbraham family. Ahead and in the centre of the house is the Staircase, the only major room to retain its mid-Georgian form, with its carved balusters and tread-ends, and very attractive provincial Rococo plasterwork. Left from here is the octagonal Ante-Room in the centre of the north front. This was the original Entrance Hall, redecorated as an Ante-Room in Regency style. The furniture is by Gillow & Co., and other important makers, and the Library and Drawing Room, which flank the Ante-Room to left and right, are of the same period. The Library has its original fitted bookcases with black portrait busts sitting on top and Gillow furniture: a perfect country-house library. The Drawing Room too has simple decoration; walls in a strong red colour, Regency furniture, and 18C portraits, mostly of the Baker family. Finally, the Dining Room, originally the Library, is by Lewis Wyatt. It is the most strongly 'architectural' of the interiors, with scagliola Ionic columns and a black marble fireplace, and a shallow segmental vault. There are Bootle Wilbraham portraits, and over the fireplace is Thomas Hudson's painting of Randle Wilbraham, the lawyer and builder of the house in the 1750s.

The park is very attractive; Humphry Repton prepared a 'Red Book' for Rode in 1790, and landscaping was eventually carried out on these lines by John Webb c 1805. The formal garden on the north side of the house was designed by W.A. Nesfield, c 1860. House and grounds are equally well-maintained, and Rode retains the character of a family home.

SB

Tabley House

2m west of Knutsford on A5033, M6 exit 19 to A556; Tabley House Collection Trust, tel. 0565 750151. Open Apr–Oct Thur–Sun and BH Mon 2–5. Refreshments.

The Tabley estate is one of many in Cheshire which has remained in the same family from the Middle Ages until recent times. The first recorded house, later known as Tabley Old Hall, was built by the Leicester family in the late 14C on an island in Nether Tabley Mere, and survived until 1927 when it suddenly collapsed because of subsidence due to salt extraction. But it was abandoned as the family's main residence when the present house was built by Sir Peter Leicester in 1761–69 on a slightly higher site on the recently purchased Over Tabley estate. His architect was John Carr of York, and the house is an impressive exercise in the neo-Palladian style, with a main block distinguished by a splendid Doric portico of the local red sandstone (originally painted white). It is approached by curving staircases, from the top of which Nether Tabley Mere can be seen to the south; two service wings, each with canted bay windows, are placed behind this block, and joined to it by curved corridors—a reduced version of the plan of Holkham Hall, Norfolk (qv.). When the bulk of the Old Hall was finally demolished in 1827–29, the detached Chapel—built in a conservative style by the antiquarian Sir Peter Leicester in 1674–77 with furnishings inspired by those of the slightly earlier chapel at Brasenose College, Oxford—was re-erected next to the west (service) block, and it is this which the visitor sees first on the approach to the house.

Tabley's chief claim to fame is the collection of pictures by British artists brought together by Sir John Leicester (later 1st Lord de Tabley), son of the builder of the house, in the early 19C. Leicester's collection was originally divided between Tabley and his London house, and was offered to the Government in the 1820s as the nucleus of a National Gallery of British Art, but the offer was turned down and a group of pictures was excluded from the ensuing sale (1827) and removed to Tabley, where it has remained largely intact; an unusual example of an early-19C country house collection devoted not to Old Masters but to contemporary pictures by native British artists. The house became a school after the Second World War, but the ground and second floors have recently been turned into residential accommodation for the elderly and the rooms on the piano nobile containing the picture collection have been expertly restored to their 1840s state.

The main rooms are arranged around a central staircase, and the tour takes the form of a circuit, starting in the Entrance Hall, chastely decorated with plasterwork by Thomas Oliver of Warrington (notice the use of the Doric entablature over the doorways and around the frieze) and woodwork by Daniel Shillito—one of Carr's frequent collaborators—and Thomas Bertram. The same craftsmen were responsible for the richer decoration in the Drawing Room (originally the dining room), the walls of which are closely hung with pictures, including portraits by William Dobson (the '1st Lord Byron', painted c 1643 during the Civil War); Lely, Opie and Lawrence. There are also works collected by the 1st Lord de Tabley, including J.M.W. Turner's 'Tabley House and Lake: Windy Day' (1808), showing the castellated round tower which can still be seen from the house, and John Martin's 'Destruction of Pompeii and Herculaneum' (1821). The more intimate Octagon Room (originally called the common parlour) has a delicate plaster ceiling, paintings of the old and new houses at Tabley by Antony Devis (c 1768–70) and Carr's original model of the present building. It leads into the Dining Room, created out of two smaller rooms in 1840–45, probably to the designs of the 2nd Lord de Tabley.

From here the route passes through the top-lit Staircase Hall to the Picture Gallery, formed c 1807, probably by Thomas Harrison of Chester, out of the four rooms on the west front of the house, but embellished by Lord de Tabley in 1840–45. Divided into three parts by low segmental arches, this impressive room has been little altered since the mid 19C, and retains furniture by Bullock and Gillow (some of whose work can be seen elsewhere in the house) and two ornate Rococo mirrors of the 1760s; there are also two early-17C virginals in playing order with painted lids. The pictures, seen to good effect against the deep red flock wall coverings, do not all live up to the quality of the setting, but they remain a valuable record of Regency artistic taste, with works by James Ward, C.R. Leslie, Benjamin Robert Haydon and other now largely forgotten artists, along with a characteristically evil-looking 'Friar Puck' by Fuseli, and Lawrence's 'Lady Leicester as Hope' (1814) occupying pride of place over the north fireplace.

GCT

Tatton Park

3½m north of Knutsford to east of A50 and A556, M6 exit 19: National Trust/Cheshire County Council, tel. 0565 654822. Open Apr–Sept daily except Mon (but open BH Mon); Oct Sat, Sun only 12–5. Garden open daily all year except Mon 10.30–6 (11–4 winter). Refreshments.

Tatton Park is essentially a late-18C and early-19C rebuilding of a late-17C house belonging to the Egerton family, whose fortunes were founded by James I's Lord Chancellor, Sir Thomas Egerton. This house superseded Tatton Old Hall, an early-16C timber structure built by the Brereton family and subsequently encased in brick, which now stands marooned in the extensive park a mile or so away (it is also open to the public). The newer house was enlarged c 1760, and in 1780 William Egerton embarked on a massive expansion which was interrupted by his death 20 years later. The architect was Samuel Wyatt, but by the time work resumed, albeit on a smaller scale, under Wilbraham Egerton in 1807, Wyatt had died and the project was placed in the hands of his nephew Lewis Wyatt, one of the lesser-known members of the celebrated architectural clan. Wilbraham Egerton was a discriminating art collector, and several of his pictures remain in the house, along with others bought in the late 19C by his grandson, the 2nd Lord Egerton. There is also an unusually good collection of furniture, especially of the early 19C, and the interiors are now sympathetically preserved and displayed by the Cheshire County Council, which has managed the house since it was given to the nation in the care of the National Trust by the 4th Lord Egerton in 1958.

As in most English country houses of its date, the main rooms are on the ground floor of the main block (which encompasses the original early-18C house), with the service accommodation placed in an attached range to one side, largely hidden behind shrubberies; a lower family wing acts as a zone of transition between the main block and the servants' quarters. The show front, essentially the work of Samuel Wyatt, faces south over the lush, largely 19C **gardens**. A giant Corinthian portico protrudes from the walls of local pink sandstone, but the house was originally entered from the north. The main reception rooms, arranged in a circuit around a central staircase, are largely the work of Lewis Wyatt; their effect is much enhanced by the superb furnishings by the cabinet-makers Gillow of Lancaster which help make the house one of the best places in which to study Regency taste in interior decoration.

The present entrance is through the family wing, and the first room to be seen is the **Card Room**, designed by Samuel Wyatt in the 1790s, and hung with pictures including Chardin's 'La Gouvernante' (1738). The **Entrance Hall** has a shallow segmental ceiling, and the Ionic columns of deep-red porphyry impart a suitable note of antique grandeur; pictures include a 'Madonna and Child with St Anne' after Murillo. The richly coloured rooms to the east reflect the influence of French taste, with several items of Boulle-revival furniture in the **Music Room**, and pieces in the Louis XV manner in the Drawing Room; they are placed in the middle of the room and not, in the outmoded 18C fashion, against the walls. Guercino's 'Absalom and Tamar' (1645) hangs in the Music Room, and in the **Drawing Room** are Van Dyck's early 'Martyrdom of St Stephen' (c 1623) and two superb Canaletto views of Venice (1730). The latter were inherited in the mid 18C, along with a large fortune, by Samuel Egerton, who had spent some time in Venice as an apprentice to the British Consul, Joseph Smith; he is depicted against a Venetian background in a portrait of c 1732 by Bartolomeo Nazzari. There are more excellent items of Gillow furniture in the **Library**, on the south front, including the bookcases filled with books going back to the 16C. The last of the main reception rooms in the **Dining Room**, decorated in the Rococo manner by Thomas Pritchard of Shrewsbury c 1763, with a series of family portraits on the walls, including one of the Jacobean Lord Chancellor over the fireplace.

The Yellow Drawing Room, in the family wing, contains a set of satinwood furniture by Gillow, and from here the route leads back to Samuel Wyatt's chastely neo-classical **Staircase Hall**—a contrast to his nephew's lavishly decorated reception rooms—with a domed rotunda further east (by Lewis

Wyatt) striking a note of spatial complexity. There are several smaller Old Master paintings here (including one by Salvator Rosa), and a series of portraits of early-18C Cheshire worthies hangs on the upper landing. The **upper floor** is given over, in the usual early-19C manner, to bedrooms and dressing rooms, two of which now contain an exhibition of architectural drawings illustrating the complicated schemes for enlarging the house in the late 18C and early 19C. The 17C Oak Staircase, brought here in the 19C, leads down to the family entrance, created in 1884 and hung with minor Old Master pictures and family portraits. From here it is possible to explore the **service wing** in an unusually thorough manner, including the cellars, before leaving via the Tenants' Hall (not always open to the public); this was added in 1935 by the 4th Lord Egerton, a noted big-game hunter, and many of his trophies are displayed on the walls, along with ethnographical curiosities collected on his travels—an odd contrast to the elegant sophistication of the remainder of the house.

GCT

CLEVELAND

Ormesby Hall

3m south east of Middlesbrough, to west of A171 Middlesbrough–Whitby; National Trust, tel. 0642 324188. Open Apr–Oct Wed, Thur, Sat, Sun, BH Mon 2–5.30. Refreshments

This neat 18C house of local sandstone lies on the edge of Middlesbrough, from which it is separated by unspoilt parkland. It was built in the early 1740s by James Pennyman (d 1743) and his wife, representatives of a family which had been at Ormesby since 1599. The rather conservative design—a plain three-storeyed box with a hipped roof—may have been supplied by the amateur architect, Col James Moyser (cf. Nostell Priory, West Yorks), a friend of the family, but the interiors seem to have been left unfinished until the 1770s, when they were fitted up by 'Wicked Sir James' Pennyman. He also built the impressive stable block (now used by the local police) in 1772, probably employing John Carr as architect. Despite some minor 19C alterations, the house remains a relatively intact example of a Georgian squire's country residence. The Pennymans continued to live at Ormesby until 1983, having given the house to the National Trust some 20 years earlier, and the comfortable interiors still retain the family pictures and furniture, and the atmosphere of a family home.

The Entrance Hall with its plaster ceiling and screens of Ionic columns at either end was decorated in a restrained early Georgian fashion c 1740, but the Drawing Room and Dining Room have plaster ceilings in the neo-classical taste, possibly by Carr, dating from the 1770s. A wooden staircase of the mid 18C leads to the upstairs rooms, arranged on either side of a corridor with richly carved wooden doorcases leading into the main bedrooms; the screen of Corinthian columns was added c 1770. The rooms, both upstairs and downstairs, are furnished with a miscellaneous collection of 18C and 19C items, and hung with an agreeable though not outstanding collection of pictures, many of them family portraits. In the former office wing, part of the previous house, there is a doorway flanked by Corinthian columns which seems to be a remnant of the Jacobean house which preceded the present one.

GCT

CORNWALL

Antony

5m west of Plymouth via Torpoint ferry on A374 2m west of Torpoint: National Trust, tel. 0752 812191. Open Apr–Oct Tues–Thur, BH Mon, Sun in June–Aug 1.30–5. Guided tours. Refreshments.

This dignified house of silver-grey granite was built in 1720–24 for Sir William Carew, descendant of an old and important Cornish family which had numbered among its members the county's first historian Richard Carew, author of *The Survey of Cornwall* (1602). It is an accomplished and rather late example of the type of gentleman's house which became popular after the Restoration, with a rectangular 'double pile' plan, two floors of equal height over a basement, a hipped roof, and pediments to the two main façades. The architect is not known for certain, though the obscure John Moyle of Exeter and the much better-known James Gibbs might both have been involved in the design.

The direct male line of the Carews came to an end in 1748, and the Antony estate was then inherited by Reginald Pole, whose family came from Shute Barton, Devon (qv.). He took the additional name of Carew, inaugurated the Torpoint ferry which linked the Antony peninsula to the flourishing naval port of Plymouth, and improved the grounds with the help of Humphry Repton. He also made some changes inside the house, eliminating the corridor which originally bisected the ground floor, but despite this, and the addition of a carrage porch to the south (entrance) front in the mid 19C, the building still retains its essentially early-18C character. Sir Reginald Pole-Carew, a successful soldier, laid out a formal garden to the north of the house and added a neo-Jacobean east wing in 1905, but the wing was demolished after the Second World War, and the gardens have been altered and beautified by Sir Reginald's son, Sir John Carew Pole; he inherited in 1924 and gave the house and grounds to the National Trust in 1962. His son now lives in the house, which has the comfortable and unostentatious atmosphere of a long-inhabited family home.

The approach from the main road leads past the estate church of St Philip and St James, designed by William White in his idiosyncratic version of High Victorian Gothic in 1863–71, and the house is entered through a formal forecourt on the south side, flanked by brick offices and closed off by a wall and iron gates—an arrangement which has not changed in its essentials since it was first depicted in a painting of c 1720. On the garden side, terraces stretch down the hillside, and artfully contrived planting of the mid 18C allows enticing vistas towards the River Lynher, one of the tributaries of the Tamar. The façades of the house are of the utmost plainness, relying for their effect on proportion rather than ornament, and the same restraint is maintained inside. The rooms are panelled in oak, and there is no elaborate plasterwork. The main interest lies in the furniture, including some pieces which have been in the house since it was first built, and the pictures, which were augmented after Sir John Carew Pole inherited the Shute estate in 1926 and subsequently married a great-niece of the American financier J.P. Morgan. There is also a good collection of oriental and English 18C porcelain.

Pride of place among the pictures in the Entrance Hall goes to a portrait of Charles I at his trial (by Edward Bower, 1648), but the anonymous picture of the county historian Richard Carew (1586) should also be noted. To the right is the Staircase, somewhat remodelled in the early 19C but still retaining its excellent wood craftsmanship with delicately turned balusters and newel posts in the form of Corinthian columns; on the lower wall is a colourful portrait by the late-16C Spanish artist Juan Pantoja de la Cruz. The Dining Room, the first of the rooms on the garden front, has a sporting picture by John Wootton (1714) showing the 4th Earl of Coventry, whose fortune, inherited by his daughter, enabled her husband, Sir William Carew, to build the present house. Beyond is the Saloon, with two excellent portraits by Reynolds of the 8th and 9th Earls of Westmorland (1762 and 1764), a sentimental 'fancy picture' by the same artist ('The Piping Shepherd Boy') and an engaging group by Thomas Beach (1793) showing the three children of Sir John Pole, cricket bats in hand, in front of Shute Barton. Some of the best furniture in the house is in the adjacent Tapestry Room, including a pair of mid-18C walnut tables with marble tops attributed to John Channon, the late-17C or early-18C tapestries, including three with the story of Diogenes, were probably made in the Soho factory, and the room retains its original marble chimneypiece with a mirror incorporated.

The Library, on the south front, contains an impressive collection of books originally housed at Shute Barton. The room is comfortably furnished, and on the walls are portraits of Carews and Poles going back to the 17C, some of them by well-known artists (Ramsay, Reynolds, Romney, etc). From here a back staircase leads up to the first floor, where several of the main bedrooms can be glimpsed and the portraits at the top of the main staircase seen, including one by Reynolds's master, Thomas Hudson, showing Sir John and Lady Pole in masquerade dress (1755). Downstairs in the east office wing, there is an excellent museum containing copies of Richard Carew's *History of Cornwall*, along with the building contract for the house and photographs of Repton's 'Red Book'.

GCT

Cotehele

On the west bank of the Tamar, off the A390: National Trust, tel. 0579 50434. Open Apr–Oct, garden, mill and quay every day 11–5.30; house every day except Fri 12–5.30 or dusk. Refreshments.

Cotehele, the medieval and Tudor house of the Edgcumbe family, lies hidden in a wooded coombe on the Cornish side of the Tamar estuary. The valley of the Tamar is tortuous and winding, so there have never been roads running up the river-side and the house has always been remote; even now, it can be difficult to find.

The Edgcumbes are an ancient Devon family. In 1353 William Edgcumbe married Hilaria de Cotehele, heiress to the manor, and their descendants owned it continuously until 1947. There was already a house here in 1353, but they added to it steadily. In 1411, Peter and Elizabeth Edgcumbe received licence to build a chapel. Their grandson Richard had a stormy career, defying Richard III and fighting for Henry Tudor at Bosworth in 1485. He held several high offices under Henry VII, including Comptroller of the Royal Household and Ambassador to Scotland, but found time to rebuild much of the house, including the gatehouse tower. He died in 1489, and his son, Sir Piers, did more rebuilding, including the present north range with the Great Hall. There were then no major alterations until 1627, when the north-west tower was added by a Flemish merchant called Sir Thomas Coteele who had fled the Spanish Inquisition—the similarity of his name to that of the house is, apparently, quite coincidental. His daughter had married Sir Richard Edgcumbe, and Coteele spent some time living here. After the death of Col Piers Edgcumbe in 1667, the family rarely resided here; finding the house to be too remote and inconvenient, they moved to Mount Edgcumbe, qv., near Plymouth. Cotehele was maintained well, but saved from change or renovation for a century and a half, preserving its 16C character by 'benign neglect'.

The Edgcumbes became Barons and then Earls, but they rarely resided at Cotehele until 1861, when the 3rd Earl died and his widow declared that she wished to retire here. A singularly tactful and restrained renovation was carried out. Lady Mount Edgcumbe lived here until her death in 1881. The family were bombed out of Mount Edgcumbe in 1941, and subsequently struck by capital taxation on the death of the 5th Earl in 1944; as a result Cotehele and 1300 acres were handed over to the National Trust in 1947, the first historic house to be acquired by the Trust in this manner.

The house stands in a romantic wooded setting, high above the Tamar. On the right-hand side of the short drive is Sir Richard Edgcumbe's barn. Ahead is the south range of the house. In essence it is 14C, plain and of rubble masonry, but the gatehouse-tower in the middle, in smoothly-cut blocks, is Sir Richard's, of c 1485–89. Through the archway is the square courtyard; to the left and right the low rubble buildings are mostly medieval; in the far left corner, the traceried window marks the position of Sir Richard's chapel. The far side of the courtyard with the Hall and Solar windows, is Sir Piers Edgcumbe's, of c 1510–20. Entering the main door, one is straightaway in Sir Piers' **hall**, with its whitewashed walls hung with arms and armour, wonderfully preserving the atmosphere of the Tudor age. The armour and the oak furniture are of the 16C and 17C.

To the left, the **Old Dining Room** is also Sir Piers' work; it is the room beneath the former Solar (now the Red and South Rooms). This room is the first of many lined with 16C and 17C tapestry. The rooms here have probably always been lined with hangings; the present ones may have replaced Tudor arras which wore out. A door behind a tapestry leads up a narrow stair into the late-15C **chapel**. It is simple and white. The barrel-vaulted ceiling has wooden ribs with the Tudor rose at the intersections, and many of the original fittings survive. The triptych on the altar of the Adoration of the Magi is Flemish, dated 1589. In the south-west corner is a very rare survival, the clock installed by Sir Richard when he built the chapel, c 1489. The clock, which is weight driven, has no face, but sounds a (replacement) bell on the chapel roof.

To the north the Old Dining Room is the **Punch Room**, hung with cheerful tapestries of drinking scenes, from the Soho factory, with early-18C furniture. From here, steep and narrow stairs lead up to the **White Room**, the lowest room in the tower, dating from 1627. It is again lined with Flemish and English tapestry, and furnished as a bedroom. The bed is of walnut and probably from Goa in India; the crewel-work hangings are also 17C. From here, you go up again to the first floor of Sir Piers Edgcumbe's buildings. The **Red Room** is dark, lined with Flemish tapestries, and dominated by an immense bed with crimson hangings. From here, a door under tapestry leads into the **South Room** formerly part of Sir Piers' Solar. There are more tapestries depicting the Foundation of Rome, and a bed with embroidered hangings of c 1680. The **upper landing** has a strangely carved pair of Welsh chairs, and, set into the wall, the Cotehele Tester. This great carved panel was the ceiling board of a 16C bed; its carved scenes have a powerful, primitive quality. From here, stairs lead back into Sir Thomas Cotehele's tower. The **Old Drawing Room** is lined with Brussels tapestry, depicting the 'History of Man', and there is Indo-Dutch ebony furniture of the 17C. A winding stair leads to the top floor of the tower, where there are two bedrooms. The smaller, called **Queen Anne's Room** for no apparent reason, is largely filled by a great bed made up of various pieces of 16C and 17C beds. **King Charles' Room** is named from the belief that the unfortunate monarch stayed here in 1644 on his way from Liskeard to Exeter. The bed is reconstructed out of 16C pieces; both these rooms are lined with tapestry.

Visitors finally emerge from the house into the little Kitchen Court, at the core of Sir Piers' buildings. On the east side is the **Kitchen**. This was in use up until 1946, but it has been restored to its early-19C appearance. The room is very high, its great hearth 10ft wide; there is an array of 18C and 19C kitchen implements. Only cooking and baking were done here; storage, preparation and cleaning of pots all took place in various pantries opening off the Kitchen Court.

The **garden** at Cotehele is largely a Victorian creation, with lush planting, at different levels on the valley-side. There are various attendant buildings in the grounds, the medieval dovecote and the Prospect Tower—probably an 18C folly. There is a fine walk by the river from Calstock, a mile and a half upstream, to **Cotehele Quay**, half a mile downstream, where the Trust has renovated the docks and some of the old warehouses. Down here is the Chapel in the Wood, built by Sir Richard Edgcumbe to mark a hiding-place where he escaped his foes in 1483. A small museum tells the story of trade on the Tamar, and the Edgcumbe Arms serves simple meals in the summer months. The Morden stream runs into the Tamar here, and half a mile up the valley is the **manor mill**, which has worked at least since the 16C. The Trust has renovated this, along with the various workshops for the estate craftsmen.

SB

Godolphin House

5m north west of Helston between Townshend and Godolphin Cross: Mrs Schofield. Open May, June BH Mon, Thur; July–Sept Tues, Thur 2–5 (also Thur in Aug 10–1). Refreshments.

This evocative granite-built house is a substantial fragment of a larger building which until the mid 18C was the home of the Godolphins, one of the leading families of west Cornwall. They derived their wealth from the local tin-mining industry, and in 1536 the traveller John Leland wrote that there were 'no greater Tynne works in all Cornwall than be on Sir William Godolcan's ground'. Sir William was a soldier who accompanied Henry VIII to the siege of Boulogne in 1544, and he may have carried out alterations to the already existing house, which consisted by the mid 16C of three ranges of building, with a crenellated wall to close off the courtyard on the north side. Further alterations were carried out at the end of the 16C by Sir Francis Godolphin, another leading promoter of the tin industry and Governor of the Scilly Isles, and the present north or entrance range may have been built by his son William in the 1630s to replace the original screen wall. The house reached its apogee in the mid 17C, and in 1689 it was said to contain about a hundred rooms. William Godolphin's grandson, Sidney, went into national politics and, as Lord Treasurer from 1702 to 1710, was responsible for financing the Duke of Marlborough's wars; he was made Earl of Godolphin and married his son to Marlborough's daughter, but he spent little time at his ancestral home, and his son went there even less. When the 2nd Earl died in 1766, the estate passed via his daughter to the Duke of Leeds and in 1805 there were large-scale demolitions, including the 16C hall. The house then became a farmhouse, and it was finally sold by the then Duke of Leeds in 1929, the family of the present owner acquiring it seven years later.

The house is hidden away among woods next to extensive farm buildings, with the remnants of old formal gardens clearly visible on the north and east sides. The long, symmetrical north range presides impressively over the entrance forecourt, with its mullioned and transomed windows of the simplified type popular in the mid 17C and its colonnade of stumpy Doric monoliths at ground level—a sign of the growing appeal of classical architecture, even in remote Cornwall. A gateway of c 1575 under the colonnade leads through the original screen wall of the 16C house and into the courtyard, where the buildings to the east and west survive intact. The east range has mullioned windows of c 1530–40, but those to the west date from the early 17C. The south or hall range has gone completely, except for its front wall and Gothic-arched porch (ex situ); foundations of more buildings have been discovered in the yard beyond (not accessible to visitors).

The spacious, uncluttered rooms exude a strong sense of the past; they are appropriately furnished with tapestries and old furniture, some original to the house and brought back by the present owner. There is a good late-16C chimneypiece in the room which now serves as the Entrance Hall, but the finest room from a decorative point of view is the Dining Room, on the ground floor of the east range. The linen-fold panelling and carved beams here date from the early 16C, and there is a picture by John Wootton (1731) of an Arab horse belonging to the 2nd Earl of Godolphin held by a nonchalant-looking man in Turkish dress. A gallery or passageway on the first floor of the north range leads to the west range, which probably contained the main reception rooms of the house in its 17C heyday. They are quite plainly decorated apart from some simple plasterwork, but the light and spacious King's Room—the original great chamber—contains an elaborately carved doorway of 1604 (possibly not in its original place) commemorating the marriage of Sir William Godolphin to a daughter of the Sidney family.

GCT

Lanhydrock House

South east of Bodmin on the Lostwithiel road (B3268): National Trust, tel. 0208 73320. Open Apr–Oct daily except Mon (open BH Mon) 11–5 (4.30 in Oct). Refreshments.

Lanhydrock means 'Valley of Saint Hydrock', and the house indeed stands in its own sequestered valley. The park runs down to the River Fowey and is thickly surrounded by plantations on all sides. Of the two entrances, the best is that from the east near Bodmin Parkway station. The long avenue climbs gently through the beautiful park; the gatehouse first appears in the distance, and then the great grey house behind it with the little church to the right, framed by the beech-woods rising behind.

In the 16C the Robartes family of Truro were prosperous merchants and bankers. In 1616 Richard Robartes was knighted, and in 1620 he bought the manor of Lanhydrock, once a possession of the Priory of St Petroc, Bodmin. He became Baron Robartes in 1624, dying ten years later. He demolished the old monastic grange, and began a new house, finished by his son, the 2nd Lord, c 1642. The 2nd Lord declared for Parliament in the Civil War, but thereafter retired from politics. He planted the sycamore avenue in 1648, and built the gatehouse in 1651. On the restoration he was received at court, and made Earl of Radnor in 1679. The earldom died out in 1740, and Lanhydrock passed via marriage twice, going to the Agar family in 1804. Thomas James Agar-Robartes became Baron Robartes of Truro in 1869; he was a model Victorian landowner, much concerned with improving the lot of the miners and farmers who provided the sources of his wealth. This life was shattered when, in 1881, Lanhydrock burnt down. Lady Robartes died of the shock, and her husband never recovered from the double blow, dying the following year. Their son, the 2nd Baron, immediately rebuilt the house as it is today, keeping the exterior almost identical to the old house. He inherited the title of Viscount Clifden in 1899; his second son, the 7th Viscount, gave the house and park to the National Trust in 1953.

The house is approached through the pretty two-storeyed gatehouse, and the house rises beyond lawns. It was originally quadrangular, but in 1780 the east range (facing the gatehouse) was removed. All of this was gutted in 1881 except for the north wing. The 2nd Lord Robartes and his architect, Richard Coad, took four years to rebuild the house, recreating the main façades exactly. It is two-storeyed and symmetrical, the windows tall and mullioned but without transoms, all in silver-grey granite. The parapets are all battlemented, and there is hardly a trace of the Renaissance anywhere. Inside, though, all the rooms except one are of the 1880s. The tour is a long one, and takes in much of the servants' side of the house, as well as the principal rooms.

The **Outer Hall** has brown panelling and Jacobean-style plasterwork on the ceiling; it is furnished as a comfortable 'lounge-hall'. Through the Inner Hall, you turn into the **Dining Room**, with excellent woodwork, and William Morris's Sunflower wallpaper between the panelling and the cornice. The Serving Room retains original fittings for keeping the food hot and from here, the tour takes in the whole ensemble of **Kitchen** quarters, including the Scullery, Dairy, Meat Larder, Fish Larder and Bakehouse. All the furnishings and equipment remain, as bought new in the 1880s; there are few places where the everyday workings of a great Victorian household can be recaptured so completely.

Visitors return via the Butler's Passage to the south wing of the house. **Lady Robartes' Room** remains as it was when she conducted the household business here. Then comes the masculine preserve of the Steward's Room, Smoking Room and Billiard Room. The Steward's Room has plans and views of the house at various stages, and the **Billiard Room** is especially handsome, with windows on three sides, and its table and fittings all complete.

The Nursery Staircase gives access to **Lord Robartes' Room**, and the huge adjacent bathroom, leading into Lady Robartes' Room. Here you are in the west wing, where the ceilings are higher; the furniture, again, was nearly all ordered new in the 1880s. Visitors next see more of the servant's side—the Housemaids' Closet, the Linen Lobby, and then a number of servants' bedrooms on the top floor. Back on the first floor, Miss Eva's Room was occupied by the Hon. Everilda Agar-Robartes, the last member of the family to live in the house. It is filled with family photographs and prints, over William Morris wallpaper. The boudoir is a grander room, looking over the courtyard, and was a retreat for the ladies. The **Oak Staircase**, the grand staircase of the house, is dominated by the great full-length portrait of Sir Richard Robartes, builder of the house. The **Morning Room** and **Drawing Room** together make a big L-shape, which could be divided by double-doors. Both have high, elaborate barrel-vaulted ceilings, and there are fine 18C portraits of the Robartes family, 18C English furniture and 17C Flemish and Mortlake tapestries.

From the Drawing Room you descend a few steps into the magnificent **Gallery**. This is one of the grandest rooms in the West Country. It occupies the whole first floor of the north wing, the only part to escape the 1881 fire. It is 116ft long, with windows on three sides and carved panelling, and the barrel-vaulted ceiling has some of the finest plasterwork of its date in England. Its 24 main panels show incidents from the Old Testament; the smaller panels have a multitude of birds and beasts. It is strange to reflect that this was made c 1640–42, while England was descending into Civil War. The gallery is richly furnished with 17C and 18C furniture, and with family portraits of the same period.

The **church** of St Hydroc, close by the north west corner of the house, was restored in the 1880s; there is a Celtic cross outside, perhaps of the 13C. Immediately around the house are formal **gardens** with clipped yews and roses. The bronze urns are French, made for Louis XIV's Versailles by his goldsmith, Ballin. In the woods above the house are extensive gardens with lush late-19C planting, rich in flowering trees and shrubs.

SB

Mount Edgcumbe

2m west of Plymouth at Cremyll on B3247 or via Stonehouse–Cremyll foot ferry. City of Plymouth/Cornwall County Council, tel. 0752 822236. Open Apr–Oct Wed–Sun, BH Mon 11–5.30. Gardens open every daily all year. Refreshments in park.

Mount Edgcumbe is one of the earliest English country houses—as opposed to fortified castles—to be sited so as to 'command a prospect': in this case a spectacular view of Plymouth Sound, one of the finest natural harbours in England. The estate, comprising the Rame peninsula and what was then known as West Stonehouse, came by marriage in the early 16C to Sir Piers Edgcumbe, whose family seat was Cotehele (qv.), ten miles away to the north. He created a deer park in 1539, and in 1547 his son, Richard, signed a contract with a local mason, Roger Palmer, to build a house or lodge on a new site high up on the hillside overlooking the harbour, according to a 'plat' (plan) supplied by an unknown third person—possibly someone connected with the King's Office of Works. The plan eschewed the sprawling courtyard layout of houses like Cotehele in favour of a compact rectangular arrangement with corner towers and a top-lit hall in the centre. By breaking so decisively with medieval precedent, Mount Edgcumbe deserves a more important place in English architectural history than it has usually been given.

Richard Edgcumbe's house underwent many later changes, and today only the general layout and some of the stonework survive. Mount Edgcumbe became the main family seat when the Edgcumbes abandoned Cotehele in the late 17C, and there was much internal remodelling and some external rebuilding in the 18C and early 19C. The circular corner towers were given their present octagonal form in 1749 in the time of Richard, 1st Lord Edgcumbe, a political crony of Sir Robert Walpole, and further changes occurred in 1818 and in the early 1840s. Far more important was the transformation of the grounds carried out by Lord Edgcumbe's son, an admiral who became 1st Earl of Mount Edgcumbe in 1789, and his grandson. They succeeded in turning Mount Edgcumbe into one of the finest and most celebrated of all English landscape gardens, vying in the minds of the cognoscenti with Stowe and Stourhead. The gardens still survive largely intact, but the house was gutted by German bombs in the Blitz on Plymouth in 1941 and it remained a ruin until 1958, when the 6th Earl of Mount Edgcumbe employed Adrian Gilbert Scott, a member of the well-known family of architects, to rebuild it (with a steel frame and concrete floors). In its present form, therefore, Mount Edgcumbe provides an example rare among English country houses open to the public, of post-War taste in interior design. The house and 865 acres were purchased jointly by Plymouth City Council and Cornwall County Council in 1971, and the land was turned into a country park. The 8th Earl moved out of the house in 1987, and the current owners are now engaged on a programme of refurnishing it.

The best approach is by the broad avenue leading up from the Cremyll ferry, from which the symmetrical turreted house is seen from below, as intended, with woods crowning the hillside behind it. A late-17C wing was demolished after the Second World War and it was then unfortunately decided not to rebuild the pinnacled top storey over the hall, which gave much-needed height to the centre of the building. At the same time rendering was removed from the walls, which are of red sandstone with granite dressings. Most of the external detailing seems to date from the early 19C, but the entrance portal, at the centre of the north front, retains the original mid-16C doorway enfolded by rather lumpy Doric pilasters and a pediment, probably of the late 17C.

The interior is neo-Georgian in character, and has something of the comfortable yet semi-public atmosphere of an embassy or a vice-regal lodge. The most impressive room is the Hall, cleverly rebuilt by Scott to provide an imposing staircase at the east end and a gallery at first-floor level. A large part of the family's collection of pictures and furniture perished in the Blitz, and today some of the rooms feel a little empty. There are two Van de Velde seascapes in the Drawing Room, overlooking a formal 19C garden, along with a Boulle desk and Reynolds's portrait of the 2nd Lord Edgcumbe, the only one among several pictures by this locally-born master to have survived the Blitz (on account, it is said, of the subject's addiction to gambling and other pleasures, which caused the picture to be relegated to the basement by his more respectable successors). There is a 19C picture of a tenants' dinner in the hall at Cotehele in the Library, and in the Dining Room (on the site of the 16C kitchen) are two 16C Flemish hunting tapestries brought from that house. Upstairs there are a number of comfortable bedrooms, complete with bathrooms, and there is also a small chapel commemorating the only son of the 6th Earl, who was killed in the War—a poignant appendage to a house whose main raison d'etre now seems to have largely vanished.

The tour of the grounds comprises enough vistas and visual surprises to satisfy the most demanding seeker after picturesque variety. In the immediate proximity of the house there is a formal mid-19C garden, but further away to the north of the house there are gardens created in the Italian, French and English styles in the early 19C, complete with their appropriate architectural adornments. Further east there is a mid-18C circular temple dedicated to the poet Milton close to an amphitheatre hollowed out from the hillside, and, to the south of that, a sham ruin poised dramatically on a hillside overlooking Plymouth Sound. Beyond is that most 'sublime' and awe-inspiring of all natural phenomena: the sea.

GCT

Pencarrow

4m north west of Bodmin on A389 Bodmin–Wadebridge: Lt Col. Sir Arscott Molesworth-St Aubyn, Bt, tel. 020884 369. Open Easter–mid Oct Sun–Thur (gardens daily) 1.30–5 (June–mid Sept, BH Mon 11–5). Guided tours. Refreshments.

This large 18C house stands in sheltered, wooded country to the west of Bodmin Moor, and the presence of an Iron Age encampment along the mile-long drive is proof of its attractiveness as a place of habitation over many centuries. The Molesworth family first came to live here in the late 16C, and they subsequently enriched themselves with the profits of colonial trade and the proceeds of prudent marriages. Sir Hender Molesworth was Governor of Jamaica in the 1680s, in recognition of which he was given a baronetcy by William III which passed on his death to his elder brother Sir John Molesworth of Pencarrow, Vice-Admiral of north Cornwall. The present house was begun, probably on older foundations, by Sir John's grandson, the 4th Baronet, and was finished by his son after his death in 1766; the architect was a Yorkshireman, Robert Allanson. Internal alterations were carried out in the 1840s by Sir William Molesworth, the 8th Baronet, who was sent down from Cambridge for challenging his mathematics tutor to a duel. He was subsequently educated at Edinburgh and in Germany, becoming a Radical politician, finally achieving ministerial office in the 1850s as First Commissioner of Works and then as Colonial Secretary, He laid out the formal garden to the south of the house and planted the surrounding woodland gardens, which were said to contain examples of all but ten of the types of conifer then known to man, including the first monkey-puzzle to be planted in England.

When Molesworth died childless in 1855 the house was left first to his widow and then to his sister, and little was done to it until 1919, when some internal alterations were carried out by Sir Ernest Newton for Sir Hugh Molesworth-St Aubyn, 13th Baronet. He came from a younger branch of the family which had inherited some of the pictures and property of the St Aubyns, an important family in west Cornwall (cf. St Michael's Mount), two of whose daughters had married Molesworths in the 18C. Today the interest of Pencarrow is enhanced by the mingling of the possessions of these two families.

The house has two main **façades**, both of them stuccoed, with roofs of the local slate; one (which may have been intended as the original entrance) looks south over the splendid formal garden created by Sir William Molesworth in the middle of the 19C, and the other faces east, where the entrance is now. Both are dignified enough, though neither show any great architectural inventiveness. The interiors are more interesting than might be expected from the outside, due in part to the quality of the decoration, in part to the excellence of the contents, and in part to the slightly faded charm which accompanies houses which have remained in the same family for a long time and have not fallen prey to ambitious 20C interior decorators.

The **Entrance Hall**, which doubles up as a library, has early-18C wood panelling brought by Sir William Molesworth in the 1840s from Tetcott (Devon), which came to the family as a result of one of their several marriages to heiresses. Tetcott was the home of the Arscott family, and portraits of 18C Arscotts look down into the room from above the bookcases; there is also good K'ang Hsi porcelain. To the north is the **Music Room**, with Rococo plasterwork on the ceiling and a splendid Rococo frame for the overmantel picture of Roche Rock by the early-19C Plymouth artist Samuel Cook. The niche in the north wall was originally contrived by Sir William Molesworth and his architect George Wightwick of Plymouth for an organ, but now contains a copy of the 'Medici Venus' apparently brought back by Sir William from Rome in about 1830—an effective visual *coup de théâtre*.

The **Drawing Room**, on the south front, was not altered significantly in the 19C, and retains its Palladian-style doorcases, some late-18C gilt furniture, and curtains made out of damask captured from a Spanish treasure ship in 1762. It leads into the **Inner Hall**, remodelled in the 19C and now hung with pictures which include seascapes by Charles Brooking and two splendid views of the Pool of London with the Tower and Old London Bridge by Samuel Scott (1755). At the foot of the **staircase**, which is lit by a Venetian window, is an extraordinary early-19C cast-iron stove surmounted by lamps, and on the walls are more family portraits, including one by Raeburn of the 7th Baronet, who had married a Scottish wife; there is also a portrait by Edward Bower of Charles I at his trail which probably came to Pencarrow through the marriage of the 4th Baronet—the builder of the house—to the heiress of the Morice family of Werrington (now in Devon). Other portraits from the same source hang in the Pink Bedroom, together with works by Catharine St Aubyn, a pupil of the local artist John Opie, and in the Boudoir, also on the first floor, there are 17C Dutch paintings including a Dutch interior by Pieter Neefs and a pastel by Rosalba Carriera.

The ground floor is reached again by a back staircase, hung with 18C views by an unknown local artist and more portraits, including representations of the politician Sir William Molesworth and his wife (described as 'a dark, experienced beauty'). This leads into the **Dining Room**, balancing the Drawing Room at the other end of the south front, and also plainly decorated, but with a good chimneypiece incorporating a scene from Aesop's fables. The main interest, though, lies in the superb early series of portraits by Sir Joshua Reynolds, dating from the period when he was still largely relying on patronage from his native south-west England, and including three (one of them over the fireplace) of the 5th Baronet, who completed his father's building of the house. Last comes the exquisite

Ante-Room (possibly the original entrance hall), with more good 18C pictures, among them a conversation piece by Arthur Devis (1754) showing four sisters standing in a garden with St Michael's Mount in the background, more portraits of the 1760s by the Dutch artist J.S.C. Schaak, and two landscapes by Richard Wilson, one of them showing the River Thames at Marble Hill, Greater London (qv.). The walls are covered in linen with a Chinese pattern, there is a lacquer cabinet and blanc de Chine porcelain and, on a table in the middle, a most unusual Ch'ien Lung bowl of c 1765 with a view of Pencarrow painted on it. From here visitors can proceed into the Italianate **garden** created by Sir William Molesworth, and beyond that to the rock garden—whose granite boulders were supposedly dragged here from Bodmin Moor by grateful tenants—a lake and other delights.

GCT

Prideaux Place

At Padstow 7m west of Wadebridge: Peter Prideaux-Brune, tel. 0841 532411 or 532945. Open two weeks after Easter then Spring BH–Sept Sun–Thur 1.30–5. Guided tours. Refreshments.

Originally called simply Place, Prideaux Place derives its present name from the family which has lived here since 1592. The estate, with its deer park which claims to be the oldest in England, belonged to Bodmin Priory in the Middle Ages, and was acquired after the Reformation by a lawyer, Nicholas Prideaux. His great-nephew, another Nicholas, built the house in a beautiful situation on a hillside above the small fishing port of Padstow in 1592, and ten years later Richard Carew wrote in his *Survey of Cornwall* that 'from his new and stately house [he] taketh a full and large prospect of the town, haven and country adjoining, to all which his wisdom is a stay, his authority a direction'. The view of the town has since been obscured by planting, but the front of the house would still be easily recognisable to Nicholas Prideaux, as would the prospect of the estuary of the River Camel.

Alterations to both house and grounds took place in the time of Edmond Prideaux, who inherited the estate from a cousin in 1728. He went to Italy in the 1730s, and soon afterwards built or remodelled the south wing which projects from the parlour end of the main block, giving the house an L-shape; he also constructed ornamental buildings in the gardens, some of which still survive. His son Humphrey, who succeeded him in 1745, landscaped the grounds and gave the east (entrance) front its present appearance by removing the gables from the wings at either end and building the toy-like castellated wall in front. More Gothickry followed in the time of the Rev. Charles Prideaux, who inherited in 1793 and took the additional name Brune on being left the Dorset estates of his mother's family; the results of his efforts (for which no architect has been discovered) can be seen both inside and outside the south range, which was given its present form in 1810, and in the stable block to the north. The house has since remained structurally unaltered, and the present owner has carried out an ambitious programme of restoration and internal redecoration, which is still continuing.

The main front follows the conventional Elizabethan E-shape, but the rugged granite walls and small mullioned windows are typically Cornish. Around the corner to the left is the castellated south front, much as the Rev. Charles Prideaux-Brune left it in 1810 apart from a reduction in the height of the central tower, a second pinnacled tower to the left remains untouched. The Ionic temple next to this was built by Edmond Prideaux in 1739, and there is another monument to his enthusiasm for the Antique in the form of an alcove at the south end of the lawn containing carved inscriptions collected in Italy, while on the hillside there is a 9C Celtic cross.

The house is entered through a screens passage, which leads into the single-storeyed hall (now the Dining Room), with a portrait of Sir Nicholas Prideaux, the builder of the house, over the fireplace. Despite 18C and 19C alterations, much of the original Elizabethan panelling survives, along with more which was brought in during the 19C, notably the screen with its fine inlaid work, possibly of Spanish origin. The Morning Room occupies the site of the Elizabethan parlour, but was panelled in the early 18C and now contains good 17C and 18C pictures, including two rustic scenes by the younger Teniers, a pastel of Humphrey Prideaux by the Italian woman artist Rosalba Carriera (who wrote him a love letter which was later found behind the frame), and several works by John Opie, 'the Cornish Reynolds', who grew up on the estate and was helped in his early years by Humphrey Prideaux; they include a self-portrait and two pictures of the family's dogs. Next comes the spacious early-19C Drawing Room, which occupies the bow at the centre of the south front and contains good late-18C satinwood furniture; at the time of writing (1992) the walls were about to be decorated with frescoes by Alec Cobbe (cf. Hatchlands, Surrey). The adjacent Grenville Room is named after the Grenville family, cousins of the Prideaux, from whose magnificent house at Stow, near Bude, the late-17C panelling came, together with the paintings by Verrio over the doors and fireplace, after it was demolished in 1739. Edmond Prideaux enriched the room further by introducing the ornate gilded mirror, table and pedestals at the west end, and there is also some good 18C furniture and porcelain.

There is a return to Regency Gothic in the Library, which occupies the tower at the end of the south range and is covered with a plaster ribbed vault. Some of the original Gothic furniture of c 1810 still survives, and the heraldic stained glass in the windows imparts an appropriate sense of ancient possession. The space between the two wings of the house is occupied by an unexpectedly impressive Staircase Hall, also of c 1810, hung with family portraits, and embellished with delicate Gothic decoration in plaster (note the niches containing busts of Pitt and Fox); some 18C English and Chinese export porcelain is also displayed in cases. The cantilevered staircase leads up to the 16C Great Chamber over the hall, panelled in the early 18C and hung with family portraits mostly of that date, but still retaining its original barrel-vaulted ceiling and its exuberant plasterwork of the late 16C or early 17C, probably carried out by the team of Devon plasterers which worked at Lanhydrock (qv.); note especially the pendants hanging from the ceiling (a speciality of south-west England) and the lively panel of 'Moses striking the rock' on the north wall.

GCT

St Michael's Mount

At Marazion, south of A394 Penzance–Helston: National Trust, tel. 0736 710507. Open Apr–Oct Mon–Fri (and some weekends) 10.30–5.30. Refreshments.

Ever since prehistoric times there have probably been buildings on the island which emerges so dramatically from the waters of Mounts Bay, but it was not until the 17C that the mount became the site of a country house, albeit one of a highly unusual character. The oldest buildings date back to the 12C, following the establishment in 1135 of a Benedictine priory on the top of the mount as a dependency of the comparable (though much larger) monastery of Mont St Michael in Normandy. But apart from the monastic church, which was rebuilt in the late 14C, the refectory, and a detached Lady Chapel of 1478, little survived the Dissolution. The island then passed into the hands of the King, who turned it into a garrison, but it was sold in 1599, and thereafter successive 'captains' or governors lived for short periods in a fort which was created out of the monastic buildings, the church meanwhile falling into disrepair.

The last Captain of the Mount was John St Aubyn of Clowance, near Camborne. He was appointed by Parliament after the island was surrendered by the last Royalist governor, and in 1659 he bought the island outright. His son was given a baronetcy and his grandson the 2nd Baronet stayed on the mount on occasion in the early 18C 'for melancholy retirement and as an asylum from the world and its follies'. The 3rd Baronet began to restore the house in the 1730s and his son the 4th Baronet created two Gothic rooms in the former Lady Chapel in the early 1750s, presumably for occasional visits from Clowance. Otherwise little was done until after Sir John St Aubyn, the 5th and last Baronet, died without legitimate children in 1839. The main family estates then passed to his nephew, from whom they descended in time to the Molesworth-St Aubyns of Pencarrow (qv.). But the mount, together with some of the property on the mainland, went to the oldest of his fifteen illegitimate children, and in 1873–78 Sir John St Aubyn, later 1st Lord St Levan, employed his cousin Piers St Aubyn, an architect best known for his many church restorations in Cornwall, to remodel the older buildings on top of the mount and to build a completely new family wing (not open to the public) lower down on the slope. The whole mount was given to the National Trust in 1954, but the family have continued to live in the Victorian wing, leaving the older parts of the house as a popular resort for visitors in search of the old, the strange, and the picturesque.

The island is approached either by boats which run regularly from Marazion, or, at low tide, on foot by an ancient causeway. From the harbour a steep path winds up to the top of the hill, from which point there are spectacular views across Mounts Bay (note also the ancient Celtic cross which existed before the Benedictine monastery was founded, and the later gun emplacements). The house is wrapped around the formerly monastic church, whose tower is the most prominent landmark from a distance, and the entrance is from the west, through a largely 16C building which formerly served as the residence of successive Captains of the Mount; the trim-looking stonework of the battlements, chimneys and window mullions bears witness to the thoroughness of Piers St Aubyn's restoration (the date 1878 is carved on the top floor of the wing to the left of the entrance), but the detailing is generally accurate and the rugged architecture still conveys a strong flavour of the island's turbulent past.

The first impressive room to be seen is that known for some time as the Chevy Chase Room, after a series of hunting scenes, supposedly based on the ancient ballad of that name, on the plaster frieze, which carries the date 1641. The room formerly served as the monastic refectory, and the much-restored arch-roof dates from the 15C, but the ecclesiastical-looking chairs were, with one exception, made in 1800, and other Gothic embellishments may date from about the same time. Visitors emerge from here onto a terrace over the Victorian family wing, and from here the route leads past the east end of the impressive though much-restored church to the former Lady Chapel, turned into an ante-room and two drawing rooms by an unknown architect and craftsmen in the mid 18C (the work was completed by 1755, but the vestibule and external embellishments date from c 1770). The surprisingly untouched interiors are an excellent example of Rococo Gothic at its most delicate and insouciant, with excellent plasterwork and furniture (especially chairs of 1760 in the Chippendale Gothic manner), and the walls are hung with 18C pictures by Hudson, Gainsborough and the 'Cornish Reynolds' John Opie (a view of the Mount by moonlight, 1796, and portraits of the wicked though popular 5th Baronet and his attractive wife, a local farmer's daughter). The tour concludes downstairs, where a museum has been created in the former Kitchen.

GCT

Trelowarren

6m south east of Helston off B3293 at St Keverne: Sir John Vyvyan/the Trelowarren Fellowship, tel. 032622 366. Open mid Apr–early Oct Wed, BH Mon 2–5.30. Guided tours.

Situated in a hollow at the end of an unusually long drive in lushly wooded country to the south of the Helford river, Trelowarren is a large, much-remodelled house whose origins go back to the 15C, when the Vyvyan family—one of the oldest and most illustrious in Cornwall—came into the estate by marriage to an heiress. In its present form, the house consists of a main block with two long wings projecting to the west, one of them containing a chapel and the other family quarters (not open to the public). The oldest part of the chapel dates from the 15C, and there is some 16C masonry in the east range, but the building did not begin to take on its present form until 1662, when Sir Richard Vyvyan, who was made a baronet in recognition of his support for the Royalist cause, reconstructed the east range as a 'double pile' house. The stable block to the west of the house, was built in 1698 by the 3rd Baronet, who was later imprisoned in the Tower of London for supporting the Jacobites in the 1715 rebellion, and the main part of the house was altered internally by the 5th Baronet in 1753–60 to the designs of Thomas Edwards (cf. Trewithen). The chapel, which takes up the whole of the long south wing, was redecorated in a Wyattesque Gothic manner in the 18C or early 19C, possibly in the time of Sir Vyall Vyvyan, who was responsible for landscaping the grounds, and the north wing was reconstructed *de novo* by his son Sir Richard Vyvyan, who succeeded him in 1820. Sir Richard also carried out further alterations to the interior of the main (east) block in 1831, and turned the chapel into a music room.

Since then there have been few changes to the structure of the house, but the character of the interior changed drastically when the family retreated to the north wing after the Second World War, taking their furniture (but not the family portraits) with them. In 1974 the main part of the house was leased to a Christian fellowship, which has reinstated the chapel, and the stable block is now used for craft workshops and similar activities.

The first glimpse of the stone-built house is highly picturesque, with the two-storeyed east range, crenellated and with mullioned windows, rising above the long wings which stretch forward to embrace the visitor. The house was originally entered through the open forecourt formed by these wings, but in 1818 the entrance was moved to the further side of the east range and the forecourt was grassed over. The tour takes in all the main reception rooms, which are used regularly by the Trelowarren Fellowship and have, perhaps inevitably, a slightly institutional air. Some of the rooms, notably the Staircase Hall (now the entrance hall) and an upstairs room used for occasional exhibitions, have delicate mid-18C Gothic decoration, but most were decorated in the 19C. They are hung with a good set of Vyvyan portraits stretching back to the 17C, including works by William Dobson and Cornelius Johnson. More impressive is the Chapel, late-Gothic outside (note the curious round-arched windows with their Perpendicular tracery), and internally little changed since the late 18C or early 19C, when a profusion of plaster pinnacles, crockets and ogee arches was introduced by an unknown architect and craftsmen, making it a largely untouched example of the pre-Pugin Gothic Revival at its most attractive.

GCT

Trerice

3m south east of Newquay to south of A3058 Newquay–St Austell at Kestle Mill: National Trust, tel. 0637 875404. Open Apr–Oct daily except Tues 11–5.30 (11–5 in Oct) Refreshments.

Trerice is a beautifully textured Elizabethan house built of silvery limestone and hidden away among the deep lanes of rural Cornwall, far removed in spirit from the holiday commercialism of nearby Newquay. Though parts of an older building are incorporated into the south wing, the bulk of the house was built c 1570–73 by Sir John Arundell, a member of one of Cornwall's leading families and a man who, in the words of his son-in-law Richard Carew the county historian, 'for frank, well ordered, and continual hospitality...outwent all show of competence'. The Arundells remained in possession until the death of the 4th Lord Arundell in 1768, after which the house passed first to the Wentworth and then to the Acland families (cf. Killerton, Devon), and for much of the late 18C and 19C it was let out, like many other houses of its type and date, to tenant farmers. The estate was sold by the Aclands in 1915, by which time the north part of the house had been largely demolished. The house and grounds then went through several ownerships before being bought by the National Trust in 1953 with the proceeds of funds bequeathed for the purchase of property in Devon and Cornwall. The Trust has since rebuilt the north range, using some of the old stonework which had fortunately been preserved, and has furnished the formerly empty rooms.

The house is now approached from the south, but the main front faces east, and there is still a walled garden here fronting a lane, with sturdy gate-piers, and a pair of stone lions (originally at another of the Arundells' Cornish houses) guarding the pathway which leads to the entrance. The façade is a highly pleasing composition, with wings projecting at each end and a porch in the centre, all surmounted by fancifully carved gables of Flemish inspiration—an unusual feature to be found at such an early date in so remote a part of the country. There are more gables of rather different design on the main block, and the presence of a hall of the traditional kind is indicated by a large mullioned and transomed window to the left of the porch.

The entrance leads through the usual screens passage (the original screen has gone) and into the white-painted Hall, sparsely furnished as it doubtless always has been, and bathed in light from the huge window. The flat late-16C ceiling with its plaster ribs and globular pendants was restored by Sir Thomas Dyke-Acland c 1840, and he also introduced the long oak table, the only piece of furniture in the house at the time the Trust acquired it. The Drawing Room occupies the ground floor of the pre-Elizabethan range to the south of the main house, but the bay window was introduced by Sir John Arundell in the late 16C and there were major alterations in the early 19C; the room is well furnished with 18C and early-19C pieces, and the pictures include works by the Cornish artist John Opie—note especially the striking self-portrait and the portrait of his second wife. Above is the Great Chamber, with a lavish plaster overmantel dated 1573 and an equally splendid barrel-vaulted plaster ceiling of the same date; the largely 18C furniture includes some Chippendale armchairs originally at Coleshill House (Berkshire), and there is a large 17C Aubusson tapestry of Judith and Holofernes on loan from the Victoria and Albert Museum. More late-16C plasterwork survives in the upstairs corridor or Gallery which leads along the west wall of the hall from the Great Chamber to the 'minstrels' gallery' over the screens passage, there are also some good pictures here, including an 'Ecce Homo' by Vincenzo Foppa. The rooms on the first floor of the remodelled north range are attractively furnished with late-17C and 18C pieces, and from here a subsidiary staircase leads down to the former service courtyard on the west side of the house, overlooked by a massive barn in the local vernacular style (now the NT refreshment room).

GCT

Trewithen

East of Probus on A390 Truro–St Austell: Michael Galsworthy. Open Apr–July Mon, Tues, Aug BH Mon 2–4.30 (gardens March–Sept daily except Sun 10–4.30). Guided tours.

Trewithen is a moderately sized 18C squire's house set amidst an attractive woodland garden (the name means 'house in the spinney'). The house was built and decorated by three generations of the Hawkins family, starting with Philip Hawkins, a younger son of a rich lawyer and MP for the local rotten borough of Grampound. He purchased the estate in the early 18C and, in the words of Thomas Tonkins's *Parochial History* (1730), 'much improved this seat, new built a great part of the house, made good gardens etc'; the architect was Thomas Edwards of Greenwich, a self-educated man who built up a practice in Cornwall, where he had interests in the flourishing tin mines. Work continued after Philip Hawkins's death in 1738, and c 1763–64 his nephew Thomas, who married the daughter of a London cloth merchant, called in a much better-known metropolitan architect, Sir Robert Taylor, to carry out some internal remodelling. Hawkins also landscaped the grounds and created the present entrance forecourt, but he died after being inoculated for smallpox in 1766 (there is a good monument to him in Probus church). His son, Christopher, a keen promoter of the local lead-mining and china-clay industries, carried out relatively minor internal alterations to the house in the late 18C or early 19C, and since then there have been very few structural changes. The gardens, with their splendid exotic trees and shrubs, are largely the creation of George Johnstone, who inherited the estate in 1904 after the male line of the Hawkins family had died out. His wife was descended from the sister of Sir Stamford Raffles, the founder of Singapore, and the present owner is their grandson.

From the outside Trewithen is modest and unassertive, but the interiors are surprisingly sophisticated—a reminder that London's influence was strong even in remote Cornwall in the 18C. The original house bought by Philip Hawkins was a five-bay brick building, but he extended it by two bays on either side, covering the north side (the present entrance front) with plaster. The more dignified south façade of the local grey Pentewan stone was probably begun to the designs of Thomas Edwards in 1738, the year of Hawkins's death; it now looks on a lawn surrounded by trees planted by George Johnstone.

The house is approached through an open courtyard, flanked by detached service blocks of the 1750s and overlooking an attractive 18C pastoral landscape with the main road conveniently removed from the immediate vicinity. The tour takes in the main reception rooms, which are all placed on the ground floor: the largely late-18C Library; the Oak Room, with dark panelling of the 1720s and a chimneypiece surmounted by a mirror incorporating an idealised early-18C landscape painting, the Drawing Room, with a canted bay window and Palladian-style woodwork of c 1758, the rather cramped late-18C Staircase Hall, lit from above through a glazed dome, and the unexpectedly lavish Dining Room on the south front, created by Sir Robert Taylor on the site of the former entrance hall in the 1760s, the ends with miniature groin vaults screened off by arcades supported on Ionic columns and entablatures—a device which he later used in the Bank of England—the fireplace wall lavishly decorated with floral garlands in stucco and a Rococo-style fireplace (an oval portrait of Philip Hawkins, the founder of the family fortunes, has pride of place over the fireplace).

Several excellent items of 18C and early-19C furniture are scattered through the rooms, and there is also a good collection of blue-and-white porcelain and of pictures by foreign artists, among them Van de Velde and Hondecoeter. But the greatest interest of the collection lies in the assembly of 18C British portraits, with some works by Allan Ramsay and others by artists born in south-west England, including the Cornishman John Opie, the Devon-born James Northcote (including a self-portrait), and, above all, Sir Joshua Reynolds, who was born at Plympton, just outside Plymouth. Most notable of the Reynolds portraits are two in his most sympathetic and intimate vein of his teacher and patron Dr Zachariah Mudge—a friend of Samuel Johnson—and his wife, they now hang in the Dining Room, having come to Trewithen through the family of the present owner's grandmother in the early 20C.

GCT

CUMBRIA

Appleby Castle

Appleby Castle Conservation Centre, tel. 07683 51402. Early Apr–Oct daily 10–5. Refreshments.

Appleby is a pretty northern market town on a hill above the river Eden. There is one long, wide main street, Boroughgate. At its foot is the parish church, and at the top are the castle gates. The Normans built a motte-and-bailey fortress on top of the hill here. Ralph de Briquessart built the square stone keep, c 1100, which still dominates the castle, which passed by marriage to the great house of Clifford in the later 13C. The Cliffords, one of the great northern dynasties of medieval England, also held the nearby castles of Brougham, Brough and Pendragon, as well as Skipton in Yorkshire. Roger de Clifford probably added the residential range here c 1383. The Cliffords became Earls of Cumberland, but the direct line died out in the 17C; the last of the family, Lady Anne Clifford (1590–1676), was a redoubtable figure. After two unhappy marriages, to the Earls of Dorset and Pembroke, and after a long lawsuit to inherit her farther's estates, she retired north in 1649. She rebuilt her castles, which Cromwell had slighted, and built much else. At Appleby, as elsewhere, she rebuilt everything in the traditional style. On Lady Anne's, death her great estates were divided between her daughter's families, Appleby passing to the Tufton family, Earls of Thanet. They rebuilt the residential ranges in a more modern style, c 1686–96. The castle passed by descent until recently; it is now owned by the company Ferguson International Holdings plc, which has opened it to the public and maintain a Rare Breeds Survival Trust centre in the grounds.

The castle has an inner bailey surrounded by medieval walls and towers. Outside this there are the remains of at least two outer baileys, surrounded by earth mounds. The curtain walls of the inner bailey are of the late 12C although the towers are mostly later. The Keep, christened Caesar's Tower by Lady Anne, rises free-standing in the west part of the courtyard; the pretty little turrets on top are probably of the 1780s. Its interior is accessible. On the first floor there is some medieval furniture. The second floor houses pieces of 17C furniture, and on the third floor there is a collection of 19C bicycles. From here you reach the roof, with spectacular views over the whole Eden valley.

At the east end of the bailey is Roger de Clifford's hall range, rebuilt by the Earl of Thanet in the 1680s. It now appears as a stately piece of Carolean architecture. The one room open here is the Hall itself. It goes through two storeys, and has a coved ceiling, with simple early-19C plasterwork. There is more fine 17C furniture here, and blue and white Nanking china recovered from a 17C shipwreck is on display. There are also various Clifford portraits, but the whole room is dominated by that hanging on the north wall. This is Lady Anne's 'Great Picture', a huge triptych she commissioned in 1646 from a Flemish artist, Jan van Belcamp. The central panel depicts her parents and siblings. The side panels both depict herself, aged 15 and aged 56; an extraordinary demonstration of her family pride.

Outside, the 27 acres of grounds house a collection of many rare speCies of birds, and also sheep, goats, pigs, cattle and deer. Halfway down Boroughgate, the arms of Clifford also appear on St Anne's Hospital, almshouses built by Lady Anne in 1651. She also renovated the fine

Perpendicular parish church of St Michael, at the bottom of the hill. Inside are fine tomb monuments to the Lady Anne (1676), and to her mother, the Countess of Cumberland (1617).

SB

Conishead Priory

2m south of Ulverston on A5089 coast road to Barrow-in-Furness: tel. 0229 584029. Open Easter–Sept Sat, Sun, BH Mon 2–5. Guided tours. Refreshments.

Conishead is one of the most unusual English country houses open to the public, both in its architecture and its current use. Its name derives from a house of Augustinian canons situated on the eastern side of the Furness peninsula, above the muddy shores of Morecambe Bay. A house was built on the site of the monastery in Elizabethan times, but this was in turn replaced in 1821–36 by the present huge and extravagantly Gothic pile designed by Philip Wyatt, son of the more famous James Wyatt. The owner was Thomas Bradyll, a colonel in the Coldstream Guards and son of one of George III's grooms of the bedchamber. The house was built with lavish entertaining in mind, but this proved to be Bradyll's undoing, and he was forced to sell in about 1850. Having served for a time as a 'hydropathic establishment' and then as a convalescent home for Durham miners, the house was acquired in 1976 by followers of the Dalai Lama, who have turned it into a Buddhist monastery and teaching centre under the name of the Manjushri Institute. A programme of repairs is currently under way.

The architecture of Conishead Priory alludes romantically to the monastic origins of the site. Pointed arched windows abound, and the skyline bristles with turrets, though from the garden side a quieter and more domestic-looking neo-Elizabethan takes over. Pugin would no doubt have loathed the meretricious mixing of styles for effect, and would certainly have condemned the use of stucco to cover the brick construction, but for the modern visitor the building exudes a melancholy charm which is enhanced by the enigmatic presence of the Buddhist occupants.

The tour of the interior starts in the tall ecclesiastical-looking Entrance Hall, apparently on the site of the north transept of the monastic church. After passing through an impressive vaulted corridor running along the spine of the building, visitors are taken up a gargantuan staircase with stained-glass windows by Wailes to a former bedroom decorated with re-used early-17C panelling from Samlesbury Hall, Lancashire (qv.); this is of a richness and complexity unusual even for that exuberant age. From a gallery outside this room it is possible to see the vaulted upper part of the hall, with excellent stained glass by Willement and a 15C screen from Samlesbury. The last room to be seen is the former Billiard Room, now a Buddhist shrine.

GCT

Dalemain

3m SW of Penrith on A592, M6 exit 40; R. Hasell-McCosh, tel. 07684 86450. Open Easter–early Oct Sun–Thur 11.15–5. Refreshments.

Dalemain stands in pastoral country near the foot of Ullswater. The restrained early-Georgian façade of pink sandstone, taken from a quarry only a mile away, conceals a building of medieval origins with four ranges around a small courtyard. The oldest part, on the north side, consists of a pele-tower, probably dating from the early 15C, and a hall which was floored over in the 16C; a kitchen was later added to the east. In 1679 the estate was purchased by Edward Hasell, steward to the formidable Lady Anne Clifford, whose now-ruined castle at Brougham lies only a few miles to the east. He created the terrace garden to the west of the house, and his son Edward, an enthusiastic tree-planter and rider to hounds, built the west and south (entrance) ranges, which were completed in 1745. The house now had a new suite of reception rooms and a well-proportioned classical façade, and the older buildings, hidden from view, were turned into servants' quarters and spare bedrooms. There have been few major altera-tions since then, and the house has remained in the hands of Hasell's descendants, having recently passed through the female line.

The approach is through an outer courtyard flanked by farm buildings in the robust local vernacular style, including a two-storeyed barn which now houses a display of old farm implements and agricultural bygones. The comfortable-looking reception rooms contain a good collection of late-17C and 18C furniture and pictures. The Entrance Hall, with its cantilevered oak staircase, contains a large view of the Piazzetta at Venice by Marieschi, along with a portrait of George, Lord Aubigny, in the manner of Van Dyck, one of several bequests by Edward Rainbow, Bishop of Carlisle, to Edward Hassell. The Chinese Drawing Room, next door, has hand-painted wall-paper, probably of the 1750s, and an exuberantly Rococo wooden chimneypiece; there are portraits by Devis and Zoffany of two of the sons of Edward Hasell, the builder of this part of the house. The main Drawing Room retains its original plain wooden panelling, but the adjacent Dining Room was remodelled in 1785.

From here a spiral staircase in the old pele-tower leads up to a series of bedrooms over the medieval hall. The first (the Fretwork Room) has a plaster ceiling of the type introduced into several local houses in the late 16C and early 17C (cf. Levens Hall), and contains some interesting memen-toes of Lady Anne Clifford, including her portrait and her 'day book'. The last of the upstairs rooms is decorated as a mid-20C children's nursery, and the domestic theme is maintained by a glimpse into the former house-keeper's room. The tour ends in the old hall, with its walls of rubble stone, which now serves as the restaurant.

GCT

Holker Hall

½m north of Cark on B5278 Grange-over-Sands–Haverthwaite: Lord and Lady Cavendish, tel. 05395 58328. Open Apr–Oct Daily except Sat 10.30–4.30. Refreshments.

The Holker estate lies on the Cartmel peninsula above the mud-flats of Morecambe Bay. It belonged to the Augustinian priory of Cartmel in the Middle Ages, and after the Reformation it was bought by the Preston family, which was responsible for the restoration of the superb priory church in Cartmel in 1618–23. Nothing remains of the Preston's house, and in the 18C the estate passed twice through the female line, first to the Lowthers, one of the most powerful families in the north-west, and then in 1756 to Lord George Cavendish, a younger son of the 3rd Duke of Devonshire, whose main seat was at Chatsworth, Derbyshire (qv.). He created the nucleus of the very beautiful landscaped garden which is one of the outstanding features of Holker today, introducing one of the first cedar trees to be grown in this country. But the present house dates almost entirely from two 19C building campaigns instigated by William Cavendish, a skilled mathematician and Fellow of the Royal Society, who developed Barrow-in-Furness, not far away, as a port for the export of iron ore, and became 7th Duke of Devonshire in 1858. He employed George Webster of Kendal to remodel the existing house in a rather uninspired neo-Elizabethan manner in 1838–42, but in 1871 a serious fire gutted the main rooms, whereupon another local firm, Paley & Austin of Lancaster, was immediately called in to design the present main block, completed in 1875; this left Webster's family and service wing surviving at the back. The 7th Duke also employed Joseph Paxton to remodel the gardens, which were subsequently improved by Thomas Mawson in 1912. The 9th Duke (d 1938) gave the house and estate to his younger son, Lord Richard Cavendish, whose grandson lives here now.

Few houses open to the public convey better than Holker the sense of late-Victorian aristocratic life and taste. The house stands in an extensive park with views across to the Furness peninsula; an atmosphere of patrician ease and understated comfort takes over at the park gates and prevails throughout. Paley & Austin's house, of pink–red sandstone from Runcorn (Cheshire), is a cleverly composed building in the 'Jacobethan' style with a striking skyline and an abundance of detail, some of it derived from local houses. A carriage porch leads into the Entrance Hall, lit by Venetian chandeliers from Devonshire House, London. The rest of the ground floor is taken up by a sequence of high-ceilinged and well-lit reception rooms opening out of the Hall; they were decorated with the help of the Crace firm, and are comfortably furnished, with some particularly good 18C French pieces. First come the Library and the Drawing Room, with semi-circular bay windows to catch the sun; there is an attractive Whistlerian portrait of Lady Frederick Cavendish by Sir William Richmond over the Library fireplace, and Old Master pictures, including landscapes by Vernet and Gaspard Dughet, hang elsewhere. The Billiard Room contains two 18C views of Whitehaven, source of much of the Lowther family's fortune, and there is a Van Dyck self-portrait over the Dining Room fireplace, which is flanked by twisted 'Salomonic' columns like those in the choir screen at Cartmel Priory.

An oak staircase leads up to the main guest bedrooms, reached through a gallery over the Entrance Hall. They include the Wedgwood Dressing Room, with an unusual chimneypiece surmounted by blue and white Wedgwood ware; this, like the Renaissance-inspired chimneypiece in the Drawing Room, was purchased at the sale of Montagu House, London, demolished to make way for the Victoria Embankment.

GCT

Hutton-in-the-Forest

6m north west of Penrith on B5305, M6 exit 41: Lord and Lady Inglewood,
tel. 07684 84449. Open Easter–early Oct Thur, Fri, Sun and all BH
Sun/Mon 1–4, grounds opendaily except Sat 11–5. Guided tours.
Refreshments.

The ancient forest of Inglewood has all but disappeared, and the irregular
pink sandstone house which preserves its name now stands in pastoral
country facing east to the Pennines. The oldest part is a 14C pele-tower on
the right of the entrance front with the usual barrel-vaulted ground-floor
room through which the house is now entered. The estate was bought by
Sir Richard Fletcher of Cockermouth in 1606, and in 1641–45 his son built
a wing out to the right of the entrance courtyard, with a gallery over a
round-arched loggia (since glazed in), probably designed by the mason,
Alexander Pogmire. The medieval hall, to the south (left) of the pele, was
replaced in the 1680s by a block with an elaborately embellished classical
façade in white stone designed by another local mason, Edward Addison,
one of the 'first introducers of regular architecture into these parts'. The rest
of the house was much rebuilt in the 18C and 19C for the Vane family,
kinsmen of the Vanes of Raby Castle, Durham (qv.), who inherited from the
Fletchers in the first half of the 18C; from them it has descended to the
present owner, a member of the European Parliament. The crenellated
south-east tower and south wing were remodelled in the early 19C by
George Nixon of Carlisle and George Webster of Kendal, with the help of
Anthony Salvin, a friend of the family, who later carried out further internal
alterations. The south range overlooks terraced gardens and a lake, and a
walk leads along the west side of the house to an attractive 18C walled
garden overlooked by the Jacobean Gallery.

The main beauty of Hutton-in-the-Forest lies in the setting, the gardens,
and the romantic exterior. The interiors date mainly from the mid to late
19C (though two mid-18C rooms have been restored recently), and they
convey a strong sense of continuity and unostentatious comfort. Architecturally, the most interesting feature is the splendid late-17C staircase which
leads from the Hall to the Gallery, the most impressive room in the house;
the vestibule at the top of the staircase is hung with 17C Mortlake 'Playing
Boys' tapestries. The Drawing Room in the south-east tower has changed
little since the 1870s, when 'art furniture' was introduced by Margaret, Lady
Vane, an admirer of the aesthetic movement. The recently restored Cupid
Room, with its plaster ceiling by Joseph Rose, contains a portrait of Walter
Vane and his family by Hogarth, and in the adjoining Blue Room there are
drawings by Lady Diana Beauclerk, friend of Horace Walpole, brought here
by her great-grandson, Sir Henry Vane (d 1908). Downstairs is the Dining
Room, by Webster, with William Morris wallpaper and portraits of early
members of the Vane family brought here in 1786. The tour ends in the
panelled and antler-hung Hall.

GCT

Levens Hall

5m south of Kendal at junction of A6 and A590, M6 exit 36: C.H.V. Bagot,
tel. 05395 60321. Open Apr–Sept Sun–Thur 11–5. Refreshments.

This rugged-looking house started life, like many others in the north-west, as a semi-fortified dwelling, with a hall block attached to a pele-tower. In 1562 the estate was sold by the Redman family, who had been here for three centuries, to Alan Bellingham, deputy Warden of the Northern Marches, and his son James enlarged and modernised the house between 1586 and 1617. As a result of these changes Levens acquired some of the finest Elizabethan interiors in the north of England, and structurally the main part of the house has changed relatively little since. Bellingham's great-grandson Alan gambled the estate away, and in 1688 it was sold to a kinsman, Col James Grahme, a staunch supporter of James II and keeper of his Privy Purse. He introduced new furniture and built a new service wing joining the older kitchen block to the south of the main house. He was also responsible for the famous and little-altered topiary garden, designed by a Frenchman, Guillaume Beaumont, whose portrait hangs in the Hall. Grahme died without male heirs, and after a complicated descent through the female line, the estate eventually came to the present owner. Francis Webster of Kendal was called in to make some alterations in the early 19C, but visually they are difficult to distinguish from the original 16C and 17C work, and today the impression is overwhelmingly of that period.

The house is built of rubble stone, whitewashed in places and rendered elsewhere; with its low-pitched slate roofs and heavy chimneystacks, it has something of the solid, workmanlike character of the farmhouses of the Lake District. Visitors enter by an external staircase leading into the panelled Hall, with an embellished plaster ceiling and frieze displaying the arms of the Bellinghams and, over the fireplace, of Elizabeth I. Pictures, introduced by the Bagots, include a Madonna and Child by the Florentine Bicci di Lorenzo, and another by the 16C Flemish artist Koeck van Aelst. The adjacent Drawing Room contains some of the most elaborate woodwork and panelling in the house, including a superbly executed overmantel of 1595 made up of coats of arms framed by stumpy classical columns. In the Small Drawing Room, to the south, there is an even more elaborate chimneypiece with Mannerist-inspired figures of Samson and Hercules flanking the fireplace and sprawling on the broken pediment, and allegorical representations of the Five Senses and the Four Elements carved on the overmantel. Both drawing rooms contain excellent late-17C walnut furniture, along with other objects including a Limoges enamel cross and the gloves worn by the Duke of Wellington at the Battle of Waterloo.

A staircase hung with embossed 17C Spanish leather leads up to a series of bedrooms, some of them created by dividing up the Elizabethan long gallery in the early 19C. One of the rooms contains a group of water-colours by Peter de Wint, who stayed in the house, and in another there is a patchwork of Indian chintz dating from about 1700, reputedly the oldest in England. From here a corridor, with a display of 18C drinking glasses, leads to the late-17C main staircase, hung with drawings by Rubens, Van Dyck, Tiepolo and others. This gives access to the Hall, to the west of which are two rooms added to the medieval structure by James Bellingham: the Library (formerly the chapel), with a portrait of a child by Cuyp and a good still-life by the 17C Flemish artist Jacob van Es; and the very attractive Dining Room, with another fine wooden chimneypiece dated 1586, a contempporary plaster ceiling, walls hung with Spanish leather introduced by Col Grahme in 1692, and a set of late-17C high-backed chairs.

GCT

Mirehouse

4½m north west of Keswick on A591: Mr and Mrs Spedding, tel. 07687 72287. Open Apr–Oct Sun, Wed, and Fri in Aug 2–5.

Mirehouse stands on the northern fringe of the Lake District, under the slopes of Skiddaw and close to the eastern shore of Bassenthwaite Lake. It started life in 1666 as a two-storeyed hunting lodge built by the 8th Earl of Derby, and was sold 22 years later to his agent, from whom it passed by descent to the Storey family. Wings with canted bays were added in 1790, but after the death of Thomas Storey in 1802 the estate was left to John Spedding, a member of a family of former ship-owners and mining engineers from Whitehaven, who had been at school with William Wordsworth. Spedding employed an obscure London architect, Joseph Cantwell, to enlarge the house c 1830, and further additions were made in 1851, but since then there have been few major changes. Several 19C members of the family had serious literary interests (Carlyle and Tennyson came here often and John Spedding's younger son James edited the works of Francis Bacon), and today the literary connections, along with the beauty of the physical setting and the unusually friendly atmosphere, constitute the main attractions of a visit to the house.

The house is built of materials indigenous to Cumbria: white roughcast for the wall cladding, slate for the roofs, and local red sandstone for the dressings and the porch of Tuscan columns. The tour proceeds clockwise through the main ground-floor rooms, in some of which are displayed letters and other manuscripts from the writers associated with the house. The Dining Room of 1790 has an attractive Gothic niche for the sideboard and pictures by Vernet and Hondecoeter on the walls; while the Library, dating from the early 1830s, retains its comfortable furnishings and bookcases of dark polished wood, in which the books are arranged according to a system of classification devised by Bacon. The main Drawing Room, added in 1851, contains portraits by Hudson and Romney, a seascape by Abraham Storck and a small oil painting ('Heath House, Hampstead') by John Constable, another friend of the family; water-colours by Girtin, Turner and de Wint hang in the adjacent study. The house is set among attractive gardens and woods, through which it is possible to walk to the lake and to the 12C (though much restored) church of St Bega.

GCT

Muncaster Castle

1m south east of Ravenglass on A595: Mrs P. Gordon-Duff-Pennington, tel. 0228 717614 or 717203. Open Apr–Oct Tues–Sun and BH Mon 1–4. Refreshments.

Muncaster perches impressively on an outcrop of rock not far from the mouth of the River Esk, commanding spectacular views of the western fells of the Lake District. The site may have been occupied by the Romans, who certainly had a garrison at the nearby port of Ravenglass, but the oldest surviving part of the present building is a late-medieval pele-tower to the east of the entrance porch. This, together with an adjacent hall range (since completely rebuilt), constituted for many years the formidable dwelling of the Penningtons, a powerful and long-established family in west Cumberland. The house was extended to the west in the 16C, and c 1780 Sir John Pennington, soon to be made 1st Baron Muncaster, modernised it to the designs of a London architect, J. Watson. Hardly any of his work is visible at Muncaster today, because in 1860–64 the 4th Lord Muncaster subjected the house to a thorough rebuilding which left it structurally in its present form; the architect was Anthony Salvin, restorer of many country houses in the north of England. The direct line of the Penningtons died out in 1917, and the house passed to Sir John Ramsden, grandfather of the present owner. He laid out the magnificent gardens, rich in rhododendrons and other shrubs, and brought in numerous works of art to augment the Pennington collection.

The chief interest of Muncaster lies in its setting, its gardens and its collections. The rather gloomy house, built of pink granite rubble with red sandstone dressings, is not one of Salvin's most successful buildings. It is approached on foot by a long woodland drive, and entered through a porch next to the ancient pele-tower, commanding a splendid view of the fells. The main rooms are reached through the Hall, created by Salvin on the site of the medieval hall; it contains excellent 15C and 16C religious wood carvings bought by Sir John Ramsden, hunting pictures by John Ferneley, and a portrait of Admiral Pennington, one of Charles I's commanders, by Cornelius Johnson. The octagonal Library, next door, is the most attractive room in the house; it was created in the late 18C on the site of the medieval kitchen, but was completely remodelled by Salvin, who designed the neo-Jacobean panelling and the wooden ribbed 'vault'. The Dining Room contains late-17C furniture, an unusual Derby dinner-service of 1821, and a Cuyp 'Shepherd Girl'.

A staircase, hung with three relief panels of dancing figures by Canova, leads up to a corridor, at the end of which is perhaps the most interesting picture at Muncaster: a full-length portrait of c 1600, showing the resident family jester (who also doubled as agent to the estate), dressed in an extravagantly patterned coat and holding a long stave and a broad-brimmed hat. Some of the bedrooms were fitted up by Sir John Ramsden with 16C and 17C panelling and furniture brought from elsewhere; there are also 18C Flemish tapestries and some attractive Elizabethan needle-work panels of the Story of Sodom. The last room to be shown is the large barrel-vaulted Drawing Room made by Salvin on the site of the former servants' quarters to the west of the Hall and staircase; it is hung with Ramsden portraits, four of them by Reynolds (the best, of Lady Hertford, is to the left of the 18C marble chimneypiece, brought by Sir John Ramsden from Bulstrode Park, Bucks), and there is also a Swiss marriage-chest of inlaid wood, dated 1621. Outside, the long garden front can be seen, with a tower to the west of the Drawing Room, designed by Salvin to balance the pele; more ambitious plans for this façade were abandoned for lack of money after the death of the 4th Lord Muncaster in 1862.

GCT

Naworth Castle

2m east of Brampton off the A69 Carlisle–Newcastle road: the Earl of Carlisle, tel. 06977 3666. Open Easter–Sept Wed, Sat, Sun, Aug Wed–Sun 12–5. Refreshments.

Built to guard the wild Scottish borderland, Naworth conveys a vivid sense of the turbulent history of this lonely area, not far from Hadrian's Wall. The pink sandstone castle has undergone many vicissitudes since it was first constructed by the Lords Dacre of Gilsland in the 14C (licence to crenellate was granted in 1335); their tombs can be seen in the partly ruined Lanercost Priory, not far away to the north. The house consists of an irregular courtyard, almost collegiate in feeling, with towers at the corners, the two tallest of which flank the south (entrance) range. The vast first-floor Hall which takes up most of the east range was almost certainly built by Thomas, Lord Dacre of the North, commander of the reserve forces at Flodden, in the early 16C; his arms also appear over the detached entrance gateway. Dacre's marriage to Elizabeth de Greystoke led to a great increase in the family's territorial holdings, but in 1560 the male line came to an end, and the castle and estates went by marriage to Thomas Howard, 4th Duke of Norfolk, who settled the estate on his younger son Lord William Howard ('Belted Will'), a man of antiquarian interests. He repaired the building, which was 'in very great decay', and created a library, oratory and bedroom in one of the towers. The house has remained in the hands of his descendants ever since.

With the construction of Castle Howard (qv.) on one of the family's Yorkshire estates in the early 18C, Naworth ceased to be the main family seat; it suffered from some neglect and was gutted by fire in 1844. Its present attractive appearance owes much to sympathetic restorations by Anthony Salvin (1846–48) and C.J. Ferguson. They left the outside intact, but created new and more comfortable rooms within. The aesthetically-minded George Howard, later 9th Earl of Carlisle, commissioned Philip Webb to carry out alterations in the south range in the 1880s; Webb also designed the church in nearby Brampton, his only ecclesiastical commission. Lord Carlisle, a Liberal, disliked the principle of primogeniture, and after his death the family estates were divided, his eldest son receiving the smaller share, including Naworth; it is his descendant who lives in the house now.

Visitors enter the house through the large, spacious Hall, with its massive arch-braced roof by Salvin. It contains several interesting objects, notably four huge painted wooden heraldic beasts, probably dating from the early 16C, which apparently served as standards for the Dacres and their retainers in their numerous battles. Portraits of 'Belted Will' Howard and his wife, the Dacre heiress, are hung above the original service entrance, and there is also a very fine set of French tapestries dated 1610, purchased in the Orléans sale after the French Revolution. A staircase leads up to the Gallery, panelled by Salvin, where there is a series of family portraits and some attractive water-colours by the 9th Earl. From here we descend to the former library, designed by Philip Webb on the site of the medieval chapel destroyed in 1844; above the fireplace there is a relief carving of the Battle of Flodden designed by Burne-Jones and executed by Edgar Boehm. The neo-Elizabethan Drawing Room, also by Webb, contains some good 16C Howard portraits.

GCT

Sizergh Castle

3m south of Kendal on A6, M6 exit 36; National Trust, tel. 05395 60070.
Open Apr–Oct Sun–Thur 1.30–5.30 (gardens open 12.30). Refreshments.

Like its neighbour Levens Hall, a couple of miles away to the south, Sizergh originated as a late-medieval pele-tower and hall block. The pele was built by a member of the Strickland family in the mid 14C, and the Stricklands have lived at Sizergh ever since, although since 1950 they have been tenants of the National Trust. As at Levens, there were major alterations in the second half of the 16C, inaugurated in this case by Walter Strickland (d 1569), who was capable of mustering an armed force of 290 men in defence of the Border. They were completed by his son Thomas (d 1612), and the exceptionally elaborate woodwork, earlier and by different craftsmen than that at Levens, is among the finest of its date in England. The family, like many others in the region, suffered losses through their Catholicism and Jacobitism, but prosperity returned with the marriage of Charles Strickland (d 1770) to an heiress, Cecilia Towneley. Some alterations were carried out towards the end of the 18C, including the remodelling of parts of the entrance and garden fronts, but since then there have been no major changes.

The house is approached from the east, and from the drive the massive pele-tower, with garderobe and staircase turrets adjoining, can be seen rising above the rest of the building; luxuriantly planted terraced gardens of 1926 slope down to the surrounding pastoral country. The picturesquely jumbled entrance front faces west, with the pele to the right, the hall block, refronted in 18C Gothic, in the centre, and an Elizabethan gable to the left; the two-storeyed ranges which stretch forward to enclose the open courtyard are vernacular in character, and served as kitchens, service rooms, and 'barracks' for servants and retainers (there is a similar block at Levens Hall).

The main rooms, on the first floor, were originally approached by an outside staircase like that at Levens, but as a result of the late-18C remodelling, the house is now entered at ground level through the relocated hall screen of 1558—one of the first examples of Renaissance-inspired craftsmanship in the northwest. To the right is the barrel-vaulted ground floor of the pele (now the tea-room) and to the left is a staircase leading upstairs. The first of the older rooms to be seen is the Dining Room created in the first floor of the pele in 1564, a date which appears on the very elaborate chimneypiece. As in the adjacent chamber (now called the Queen's Room) the ceiling is decorated with a pattern of ribs in wood, rather than the more usual plaster. The walls of the Dining Room are lined with an evocative series of portraits of the later Stuarts, many of them by the French artist Hyacinthe Rigaud, given to Sir Thomas and Lady Strickland, who followed James II into exile. In the Drawing Room, created out of the Elizabethan Hall in the late 18C, dark wood panelling gives way to plain plastered walls; there are portraits of Thomas Strickland and his heiress wife by the locally-born George Romney, and the sash windows (introduced when the room was remodelled) look out over the gardens. Three older panelled rooms follow in the gabled wing to the north; one of them (the Old Dining Room) containing the finest of all the Elizabethan overmantels in the house, an extravaganza of wreaths, cherubs and arabesques set in a classical frame.

From here a staircase leads up to a corridor on the top floor and then to the so-called Banqueting Hall, part of what was once a suite of grand reception rooms at the top of the pele-tower. This large and bare room contains some outstanding pieces of Elizabethan furniture, including two armchairs of 1570 and some forms dated 1562 and carved in the sophisticated Renaissance tastes of the chimneypieces downstairs; the ceiling has alas been partially removed. The last room to be shown, the Inlaid Chamber, was once the pièce de résistance of the whole house, but in 1891 the spectacular panelling which gave the room its name was removed to the Victoria and Albert Museum in London, where it can still be seen. The splendid plaster frieze and the ceiling with stalactite-like pendants are, however, still in situ, and the columned four-poster bed has been returned on loan by the museum.

GCT

Townend

At south end of Troutbeck, 3m south east of Ambleside off A592: National Trust, tel. 05394 32628. Open Apr–Oct Sun, Tues–Fri, BH Mon 1–5.

Townend is a farmhouse rather than a country house in the generally accepted sense. There is no park and no grand drive, and the architecture is in the rough but impressive style of the Lake District vernacular, with rendered whitewashed walls, slate roofs and massive round chimneys. But in contrast to the common English practise, the house and farm remained in the hands of the same family for more than four centuries, and the rooms are still filled with their possessions. The Browne family, who first appeared at Townend in the early 16C, came from the class of wealthy farmers known in the Lake District as 'statesmen', and in the absence of large estates in the area they came to fill the role of gentry, holding local government office, acquiring a coat of arms, and sending their son into the professions. The last of the family to live in the house was Clara Browne, who died in 1943, and in 1947 the building was transferred, along with its contents, to the National Trust, which also acquired the 800-acre estate extending up onto the fells overlooking the house and village.

The house is built on the slope of a hill and looks out onto a yard with a barn and an attractive garden beyond. The centre of the house is occupied by the hall or 'fire house' (to use the local expression) dating from the late 16C or early 17C, and used for communal meals in which the family and farm-hands dined together. But there have been several subsequent additions and alterations, giving the exterior a satisfying irregular appearance. Visitors can see most of the low-ceilinged rooms, which are interesting not so much for their rather sparse decoration as for their contents. These include cooking and household implements, crockery, books, clocks, hangings, pictures, and, above all, carved wooden furniture—a speciality of north-west England—some of it dating from the 17C and 18C but much of it introduced by George Browne (d 1914), who combined amateur joinery and antiquarian research with a farming career. He not only carved much of the furniture and some of the chimneypieces, but also ensured the survival of the old interiors with their fascinating accumulation of objects into the 20C. Today therefore he is the presiding spirit of a house which to an unusual degree retains the atmosphere of the rural past.

GCT

DERBYSHIRE

Bolsover Castle

In Bolsover on A632, 6m east of Chesterfield, M1 exits 29 or 30; English Heritage, tel. 0246 823349. Open Apr–Sept daily 10–6; Oct–Apr Tues–Sun (except Christmas/New Year) 10–4.

This extraordinary house occupies a commanding site looking west over the Derbyshire coalfield towards the heights of the Peak District. A medieval castle stood here, but in its present form Bolsover is a monument to the ambitions of two generations of the Cavendish family in the 17C. The first builder was Sir Charles Cavendish, younger son of 'Bess of Hardwick', the builder of Hardwick Hall (qv.). He acquired the estate from his step-brother, the 7th Earl of Shrewsbury, in 1608, and four years later began the construction of a castellated villa or pleasure-house (the 'Little Castle') on the site of the medieval keep. This strange building was completed in 1621, and a few years later, his son Sir William Cavendish—a leading courtier, who later became Duke of Newcastle—began work on a prodigious range of state rooms on the west side of the former inner bailey, followed by an equally impressive Riding School on the south side of the courtyard. Work was interrupted by the Civil War, after which the castle sustained some damage from the Parliamentarians, but it was resumed and completed after the Restoration. With the death of the 2nd Duke in 1691 the estate passed through the female line, and in the early 18C the massive complex of buildings was abandoned in favour of Welbeck, a few miles away in the 'Dukeries'. But despite the unroofing of the state rooms, the 'Little Castle' and Riding School remained intact (though unfurnished) and in 1954 the property was acquired by the Government as an ancient monument.

Even in its present semi-ruined state, Bolsover Castle is one of the most spectacular of all 17C English houses. It is entered from the south, and from the main courtyard (the inner bailey of the medieval castle) all the main parts of the building can be seen: the 'Little Castle' towering over the other buildings to the north, the ruined state rooms to the west, and the Riding School to the south. The 'Little Castle' was probably designed by Robert Smythson, the architect of Hardwick Hall, and completed by his son John. It represents a fusion of the ideals of medieval chivalry and Renaissance romance. It is a tall but compact rectangular house with a crenellated roof-line and ogee-capped corner turrets, but the now empty rooms evoke an enclosed, sophisticated world of arcane symbolism. Some are vaulted, and most contain carved stone fireplaces derived from Sebastiano Serlio's *Architettura.* There is elaborate wood panelling (eg, in the vaulted 'Pillar Chamber' on the first floor) and copious decorative painting by unknown artists (eg, a series of erotic figures representing the Virtues in the Marble Closet on the second floor, and the adjacent Heaven and Elysium Rooms, formerly part of the duke's private apartment, in which pagan and Christian imagery is contrasted). To the south east is a walled garden with a 'Venus Fountain' and three garden rooms contrived by John Smythson out of the medieval walls.

The ruined main apartments are best seen from the west-facing terrace outside the main courtyard. The north end of the range, begun c 1627–30, is marked by a pedimented 'Dutch' gable, and other Mannerist motifs appear on the front of the former Gallery further south, notably the eccentric pilaster-like projections between the windows, their shapes supposedly symbolising cannon. The Gallery was probably completed, to John Smythson's designs, in time for a visit in 1634 by Charles I and Henrietta Maria, celebrated by the performance of Ben Jonson's masque 'Love's Welcome to Bolsover'. The more classical courtyard front of this range, comprising an entrance hall and adjoining rooms, was probably built soon after the Restoration to the designs of Samuel Marsh, the architect of Nottingham Castle, another of the Duke's houses. The south side of the main courtyard is occupied by the Riding School, built to satisfy his love of horsemanship, a subject on which he wrote a treatise. It was probably designed by John Smythson's son, Huntingdon Smythson, in the mid 1630s, but may not have been completed until after the Restoration. It consists of a large room, with a wooden tie-beam roof, and a gallery at one end, flanked by a harness room to one side and a forge to the other; there is an impressive display of Dutch gables on the roof-line and a massive doorcase of Mannerist character with a broken pediment.

GCT

Calke Abbey

9m south of Derby on A514 at Ticknall: National Trust, tel. 0332 863822.
Open Apr–Oct Sat–Wed 1–5.30.

Until it was opened to the public by the National Trust in 1989, Calke Abbey was one of the most withdrawn and secretive of English country houses. It stands on or near the site of a small Augustinian priory which came, in 1622, into the hands of a younger branch of the Harpur family, whose wealth derived from the successful legal career of Richard Harpur (d 1577). In its present form the house dates largely from 1702–4, when Sir John Harpur, who had inherited the estates of the senior branch of the family, rebuilt the existing Elizabethan or Jacobean courtyard structure in the currently fashionable Baroque taste. By this time the wealth of the Harpurs was second only in Derbyshire to that of the Cavendishes, and the ambitious rebuilding scheme may have represented a bid for a peerage which, in the event, never materialised. Sir John's great-grandson, Sir Henry Harpur (called the 'isolated Baronet' because of the social ostracism which followed his marriage to a lady's maid), also hankered after a peerage, and in 1793–94 employed the elder William Wilkins, father of the architect of the National Gallery, to remodel some of the interiors; he also added an Ionic portico to the south (entrance) front in 1806–8. His son, Sir George Harpur Crewe, carried out internal alterations in the 1840s, but since then there have been no important changes, apart from the accumulation of a large and diverse collection of objects, especially specimens of natural history, by his eccentric and reclusive successors. These strange collections still fill many of the rooms and constitute much of the interest of Calke Abbey for visitors, who are attracted by the idea of a house which has, until recently, been almost untouched by the changes of the 20C.

The isolation of the house matches that of its more recent owners. It is hidden away in a hollow, approached by a two-mile-long drive through a wooded park, interrupted only by a sinister-looking neo-classical lodge designed by Wilkins. The house is a solid-looking rectangular building with four ranges of rooms around a courtyard and the corners projecting, doubtless to reflect the usual early-18C system of 'apartments'. The walls are of local sandstone, slightly blackened in places, with pilasters of the Composite order at the corners, an enriched cornice and a balustrade on the roof-line; these features are commonly found in houses by Francis Smith of Warwick, but there is no evidence to connect him to Calke (as the local saying has it: 'Like Calke House, the thing was done, but nobody did it'). The entrance was originally at first-floor level, but since 1841 it has been through an inconspicuous doorway underneath Wilkins's portico, which leads into an equally unpretentious **Entrance Hall** lined with heads of sheep and cattle. From here an impressive wooden staircase gives access to the main reception rooms; it is hung with family portraits, obsequious illuminated addresses from 19C tenants, and equestrian pictures (notably John Ferneley's 'Council of Horses', 1850) which reflect the family's enthusiasm for rural pursuits.

The grandest room is the two-storeyed **Saloon**, which was the entrance hall until 1841; the Corinthian pilasters lining the wall date from the early 18C, but the enriched ceiling is early Victorian. There are more family portraits here, including one of the 'isolated Baronet' and his mother by Tilly Kettle over the fireplace, but the visitor's attention is easily distracted by the glass cases full of minerals and stuffed birds (and even an alligator's skull) which line the walls and take up most of the floor space.

The remaining reception rooms date essentially from the late-18C remodelling, but some have acquired a distinctly mid-Victorian decorative overlay, notably the **Drawing Room**, which was wallpapered, carpeted, upholstered and filled with furniture and knick-knacks in 1855, and now represents a rare and intact survival of a kind of interior shown in many early country house photographs. The less claustrophobically furnished Library contains a good collection of equestrian pictures by Sawrey Gilpin, Sartorius, Ferneley and others; next come the Boudoir and Schoolroom, and upstairs is the bedroom of Sir Vauncey Harpur-Crewe (d 1924), a fanatical ornithologist whose collection is displayed in the original cases in a corridor outside. The **Breakfast Room** (originally the music room), back on the main floor, contains a group of four Neapolitan views by Gabriele Ricciardelli acquired in the early 19C (the same time as the room was decorated) and a pretty landscape ('Kingsey Village near Thame', 1826) by John Linnell. Beyond is the chastely neo-classical **Dining Room**, the most complete of Wilkins's interiors, repainted by the National Trust in its original pastel shades. It stands at the corner of the west or service range, in one of the rooms of which is displayed a state bed of c 1715 with its original silk hangings, probably given to Sir Henry Harpur's bride by Princess Anne, daughter of George II, on her marriage in 1734 and never even unpacked from its case (hence its superb state of preservation).

From here the route descends to the shabby, uncomfortable kitchen and then into the courtyard, where the stonework of the original 16C or 17C house can be seen. On leaving the house it is worth looking at the red-brick **stable block**, built in 1712–14 to the designs of William Gilks of Burton-on-Trent and still containing a remarkable collection of carriages and riding gear which evoke the not-too-distant past with particular poignancy.

GCT

Chatsworth

At Edensor on A623, 4m east of Bakewell: Chatsworth House Trust,
tel. 0246 582204. Open late Mar–Oct daily 11–4.30. Refreshments.

Ever since Sir William Cavendish began building a courtyard house of
'surprising height' in the sheltered valley of the Derwent among the bleak
moors of the Peak in 1552, Chatsworth has been one of the grandest houses
in England. Cavendish, who came from Suffolk, was one of the ruthless
men who profited from the disposal of monastic land after the Reformation,
and his ambitions were furthered by his marriage to the notoriously
ambitious Bess of Hardwick (cf. Hardwick Hall), who persuaded him to
concentrate his territorial holdings in her native county, and carried on
building at Chatsworth after his death. Their younger son, who later
became Earl of Devonshire, inherited the substantial estate, and in 1686
his descendant, the 4th Earl, began a piecemeal programme of rebuilding.
By the time of its completion shortly before his death in 1707, Devonshire
had succeeded in transforming the 16C house into a Baroque palace, only
the courtyard layout and the general arrangement of the rooms surviving
to remind future generations of its earlier origins. He also laid out a
spectacular garden, parts of which (notably the cascade of water) have
survived subsequent landscaping.

The Earl was one of the grandees who invited William of Orange to launch
the Glorious Revolution in 1688, and he was rewarded with a dukedom.
The 2nd Duke was a notable collector, and the collections were further
augmented when the 4th Duke, a leading Whig politician, married the
heiress of Lord Burlington, prophet of neo-Palladianism (cf. Chiswick
House, Greater London); he also called in 'Capability' Brown to landscape
the grounds and James Paine to design the present bridge over the Derwent
(1760–64) and the monumental **stable block** (1758–63) which looms over
the visitors' car park. Further major changes were carried out by his
grandson, the 6th or Bachelor Duke, who inherited in 1811. He used his
immense wealth to build up the already substantial holdings of books,
pictures and sculpture, and to house them—and also to provide a suitably
splendid setting for the entertaining at which he excelled—commissioning
Jeffrey Wyatville to build a new wing on to the north-east corner of the
house in 1820–27. With the help of his head gardener, Joseph Paxton, he
also reintroduced a measure of formality to the grounds, and rebuilt the
estate village of Edensor. More recent dukes, though less lavish in their
purchases, have continued to add to the collection—now probably the
richest in any English country house—and with the demolition of Devonshire House in Piccadilly and the evacuation of Chiswick House in the
1920s, the family's works of art are concentrated at Chatsworth to a greater
extent than ever before.

Most visitors get their first glimpse of Chatsworth from the main drive,
with the pedimented **west range** of the 1st Duke's house (built in 1700–3 to
the designs of an unknown architect) set against a wooded background
and Wyatville's massive extension to the left, terminating in a tall
belvedere-like tower, with a hunting tower built by Bess of Hardwick on
the far horizon. The main entrance was originally in the west range, but in
1760 it was shifted to the **north range** (by Thomas Archer, 1704–7, but
altered by Wyatville); this is now approached through a monumental arch
designed by Wyatville. The **Entrance Hall**, created by Paine out of the

former kitchen, is divided by Doric columns and contains some notable sculpture, including a Roman portrait group of a mother and child dating from the 1C AD. From here a flight of steps leads to a corridor, created out of an open colonnade in the 1820s and hung with small Old Master paintings. It gives access to the **Painted Hall** in the east range, standing on the site of the hall of the 16C house; it was designed by William Talman, Comptroller of the King's Works, who acted as the 1st Duke's architect from 1687 until his dismissal in 1697. There are extensive wall and ceiling paintings by Louis Laguerre, not in his best manner, and the staircase—the third on the site—is by W.H. Romaine-Walker (1911). From the landing another staircase, with an iron balustrade by the Huguenot Jean Tijou and a ceiling painting by Verrio, leads up to the top floor, where a series of bedrooms known as the **Leicester and Queen of Scots apartments** (not always open; the names were taken over from the 16C house) survive largely intact from their remodelling by Wyatville. They contain attractive Regency furnishings and some interesting pictures, including landscapes by Gaspard Dughet (in the Green Satin Dressing Room) and portraits of Lord Burlington (by George Knapton, 1763) and the architect William Kent (by Benedetto Luti).

The 1st Duke's 'state apartment' takes up the whole of the top floor of Talman's south range. This magnificent set of rooms—dismissed by the 6th Duke as 'a museum of old furniture and a walk in bad weather'—occupies the site of the long gallery of the 16C house and was intended primarily for ostentatious display, with the rooms arranged in a set sequence and the doors in *enfilade* (the family has always lived on the floor below in rooms which are not open to the public). There have been several changes since the late 17C, notably the introduction of later furniture, some of it originally at Chiswick House and Devonshire House, and the embellishment of the walls of the State Bedroom and Music Room with gilded leather hangings by the 6th Duke c 1830. But the rooms still contain quantities of superb late-17C craftsmanship, above all wood carving by the Londoners Lobb, Davis and Young, assisted by a local man, Samuel Watson, and ceiling paintings by Verrio and Laguerre (more lively than those in the Painted Hall, especially the figures in the coves). The **State Dining Room** has a particularly attractive wooden overmantel; there is also some ponderous furniture designed by William Kent for Lord Burlington, a silver-gilt dish of 1761 with a depiction of classical ruins—one of several pieces of 17C and 18C silver on view—and an attractive early-17C portrait of a girl by Cornelis de Vos, from Burlington's collection. Mortlake tapestries of c 1635, after the Raphael Cartoons, line the walls of the **State Drawing Room**, and there are more paintings from Burlington's collection, including a family group by Paris Bordone and Luca Giordano's 'Acis and Galatea' in the **Music Room**. The **State Bedroom** follows, with more Old Masters and a rather tame 'Europa and the Bull' by Lely (the bed was a gift after the death of George II), and the much smaller **Dressing Room**, with its contemporary silver chandelier (only hung here from c 1912), and the small China Closet, hung with small 17C Dutch and Flemish low-life pictures, complete the sequence.

The corridors known as the **Sketch Galleries** were designed by Wyatville in 1834–35 to house the family's excellent collection of Old Master drawings, but they are now used to display family portraits, along with tapestries and some of the Delft vases collected by the 1st Duke. From here the ground floor is reached via the **West Staircase** (ceiling by Sir James Thornhill), hung with some of the most important paintings in the collection, among them Simon Vouet's 'Allegory of Peace', Tintoretto's 'Samson and Delilah' and Salvator Rosa's 'Jacob's Dream'; there is also a copy by Richard Wilson of a 17C view of the first house, an 18C view of the present house and grounds before the latter were remodelled by Paxton, and a bleak 'Large Interior W9' by Lucian Freud (1973) bought by the present Duke and Duchess. A corridor at the foot of the stairs contains assorted Egyptian and Roman antiquities. It gives access to the **Chapel**, one of the finest Baroque interiors in England, with a lavish alabaster altarpiece designed by Caius Gabriel Cibber and executed by Samuel Watson, who was also responsible for the carved woodwork; the paintings (apart from the 'Incredulity of St Thomas' over the altar, by Verrio) are by Laguerre. The **Oak Room**, next door, is a not very successful attempt by the 6th Duke to create a new interior making use of early-18C wood carvings from a German monastery bought at an auction in London. The corridor outside contains more of his purchases, including a Hellenistic or early Roman colossal foot in marble (the other foot is in Berlin).

Having passed through the Painted Hall for a second time, the visitor now goes up Wyatville's Oak Staircase, where a carved cravat by Grinling Gibbons, in imitation of lace, is shown. The **Library** can be glimpsed from the ante-room at the top of the stairs; it was created by Wyatville out of Talman's gallery, from which the late-17C ceiling plasterwork, by Edward Gouge, survives. From here two smaller rooms lead into the lavishly decorated **Great Dining Room** in Wyatville's north wing, hung with portraits including three by Van Dyck. This opens into the **Sculpture Gallery**, one of the finest surviving monuments to early-19C artistic taste in an English country house. It now contains the sculptures collected by the 'Bachelor Duke' in Rome in 1818–24, including works by Canova and Thorwaldsen—note especially Canova's 'Sleeping Endymion' (1819) and his seated figure of Napoleon's mother—as well as English sculptors like John Gibson and the younger Richard Westmacott; there are also Old Master paintings, including Rembrandt's 'Man in Oriental Costume'— possibly King Uzziah—(c 1639), Franz Hals' Portrait of an Unknown Man (1622) and two large canvases by Sebastiano Ricci (the 'Presentation in the Temple' and the 'Flight into Egypt'), painted in 1713 while he was in England. The former Orangery (now a gift shop) leads into the gardens, where Thomas Archer's strikingly Baroque **Cascade House** (1702) still survives above its contrived waterfall. Further south is the formal canal of the same date, with Paxton's spectacular 'Emperor Fountain', and from here Talman's magnificent **south front**, begun in 1687, can be clearly seen, its wall surfaces dignified by giant Ionic pilasters and its skyline bristling with urns—a suitably magnificent finale to a tour of Chatsworth.

GCT

Eyam Hall

In Eyam 12m west of Chesterfield off A623 Chesterfield–Stockport: R.H.V. Wright, tel. 0433 631976. Open end Mar–end Oct Sun, Wed, Thur, BH Mon 11–4.30. Guided tours.

This attractive gabled manor house of local gritstone stands in the much-visited village of Eyam in the Peak District, scene of a particularly horrendous visitation of the Plague in 1666. It dates in its present form from

1671 (the date 1676 on a rainwater-head presumably refers to its completion), and it incorporates parts of an earlier, smaller, house. The builder was
Thomas Wright, a younger son from a long-established local family, who
bought the estate for his son John and his wife, an heiress; the house has
remained in the family ever since, and has recently been sympathetically
restored by the present owner.

Eyam Hall is an excellent example of the rugged traditional architecture
of the locality, little touched by classical influences, and by metropolitan
standards distinctly old-fashioned for its date. A strong horizontal emphasis
is imparted by the string courses which mark the floor levels on the entrance
front and by the long, low mullioned windows; there is very little external
ornamentation, and the house blends well into the hilly landscape. It is
entered through the stone-flagged Hall, which faces south onto the street
and is flanked by projecting wings of the usual kind. Beyond lies the
staircase, possibly a survival from the earlier house (or conceivably brought
in from elsewhere), and in one of the wings there is a room hung with 15C
and 16C Flemish tapestries. The Library occupies the position of the
original great chamber, and the tour also encompasses a bedroom, the
Dining Room—probably on the site of the original kitchen—and the present
Kitchen, added to the house c 1700. The main rooms are appropriately
furnished with 17C, 18C and 19C pieces, and there is a good collection of
family portraits.

GCT

Haddon Hall

2m south east of Bakewell on A6 Buxton–Matlock: the Duke of Rutland,
tel. 0629 812855. Open Apr–Sept Tues–Sun (except Sun in July, Aug) and
BH Sun and Mon 11–6. Refreshments.

Haddon Hall is for many people the *beau ideal* of the English country house.
Built by several generations of the Vernon family during the Middle Ages
and relatively untouched since the early 17C, its appeal is enhanced by the
texture of the old grey limestone walls and the irregular picturesque
skyline. The Vernons first came into possession of the estate c 1170, and
the walls of the Chapel, which once served as the parish church of the now
vanished village of Nether Haddon, date from c 1195, when Richard Vernon
was given permission to build a high wall around his house. But its present
appearance is domestic rather than warlike. The Vernons, though important enough figures in the remote world of north Derbyshire, were not great
feudal barons and their house was never a castle. Its present external
appearance was fixed chiefly in the mid 14C, when much of the present
upper courtyard, including the hall range, was built by another Richard
Vernon, and in the late 15C, when a second, lower, courtyard was built by
Sir William Vernon and his son to provide extra lodgings for the household.
In 1567, on the death of Sir George Vernon, the 'King of the Peak', the house
passed to his son-in-law Sir John Manners, younger son of the Earl of
Rutland, and he carried out major alterations in the upper courtyard at the
end of the 16C, including the rebuilding of the Long Gallery in its present
form. His grandson inherited the earldom of Rutland in 1641 and in 1703
the 1st Duke of Rutland moved into the family's main seat, Belvoir Castle,
Leicestershire (qv.), leaving Haddon to fall into a long and gentle decrepi-
tude. When that irascible traveller John Byng went there in 1789 he was

allowed to walk off with a sword 'worn by the Vernons in the wars of France', and a century later Henry James, another avid country house visitor, wrote that 'of every form of sad desuetude and picturesque decay Haddon Hall contains some delightful example'. The 9th Duke (d 1940) made the house habitable again, and in its present form it still bears witness both to its long and romantic past and also to the principles of careful and 'conservative' restoration espoused by Lord Rutland, his architect, Harold Brakspear, and his craftsmen.

The house stands on rising ground above the River Wye, and the whole ensemble can be well seen from the hill above the car park. The approach is dominated by the north west tower, through which the college-like **lower courtyard** is entered, its worn paved surface of local gritstone rising up to the Hall, which stands at the centre of the house. The remaining sides are occupied by the late-15C lodgings, each with its own door, and by the much older **Chapel** which still contains many of its decorations and fittings, including 15C wall paintings and stained glass, and Jacobean pews and pulpit. A 15C porch tower occupies the centre of the hall range, with the service end to the left and the Hall itself to the right, lit by a traceried 14C window next to the chimneybreast (a later insertion); to the right of the Hall is a two-storeyed chamber block with large mullioned windows of c 1500 lighting the downstairs Parlour and the Great Chamber above. The porch gives access to the usual screens passage with three doors on the left which originally led to the pantry, the buttery and to the draughty, cavernous **Kitchen**; this still retains its much-used shelves and chopping-blocks, and some medieval cupboards are preserved in an adjoining room. The wooden roof of the **Hall** dates from 1923–25, but the 15C screen still survives, along with the early-17C gallery to ease communication between the upstairs rooms; the splendid *millefleurs* tapestry with its representations of the royal coat of arms hanging over the high table (only wide enough to seat people on one side), dates from the mid 15C, and may have been given by Henry VIII to Sir Henry Vernon, who had been treasurer to his elder brother Prince Arthur.

A doorway close to the high table leads into the **Parlour**, one of few early-16C rooms in England to survive in anything like its original state. It is especially notable for its painted heraldic ceiling and for the wooden panelling (something not found in earlier country houses) bearing the date 1545, along with the motto 'Drede God and Honor the King' over the fireplace, and relief carvings of a man and woman in early-Tudor dress close to one of the two bay windows. There is a conspicuous (and authentic) absence of furniture. The equally empty **Great Chamber**, upstairs, was the most important reception room in late medieval and Tudor times; it has an open timber roof of c 1500, a late-16C plaster frieze and 17C Flemish tapestries, more of which can be seen in the adjacent 'Earl's Apartments' overlooking the lower courtyard. The early-17C **Gallery** takes up most of the south side of the upper court, its striking beauty deriving partly from its proportions, partly from its profuse wood carving and partly from the fact that the wood has been allowed to age naturally to an unpolished silver-grey. An evocative Rex Whistler painting of 1932 over the fireplace commemorates the completion of the 9th Duke of Rutland's restoration of the house. The **Orpheus Room** (once the state bedroom but since divided up) contains a crude late-16C overmantel of Orpheus taming the beasts and an accomplished set of 16C Brussels tapestries of hunting scenes; other tapestries from the house perished in a fire in 1925. From here a doorway leads out into the terraced **gardens** which date, at least in their basic form, from the early 17C—making them among the earliest to survive in an English country house—and from this point it is possible to see the crenellated exterior of the Gallery with its large mullioned and transomed windows set against the expanse of grey creeper-clad stone.

GCT

Hardwick Hall

2m south of A617, 6½m west of Mansfield, M1 exit 29: National Trust, tel. 0246 850430. Open Apr–Oct Wed, Thur, Sat, Sun and BH Mon 12.30–5. Refreshments.

This spectacular late-16C house is inseparable, even after 400 years, from the personality of its builder, Elizabeth, Countess of Shrewsbury ('Bess of Hardwick'). The daughter and heiress of a local squire, Bess was an energetic, rapacious and aggressive woman with insatiable dynastic ambitions. She saw four husbands to the grave and, at the age of 70 used her considerable fortune to construct a magnificent new house on a site adjoining the family seat, which she had already enlarged and whose ruins survive today. The architect was almost certainly Robert Smythson, who had recently completed Wollaton Hall, Notts (qv.), a few miles away to the south, and work began in 1591. When Bess died in 1608, the house passed to William Cavendish, her second son by her second marriage. His successors kept it in repair, but fixed their main residence at Chatsworth (qv.), a few miles away to the west, and in 1958 Hardwick was acquired by the National Trust. Throughout this long period the house retained many of the costly furnishings introduced at the end of the 16C, and, with the revival of interest in the 'Old English' style in the early 19C, the collection was augmented by other items brought from Chatsworth by the 6th Duke of Devonshire. Today there is no house in England which better conveys the sense of a great Elizabethan aristocratic establishment in its heyday.

From the outside, Hardwick Hall transmits a feeling of unadorned power which clearly reflects the taste of its formidable builder. It is built of local yellow sandstone, recently cleaned and restored after generations of smoke-blackening, and makes the most of its prominent position, looking west towards the hills of the Peak District. Architecturally, it is a synthesis of medieval and Renaissance ideas. A vision of ancient chivalry is conjured up by the huge glittering windows and the tall encircling towers, each of them defiantly crested with the initials 'E.S.', but the loggia, the balustrade and much of the internal detailing show the influence of the newer foreign fashions. The accommodation is fitted into a rectangular block two rooms deep, with three storeys of gradually increasing height: entrance hall, kitchens and domestic offices on the ground floor, the everyday living-rooms and bedrooms above, and a suite of grand state rooms at the top.

The house is as noteworthy for its contents as for its architecture. The rooms are especially rich in 16C and 17C needlework and tapestries, and there is a good collection of portraits and furniture. The entrance is through the **Hall**, placed, unusually for houses of the period, across the main axis of the house. It is dominated by a stone screen of Doric columns and an elaborate heraldic plaster overmantel by Abraham Smith, a local man who did a great deal of work here; on a screen are displayed a set of needlework wall-hangings of classical heroines accompanied by representations of the Virtues, dating from c 1575. The upper floors are reached by a massive stone **staircase** hung with 16C and 17C English and Flemish tapestries. In Bess's time the largest rooms on the first floor were the 'low great chamber', where she dined with the most important members of her household and a withdrawing chamber (now the **Drawing Room**); this latter is now furnished as a comfortable sitting room, reflecting the taste of the last occupant, Evelyn, Dowager Duchess of Devonshire (d 1960). It contains late-16C Flemish tapestries, some former cushion-covers embroidered by Bess and the ladies of her household, and a Ming porcelain vessel with a gilt mount dated 1589—one of the earliest examples of Oriental porcelain in an English collection. The portraits include one of Bess's 23-month-old granddaughter, Lady Arabella Stuart, who, thanks to her grandmother's machinations, was second in line to the throne when the house was under construction.

The lofty and well-lit state rooms at the top of the house have changed relatively little since the late 16C, although much of the furniture has been brought in since Bess's time. Three rooms were provided for entertaining visitors: the High Great Chamber, the adjoining Withdrawing Chamber in the centre of the west front, and a Gallery running along the whole of the east front. When not in use, the furniture was placed around the edges of the rooms, as it is now. The **High Great Chamber** was designed to display a set of Brussels tapestries of the story of Ulysses; there is also an allegorical plaster frieze with lively hunting scenes by Abraham Smith, and a splendid alabaster and marble chimneypiece by Thomas Accres, who had worked with Smythson at Wollaton. The **Withdrawing Room** has some of the best furniture in the house, notably an elaborately carved marquetry chest of c 1570 and the extraordinary 'Sea Dog' table of c 1580, mentioned in an inventory of 1601. There is also a late-16C alabaster bas-relief of great beauty, originally at Chatsworth, showing Apollo and some demure Muses playing lutes and viols. The **Gallery** has two massive chimneypieces by Accres, some Oriental carpets placed over tables in the usual Elizabethan manner, and a canopy (formerly part of a state bed at Chatsworth) which may have replaced the 'cloth of estate' under which Bess could have sat on state occasions. The room is hung with tapestries purchased in 1592, on top of which have been hung a prodigious collection of 81 portraits, including one of Bess herself, attributed to Rowland Lockey, an apprentice of Nicholas Hilliard. The remaining rooms on this floor were bedrooms, including the **Green Velvet Room**, with a state bed of c 1740 and now hung with excellent late-16C Flemish tapestries of the story of Abraham, possibly those listed in the 1601 inventory, when the room was the best bedchamber. The richly coloured chimneypiece and doorcase of Derbyshire marble are contemporary with the house.

A subsidiary staircase leads down to the **Dining Room** (originally the low great chamber) on the first floor, now furnished in the style of the 18C, beyond which is a bedroom containing a magnificent 18C state bed by James Vardy. The adjacent 'little dining chamber' (now called the **Paved Room**) contains a plaster overmantel decorated with a figure of Ceres, more Elizabethan embroideries, notably one of the 'Judgement of Paris' dated 1574, and some needlework by Mary, Queen of Scots, who had been held captive (though not at Hardwick) by Bess and her husband; here Bess had meals in private. The plainly furnished **Chapel**, on the same floor, is hung with painted cloths—a rare survival in a country house—and from here stairs lead to the Kitchen, conveniently underneath the dining rooms, where the National Trust now serves its lunches and teas.

GCT

Kedleston Hall

3m north west of Derby near Allestree (signposted from A38/A52 crossroads): National Trust, tel. 0332 842191. Open Apr–Oct Sat–Wed 1–5.30 (gardens 11–6). Refreshments.

Kedleston is the epitome of the late-18C English country house: large, classically proportioned, rich in furniture and works of art, and set in a magnificent landscape garden. Its special character derives from the fact that it has been very little altered since it was built in 1759–65. There have been no major structural changes, and the original furniture is largely in situ, together with the pictures collected by the builder, Sir Nathaniel Curzon, who became 1st Lord Scarsdale in 1761.

There have been Curzons at Kedleston since the Norman Conquest, many of whom are buried in the medieval parish church next to the house. Lord Scarsdale was an enthusiast for classical antiquities and a collector of Old Master pictures (although there is no evidence that he ever went to Italy). On inheriting in 1758, he immediately decided to replace the existing house by Francis Smith of Warwick with one 'in attick elegance made neat'. He first consulted Matthew Brettingham, the executant architect at Holkham Hall, Norfolk (qv.), and the plan of a rectangular porticoed block flanked by lower pavilions joined to the main house by corridors obviously derives from Holkham and from Palladio's scheme for the Villa Mocenigo which inspired it (though only two of the four pavilions proposed for Kedleston were actually built). James Paine was called in to superintend the practical details in 1759, and the design for the north (entrance) front is basically his. But two years later both he and Brettingham were superseded by the young Robert Adam, who had recently returned from Italy and had already been informally consulted by Curzon. By this time the two pavilions on either side of the entrance front had been built and the main block begun. Adam's contribution lay in the decoration of the rooms and the design of some of the furniture, the design of the south (garden) front and, to a great extent, the layout and embellishment of the grounds. Kedleston was his first major commission, and for this reason alone it occupies an important place in the history of English taste. The decoration of the interior lasted into the 1780s.

Approached across an artificial lake and with its backdrop of woods, the house exudes an air of calm patrician confidence. The **central block**, built of a creamy local limestone, is articulated by a Corinthian portico resting on a rusticated base; above it rises a low dome covering the Saloon at the centre of the garden front, while on either side curved wings link the main block to the pavilions, one of which contained the kitchens and domestic offices and the other a private suite of rooms. When Dr Johnson visited Kedleston he said that it 'would do excellently for a town-hall', and the design was indeed echoed in government buildings in America and other former British colonies. The **garden front** represents Adam's most important contribution to the exterior. The centre, with its free-standing columns, echoes the triumphal arches of the Romans, and the curved staircase and the play of light and shadow on the façade show his skill in introducing what he called 'movement' into domestic architecture.

The vast **Entrance Hall** sets the tone of slightly chilly magnificence which pervades the house. It derives its character from the Vitruvian idea of the 'Egyptian Hall': a rectangular space surrounded by a continuous colonnade. Here, columns of local alabaster support a coved ceiling embellished with delicate stucco grotesques and arabesques designed in 1775–77 by Adam's draughtsman, George Richardson; the effect of imperial splendour is enhanced by the copies of classical statuary which fill the niches along the walls. From here the tour proceeds in a clockwise direction, starting with the **Music Room** and **Drawing Room**, which were started by Brettingham and Paine before Adam came on the scene. Their decoration is still fundamentally Palladian in character, but Adam's hand is shown in the subtle choice of colours. The pictures were collected by the 1st Lord Scarsdale on the advice of the dealer William Kent (no relation of the architect) and most of them still hang in their intended places; note especially Luca Giordano's 'Triumph of Bacchus' and Matteo Rosselli's 'Triumph of David' (with the participants playing musical instruments) in the Music Room, and the Cuyp 'Landscape in the Rhine Valley' which hangs in the Drawing Room along with large canvases by 16C and 17C Italian artists including Lodovico Carracci, Bernardo Strozzi and Benedetto Luti. There are also several very fine pieces of furniture, including a chamber organ with a case by Adam in the Music Room and two pairs of extravagantly lavish sofas by John Linnell of c 1762–65 in the Drawing Room, with legs in the form of dolphins, mermen and mermaids, supposedly to celebrate recent British victories in the Seven Years War.

The first of the rooms entirely by Adam is the **Library**, with its Doric doorcases and frieze, and pictures by Salvator Rosa ('A Philosopher') and Rembrandt's follower Saloman Koninck ('Daniel before Nebuchadnezzar'). Next comes the circular **Saloon** with its coffered dome lit by a Pantheon-like opening at the apex. This was originally intended as a sculpture-gallery, like that at Newby Hall, Yorkshire (qv.), but in the event the niches were filled with iron stoves surmounted by urns; the pictures of classical ruins over the doors were commissioned by Lord Scarsdale from William Hamilton. A door leads into the State Apartment, starting with an **Ante-Room** and **Dressing-Room** divided by a screen with details copieD from the Emperor Diocletian's palace at Split in Croatia, on which Adam published an influential book; a portrait of the 1st Lord Scarsdale and his wife by Nathaniel Hone (1761) hangs over the fireplace. The lusciously palmy mirror is by James Gravenor, who also designed the even more extravagant gilded bed of 1764 in the **State Bedroom** next door; portraits here include two by Lely of James II and his second wife, Mary of Modena.

The **Dining Room**—the last room on the piano nobile—displays Adam's art at its most delicate, although some of the original sense of space has been lost by the placing of furniture in the centre of the room. The apsidal projection at the north end contains serving-tables designed to display Lord Scarsdale's collection of 17C Italian plate at meal-times, and his neoclassical sympathies are shown in the ormolu perfume burner in the form of a classical tripod, designed by James 'Athenian' Stuart, and the unusual urn-like plate-warmer of gun-metal and ormolu, probably also designed by Stuart in 1760. The adjoining corridor contains portraits and other mementoes of the statesman George Nathaniel Curzon, uncle of the present Lord Scarsdale, while a ground-floor **museum** houses some of the many objects he collected on his travels in the East and when he was Viceroy of India in the early years of this century. There are several ornamental buildings in the well-maintained **park**, including a Fishing Room (1770–72) by Adam on the upper lake, flanked by boathouses, with a cold bath below.

GCT

Melbourne Hall

At east end of village of Melbourne, 1m south of A514 Derby–Ashby: Lord Ralph Kerr, tel. 0332 862502. Open Aug (not Mon except BH) 2–5. Guided tours (not Sun). Garden open Apr–Sept Wed, Sat, Sun, BH Mon 2–6. Refreshments.

This attractive though architecturally modest house stands close to the magnificent Norman parish church of Melbourne—one of the finest of its date in England—overlooking a beautifully-preserved example of an early-18C formal garden. It occupies the site of the rectorial manor-house of the medieval Bishops of Carlisle, from whose successors Sir John Coke, Secretary of State to Charles I, took a lease of the estate in 1628. He took over, and possibly rebuilt, an L-shaped house of stone, little of which survived an ambitious programme of improvements inaugurated by his great-grandson Thomas Coke, Vice-Chamberlain to Queen Anne and George I. The royal gardener, Henry Wise, supplied shrubs and trees for the gardens, which were laid out to Coke's own design, and Coke also prepared plans for a new east wing containing reception rooms overlooking the gardens. Work began in 1725–26 under the supervision of Francis Smith of Warwick but was not finished until 1744, when the pedimented east façade was completed by his son William. The house subsequently passed by inheritance to the Lamb and Cowper families before settling into the possession of the Kerrs, Marquesses of Lothian. These later owners introduced new furniture and altered most of the Smiths' interiors, but the fabric of the building was left largely untouched.

The house is best understood and enjoyed if the gardens are seen first. From here William Smith's east front of smooth ashlar can be viewed in the context of the formal alleys, yew hedges and statuary it was designed to complement (note especially the fanciful wrought-iron arbour by Robert Bakewell of Derby at the end of the main vista). The entrance to the house is through a conservatory-like Outer Hall in the narrow space between the east and west wings, containing a collection of formal early-18C royal portraits which presumably counted among Thomas Coke's perquisites of office. Beyond lies the Dining Room—the hall of the original house—with an overmantel of 1596 brought from elsewhere and 17C and 18C family portraits, including one of Sir John Coke by Cornelius Johnson and two good double portraits by Lely. The 18C west wing contains three main rooms: the Hall, with a wooden staircase characteristic of Francis Smith's work of the 1720s (note the portrait of Sir Thomas More attributed to Holbein, several good Jacobean portraits and a large and sentimental early-18C portrait by Huysmans of the children of Col. John Coke); the Library, furnished as a comfortable living room and hung with pictures collected in the 18C, including an architectural fantasy by Pannini, a Nativity and 'Moses striking the Rock' by Bassano, and drawings by Gainsborough and others; and the Drawing Room, overlooking the gardens and attractively furnished with 18C pieces.

GCT

Sudbury Hall

6m east of Uttoxeter on A50 Derby–Stoke and A515 Lichfield–Ashbourne:
National Trust, tel. 0283 585305. Open Apr–Oct Wed–Sun, BH Mon 1–5.30
(gardens open 11–6). Refreshments.

Sudbury Hall is one of the best-preserved post-Restoration houses in
England. Its builder, George Vernon, was descended from the Vernons of
Haddon Hall (qv.), one of the most important families in the county, and he
began building soon after marrying an heiress and inheriting the estate in
1660, the year of Charles II's return—an event which he must have
welcomed, since he was described shortly afterwards as being 'loyal and
very orthodox'. The body of the house was finished by 1670, but the
decoration of the interior lasted until the 1690s, and it is this which
constitutes Sudbury's chief claim to fame. Vernon's grandson was ennobled
as Lord Vernon in 1762, and the house remained in the family's possession
until 1967, when it was presented to the National Trust. George Devey made
made discreet additions to the service end in 1874–83, but otherwise the
building remains remarkably intact.

The house stands in a pastoral setting on the edge of the estate village.
In some respects it is a rather old-fashioned building for its date. The walls
are of red brick, with criss-cross patterning in blue brick, more reminiscent
of early Tudor architecture than of the reserved style favoured by many of
Vernon's more sophisticated contemporaries. The large mullioned and
transomed windows, some of them with curious tracery, must also have
appeared somewhat dated to connoisseurs of classical architecture, and the
plan—a double-pile block with two slightly projecting wings, a Hall entered
through a screens passage and a Long Gallery on the first floor—harks back
to Jacobean houses like Aston Hall, West Midlands (qv.). But the hipped
roof, cupola and tall chimneys show that Vernon—who may have acted as
his own architect—was not totally out of touch with contemporary devel-
opments (the original balustrade on the roof ridge was removed by
E.M. Barry in 1872, to the detriment of the general appearance). The
entrance, on the north side, is through a two-storeyed porch, with pairs of
superimposed columns of the local yellow sandstone carrying segmental
pediments—an effect reminiscent of the Canterbury Quadrangle at
St John's College, Oxford, built some 30 years before; the sculptural
enrichments were carved by the Leicester-born mason William Wilson in
1670. The garden front is plainer, and because the formal gardens were all
landscaped away in the 18C (they are shown in a view of 1681 inside the
house) the effect is more gaunt than was originally intended.

The main interest of Sudbury Hall lies in its superb plasterwork and wood
carving, with work by some of the leading craftsmen of the day displayed
in a series of light and, to a large extent, empty rooms, the clutter of later
furnishing having been removed after a series of sales and a prolonged
period of letting in the early 20C. The first room to be seen is the Hall, with
a mural painting of 'Industry and Idleness' by Louis Laguerre over the
fireplace. The decoration here is restrained, but the same cannot be said of
the spectacular Staircase, with its wooden balustrade richly carved by the
sculptor Edward Pierce, one of Christopher Wren's collaborators, in
1676–77; this was painted white (the original colour) as part of an ambitious
programme of redecoration carried out by John Fowler for the National
Trust in 1968–70. The sumptuous effect is reinforced by the exuberant

contemporary plasterwork on the ceiling (and even underneath the upper flight of stairs) by Robert Bradbury and James Pettifer, and by Laguerre's mythological paintings introduced in the 1690s when he was working at Chatsworth (qv.). The Saloon (originally called the parlour) has more first-rate woodwork and plasterwork, and the effect was made even richer in the 1740s when the 1st Lord Vernon introduced a series of full-length family portraits into the segment-headed aedicules which line the walls; the smaller portrait of George Vernon, the builder of the house, over one of the doors is by John Michael Wright, one of the best British portraitists of the era, who supplied a number of pictures for the house in the 1660s. The adjacent Drawing Room contains another plaster ceiling by Bradbury and Pettifer and an overmantel with delicately carved festoons of fruit, flowers and game by Grinling Gibbons, and the Library contains some Greek vases acquired by the 5th Lord Vernon in 1843; the remaining ground-floor rooms are plainer and have undergone more alterations.

The first floor is reached by a staircase in the east part of the house. It leads to the Gallery, which takes up the whole of the garden front, 'commanding the prospect' over the grounds and the surrounding countryside. This magnificent room, now once again largely empty of furniture as it would have been in the 17C, is lined with a series of family portraits, including some by Wright, but the pièce de résistance is the amazingly inventive plaster ceiling by Bradbury and Pettifer. From here the route passes via the upper landing of the main staircase to a bedroom called the Queen's Room after William IV's widow Queen Adelaide, who leased the house in the early 1840s. The decoration here slightly pre-dates that of the other rooms, and the craftsmanship is correspondingly less inventive, with plasterwork by Samuel Mansfield of Derby, and a rather stodgily carved chimneypiece by William Wilson enclosing an attractive Italianate garden scene by the contemporary Dutch artist Hendrick Danckerts.

GCT

DEVON

Arlington Court

North east of Barnstaple on the east side of the Lynton Rd (A39): National
Trust, tel. 0271 850296. Open Apr–Oct daily except Sat 11–5.30, last
admission 5. Open Sat on BH weekends. Refreshments.

The Chichester family first settled at Arlington in 1384. They lived quietly,
marrying among the Devonshire gentry and expanding their estates. In
1783 Col John Palmer Chichester succeeded, and wanted a more up-to-
date residence. He demolished the old house, and built a large, plain
three-storeyed one in the park south of the church in 1790. It was evidently
not built very well, for in 1820 it too was demolished, and the Colonel began
the present house to designs by Thomas Lee of Barnstaple. He died in 1823
before this second new house was complete. His son, John,was created a
baronet, completed the house, made the lake and planted most of the
woodlands, dying in 1851. His son, Sir Bruce, came of age in 1863, and
extended the house, but his lavish hospitality cost the estate dearly. On his
death in 1881 his widow and only daughter, Rosalie, were left with heavy
debts, and much of the estate had to be sold. Miss Rosalie Chichester lived
at Arlington until 1949, suffusing the house and estate with her warm and
sympathetic personality. She was a capable painter and photographer,
interested in botany, zoology and the sea. She turned the park and much
of the estate into an animal sanctuary, providing a haven for local wildlife.
On her death in 1949 she bequeathed the house and the whole estate of
3471 acres to the National Trust.

The house is sequestered in well-wooded parkland, with the group of
church and estate buildings nearby. It is Greek Revival in style, a simple
free-standing rectangle, faced with white stucco, and quite plain except for
Tuscan pilasters at the corners and a semicircular Doric porch on the east
(entrance) front. Originally the service rooms were all in the basement, with
two main floors above. Sir Bruce removed the rooms on the north side on
both floors, creating a big galleried staircase hall. He added a large new
wing to the north, to house extra bedrooms, new kitchen and servants'
quarters, and built the stable block near the church, dated 1864.

The Entrance Hall contains plaster reliefs of Sir John Chichester and his
wife. To the left is the Morning Room. This is really only a section of one
great room, 70ft long, running the whole length of the south front, and
divided into three parts by Ionic columns. The three sections can be divided
by great doors or panels, which slide back into the walls, and all three have
elaborate Greek Revival ceilings. The furniture, here as elsewhere in the
house, is eclectic, reflecting the family's history and Miss Rosalie Chichester's taste. In the Ante-Room are collections of spoons, jade, glassware, and
a most remarkable painting by William Blake 'The Four Ages of Man',
rediscovered on top of a cupboard when the National Trust took over the
house in 1949. The White Drawing Room, the final part of this long room,
contains English, French and Chinese porcelain and snuff boxes

The boudoir has papier-mâché furniture, and a strong atmosphere of the
mid 19C. The Pewter Room contains part of Miss Rosalie Chichester's large
collection of Roman to 19C pewter and the big Hall contains many paintings
and models of ships, including one of Sir Francis Chichester's Gypsy Moth
IV. Upstairs, in the Blue Bedroom, is a collection of dresses worn by ladies

of the family between 1830 and 1910. The other bedrooms remain very much as they were in Miss Chichester's day.

Outside, there is a good collection of 19C vehicles in the Stables; between this and the house is a pretty Victorian flower garden and conservatory. The park is extensive and well-wooded, with deer, donkeys, Shetland ponies and a duck sanctuary on the lake.

SB

Bickleigh Castle

4m south of Tiverton off A396 at Bickleigh Bridge: O.N. Boxall, tel. 0884 855363. Open Easter week, then Wed, Sun, BH Mon to Spring BH, then daily except Sat to early Oct 2–5.30. Refreshments.

Beautifully situated among woods in the valley of the River Exe, Bickleigh Castle is the surviving part of an important medieval fortified house slighted in the Civil War but never totally abandoned. The house is hidden away some distance from the village at the centre of a complex of buildings of different dates, by far the oldest of which is a chapel with a 12C doorway and a 15C wagon roof, claimed to be the oldest complete building in Devon. This must have served the house of the Bickleigh family, which lived here in the early Middle Ages, but in the early 15C the estate passed to a junior branch of the Courtenays of Powderham (qv.), and the impressive stone gatehouse which represents the main survival of the medieval domestic buildings was probably built by them. It is three storeys high (but only two storeys on the courtyard side), with a rib-vaulted passageway on the ground floor, flanked by an Armoury, containing a collection of armour, and a Guard Room, with mainly 17C furniture and portraits, including one of Queen Henrietta Maria in a carved frame of 1637. Upstairs is a spacious chamber (the present Great Hall) lit by late-16C or early-17C mullioned windows, with more 17C furniture and a screen brought in in the 20C. At the time of its construction the gatehouse led into a courtyard with a hall and the usual ancillary buildings, but their precise location has not been established.

In the early 16C the castle went by marriage to Sir Thomas Carew, a member of another important West Country family, and his descendants lived at Bickleigh until the Civil War, when they took the Royalist side and paid for it by seeing the bulk of the residential buildings around the courtyard destroyed by General Fairfax's soldiers. Sir Henry Carew repaired the gatehouse after the Restoration, and the picturesque thatched building which now stands on the north side of the former courtyard was built at about the same time; it now contains 16C and 17C furniture and in the Garden Room beyond, there is an unusual carved overmantel of 1626, probably brought from one of the demolished parts of the house. When Sir Henry died in 1681 the property went to his daughter and her husband (and distant cousin) Sir Thomas Carew of Haccombe, and for the next two centuries or more parts of the castle were used from time to time as a residence for younger sons of the family who served as rectors of Bickleigh church, the rest serving as cottages and farm stores. The house was finally sold in 1923, and the present gardens—including surviving parts of the original moat—were then laid out, with an attractive set of 18C Italian gates by the side of the road. The present owner, who bought the property in

1970, has also created a 'museum of domestic objects' in a thatched barn nearby, together with a display of World War II espionage and escape equipment.

GCT

Bradley Manor

1m from Newton Abbot station, approached from A381 Newton Abbot–Totnes: National Trust/Commander and Mrs A.H. Woolner. Open Apr–Sept Wed 2–5.

The front of this largely 15C house, with its white-washed roughcast walls, wide gables and irregularly spaced windows, makes a memorable impression in its wooded valley setting, seemingly far removed from the bustle of modern urban life. The east wing of the building dates from some time after 1402, when Richard Yarde married the heiress of the Bushels, lords of the manor since the 13C, and built a hall flanked by the usual service rooms and parlour. The domestic chapel, which projects from the parlour, was licensed in 1428, and at some time towards the end of the 15C the façade was given its present appearance by Richard Yarde's grandson, another Richard; this involved hiding the front wall of the hall behind a gabled structure containing a passageway on the ground floor and two small rooms above—a most unusual arrangement for its date. Since then the front has remained virtually unchanged, save for the removal of a high enclosing wall with a gatehouse in the 19C (it was shown in an engraving of 1822). But two of the three sides of the courtyard behind the hall block have completely disappeared, leaving only the south range which contains remnants of an earlier 13C building. The Yarde family remained at Bradley until 1751, and the house subsequently passed through several ownerships before being bought in 1909 by Cecil Firth, a descendant of the Yardes. He restored the building and left it to his daughter, Mrs Woolner, who gave it with the surrounding woodland to the National Trust in 1938; her family still live there as tenants of the Trust.

The low, spreading front of the house makes an unusually satisfying composition. There are three gables in the centre, each with a first-floor window corbelled out from the wall surface, while another gable is set back to the left and the Chapel, with its three-light Perpendicular east window, projects to the right. The porch, underneath the middle gable, leads in to the Hall via a screens passage (the wooden screen was brought from an inn in Ashburton in the early 20C), and to the right is another passage—part of the late-15C extension—serving as an ante-chapel. The Hall retains its early-15C arch-braced roof, and there is a painting of Elizabeth I's coat of arms on the north wall over the place where the high table would once have been. Close to this is a splendid wooden screen dated 1534 with linenfold panelling below and Renaissance ornament above; it leads via the ante-chapel passage to the Chapel, with a wagon roof of the kind often found in Devon churches, adorned with carved wooden bosses. Some early decoration survives in some of the upstairs rooms, including the one over the buttery at the 'lower' end of the Hall, with a late-16C plaster overmantel and another in the south wing with some late-15C or early-16C wall painting; another room in the south wing has good late-17C panelling and an elaborate plaster cornice.

GCT

Buckland Abbey

6m south of Tavistock off A386 Plymouth–Tavistock at Yelverton: National Trust/Plymouth City Council, tel. 0822 853607. Open Apr–Oct daily except Thur; Nov–Mar Sat, Sun 2–5.30 (2–5 in winter). Refreshments.

Buckland is one of the many English country houses formed out of monastic buildings after the Reformation, but in this case the house was built not around the former cloister but within the church: an unusual, though not unique, occurrence which has left its mark on the building down to the present day. The Cistercian abbey was founded in 1278 in a characteristically remote site in a steep valley leading down to the River Tamar to the west of Dartmoor, and details from the original church can be seen both outside and inside the present house. In 1541 the site was sold to Sir Richard Grenville, former High Marshal of Calais. His grandson, another Richard Grenville, one of the most important of the Elizabethan naval commanders, completed the conversion into a house in 1576, only to sell it five years later to an even more celebrated figure in English history, Sir Francis Drake, newly returned from his famous voyage round the world.

Drake seems to have done little to the house, and when he died in 1596 it was inherited by his brother, in the hands of whose descendants it remained until the end of the 18C. For much of this time it was let out to tenants, but it was repaired in the 1770s and again after 1794, when it passed by descent to the 2nd Lord Heathfield, who employed Samuel Pepys Cockerell to fit it up 'for an occasional residence for a month or two at a time' in 1796–1810. More alterations were carried out after 1915 by Elizabeth Fuller-Elliot-Drake and her husband Lord Seaton, but in 1938, the year after her death, there was a fire which gutted much of the interior. The house was given to the National Trust after the Second World War, and it later proceeded, in conjunction with the City of Plymouth, to turn it into a museum concentrating on the life and times of Sir Francis Drake. The present display was created in 1988, the 400th anniversary of the Spanish Armada.

Nestled away in its valley, the house cannot be seen from a distance, and it is approached from the higher ground to the east through the former monastic guest house; this stands close to a set of farm buildings (now used as craft workshops, tea rooms, etc), some of them dating from the late 18C, when the property was leased to the agricultural economist William Marshall. The least altered, and most impressive, of the monastic survivals is the splendid 15C stone barn with its arch-braced timber roof, and to the west of this is the house. It is dominated externally by the crossing tower of the monastic church, which Sir Richard Grenville allowed to survive over the newly-created hall (the wavy cresting dates from his time). The church was an aisleless cruciform building, but Grenville demolished the south transept (the north transept was pulled down in the 18C) and built out a kitchen wing to the south of the chancel. The roofs of the church were also lowered and windows and chimneys inserted to light and heat the new rooms. But despite this the ecclesiastical origin of the building is quite obvious, as is the cavalier way in which Elizabethan Protestants like Grenville and Drake treated the legacy of the monastic past.

It is difficult now to understand the interior as it was in Elizabethan times, partly because of later alterations, partly because some of the most important rooms have been turned over to museum use. The house was originally entered through a porch leading into the hall, but now the hall is not seen until the end of the tour. The entrance is through the former kitchen wing, from which an 18C staircase leads up to a room on the second floor under the tower; the tracery of a large 14C window can be seen here, along with other features from the church and a late-16C chimneypiece with Drake's coat of arms. The top floor of the former nave, gutted in 1938, now contains a display relating the history of the house, and from here stairs lead down to the Drake Gallery, also arranged museum-fashion with an excellent display of pictures and objects, most of them from the City of Plymouth's collection (Drake was Mayor of the town in the 1580s). They include the drum celebrated in the well-known patriotic poem by Sir Henry Newbolt, a standing-cup of c 1595 by a Zurich craftsman with a map engraved on it, and pictures of Queen Elizabeth (by Zucchero), Drake (by Marcus Gheeraerts) and his wife (attributed to George Gower).

The Drake Chamber, to the west, retains its late-16C panelling (though not the plaster ceiling which was destroyed in the fire) and is hung with 16C portraits, including an unflattering representation of the Queen in old age (over the fireplace) and one of Sir Henry Palmer (by Gheeraerts, 1586). The Dining Room, by contrast, on the other side of the Drake Gallery, was remodelled by a local craftsman, Thomas Rowe, in 1772, and has changed little since then; the portraits include an early work (Miss Knight) by the Plympton-born Sir Joshua Reynolds and a picture of Ann Drake, the heiress who married Lord Heathfield, by Allan Ramsay. This room occupies part of the space of the crossing of the medieval church, and underneath it is the Hall, by far the most impressive room in the house from a decorative point of view, largely because of its splendid plaster ceiling embellished with plaster ribs and pendants in the style popular in south-west England in the late 16C (cf. Lanhydrock, Cornwall, etc). There is also decorative plasterwork over the fireplace bearing the date 1576 and on the upper part of the east and west walls; the latter depicts a pastoral scene with a knight (Sir Richard Grenville?) resting under a vine—a favourite Elizabethan conceit. To the west is a Chapel created in 1917 by Lady Seaton on the site of the former high altar.

GCT

Cadhay

1m north of Ottery St Mary on B3176, south of A303 Exeter–Honiton: Lady William-Powlett, tel. 0404 812432. Open July–Aug Tues–Thur, Spring and Summer BH Sun, Mon 2–6. Guided tours.

Cadhay is a largely 16C stone courtyard house set among meadows not far from the small town of Ottery St Mary, best known for its splendid medieval collegiate church. Most of the house as we see it today was built by John Haydon, a local lawyer who married the heiress to the estate in 1527, acted as legal adviser to the city of Exeter and was involved in the sale and dispersal of Church land after the Reformation. Work may have started in the later 1540s, when he became one of the 'governors' of Ottery church (his tomb can still be seen there), and some of the stonework from the superfluous buildings of the collegiate priests was probably incorporated into the new house, which originally had the standard plan of a hall block flanked by projecting wings. John Haydon's great-nephew Robert, who succeeded him in 1587, built a new range with a gallery to link the ends of the two wings, thus creating a courtyard which was embellished in an unusually attractive way c 1617, and since then the house has remained the same size.

The Haydons fell on hard times in the late 17C and the house was sold in 1737 to William Peere Williams, who altered most of the rooms and refaced the entrance front in a restrained Georgian manner. It subsequently passed through the female line, was denuded of its pictures and furniture and was divided into two dwellings. It was finally sold in 1909 to Dampier Whetham, a scientist and Fellow of Trinity College, Cambridge, and he cleared away the farm buildings on the site of the present gardens and called in H.M. Fletcher to carry out a tactful restoration on 'conservative' principles. In 1935 the house and the adjoining farm were sold to Major William-Powlett, whose family have furnished it attractively and lived here ever since.

The house is approached from the east, and the first sight is of the largely mid-16C east front of Salcombe sandstone with a gabled polygonal projection for a staircase in the centre (the small window on the ground floor may have come from the dissolved College at Ottery St Mary). The plain south front, overlooking the 20C gardens, dates from the late 16C, and the north-facing entrance front with its sash windows and pedimented doorway is of the mid 18C (the stepped gables may be later). This was the hall range of the 16C house, and is now approached by visitors through the courtyard via the garden entrance in the south range. In contrast to the relatively restrained exterior of the house, the courtyard is elaborately decorated with a chequerboard pattern of flint (a common building material in east Devon) and small blocks of stone. Some of the original small mullioned windows remain, and over each of the doorways are crudely carved figures of Tudor monarchs set within niches flanked by Corinthian columns and surmounted by strapwork ornament (the date 1617 appears under Queen Elizabeth).

A vestibule on the site of the 16C screens passage leads into the Hall, which was originally open to the roof but was given its present coved plaster ceiling in the mid 18C. The original wooden roof survives and can be seen at the end of the tour, and the stone chimneypiece, still late-Gothic in character, with a frieze of shields over a flat pointed arch, also remains from John Haydon's house, having been uncovered in the 1910 restoration. The rooms in the east range were originally parlours leading off from the hall, but they too were remodelled in the 18C with plain white-painted panelling, and are now comfortably furnished with mainly 18C pieces; a 16C chimneypiece survives in the Library, next to the Hall. The first floor is reached by a mid-16C spiral staircase which leads first, via a corridor, to the Gallery—really a passageway linking the two ends of the house—and then to the room over the Hall, where the open timber roof of the Haydons' house can be seen at close quarters. It is of the arch-braced type common in the West Country, and might be a survival from a previous house on the site. Outside, well-tended gardens lead to lakes which might have been medieval fish ponds.

GCT

Castle Drogo

15m west of Exeter, south of the A30 near Drewsteignton: National Trust,
tel. 064 743 3306. Open Apr–Oct daily except Fri 11–5.30, last admission 5.
Refreshments.

Despite its ancient-sounding name, Castle Drogo is the newest house
described in this book, and almost certainly the last house that will ever be
built on such a scale in Britain. It was built from 1911 to 1930, and was the
brainchild of two men, Julius Drewe and Edwin Lutyens.

Julius Drewe was born in 1856, the son of a clergyman, and because his
family were genteel but poor he left school at 17 to work for a grocery firm
owned by relations of his mother. Sent to China as a tea-buyer, he realised
that huge profits could be made by retailers who bought goods directly from
the country of origin, cutting out the middleman. In 1878 he opened his first
grocery in Liverpool; his business grew fast, under the name of the Home
and Colonial Stores, and in 1889 he retired from active involvement. In 1899
he bought Wadhurst Hall in Sussex with all its contents, many of which are
now at Castle Drogo. At some point he and his brother consulted a
professional genealogist, who convinced them that they were descended
from Dru or Drogo, a companion of the Conqueror, whose descendants
settled at Drewsteignton (Drew's town on the Teign), in Devon. Julius
resolved to build a castle there, and in 1910 he bought the first 450 acres
of what became a 1500 acre estate. It included a superb site, a granite
outcrop soaring over the Teign valley. Drewe hired Edwin Lutyens, and the
foundation stone was laid in April 1911, with Drewe specifying a budget
of £50,000 for the house and £10,000 for the garden. Architect and client
got on well, but the castle as built is much scaled down from Lutyens'
gigantic original scheme. It rose slowly with a small workforce; every stone
in the building was laid by two local masons, Doodney and Cleave. Drewe's
eldest son Adrian was killed in the Great War, and the design was scaled
down again, but it was still not ready for them to move in until 1927, and
work went on until 1930. Julius Drewe died the following year. His family
gave the house with 600 acres to the National Trust in 1974, but happily
still live here.

Castle Drogo is visible from miles away, but the entrance is low-key. The
drive winds for over half a mile, with extensive views southwards, but the
house does not come into view until the last moment. The drive spills into
a forecourt; north and west the land falls away sharply below a parapet, to
the wooded gorge and the Teign. South and east is the house, in two wings
at an angle of about 160 degrees. The floors change level between the
wings, giving Lutyens many opportunities inside for the sort of spatial
effects he loved. Everything is in granite, laid in big, long blocks. The
windows are huge Elizabethan-looking grids of mullions and transoms, but
the broad shapes of the house and its battlements hint more at the 13C.

The character of the **Hall** is determined by the bare granite walls and
unpainted timber which recur in much of the house. Hall, staircases and
passages are simply furnished with Flemish tapestries, oriental rugs and
Spanish furniture. Straight ahead, the **Library** is an L-shaped room, with
more exposed granite and oak bookcases, and views east. The **Drawing
Room** stands at the south end of the house, with windows on three sides;
the 17C-style panelling is painted a soft green, in deliberate contrast to the
austerity elsewhere. The ground falls away so steeply that there are two
floors beneath the roof, and superb views over the Teign valley to Dartmoor.

The furniture is mixed, but chiefly English and early Georgian. In one of Lutyens' favourite conceits, two windows here look down over the main staircase, lit by the huge staircase window. With its granite walls, colossal window in the east wall, and Drawing Room windows high overhead, the **staircase** is a memorable space. There is a huge, if rather wooden, portrait of Julius Drewe at the half-landing; Lutyens' verdict on the artist was 'at least he could paint boots'. The stairs lead to the **Dining Room** a low room with dark mahogany panelling and a heavy plasterwork ceiling, all in late-17C style; it is probably the least successful of the main rooms.

From here a wide service corridor leads to the Pantry, beneath the Library, lined with china cupboards, with sinks under the window, all designed by Lutyens. The house is built on rising ground, so the **Kitchen** is semi-underground. This is in the north wing of the house, housing the service rooms and family bedrooms on its upper floors. The Kitchen is an impressive space, top-lit from a circular lantern in its roof. Underneath is a great circular table designed by Lutyens, and all the Kitchen equipment is intact; the Dining Room is about 50 yards away. The Scullery and Larder are further underground, top-lit and dramatic.

The north wing contains the family's private rooms. **Adrian Drewe's room** at the end of the corridor was arranged by Mrs Drewe after her son's death in Flanders in 1917 as a family memorial to him, of a kind common at the time, but a rare and touching survival now. A flight of steps underneath the Entrance Tower in the forecourt lead down to the **Chapel**. This was going to be the undercroft of a huge hall, which was never built, so its roof is now a terrace. The Chapel itself is of granite, with pillars and low arches, and quite plain. From here the **Gun Room** is entered. This is the vaulted basement under the Dining Room, and it now houses a display of Lutyens' drawings for the castle.

There is much else to see, for the castle has extensive grounds with fine walks. The **formal garden** is kept out of sight of the house; terraces are created with massive granite retaining walls, and the yew hedges give it a strongly architectural character.

SB

Compton Castle

3m west of Torquay, 1m north of Marldon off A3022: National Trust/ Mr and Mrs G.E. Gilbert, tel. 0803 872112. Open Apr–Oct Mon, Wed, Thur 10–12.15, 2–5.

Despite being called a castle, Compton is in fact a fortified late-medieval manor house hidden away in a wooded valley not far from Torbay. The nucleus of the building is a hall built c 1340 by Geoffrey Gilbert, MP for Totnes, after his marriage to the heiress of the estate; it was flanked by a wing containing a great chamber (solar) on one side and a service wing on the other. Fortification began in the mid 15C, when Otho Gilbert—whose tomb can be seen in the church at Marldon—added a tower onto the chamber wing, which he also rebuilt and extended by the addition of a domestic chapel. This was a foretaste of a more thorough fortification programme undertaken by his son John c 1520, possibly inspired by the fear of French raids, but also no doubt by the family's wish to impress their neighbours with a show of quasi-feudal splendour. The work involved rebuilding the service end and detached kitchen, with towers added to each, and building a high curtain wall around the whole enclosure, with more towers and a gatehouse in front of the hall, a walled forecourt, and a dry moat around the remaining three sides. The house thus acquired a spectacular external appearance which has remained unchanged in its essentials ever since.

Sir Humphrey Gilbert, the half-brother of Sir Walter Raleigh, played an important part in the maritime ventures of the late 16C and early 17C (he was drowned at sea after annexing Newfoundland for the English Crown in 1583), but his descendants subsequently settled down as country squires and abandoned Compton in the 18C for a house more in keeping with contemporary ideas of comfort and fashion. By 1750 the hall was in ruins, with parts of the rest of the building in use as a farmhouse, and in the late 18C the whole property was sold. But in 1930 it was purchased by Commander Walter Raleigh Gilbert, the direct descendant of the original builders, and he set about restoring the dilapidated, ivy-covered exterior: in 1954–55 he rebuilt the hall and reinstated the main rooms in the west wing as a dwelling, having given the house and the surrounding land to the National Trust in 1951. His son and daughter-in-law live here now.

Few English houses of Compton's size and date have a more impressive exterior, with the walls of the early Tudor fortifications on the north or entrance front completely masking the residential quarters behind. There are towers at each corner and an impressive gatehouse with a crenellated top punctuating the curtain wall at the centre, while to the right a four-light window with Perpendicular tracery protected by an iron grille indicates the presence of the Chapel; the towers contained rooms for members of the household, in the usual medieval fashion, and the corbelled projections at the upper levels were for privies. The gateway leads into a narrow enclosed courtyard in front of the Hall, reconstructed in the 1950s (architect: F.A. Key of the Ministry of Works) with a plain arch-braced roof, medieval-style hooded fireplace, two-light windows of 14C character, and wood panelling upon which portraits of the Gilbert family are hung. The other rooms shown to visitors are the 15C chamber or Solar, reached by a spiral staircase at the 'upper' end of the Hall, the adjacent Chapel, and the barrel-vaulted Kitchen dating from the 15C or 16C. The remainder of the highly picturesque exterior can be seen from the courtyard behind the Hall.

GCT

Flete

11m east of Plymouth on A379 Plymouth–Kingsbridge: Country Houses Association. Open May–Sept Wed, Thur 2–5. Guided tours.

Though relatively little known, even to enthusiasts for Victorian architecture, Flete is one of the most impressive of the country houses designed by Richard Norman Shaw, arguably the most gifted domestic architect in late-19C Britain. It is superbly situated above the wooded valley of the River Erme, not far from the sea, with the hills of Dartmoor closing the vista to the north, and it incorporates an older and smaller house built by the Hele family in the late 16C. In 1716 the estate passed to the Bulteel family, who made various additions and alterations to the house, but it was sold in 1863 to a retired Australian sheep-farmer, and again in 1876 to Henry Mildmay, a partner in Baring's Bank. He married a Bulteel and built up a large estate in the area, and in 1879–83 he employed Shaw, who had designed Barings' offices in the City of London, to transform the house into a substantial country seat suitable for grand house-parties. It was used as a maternity hospital during the Second World War, and was subsequently vacated by the Mildmay family in favour of a less grandiose 18C residence nearby, but in 1961 it was leased from the Mildmay estate by the Mutual Households Association (now the Country Houses Association) and converted into self-contained flats, the main rooms on the ground floor surviving intact for use in common by the residents.

The house is approached by a long drive, with a lodge designed in 1887 by the Arts and Crafts-inspired architect J.D. Sedding (who was also responsible for the excellent restoration of the estate church at Hoilbeton) at the entrance. The first view of a castellated tower and sundry neo-medieval projections rising above the surrounding woodland is reminiscent of Haddon Hall, Derbyshire (qv.), and this genuinely medieval house may well have inspired Shaw at Flete. The exterior, with its walls of Cornish granite and large mullioned and transomed windows, is free of the mock timber framing, tile hanging and other affectations commonly found in Shaw's houses, and what it lacks in coherence—partly a result of the need to incorporate the earlier, gabled house—it gains in picturesqueness. There are well-maintained gardens, some of them (eg, the water garden by Russell Page) created between the Wars, and the whole ensemble effectively complements the beautiful natural surroundings.

The interior is unexpectedly magnificent, its effect enhanced by the excellent Renaissance-style craftsmanship in wood and stone, some of it designed by Shaw's Devon-born assistant W.R. Lethaby, and by the presence of some portraits of the Mildmay family. The entrance leads through an enormous granite arch into a spacious, dimly lit Staircase Hall with armorial stained glass in the windows over the carved wood staircase with its half-landing from which the lady of the house could descend to greet her guests. On one side is the Morning Room (formerly the dining room) incorporating neo-Jacobean features of 1835 from the previous house, and on the other the Library with a particularly good chimneypiece incorporating an inglenook—a favourite Shavian motif—lit by stained glass windows designed by Burne-Jones. Ahead lies the former gallery or billiard room (now the Dining Room), a long and spacious room created by Shaw and Lethaby out of the hall of the 16C house. Next to this is the Drawing Room, with a bow window looking out onto the gardens and another good chimneypiece of alabaster.

GCT

Fursdon

9m north of Exeter off A3072 near Cadbury: E.D. Fursdon, tel. 0392 860860. Open Easter–Sept Thur, BH Mon 2–4.30. Refreshments.

The Fursdon estate is unusual in having passed through the same family in direct male succession from the mid 13C to the present day. The Fursdons have always been country squires rather than great landed magnates, and the house reflects their modest prosperity over many generations. It stands high up in attractive countryside, commanding extensive views to the south. From the outside the classical proportions, hipped roofs of local slate, and grey cement-rendered walls reflect remodellings in the 18C and early 19C by local builders and architects, using the materials the locality provided, but structurally the house probably dates back to the time of George Fursdon (d 1629). He built a house on an H-plan, with a central hall flanked by parlour and service wings; a surviving overmantel carries the date 1601. In 1723 another George Fursdon called in Richard Strong, a builder from Minehead (Somerset), to rebuild the main front, and in 1792 the hall was floored over. Finally in 1813–15 a library was added onto the west wing, and in 1818 a Doric colonnade was built in front of the central hall range, to the designs of the county surveyor James Green. Since then there have been very few changes to the exterior.

The interior is arranged as a comfortable family home, with pictures and objects accumulated over the centuries. There is some re-used Jacobean panelling in the Dining Room, on the site of the parlour of the early-17C house, but the predominant impression is of the early 19C, especially in the Library (also used originally as a ballroom), which retains much of its original Regency furniture. A selection of memorabilia relating to the house and family is displayed in the Billiard Room (on the site of the former dairy), and, in the former game larder and brewhouse behind the main house, there is a display of costume, including some particularly good 18C items.

GCT

Hartland Abbey

15m west of Bideford near Stoke on B3248, 5m west of A39: Sir Hugh Stucley, tel. 0237 441264. Open May–Sept Wed, Sun in July, Aug, early Sept, all BH Sun/Mon 2–5.30. Refreshments.

Hartland Abbey lies in one of the most remote and beautiful parts of southern England, close to the high cliffs of the Atlantic coast at Hartland Point. An Augustinian priory was founded in a wild though sheltered valley in 1169, near the site of an earlier religious house, and not far away from the parish church at Stoke, magnificently rebuilt in the late 14C and 15C. At the Dissolution the monastic buildings (which then housed only four canons) were granted to William Abbot, sergeant of Henry VIII's wine cellar, and he turned the west range, comprising the prior's lodgings, and some of the other residential quarters into a house, retaining part of the cloisters. The estate subsequently passed through the female line, first in 1600 to the Luttrells of Dunster Castle, Somerset (qv.), then in 1704 to the Orchard family of Kilkhampton (Cornwall), and finally in the early 19C to the Stucleys, with whom it has remained. Paul Orchard carried out some alterations soon after marrying the Luttrell heiress in 1705, but more drastic changes were made in 1779 by his son, another Paul Orchard. He employed the London architect John Meadows to rebuild the main west range, providing a fashionably Gothic exterior and suite of new reception rooms inside, but entailing the demolition of much of the medieval and 16C houses, including the hall and chapel. Several of the rooms were given a neo-Tudor remodelling by Sir George Stucley, great-grandson of the last of the Orchards, in about 1845, and in 1862 George Gilbert Scott was called in to remodel the north end of the house in the High Victorian Gothic style of which he was a master. Since then there have been no major changes.

The house stands among lawns which replaced the earlier formal gardens in the late 18C. Externally the predominant impression is of the Gothic remodelling of 1779, with a dour façade covered in grey rendering looking west towards the sea and the east front (originally the entrance) enlivened with pointed windows. In 1862 the entrance was moved to the north, and it is from here that the tour begins. Gilbert Scott's Inner Hall contains panelling taken from the hall of the 16C house when it was demolished, and leads to the three main reception rooms created in 1779 but remodelled in the mid 19C. The Drawing Room has a heavy neo-Jacobean chimneypiece and doorcases, linenfold panelling influenced by Pugin's work in the House of Lords, and a painted frieze of 1852 by an unknown Exeter artist depicting events in the history of the Stucley family. Next comes the Billiard Room, originally the entrance hall, and now containing a portrait of Catherine, Lady Bampfylde by Hudson (1776). There is some more late-16C panelling in the adjacent Dining Room, but once again the predominant impression is of neo-Jacobean woodwork; the early portraits are of members of the Grenville family, whose demolished house at Stow was just over the Cornish border, and there are 18C portraits by Reynolds and others. The wood-panelled Little Dining Room, in the part of the house built by Paul Orchard in 1705, has a portrait by Kneller of the antiquarian William Stukeley (1726), and from here the route leads through the Upper Corridor to the Alhambra Corridor, part of the 18C house but splendidly redecorated with a painted vault by Gilbert Scott in 1862, apparently commemorating a visit to Granada by Sir George Stucley. Pictures showing the house before the 1779 rebuilding are on display here, and in another room is a selection of documents dating back to the 12C.

GCT

Killerton House

7m north east of Exeter to west of B3181 Exeter–Cullompton: National Trust, tel. 0392 881345. Open Apr–Oct daily except Tues 11–5.30 (garden open all years in daylight hours). Refreshments.

Killerton is a modest late-18C house built and subsequently extended by one of the oldest Devon landed families, the Aclands. It occupies an attractive site beneath the slopes of Dolbury Hill, a prominent local landmark. The Aclands originated in north Devon, but a younger son acquired the Killerton estate, along with its Elizabethan manor house, in the late 16C, and in the 1775 Sir Thomas Dyke Acland, 7th Baronet, commissioned James Wyatt to draw up plans for an impressive new house to be built on the top of the adjacent hill. They were shelved after the untimely death of Acland's son, and in their place he commissioned a less well-known architect, John Johnson, to build a much smaller house as a temporary residence in 1778–79, meanwhile employing the Scotsman John Veitch to lay out the grounds in the natural style made fashionable by 'Capability' Brown. The 'temporary' house soon became permanent, and in about 1830 an east extension (architect unknown) was made by the 10th Baronet, a leading local politician. Soon afterwards, in 1838–41, C.R. Cockerell was brought in to design a new chapel in the woods behind the house. Some relatively minor alterations were made by the 12th and 13th Baronets in the early 20C, and the gardens close to the house were laid out with the advice of William Robinson, the apostle of the herbaceous border. In 1943 the socially conscious 15th Baronet, leader of the since-defunct Commonwealth party in Parliament, gave all his Somerset and Devon estates, amounting to 17,000 acres, to the National Trust. For 30 years Killerton was used for institutional purposes, but it was finally opened to the public in 1977, and is now once more furnished as a comfortable and unusually welcoming family home.

The influence of the Killerton estate is clearly seen in the neat colour-washed thatched cottages of the nearby villages, and the approach to the house is through an impressive stone-built stable block built to the designs of John Johnson in 1778–80. The horses were housed in more stately surroundings than the family, and although the house is larger than it first seems—mainly because of the generously-planned service quarters at the back (which visitors do not see)—it is nevertheless a remarkably modest building. The Aclands were not great connoisseurs of the arts, and they were confident enough of their place in local society not to need to flaunt their wealth. The main part of the house, with its severely plain elevations and flat roof, could almost be a London merchant's villa, were it not for the spacious setting. The entrance, to the east of the main block, was created by Randall Wells in 1924, and leads into a spacious Music Room, the most attractive room in the house, dating in its present form from c 1830, with neo-Georgian ceilings of c 1900. There is a grand piano and a chamber organ (which organists are encouraged to play), and on the walls are family portraits, including an excellent one by Lawrence of Lady Acland and her sons (1814). The other impressive rooms are the Library and the Dining Room on the west side of the house, both of which retain their late-18C appearance; the Library contains a race cup of 1774 and a pair of terracotta roundels by Thorwaldsen, bought by the 10th Baronet in Rome. Upstairs, the former bedrooms are now given over to a well-organised display of costumes, and in the gardens there are woodland walks leading to, *inter alia*, a thatched early-19C summerhouse, a monument to the 10th Baronet, and Cockerell's impressive neo-Romanesque chapel.

GCT

Knightshayes Court

2m north of Tiverton off A396 Tiverton–Bampton: National Trust, tel. 0884 254665. Open Apr–Oct daily except Fri 1.30–5.30 (garden open daily 10.30–5.30). Refreshments.

Knightshayes is the only English country house designed entirely by that most inventive and exuberant of Gothic revivalists, William Burges (his better-known houses for the 3rd Marquess of Bute are in Wales). The patron was Sir John Heathcote-Amory, owner of a flourishing lace-making business removed from Nottingham to Tiverton by his grandfather, and the house was built on a prominent site overlooking the town in 1869–74. Burges also drew up schemes of overwhelming richness for the decoration of the interior, but they were set aside and a more restrained scheme by J.D. Crace (cf. Longleat, Wilts) was adopted instead, work finishing in 1883. This in turn fell victim to subsequent changes in taste, and when Knights-hayes was bequeathed to the National Trust after the death of Sir John Heathcote-Amory, a notable art collector, in 1972, the interior had lost much of its original character. Since then the Trust has gradually restored the main rooms wherever possible to their late-19C appearance, using objects brought from elsewhere where necessary, so that today the house conveys an impression of a large late-Victorian establishment in its prime, solid and impressive, yet at the same time agreeably welcoming.

Much of the appeal of Knightshayes derives from its setting, high on a wooded hillside. The house stands among beautiful **gardens** first created in the 1870s by Edward Kemp, a pupil of Joseph Paxton, but transformed, softened and replanted by the present Lady Heathcote-Amory, starting in the 1950s. The approach leads past the **stable block**, in which Burges struck the note of playful, dream-like medieval fantasy which he could evoke better than any other Victorian architect; note especially the archway and conical turret on the side facing the house, redolent of Grimm's fairy tales. The house itself is less whimsical, and the **north (entrance) side** can be interpreted as a 'muscular' reworking of the standard late-medieval country house type, with a central hall lit by large windows and flanked by higher blocks on either side; the massive effect derives from the use of large blocks of the local red sandstone for the walls, the simple forms of the chimneys and gables, and the employment of French early-Gothic plate tracery—a Burges speciality—for the windows. The **garden front**, by contrast, is a High Victorian Gothic reworking of the typical 16C English country house façade, almost symmetrical, with large windows to light the south-facing reception rooms. From here there is a view down to Tiverton, with the Heathcote-Amory factory rising above the roofs of the market town.

The projecting porch on the north side of the house leads into the **Hall**, an impressive piece of romantic medievalism designed 'to be used for the reception of the owner's tenantry'. There is an arch-braced wooden roof of a kind commonly found in English late-medieval houses, and, at the far end, is a screen of Gothic arches on marble columns hiding the main staircase and supporting a balcony from which the 'tenantry'—ie, the lace-factory workers on their summer outings to the house—could, when necessary, be addressed. Opposite, on the wall over the entrance, is a portrait of Sir John Heathcote-Amory, the builder of the house. Examples of Burges's inventive imagination can be seen in the corbels supporting the roof beams, carved by his regular collaborator Thomas Nicholls (note also the animals and grinning clerics under the stairs), and at the foot of the **staircase** there is a huge painted bookcase which he designed for his London house c 1860, with panels painted by Burne-Jones and others. One of the comfortably furnished upstairs rooms, the Boudoir, has a restored ceiling by Crace, and in the **Billiard Room**, part of a 'male domain' to the east of the Hall, there are corbels of the Seven Deadly Sins (the Virtues which were to complement them were never executed); the sideboard, by Burges, was made for the hall of Worcester College, Oxford.

Although the architecture of Knightshayes is inspired by that of the Middle Ages, the planning is not, and the main reception rooms are placed in a row on the south front behind the Hall, as in many 18C houses (even the doors are in line with each other). First comes the wood-panelled **Dining Room**, suitably dark and beefy, with a ceiling by Crace and a frieze made up of quotations from Robert Burns to add the requisite note of sentimentality; there are pots by William de Morgan over the fireplace and pictures by his wife Evelyn on the walls. The octagonal **Morning Room** is notable mainly for the excellent 16C and early-17C Italian maiolica pottery acquired by the last Sir John Heathcote-Amory in 1946 (note especially the dish of c 1545 showing a battle of the Romans and Samnites, probably made in Urbino). Some of the larger pictures from Sir John's collection are displayed in the adjacent **Library**, in particular a group of the Madonna and saints by the 15C Italian master Matteo di Giovanni and Claude's 'Apollo and the Cumaean Sibyl'; the original bookcases were removed in the 20C to accommodate the pictures, but the brightly-coloured ceiling designed by Burges has recently been restored. Recent restoration has also uncovered some of the original features of the **Drawing Room**, including the ceiling, and the ensemble has been enhanced by the introduction of the marble chimneypiece from Worcester College and an assortment of 19C furniture, including items designed by Salvin, Burges and the Gillow firm. Pride of place must go to the pictures, including works by Holbein ('Lady in a White Cap'), Cranach, Rembrandt, Constable, Turner (a version of his 'Sun of Venice going to Sea') and Bonington ('Landscape in Picardy'). From here a door leads into that most Victorian of adjuncts to a country house, the Conservatory, and then to the gardens.

GCT

Powderham Castle

8m south of Exeter off A379 Exeter–Dawlish at Kenton: Lord and Lady Courtenay, tel. 0626 890243. Open Easter–Oct daily except Sat 9.30–6. Guided tours. Refreshments.

The Courtenay family have been lords of the manor of Powderham since the early 14C, and the core of the present house was built on a commanding site overlooking the estuary of the River Exe by Sir Philip Courtenay, younger son of the 2nd Earl of Devon, c 1390–1420. It was a fortified house rather than a true castle, with a central hall block flanked by towers and a courtyard entered through a gatehouse on the east side facing the river. Much of the masonry of the late-medieval house still remains, but the house was transformed, especially internally, in a series of 18C and 19C remodellings. The senior branch of the Courtenays died out in 1556, and the earldom of Devon went into abeyance, but the Courtenays of Powderham did not inherit their estates, and little seems to have been done to the house until c 1710–27, when a local builder, John Moyle of Exeter, carried out some work. Next, Sir William Courtenay transformed the interior in 1754–55 by creating a spectacular new staircase within the walls of the medieval hall, employing another Exeter man, James Garrett, to supervise the work. Sir William was made Viscount Courtenay in 1762, and his son, the 2nd Viscount, remodelled the east side of the house, facing the river, in a mildly Gothick style and redecorated several of the rooms in the Rococo style in 1766–70; at about the same time the remains of the old entrance courtyard on this side of the house were demolished.

The 3rd Viscount, a close friend of the connoisseur and debauchee William Beckford, also made his mark on the building by employing James Wyatt to add a magnificent music room onto the east front in 1794–96. His scandalous life-style forced him to flee the country in 1810, but he managed in 1831 to reclaim the dormant title of Earl of Devon. He was succeeded by a respectable cousin who, as 10th Earl, employed yet another Exeter architect, Charles Fowler, to add a new entrance forecourt on the west side of the house in 1837–48, and to build a new dining room facing it in 1847–60. This was completed by the 11th Earl, who also turned a detached outbuilding on the east front into a chapel; since his time there have been few important changes. Powderham is now the home of the son of the current Earl of Devon, who still lives on the estate.

The house stands on high ground overlooking meadows reclaimed from the River Exe (in the 16C it was, in the words of Leland, 'on the haven shore'), with wooded parkland to the north. The initial view, from the west, is dominated by Charles Fowler's rather heavy-handed castellated Gothic, but closer inspection reveals the granite and sandstone walls of the late-medieval house rising above the later accretions. The east or **garden front** is different in character, with the rendered walls and toy-like castellations of the 18C Gothic additions almost completely hiding the walls of the medieval hall block. To the left is the **chapel**, largely of 1861, but with a late-medieval arch-braced roof and some old bench-ends. The 19C formal gardens replaced late-18C lawns, which were in turn a replacement of the medieval entrance forecourt. The gardens command superb views of the river estuary, and are now the summer residence of an ancient tortoise.

The note of long family possession which pervades Powderham is immediately struck in the **Dining Hall**—paradoxically, despite its baronial appearance, the newest part of the building. It was clearly intended by the 10th Earl of Devon to celebrate the family's recovery of the title and to evoke the vanished grandeur of the genuinely medieval hall against whose outer wall it was built, and the lavish linenfold panelling, open timber roof and ubiquitous heraldry convey a sense of family pride and 'ancient hospitality'. Among the many family portraits is a large canvas of the 1st Viscount Courtenay and his family by Hudson—more ambitious than most of this artist's pictures (1756). The adjacent **Ante Room** is in the medieval part of the house, but it was completely remodelled in the 1760s (note the chimneypiece and Rococo plaster ceiling) and is now dominated by a superb pair of rosewood bookcases with broken pediments made in 1740 by the Exeter-born John Channon. The **First Library**, which follows, was created within the walls of the medieval chapel and redecorated in the 1760s (the bookcases are early 19C). From here there is a view through to the adjoining Second Library, added by John Moyle as a new chapel in the early 18C, but before seeing it visitors are taken into James Wyatt's domed **Music Room**, one of the finest and best-preserved rooms of the 1790s in any English country house. The 3rd Viscount Courtenay, whose portrait in masquerade dress by the Devon-born Francis Cosway (1792) hangs over the fireplace, was an enthusiastic musician, and musical motifs can be seen on the frieze and on the marble fireplace (by the elder Richard Westmacott)—the organ of 1769 was brought from the former chapel (now the Second Library). The frieze rests on yellow scagliola pilasters, and the turquoise-coloured wall surfaces are broken up by niches housing alabaster urns; the set of gilded furniture was skilfully copied in 1991–92 from the originals by Edward Marsh and C.H. Tatham, best know for their work for the Prince Regent. There is an Axminster carpet contemporary with the room. The **Second Library** contains more furniture attributed to Marsh and Tatham, along with portraits by Hudson and Cosway.

The top-lit **Staircase Hall**, reached through a small ante-room now used to display china, is one of the most striking Rococo interiors in England; not only because of its exuberant plasterwork (by the otherwise unknown John Jenkins) on the unexpectedly vivid (but authentic) blue wall surfaces and even the undersides of the stairs, but also because of its vertiginous proportions, dictated by the need to squeeze the carved wooden stairs into the high walls of the narrow medieval hall. Until the end of the 18C some of the most important rooms at Powderham were upstairs, including one with a late-medieval fireplace, and another (the **Gold Drawing Room**) which was originally the library and still retains its splendid fireplace and overmantel of c 1740, probably by the J. Channon who made the bookcases now in the ante-room downstairs.

Back on the ground floor, the **Marble Hall** occupies what was the 'lower' end of the medieval hall, but unlike the adjacent staircase hall it retains some pre-18C features, notably the three medieval doors which once led to the buttery, pantry and kitchen, and a chimneypiece dated 1553. The Jacobean-style panelling was introduced in the 19C as a counterpart to the early family portraits, which include one of Edward Courtenay, 9th Earl of Devon, who died in the Tower of London in 1556, and two attributed to Cornelius Johnson. There is also a 17C Brussels tapestry after Teniers and a splendidly ornate clock made in Totnes in 1743–47. The last room to be seen is the more intimate **Pink Drawing Room**, with more of the attractive Rococo plasterwork which is so notable a feature of Powderham; this forms part of the additions made to the garden front (originally the main entrance to the house) in the 1760s.

GCT

Saltram

3½m east of Plymouth between A38 Plymouth–Exeter and A37 Plymouth–Kingsbridge: National Trust, tel. 0752 336546. Open Apr–Oct Sun–Thur 12.30–5.30 (garden and kitchen open 10.30). Refreshments.

The plain white elevations of Saltram mask a 16C courtyard building which was transformed into one of the finest 18C houses in the west of England. The responsibility for the transformation rests with two generations of the Parker family. The original house was built by the Bagg family, but their last representative at Saltram was banished to the West Indies during the Interregnum and in 1660 the estate was acquired by Sir George Carteret, who probably remodelled the centre of the west range in its present form. In 1712 the property was purchased by George Parker, former MP for Plymouth and owner of the neighbouring estate of Boringdon, and, when he died in 1743, his son John decided to fix his main residence at Saltram, employing an unknown architect to rebuild the south and east ranges c 1746–49; the guiding spirit behind the alterations seems to have been John Parker's wife Lady Catherine. His son, another John, succeeded him in 1768, having made a Grand Tour and became Lord Boringdon in 1784; he was largely responsible for amassing the collection of Old Master and 18C English pictures which can still be seen in the house today. In 1768–72 he employed Robert Adam to create magnificent new rooms in the east range, which had probably remained undecorated (more grandiose plans for the west range were also aired but rejected). Some minor alterations were carried out by the Plymouth architect John Foulston for Lord Boringdon's son, the 1st Earl of Morley, in 1818–20, but since then the house has remained remarkably unchanged, its contents largely intact and interiors little altered. When the 4th Earl died in 1951 the house, contents and park were conveyed to the Treasury in lieu of death duties, and six years later they were transferred to the National Trust.

The house stands among lawns and parkland on the edge of Plymouth, its seclusion broken only by distant views of the city's factories and housing estates and the dull roar of traffic on the A38 road. It is approached through extensive 18C and early-19C stable buildings, and the bland stuccoed exterior gives no foretaste of the magnificence within. The south or entrance front has canted bay windows at the ends—a favourite motif of the mid 18C—while at the centre is a stone carriage porch (added by Foulston) with stumpy Greek Doric columns; Foulston was also responsible for the incised Grecian ornamentation surrounding the windows above. A second front faces west and comprises a late-17C hipped-roofed block in the centre joined to pedimented pavilions at the ends by low wings with Palladian windows of both the 'Diocletian' and Venetian variety, part of John Parker's alterations of the 1740s; above the roofs can be seen some chimneys and turrets from the original house.

Internally, the interest of Saltram derives from the superb Rococo and neo-classical decoration, and the excellent quality of the pictures and furnishings. Though undoubtedly grand, the house is less pompous than many others of its date, partly because of the Parkers' decision to dispense with a piano nobile, partly because of the National Trust's admirable policy of presenting the house so that 'the caller should feel like a private visitor who has arrived while the family is out'. The **Entrance Hall** is the first of a series of reception rooms on the south front dating from the mid 18C and adorned with exuberant Rococo plasterwork by craftsmen whose identity has remained tantalisingly undiscovered; the chimneypiece is by Thomas Carter, and there are portraits by Thomas Hudson, including one of Lady Catherine Parker in masquerade dress. The **Morning Room**, to the right, is closely hung with pictures in the 18C fashion, including five by Sir Joshua Reynolds, who was born in the neighbouring parish of Plympton and advised the 1st Lord Boringdon on the purchase of the Old Masters in his art collection; they include portraits of Boringdon casually resting against a field gate, gun in hand, one of his son and daughter (over the fireplace), and one of the engraver Francesco Bartolozzi. The Old Masters are, taken together, a representative example of conventional 18C artistic taste; several are studio copies, but there is a genuine Guido Reni ('St Faith'). More pictures are hung in the **Velvet Drawing Room**; they include a tavern scene by Pieter de Hooch and 'cabinet pictures' by assorted Netherlandish and Italian masters. The eye is caught more, however, by the sumptuous red wall hangings (not the original ones), the furniture, including a set of gilded chairs bought for the room in the 1770s, the plasterwork, and the screen of Corinthian columns which frames the entrance to the Saloon beyond, flanked by mirrors and pier-glasses designed by Adam.

On entering the **Saloon** the grandeur of Robert Adam's imagination is immediately revealed. It was designed in 1768–72 as a spacious 'great room' for entertaining guests, and the proportions and details, some of them taken from the Emperor Diocletian's palace at Split (which the Adam brothers had studied in situ and subsequently published) proclaim its semi-public character. The fittings, even down to the door-handles, were designed by Adam, and the ensemble is enhanced by the splendid Axminster carpet, the furniture—including chairs and sofas probably by Chippendale—the chimneypiece (by the younger Thomas Carter) and the candelabra at the corners of the room by Matthew Boulton; the pictures include works by Gheeraerts and Reynolds and copies of well-known Old Masters (Raphael, Correggio, Titian, etc). The **Dining Room** is in a different vein, lower, more intimate and more delicate; it was built by Adam as a library but was converted by him to its present use in 1780–81 after the kitchen had been re-located on the north side of the house following a fire. There is more excellent neo-classical craftsmanship here, with paintings by Zucchi on the ceilings and over the doors, plasterwork by Joseph Rose and vases and pedestals (no doubt once housing the obligatory chamber-pots) designed by Adam; the classical landscape over the fireplace is by Zuccarelli, and there are Wedgwood vases on the mantelpiece.

From here a corridor lined with drawings, including some by Adam, leads to the main **Staircase Hall,** behind the south range. Here we are back in the mid-18C part of the house, and the wooden staircase is of the conventional early-18C type with twisted balusters; putti disport themselves on Rococo curlicues on the plaster ceiling. At the foot of the stairs are a Boulle writing desk said to have been given to Sarah, Duchess of Marlborough, by Louis XIV and a bust of the 1st Earl of Morley by Nollekens (1806), and several of the finest pictures in the collection hang on the walls, including a colourful 'Madonna and Child' by the 16C Bolognese artist Orazio Samacchini, a portrait of Sir Joshua Reynolds by Angelica Kauffmann, a view of Caserta with Vesuvius in the background by Jacob Philipp Hackert, and, on the top landing, a Rubens portrait once in the collection of Charles I. The **Chinese Dressing Room** and Bedroom, at the top of the stairs, are hung with early-18C Chinese wallpaper, and in the bedroom there is an excellent collection of mid-18C 'Chinese Chippendale' furniture (the bed may be by Chippendale himself), along with painted mirrors with Rococo frames and, on the mantelpiece, items of *blanc de Chine* porcelain. The remaining upstairs rooms were altered in the 19C, as was the **Library,** which occupies the ground floor to the west of the entrance hall. In its present form it dates from 1818, when John Foulston ran two rooms together to create a comfortable living room of the sort popular in the Regency period, with a screen of Ionic columns in scagliola in place of the dividing wall. The family portraits include works by Reynolds, Angelica Kauffman, and Gilbert Stuart.

Next, in the west range, comes the **Mirror Room**, so named from its 18C Chinese mirror paintings, one of them dated 1756, but notable mainly for an excellent collection of mid-18C porcelain displayed in a case, including pieces from Meissen (note the cat with a mouse in its mouth) and Chelsea. The **Garden Room**, in the late-17C part of the house, contains two equestrian pictures by Sartorius and some 18C and early-19C views of the estate, and from here it is possible to go either into the courtyard, where the remnants of the 16C house can be seen, or into the gardens and from there to the impressive, airy **Kitchen** of 1788 on the north side of the house.

GCT

Shute Barton

3m west of Axminster to south of A35 Honiton–Dorchester: National Trust, tel. 0297 34692. Open Apr–Oct Wed, Sat 2–5.30. Guided tours.

A barton in Devon means a large farmhouse, and for a third of its life this formidable building served that purpose. It was built c 1380 as the residence of Sir William Bonville, whose family became one of the most important in Devon, and in the 1530s it was described by the traveller John Leland as 'a right goodly manor house' surrounded by a park. By this time it had passed by marriage into the hands of the Grey family, Marquesses of Dorset, and it was enlarged by them, probably at the end of the 15C. They lost possession in 1554 when Henry Grey, by then Duke of Suffolk, was executed by Mary Tudor, and in 1560 William Pole of Colyton took a long lease of the estate from the Crown. His son, Sir William Pole, an enthusiastic antiquary and local historian, extended the house and built the attractive detached gatehouse in the late 16C, but Shute did not become the main seat of the Poles until after the destruction of the nearby Colcombe Castle in the Civil War. The house was then repaired by Sir Courtney Pole, who inherited in 1658, but it was much reduced in size in 1787, when Sir John Pole built a new house (not open to the public) on higher ground a quarter of a mile away. Here, according to his monument in the parish church, 'with manners fresh and courteous and sincere he received his Friends with liberal Hospitality and relieved the Indigent with unbounded Charity'.

For the next 175 years the largely medieval remnant of the older building was occupied by farmers. In 1956, Sir John Carew Pole of Antony, Cornwall (qv.), who had inherited the estate when the senior branch of the family died out, thoroughly repaired the house and gave it three years later to the National Trust. It is now occupied by a member of the Pole family, in accordance with the wishes of the donor, which gives precedence for the tenancy to direct descendants of the family; the gatehouse has been leased separately to the Landmark Trust, which lets it out as a holiday home.

The house stands in rolling, pastoral country only a few miles from the sea, and is approached from the north through the pretty late-16C gatehouse of the local Beer stone, still medieval in spirit, and linked by crenellated walls to detached pavilions on either side. The village is spread out in front of the gatehouse, and the largely 14C church, with some good monuments to the Poles, stands on the hillside to the left. The house as we now see it is an L-shaped building, mostly of flint, approached through an open courtyard. In front is the late-14C hall block, mentioned in the will of Sir William Bonville (d 1408), while to the right is a low 15C gateway. The long wing to the left was partly built in the 15C, and was extended by the Poles in the early 17C; before the 1780s it formed one side of a second courtyard aligned on the Elizabethan gatehouse.

The hall block seems originally to have consisted of a single room open to the roof, with a solar, approached by a spiral staircase, at one end, but in the mid 15C the solar was extended across the full length of the Hall, and another floor was inserted by Lady Cecily Bonville, first Marchioness of Dorset, c 1485. The mammoth fireplace seen to the right on entering was inserted when the Hall was divided in the mid 15C; it extends the full width of the house and is reputedly the largest in the United Kingdom. The two other rooms of most interest to visitors are the room at the top of the hall block, with its fine original arch-braced roof, and the Drawing Room, panelled at the time of the Restoration, and the only one of the main reception rooms of the Poles' house to have survived the late-18C alterations (note the picture showing the house in its pre-1787 form). To see the portraits of the Poles it is now necessary to go to Antony; at Shute the overwhelming mood is one of vanished splendour.

GCT

Torre Abbey

On the sea front at Torquay, 1/4m from Torquay station: Torbay Borough
Council, tel. 0803 293593. Open Apr–Oct daily 10–5, gardens all year.

Though now engulfed by the sprawl of the Torbay holiday resorts, Torre
Abbey is a country house formed in the 17C and 18C out of the remains of
a Premonstratensian abbey founded in 1196. The site chosen was then a
remote one, near the sea and far from any town or village. The round-
arched 12C entrance to the chapter house still survives, but the church and
most of the other monastic buildings have either been swept away or
remodelled. Following recent archaeological excavations, the foundations
and surviving walls of the abbey church have been uncovered, but the most
impressive monastic survivals are a tithe barn, the rendered tower of the
Abbots' lodgings, and a 14C gatehouse of rubble stone with bright red
sandstone dressings, paid for by the Mohun family of Dunster Castle,
Somerset (qv.); this now forms the main entrance to the house from the west.

There were several owners after the Dissolution of the Monasteries, and
the remaining monastic buildings, by now much reduced in scale, do not
seem to have been turned into a house until after 1598, when Thomas
Ridgeway of Torwood, owner of the surrounding land, 're-edified the almost
decayed cells'. He did not use the house as his main residence, and it was
not until after it was purchased by Sir George Cary in 1662 that it began to
take on its present appearance. He came from a local Catholic family which
had lost much of its land as a penalty for backing the wrong side in the Civil
War, and the acquisition of Torre gave him the opportunity to create a new
family seat in what had been a bastion of the old Faith. A new residential
range was built within the walls of the former refectory on the south side
of the cloister, and this was heightened and extended by his descendant
George Cary in 1741. The growth of Torquay as a seaside resort in the 19C
removed the rural seclusion of the site, and in 1842 the landscaped park
was cut off from the sea by the building of the present road. The Carys
entered into the development of the town by building villas on their
farmland in the later 19C, but they continued to live at the Abbey until after
the First World War, when first the grounds and then the house were
purchased by the local authority. Many of the rooms fell into disrepair, but
much of the interior has recently been restored to its 18C and 19C appearance and is now used to display items from the Borough's collections.

The rather gaunt south-facing exterior is made up of the late-17C house
of the Carys flanked on either side by mid-18C extensions with castellated
rooflines like those of Ugbrooke (qv.), not very far away; the west extension
incorporates the remnants of the monastic kitchens. Behind this is the west
range of the monastic buildings, containing the former guest-hall, used as
a laundry for many years but converted into a chapel after the Catholic
Relief Act of 1778. Inside the main house there are some medieval under-
crofts, but most of what can be seen is of the 18C, including the Staircase,
a spacious Dining Room with a plaster frieze, coved ceiling and marble
chimneypiece, and the Chapel with its 15C wooden roof, Gothic windows
and monuments to the Cary family; some of the rooms in the south-west
wing have also been restored to their 19C appearance. Elsewhere there are
paintings by 19C English artists, including Holman Hunt ('The Children's
Holiday'), sculptures by Frederick Thrupp, and collections of drinking

glasses and pottery. A room in the Abbot's Tower has been set aside as a memorial to Agatha Christie, who was born in Torquay.

GCT

Ugbrooke House

Near Chudleigh to west of A380 Exeter–Torquay: Lord Clifford, tel. 0626 852179. Open Spring BH weekend and late July–late Aug Sun, Tues, Wed, Thur and BH weekend 2–3.45. Guided tours.

Ugbrooke is a largely 18C house standing in hilly country to the south east of Dartmoor, but the origins of the house and its owners go back a good deal earlier than the 18C. The estate belonged to Exeter Cathedral in the Middle Ages, but was secularised at the Reformation and later passed by marriage to Anthony Clifford, whose descendants have lived here ever since. The Cliffords of Ugbrooke were the junior branch of an old and illustrious family which ruled large tracts of land in the north of England; they became the senior male branch in the 17C, and in 1672 Thomas Clifford was created Lord Clifford or Chudleigh. He was a Roman Catholic sympathiser and exercised great influence as a member of Charles II's notorious CABAL ministry, but in 1673, the year after becoming Lord Treasurer, he resigned under the provisions of the Test Act, and died later in the same year.

As staunch Catholics the later Cliffords were cut off from high political office, and their architectural ambitions were modest compared with those of the leading Protestant gentry and nobility of Devon. The 1st Lord Clifford made provision in his will for the building of a new house to replace the existing 16C building, but it was not until the time of the 4th Lord that anything significant was done. He employed Robert Adam to rebuild that house in 1763–68, and he also brought in 'Capability' Brown to landscape the park, but most of Adam's schemes for the interior were set aside on the grounds of economy. Certain important alterations were made in the 19C, notably in the time of the 8th Lord, who was largely responsible for the highly Ultramontane interior of the chapel (c 1866). The house fell into disrepair after the Second World War, when several of the main reception rooms were used as a grain store, but it was rescued by the late (13th) Lord Clifford, and today the rooms are used to display a good collection of pictures, tapestries and furniture, including several items which have belonged to the family since the 17C.

Ugbrooke must be the plainest of all Adam houses, and it was certainly the first to employ the austere castellated style which he later developed to great dramatic effect in his native Scotland. The rendered, symmetrical elevations conceal considerable remains of the original 16C stone house, as can be seen from inside the open courtyard through which the building has been entered since the mid 19C. From the outside, the house appears like a greatly enlarged child's toy fort, with crenellated turrets at the four corners, and a wing containing the chapel to one side. Mid-19C alterations to the ground-floor windows did not improve the appearance of what was already a rather forbidding exterior, but the chapel wing with its bow front remained unchanged, and here the house appears in a more sympathetic light. The house was designed to be seen in the context of its park, but to appreciate this it is necessary to descend to the two lakes which Brown created as the central features of his new landscape.

The present Entrance Hall is a plain room hung with splendid tapestries including two given to the 1st Lord Clifford by Cosimo de' Medici in 1669. It leads into the domed Staircase Hall, where an ornate silver-gilt dish and ewer made in Augsburg and given by Charles II to his godson Charles Clifford is displayed in a case. The original entrance hall is now used as the Morning Room; it has lost its original colouring, but contains some good furniture, including a bookcase made by the Gillow firm to a design by Chippendale. The Drawing Room is mainly notable for its pictures, including some by Lely (James II as Duke of York, his first wife Anne Hyde, and Charles II's ill-fated illegitimate son, the Duke of Monmouth); there are also three well-preserved Elizabethan needlework panels. More pictures hang in the Dining Room, on the west front overlooking the park, including Lely's portrait of the 1st Lord Clifford as Lord High Treasurer of England in contemplative mood, book in hand, a genre picture by the Flemish master J. van Schooten (1621) and a large farmyard scene by Jan Siberechts (1661); a good collection of Chinese armorial export porcelain with the Clifford coat of arms (c 1745) is also displayed.

The first floor is reached by the main staircase, hung with family portraits including one of the formidable 17C Lady Anne Clifford (cf. Appleby Castle, Cumbria). A bedroom contains vestments and other memorabilia connected with Thomas Weld, who became a cardinal in 1830 after his wife had died and his daughter had married the 7th Lord Clifford (who later settled in Rome). Pictures on the walls include some by the Devon-born painter Francis Towne, who taught the 6th Lord, an amateur artist. The tapestries in the Tapestry Room include some 17C Mortlake pieces taken from the Raphael Cartoons and some of Eucharistic subjects from a set by Francis Poyntz; the bed, from a Chippendale design, has hangings of c 1720 made by the Duchess of Norfolk. From here a corridor lined with late-18C and early-19C English watercolours, including some by the 6th Lord Clifford, leads to the Conservatory, unusually placed over the archway into the entrance courtyard, and then to the chapel wing, which contains the Library, with delicate, though still very simple, Adam decoration. The Chapel itself, by contrast, though originally designed by Adam, was enlarged and completely remodelled with sumptuous enrichments in differently coloured marble by the 7th and 8th Lords Clifford in the 19C, and still conveys a strong feeling of the Catholicism which has been the Clifford family's main distinguishing characteristic over the past three centuries.

GCT

DORSET

Athelhampton

1m east of Puddletown on A35 Dorchester–Bournemouth: Patrick Cooke, tel. 0305 848492. Open Easter–Oct Wed, Thur, Sun and Tues May–Sept, Mon, Fri in Aug, BH Mon 12–5. Refreshments.

From the outside Athelhampton presents as pleasing an assemblage of worn stone walls, tiled roofs and picturesquely irregular surfaces as can be found in any house in the south of England. The late-15C hall range, which constitutes the core of the house, was built by Sir William Martyn (d 1504), Lord Mayor of London in 1493 and representative of a local family which had acquired the manor, on the banks of the River Piddle, in the 14C. It survives virtually intact, with its crenellated porch at the east or service end (to the right as first seen by visitors) and oriel window at the 'upper' or high-table end. The gabled and beautifully-detailed parlour wing which projects at an unusual angle from the 'upper' end was added in the second quarter of the 16C by Robert Martyn (d 1550), and the service range which stretches north from the opposite end of the hall was remodelled and heightened in the 17C. Until 1862 there was also a detached gatehouse closing a courtyard to the south bearing the coat of arms of Robert Martyn and, like the parlour wing, contained carved detailing in Ham Hill stone reminiscent of contemporary work at Sandford Orcas Manor (qv.) and elsewhere.

The family estates were divided among four daughters after the death of Nicholas Martyn in 1595, and in 1665 the house was sold to Sir Robert Long, under whose descendants it entered into a long period of decline, finally becoming a farmhouse before being sold in 1848 to George Wood. He restored the hall range (employing members of the family of Thomas Hardy, who immortalised the house in two of his poems), but demolished the gatehouse. Final deliverance came in 1891 when the house was sold to Alfred de Lafontaine, an enthusiastic antiquarian. More restoration of the interior was carried out under his direction, the rooms were filled with antique furniture and, where appropriate, new panelling and plasterwork were introduced. A new (private) wing was also added to the north of the hall range and, more importantly, Inigo Thomas, co-author (with Reginald Blomfield) of *The Formal Garden in England* was employed to create a new garden setting made up of a series of Renaissance-inspired 'outdoor rooms' in place of the existing 'cowsheds and dilapidated buildings'; these rank among the most beautiful gardens of their date in England, and in themselves justify a visit to Athelhampton. Since Lafontaine's time the house has been sold on two more occasions, most recently in 1957 to Robert Cooke, who introduced much of the furniture now on view and further improved the gardens, a process which has been continued by his son and by his daughter-in-law.

The finest room at Athelhampton, as in so many houses of its date, is the Hall, entered through a screens passage (the screen is not the original one), retaining its superb wooden roof with boldly cusped arch braces—an unusual feature—and its equally richly detailed oriel window, complete with some of the original stained glass. A large mid-16C Flemish tapestry of Samson killing the Philistines hangs over the fireplace at the upper end, and there is also a good selection of 19C metalwork, including a pair of

French bronze candelabra of c 1830 and a pair of fire-dogs attributed to A.W.N. Pugin, along with several earlier items of furniture. The remaining rooms have been altered on more than one occasion in the 20C and lack the carefully recreated patina of age aspired to by Lafontaine and so well preserved at the somewhat comparable Lytes Cary Manor (qv.), not far away in Somerset. The Great Chamber (originally the main parlour), on the ground floor of the 16C wing, contains some original stained glass, as well as a good collection of mainly early-18C furniture; the late-16C-style ceiling carries the date 1905 and the panelling was introduced soon after *Country Life* photographed the house in the following year. In many ways as impressive as the house are the well-maintained gardens which encompass it, especially the circular Corona and the Great Court with its terrace and pointed-roofed gazebos to the south east and the lawn with its circular early-16C dovecote to the west.

Note. At the time of writing the rooms in the east range were closed to the public because of fire damage.

GCT

Chettle House

6m north east of Blandford, to north of A354 Blandford–Salisbury: J.P.C. Bourke, tel. 025889 209. Open Easter–early Oct daily (not Tues or Sat) 11–5.

This unusual early-18C house is one of the most striking, though least-known, examples of that elusive phenomenon, the English Baroque. It was built c 1710–15 by George Chafin, whose ancestors had been lords of the manor of Chettle, in Cranborne Chase, since the late 16C, and the architect was almost certainly Thomas Archer, who lived 15 miles away over the Hampshire border. Archer had travelled in Italy, where he had imbibed the highly original style of Borromini and his followers. Borromini had made great play with curves in his buildings, and, uniquely among English country houses, Chettle is shaped not as a rectangle but as an ellipse, with curved corners and another curved projection in the middle of the west (originally the entrance) front. The red-brick walls are also enlivened with what are by English standards very eccentric details, including the peculiar capitals (of Chilmark stone) at the tops of the pilasters.

The house faces east over lawns in which the terraces of the early-18C garden can be easily traced. Visitors usually enter through the Stone Hall, on the west side of the house, with its original Doric pilasters and frieze; the classical plaster reliefs over the doorways are attributed to the sculptor Alfred Stevens, whose father, a Blandford man, was employed to redecorate the interior for a local banker, Edward Castleman, in 1846–50, the Chafin family having died out 30 years earlier. Beyond this is the spectacular early-18C Oak Hall, the most striking feature of which is the unusual double staircase of carved wood, with the top flight funnelled mysteriously into an arched opening in the west wall—an example of Baroque spatial manipulation (some might say waste of space), rarely paralleled in English country house architecture. The Drawing Room, the only other room shown to visitors, was remodelled in the mid 19C.

GCT

Forde Abbey

4m south east of Chard to south of B3162 Chard–Bridport: Trustees of
Forde Abbey, tel. 0460 20231. Open Apr–Oct Wed, Sun, BH Mon 1–4.30
(gardens daily all year 10–4.30). Refreshments.

This picturesque and beautifully textured house of lichen-covered brown
Ham Hill stone originated as a Cistercian abbey founded on the banks of
the River Axe in 1141 and dissolved in 1539. Several of the monastic
buildings have survived to the present day, including the long, low 13C
dormitory (the first part of the building seen by visitors as they approach
the house) the chapter house (now the Chapel), the refectory, and the Hall
and porch built as part of a grandiose expansion of the abbot's lodgings by
the last abbot, Thomas Chard, in the early 16C. The church, which stood
to the south of the cloister, was demolished after the Reformation, and the
remaining buildings went through several hands before coming in 1649 to
Sir Edmund Prideaux, a staunch Parliamentarian, Attorney-General under
Oliver Cromwell and promoter of a weekly postal service. He made major
alterations, which were largely finished by the time he died in 1659. Since
then there have been remarkably few changes to the building, as can be
seen from looking at Buck's engraving of 1734. The house remained in the
hands of Prideaux's descendants until 1846, when it was sold and most of
the contents dispersed. There was another sale in 1864, to Mrs Bertram
Evans, and her descendant, Mark Roper, lives here now.

The house faces south towards an attractive garden first created in the
early 18C—the original ponds, terraces and cascades can still be seen to
the south west—and were further improved by the Roper family in the 20C.
To the left (west) of the long sprawling complex of buildings is the early-16C
Hall, its two west bays remodelled as a private wing in the 1650s. Then,
moving east, comes the tall gatehouse built by Abbot Chard in 1528, next
to a remodelled late-medieval block, and beyond it the north walk of the
medieval cloister with the former chapter house on the extreme right; the
rest of the cloister was presumably demolished in the 16C, at the same time
as the church.

The house is entered through the gatehouse tower (note the delicate
late-Gothic carving around the oriel windows over the doorway), and, after
passing through the screen (of the 1650s), visitors emerge in the Great Hall,
larger even in its truncated form than those of many Oxford and Cambridge
colleges, its interior flooded with light from the Perpendicular windows on
the south side. The windows on the north side were blocked in the 1650s,
when Sir Edmund Prideaux and his team of unrecorded craftsmen created
the present Staircase leading to new reception rooms on the east side of
the house. It is a splendid wooden construction, not unlike that of Ham
House, Greater London (qv.), though lacking the delicacy of the best
metropolitan work. It has a hefty balustrade of stylised floral motifs (echoed
in trompe-l'oeil form on the painted walls) and vases of fruit carved on the
newel posts; there is rich plasterwork of a similar kind by local plasterers
on the ceiling, which carries the date 1658. The grandest of Prideaux's
rooms is that now known as the Saloon, facing south towards the gardens;
there is an even more elaborate plaster ceiling here, with naïve depictions
of scenes including the Sacrifice of Isaac, and the contemporary wood
panelling has also survived, with giant Composite pilasters and circular and
oval frames for paintings which break jarringly into the frieze. The five

Mortlake tapestries after the Raphael Cartoons (with unique borders attributed to Francis Cleyn c 1640–50) were ordered by Sir Edmund Prideaux for the room but were confiscated by the Crown at the Restoration and did not take their place here until the early 18C, when they were given by Queen Anne to her Secretary-at-War, Francis Gwyn, who married Prideaux's granddaughter.

A passage hung with 16C Flemish tapestries leads to a Library created in the 19C out of the upper part of the monastic refectory, which still retains its 15C arch-braced roof. A series of bedrooms over the north walk of the cloister retain their mid-17C plaster ceilings, but were otherwise remodelled in the 18C. There is a painting of peasant girls possibly by Le Nain, over the fireplace of the Oak Room, and the adjoining room is named after the philosopher Jeremy Bentham, who rented the house from 1815–18. From here the route passes through the monastic dormitory (divided up for servants' bedrooms in the 19C) and then down to the north walk of the cloister, another of Abbot Chard's building works, but left unfinished at the Reformation and now covered by a 19C plaster vault. The last room to be seen is the Chapel, with its 12C rib vault, early-16C east window and mid-17C woodwork, and, on emerging, visitors can refresh themselves in the tea room in the vaulted undercroft of the monks' dormitory.

GCT

Ilsington House

In Puddletown on A35 Dorchester–Bournemouth: Mr and Mrs P. Duff, tel. 0305 848454. Open May–Sept Wed, Thur, Sun, BH Mon 2–6.

Ilsington House stands on the edge of the village of Puddletown, not far from Athelhampton (qv.). There was a hunting lodge here belonging to the Hastings family, later Earls of Huntingdon, in the Middle Ages, but the present house was built c 1690 by the 7th Earl to the designs of an unknown architect. The north or entrance front makes a handsome composition, with a long central block and projecting wings, hipped roofs, tall brick chimneys, stone quoins and a projecting wooden cornice. The brick walls were covered in rendering in 1837, and at the same time the south front was remodelled with larger windows and Tuscan pilasters. By this time the house had passed by marriage to the Earls of Orford, descendants of the early-18C Prime Minister Sir Robert Walpole, but they spent little time here and, from 1780–1829, the house was leased to George III's principal equerry, Thomas Garth, who seems to have carried on an illicit relationship here with one of the King's daughters on their frequent visits to their ailing and often distracted father at Weymouth. The estate was sold to a local man, John Brymer, in 1862, and he subsequently added a new porch, billiard room and conservatory. The present owners bought and refurnished the house in 1979, and they have also carried out an extensive restoration of the gardens. The Hall retains its late-17C bolection panelling and its attractive wooden staircase with twisted balusters, which leads up to the main reception rooms, at first-floor level, including the Drawing Room, with late-18C plasterwork introduced by Thomas Garth, and a bedroom used by the princesses.

GCT

Kingston Lacy

1½m west of Wimborne on B3082 Wimborne–Blandford: National Trust, tel. 0202 883402. Open Apr–Oct Sat–Wed 12–5.30. Refreshments.

Kingston Lacy is one of only two surviving country houses designed by the amateur architect Sir Roger Pratt, perhaps the most talented country-house architect of the post-Restoration period. It was built in 1663–65 for Sir Ralph Bankes as a replacement for Corfe Castle on the Isle of Purbeck, bought by his father, Chief Justice to Charles I, in 1635 and left a ruin by Parliamentarian troops during the Civil War. Bankes and Pratt had both been to Italy during the Interregnum, and the new house, which was built of brick, represented a synthesis of Renaissance planning and proportions and the comforts thought appropriate for a prosperous English country gentleman. Changing ideas of comfort induced Bankes's descendant, Henry Bankes, an enthusiast for classical antiquities and trustee of the British Museum, to make extensive internal alterations in the 1780s, with Robert Furze Brettingham as architect. There were even more sweeping changes in the time of his son William Bankes, a compulsive traveller and collector who employed Charles Barry to encase the house in Chilmark limestone and to carry out extensive internal and external alterations in 1835–41. Bankes was subsequently involved in a homosexual scandal and retired to Italy, where he employed a team of highly talented craftsmen to design new interior decoration as a framework for his superb collection of pictures. Today his taste pervades the house, which remained in the family until it was bequeathed to the National Trust, along with the ruins of Corfe Castle, in 1981.

Since its 19C remodelling, the influence of Italy has been omnipresent at Kingston Lacy, both inside and outside the house. The approach, from the north, is through parkland, but the most impressive front faces south across terraces and a lawn to an obelisk of c 1313–1296 BC, brought from Egypt by William Bankes and erected here in 1839. Barry retained the basic structure and proportions of the 17C house, but he successfully enriched the exterior by introducing tall chimneystacks at the corners, placing dormer windows in the hipped roof, inserting an arched loggia lighting the main staircase on the east front, and raising the central three bays of the south front to form at attic storey. The house rests on a basement and was originally entered at first floor level, but Barry made a new north entrance through the basement, and it is through this that visitors now gain admittance.

The **Entrance Hall** establishes the mood of marbled magnificence which pervades the whole house. The **main staircase** occupies the site of the 'great backstairs' of the 17C house, but a new staircase was created here in 1783, and Barry rebuilt it in its present highly impressive form, strongly influenced by the Roman Renaissance, with marble balusters and rich plaster decoration on the ceiling. Glazed arches on the first landing allow vistas to the formal east garden—a masterly stroke—and niches house bronze statues by the Turin-born sculptor Baron Marochetti, of Sir John and Lady Bankes (the latter holding the key of Corfe Castle) and Charles I, commissioned by William Bankes, but not placed here until after his death in 1855. The keys of the castle itself are preserved over the fireplace of the **Library**, which dates in its present form from the 1780s; several books survive from the 17C collection of Sir John Bankes, and above the cases are family portraits. These include some by Lely in his best manner, of Sir Ralph Bankes and members of his family, some of them in their original 'Sunderland frames', a portrait by Massimo Stanzione of Sir Ralph's younger brother Jerome, painted in Naples c 1655, and Batoni's portrait of Henry Bankes on the Grand Tour in 1779.

The **Drawing Room**, on the site of the parlour of the original house, is lavishly furnished in the taste of the late 19C and contains more family portraits, including works by Van Dyck (Lady Borlase, daughter of Sir John Bankes, and her rather ineffectual-looking husband—better seen from the other side of the room, entered later in the tour), Romney and Lawrence. Next comes the **Dining Room**, created by Barry in place of the former main staircase; much of his decoration perished in a fire, but the plaster ceiling (based on one in the vanished Coleshill House, Berkshire, another Pratt house) survives, as do the superbly carved early-Renaissance-style box-wood doors made in Venice in 1849–53. The most important pictures are Palma Giovane's 'Allegory of Prophecy' and a huge and unfinished 'Judgment of Solomon' (c 1505–10) bought by William Bankes as a Giorgione but now attributed to Sebastiano del Piombo.

The cream of the picture collection is displayed in the **Saloon**, created out of the entrance hall of the original house in the 1780s, with a barrel ceiling decorated in a Wyattesque taste, probably by a little-known painter, Cornelius Dixon, and a chimneypiece by Flaxman. The pictures include some collected by Sir Ralph Bankes in the 1650s and '60s, including works by Sébastien Bourdon, Nicholas Berchem, Lely ('Mary Magdalen') and a self-portrait by Edward Altham, dressed as a hermit, in the manner of Salvator Rosa. But the finest works were bought by William Bankes in the early 19C; they include, on the west wall (to the left on entering), an early-16C 'Holy Family', possibly by Giulio Romano, a splendidly confident male portrait by Titian of c 1545, and a pair of portraits by Rubens of the sumptuously dressed Marchesa Maria and Caterina Grimaldi (1606), the former accompanied by her dwarf. William Bankes was also, rather unusually for his time, an enthusiast for Spanish art, and he decorated the **Spanish Room** to the west of the Saloon as an exquisite setting for his Spanish pictures, with a painted ceiling taken from the Palazzo Contarini degli Scrigni in Venice and walls hung with leather in the Spanish manner; the attributions of the pictures, which he bought in Spain after the Napoleonic Wars, have not all stood the test of time, but there is one indisputable masterpiece in the shape of a portrait by Velasquez of Cardinal Camillo Massimi, painted in Rome in 1649–50, wearing blue robes and not the usual scarlet; there is also an early copy of one of Velasquez's most famous paintings, 'Las Meninas' (the original is in the Prado, Madrid).

After passing through the somewhat gloomy State Bedroom on the other side of the Saloon, the route continues up the main staircase to the **second floor**, where Barry's magnificent plaster decorations can be observed more closely (note also the 16C Venetian ceiling painting). The White Bedroom was furnished at the beginning of the 20C, and there is a conversation piece by Zoffany ('The Woodley Family') in the South-East Bedroom, along with a small selection of Old Master Drawings in the adjoining Dressing Room. A less imposing staircase mounts to the attic floor, where Barry's cupola can be seen at close quarters (the original cupola having been removed in the 18C), and from here visitors descend to the basement, where William Bankes's Egyptian collection is displayed in the former **Billiard Room**. A doorway leads out into the service courtyard created in 1775–76 and still containing its laundry and drying room. The west front of the house, which can be seen from here, still retains its 17C mullioned and transomed windows.

GCT

Lulworth Castle

7m south west of Wareham, in East Lulworth village on the B3070, south from the A352: English Heritage. It is planned to open the Castle to the public regularly in 1994.

Lulworth Castle is a ruin, without any contents, but it demands mention as an especially dramatic and important work of architecture. It is not a medieval building, but a mock castle, built early in the 17C. Like a few other such buildings (eg, Bolsover in Derbyshire, Cranborne Manor in Dorset and Longford Castle in Wiltshire) it relates to the chivalric literature of the age, such as Spenser's 'Faerie Queene' and Sir Philip Sidney's 'Arcadia', and to the elaborate tournaments and spectacles which the Elizabethan and Jacobean courts loved.

Thomas Howard, the 3rd Viscount Bindon, was a relatively junior member of the enormous Howard clan, who were much in favour at James I's court. He had a principal seat nearby at Bindon Abbey and built Lulworth c 1607–10 as a hunting-lodge, although it must always have been a particularly large and grand one. Bindon gave credit for the idea to Robert Cecil, Earl of Salisbury, head of the government and builder of Cranborne Manor:

'If the little pile in Lulworth park shall prove pretty or worth the labour bestowed on the erecting of it, I will acknowledge as the truth is, that your Lordship's powerful speech to me at Bindon, to have laid the first foundations of the pile in my mind.'

During the Civil War, the Castle was badly damaged, while Bindon Abbey was burnt out and left uninhabitable. A rich Londoner, Humphrey Weld, bought the estate in 1643. The Weld family made the Castle their principal residence, remodelling the interior at various points in the 18C and 19C; we have no clear idea what the original interiors looked like. In 1929 a disastrous fire destroyed the Castle, which has been a shell ever since. The Weld family still own and run the estate, and live in a handsome new house in the park, built in 1975 in late-Georgian style by Anthony Jaggard. The Castle ruins are in the guardianship of English Heritage, which is carrying out a major programme of restoration.

The castle is a spectacular ruin. It is a solid square block, three storeys high over a basement, with great round towers a storey higher, at the corners. There was a central tower, which is being rebuilt as part of the current restoration. The windows are tall and mullioned, and the parapets are all battlemented. The front door on the east side, and that on the west side, are 18C, as is the balustraded terrace. English Heritage is in the process of re-roofing and re-glazing the whole building—which will secure its long-term future—and display the shell in such a way that the various stages of its development are visible. The castle has a wonderful setting in beautiful parkland with views to the Channel.

In the park is the Catholic church of St Mary, designed by John Tasker and built by Thomas Weld in 1786–87. There is a family tradition that Weld only received permission to build the church on condition that it did not resemble one—so it is neo-classical, and resembles a very big garden temple. The interior has a domed centre, with four big apses opening off it with half-domes. It is a most beautiful space and retains nearly all of its original fittings, in particular the marble altar ordered from Rome.

SB

Milton Abbey

7m south west of Blandford to west of Milton Abbas, north of A354 Blandford–Dorchester: Milton Abbey School. Open Easter week and summer holidays (mid July–end Aug) 10–6.30. Refreshments.

This severe-looking house, one of the largest in Dorset, is beautifully situated amid lawns in a fold of downland country next to the magnificent 14C and 15C church of the Benedictine abbey of Milton. The church and estate were acquired after the Reformation by Sir John Tregonwell, who formed a house out of the former monastic buildings, incorporating the splendid hall built by Abbot Middleton (d 1525), which still survives; the church meanwhile was turned over to parochial use. But, in its present form, the house is a monument to the ambitions of Joseph Damer, great-nephew of a notorious money-lender in Ireland. He bought the estate from the descendants of the Tregonwells in 1752, was raised to the Irish peerage as Lord Milton in the following year, and married a daughter of the 1st Duke of Dorset (cf. Knole, Kent). The rambling, picturesque house depicted in Buck's engraving of 1733 was clearly not grand enough to satisfy his sense of his own importance, and in 1771 he called in Sir William Chambers to design a new one. Chambers was one of the most accomplished classical architects of his age, and it seems highly likely that the style, and possibly even the design, of what he called this 'Cursed Gothick house' was forced on him by Lord Milton, whom he described as an 'unmannerly Imperious Lord' (Horace Walpole said that he was 'moderately sensible, immoderately proud'). Chambers resigned the commission in 1774 after an argument, and the decoration of the interior was completed by James Wyatt in 1775–76. Lord Milton died in 1798, having been made Earl of Dorchester (the Dorchester Hotel in London stands on the site of his town house), but when his son died ten years later the earldom became extinct and in 1852 the property was sold to the Danish merchant banker Baron Hambro. In 1933 the Hambros sold the house and grounds to the Ecclesiastical Commissioners, and in 1954 it became a boys' public school.

Until the 1770s the house and church stood in close proximity to the small town of Milton, but in 1774–80 Lord Milton, who had already employed 'Capability' Brown to landscape the grounds, constructed a new estate village—nearly a mile away to the south east—following Brown's designs, with thatched cottages (designed by Chambers) neatly arranged on either side of a broad street climbing up the hillside. The old town was obliterated, and the house now stands isolated next to the church, which serves as an unusually magnificent school chapel, containing a dramatic monument to Lady Milton (d 1775) in the north transept by Robert Adam and Agostino Carlini, with Lord Milton propped up on an elbow on the tomb-chest gazing disconsolately at the body of his wife—a gesture that goes some way to redeem his memory.

The house stands to the north of the church and is arranged around a quadrangle, with the medieval Hall of Abbot Middleton occupying most of the south side and the main carriage entrance from the north aligned on its porch. Chambers's main elevations, to the west and north, are in Portland stone, but the detailing is repetitive and mechanical, and at close quarters the building conveys a somewhat dour, almost barrack-like impression. The bleak feeling is maintained inside the courtyard, faced in flint with horizontal bands of stone. By far the most attractive interior is the Hall, with its magnificent hammer-beam roof—a rarity in this part of the country—enlivened by carved figures of angels holding shields, and its extravagantly carved movable screen—another rarity—with a dining recess at the high table end; a sumptuous setting for entertaining by an Abbot who presided over a community of no more than a dozen monks at the time of the Reformation. Visitors proceed from here to the 18C house, where four of the main reception rooms are shown, long denuded of their fittings. The King's Room (formerly the dining room) and the Drawing Room, on the ground floor, were both decorated by Chambers before his row with Lord Milton. The former has a display of portraits of 18C personages which always seem to have been in the house, and the latter has a ceiling inspired by a plate in Wood's *Ruins of Palmyra*. Chambers's staircase, hung with family portraits of the Damers, including two from the studio of Angelica Kauffmann, leads up to the largest of the 18C rooms, the Ballroom, designed by Wyatt as a picture gallery, with characteristically spindly neo-classical decorations on the barrel-vaulted ceiling.

GCT

Parnham

1m south of Beaminster on A3066 Beaminster–Bridport: Mr and Mrs John Makepeace, tel. 0308 862204. Open Apr–Oct Wed, Sun, BH Mon 10–5. Refreshments.

From the outside this gabled stone house immediately proclaims its 16C origins. But since it was first built on the site of an earlier building by Robert Strode (d 1558) there have been many changes. The Strodes were an old Dorset family who acquired the estate by marriage in the 16C, and they remained in possession until 1764, when the property passed by marriage to Sir John Oglander of Nunwell in the Isle of Wight (qv.). Like many others of its type, the house was neglected in the late 18C, but in 1807–11 Sir William Oglander decided to reinstate it as a second home, and brought in John Nash, who had already worked for him at Nunwell, to add a new dining room, embellish the exterior and remove sundry Georgian altera-tions. He also remodelled some of the interiors, but most of his work inside the house vanished in another remodelling by Vincent Robinson, who bought the house in 1896. He was a collector, 'equipped not merely to furnish a Parnham but to fill a Knole or Hatfield', and in his time the house took on the character of a sumptuously decorated furniture showroom. More changes were carried out by his successor, Hans Sayer, who lived at Parnham from 1910–14 and reinstated the Tudor character of the interior, using woodwork brought in from elsewhere; he also laid out the formal gardens. After being a country club and a private residence, the house was requisitioned in the war, and part of the planning for the invasion of Europe in 1944 took place here. Having served for a time as an old peoples' home, it was bought in 1976 by the present owner, a well-known furniture-maker, who has restored the gardens and interior and established his own workshop and the world-famous Parnham College of wood craftsmanship in the grounds.

The house stands in wooded, hilly country, and is built of the local golden-brown lichened Ham Hill stone. It is approached through a formal walled courtyard like that of Montacute, Somerset (qv.), but dating from the early 20C. The east (entrance) front retains its mid-16C scale and relaxed asymmetrical proportions, but there was a good deal of refacing by Nash, and he was also responsible for adding the pinnacles, battlements and copings of the gables. The central hall block is entered through a three-storeyed porch with oriel windows over the entrance; to the right is the former service end, remodelled in the 17C, and to the left is the hall, lit by large mullioned and transomed windows (the centre one is by Nash), with a gabled wing for the main reception rooms projecting beyond it (more of Nash's work can be seen on the garden front of this wing).

The interior is now arranged as a series of galleries displaying furniture made by John Makepeace, along with other, mostly 20C objects. The Hall dates in its present form from the restoration of 1910, when Hans Sauer brought it back to something like its original appearance, exposing the wooden ceiling and bringing in the late-16C wooden screen. Some of the original 16C glass survives in the windows, and the late-15C overmantel probably came from an earlier house on the site. The Drawing Room retains some late-17C woodwork around the doors and overmantel, and next to it is a 17C staircase with walls painted in 1936, leading to a bedroom with a plaster ceiling, a crudely carved wooden overmantel with a representation of Joseph and Potiphar's wife and a four-poster bed by Makepeace. The Oak Room, at the service end to the north of the Hall, has early-16C linenfold panelling and a splendid frieze of early Renaissance-style arabesques and roundels. Outside, there is a restaurant and also a shop selling products made in the Parnham workshop.

GCT

Purse Caundle Manor

1m east of Milborne Port to south of A30 Sherborne–Shaftesbury: Michael de Pelet, tel. 0963 250400. Open Easter Mon, May–Sept Thur, Sun, BH Mon 2–5. Guided tours.

This grey stone house stands in the village street in the pastoral countryside of Blackmoor Vale, close to the Somerset border. It dates fundamentally from the late 15C, when the manor belonged to the Long family, some of whom are buried in the nearby church. The Longs were succeeded by the Hannams, who carried out some alterations in the second half of the 16C and built a new service wing in the early 17C. Since then there have been few structural changes, and today, despite having passed through several ownerships in the 20C, the building survives intact as a good example of a moderately sized West Country squire's house of medieval origin.

The architectural evolution of the house is somewhat complicated. The hall range faces east towards the street, with a wing projecting on the south side, on the upper floor of which is a 15C oriel window lighting the great chamber. The entrance is on the west side, where the large traceried window (a relatively recent replacement) announces that the house still retains its 15C open hall; to the left is a 17C projection housing the main staircase, and to the right (south) is a much longer wing, also of the 17C, containing the kitchens. This joins onto the 15C great chamber wing, and has its own long and rather plain 17C façade to the garden.

The entrance leads via the usual screens passage into the Hall, with an open timber roof of a hybrid type featuring tie beams and crown posts as well as the arched braces found commonly in the area (cf. Lytes Cary Manor House, Somerset); the wind-braces are decorated with quatrefoil patterns. No doubt there was originally an open central hearth, but at some time in the 16C the present fireplace was built on the east wall and two rooms built out on either side, possibly during the tenure of William Hannam (d 1576), whose initials appear over the doorway to the right. The tour takes in the 15C service rooms, the panelled Parlour, several bedrooms on the first floor and the former Great Chamber, with its barrel ceiling. The house is lived in as a family home, and the rooms are appropriately furnished with period items.

GCT

Sandford Orcas Manor

2½m north of Sherborne: Sir Mervyn Medlycott, tel. 0963 220206. Open Easter Mon, May–Sept Sun 2–6, Mon 10–6. Guided tours.

Sandford Orcas is a complete and well-preserved example of a smaller manor house of the mid 16C. It was built of the local Ham Hill limestone, probably by Edward Knoyle, who inherited the property in 1533. Several of the details echo those to be seen at Athelhampton (qv.), and it seems likely that the same highly skilled masons worked on both houses. The family remained in occupation until 1701, although mounting debts (they were Roman Catholics and Jacobites) forced them to sell the estate to a creditor. The house became a farmhouse after the land was purchased by the Hutchings family in 1736, but in 1873 it was restored by Hubert Hutchings, who left it to his cousin Sir Hubert Medlycott of Ven House, a large 18C house (not open to the public) just over the Somerset border. He moved to Sandford Orcas and furnished it with items from Ven, which are still in the house along with portraits and other family memorabilia.

The house is situated in the rolling countryside of the Dorset/Somerset border (it was in Somerset until 1896) and is approached from the village past the church and through a gateway projecting from the north range; this has a flattened Gothic arch and beautifully carved Gothic mouldings, an indication of the continuing vitality of medieval building traditions in the south west in Tudor times. The house stands in an attractive, largely 19C, garden, separated from the stable yard (the original farmyard) by a low wall. The pleasing asymmetrical main front faces east, its walls faced with ashlar—an important status symbol in the mid 16C—and its roof-line diversified by two gables (the left-hand one a late-19C replacement) surmounted by heraldic beasts; a large mullioned and transomed bay window of typically mid-16C design lights the Hall, to the left of the projecting porch, and there is a similar window on the south wall. In keeping with the usual mid-16C practice, the Hall is one storey, with the Great Chamber placed over it; the Parlour is to the right of the porch, and the service quarters are placed in lower buildings at the back, on the other side of a small courtyard—an unusual but effective arrangement which allowed the main east block to be used exclusively by the family and their guests. The entrance is through a wooden early-17C screen surmounted by strapwork cresting, leading into the well-lit Hall, now furnished as a drawing room, with armorial glass in the upper lights of the windows; at the former high table end the original mid-16C spiral staircase leads up to the Great Chamber (now a bedroom), and a similar staircase leads back down from the room over the parlour to the screens passage and the Parlour itself. These rooms are attractively furnished with 17C and 18C pieces, and there are some 17C Dutch and Flemish genre paintings on the walls.

GCT

Sherborne Castle

On the south edge of Sherborne, ½m from town centre: Simon Wingfield Digby, tel. 0935 813182. Open Easter–Sept Thur, Sat, Sun, BH Mon 2–5.30 (grounds open 12.00). Refreshments.

This curious, romantic house started life as a lodge built in 1594 by Queen Elizabeth I's favourite Sir Walter Raleigh in the park of the medieval castle of the Bishops of Salisbury. He acquired the lease of the castle from the Queen in 1592, having seen and admired it en route from London to his native West Country, and, according to a 17C account, he 'began very fairly to repair [it]; but, altering his purpose, he built in the park adjoining to it...a most fair house, which he beautified with orchards, gardens and groves, of such variety and delight that...it is unparalleled by any in these parts'. The gardens have not survived, but Raleigh's compact lodge is still the centre of the present building. The estate reverted to the Crown when Raleigh fell into disgrace under James I, but in 1617 it was acquired by Sir John Digby, a younger son from a Warwickshire family, who served as ambassador to Spain. He was raised to the peerage as Earl of Bristol in 1622, and three years later he turned the house into a full-sized country seat by throwing out wings from the four corners of the original building, thus giving it a striking, though no doubt always inconvenient, H-plan. Not long afterwards, in the course of the Civil War, the old castle was ruined (it is now maintained by English Heritage).

When the 3rd Earl of Bristol died in 1698, the estate passed to the senior branch of the family, but in the mid 18C, Henry, 7th Baron and 1st Earl Digby, abandoned the old family seat at Coleshill in Warwickshire and settled at Sherborne, where he carried out some internal remodelling. He also employed 'Capability' Brown to create a new landscape setting, which survives largely unaltered. His son, the 2nd Earl, left the estate in 1856 to a nephew, George Wingfield Digby, who employed P.C. Hardwick to carry out a thorough, and generally sympathetic, restoration in 1859–60; the title meanwhile passed to another branch of the family. Since then there have been few major changes. The family ceased to live regularly in the house after the Second World War, but it has been well maintained, and the collections of portraits and furniture have been augmented by an unusually good display of oriental porcelain largely brought together by the art-historian George Wingfield Digby.

The house stands on a hill to the south of the ruined medieval castle, and separated from it by a lake formed as part of Brown's landscape improvements. The lodge built by Sir Walter Raleigh was a three-storeyed rectangular building with corner turrets and chimneys clustered on the roof-line. The 1625 additions were in a similar style, though there are only two storeys, and externally the house has changed little since the 1620s except for the addition of pedimented frames to windows on east side, probably in the late 17C or early 18C. Its surprisingly gaunt appearance derives from the absence of the gables so often found in Elizabethan and Jacobean houses, and from the rather unattractive rendering with which the rubble-stone walls have always been covered; the dressings are of dark brown Ham Hill stone, and there is little in the way of carved detail to divert the eye from the overall plainness.

The house was originally entered through the hall of the original lodge, but visitors are now channelled first into a small lobby in a turret at the corner of the south-east wing. This gives access to the **Library**, created in a whimsical Rococo Gothick style as part of the improvements undertaken by the 1st Earl Digby after inheriting the house in 1757. There are busts of classical worthies in niches, and over the fireplace, in an ogee-arched plaster overmantel, is a portrait after Van Dyck of the 17C savant and naval commander Sir Kenelm Digby. The **Solarium**, which follows, was created as a dining room in the neo-Jacobean manner by P.C. Hardwick out of the parlour of Raleigh's house, and is hung with portraits of 19C members of the Wingfield and Digby families; its unusual shape is explained by the incorporation of the former corner turrets. Next comes the **Red Drawing** Room, in the north-east wing, with a chimneypiece and plaster ceiling of c 1625 and some excellent early portraits, including Robert Peake's famous and much-reproduced picture (originally at Coleshill) of Queen Elizabeth being carried in procession on the shoulders of some of her leading subjects (c 1600). There are also works by Cornelius Johnson and Lely, and some attractive pieces of late-17C and early-18C inlaid furniture.

A narrow staircase in the north-east tower leads up to the **Porcelain Room**, where superb Japanese Imari and Kakiemon items and Chinese pieces of the Transitional and K'ang Hsi periods are shown in well-lit display cases. The **Green Drawing Room**, like the Solarium underneath, is in the part of the house built by Raleigh, but the lavish chimneypieces are of c 1625 and the curtains (by Owen Jones) and the wallpaper were introduced at the time of the 1859–60 restoration. There are portraits by Mytens, Kneller and Reynolds, and some good items of mid-18C French furniture, including a pair of commodes by Pierre Langlois; a dispatch box is also displayed as a memento of the abortive attempt to marry Charles I (then Prince of Wales) to the Spanish Infanta, the failure of which led to the 1st Earl of Bristol's disgrace at court. The adjacent **Blue Drawing Room**, in the south-east wing, dates mainly from c 1860, although a marble chimneypiece and some contemporary chairs survive from a late-18C remodelling; the pictures include a copy of Van Dyck's famous dual portrait of the Earls of Bristol and Bedford at Althorp, Northants (qv.), and a Gainsborough of the 1st Earl Digby. More excellent oriental porcelain is displayed both here and in the adjacent **Boudoir**, where good items of Chelsea porcelain and 17C and 18C ebony and Boulle furniture are also shown.

From here the route passes back through the Green Drawing Room to **Lady Bristol's Bedroom**; this is above the hall of Sir Walter Raleigh's house, and is hung with early-18C tapestries, including some with an arabesque pattern woven at the Soho factory after a design by Clermont. The **Hall** itself is at the bottom of the main staircase and retains its original pointed-arched doorways, although the floor level was raised and the screen removed at an early date; a late-medieval tilting helmet is kept here, along with a small portrait of Raleigh supposedly painted while he was in the Tower of London. One of the original outer windows of the house can be seen just before entering the adjacent **Small Dining Room**, which contains an outstandingly good collection of late-16C and 17C miniatures, including works by Nicholas Hilliard and Isaac and Peter Oliver (note the portrait of the well-known beauty, Venetia, wife of Sir Kenelm Digby, on her death-bed). The last important room is the **Oak Room**, in the north-west wing, much altered since it was built in 1625, but still retaining two richly-carved internal porches. Visitors leave the house through the basement, where a **museum** has been created in the former kitchen containing Raleigh memorabilia, including his pipe. Outside, an 18C Gothic dairy, now the tea room, contains a Roman tessellated pavement, and a path around the lake affords good distant views of the house.

GCT

Wolfeton House

1 ½m north west of Dorchester on A37 Dorchester–Yeovil: Captain N.T.L. Thimbleby, tel. 0305 263500. Open May–Sept Tues, Thur, BH Mon 2–6.

Described by Thomas Hardy as 'an ivied manor house, flanked by battle-mented towers, more than usually distinguished by the size of its many mullioned windows', Wolfeton is a substantial fragment of the early Tudor and Elizabethan house of the Trenchards, once one of the leading Dorset families. The estate came by marriage to John Trenchard in 1480, and he and his son, Thomas, built a compact courtyard house which played host in 1506 to the Archduke Philip of Austria and his wife Joanna when they were forced ashore at Weymouth en route for Spain. In the late 16C, Sir George Trenchard (d 1630) extended the south range, and he subsequently built one of the first purpose-built riding-houses in the country close by (not open to the public). The house probably reached its zenith in his time, but in the late 18C his descendants abandoned it, and it was later sold to cousins. The chapel in the north range was in ruins by 1800, and more of the house was demolished in 1822–28. The remaining buildings were repaired and somewhat modified by W.H.P. Weston, who bought the property in 1862, and since 1973 more work has been done by the present owner, a kinsman both of the Trenchards and of the Mohuns who preceded them at Wolfeton.

The house is approached through the gatehouse which originally led into the small courtyard of the Trenchards' house. It is flanked by two round towers, one of which still serves as a dovecote, and in the small room to the right, now known as the Chapel, there is a remarkable series of early-16C carved wood panels representing the Signs of the Zodiac and the Occupa-tions of the Months, brought from the main house when it was reduced in size. The gatehouse is now detached from the main building, but old illustrations show that it was originally joined to the north and south ranges of the early Tudor house, both of which have been demolished. In its present form the house—best seen from the south or garden side—consists of the south-west corner of the original building, including the Hall with its crenellated stair turret and elaborately carved mullioned windows, and the plainer three-bay Elizabethan extension to the west, with a small garderobe projection between the two. These buildings, together with the gatehouse, make a highly satisfying composition in their own right.

The house is entered from the north through a groin-vaulted passageway lined with linenfold panelling and giving access to the Elizabethan stone staircase, one of the finest of its type and date (c 1580) to survive in England. To the east is the Hall, entered through a lavishly carved doorway—one of several in the house—but internally much altered in the 19C; some more curious early-16C panels can be seen here, including some with apes in human dress, and 17C portraits hang on the walls. The two main ground-floor rooms of the Elizabethan wing to the west contain magnificent carved wooden doorways and chimneypieces dating from the late 16C or early 17C, and plaster ceilings of the same date. The overmantel in the Parlour has figures of Hope and Justice guarded by a knight, a squire and a servant (representing the degrees of society and relating to the King and Queen carved over the door). The Dining Room overmantel, which is of plaster, was possibly designed by William Arnold (cf. Montacute, Somerset), and depicts Paris presenting an apple to Aphrodite (note also the carving of a chained ape c 1500 inserted into later woodwork to the west). In Elizabethan times there was a sumptuously decorated great chamber or Gallery above these rooms, reached by the main staircase, which probably resembles the original staircase at Longleat, Wiltshire (qv.). But although the surprisingly classical stone doorcase at the head of the stairs still survives, possibly designed and carved by Allan Maynard, who also worked at Longleat, the room itself was subsequently divided up and has lost its barrel ceiling of plaster. The present owner has removed the later subdivisions, and it is now once again possible to appreciate the proportions of the room, with its magnificent stone chimneypiece incorporating figures of native Americans, possibly inspired by tales told by Sir Walter Raleigh, who is known to have visited Sir George Trenchard from his own house, Sherborne Castle (qv.), not far away.

GCT

COUNTY DURHAM

Auckland Castle

In Bishop Auckland, entered from market-place: The Church
Commissioners, tel. 0338 601627. Open May–Sept Sun, Tues, Wed,
Thur, Sat in Aug, all BH Mons 2–5 (also Tues 10–12).

Ever since the Middle Ages, Auckland Castle has been the main country
residence of the Bishops of Durham. Durham was one of the richest sees in
England, and the medieval bishops shared with the Nevills of Raby (qv.)
and the Percys of Alnwick, Northumberland (qv.) the responsibility of
securing the north-east of England against the Scots. As 'prince-bishops'
they enjoyed political powers unparalleled in Britain and their houses were
built on the grandest scale. Since then Auckland Castle has undergone
many alterations, notably in the 1660s and in the second half of the 18C,
and today, like Durham Castle a few miles to the east, it vividly conveys a
sense of the power and dignity of the bishopric in its pre-19C heyday.

Despite its name, Auckland Castle is not, and probably never was,
fortified. It stands in a wooded park overlooking the River Wear, and is
approached through a Gothic Revival gateway. This was designed in 1760
by Sir Thomas Robinson of Rokeby Park (qv.), leader of the local architectural cognoscenti, as part of a series of alterations instigated by Bishop
Richard Trevor, a wealthy and ambitious cleric who supposedly consoled
himself for his disappointment in not being offered Canterbury by embarking on the reconstruction of Auckland Castle and its surroundings; his
Gothic deercote, dating from 1767, can still be visited in the park. The
remodelling, interrupted by his death, was continued by Bishop Shute
Barrington, who in 1794–96 placed the building in the hands of James
Wyatt, and it was Wyatt who designed the highly effective Gothic screen
to the entrance courtyard. The house is an L-shaped building, with the
medieval hall range facing the visitor to the north and the residential
apartments, greatly altered and expanded in the 18C, on the left. It is built
of the ubiquitous local yellow sandstone, still blackened in parts by the
smoke of now-defunct industries. The aisled Hall, built by Bishop Hugh
Pudsey in the second half of the 12C, is the oldest part of the building to
survive, but it was greatly altered in 1662–65 when it was turned into a
Chapel by the high church Bishop John Cosin, as part of his plans to restore
the magnificence of the see after the depredations of the Interregnum. The
alterations were entrusted to a local mason, John Langstaffe, and entailed
the addition of a clerestory and the refacing of the exterior in a curious
quasi-Mannerist way, with embellished blocks of masonry. Inside, there is
an abundant display of contemporary woodwork in dark oak, and the
ensemble remains one of the best surviving examples of the neo-medieval
style associated with Cosin, also found in Durham Castle and Cathedral as
well as in several local churches.

The house is entered through Wyatt's porch, from which a ceremonial
route leads up to the state rooms on the first floor of the west block. Wyatt
redecorated these rooms, which occupy the site of the medieval great
chamber, and they survive intact as one of the best sequences of late-18C
Gothic rooms to be seen in England. Two large late-17C paintings on the
landing at the top of the staircase show the house before the Georgian
improvements, and from here a large Gothic window allows the visitor to

'command the prospect' of the Wear valley below. The octagonal Ante-Room with Gothic niches and a plaster vault, leads into the spacious Throne Room, lined with portraits of bishops, including Bishops Barrington and van Mildert by Lawrence, and still containing Wyatt's throne in its ogee-topped niche. A door in the south wall gives access to the Dining Room, added in the early 16C but with decoration dating from Bishop Trevor's alterations of c 1760 (his coat of arms can be seen in a Rococo cartouche on the ceiling). The walls are hung with a series of large and exotic canvases by Zurbaran showing Jacob and his sons. These superb pictures, which alone justify a visit to Auckland Castle, were painted in 1640 and were acquired by Trevor from a Jewish trader in 1756 after having been seized by pirates en route for South America.

GCT

Raby Castle

1m north of Staindrop on A688 Barnard Castle–Bishop Auckland road: Lord Barnard, tel. 0833 60202. Open Easter weekend,May, Jun Wed, Sun; July–Sept daily except Sat 1–5 (gardens open 11–5.30). Refreshments.

In the late Middle Ages the Nevills of Raby were among the most powerful magnates in the north of England. Starting in the early 14C, they built a massive and a formidable fortified residence, for which licence to crenellate was granted in 1378 to the 3rd Lord Nevill. In its completed form the house consisted of a first-floor hall, built over a lower hall, with a fortress-like keep tower, probably for retainers, adjoining it, and a massive encircling wall punctuated by nine towers of varying size and height: these contained the Chapel and Kitchen, both of which still survive, and further residential accommodation. The plan is confusingly irregular, possibly following that of earlier buildings, and the external aspect grimly powerful.

The Nevills lost Raby after taking a leading part in the Northern Rising of 1569. After some years in the hands of the Crown, the castle was sold in 1626 to Henry Vane, a lawyer and politician who became Charles I's Secretary of State in 1640, but subsequently transferred his loyalty to Parliament. His son, a leading politician during the Interregnum, was executed after the Restoration, and his grandson, raised to the peerage as Lord Barnard, tried to demolish the castle to spite his son. He was forced to desist by an order in Chancery in 1716, and in the 1740s the 2nd Lord Barnard employed Lord Burlington's draughtsman, Daniel Garrett, to design new state rooms on the north and west sides of the building; these rooms survive, but are not open to the public. The work was continued by James Paine for the 3rd Lord Barnard, later 1st Earl of Darlington, and in 1781–85 the 2nd Earl, a leading agricultural improver, brought in another prominent northern architect, John Carr of York, to design a spectacular new Gothic entrance hall; Carr also designed the stable courtyard. The 3rd Earl, a well-known Whig, sportsman and bon-viveur, was created Duke of Cleveland in the aftermath of the Reform Act of 1832, and in 1845–49 his son, the 2nd Duke, lavished a great deal of his considerable wealth on the creation of another suite of state rooms, this time on the south side of the house. His architect was William Burn, and as a result of his activities, which extended to the remodelling of the medieval hall and chapel, the interior now bears the strong and pervasive imprint of early-Victorian taste. The 4th Duke of Cleveland died without issue in 1891, and the house went to a cousin, who retained the Barnard title; from him the house went in direct male line to the present owner.

Raby Castle lies in a sheep-strewn park, and it makes sense to make a circuit of the outside before seeing the interior. The moat has been drained and the south front rebuilt (by Burn), but otherwise the exterior has preserved its medieval appearance largely intact. Carr made a new carriage entrance into the castle through the base of the Chapel Tower, but today the entrance is through the impressively machicolated (though restored) **Nevill Gateway** on the west side of the building, from which a lierne-vaulted passage leads into a confined courtyard dominated by the hall block and adjoining keep tower.

The suite of state rooms starts with the mid-18C **Small Drawing Room**. It has a plaster ceiling, possibly by Thomas Perritt of York, and is hung with a good collection of sporting and equestrian pictures reflecting the enthusiasms of the 2nd Earl of Darlington and his son; artists include Ben Marshall, J.F. Herring, Sartorius and John Wootton. The **Library**, next door,

The entrance to Raby Castle, Nevill's Gateway from inside the Castle, late 14C

retains its original early-18C wood panelling, but has been subsequently much altered. There are attractive ruin pictures and harbour scenes by Sebastiano Ricci and Antonio Joli over the fireplaces, as well as a portrait of Nell Gwyn by Lely and two very tall 18C Chinese porcelain pagodas. A bay at the end of this room contains a splendid mid-17C North Italian inlaid cabinet known as the 'Temple of Hymen', and also some of the best pictures in the house, collected by the 2nd Duke of Cleveland. These comprise two Dutch interiors by Pieter de Hooch, an 'Artist's Studio' by the younger Teniers, a genre scene by Willem van Mieris and a harbour scene attributed to Claude. The richly decorated octagonal **Drawing Room** by Burn, its walls hung with yellow silk brocade, is a virtually unaltered example of the opulent taste of the 1840s, with motifs drawn from Jacobean and Rococo sources. In the adjacent **Dining Room**, by contrast, the predominant colour is a deep red. There is furniture by Gillow, and pictures by Leonardo Bassano (a 'Vegetable and Fruit Market by Night'), Luca Giordano, Reynolds—in his more sentimental vein—and a good Kneller of Alexander Pope.

Tortuous corridors lead from here to Carr's magnificently gloomy **Lower Hall**, justly called 'the first truly dramatic interior of the whole Gothic Revival'; it was designed for carriages to pass through into the medieval courtyard. The room is aisled, with vaults supported on piers faced with red scagliola, and among the usual trophies and armour stands the 'Greek Slave', a chained female nude sculpted by the American Hiram Powers and shown to admiring crowds at the Great Exhibition of 1851. The huge **Barons' Hall**, above the Lower Hall, is one of the largest and least usable rooms in any country house. It shows little sign of its medieval origins, the floor having been raised 10ft by Carr and the south end extended 52ft by Burn when he created the Drawing Room underneath. Burn was also responsible for the creation of the clumsy wooden ceiling in place of its medieval predecessor. The room contains quantities of 19C furniture, including tables attributed to Pugin, some gargantuan Meissen figures of birds, and numerous family portraits. The **Chapel**, reached from the former lower end of the Hall, was totally remodelled by Burn and again in 1901 by the 9th Lord Barnard, but the vaulted 14C **Kitchen** in the base of Clifford's Tower remains almost untouched as one of the finest surviving examples of a medieval kitchen in England. From here a passage leads to the servants' hall (the former medieval guard-room) and then out of the castle.

GCT

Rokeby Park

2m south east of Barnard Castle, off A66 at Greta Bridge. Open endMay–early Sept Mon, Tues and May BH Mon 2–5.

Rokeby is an early and complete example of the Palladian revival in 18C English architecture. It was designed by its owner, Sir Thomas Robinson, in the late 1720s, and was completed in 1731 soon after his return from a two-year tour of the Continent. Robinson was a son-in-law of the Earl of Carlisle, the builder of Castle Howard, Yorkshire (qv.) and numbered Lord Burlington among his friends. The design has the stark cubic simplicity of Burlington's own buildings. It follows the pattern of some of Palladio's villas, with a square three-storeyed main block covered by a pyramid roof flanked on the north side by towers, and lower wings on either side; the main block is faced in stone to the south, but the wings are stuccoed. The austere effect was intended to convey a sense of Roman gravity, appropriate in view of the fact that Robinson had a large collection of Roman inscriptions and statuary. But the austerity has always been mitigated by the Arcadian beauty of the surrounding landscape which Robinson did much to restore.

The interiors were not finished until after Robinson had returned from serving a spell as Governor of Barbados from 1742–47. He subsequently became Master of Ceremonies at the ultra-fashionable Ranelagh pleasure gardens in London, but he dissipated his fortune and was forced to sell the estate to J.B.S. Morritt in 1769. He and his descendants made few structural alterations to the house, but they introduced some superb pictures, including the 'Rokeby Venus' by Velazquez, now in the National Gallery, London. J.B.S. Morritt, the collector of the Velazquez, was a friend of Sir Walter Scott, who in his poem 'Rokeby' paid tribute to the scenic qualities of the surroundings, qualities which also attracted painters like Cotman.

The house was designed to be approached from the north, through the stable courtyard, but the entrance is now on the south side. The main rooms are on the piano nobile, and Robinson planned a staircase to lead directly to a first-floor hall (now the Saloon), but this was never built and the house is now entered through a Tuscan colonnade at ground-floor level, probably built after Robinson's return from the West Indies. The interior is furnished as a family home, and conveys a greater sense of comfort than the better-known Palladian villas near London. The low ground-floor rooms were not originally intended for everyday use and have less architectural enrichment than the grand rooms above. There is a copy of a Roman bas-relief from the Villa Borghese over the Hall fireplace, and in the Library there are two 18C pictures of Robinson's town house in Whitehall. The Breakfast Room to the left of the Hall was originally designated by Robinson as a 'bagnio' or bathroom, but was subsequently decorated as a 'print room'; it now contains an impressive Italian *pietra dura* cabinet of c 1700.

A vestibule on the north front leads to the staircase, hung with remarkable needlework pictures by Anne Morritt (d 1797), sister of the purchaser of the house. The centre of the piano nobile is taken up by the lofty Saloon, with a coved ceiling painted in a Raphaelesque manner in the mid 19C and a splendid Kentian 'tabernacle frame' around the main doorway inscribed with the Rabelaisian motto 'Fay ce que vouldras'—advice which Sir Thomas Robinson seems to have taken to heart throughout his life. The Rokeby Venus, which originally hung here, is now represented by a copy, but by way of compensation there is a good Reynolds 'fancy picture' ('Hope nursing Love'), and also Benjamin West's portraits of J.S. Morritt and his wife, two late-18C views of the house and grounds, and two free-standing sculptures by the younger Westmacott. The adjacent bedroom contains the best picture remaining in the house, a 'Venus disarming Cupid' by the 18C Venetian artist, Antonio Pellegrini. The tour ends in the spacious Dining Room created in the north west wing by J.S. Morritt in the 1770s, almost certainly to the designs of John Carr of York; it is adorned with delicate plaster enrichments in the neo-classical manner, both on the ceiling and in the apsidal projection which houses the fireplace. The pictures here include an 18C view of the Roman ruins at S. Rémy in Provence, a portrait of Queen Caroline by William Kent and some 18C views of the house and estate.

ESSEX

Audley End

West of Saffron Walden on B1383: English Heritage, tel. 0799 522399.
Open Good Fri or Apr 1–end Sept Tues–Sun (except BH) 1–6.
Refreshments.

Audley End is a very large and imposing Jacobean house just outside
Saffron Walden, now in the care of English Heritage. Impressive though it
is, the present house is a small part of what was once one of the largest
palaces in Britain. The medieval abbey of Walden was given by Henry VIII
in 1538 to Sir Thomas Audley, then Speaker of the House of Commons. Sir
Thomas adapted the monastic buildings to make a country house, known
as Audley Inn, or End. It passed to his daughter and her husband, the 4th
Duke of Norfolk, who was executed for treason in 1572. Their second son
Thomas Howard eventually inherited Audley End. He re-established his
position at the Elizabethan court as a naval commander, and in 1597 he was
created 1st Lord Howard de Walden. The Howard clan prospered in the
reign of James I; Thomas Howard became 1st Earl of Suffolk, Lord
Chamberlain and, in 1614, Lord Treasurer. Like other leading members of
the government, he helped himself freely to public funds, eventually
exceeding even the lax standards of the Jacobean court; in November 1619
Lord Suffolk and his wife were found guilty of embezzlement. He was fined
heavily, and retired to Audley End, where he died in 1626.

Between 1605 and 1614, Lord Suffolk spent about £200,000 on a colossal
new house. King James I is supposed to have remarked that it was too large
for a king, but about the right size for a Lord Treasurer. The new house
surrounded two square courtyards. The smaller court was flanked on three
sides by three-storey buildings and on the fourth (west) side by the Great
Hall. West of this was the much bigger front courtyard, with a grand arched
entrance on its west side. It was indeed a building with royal pretensions,
and fortunately was recorded in very good drawings and plans by Henry
Winstanley in 1667.

This vast house was obsolete almost as soon as it was completed; the Earls
of Suffolk never recovered from the 1st Earl's disgrace and the cost of
building Audley End, and they could never afford to maintain it properly.
In 1666 King Charles II took a liking to the house—it was near to Newmarket racecourse—and he leased it from them. But Audley End was not
a success as a royal residence, and its condition declined further, being, as
Sir Christopher Wren put it 'built after an ill manner rather Gay than
substantiall'. The house was given back to the 6th Earl of Suffolk in 1701.
There followed a series of demolitions and alterations, starting in 1708, as
the Howards and their successors tried to reduce and convert Audley End
to a manageable size and shape. This makes the house architecturally very
interesting, and also rather confusing.

In 1745, the 10th Earl of Suffolk died without direct heirs, and the estates
were divided. A distant relative, the Countess of Portsmouth, bought the
house and left it, in 1761 to her nephew, Sir John Griffin Whitwell, a
distinguished soldier, on condition that he change his name to Griffin
Griffin. Sir John engaged Robert Adam to design a new suite of reception
rooms on the ground floor. Sir John became Lord Howard de Walden, and
then Baron Braybrooke; on his death in 1797 his estates and title passed to

a cousin, Richard Neville. The Neville family, Lords Braybrooke, lived here, carrying out various internal alterations, until in 1948 the 9th Lord sold the house to the Ministry of Works. It is now in the care of English Heritage, but many of the contents still belong to the Hon. Robin Neville, who still lives on the estate.

The grand symmetrical entrance façade, seen from the road, faces west. In the middle are the tall windows of the great hall, flanked at either end by very elaborate Renaissance porches. On either side of these are big three-storey wings. This façade once looked over the square outer court-yard, entirely demolished between 1708 and 1770. Visitors enter the screens passage, known as the Bucket Hall from the leather fire buckets hanging from the ceiling, and then the **Great Hall**. Although its appearance is convincingly Jacobean, much of this dates from a restoration of 1825; the greatest original feature is the carved oak screen, one of the finest pieces of Jacobean woodwork in the country. The room is given a dramatic appearance by the great stone screen at the far end, behind which stairs rise to the Saloon; this, or at any rate its lower half, is probably by Sir John Vanbrugh, called in to advise on the first stage of the house's remodelling in 1708. The Hall is hung with a wealth of armour and fine portraits.

The tour goes through the **Adam apartments** on the ground floor of the south wing, remodelled in the 1760s for Sir John Griffin Griffin. There is an Ante-Room, a Dining Parlour, Vestibule and the Great Drawing Room. Although lower than most Adam interiors, they are richly decorated; the splendid crimson silk in the Great Drawing Room was rewoven to the original design in 1962. The Little Drawing Room, beyond, is decorated with jewel-like richness, with brightly painted panels of garlands and cherubs by Biagio Rebecca. At the east end of the south range, Adam created a library; this was subdivided into smaller rooms in 1825; the Tompkins Room is hung with views of the house, mostly painted by William Tompkins in the 1780s. Visitors return along a corridor by the foot of the Jacobean South Stairs, to the **Lower Gallery**. Until 1863 it was an open cloister, but in that year it was glazed in and now has a Victorian character, filled with stuffed birds and animals. Visitors now ascend the North Stairs, also authentically Jacobean, and see the first floor of the North Wing. Around 1736, two bedroom suites were created here. The **State Dressing Room** retains its original Jacobean ceiling and frieze, and has fine Georgian furniture. The **State Bedroom**, next, has a magnificent State Bed of 1786. Next are the Lady's State Dressing Room, and the Neville Dressing Room, both of which have a more 19C character. The **Neville Bedroom** has another great bed, made for the house in 1766, and more Georgian furniture and portraits. Finally, Lady Braybrooke's Sitting Room has an eclectic, Victorian character.

Back across the North Stairs landing is the Chapel Lobby and the **Chapel**. This is of 1768–72, the work of a joiner called John Hobcraft. It is a complete and delightful example of 'Strawberry Hill Gothic'; the fine painted window, representing the Last Supper, is by Biagio Rebecca. Visitors now proceed along the **Picture Gallery**, created by Sir John Griffin Griffin in 1762. It houses more of the 4th Lord Braybrooke's stuffed birds, and a great many portraits of the Cornwallis family. The South Lobby at the far end is lined with portraits by Lely.

Next follows the first floor of the south wing. The first four rooms were created in 1825 by the 3rd Lord Braybrooke as a suite of grand reception rooms, to replace the Adam rooms downstairs, and the rich Jacobean decoration is nearly all of this period. The impressive **Dining Room** has early 19C furniture, and very fine 17C and 18C portraits. The **Library**, a big room looking east, was redecorated and furnished in Jacobean style in the early 19C, befitting its use as a family sitting room. Beyond is the **South Library**, with a fine portrait of Sir John by Benjamin West. Lord Braybrooke's **Sitting Room**, beyond, is a comfortable Victorian living room, again with Jacobean-style decoration of 1825, and the best of the house's pictures, including works by Van Goyen, Canaletto and Jordaens. At the far end is the **Saloon**; when the house was first built, this would have been the King's Great Chamber, and the fine ceiling with its pendants dates from this period. The richly carved panelling is partly original to the room, partly brought in when the Long Gallery was demolished in 1753. Sir John Griffin Griffin redecorated the room in 1784, installing the series of full-length portraits of his ancestors here and painting and gilding the panelling. Some of the fine furniture was bought for the room in this period. From here, visitors descend the grand **staircase** behind Vanbrugh's screen, and are back in the Great Hall.

The beautiful landscape **park** around the house was designed by 'Capability' Brown in 1762, involving the damming of the River Cam to make the lake. Robert Adam designed the bridge over it, and the Temple of Concord to the east. Work is in hand to restore the elaborate Victorian parterre below the east front. Finally, to the north west of the house, the Elysian Garden is a landscaped grove with a Cascade and the Tea House Bridge, both by Robert Adam.

SB

Castle House

Just outside Dedham village, 2m off the A12: The Munnings Collection, tel. 0206 322127. Open May–early Oct Sun, Wed, BH Mon 2–5; Aug Thur and Sat.

Castle House, a pretty stuccoed house like a generous country rectory, was the home from 1919 to 1959 of the artist Sir Alfred Munnings, President of the Royal Academy and renowned painter of horses and of English country life. It now houses the Munnings Museum, with permanent displays of his varied work.

Castle House began as a Tudor timber-framed house in an L-shape, expanded to its present roughly square shape in the early 19C; the pretty Gothick staircase dates from the latter period. The house is attractively furnished with the English pieces bought by Sir Alfred and Lady Munnings, and with a great variety of his paintings. The core of these is the permanent collection left on his death, but this is supplemented by loans from other collections. The principal themes of Sir Alfred's work are hunting, horse-racing and English country life. He enjoyed sketching in the hunting field, or in the paddock or at the starting-gate at Newmarket, and many of his remarkably fluent oil sketches are on display.

Outside in the garden is Sir Alfred's thatched studio, where one sees his artist's materials, his easel and hunting-pink. His work exemplifies English reasonableness in its tone, but also has an elegiac quality in commemorating a rural way of life which survived briefly into the postwar period, but has now gone for ever.

SB

Gosfield Hall

In Gosfield village, west of Halstead on the A1017 Braintree/Haverhill road: Country Houses Association. Open May–Sept Wed, Thurs 2–4.30.

Gosfield is a fascinating house; its architectural history is evidently very complex, and has never been fully elucidated. It was built c 1545 by Sir John Wentworth, a wealthy landowner, formerly in Wolsey's household. He built a symmetrical courtyard house of brick, of two fairly tall storeys with large mullion and transom windows with cusped lights, and he entertained Queen Elizabeth here in 1561, but his wastrel grandson, also Sir John, sold the estate to Sir John Garrard in 1631.

Gosfield then passed through several hands, including those of Forde, Lord Grey, the builder of Uppark in Sussex (qv.). In 1691 he sold it to Sir Thomas Millington, a distinguished academic who was physician to William and Mary. Sir Thomas remodelled much of the house, but he died in 1704, and in 1714 his daughters sold the house to John Knight, a financier and merchant and one of the few who made a fortune from the South Sea Bubble fiasco of 1720–21. He apparently remodelled the north side of the house, creating the magnificent Ballroom. On his death in 1733, his fortune passed to his wife, Anne. She raised an elaborate monument to him in Gosfield church, and in 1736 married an impecunious Irish nobleman, Robert Nugent; they made Gosfield their main seat. Anne died in 1756, and Nugent later remarried and was made an earl. On his death in 1788, his estates passed via his daughter to her husband, George Grenville, Marquess of Buckingham, of Stowe in Buckinghamshire (qv.) and Gosfield was occupied by various French emigrés during the Revolutionary period, including Louis XVIII himself (1807–9), who surprised the locals by continuing his habit of dining in public once a week. Thereafter the house was let, and in 1825 the debt-ridden Grenvilles sold it again.

Later owners, who included the textile magnate Samuel Courtauld, did very little to alter the house, which was let in the 1920s to the conductor Sir Adrian Boult. The house narrowly escaped demolition after 1947, and in 1958 it was rescued by the Mutual Households Association (now the Country Houses Association), and sensitively converted into retirement apartments; the main rooms remain intact, and are furnished with appropriate furniture and pictures.

The house retains the basic form—four ranges around a square court-yard—given to it by Sir John Wentworth. From the outside, only the west side, with the gatehouse, remains as he left it, apart from the projecting wings at either end, added in matching brickwork c 1813. The inner sides of the courtyard, on the other hand, all seem to be intact 16C work, with the original windows. The Hall was probably in the east wing, where the Saloon now is, and one of the most puzzling features is the high extra storey rising above the centre of this range, with apparently authentic 16C windows, possibly a Great Chamber or 'Prospect Room'. The east front is nearly all Sir Thomas Millington's, ie, 1691–1701. It is broad, with wings projecting at either end, of excellent brickwork, with sash windows and a hipped roof. In the middle are the tall Saloon windows and a magnificent doorcase, but above this, most disconcertingly, rises the extra storey with its big Tudor-looking windows. Sir Thomas may have rebuilt the north and south fronts of the Tudor house at the same time, but the brickwork of these fronts is now entirely hidden under cream-painted stucco. The north front has an impressive seven-bay centrepiece, which may have been added by

John Knight, c 1720. This has blocked rustication and square windows on the ground floor, and two large doorcases. On the first floor are very tall windows, divided by Corinthian pilasters, with banded rustication. The south front is somewhat similar, with another elaborate centrepiece, seven bays wide and slightly French in style.

Visitors enter by one of the north front doors, which leads into a spacious panelled stairwell. Ahead, a paved corridor runs along the courtyard-side of the east range, opening out into a much grander staircase-hall, with a 'flying' staircase of c 1700. The Saloon, entered from here, is a splendid room, retaining all of its original panelling and fittings. There is a fine marble chimneypiece with entwined figures of 'mer-boys', and a grand Baroque ceiling painting, said to be by Sir James Thornhill. The Library occupies the centre of the south front, and commands a splendid view over a Victorian parterre to a big lake amongst trees. The bookcases are divided by Corinthian pilasters, all grained to resemble walnut and oak, and there is also a fine Elizabethan chimneypiece, with Ionic columns and grotesque masks. The Long Gallery occupies the first floor of the west range over the entrance-arch. It seems virtually unaltered since it was built by Sir John Wentworth, and is lined with beautiful, very well-preserved linenfold panelling. A short passageway leads into the Ballroom, in the centre of the north front. This is a splendid Baroque room, with heavy, grained panelling and enormous, very old mirrors. The sumptuous plasterwork of the ceiling is hard to date, but the stencilled decoration is presumably mid 19C.

Outside, there is an immense covered well with a 19C donkey-driven pump (all the machinery still in place), and well-maintained gardens, with beautiful views over the former park. Gosfield church, a short walk across fields, houses the plain Perpendicular-style tombs of Sir John Wentworth and his daughter, and in the Sacristy is the immense Baroque monument raised to John Knight by his widow, with an epitaph by Pope.

SB

Ingatestone Hall

Just south of Ingatestone village, off the A12, 4m south west of
Chelmsford. The Lord Petre: tel. 0277 353010. Open Easter–Sept Fri, Sat,
Sun and BHs 1–6, also Wed and Thur in late July and August.
Refreshments.

The Petre family (pronounced 'Peter') is one of the most consistent and most distinguished of England's Catholic dynasties. Ingatestone has belonged to them since 1539, when it was acquired by Sir William Petre from the lands of the Abbey of Barking. He was an able young lawyer from Devon, who rose in the world as a tutor to the Boleyn family, and then as Proctor, or assistant, to Thomas Cromwell, in the Dissolution of the Monasteries. He bought the manor for £849 12s 6d and, dissatisfied with the existing Steward's House, he built the present mansion. To satisfy his conscience he obtained a Bull of exoneration from the Pope, which required him to found almshouses in compensation; they still exist in the village, although since rebuilt. His son, John, moved to Thorndon Hall near Brentford, and became the 1st Lord Petre in 1603; he was eminent as a patron of the great composer and fellow-recusant, William Byrd. The family suffered sequestration of their estates under the Commonwealth, but recovered to a position of great wealth in the 18C. At some point early in the 18C, Ingatestone was modernised, with Georgian panelling and sash windows. In the 1760s, the 9th Lord rebuilt Thorndon Hall to the designs of James Paine, but after the death of the 16th Lord (1915), his widow felt unable to remain at Thorndon, and moved back to Ingatestone, carrying out a careful programme of renovation which lasted until 1937, returning the house to its Tudor appearance. The present, 18th Lord Petre, inherited the title in 1989, and renovated the house in order to open it to the public; he lives nearby, and his son lives in the south wing of Ingatestone.

The house is approached via a lime avenue. Visitors go under a clock tower in a picturesque range of outbuildings, 16C timber-framed work refaced in the 18C. The main house appears at the end of smooth lawns. Sir William Petre built a fairly regular square, quadrangular house, of two storeys, all of the local dark russet brick, with brick mullion and transom windows. In the 18C the east, or hall range was demolished. Visitors cross the site of the hall to enter by a modest doorway in the west wing. Inside, the first room seen is the Stone Hall, created from a number of smaller rooms in the 1930s, but convincingly done with a stone floor and good panelling. It has good English furniture, and the first of the house's very fine collection of portraits. Those of the Earls of Derwentwater commemorate the 3rd Earl, whose daughter married the 8th Lord Petre, and who was executed for his part in the 1715 Jacobite uprising. At the far end of the Hall, you enter the Drawing Room, a long low panelled room, with more interesting pictures, notably two by Stubbs, and two fine portraits of Henry VIII and Prince Edward from the studio of Holbein. From the Study, you can see one of Ingatestone's two Priest Holes, rediscovered in 1937.

Visitors can see the Main Staircase (but cannot ascend it, for the family occupies the first floor of this wing), which has more interesting portraits. Next is the Dining Room, with linenfold panelling and good tapestries, in particular an unusual portrait in Mortlake tapestry of Sir Francis Crane, owner of the factory. Beyond the Dining Room, the picturesque Old Kitchen houses the tea room. Visitors retrace their steps through the Drawing Room to ascend a spiral staircase. The bedroom at the top was described in 1600 as My Master's Lodging; Lord Petre's peer's robes are on display, and there are some 17C Dutch School pictures. The Queen Anne Room is one of the few in the house to retain its 18C decor, with deal panelling (unfortunately left in its stripped state) and a sash window. The furniture includes a splendid carved and gilded table, and there are early 18C portraits. The Gallery is 95ft long. Although it has lost its panelling, its basic form has remained the same since the house was built. It houses the bulk of the family portraits—over 40 of them—going from fine 16C likenesses of Sir William Petre and the 1st Lord up until the present generation. There are also cases with a variety of interesting objects on display—family documents, miniatures, plate from the family chapel, and the clothes worn by the 3rd Earl of Derwentwater at his execution.

SB

Layer Marney Tower

6m south of Colchester, from the B1022: Mr Nicholas Charrington, tel. 0206 330784. Open Apr–June 30 and Sept Sun, Thur 2–6; July–Aug Sun–Fri 2–6. BH 11–6. Refreshments.

Layer Marney Tower is a giant of a gatehouse, set between lower ranges of lodgings, in warm red brick. It represents all that was ever built of a great mansion, the brain-child of Henry, first Lord Marney. The Marney family, of French origin, were established here in the quiet coastal lands south of Colchester at least by the 1160s. They lived as country squires until the time of the 1st Lord. He inherited when very young, in 1463. He backed Henry VII's bid for the throne, and rose in the royal service as a result, fighting in battles to establish the new dynasty. He gained a string of important and profitable offices, and in 1520 he accompanied Henry VIII to the Field of the Cloth of Gold. In 1523 he was created Lord Marney, but he died a few weeks later. It is not known exactly when he started work on his own house, but by the time of this death he had built more or less what you see today. It is the front or entrance range of what would presumably have been a square courtyard-house, possibly even a two-courtyard house. He also demolished the old Norman church close by, and replaced it by the present handsome brick edifice.

His son, John, the 2nd Lord, only survived him by two years. He doubtless carried on work on the house, for his and his wife's initials appear at the top of one of the turrets. His executors sold Layer Marney to Sir Brian Tuke for £2000. Layer Marney then passed through various families, none of which apparently had the money or perhaps the desire to change the house much, until the early 20C. The north-west wing was added in 1900, and shortly afterwards a Mr de Zoete carried out a general renovation. He filled in a gap in the buildings which had appeared just east of the tower, laid out the gardens and generally made it a convenient country residence by the standards of the times. In 1959, the Charrington family bought the house, and it is theirs still.

The house is approached through a maze of winding lanes; the drive leads to the back of the gatehouse, or what would have been the courtyard-side had the house been finished. The archway was filled in to create an entrance hall in Edwardian times; the visitor enters here, and climbs a spiral staircase to the upper floors of the great tower. There are no historic contents to speak of, but there are displays on the history of the manor, and a new model of the house as it might have appeared had the Marneys completed their work. Recently, Mr Charrington has restored the ceiling of one of the big upper rooms in oak, with 24 carved and gilded bosses. From the roof there are panoramic views to the sea. A major feature of the house is the original, very early terracotta decoration; the terracotta parapet at the top has a pattern of shells and dolphins. The window-mullions are also of terracotta, in early Renaissance style with winged cherubs' heads.

The gallery, outside, is largely an Edwardian creation; it used to house stables below and lodging above. Just to the south east of the house is the parish church, also built by the 1st Lord Marney. It is all of brick, with Perpendicular-style windows created in brickwork; there was plaster rendering around these to simulate stonework, but this has worn away. Inside, there is a wagon-roof over the nave, and a flat panelled ceiling over the Marney Chapel. This stands on the north side of the chapel; the splendid Renaissance tombs of Sir William Marney, and of the 1st and 2nd Lords, with more early terracotta ornament, should not be missed. Emerging from the church, the great gatehouse dominates the view. It is similar in plan to those at the Cambridge colleges, only much bigger at over 80ft high, and much more ornate. It is extraordinary to find such architecture somewhere so remote, and the mind boggles as to how grand the rest of the house would have been, if it had been built.

SB

Paycocke's

On West St, Coggeshall, A120 between Colchester and Braintree:
National Trust, tel. 0376 561305. Open early Mar–early Oct Tues, Thurs,
Sun, BH Mon 2–5.30.

Paycocke's House is a handsome timber-framed town-house, standing hard
by the street-side in the large village of Coggeshall. It shows, as well as
anywhere, how a prosperous English merchant lived at the end of the
Middle Ages. It was built by John Paycocke for his son Thomas, on the
occasion of Thomas' marriage, and was probably completed by John's
death in 1505. Thomas Paycocke was a clothier; his business covered all
the activities from shearing the sheep, combing and spinning the wool, to
weaving and fulling the cloth. Coggeshall was an industrial town in the
early 16C, and this house was as much a place of business as a home.
Paycocke's and Coggeshall declined with the wool trade. The house was
divided into tenements in the 18C, and nearly demolished in the 19C. It
was saved by the awakening interest in English vernacular architecture,
and bought by Lord Noel Buxton, who carried out a full restoration, and in
1925 gave it to the National Trust. Lord Buxton was a descendant of the
Buxton family, who owned the house from the late 16C to the 18C.

The house stands on the High Street; the Fleece Inn immediately to the
right was also built by the Paycocke family. Paycocke's is roughly U-shaped,
and the street façade represents the bottom bar. The two wings extending
towards the garden are earlier. The impressive street façade is John
Paycocke's rebuilding of about 1500. Some of the wood-carving is from the
restoration of 1905, but the appearance of the house is probably authentic.
It is two storeys in height, the upper storey projecting. On both floors there
are slightly projecting oriel windows. The timbers of the frame are closely-
spaced, not because they needed to be, but as a demonstration of wealth.
There is some reason to think that there may originally have been a third
storey on top.

The Hall has been rearranged since Thomas Paycocke's time, but the
superb ceiling, with the beams all carved with Gothic tracery, is original.
The walls were left plain, not panelled, so were probably originally hung
with tapestry. To the left, the Dining Room has another fine carved ceiling
and excellent linenfold panelling. This may well have been Thomas
Paycocke's business-room, with its own entrance. On the other side of the
Hall is the Small Sitting Room, a more private room, but with the same
moulded ceiling-joists, and embattled carving on the wall plates; there is
a small permanent display of Coggeshall lace. Ascending the staircase (a
20C restoration), two bedrooms are on view, looking over the street. Both
have wonderful ceilings, with carved beams, and oak boards laid over
these, and oak arches to the doors. The garden was formerly a tentering
yard, where lengths of cloth were laid out to dry after fulling. In its present
form it was designed by Mrs Conrad Noel, wife of a vicar of Thaxted and
one-time tenant, and is the perfect foil for the house, with roses, wisteria
and lavender-beds.

SB

St Osyth's Priory

In St Osyth's, 12m south east of Colchester via B1027: Mr Somerset de
Chair, tel. 0255 820492. Open Easter weekend, then daily May–Sept;
gardens and ruins 10–5, art collection (not Sat) 10.30–12.30, 2.30–4.30.

St Osyth's Priory is a complex group of buildings and ruins, the work of
many centuries, created from the remains of an Augustinian priory. It
houses some major works of art, and is surrounded by beautiful gardens.

In Saxon times there was a nunnery here, of which Osyth, the daughter
of Frithwald, King of the East Angles, was the abbess. In 653 the Vikings
captured and plundered the nunnery, and Osyth herself was murdered. A
spring or fountain burst forth on the site of her martyrdom, which swiftly
gained a reputation for curing all manner of ills. Between 1108 and 1120,
an Augustinian priory was founded here, and became a wealthy
establishment, with relics which included St Osyth's arm. Much rebuilding
went on, and as late as 1527 Abbot Vytner was remodelling the Abbot's
Lodgings. In 1539 the property passed to Sir Thomas D'Arcy, Master of the
Ordnance in Henry VIII's reign and Vice-Chamberlain to Edward VI. He
seems to have demolished the church and much of the cloister buildings,
converting the north cloister range and the Abbot's House just to the north
west into a residence. It was good enough for his son, the 2nd Lord D'Arcy,
to entertain Queen Elizabeth there twice. The 3rd Lord D'Arcy had no son;
his daughter Elizabeth married Sir Thomas Savage, later Earl Rivers, and
she inherited the proprty.

During the Civil War, a mob of ardent Parliamentarians and reformers
sacked and looted the house, and it was not used as a main residence again
until about 1720, by which time it had passed to the Earls of Rochford. The
3rd Earl of Rochford added a large, fairly simple new wing to the house, to
make it a convenient modern residence. The 5th and last Earl of Rochford
left it to an illegitimate son early in the 19C, and after that it passed through
a number of hands. In 1954 it was bought by Mr Somerset de Chair, writer
and Member of Parliament, who has carried out careful repairs and
renovation of the buildings. He has filled St Osyth's with fine furniture and
paintings, and there are also very important paintings from the collection
of the Earls Fitzwilliam, which have come here through the Lady Juliet de
Chair.

St Osyth's is a pretty coastal village, with a pleasantly remote air. The
Priory stands just on one side, and is announced by the magnificent 15C
gatehouse, one of the grandest pieces of monastic architecture to survive
in Britain. The whole façade is covered in elaborate flushwork, a pattern
like window-tracery in limestone with the spaces between filled with
knapped flint. Over the arch are vigorous carvings of St Michael and the
Dragon, and the archway itself has very fine stone vaulting. Through this
is a very large courtyard, with level lawns surrounded by walls and
buildings of various dates, a little like an Oxbridge college or a cathedral
close. To the right is the site of the abbey church and the cloister, much of
it now occupied by two walled gardens, the Rose Garden and Topiary
Garden. On the north side of the Topiary Garden are the remains of the
D'Arcy house. The dominant feature is the 16C D'Arcy Tower, with its
octagonal corner turrets; there are fine views from the top. Adjoining this
is a large part of the original cloister-range, with a 13C vaulted interior,
fitted up as a chapel in the 19C, and nearby there are more ruined elements
of the 16C buildings.

The present house is L-shaped. The smaller, south wing (the Cellarer's Range) is of medieval and 16C construction. The larger north wing has three elements. There is part of the Abbot's Lodging, built in 1527 by Abbot Vytner, most notably the oriel window. This was incorporated into a plain Georgian house of brick, built by the 3rd Earl of Rochford. A large extension in Tudor style was added in the late 19C by Sir John Johnston. Visitors see a number of rooms in the Rochford wing. The finest paintings here come from the collection of the Earls Fitzwilliam, and were formerly at Wentworth Woodhouse in Yorkshire. The Whistlejacket Room is named after the famous life-size painting, by George Stubbs, of the stallion of that name, painted for the 1st ·Marquess of Rockingham; there is also a full-length portrait of Lord Rockingham by Reynolds, and fine Georgian furniture, in particular a set of Chinese Chippendale pieces. Abbot Vytner's Hall has early 16C panelling, moved from elsewhere in the Priory, and pictures by Stubbs, portraits by Honthorst and Lely, and Van Dyck's great double portrait of Strafford and his secretary. The Library has two more important paintings by Stubbs; other works of art include Chinese paintings of Ming dignitaries, and there are memorabilia of the de Chair family, in particular of Mr de Chair's role in the capture of Baghdad in 1941. The Colchester Dionysos is one of the finest Roman bronzes to have been found in Britain. The Banqueting Hall has more fine portraits, including a version of Van Dyck's of Strafford. Mr de Chair acquired the fine Tudor fireplace from the estate of William Randolph Hearst. Finally, the State Drawing Room lies behind the immense oriel window which dominates the façade of the main house, bearing 180 coats of arms. The big tapestry of the Battle of Issus is Flemish, of the 17C, and the room is filled with a great variety of objects, from a collection of historic letters, to a Red Indian head-dress.

SB

Shalom Hall

On the south side of Layer Breton village, 7m south west of Colchester, 2m from the A12: Lady Phoebe Hillingdon. Open Aug Mon–Fri 10–1, 12.30–5.30.

Shalom Hall is a pleasant early-19C house of yellow brick, the façade covered in yellow stucco, in scale and appearance like a comfortable country rectory. It houses the Hillingdon family's small but fine collection of French and English furniture and predominantly English paintings. The stove-paved Hall has English chairs, and is dominated by a long-case Louis XV clock, with Sèvres china of the same period. The Drawing Room, to the right, has English 18C portraits, with Gainsborough, Reynolds and Sir William Beechey all well represented. The Dining Room has mostly Regency furniture, and portraits by Reynolds and Gainsborough and a superb Louis XV clock in the style of Caffieri. A nearby Sitting Room has more French 18C furniture, and an interesting 17C portrait of Cosimo III as a boy, probably by Justus Sustermans. Finally, up the staircase is a superb Dutch portrait of a woman in black and white, worthy of Rembrandt or Hals, in fact by Moreelst.

SB

GLOUCESTERSHIRE

Berkeley Castle

Midway between Gloucester and Bristol, just off the A38. M5 exit 13 or 14:
Mr and Mrs R.J. Berkeley, tel. 0453 810332. Open Apr Tues–Sun 2–5;
May–Sept Tues–Sat 11–5, Sun 2–5; Oct Sun only 2–4.30; BH Mon 11–5.
Refreshments.

Of all inhabited English castles, Berkeley best preserves the character of a
medieval fortress-home of a great feudal lord and his household. The first
castle on the site was erected by William FitzOsborn, Earl of Hereford, soon
after the Norman Conquest, in order to command the flat meadowland
between the River Severn and the Bristol–Gloucester highway—strategically one of the most important sites in the south of England. The original
buildings were almost certainly of timber, and the nucleus of the present
formidable pile of dark red and grey sandstone is the shell keep constructed
around (not, unusually, on top of) the Norman motte in 1153–56 by Robert
FitzHardinge, the founder of St Augustine's Abbey in Bristol (now the
cathedral) and ancestor of the Berkeley family, which has retained possession of the castle ever since. Robert's son Maurice (d 1190) built the
fore-building protecting the approach to the keep and also constructed a
curtain wall around the bailey, and in the mid 14C his descendant, another
Maurice, rebuilt the hall, the kitchen and the main domestic quarters, all
of which survive largely intact.

By this time the castle had achieved notoriety as the place in which
Edward II was imprisoned and murdered in 1327 in a peculiarly brutal and
unpleasant manner (his magnificent tomb can be seen in Gloucester
Cathedral, partly rebuilt out of the proceeds of the cult which grew up
around his remains), but its subsequent history was relatively uneventful.
The castle passed through the female line in the 15C, and subsequently
came briefly into the hands of the Crown before being recovered by the
family in 1553. There was some damage during the Civil War, when it
changed hands twice, but it avoided being slighted by the Parliamentarian
troops and when George, Lord Berkeley, resumed possession, the medieval
buildings were still largely intact. His son, an important promoter of the
East India Company, was made Earl of Berkeley by Charles II in 1679, and
during the remainder of the 17C and 18C, succeeding Earls introduced a
varied collection of pictures, furniture and tapestries, which were
augmented in 1773 by items belonging to the Berkeleys of Stratton, a
distant branch of the family.

The Earls of Berkeley refrained from carrying out the large-scale structural alterations which took place at other medieval castles like Warwick
(qv.), but there was some internal remodelling in the time of William, Lord
FitzHardinge, who inherited the castle (but not the Berkeley title) in 1810.
The effect of these changes was largely obliterated between the two World
Wars by the 8th and last Earl, in whom the castle and the title were briefly
reunited. He was both a distinguished scientist and a well-informed
antiquary, and, with the help of Messrs. Keeble, a firm of architectural
decorators, he modified the exterior and successfully transformed the
interior by bringing in medieval and later fittings and architectural details,
both from elsewhere in the castle and from further afield (even from
abroad). When he died in 1942 the castle passed to a cousin, whose son

lives here with his family today and who is a direct descendant in the male line of the 12C Robert FitzHardinge.

The castle stands on the edge of the small town of Berkeley, from which it was, until recently, entered through a gateway leading into the **Outer Bailey**, whose walls were demolished during the Civil War. To the north of the bailey is the magnificent parish church, with an excellent collection of medieval tombs of the Berkeley family, while to the south are the terraces of the 17C **gardens**, overlooking a pastoral landscape and the castellated stables, dating from the mid 18C, built to house the kennels of the famous Berkeley Hunt. It is possible to walk around the circuit of the castle from the foot of the terraces, and from here the largely intact medieval structure can be seen, with huge buttresses projecting from the grim, unadorned walls.

The **Inner Bailey** is entered through a gatehouse squashed up against the massive 12C shell keep, a substantial part of which (to the left of the gatehouse) was blasted away during the Civil War and was never rebuilt. The 14C Hall, lit by tall square-headed traceried windows, lies at the further (east) end of the courtyard, with the original porch to the left and another porch at the 'upper' end to the right, added by the 8th Earl in the 1920s and incorporating French 15C stone carving around the doorway. The tour begins in the **Keep**, reached by a stone staircase in the mid-12C fore-building and entered through a round-arched doorway of the same date. Here Edward II spend his last days, having been 'courteously received' by Lord Berkeley, according to the author of the 17C *Lives of the Berkeleys*, but subsequently 'grievously tormented many days together' before being barbarously despatched by the henchmen of Berkeley's father-in-law, Roger Mortimer, leader of the opposition to the King, Lord Berkeley himself having been sent away. A bare room said to have been used by Edward II is shown to visitors, but the interior of the Keep was much altered by later generations, and it is now notable mainly for a selection of early portraits, including two by Paul van Somer of James I's son Prince Henry and his daughter Elizabeth, the 'Winter Queen'.

From here a 14C ogee-arched doorway leads through a room containing 17C ebony furniture—a reminder of the 1st Earl's interests in India—and then out of the Keep and into a plainly decorated **Picture Gallery** containing paintings by Van de Velde reflecting the seafaring interests of the Berkeleys in the late 17C, and others celebrating the enthusiasm of later members of the family for rural pursuits, notably a fine Stubbs ('Groom and Horses') and Ben Marshall's 'Old Berkeley Hounds'. There are also several good items of late-17C furniture, including marquetry tables, lacquered chairs and blue and white porcelain. The **Dining Room** below, originally part of the medieval service quarters, is hung with family portraits, including 20C members of the family, by Orpen and others, in their characteristic yellow (as opposed to the usual pink) hunting coats. From here passages lead to the magnificent hexagonal mid-14C **Kitchen** with its timber roof, and to the Housekeeper's Room, abutting onto the screens passage, with an 18C Gothic fireplace, a selection of 17C pictures mostly by Dutch and Flemish masters (eg, Michael Sweerts 'Interior of a Roman Workshop') and the 'Godwin Cup', traditionally said to have belonged to the Anglo-Saxon Earl Godwin, father of King Harold, but with an early-16C cover.

The finest interiors at Berkeley Castle are the Hall, dating from c 1340–50, and the chapel (now the Morning Room) of about the same date. The **Hall** retains its arch-braced timber roof, one of the best to survive in a medieval castle, but the painted 16C screen was brought in by the 8th Earl from Cefn Mably (Glamorgan). 17C Flemish tapestries of the story of Queen Esther are displayed at the high-table end, and over the fireplace (also a later addition) is an improbably elegant-looking Admiral Berkeley on a storm-tossed beach, by Gainsborough. A curious 14C stone arch of the so-called 'Berkeley' type (one of several in the castle) leads to a wooden staircase of 1637 and then to the **Morning Room**, with its painted timber roof containing verses from a translation of the Book of Revelation made by John Trevisa, one of the castle chaplains, in 1387; the arches leading into the narrow aisle formed within the thickness of the outer wall are exquisitely embellished with ogee-shaped cusps, characteristic of the late, ultra-refined period of English Decorated architecture. The rarified quality of the room was enhanced by the introduction of a French 15C fireplace and doorway by the 8th Earl, along with 16C and 17C wooden furniture and more excellent 17C tapestries. In medieval times the rooms to the west served as a great chamber and withdrawing chamber, but both have since been much altered. The former (now called the **Long Drawing Room**) is entered underneath the 15C carved wooden family pew from the former chapel, removed here by the 8th Earl, and contains an impressive set of gilded chairs, tables and mirrors of the 1720s and 1750s, while the latter (now the **Small Drawing Room**) contains more fine tapestries, this time by the 17C maker Jan Cobus, of scenes from Ovid's *Metamorphoses*; in the lobby between the rooms is an elegant 15C alabaster Madonna and Child. The rooms further west (the private apartments of successive lords of Berkeley Castle) are not open to the public, and visitors now retrace their steps to the main staircase, which leads down to a vaulted cellar under the former chapel, and then, via a passage, to the vaulted 14C porch to the Hall, through which the courtyard is regained.

GCT

Chavenage

2m north of Tetbury to west of B4014: D. Lowsley-Williams, tel. 0666 502329. Open Easter Sun, Mon and May–Sept Thurs, Sun, BH Mon 2–5. Guided tours.

Hidden away among narrow lanes in one of the less frequented parts of the Cotswolds, Chavenage is an old stone manor house dating for the most part from 1576 (the date on the porch) but almost certainly incorporating the remains of an earlier building. The builder was Edward Stephens, who bought the formerly monastic estate out of the profits of sheep farming in 1564, and had his initials carved on the porch together with those of his wife. There were some internal alterations in the early 17C, but the Stephens family never became unduly grand, and the house retained its Elizabethan and Jacobean character substantially unimpaired, save for some remodelling by Henry Willis Stephens in the late 18C or early 19C. The heavily mortgaged property was sold to the family of the present owner in 1891, and in 1904–5 George Hoole-Lowsley-Williams employed J.T. Michlethwaite to add a ballroom. Since then there have been few major changes.

The house faces east towards the road, and consists of a hall block with a porch projecting from the centre and two gabled wings; the classic 16C E-shaped plan. The walls are of grey rubble stone and the roofs of stone tiles, and there are tall mullioned and transomed windows lighting the Hall to the left of the porch, which has a Gothic first-floor window possibly salvaged from an earlier building. The south front, around the corner to the left, is more irregular, with the early-19C Billiard Room projecting at one end and the Arts and Crafts-influenced Ballroom at the other, next to the largely 19C Chapel with a west tower built originally as a folly.

The entrance leads through the usual screens passage into the Hall, extending the full height of the house, with fragments of medieval stained glass in the windows and an impressive classical chimneypiece on the west wall, dating from the second half of the 17C and adorned with coats of arms and marble panels. A staircase at the former 'upper' end leads to two bedrooms on the first floor of the south wing, named after Oliver Cromwell and Henry Ireton, who are said to have visited the house in 1648 in order to persuade the then owner, Nathaniel Stephens, MP for Gloucestershire and one of Cromwell's relatives by marriage, to agree to Charles I's execution—a visit which led to one of the best of all country-house ghost stories, told with relish on the guided tour. Both rooms retain their 17C character to a marked degree, due largely to the excellent state of preservation of their tapestry hangings (note especially the early-17C Flemish 'verdure' tapestries with their original borders in the Cromwell Room). The Library on the ground floor has largely lost its original character, but the adjacent Oak Room—the original parlour—contains gilded panelling bearing the date 1627, including four reset panels supposedly depicting the Four Muses below the Tree of Life. Leading out of the Library is the early-19C Billiard Room, originally built as a dining-room and hung with portraits and copies of Old Master paintings, and beyond the present Dining Room and Ballroom of 1905 is the Chapel, to which a spectral monk is said to be an occasional visitor.

GCT

Little Dean Hall

At Littledean, 2m east of Cinderford, off A4151: D.M. Macer-Wright, tel. 0594 824213. Open Apr–Oct daily 11–5.30. Refreshments.

The Forest of Dean contains fewer country houses than the more squire-archical Cotswolds to the east, and few of those that exist are of any great moment from an artistic or architectural point of view. Little Dean Hall is an unassuming building both internally and externally, but it stands on a site of great archaeological interest and contains what may be the remains of an Anglo-Saxon hall embedded into the later structure. The house stands on high ground to the west of the River Severn, close to the recently excavated remains of a Roman temple. It is a rambling, irregular stone building arranged around an irregular courtyard, with the main rooms in a north-facing range which seems to date from after 1612, when the manor was bought by Charles Bridgeman. Some of the interiors were remodelled by members of the Pyrke family, which bought the estate from the Bridgemans in 1664, and in 1852 the exterior was remodelled in a neo-Jacobean style by Duncombe Pyrke, with a row of small gables and mullioned and transomed windows. There is a good deal of 17C and later panelling inside the house, and items found in excavations on the site are on display. The cellar, which may represent the surviving part of the sunken Anglo-Saxon hall, is also shown to visitors. If it is indeed what it is claimed to be, it must be the oldest room in any English country house open to the public.

GCT

Owlpen Manor

1m east of Uley off B4066 Stroud–Dursley: Mr & Mrs Nicholas Mander, tel. 0453 860261. Open Apr–Sept Tues, Thur, Sun, BH Mon 2–5.30.

Few English houses are more seductively beautiful than this manor house of grey limestone, tucked away in a deep, wooded valley near the western escarpment of the Cotswolds. There was a house here in the Middle Ages, and some of its structure survives in the east wing of the present L-shaped building. In 1464 the estate came by marriage to the Daunt family, and at some time between 1542 and 1573 the present south-facing hall range was built, probably on the site of the medieval hall, with mullioned windows and a wide triangular gable on the top floor. The bay-windowed parlour wing to the west carries the date 1616 and the initials of Thomas Daunt. In 1719–21 another Thomas Daunt remodelled the service end to the east of the hall with new sash windows outside and Georgian panelling within. The main façade thus acquired the agreeably varied appearance which to modern eyes constitutes a large part of its charm. Daunt also laid out a formal garden to the south of the house, with terraces and yew hedges which later grew to a great height; they figure prominently in an engraving by the 20C artist F.L. Griggs which can be seen in the house.

For a century and a half after the 1770s, Owlpen was virtually abandoned by the Daunts, who had estates in Ireland, and by their successors the Stoughtons. The house thus escaped the 19C zeal for 'improvement' and restoration. It was 'discovered' by aficionados of picturesque Cotswold manor houses in the early 20C, but by then it was rapidly falling into decay. Salvation came from Norman Jewson, a follower of the Arts and Crafts-inspired architect and furniture designer Ernest Gimson; he bought the house in 1925 and restored it as his own residence, employing the 'conservative' principles first adumbrated by William Morris. After two more sales it was acquired in 1974 by the present owner, a descendant of the Manders of Wightwick Manor, Staffordshire (qv.). He and his wife have sympathetically maintained the interior much as Jewson left it, introducing appropriate furniture and pictures, and they have also recreated the 18C formal garden to the south.

The house is part of a 'manorial complex' which includes the church—a largely 19C building with lavish mosaics and stained glass—a medieval barn, a mill with a curious cupola, and sundry outbuildings, some of which are now used as holiday cottages. The entrance is through the east (service) wing, and before exploring the interior it is worth walking through the Hall to see the south front and the walled garden sloping down to the valley, with a pair of early-18C gate-piers and a stream beyond. Inside, there is workmanship of different dates co-existing harmoniously in the manner prized by the Arts and Crafts movement. The Hall contains good, solid 17C furniture, plasterwork by Gimson and a settle by Jewson's father-in-law Sidney Barnsley. A doorway with an elaborate classical frame of 1719–21 by Henry Fryer of Bristol leads into the Little Parlour, furnished with 18C English pieces. There is some early panelling in the Oak Parlour on the other side of the Hall, and upstairs, in the former great chamber (now a bedroom), there is a set of late-17C 'painted cloths', once very common in smaller country houses, depicting the story of Joseph from the Old Testament. They have always been in the house, and their survival adds to the sense of timelessness which pervades it.

GCT

Sezincote

1½m west of Moreton-in-Marsh to south of A44 Chipping Norton–Evesham; Mr and Mrs D. Peake. Open May–July and Sept Thurs, Fri 2–6 (gardens same days and BH Mon throughout year except Dec 2–6). Guided tours.

This extraordinary house represents the high water mark of Indian influences on English country house architecture. Sezincote (the name probably derives from the Anglo-Saxon word for gravel) was bought in 1795 by a 'nabob', Sir Charles Cockerell, and about ten years later his younger brother Samuel Pepys Cockerell, a successful London architect and Surveyor to the East India Company, designed the house with the help of the much-travelled topographical artist, Thomas Daniell. Daniell also gave advice on the architectural embellishment of the gardens, in the design of which Humphry Repton also played a part. The estate was sold to James Dugdale in 1885, and in 1944 his daughter-in-law sold it to Sir Cyril Kleinwort, whose daughter lives here now with her husband. Both house and grounds are immaculately kept up, and together they represent one of the most attractive surviving examples of an early-19C country house in its original setting.

The house stands high up in the shelter of the Cotswolds, commanding an expansive pastoral view to the east. Both house and setting embody the aesthetics of the 'picturesque' which Repton and his contemporaries publicised so effectively. Visitors pass first, by means of an Indian-style bridge, over a steep valley planted with exotic trees and shrubs, with a shrine to Suriya, the sun-god, overlooking a pool at the head. First seen at an oblique angle, the house itself is asymmetrically planned, with contrasting façades of honey-coloured stone, quarried locally and possibly artificially stained to make it look more authentically Indian. There is abundant use of Indian decorative devices (both Muslim and Hindu), in particular the projecting *chujja* or cornice and the turrets or *chatris* at the corners, topped with domes like solar topees. At the top of the house is a larger, onion-shaped dome anticipating those added to the Royal Pavilion at Brighton about ten years later, after the Prince Regent had been to Sezincote. To the south is a curved semicircular wing housing the conservatory and ending in an octagonal pavilion; it enfolds a formal garden of the type which Repton often advocated as appropriate for the immediate surroundings of the house (but actually created by Lady Kleinwort in 1968), while to the east ruminant cows graze on the other side of a ha-ha.

Though Indian from the outside, Sezincote is, as John Betjeman remarked in his verse autobiography *Summoned by Bells*, 'coolest Greek within'—a contrast which would have seemed less remarkable in the early 19C than it does to us now. Unusually for an early-19C house, the main rooms are placed on a first-floor piano nobile; they are reached by a double-flight staircase resting on exposed iron girders and lit by lunette windows under the dome, and there are panels of Aubusson tapestry on the walls. The most impressive room is the Drawing Room, with splendidly lavish draped curtains around the bow window overlooking the formal garden. One of the bedrooms contains a bed with a canopy resting on 'spears' taken from Sir Charles Cockerell's tent room at the end of the north or service wing, and the Dining Room downstairs has been appropriately decorated with exotic wallpaper by George Oakes which admirably captures the spirit of this singular house.

GCT

Snowshill Manor

3m south west of Broadway: National Trust, tel. 0386 852410. Open Apr and Oct Sat, Sun 11–1, 2–5; May–Sept Wed–Sun, BH Mon 11–1, 2–6.

This strange house, well situated in an unspoilt though much-visited village in one of the most beautiful parts of the Cotswolds, owes its present character to the obsessive collecting habits of its last private owner. The house itself is a good example of a small Cotswold manor house, with a late-medieval hall range 'floored over' in the late 16C and a hipped-roofed entrance front dating in its present form from the early 18C, all built in the local limestone with roofs of stone slates. During the Middles Ages, the manor belonged to the Benedictine Abbey of Winchcombe, not far away, and after the Dissolution it passed through several families before settling in the hands of William Sambach in 1712. He created the new entrance front—architecturally the most memorable part of the building—by widening and reroofing the formerly gabled south end of the existing house, but the estate was sold in 1759, and from the end of the 18C the house was occupied by a succession of tenant farmers.

In 1919 it was bought by Charles Paget Wade, an architect who had worked for a time in the office of Raymond Unwin, and while there had imbued the artistic philosophy of the Arts and Crafts movement. He subsequently restored it in the 'conservative' manner expounded by the movement's founding father, William Morris, brought in his fellow-architect M.H. Baillie-Scott to help create a new garden, and filled the house with an increasingly diverse collection of craftsmanship which, as time went on, gave it a character far removed from the wholesome rustic simplicity shown in photographs taken in the early years of his tenure. In 1951 he gave the whole property to the National Trust and retired to the West Indies, where he owned a sugar plantation.

The house is approached from the south by a pathway leading through chunky 18C gate-piers to the entrance front, an attractive though lopsided composition with sash windows to the left, mullioned and transomed windows to the right and the doorway slightly off-centre—a discrepancy explained by the fact that the façade represents an enlargement of an already existing building. A longer front, containing the original hall, faces west, partly hidden by the smaller 'Priest's House', with the terraced gardens, like those of many Arts and Crafts-inspired houses, descending the hill slope below. After this homely, well-mannered prelude, the dark interior, pervaded by the omnipresent ticking of clocks, comes as something of a shock. Charles Wade intended it not so much to please in any conventional way, or to evoke a particular period of the past, as to express his own philosophy of craftsmanship and design. Objects ranging from ship models to lacquered cabinets and Japanese Samurai armour, from old bicycles and musical instruments to looms and other relics of vanished rural crafts, are arranged together in rooms which have lost all semblance of ever having been lived in. The Priests' House, in which Charles Wade lived a Spartan life, is if anything even odder, calling to mind the observation of Queen Mary in 1937 that the most remarkable part of the collection was its owner.

GCT

Stanway House

10m north west of Stow-on-the-Wold on B4077, 1m east of junction with B4632 Cheltenham–Broadway: Lord Neidpath, tel. 038673 469. Open June–Sept Tues, Thurs 2–5.

Stanway is beautifully situated at the foot of the western Cotswold escarpment, with the hills rising steeply behind the ochre-coloured stone house and the vale of the Severn stretching away towards the Malvern Hills in the west. The manor was part of the large holdings of Tewkesbury Abbey in the Middle Ages, and at the Dissolution of the Monasteries it was purchased by Richard Tracy, a younger son from a local family living at Toddington, a mile away. He adapted the 'fair stone house' of the Abbots as his home, and this was greatly extended by his three successors, starting with his son Paul, who inherited in 1569 and was made a baronet by James I, and finishing in the time of the 3rd Baronet after the Civil War. There was some internal remodelling in the 1720s, and a garden was subsequently laid out on the hillside behind the house, culminating in 1750 with an impressive pyramid above a cascade of water which the present owner is beginning to restore. Since then there have been relatively few changes.

When the last of the male Tracys died in 1773, the estate passed to two daughters in succession, the second of whom married the son of the 7th Earl of Wemyss in the Scottish peerage, and for the last hundred years the house has usually been occupied, as it is now, by the eldest son of the current Earl. Lord Elcho (later the 11th Earl) and his wife, who lived at Stanway from 1883 to 1937, were leading luminaries of the self-consciously intellectual aristocratic group which called itself 'The Souls', and the house appears in several of the memoirs of the period as a setting for their house-parties. There were some demolitions after the Second World War, but the main part of the house remains intact.

The usual approach is from the south, and the first part of the house to be seen is the gatehouse, a splendidly extravagant structure of c 1630 placed, most unusually, at right angles to the house, and surmounted by three elaborately shaped gables with a Gothic archway enclosed within a classical frame. Visitors do not enter through here, but proceed past the parish church (which contains a war memorial with lettering by Eric Gill) to a separate entrance next to a magnificent 14C tithe barn. From here the main (west) front of the house can be seen, probably dating from the 1580s, with four regularly spaced gables and a huge mullioned and transomed bay window at the south end lighting what was the high-table end of the Hall; a most satisfying composition which can vie with anything in late-16C

English domestic architecture. To the left (north) is the stable block, designed by the Scottish architect William Burn in 1859–60 (and very restrained in character), and around a corner to the right of the bay window is a two-storeyed south-facing range, probably started in the 1630s but possibly interrupted by the Civil War and not finished until 1670, a date which appears on rainwater heads. It contains the main reception rooms leading off from the 'upper' end of the Hall and has a symmetrical façade, with mullioned windows of the traditional kind and ornamental cresting on the roof-line instead of the more usual gables—a clear attempt by the mason-architect (possibly one of the Strong dynasty) to come to terms with new fashions. Until 1948 there was also a north range at the opposite side of the hall block, but this has gone and the house is now L-shaped.

The entrance is at the service end of the house, and the first room to be seen is the Audit Room, where house and farm tenants still pay their rents in person. There are several family portraits here, together with a somewhat naïve view of the house from the east in 1748 with a rectangular canal in the foreground (it has since been drained), and a Chelsea dessert service of c 1755 with attractive designs of plants and insects. The lofty and spacious Hall, entered through a Doric screen in place of the former passage, is flooded with light from the huge bay window, and contains a long shuffleboard table of c 1620 and some early-18C Brussels tapestries. Next, up some stairs in the south range (built on a slope, contrary to external appearances) comes the wood-panelled Drawing Room, with a neo-Jacobean plaster ceiling introduced in the 19C. The two extraordinary day beds of c 1760 with Chinese canopies were made, almost certainly by Chippendale, for Amisfield House in Scotland, then home of the 7th Earl of Wemyss. His son Francis, Lord Elcho, married Susan Tracy, and her portrait by Romney hangs in the room, along with another by the same artist of her three children (over the fireplace), one by Raeburn of Francis, Lord Elcho, and two erotic fantasies of c 1770 by the French artist L.-J.-F. Lagrenée. The Old Library, with a Gothic overmantel, contains an unusual early-18C double portrait of Robert and John Tracy, and in Lady Elcho's Sitting Room there are portraits by Sargent and Leighton, and one by Poynter (1886) of a soulful Lady Elcho, whose 'charm, humour, humanity and vagueness' are, it is said, still warmly remembered at Stanway. These constitute what James Lees-Milne has aptly called 'a nostalgic little museum of a recent but totally vanished phase of British civilization'. More late-19C portraits hang upstairs in two bedrooms, including one of Lady Elcho as a girl (by Val Prinsep, 1879) and another by G.F. Watts of Lady Granby, painted in the same year.

GCT

Sudeley Castle

East of Winchcombe on B4632 Cheltenham–Stratford: Lord and Lady Ashcombe, tel. 0242 602308. Open Apr–Oct daily 12–5 (grounds 11–5.30). Refreshments.

Sudeley is not so much a castle as a large 15C and 16C nobleman's country house which has had an unusually chequered history. It was first built c 1442, around two courtyards, by Ralph Boteler, Lord Sudeley, a leading follower of the Lancastrian kings who had been Admiral of the Fleet in the French wars of Henry V and VI. In 1469 he was obliged to sell it to the

Yorkist Edward IV who conveyed it to his brother Richard, Duke of Gloucester, later Richard III. Richard rebuilt the south or inner courtyard, including the hall, in a suitably magnificent manner, and the house remained Crown property until Edward VI gave it in 1547 to Thomas Seymour, newly created Lord High Admiral, on his marriage to Catherine Parr, the last of Henry VIII's wives. They lived here in great splendour, but Catherine died in the following year and in 1549 Seymour was executed by order of his brother the Lord Protector Somerset, who shortly afterwards followed him to the block. In 1554 the house was granted by Queen Mary to Sir John Brydges, 1st Lord Chandos, lieutenant of the Tower of London and formerly constable of Sudeley; and his son, the 2nd Lord, made extensive alterations, especially to the outer courtyard, c 1572. The house became a Royalist headquarters during the Civil War and, after a series of sieges, it was slighted by order of Parliament in 1649. It later passed by marriage to the Pitts of Stratfield Saye, Hampshire (qv.), and, as ruins became fashionable in the 18C, it became a favourite destination for sightseers, including George III, who fell down one of the staircases and was caught by the housekeeper.

The restoration of Sudeley resulted from its acquisition in 1837 by two antiquarian-minded glove makers from Worcester, John and William Dent. They immediately set about transforming the dilapidated buildings into a romantic recreation of a Tudor country house, employing as their architect a Worcester man Harvey Eginton, grandson of the well-known glass painter Francis Eginton; they also furnished the house with appropriate historical items, including several purchased at the sale of the contents of Horace Walpole's Strawberry Hill in 1842. Their nephew, John Coucher Dent, who inherited in 1855, created the present formal gardens and in 1859–63 brought in Gilbert Scott and his draughtsman J.D. Wyatt to restore the adjacent church (ruined in the Civil War), where Catherine Parr is buried; Wyatt subsequently made still more alterations to the house. When Dent died the house passed to his widow and then to their nephew, from whom it has descended to the present owners. The interior has again been remodelled in the 20C, and the picture collection augmented by works originally acquired in the early 19C by James Morrison of Basildon Park, Berks (qv.), and inherited by Lady Ashcombe.

The present house occupies the north, or outer courtyard, originally given over to lodgings and dating largely in its present form from the 2nd Lord Chandos's rebuilding in the 1570s. Before entering, it is worth seeing the much-restored 15C **church** to the east containing J.B. Philip's beautiful effigy of Catherine Parr (1859), and also the Victorian formal garden close to the shell of the magnificent late-15C great chamber or Banqueting Hall in the **south (inner) courtyard**. This, together with the hall (probably in the vanished south range), was the ceremonial centre of the life of the house until its destruction in the Civil War, and was lit by huge Perpendicular-traceried windows high up on the walls. The opposite (west) side of the inner courtyard contained the service area (now the restaurant and shop), flanked by the fortress-like Portmare Tower, believed to be named after a ransomed French admiral, and Dungeon Tower (now housing craft work-shops and a design exhibition) of c 1442.

The house was originally entered through a gatehouse still visible in the centre of the north front, but the present entrance is through a tower of 1889 at the north-east corner of the outer courtyard. This leads into the **North Hall** containing landscapes by Jacob van Ruisdael and Cuyp, Parmigianino's 'Mystic Marriage of St Catherine', a bust of Oliver Cromwell by Edward Pierce, and a waistcoat said to have belonged to Charles I. A staircase leads from here to the first floor, from which the courtyard can be seen, and also the **Drawing Room** over the gatehouse, with pictures by Rubens and others. A Victorian bedroom suite follows and then the **Oak Lobby**, with 16C and 17C stained glass in the windows and two poetic Turner landscapes, of Stourhead, Wilts (qv.), and Pope's villa at Twickenham on the walls. A nearby bedroom contains a massive four-poster said to have belonged to Charles I. The **Queen's Bedroom** contains another grand four-poster furnished with an Aubusson bedcover and hangings formerly belonging to Marie Antoinette. On the far wall is a remarkable picture of the family of Henry VIII, attributed to Lucas de Heere and commissioned by Elizabeth c 1570–75 to present to Sir Francis Walsingham; it shows doll-like figures of the King flanked on one side by Queen Mary, her husband Philip II of Spain and Mars, God of War, and on the other by Queen Elizabeth with the Goddesses of Peace and Bounty. Also displayed in this room are Elizabeth's christening robe, Catherine Parr's prayer book and the love letter she addressed to Thomas Seymour accepting his hand in marriage. At the end of the corridor is the shrine-like **Catherine Parr Room**, an untouched early- Victorian period-piece with excellent woodwork and stained glass by Thomas Willement and others, and a splendidly ornate plaster ceiling.

The south staircase, with a stained-glass portrait of Elizabeth, leads down to a corridor, containing copies of Holbein drawings at Windsor made by the antiquarian George Vertue and hung by Horace Walpole in the Holbein Chamber at Strawberry Hill. The **Library** contains Charles I's dispatch case, and also a magnificent late-16C floral tapestry (probably intended as a table cloth), made at the Sheldon factory at Barcheston, Warwickshire, with roundels showing the Expulsion from Paradise, and personifications of Justice, Temperance, Providence and Charity against a floral background. The classical fireplace with the initials of the 2nd Lord Chandos and the date 1560 was originally in an upstairs room; on either side of it are hung Van Dyck's 'Infant Jesus with St John' and Jan Steen's tender 'Grace Before Meat'. A display of lace and embroidery, including some reputedly made by Anne Boleyn, is housed in a corridor, now entered through the former Garderobe Tower, linking the east and west ranges.

GCT

Whittington Court

4½m east of Cheltenham on A40 Cheltenham–Oxford:
Mrs R.J. Charleston, tel. 0242 820218. Open 16 days after Easter Sat and 17 days in August leading up to and including BH Mon 2–5.

This attractive manor house of Cotswold ashlar stone stands within the remains of a medieval moat, next to a small parish church of Norman origin and close to the site of a Roman villa. The builder was probably John Cotton, whose father acquired the freehold of the estate in 1545, and it is assumed that the house was ready for Queen Elizabeth to visit it en route for Sudeley Castle (qv.) in 1592. There were important changes in the 17C, notably the addition of a staircase onto the south side in or before 1657 and the rebuilding of the east range (to the left of the present entrance), which has a hipped roof in contrast to the gables of the 16C hall block; there may also once have been a range to the west, but if so it has long disappeared. As a result of these alterations the house now has an irregular and somewhat lopsided, though undoubtedly picturesque, appearance which has changed little over the last 300 years. The estate was sold in the mid 18C, and, with the house, which by then had probably become a farmhouse, became part of the larger Sandywell Park estate nearby. It became a gentleman's residence again in the later 19C, and for most of the 20C was occupied by members of the Lawrence family of Sandywell and Seven-hampton Manor, the last of whom bequeathed it in 1985 to the present owner, along with a collection of portraits and furniture going back to the 17C and removed here at different dates from the family's other homes.

The house now has a welcoming atmosphere, and the furnishings are sympathetically displayed in a series of light, spacious rooms, notably the Hall in the main block, and the Library in the east wing, with a massive late 16C stone chimneypiece based on a design in Serlio's *Architettura*, and splendid bookcases, made originally for Sandywell and attributed to the Gillow firm. The handsome wooden staircase still retains its original gate to prevent dogs (and small children?) from ascending to the first floor, but the finials on the newel posts were apparently removed in the 19C when sacks of grain were stored on the top floor, and the upstairs rooms, where there are more handsome late-16C chimney-pieces, have been much altered and divided up. Outside there is a good collection of farm buildings, including a barn with the date 1614 inscribed on it.

GCT

Woodchester Park

½m from Nympsfield, off B4066 Stroud–Dursley· Woodchester Mansion Trust, tel. 0453 860531 or 750455. Open first weekend in each month, BH weekends and one week in July. Guided tours. Refreshments.

Even in its uncompleted state, Woodchester Park is one of the major monuments of the Gothic Revival in England. The house stands at the end of a long drive in a secluded valley near the western Cotswold escarpment, on land which was bought in 1845 by William Leigh from the 2nd Lord Ducie. The son of a Liverpool merchant, Leigh was a recent convert to Roman Catholicism, and soon after buying the estate he commissioned his fellow convert Augustus Welby Pugin to produce designs for a new house and also for a Dominican priory to be built near the village of Woodchester, some distance away. Pugin's schemes were set aside, mainly on the grounds of cost, and the priory was eventually built in 1846–49 to the designs of C.F. Hansom, President of the Bristol Society of Architects (the church survives, but the monastic buildings have been demolished).

Work on the house did not begin until 1854, by which time Pugin had died. Leigh, who was living in another house on the estate, chose as his architect one of Hansom's assistants, the 21-year-old Benjamin Bucknall, who had been born only two miles away. He was fascinated by Gothic construction, and later struck up a friendship with the French architect and theorist, Eugne Viollet-le-Duc, whose publications he read before design-ing the house. Work proceeded slowly, and in 1868, for reasons which have never been satisfactorily explained, it came to a complete halt, with the walls and roofs completed but the rooms still empty shells and many of the floors not laid. Leigh died in 1873, and his descendants chose not to finish the house, but not to demolish it either. It was sold in 1938, and was kept in good repair until the 1980s, when accelerating decay and vandalism prompted the local authority to buy and repair it with the help of a grant from English Heritage. It is now managed by a charitable trust which plans to use it as a centre for the study of stonemasonry and building conservation.

The house is built of the superb cream-coloured local limestone, and it is vaulted in stone throughout, with wood being used only for the rafters (it would also have been used for some of the upper floors and ceilings, had they ever been completed). The result is a *tour de force* of building construction. The house is built around a courtyard, with the main rooms in a tall, gabled south-facing block lit by large mullioned and transomed windows between projecting buttresses to counteract the outward thrust of the stonework within; the fanciful-looking gargoyles serve the functional purpose of draining water from the roof. A vaulted Chapel with an east window of Decorated Gothic tracery projects from the east range, and a tower rises from the courtyard side of the west or entrance range.

Inside, there is much of interest, despite the fact that only two rooms—the Drawing Room and Chapel—are in anything like their completed form. When work ceased in 1868 the builders simply abandoned the site, and some of their ladders and even the wooden centerings for the stone arches remain where they were left. There are some impressive spaces—especially the main Staircase which rises on the inner side of the south range—and also some quirky details, like the water outlets in the shower room, in the form of leopards' heads, and the massive bath carved from a single block of stone. These combine to make Woodchester one of the most memorable, and also one of the most beautiful houses of its date in England.

GCT

HAMPSHIRE

Avington Park

4m north east of Winchester to south of B3047: Mr and Mrs J. B. Hickson, tel. 0962 779260. Open May–Sept Sun, BH Mon 2.30–5.30. Guided tours. Refreshments.

This large brick house occupies an idyllic site in the lush meadows of the Itchen valley, praised by the often critical William Cobbett as 'one of the prettiest places in the country'. The land belonged to Winchester Cathedral during the Middle Ages, and was seized by the King at the Reformation before being sold to Edmund Clerk, whose descendants lived here until 1665. The manor was then bought by George Brydges (d 1713), one of Charles II's courtiers, and the façade of the house as we see it today is essentially his. At the centre is a giant Tuscan portico, not unlike that of The Vyne (qv.), and on either side are four-bay wings; the two bays on either side of the portico may stand on the site of the wings of the previous house, but the outer bays are entirely of Brydges's time. The work could date from the 1670s, with some alterations (eg, the segment-headed sash windows) following the early 18C, but there is no firm evidence, and the architect remains unknown.

When George Brydges's son died in 1751 the estate passed to his cousin, James Brydges, Marquess of Carnarvon and, from 1771, 3rd Duke of Chandos. He carried out major alterations, adding the three lead statues on top of the portico, remodelling the sides of the wings, and transforming the interior. He also built the attractive parish church (1768–71) overlooking the south lawn, and this remains almost untouched with its box pews, three-decker pulpit and family monuments; there is also a fountain on the lawn which is said to have come from the family's magnificent house at Cannons, Middlesex, demolished in 1747. The title died out on the death of the 3rd Duke in 1789, but it was revived for his son-in-law, who became Duke of Buckingham and Chandos in 1822. He and his wife lived mainly at the new Duke's ancestral seat at Stowe, Bucks (qv.), using Avington as a secondary residence to which the Prince Regent and Mrs Fitzherbert were frequent visitors, but the estate was sold by the 2nd Duke in 1848 as a result of the financial disaster which also caused the dispersal of the contents of Stowe. The new owner was Sir John Shelley, younger brother of the poet Percy Bysshe Shelley, and he built two spectacular iron and glass conservatories onto the south front c 1850. The house remained in the Shelley family until 1952, when it was sold to the present owners, the contents having been dispersed at auction. Much of the building has since been divided into flats, but a small number of the main reception rooms have remained relatively untouched and are now shown to visitors.

The two-storeyed house sits firmly on the low-lying ground among extensive lawns, overlooked by the church on a hillside to the south. The exterior is a satisfying study in brick craftsmanship, the brownish colour of the walls contrasting with the deep red of the window surrounds and the white paint of the sash bars, balustrade and portico. The rich though somewhat chilly interiors, dating mainly from the later 18C and 19C, owe more to Continental than English decorative fashion. The Entrance Hall, with ceiling paintings by Clermont (c 1780), leads to the main staircase, and this gives access to the large, empty Ballroom, over the Hall, with late-18C gilded pier-glasses, ceiling paintings attributed to Vicenzo Valdré, who also worked at Stowe, and some earlier painted panels which may survive from the late-17C house. Next door is the Red Drawing Room, also dating fundamentally from the late 18C, but modified in the first half of the 19C, when costumed figures of medieval and Tudor royalty in fanciful surrounds were painted onto the walls; there is also some Empire-style furniture of the same period. The tour concludes in the less grandiose Library, on the ground floor of the south wing, which retains some late-18C Pompeian-style paintings on black backgrounds on either side of the fireplace. The present owner has introduced mementoes of his military career in Africa and the Far East, including a flag captured from the Japanese during the Second World War. From here a door leads out into the first of the two south-facing conservatories built against a wall hiding the service quarters.

GCT

Beaulieu Palace House

In Beaulieu, 7m south east of Lyndhurst on B3054/B3056: Lord Montagu of Beaulieu, tel. 0590 612345. Open all year daily (not Christmas) 10–5 (Easter–Oct 10–6). Refreshments.

For most visitors to Beaulieu the great attraction is the excellent National Motor Museum established by the present Lord Montagu. The house is a much smaller and more modest building standing on the edge of the museum grounds, close to the village and Beaulieu River. A large Cistercian abbey was established here in 1204 on the site of a royal hunting lodge in the New Forest, but in 1538 is was suppressed and the property acquired by Thomas Wriothesley, a protégé of Thomas Cromwell who was later made Earl of Southampton. He demolished the monastic church and many of the ancillary buildings, leaving intact only the early-13C refectory, which became the parish church, the outer gatehouse, the massive 14C inner gatehouse, which form the core of the present Palace House (the name goes back to the 16C), and the lay brothers' dormitory building, which is now a Banqueting Hall and houses an exhibition on the history of the abbey; the foundations of the church and the ruins of some of the other monastic buildings can be seen nearby.

The Earl established his main residence at Titchfield, another former monastery, and for another three centuries the house at Beaulieu was used as an occasional residence and as a centre for administering the estate. When the 4th Earl died in 1667 the estate passed to his youngest daughter, who married the 1st Duke of Montagu (cf. Boughton, Northants). It then followed the descent of Boughton to the Dukes of Buccleuch, but in 1867 the 5th Duke settled it on his second son Lord Henry Scott, the grandfather of the present owner. He employed Sir Arthur Blomfield to restore and enlarge the house in 1871–74, and it has since remained much as he left it, except for some refurbishment after the Second World War.

The first view of the house, from the west, is of a largely late 19C building in the 'Old English' style with the jumbled assortment of gables and mullioned and transomed windows found in many houses of the period. Closer inspection reveals that the south (right-hand) part of the building is made up of the medieval abbey gatehouse, with the original Gothic-arched windows set in the rubble-stone walls and a pair of parallel gabled roofs added in the 16C or 17C. The tour takes in the main rooms in the older part of the house (the family live in the Victorian service wing at the back), but it starts in the Entrance Hall and Picture Gallery (formerly the Library), to the left, both of which were part of Blomfield's additions; the latter contains a selection of Wriothesley and Montagu portraits, including one of the 1st Earl of Southampton (over the fireplace). In monastic times the passage through the gatehouse was vaulted in stone, and the main Dining Room and the adjacent Lower Drawing Room, which were formed out of this passageway, still have impressive rib-vaulted roofs which may or may not be original; the vaults were certainly there in the early 19C, but the rest of the detailing, including the hefty stone chimneypieces, is clearly Blomfield's. Items on display include a 14C bread cupboard in the Dining Room and a selection from a series of views of Italy by Antonio Joli painted c 1759 for Lord Brudenell, an enthusiastic Grand Tourist whose father, the 4th Earl of Cardigan, owned the estate in the later 18C. The first floor consisted of two chapels in monastic times, and the piscina is still visible in the Upper Drawing Room, next to the east window with its Decorated tracery, but the decoration is largely by Blomfield, as is that of the Private Dining Room; more of Joli's views are hung under the gaze of Lord Brudenell, whose Grand Tour portrait by Anton Raphael Mengs (1758) is over the fireplace (another, by Pompeo Batoni, can be seen at Boughton).

GCT

Breamore House

3m north of Fordingbridge off A338 Bournemouth–Salisbury: Sir Westrow Hulse, Bt, tel. 0725 22468. Open Apr Sun, Tues, Wed; May–Sept daily except Mon, Fri (daily in Aug) 2–5.30. Guided tours. Refreshments.

People have lived at Breamore (pronounced 'Bremmer') since at least the 10C, when the core of the parish church—one of the best surviving Anglo-Saxon churches in the south of England—was built on sloping ground overlooking the Avon valley to the north of the New Forest. In the Middle Ages the site of the present Breamore House was Crown property, but the manor was sold by Queen Elizabeth to her favourite Sir Christopher Hatton, and he conveyed it in 1580 to another courtier, William Dodington, who built the present red-brick house on a commanding position looking south over the valley. He later committed suicide by throwing himself from the tower of St Sepulchre's church in London, and in 1660 the estate passed by the marriage to the 4th Lord Brooke of Warwick Castle (qv). The house then became a secondary residence and therefore escaped alteration until after 1748, when it was sold to George II's physician Sir Edward Hulse. Popularly known as the 'Whig doctor', he had married the daughter of one of the directors of the Bank of England and had been made a baronet, and he promptly turned the house and estate over to his son and daughter-in-law, who carried out internal alterations c 1750; since then they have passed by descent to the present owner. A fire destroyed most of the remaining Elizabethan interiors in 1856, but many of the contents, amassed through a series of marriages to heiresses, were saved, and the house itself was tactfully rebuilt soon afterwards. There have been few major changes since.

The house is approached from the south west through a farm courtyard, part of which has been adapted as a museum of rural life and crafts. From here a path leads up through the park to the house, past the flint-built church (which should not be missed) and the original E-shaped entrance front, which now looks out onto a private garden. It is clear from old pictures, some of which can be seen in the house, that the unknown Victorian architect in charge of the rebuilding resisted the temptation to 'improve' the Elizabethan original, and today the sober, well-proportioned exterior looks much as it did when work finished in 1583. The main alteration was to the north side, where the hall block was doubled in width so as to create a new entrance hall and staircase. An Elizabethan wing with its own porch projects to the north from here, giving the house an L-shape, and there is also an 18C stable block—now housing a collection of carriages—and an octagonal Victorian clock tower.

The tour starts in the Dining Room, with its ornate late-16C stone chimneypiece (possibly brought from elsewhere in the house), and four canvases of dead game by Peter Rysbrack, son of the sculptor of the same name. The Great Hall, like the Dining Room, dates essentially from the 19C, but the panelling and plaster ceiling may reflect what was there before the 1856 fire, and the chimneypiece is genuinely Elizabethan. The room was greatly enlarged after the fire by taking in the space formerly occupied by the screens passage, staircase and parlour, and now the character is that of a long gallery. There is a good collection of portraits at Breamore, and several of the earlier ones can be seen here, including works by, or attributed to, Marcus Gheeraerts and Cornelius Johnson. Other works of art include a large, rollicking peasant scene by the younger Teniers ('The Coming of the Storm') and there is also some unusual 17C furniture, including an ebony and ivory cabinet decorated with scenes of Noah's Ark and a Mexican alabaster table. The two drawing rooms which follow were redecorated in the plainest style after the fire, and now contain excellent early-18C Dutch marquetry furniture and Rococo mirrors commissioned by the 2nd Baronet. There are also family portraits by John Riley and Francis Cotes, and another portrait by an unknown artist of a boy, Walter Fawkes, holding a cricket bat (c 1760). Next comes the Inner Hall, part of the 19C additions to the house, with memorabilia connected with Sir Samuel Hulse, a successful soldier who became aide de camp to the Prince Regent and subsequently Field Marshal and Treasurer of the Royal Household.

From here the 19C staircase, hung with Dutch paintings and a very early English carpet dated 1614, leads up to a lobby containing various items of booty brought back from the Caribbean in the late 17C; they include an extraordinary series of paintings of *mestizos* (half-breeds) attributed to an illegitimate son of the Spanish master Murillo who worked in Mexico, and a 17C fan made by Mexican Indians. An excellent series of pastel portraits by Francis Cotes hangs in the Blue Bedroom, over the hall, and the tour concludes in the north wing, where two more bedrooms were created at an early date out of what might have been a long gallery in Elizabethan times. They contain early-17C beds with their original embroidered hangings and some attractive Flemish tapestries of c 1630. Downstairs is the old Kitchen with an impressive display of well-polished pots and pans.

GCT

Broadlands

8m north of Southampton on the south edge of Romsey, approached from
A31: Lord and Lady Romsey, tel. 0794 516878. Open Easter–late Sept daily
except Fri (but open Good Fri and Fri in Aug) 10–5.30. Guided tours.
Refreshments.

The broad lands which provide the setting for this dignified 18C house
belonged in the Middle Ages to the Benedictine nunnery of Romsey, whose
splendid, largely 12C, church still presides over the town to the north. The
estate was bought after the Dissolution by Sir Francis Fleming, who built
the first known house on the site, in the form of 'a half Roman H' (Celia
Fiennes's words) with a lofty hall in the central block and a long gallery on
the top floor. The estate later passed through the female line to the St Barbe
family, before being sold in 1736 to Henry Temple, a kinsman of the
Temples of Stowe, Buckinghamshire (qv.) and 1st Viscount Palmerston in
the Irish peerage. He began landscaping the gardens, but the Elizabethan
house remained largely unaltered until 1765–74, when his grandson the
2nd Viscount called in 'Capability' Brown to rebuild it in its present form;
at the same time Brown completed the transformation of the gardens into
an arcadian park, with lawns stretching down from the house to the River
Test, and views of the low hills rising beyond. Further alterations to the
house took place in 1788–92 under the supervision of Brown's son- in-law,
Henry Holland, and it now remains much as he left it. The 2nd Viscount
was a notable virtuoso, returning from his first Grand Tour in 1764 with
525-worth of antique and neo-classical statuary; he also bought Old Master
and contemporary paintings (many of which have since been sold) and
commissioned new furniture, some of which can still be seen in the
comfortable rooms created by Brown and Holland.

Broadlands is best known today for its association with two men who
played an important part in British 19C and 20C history: the 3rd Viscount
Palmerston, twice Prime Minister in the 1850s and 60s, and Queen Victoria's
great-grandson, Lord Louis Mountbatten, who followed a distinguished
naval career during the Second World War by becoming the last Viceroy of
India and, as Earl Mountbatten of Burma, Admiral of the Fleet from 1956
to 1965. Both men left their mark on the house, but neither removed its
essentially 18C character. Palmerston employed T.L. Donaldson to add a
wing onto the house and carry out other relatively minor alterations in 1859,
and Mountbatten made some discreet changes to the interior and demolished the Victorian wing in 1954. His connection with Broadlands derived
from his marriage in 1922 to Edwina Ashley, whose grandfather had been
left the estate by Lord Palmerston's stepson William Cowper, later Lord
Mount Temple, a minor politician who served as First Commissioner of
Works for much of the 1860s. Mountbatten was killed by an IRA bomb in
1979, and the house was then inherited by his grandson, the present owner,
who brought in his uncle, the fashionable interior designer David Hicks, to
redecorate the interior during the 1980s.

The approach to the house leads through the former dairy, a modest
building with Tudor-Gothic windows, and the first view of the house itself
is of Brown's **north and west fronts** rising straight from the lawns overlooking the widened river—a largely unaltered expression of his ideal of
juxtaposing classical architecture with 'improved' nature. The house is built
of grey brick, possibly suggested by the 2nd Lord Palmerston's admiration
for the recently-completed Holkham Hall, Norfolk (qv.), and there is little

embellishment apart from the giant Ionic portico on the west or river front, on the site of the hall range of the 16C house. The **entrance** is on the east side, through another Ionic portico in antis, built by Holland to link the remodelled wings of the original house; the attic storey over the top was added by Donaldson to provide more bedrooms. Holland also filled in the former open courtyard behind the portico with an octagonal top-lit entrance vestibule, and it is through this that the interior is reached.

The tour starts in the **Sculpture Hall**, created by Brown in 1768–69 to house the cream of the 2nd Lord Palmerston's still largely intact collection of antiquities and later sculptures. The most important of the genuinely Roman pieces is the relief of the Hunt of Meleager, from a sarcophagus, on the west wall, and there are also some excellent neo-classical pieces, including a 'Boy on a Dolphin' by Nollekens (1765) and some marble vases of about the same date designed by Piranesi, standing on marble-topped tables made for the room. The **Dining Room** (not always open to the public) dates from Holland's time and is sparingly decorated in the neo-classical taste; some visitors may find David Hick's choice of colours a little startling. The pictures include three Van Dycks bought by Lady Mountbatten's maternal grandfather, Sir Ernest Cassel, of which the finest is 'Madame Vinck', from his Flemish period, and, in the sideboard alcove, a portrait by Lawrence of Emma, Lady Hamilton, painted onto an earlier flower picture by Monnoyer.

Brown's garden front, overlooking the river, is taken up by three spacious, well-proportioned reception rooms, of which the best-preserved, and also the most beautiful, is the **Saloon** in the centre. This contains some good porcelain including Sèvres and Meissen pieces, arranged by Mountbatten's brother-in-law, King Gustav of Sweden, and the furniture includes two commodes probably by Ince and Mayhew. But the most striking feature is the gilded plaster decoration of the walls and ceiling, by the elder Joseph Rose, with arabesques and wreaths of foliage arranged in a flowing style influenced by contemporary France. To the south (left on entering) is the **Drawing Room**, used by the family as a living room and containing the original neo-classical pier-glasses, while to the north is a room originally known as the book room and now called the **Wedgwood Room** after the excellent collection of Wedgwood ceramics bought by the 2nd Lord Palmerston and augmented by later owners. Most of the delicate plaster-work is by Rose, but the bookcases and mirror were introduced by Holland, who may also have designed some of the furniture, and the room also contains some Lely portraits of court beauties.

The remaining rooms are more interesting from a historical than from a purely aesthetic point of view. A back staircase, hung with portraits of Lord Mountbatten's German forbears from the House of Hesse, leads up to the **Oak Room**, turned into a cinema by Mountbatten. The late-17C panelling may possibly have been part of the decoration of the hall or the pre-18C house, and there are some early portraits, including one by Lely of Lady Dorothy Sidney in the elaborately carved overmantel. A back staircase leads down to the ground floor, where a passage contains a series of models of ships on which Lord Mountbatten served. The last major room, the **Palmerston Room**, contains a Grand Tour portrait by Angelica Kauffmann of the 2nd Viscount with Vesuvius in the background, and portraits of the Victorian Prime Minister, together with memorabilia of his career, including letters selected from his extensive archives, now mainly housed in the University of Southampton. A 17C brick former stable block to the north of the house has been turned into an extensive **museum** of the life of Lord Mountbatten.

GCT

The Grange

4m north of New Alresford off B3046 Alresford–Basingstoke:
English Heritage, open any time.

This gaunt, deserted pile is one of the key monuments of the Greek Revival in England. The house was first built for Sir Robert Henley c 1670, but in 1787 his descendants sold the estate to the Drummonds, whose fortune derived from banking, and in 1804 the 18-year-old Henry Drummond, recently returned from Greece, called in the young Cambridge don, William Wilkins, who had also travelled in Greece, to remodel the exterior in a manner which would appropriately express the philhellenism which they both shared. The result is awe-inspiring—or, to use a work much banded-about in the aesthetic discourse of the age of Romanticism, 'sublime'. The house stands quite alone in its landscaped park, and 'reads' like a Greek temple, with a massive projecting portico of baseless Doric columns on the east side and a Doric frieze continued around the building—an idea which Wilkins seems to have taken from a project for a house in the Greek style published by Robert Mitchell in 1801. Steps lead down from the portico to the lake in the valley below, and a temple-like podium obscures the original basement. The brick walls of the original house were meanwhile encased in cement to give a fashionably smooth appearance, but, Wilkins left the existing windows undisturbed, except for those of the servants on the top floor, which were blocked out by the new frieze. Drummond sold the still unfinished house in 1817 and moved to Switzerland, returning eventually to found the Catholic Apostolic Church (cf. Albury Park, Surrey).

His successor at the Grange was Alexander Baring (later Lord Ashburton), another leading banker, and he employed first Robert Smirke and then C.R. Cockerell to extend the house to the west and to build a new conservatory with an exquisite Ionic portico, the latter completed to Cockerell's designs in 1825. These additions doubled the size of the house, which remained the home of the Barings until the Second World War. It was then abandoned, but, after a public outcry, was saved by the government from the final indignity of being blown up in 1975. A decision was then taken to demolish Alexander Baring's additions, save only for the Conservatory, and to restore the exterior (but not the interior) of the main house as Wilkins left it. Visitors can now wander around the outside of the building, but the interior is locked up, bereft of furniture and decoration, like a mausoleum to a long-dead hero. But on a fine summer's day it is still possible to recapture the enthusiasm of C.R. Cockerell when he first saw the house in the 1820s: 'Nothing can be finer, more classical or like the finest Poussins. It realises the most fanciful representations of painters' fancy or the poets' description...There is nothing like it on this side of Arcadia'.

GCT

Highclere Castle

4½m south of Newbury on A34 Newbury–Southampton: the Earl of
Carnarvon, tel. 0635 253210. Open July–Sept Wed–Sun, Easter, May,
Aug BH Sun Mon 2–6. Refreshments.

Though called a castle, Highclere is a Georgian house remodelled and
transformed in the spirit of Victorian romanticism. The man responsible for
the transformation was Henry Herbert, 3rd Earl of Carnarvon and great-
great-grandfather of the present owner. He was descended from the
Herberts of Wilton, Wiltshire (qv.), a younger branch of whom inherited the
estate under the will of Sir Robert Sawyer (d 1687). The first of the family
to live at Highclere was Robert, younger brother of the 9th Earl of
Pembroke, the designer of the Palladian bridge in the gardens at Wilton.
His nephew, who was given an earldom by George III for calming the mob
during the Gordon Riots, remodelled the existing brick house in a conventional Palladian manner in 1774; he also employed 'Capability' Brown to
landscape the grounds, and his lawns still encompass the house. The
building was too bland for the taste of the 3rd Earl, and in 1838 he
approached Charles Barry, the newly-appointed architect of the Houses of
Parliament, to give it a face-lift in stone. Barry's first designs were in the
Italianate style, in which he excelled (cf. Cliveden, Bucks), but in the end
it was decided to impart, in his own words, 'something more of a feudal
character', and, with this in mind, the Elizabethan style was chosen instead.
Work started in 1842, but Barry's schemes for the interior remained largely
unimplemented, and the 4th Earl, Colonial Secretary in several Tory
governments, turned to Thomas Allom, best known as an architectural
illustrator, to complete the redecoration of the interior in the 1860s. There
were further alterations by the 5th Earl in the 1890s, but there have been
few changes since, and Highclere now remains a largely unaltered
example of a nobleman's country house of the Victorian era.

The most dramatic of Barry's alterations to Highclere was the addition of
a staircase tower to impart a new sense of drama and verticality to the
house, and it is this tower which both makes the biggest impact on arrival
and remains longest in the memory after leaving. Sometimes compared to
the tower of Wollaton Hall, Notts (qv.), though in fact much more slender
and graceful, it dominates the surrounding wooded country, and it is echoed
in the four smaller towers attached to the four corners of the house. Barry
had a good understanding of the value of an interesting skyline, as the
Houses of Parliament show, and the roof-line is broken up by characteristically delicate pinnacles and strapwork crests; otherwise the external
detailing is sparingly applied over the regular, symmetrical façades
inherited from the earlier house (even the windows preserve their original
proportions).

The house is square in plan, and the rooms are grouped around a central
top-lit Saloon. The lierne-vaulted Entrance Hall, on the north side of the
house, is one of the only two interiors completed to Barry's designs, though
not until after his death, its Gothic character contrasting with that of the
Elizabethan exterior. There is another change of style in the Library, largely
by Allom and divided into two by a screen of Ionic columns; it is comfortably
furnished with an assortment of pieces including a desk and chair with
Egyptian decoration, made for the exiled Napoleon on St Helena. The
remaining rooms were, with the exception of the Saloon, also designed

more for comfort than for show. The Drawing Room, on the south front, was redecorated at the end of the 19C in the then-fashionable style of the French Rococo. The pictures include a lively family group of the children of the 1st Earl by Beechey, several of whose portraits hang in the house. There is a bureau of 1765 by Pierre Langlois in the Boudoir, on the same front, and from here the back stairs lead up to a series of bedrooms opening onto the gallery of the Saloon, which was decorated by Allom in the Tudor-Gothic style with a copious use of heraldry and military trophies to emphasise the long and distinguished history of the family. One of the bedrooms has been given over to an excellent exhibition of the architectural evolution of the house, including several of Barry's drawings.

Barry's spacious, well-lit main staircase leads down from the gallery, past Reynolds's painting of Mrs Musters as Hebe, the cup-bearer of the gods (there is another version at Kenwood, Greater London, qv.) to the ground-floor Saloon, where the 17C Spanish leather wall-hangings and the ebony cabinets of c 1700 should be noted. The last room to be seen is the neo-Tudor Dining Room, to the west of the Entrance Hall, with beefy wooden furnishings of a kind found in many Victorian dining rooms, including a pair of cupboards by George Bullock; there is also a collection of 17C and 18C family portraits, including a copy of Van Dyck's famous equestrian portrait of Charles I. Visitors leave the house through the service quarters in the basement, where there is a display, unparalleled in any other English country house, of ancient Egyptian items. They include the contents of the tomb of the pharaoh Amenophis III found by the 5th Earl, a keen archaeologist who, together with Howard Carter, discovered the tomb of Tutankhamun in 1922.

GCT

Hinton Ampner

8m east of Winchester on A272 Winchester–Petersfield: National Trust, tel. 0962 771305. Open Apr–Sept Tues, Wed, also Sat, Sun in Aug (gardens Sat, Sun, Tues, Wed, BH Mon) 1.30–5. Refreshments.

Though standing on an old site, close to a church which contains Anglo-Saxon masonry, Hinton Ampner is a 20C neo-Georgian house built and furnished with great sensitivity by Ralph Dutton, latterly the 8th Lord Sherborne, a notable collector and writer on English and French country houses and interiors. The Dutton family came from Sherborne in the Gloucestershire Cotswolds, and acquired the Hinton estate by marriage in the early 19C. It was settled on a younger son, John Thomas Dutton, and in 1864 he employed a local architect, to enlarge the existing modest house in a stodgy Tudor-Gothic manner. It was this unremarkable building which the aesthetically-minded Ralph Dutton inherited from his father in 1935, and in the following year he began to rebuild it to the designs of his friend Gerald Wellesley, later 7th Duke of Wellington (cf. Stratfield Saye) and Trenwith Wells. He furnished the remodelled house with a notable collection of pictures and furniture, but in 1960 there was a disastrous fire which left the house an empty shell and decimated the collection. Rebuilding began almost immediately, and at the same time the 62-year-old Ralph Dutton set about forming a new and equally outstanding collection of British and Continental pictures and furniture. This now survives in the beautifully maintained house, which was completed in 1963 and left, together with the gardens and the surrounding estate, to the National Trust on his death in 1985.

The house is set among semi-formal gardens from which there are vistas of the attractive undulating countryside beyond. Externally the house is a virtual replica of its 1930s' predecessor, save for a reduction in the height of the attic storey. The brick elevations are dignified and restrained, but the interiors are unexpectedly rich and splendid. Ralph Dutton was a member of the generation which rediscovered the delights of Regency and 'Empire-style' art and architecture, and, while more conventional in his taste than the Sitwells or John Betjeman, he had a marked predilection, perhaps developed in Oxford during the 1920s, for gilded furniture and objects made out of hard stones. These can be found in all the main rooms, together with a collection of pictures bought, one senses, not primarily for their monetary worth or art-historical 'importance' but because the purchaser liked and understood them. The result is a house which was designed to give pleasure to the owner and his guests (see the memoir by Sir Brinsley Ford in the excellent National Trust guidebook), and which is as interesting in its way as the better-known collectors' houses of the 18C and 19C.

The tour takes in all the main ground-floor rooms, starting in the Entrance Hall, which occupies the whole width of the previous 18C house. This is a light and cheerful room with a porphyry chimneypiece of c 1800 from Hamilton Palace in Scotland (one of several furnishings at Hinton bought from altered or demolished country houses) surmounted by porphyry ornaments. Other furnishings include a pair of 18C gilded Italian *torchres* and a table with a 17C *pietra dura* top. On or around the walls there are 17C Italian marble and porphyry busts and Italian Baroque paintings, including Pellegrini's 'Selene and Endymion' (over the fireplace) and an odd allegorical portrait of the 1st Earl of Macclesfield by the Florentine artist Giuseppe Grisoni (c 1718–21: only visible from the staircase). From here visitors proceed into the Drawing Room, curtained and carpeted in the Regency manner, with two marble chimneypieces from Ashburnham Park, Sussex, and 18C English and Italian pictures; the furnishings include Rococo mirrors and a marble-topped ebony table from Lowther Castle, Cumbria. The Library, on the garden front, is arranged as a comfortable living room, with solid Regency furniture, but a note of the exotic is introduced by the porphyry pilasters and chimneypiece, the latter with the initials 'N' for Napoleon. The Sitting Room, next door, is mainly notable for its paintings, with works by Gaspard Dughet, Marco Ricci (a pair of oval landscapes), Zuccarelli and Henry Fuseli (two scenes from Shakespeare's 'A Winter's Tale'), and for a 17C porphyry portrait bust and a relief carving in the same material. Last comes the Dining Room, with a ceiling copied from one by Robert Adam in 38 Berkeley Square, London, an Adam mirror of 1773 (also from a London house), which forms a pair with one in the library at Basildon Park, Berkshire (qv.), and a massive early-19C English sideboard bought by Ralph Dutton for £8 during the Second World War. The portraits on the walls are of members of the Stewkeley and Stawell families, from whom the Duttons were indirectly descended; monuments to these families can be seen in the modest church nearby, discreetly restored by Ralph Dutton, which is now his burial place.

GCT

Mottisfont Abbey

4½m north west of Romsey off A3057 Romsey–Andover: National Trust,
tel. 0794 41220/40757. Open Apr–Oct Tues, Wed, Sun 1–5 (Whistler Room
& 'cellarium' only; guided tours); garden Sat–Wed 12–6; June 12–8.30.
Refreshments at local Post Office.

The small Augustinian priory of Mottisfont was founded on the banks of
the River Test in 1201 close to a *fons* or spring which can still be seen. It
was acquired in 1536, after the Dissolution, by William, Lord Sandys, one
of Henry VIII's courtiers, in exchange for the manors of Chelsea and
Paddington on the edge of London. Sandys had already built extensively
at The Vyne, near Basingstoke (qv.), and he soon began to turn the
redundant monastic buildings of Mottisfont into a second grand house; a
contemporary correspondent remarking in 1538 that 'he makes a goodly
place of the priory and intends to lie there most of his life'. The work
involved turning the refectory into a hall, building a base court in front of
it, and turning the remaining buildings around the cloister into a second
courtyard; one side was occupied by the nave of the church, which now
became a two-storeyed residential range with the main rooms on the upper
floor. The descendants of Lord Sandys lived at Mottisfont until 1684, when
the house was passed to Sir John Mill, whose son Sir Richard Mill carried
out major alterations in the 1740s. These involved demolishing most of Lord
Sandys' sprawling house except for the range made out of the former nave
of the monastic church and the wings on either side which formed part of
the inner courtyard; this remnant was then refaced, new windows were
inserted and new interiors created, thus giving the building a largely
Georgian appearance which it has retained to the present day. Externally,
little has changed since then, but there was a major internal alteration in
1938, when Gilbert Russell, who had recently bought the house from the

*The Saloon at Mottisfont showing Rex Whistler's Rococo Gothick
trompe l'oeil paintings*

Mills, brought in the painter Rex Whistler to redecorate the former entrance hall in a characteristically frothy Rococo Gothic manner. The Russells also beautified the gardens, and in 1957 Mrs Russell gave the house and estate to the National Trust.

The house stands among tree-studded lawns with the river flowing idyllically by to the east. Some details from the medieval monastic church can still be seen on the north and east fronts of the present house, but the outside of the long main façade, which faces south over the gardens, dates mainly from the 1740s. The pedimented brick central portion is flanked by Tudor projections, and beyond them are wings terminating in canted bays—a favourite mid-18C motif. The Tudor hall, and the monastic refectory before it, stood on the site of the present lawn. Inside, the only rooms shown to visitors are the vaulted monastic cellar under the west wing, little altered since the 13C, and Rex Whistler's spectacular Saloon above it. This spacious and beautifully furnished room, with its trompe l'oeil paintings on a pink background, was conceived as a tongue-in-cheek tribute to the world of Batty Langley and his contemporaries (note the small paint pot and brush wittily left on the cornice at one end of the room); to aficionados of the taste of the 1930s, it will in itself justify an excursion to Mottisfont. To the west is an impressive red-brick stable block of 1836, and beyond it a walled rose garden created by the National Trust in 1972–73.

GCT

Rotherfield Park

At East Tisted, 4½m south of Alton on A32 Alton–Fareham: Lt Col Sir James and Lady Scott, tel. 042058 204. Open first seven days of June, July and Aug, Sun and Mon of BH weekends 2–5. Gardens only Easter–Sept Sun and Thurs. Refreshments when house open.

The first sight of this large Regency and Victorian house is of a romantic array of medieval-looking turrets perched on the slope of a hill overlooking the estate village of East Tisted and the undulating countryside to the east. The largely intact ensemble of house and village was created by successive members of the Scott family, starting with James Scott, the son of a building contractor in London, who bought the estate from the Marquess of Winchester in 1808. The house was designed by Joseph Parkinson, architect of the façades of Bryanston Square in the West End of London, in 1818–21, and the pretty estate cottages along the main road date from about this time. In one of his *Rural Rides*, written in 1822, William Cobbett, who was born just over the county boundary in Farnham, Surrey, said that Scott had 'quite metamorphosed the village of East Tisted' and 'really and truly improved the whole country just round about here'—a comment which still holds good. Later alterations did not destroy the basic unity of the ensemble. The village church was rebuilt in 1846, the rooms in the house were redecorated in the 1860s, and the whole building was faced in stone some 20 years later, when most of the towers which enliven the exterior were added to the designs of an unknown architect; meanwhile a large garden was created, with formal terraces near the house and paths through the trees (depleted alas by recent gales) beyond.

Taken together, the house and its setting are a textbook example of the influences of the 'Picturesque' aesthetic which did so much to shape 19C (and modern) taste. The house is grouped against a wooded backdrop, commanding a view over the village and the country beyond. The exterior, especially as improved in the late 19C, is as irregular as it could possibly be, with sundry projections and recessions, towers and chimneystacks to break the skyline, and Tudor-Gothic details to evoke the past. The approach leads over a bridge to the front porch, with the service courtyard and towers concealing the meat larder and laundry chimney to the right. On the opposite (south) side of the house there is another tower, of brick (1887) over the stables, linked to the main body of the house by a lower wing.

The interiors have changed relatively little over the last hundred years, apart from the inevitable moving around of furniture and pictures. The finest room is the top-lit Staircase Hall, around which all the other rooms are grouped; there are marble busts of the Duke of Wellington and other worthies, and Joseph Parkinson's perspective view of the house hangs over the fireplace, showing the building before the Victorian alterations. The kitchen (formerly the Library) and the Dining Room face east over the valley, the latter containing some of the original Regency furniture, along with family portraits and copies of Old Master paintings, of which there are several in the house. There are more pictures in the two south-facing Drawing Rooms, including two family portraits by Zoffany, and one by Francis Cotes of Susannah Thrale, sister-in-law of Dr Johnson's confidante, who married the uncle of the builder of the house. But the overwhelming impression of Rotherfield is not so much of individual works of art as of a welcoming and well-preserved example of a 19C squire's country residence carefully maintained by a descendent of the first builder.

GCT

Stratfield Saye

6m north of Basingstoke off A33 Basingstoke–Reading: the Duke of Wellington, tel. 0256 882882. Open May–Sept daily except Fri 11.30–4.00. Refreshments.

Stratfield Saye is inseparable from the memory of Arthur Wellesley, 1st Duke of Wellington. He acquired the estate in 1817 with money voted by Parliament after his victories in the wars against Napoleonic France. However, unlike an earlier military hero, the Duke of Marlborough at Blenheim, Oxfordshire (qv.), he finally chose not to build a great palace but instead to adapt the existing house, making it, in his own words, 'a very fair house and as magnificent as it ought to be'. It was built of brick, probably in the 1630s, by Sir William Pitt, former Comptroller of the Household to James I, or by his son, and it is still structurally intact, with its long 'double pile' central block and its two Dutch-gabled cross-wings. The interiors were all remodelled, and the exterior covered in stucco (originally white but now ochre-coloured), by George Pitt, who inherited in 1745 and went on to become Ambassador to the court of Turin and finally, in 1776, Lord Rivers. Most of this work was carried out c 1755, probably with the advice of his uncle John Pitt of Encombe, Dorset, who also may have designed the impressive classical parish church in the park in 1754–58. Rivers later built a new dining room onto the already very long east (garden) front, and Wellington lengthened it further by adding a conservatory in 1838, he also widened the wings on the west (entrance) side in 1846, but otherwise his alterations were mainly internal. He remodelled several of the main rooms in 1822 with the help of Benjamin Dean Wyatt, and went on to introduce central heating and hot water. The house remained very little altered after his death in 1852, and it subsequently fell into neglect, from which it was rescued after the Second World War by the 7th Duke, who, as Gerald Wellesley, had practised as an architect between the Wars and had been one of the pioneers in the revival of interest in the architecture and decoration of the Regency period. It was he who restored the interiors and designed the cupola on the roof.

The long, low house stands in surprisingly remote and unspoiled country, despite its proximity to Reading and Basingstoke, and the surroundings bear the marks of careful estate management. It is approached from the west, with low stable blocks on either side of the drive, one of them housing a well-organised **exhibition** of memorabilia relating to the life and military career of the 1st Duke, including a prototype Wellington Boot, some neo-Elizabethan costumes from George IV's coronation, and the spectacular funeral carriage on which the Duke's coffin was carried to its final resting-place in St Paul's Cathedral, London. In the forecourt is a bronze group of a horse and dragon by Matthew Cotes Wyatt, originally commissioned by George IV.

The house is entered through the **Hall**, and the tour proceeds anti-clockwise through all the main reception rooms, which, following the usual late-18C and early-19C fashion, occupy the ground floor. For a ducal residence, they are remarkably lacking in pomposity, and the atmosphere of the house, which is still the family home of the present Duke, is noticeably friendly. The Hall, with its Ionic colonnade supporting a gallery, received its present form in the 1750s, but it was refurnished by the 1st and 7th Dukes of Wellington, and it is their taste which now predominates. Much of the French 'Empire style' furniture which can be seen here and elsewhere in the house was bought in 1816 from the collection of Napoleon's uncle Cardinal Fesch, and the antique and pseudo-antique busts on pedestals came from the same source. The tricolour flags bearing the initial N in laurel wreaths and the symbol of the bee (for Bonaparte) were given to the 1st Duke when he entered Paris after the Battle of Waterloo, and the green malachite *tazza* came from Alexander I of Russia. On the floor are Roman mosaic pavements from the abandoned town of Silchester, whose walls still stand isolated in the fields only a couple of miles away. The **Library**, to the right, is also fundamentally a mid-18C room, with a coffered ceiling and an enriched frieze and cornice, but the masculine, clubby atmosphere comes largely from the comfortable furniture introduced by the 1st Duke. A 'Resurrection' attributed to Tintoretto hangs over the fireplace, and there are also portraits of George Washington and Napoleon, while in the **Music Room**, divided from the Library by a screen of Ionic columns, are sporting and animal pictures, including several of the 1st Duke's favourite charger Copenhagen, who was buried in the grounds.

The remaining reception rooms are reached through the **Staircase Hall**, with mid-17C stairs and a mid-18C Rococo ceiling. There is a similar ceiling in the drawing room known as the **Lady Charles Room**, and the curvaceous chimneypiece is of the same style and date; the pictures by 18C English artists of members of the Pierrepont family (cf. Holme Pierrepont, Notts) were inherited by the 1st Duke's daughter-in-law, and the room was one of several redecorated by John Fowler in 1973. The **Print Room** next door was decorated in the time of the 1st Duke, and there are more prints pasted onto the walls of the adjacent **Gallery** at the centre of the garden front. This is now the most impressive room in the house, due largely to the superb furnishings and statuary introduced by the 1st Duke. They include items of 18C Boulle and Boulle-style furniture specially purchased from a French dealer, a commode by Carlin and a series of nine bronze busts of monarchs and military heroes (including 'Le Grand Condé' and a Roman emperor with features suspiciously like those of Napoleon) dating from the 17C to the early 19C and standing on Boulle pedestals of ebony whose black and gold colouring adds to the feeling of richness.

Next come two more **Drawing Rooms**, the first of which contains a Hogarth conversation piece of the 1st Duke's grandfather, Lord Mornington, with his family and James Thorburn's well-known picture of the Duke himself with his grandchildren, painted in the last year of his life. The second and larger room has some inventive mid-18C Rococo decoration in wood and plaster, gilded in the French manner and possibly designed by Giovanni Borra (cf. Stowe, Bucks); note especially the trophy of musical instruments over the south door, similar in character to work in Norfolk House music room in London (now in the Victoria and Albert Museum), also associated with Borra. There is more 18C French furniture here, including an excellent Boulle cabinet, and the walls are hung with pictures by minor Dutch and other masters captured by the 1st Duke from Joseph Bonaparte, Napoleon's puppet king of Spain, as he fled from the field of Vitoria in 1813 (the cream of the collection is in Apsely House, London, where it can still be seen, but the cases in which the pictures were found are displayed in the museum in the stables). The last important room is the **Dining Room**, built on to the house by Lord Rivers c 1775, with a ceiling of the 'Palmyra' type and a set of Wellesley family portraits on the walls, including works by Hoppner and Lawrence. Part of the 'Deccan Service', given to the 1st Duke in 1806 by his fellow-officers of the Indian campaign, is displayed on the table (note the elephants and other Indian motifs). From here visitors pass into a **corridor** leading back to the Hall; the pictures here include a good portrait of the 1st Duke by Benjamin Robert Haydon and a set of designs by Benjamin Dean Wyatt, C.R. Cockerell and C.H. Tatham for a 'Waterloo Palace' which it was originally intended would replace Strattield Saye. There is also a collection of porcelain from the 1st Duke's time, including some Meissen pieces depicting Spanish towns.

GCT

The Vyne

4m north of Basingstoke on Bramley–Sherborne St John road: National Trust, tel. 0256 881337. Open Apr–Oct daily except Mon, Fri, but open Good Fri and BH Mon (closed Tues following BH Mon) 1.30–5.30 (garden opens 12.30). Refreshments.

The name of this large and fascinating house may allude to a medieval or even Roman vineyard on or near the site, but the building owes its origin to William, Lord Sandys, a soldier and follower of Henry VIII who became Treasurer of Calais and played a leading part in the festivities of the Field of the Cloth of Gold in 1520. The house dates in its present form from the first quarter of the 16C and is built, like the early Tudor royal palaces, of red brick, with the usual blue criss-cross patterning. The rooms are arranged around three sides of a quadrangle; the fourth or entrance side, if there ever was one, has disappeared, along with a second courtyard to the north which may have contained the main domestic quarters. There are low towers at the ends of the hall ranges (two other towers at the ends of the wings were demolished in the 19C), and a chapel projects to the east. The superb interior of the chapel is still largely intact, as is the gallery in the west range, one of the earliest to survive in an English country house.

Much of the interest of the house today derives from two later remodellings, in the mid 17C and the mid 18C. The Sandys family fell on hard times during the Civil War and retired to Mottisfont Abbey (qv.), their other Hampshire estate, and in 1653 the Vyne was purchased by Chaloner Chute, a lawyer who prospered under both the Royalist and Cromwellian regimes and became Speaker of the House of Commons just before his death in 1659. He employed Inigo Jones's pupil John Webb to modernise the interiors and to add a portico—the first in any English country house—onto the north side of the hall range in 1654–57. More major changes took place in the time of John Chute, a friend of Horace Walpole and member of the 'Committee of Taste' which planned Walpole's Gothic villa at Strawberry Hill. He inherited the Vyne in 1754, and in the years before his death in 1776 he carried out sundry alterations in the Gothic and Rococo tastes and built a splendid new classical staircase, perhaps out of deference to John Webb, in the centre of the house. William Wiggett Chute did some internal remodelling after inheriting the property in 1827, but since then there have been few major changes. In 1956 the house was given to the National Trust, together with the surviving contents, including objects accumulated by John Chute on his foreign travels in the 1740s, and furniture commissioned by him.

The first view of the house is of the Tudor **hall range** with the two surviving wings of the original building stretching forward to form what may have been the 'fair base court' mentioned by Leland c 1540. while much of the Tudor brickwork remains, the windows were replaced by John Webb in the 1650s and sashed in the 18C. More alterations are visible on the north or **garden front**, notably Webb's noble Corinthian portico of stuccoed brick, with the capitals carved by Edward Marshall. To the left is the chapel, and beyond it a rather ungainly circular brick garden pavilion, of Webb's time but possibly not by him, while to the north is a lake formed by John Chute c 1755–76 as part of his improvements to the gardens; there is an excellent view of the whole north front from the opposite side.

The house is entered through the **Stone Gallery** in the west wing, used in the 18C as an orangery; a terracotta bust of the Emperor Probus (who authorised the introduction of vines into Britain) may date from the time of the 1st Lord Sandys, who would have been familiar with the similar busts at Cardinal Wolsey's Hampton Court (qv.). The main living rooms, in the north range, have been much altered since the 16C. The first two, both of them drawing rooms, were remodelled by John Chute, and still retain their red damask wall hangings and Rococo plaster ceilings. Chute's portrait (by Gabriel Mathias, 1758), hangs to the right of the fireplace in the **Further Drawing Room**, with an unexecuted Gothic design for the house in his left hand, and many of his furnishings still survive, including the striking circular mirror with a mask of Apollo emitting sun rays over the fireplace and some Chinese Chippendale tables supplied in 1765–68; a picture by J.H. Muntz, a popular artist in the Walpole circle, shows the house as it was in 1755, just after he inherited. The small **Ante-Room** next door contains some of Chute's Italian purchases, notably a set of enamelled 'Lattimo' glass plates bought in Venice in 1741 and a delicate *pietra dura* casket made in

Florence and probably bought while he was staying there with the English consul, Horace Mann, in the 1740s; the fanciful stand, with horned satyrs' heads at the corners, was made in the 1750s, probably by William Vile, partner in the firm of Vile & Cobb which supplied other items of furniture in the house. There is more good furniture in the **Large Drawing Room**, including a set of chairs with faintly Gothick details and a pair of commodes in the Louis XV manner by Pierre Langlois, and on the walls is a pastel by Rosalba Carriera of Francis Whitehead, who went to Italy with John Chute and Horace Walpole in 1741.

The **Dining Room**, on the other side of Webb's portico, probably occupies the site of the hall of the Tudor house, but has been much altered, even in relatively recent times, as can be seen from a Victorian watercolour painted by Mrs Wiggett Chute, one of several by her hanging in the house. The stone chimneypiece must date from the 1650s, and on either side of it are pastiche landscapes by Muntz in the manner of earlier masters. Next comes the **Chapel Parlour**, in the tower at the end of the north front; this has also been much rearranged, but it retains its original linenfold panelling and is now hung with 16C and 17C portraits. The **Ante-Chapel** is largely the creation of John Chute and his fellow-members of the Strawberry Hill committee, but the **Chapel** itself, which Horace Walpole gushingly called 'the most heavenly Chapel in the world', has been very little altered since it was built in 1518–27. The east windows are filled with outstanding stained glass (probably Flemish) showing, inter alia, Henry VIII and Catherine of Aragon; the tiles in front of the altar may have been made in a workshop set up by an Italian craftsman in Antwerp in 1512, and the wooden stalls are carved with Renaissance motifs popularised by the craftsmen working for Henry VIII and Wolsey. To the south (right) of the chancel is a mortuary chapel designed and built by John Chute c 1770 and containing an effigy of his ancestor Chaloner Chute in 17C dress and in pensive mood by Thomas Carter (1775–76); this can vie with anything in late-18C British sculpture.

Visitors now retrace their steps to the centre of the house, once occupied by the screens passage but now by John Chute's spectacular **Staircase Hall**, Roman in its detailing and exuberantly Baroque in its layout and overall effect, with screens of Doric columns on the ground floor and Corinthian upstairs enclosing the central space through which the stairs rise enticingly upwards: an effect of great grandeur in miniature. A pair of Rococo side tables and an excellent Italian cabinet of ebony stand on the top landing, which leads into the **Library**, largely dating from the 1830s or '40s but with a Webb chimneypiece. The **Tapestry Room**, in the west tower next door, was called the Queen's Great Chamber in a 1541 inventory, but was much altered later and is now mainly notable for a set of tapestries of oriental scenes woven by John Vanderbank at the Soho works c 1720. Beyond, occupying the whole length of the west range, is the **Oak Gallery**, panelled throughout in linenfold and enlivened by small carvings of badges and heraldic devices of Lord Sandys, his family and other early Tudor notables. The classical chimneypiece was almost certainly designed by John Webb and carved by Edward Marshall, the furniture was brought in and the plaster ceiling designed by John Chute and the busts on pedestals were mostly acquired by William Wiggett Chute. These disparate elements combine to create an unusually satisfying and memorable interior.

GCT

HEREFORD AND WORCESTER

Berrington Hall

3m north of Leominster on A49 Leominster–Ludlow: National Trust,
tel. 0568 615721. Open Apr–Oct Wed–Sun and BH Mon 1.30–5.30 (4.30 in
Oct). Grounds open 12.30. Refreshments.

This compact house of local red sandstone is the finest accessible example
of the architecture of Henry Holland, one of the most accomplished domestic architects of the late 18C. The builder was the Hon. Thomas Harley,
younger son of the 3rd Earl of Oxford and Mortimer, who lived not far away.
Harley made his fortune in London as a government contractor, supplying
the clothing for the British army in America, and subsequently was elected
MP for Herefordshire. He purchased the Berrington estate c 1775, choosing
the site with the assistance of 'Capability' Brown, who subsequently laid
out the park. Holland was Brown's protégé and son-in-law, and had
collaborated with him at Claremont, Surrey (qv.); at Berrington, however,
he had a free hand, and in the five years from 1778–83 he created a building
whose logical layout, beautifully proportioned façades and elegant interiors make it one of the most satisfying houses of its date in England. When
Harley died the estate went to his daughter, who married the son of the
naval hero, Lord Rodney. The 7th Lord Rodney sold the estate in 1901 to
Frederick Cawley, who subsequently served in Lloyd George's wartime
coalition government and was ennobled as Lord Cawley. On the death of
his grandson, the 3rd Lord Cawley, in 1957, the house and park were
conveyed to the National Trust.

The house stands alone on rising ground near the village of Eye, and is
approached from the north east through a stone arch typical of the plain
and refined classicism which characterises all the exteriors. From here the
service quarters—stables, laundry, dairy and servants' hall—can be seen,
carefully arranged in a courtyard behind the house as an integral part of
the overall design. The main entrance faces west and commands a broad
view looking west towards Radnor Forest and the Welsh border, with the
lawn coming right up to the house in the typical Brown manner. It is
dominated by a massive Ionic portico stretching the whole height of the
house, but with an unusually wide gap between the two central columns
so as to allow adequate light into the rooms.

In typically late-18C fashion, the reception rooms are wrapped around a
central top-lit staircase, the scenic potential of which Holland exploited to
the full. Holland was well-known for his Francophile tastes, but the influence of the 'Adam revolution' in interior design can also be detected in
some of the rooms at Berrington. The finest interiors are the Entrance Hall,
with its ceiling resting on pendentives in a manner later developed by
Soane, who was in Holland's office when the house was designed; the
Boudoir, a small room made to look larger by the ingenious device of a
curved screen of blue scagliola columns closing off an apsidal extension;
the Staircase Hall, with a massive archway supporting the landing, paired
Corinthian columns of yellow scagliola masking the corridors at bedroom
level, and a glazed dome; and the Library, with the fireplace and bookcases
framed by attenuated pilasters and a ceiling made up of roundels with the
heads of famous literary figures, painted by Biagio Rebecca, who may also

have been responsible for some of the decorative painting in the Drawing Room on the other side of the Entrance Hall.

There are good marble chimneypieces in the main rooms, but few of the original pictures or furnishings survive, apart from the four large paintings of Admiral Rodney's naval battles (1785) by Thomas Luny and others in the Dining Room. The attractive colour schemes date from the time of the 1st Lord Cawley, and he also introduced the French neo-Rococo tapestries from the Aubusson factory in the Entrance Hall and Staircase Hall, which still exude an atmosphere of Edwardian comfort. Some of Cawley's furniture is still in the house, but the excellent 18C French items in the Drawing Room and Boudoir form part of a collection brought together by the Hon. A.E. Digby and given to the National Trust in 1981.

GCT

Burton Court

Off B4457 to south of Eardisland, 5m west of Leominster: Mr and Mrs R.M. Simpson, tel. 05447 231. Open Spring BH–late Sept Wed, Thur, Sat, Sun and BH Mon 2.30–6. Refreshments.

The largely 19C and early-20C front of Burton Court hides a house whose origins go back to the early 14C, when a timber-framed hall was built on a site close to an Iron Age encampment, not far from the village of Eardisland, one of the most attractive in a county justly famous for its unspoiled villages. The house and the small estate attached to it passed through several families, including the Crofts of Croft Castle (qv.), before settling in the mid 17C with the Brewsters, whose descendants remodelled the house in brick in the early 19C and sold it in 1865 to John Clowes, a local MP. He immediately employed the Hereford architect Frederick Kempson to carry out further alterations, and in 1912 his son Col. Peter Clowes brought in the young Welsh architect Clough Williams-Ellis—then at the outset of a career which was to culminate in the creation of the bizarre seaside fantasy of Portmerion in Wales—to remodel the entrance front in its present form. The estate was sold off in 1950, and in 1960 the house was bought by the present owner, who runs a soft-fruit farm on the surrounding land.

The east or entrance front is an interesting example of early-20C taste in country-house design, eclectic in character and agreeably irregular in appearance. Clough Williams-Ellis was responsible for the projecting porch, broadly Jacobean in character, the large mullioned and transomed windows on either side, and the window to the right which lights the medieval Hall; the bow-windowed wing to the right dates largely from the 1860s, but its south front, facing the garden, was altered by Williams-Ellis. Inside, the most important room is the early-14C Hall, an unexpected survival in such a recent-looking house, with its open arch-braced roof still intact and a richly-carved wooden chimneypiece of 1654 with terminal figures on either side of the fireplace. Visitors also see the Billiard Room and the old Dining Room, and the present Dining Room (originally the drawing room) and the Library are open on request. Historic costumes are displayed on dummies scattered through the rooms, and visitors can also see a model fairground and collections of ship models and stuffed animal heads.

GCT

Croft Castle

5m north west of Leominster on B4362: National Trust, tel. 056885 246.
Open Apr, Oct Sat, Sun; May–Sept Wed–Sun, BH Mon 2–6 (Apr, Oct 2–5).

Croft Castle stands in a wooded park in the beautiful remote country of the
Welsh borders, not far away from the Iron Age hill fort of Croft Ambrey,
which commands wide views into Wales. A fortified house was built here
in the late 14C or 15C by a member of the long-established Croft family,
but little now survives apart from the basic structure of the walls and the
four circular towers at the outer corners. Major reconstruction took place
in the late 16C, probably at the instigation of Sir James Croft (d 1590),
Comptroller of the Household to Queen Elizabeth. However, most of the
interest of the house today derives from alterations carried out in the 18C,
after the estate had been sold by the profligate Sir Archer Croft to his main
creditor the ironmaster Richard Knight, uncle of Richard Payne Knight of
nearby Downton Castle, one of the apostles of the Picturesque. When
Knight died in 1765, his son-in-law Thomas Johnes employed the Shrewsbury architect Thomas Pritchard—best-known as the designer of the Iron
Bridge in Coalbrookdale (Shropshire)—to remodel some of the interiors in
a delicate Gothic style influenced by Batty Langley's famous pattern-book.
   Johnes's son sold the house c 1785 in order to pay for improvements to
his house and gardens at Hafod (Dyfed), now alas destroyed, and the
descendants of the new owner, Somerset Davies, continued in possession
until 1923, during which time the house was relatively little altered. The
Croft family meanwhile lived on in Herefordshire in a somewhat reduced
style, and in 1923 Sir James Croft, 11th Baronet, moved back into the house.
From him it passed to a cousin, the 1st Lord Croft, and then in 1957 to the
National Trust. The 2nd Lord Croft still lives in the house, and many of the
family's pictures and possessions are on display.
   The house is approached through a castellated late-18C stone gateway
at the end of an avenue of old trees. It stands next to the modest parish
church of c 1515—in effect a family chapel—with its strangely East-Euro-
pean-looking bell turret, and a well-preserved monument to Sir Richard
Croft (d 1509) and his wife close to the altar. The exterior of the house bears
the marks of repeated alterations. The east or entrance front was originally
open in the centre, but the gap was filled in with a new entrance hall
flanked by rooms with canted bay windows in the Gothick style in 1765;
they were altered in 1913, when the present Entrance Hall was created by
a little-known architect, Walter Sarel. The medieval hall occupied most of
the west range, but all trace has now been lost and this façade, like that to
the south, is now lit by Georgian sash windows. There have been fewer
changes to the north or service range, which has been little altered from
the late 16C.
   The main rooms are all on the ground floor, with a Dining Room and
staircase on the site of the medieval hall and a series of reception rooms
occupying the whole of the south range, flanked by a corridor made along
the side of the brick-fronted courtyard as part of the 18C improvements.
The panelled Entrance Hall and the neo-Georgian Dining Room both date
essentially from 1913. They contain Croft family portraits, and the corridor
is lined with attractive 18C Gothic chairs. The finest of the interiors is
Pritchard's Staircase Hall, recently repainted in its original colours, with
delicate ogee arches in plaster on walls and ceiling. This occupies a narrow

space between the Dining Room and the Oak Room (the former parlour), which contains an architectural fantasy by the 17C Italian painter, Viviano Codazzi. The Blue Room, to the south, has an exuberant Rococo fireplace and overmantel by Pritchard framing an early Gainsborough portrait of Elizabeth, Lady Croft (c 1759); this is complemented by the 17C panelling installed by Thomas Johnes from another of his houses, and painted blue with gilded rosettes. Both this room and the Drawing Room contain good late-17C furniture. There are books by Herbert Croft, the late-17C Bishop of Hereford, and scores by the 18C composer William Croft, in the Library, along with an ingenious desk and filing cabinet called 'the Croft' made by the cabinet-maker George Seddon; and in the small ante-room next door there is a splendid Gothick overmantel, some Gothick pier-glasses and contemporary chairs in the Chinese taste. Two small rooms to the north of the Entrance Hall contain prints and water-colours of the Hafod estate by John 'Warwick' Smith and others.

GCT

Eastnor Castle

2m east of Ledbury on A438, M50 exit 2: James Hervey-Bathurst, tel. 0531 633160 or 632302. Open Easter–Sept Sun, BH Mon, Aug daily except Mon 12–5. Refreshments.

This massive, intimidating house, built in 1812–20, stands at the southern end of the Malvern Hills. The builder, John Cocks, 2nd Baron (and 1st Earl) Somers, came from a long-established family of local gentry which was raised to the peerage in 1736 after inheriting some of the estates of the early-18C Whig politician and Lord Chancellor Lord Somers, who is commemorated by an obelisk on the hills close by. Financed in part by the profits of the family banking firm of Cocks, Biddulph & Co., the new residence replaced the old family home, Castleditch, whose site is now occupied by an island in the ornamental lake to the south, and the choice of the fashionable castellated style may have been influenced by the romantic surroundings, complete with a 'British Camp' on Herefordshire Beacon nearby.

Begun during the Napoleonic Wars, Eastnor Castle reflects the somewhat edgy self-confidence of a great landowner at a time of political and social upheaval; Lord Somers was nominally a Whig, but he wrote a pamphlet attacking universal suffrage in 1817. The architect, Robert Smirke, is best known for his classical buildings (he designed the British Museum), and the symmetrical plan, the regular massing of huge, simple forms and the choice of smooth grey ashlar from the Forest of Dean, betray his classical training. Smirke was also a pioneer in the use of the new materials furnished by industry, and the house is one of the first in England to have iron roof-trusses (invisible inside) and iron chimneys. But externally the effect is of awesome 'sublimity', with heavily machicolated round turrets at the corners and a massive lantern tower over the central hall; these features give the house its character of brooding power.

Contemporary drawings show that the interior was still bare and relatively unfurnished when Lord Somers died in 1841, but the 2nd Earl called in A.W.N. Pugin and J.G. Crace (collaborators in the internal decoration of the new Houses of Parliament) to decorate the Drawing Room. His successor, the 3rd Earl (d 1883), a Lord-in-Waiting to Queen Victoria, employed

G.F. Fox to remodel the rest of the main rooms in the manner of the Italian Renaissance. He was an enthusiastic collector, and introduced most of the interesting furniture and works of art in the house today, as well as a superb collection of historic armour. He was also responsible, with Fox, for making the terraces on the garden side of the house, and for planting the numerous conifers in the grounds. The present owner has recently restored the interior to its late-19C splendour and has opened up more rooms to the public.

The house is entered through a *porte-cochre* which leads into the huge top-lit **Hall** with Norman detailing. This has been redecorated as a 'living hall' of the type popular in the late 19C, and is now hung with family portraits, including one by Reynolds of Elizabeth Eliot, later Lady Somers, as a child. The benches were designed by Smirke for the house, and there is a massive 17C Flemish ebony cabinet presented to Lord Somers in the early 18C. The adjacent **Inner Hall** provides an appropriately gloomy setting for the 3rd Earl's collection of armour, one of the best in the country, most of it European of the 15C, 16C, and 17C, but with some specimens from Asia and Africa. The main reception rooms are arranged in a circuit around the hall. The **Dining Room**, little altered since the 1820s except for the painting of the ceiling (possibly by Pugin), contains portraits of the Stuarts after Van Dyck and works by Kneller, Lely (the Lord Chancellor, Lord Somers) and Romney. The sumptuous **Drawing Room** is a complete contrast, with its plaster Gothic 'vault' by Bernasconi dating from the 1820s, and rich and colourful fittings added by Pugin and Crace in 1849–50: panelling in wood, a chimneypiece and wall-paintings heavy with heraldry, a many branched metal chandelier, and furniture to match. The walls are hung with excellent late-17C Brussels and Gobelin tapestries introduced by the 2nd Earl. The recently redecorated **Octagon Saloon**, at the centre of the garden front, contains some early-19C furniture, but the main interest lies in the collection of portraits by G.F. Watts, a frequent visitor to the house in the 1850s. The 3rd Earl Somers was a friend of Tennyson, and his portrait hangs here, along with those of the actress Ellen Terry and her sister, and of Lady Somers.

The magnificent **Library**, next door, is an impressive reminder of the mid-Victorian fascination with the early Italian Renaissance; much of the inlaid woodwork was made in Venice and Verona to Fox's designs, as were the marble chimneypieces which closely followed quattrocento models. The furniture and well-preserved French tapestries of c 1620 brought from Fontainebleau after the 1848 Revolution (notice the contemporary buildings and formal gardens in the background) combine in this setting to create an impression of civilised and privileged comfort. The books include items from the collection of Dr Nash, the Worcestershire historian, and a small room in the south east turret contains photographs of the family by Julia Margaret Cameron, sister-in-law of the 3rd Earl. The Italian Renaissance theme is taken up again in the **Billiard Room**, where some of the 3rd Earl's pictures, including anonymous portraits of the poet Tasso and his patron, the Duchess of Urbino, and more works by Watts, are displayed against a background of walnut panelling from Sienna dated 1646; the carving around the mirror over the fireplace is in the manner of Grinling Gibbons, and came from Reigate Priory, Surrey. The grey and gloomy **Staircase Hall** is hung with more good pictures, notably Salvator Rosa's 'Empedocles on Etna', an early (late 1660s) instance of the 'sublime' sensibility, together with three 17C Bruges tapestries; the furnishings include a wooden chandelier from the Corsini Palace in Florence. More

Italian furniture and pictures can be dimly seen in the tenebrous north-facing **State Bedroom**, notably a 'Last Supper' by Jacopo Bassano and a Tintoretto 'Baptism of Christ'.

The first floor affords views down into the Hall through colonnades of differently coloured marble. Some of the **bedrooms** have been recently restored, including one with Chinese wallpaper and another with a picture by Hondecoeter over the fireplace. There are views out to the Malvern Hills, but the **Chapel**, over the Octagon Saloon, exudes a dim religious light through its late-19C stained-glass windows. Outside, in a corridor, is a view of Naples (1783) by Jacob Philipp Hackert.

GCT

Hanbury Hall

4m east of Droitwich to north of B4090 Droitwich–Alcester: National Trust, tel. 0527 821214. Open Apr–Oct Sat–Mon 2–6. Refreshments.

This large red-brick house was built in the first decade of the 18C for Thomas Vernon, representative of a younger branch of the Vernons of Haddon Hall and Sudbury Hall, Derbyshire (qv.), whose grandfather had purchased the estate 70 years before. Vernon was a successful barrister who subsequently became MP for Worcester, and the house is a monument to his social and political ambitions. It stands in open parkland at the end of an avenue, well away from the village with its hilltop church containing a good collection of family tombs. From a distance it looks conventional enough, with its hipped roof, dormer windows and cupola, but the squareish ground-plan is unusual for its date (it only emerged after several changes of mind on the part of the builder) and the entrance front has a striking central feature in the form of a pediment resting on a pair of giant engaged Corinthian columns. There was a similar feature at Ragley Hall, Warwickshire (qv.), not far away, but although three elevations by obscure local architects are preserved in the house, none is identical to any of the present façades, and the identity of the designer has eluded detection.

Some internal alterations were carried out by Anthony Keck for Emma Vernon and her husband (who later became the Marquess of Exeter) c 1776, and the original formal gardens were landscaped away at about the same time. R.W. Billings created the attractive formal entrance forecourt at the entrance in the 1850s, but since then there have been few major changes. The house remained in the hands of the Vernons until 1962, when it was conveyed virtually empty to the National Trust. Since then the original portraits and some items of furniture have returned, and other items have been introduced, including an excellent collection of English porcelain given to the Trust by R.S. Watney. There was a major overhaul in 1990–91, and the house is currently available on weekdays for meetings and for private and corporate entertaining.

The outstanding internal feature of Hanbury Hall is the early-18C staircase, one of the finest of its date in England. It rises out of the Entrance Hall without any visual interruption; and the wooden stairs with their delicately carved balusters are cantilevered out from the walls, painted by Sir James Thornhill c 1710 with representations of the story of Achilles set in an architectural framework. Note especially the exuberantly Baroque figure of Mercury tumbling over the cornice on the west wall, his finger pointing to a picture of the Tory Dr Sacheverell about to be burnt by the Furies—an allusion to the politics of Thomas Vernon, whose bewigged bust is over the Hall fireplace. There are two ceiling paintings by Thornhill in the otherwise remodelled Dining Room, which is hung with portraits of the Vernons, and contains Bow and Chelsea porcelain figures from the Watney collection. More porcelain can be found in the Parlour and behind the Hall. In the bedroom above the Hall there is a bed with its original wool damask hangings of the 1720s. The long west range (now housing the tea rooms) looks out over a broad expanse of lawns, in which traces of the original formal layout can be discerned; an early-18C Orangery and Gallery also survive in the grounds.

GCT

Hartlebury Castle

5m south of Kidderminster to west of A449 Kidderminster–Worcester: The Church Commissioners, tel. 0229 250410. Open Easter–early Sept Wed and 1st Sun in month 2–4.

Hartlebury has belonged to the see of Worcester since at least the 10C, and there has been an episcopal residence on the present site since the middle of the 13C, when a fortified house was built in which Edward I was entertained on his way to crush the Welsh in 1282. The nucleus of the present large and impressive house is the red sandstone hall block, built by Bishop Carpenter (1458–62). The building was sacked by Parliamentary troops in 1646, but Bishop Fleetwood (1675–83) restored it and built the hipped-roofed extensions on either side of the site of the medieval service and parlour wings. Henry Keene, the surveyor to Westminster Abbey, was employed by Bishop Maddox c 1750 to embellish the medieval chapel next to the south wing in the newly fashionable Gothic manner; and soon after his enthronement in 1759 Bishop Johnson introduced the pointed windows in the hall block and wings and created the Saloon next to the Hall, possibly with the help of the carpenter-architect, Stiff Leadbetter. The façade has been little altered since, but in 1781–82 Bishop Hurd built a Library on to the west side of the Hall to the designs of a local architect, James Smith of Shifnal (Shropshire), with Adamesque decoration carried out by Joseph Bromfield of Shrewsbury.

The late-17C walled forecourt still survives in front of the unusually long façade, with its Rococo Gothic clock turret in the centre. A porch of c 1675 with the arms of Bishop Fleetwood leads into the Hall, which retains its 15C arch-braced roof. There is an impressive array of episcopal portraits going back to the 15C, including the future Pope Clement VII—an absentee Bishop of Worcester in the early 16C—the Protestant martyr Hugh Latimer and the Elizabethan Archbishop of Canterbury, John Whitgift. The Saloon, to the south was decorated c 1759 with Rococo embellishments in *papier mâché* and now contains copies of Gainsborough's portraits of George III and Queen Charlotte, commemorating a royal visit in 1788. The Chapel has been little altered since the 18C and still contains its Gothick furnishings and absurdly unconvincing plaster fan-vault; this is one of the best though least-known ensembles of its kind and date in the country. Equally fine is the Library, a delicately neo-classical room divided into three by Ionic columns in scagliola, and looking west over the surviving fragment of the medieval moat. It contains all its original fittings, as well as Bishop Hurd's collection of 7000 books, many of them formerly belonging to the poets Pope and Addison, with their notes in the margins, and a portrait of Hurd by Gainsborough. The north wing now serves as the County Museum (different opening times).

GCT

Harvington Hall

3m south east of Kidderminster near Mustow Green at intersection of A450 and A448: R.C. Archdiocese of Birmingham, tel. 0562 777267. Open Mar–Oct daily (not Good Fri) 11.30–5.30. Refreshments.

This moated red-brick building, hidden away among winding lanes, stands on the site of a medieval timber house which was bought in 1529 by John Pakington, a successful lawyer who built up a large estate in north Worcestershire. He left Harvington to his nephew, whose son Humphrey Pakington, a Catholic recusant, built most of the present house c 1580. He was succeeded by his daughter, Mary Yate, from whom the house was inherited at the end of the 17C by the Throckmortons of Coughton Court, Warwickshire (qv.). Rarely used during the 18C, the building sank into decline and was later leased out to tenant farmers and stripped of its fittings. Because of its recusant associations it was given to the present owners in 1923, and a major restoration began six years later.

In its present form Harvington Hall is a highly irregular and puzzling building. The east range, which faces the visitor on arrival, has a plain two-storeyed centre (probably including part of the medieval house) with a taller gabled block of c 1580 on the left and another tower-like block on the right, added in the second half of the 17C. A passage leads into a confined courtyard, with Humphrey Pakington's chamber wing on the site of the medieval hall to the left (south), on to which the Throckmortons added three gables c 1700, partly carried on a curious stone arch. The Throckmortons also demolished most of the wing on the west of the courtyard, which may have contained the hall of the Pakingtons' house. Two timber-framed and brick outbuildings survive beyond the courtyard, one of which was used as a Catholic chapel in the 18C, and has recently been restored.

The house is a warren of empty or partially furnished rooms, with a bewildering number of staircases connecting the different levels. Some rooms, like the Great Chamber on the first floor of the south range, have lost their panelling, and the main staircase is a replacement of the original which is now at Coughton. The pictures and mementoes of Catholic priests sheltered here, together with the plethora of priest-holes and the chapel on the top floor painted to represent the blood of Christ's Passion, vividly evoke the beleaguered recusant community of the 16C and 17C. From an artistic point of view, the main interest of the house lies in a series of highly sophisticated though fragmentary late-16C wall paintings in monochrome, uncovered when the house was restored; note the arabesques in a first-floor passage and the 'Nine Worthies' in a passageway on the floor above.

GCT

Hellens

East of Much Marcle (entrance opp. church) on A449 Ledbury–Ross: the
Pennington-Mellor-Munthe Trust. Open Easter–Sept Wed, Sat/Sun and
BH Mon 2–6. Guided tours.

Hellens derives its name from the Helyon family, stewards of the manor of
Marcle Audley in the parish of Much Marcle in the 14C. Thomas Walwyn,
several times sheriff of Herefordshire, purchased the estate in 1403, and,
except for a short period in the 1930s, it has remained in the hands of
descendants ever since. The house, like most others in the county, probably
originated as a timber-framed building, but it was encased in brick in the
1450s. The Walwyns, who were Roman Catholics, fell upon hard times after
getting involved in a damaging law-suit early in the 16C, and in 1619 the
house was described as ruined. It was restored and enlarged by Fulke
Walwyn shortly before the Civil War, but after the death of his son in 1695,
it went through a bewildering succession of heiresses and co-heiresses
which led to long periods of neglect and the demolition of some of the 17C
additions. It was sold in 1930, and restored after the Second World War by
Hilda Pennington-Mellor, wife of the Swedish writer, Axel Munthe
(cf. Southside House, Greater London). She was descended from the
Walwyns, and she and her family have refurnished the house and
introduced an unexpectedly good collection of pictures.

The L-shaped house stands in remote pastoral country, and consists of a
medieval north range (seen first) and a brick cross-wing almost certainly
built by Fulke Walwyn, whose initials appear with the date 1641, the year
of his marriage, on the attractive dovecote nearby. The house is entered
from a small courtyard through a door next to a 16C staircase turret, giving
access to the medieval hall, now known as the Court Room.

The main rooms exude a strangely contrived feeling of age. The White
Drawing Room, on the ground floor of the older range, contains some
interesting Jacobean portraits of children, and a version of one of Reynolds's
'fancy pictures', the 'Laughing Girl', while the downstairs rooms of the
cross-wing (the Staircase Hall and the Music Room) retain their original
wood panelling and rustic plasterwork. In one of the upstairs rooms (the
Cordova Room), hung with Spanish leather, there is a good early-17C
chimneypiece attributed to the local carver John Abel, a portrait of a
sultry-looking Catherine of Braganza, and a mahogany stool supposedly
given by her to one of the Walwyns. The adjacent Queen's Bedroom has a
mid-16C ribbed plaster ceiling and a plaster overmantel with the initials of
Mary Tudor, commemorating the family's adherence to her cause; there are
also pictures attributed to Perugino and Tintoretto. The last rooms to be
seen are in a recently built range to the west of the courtyard; they contain
portraits by Gainsborough, Raeburn and Hogarth (the actress Kitty Mark-
ham), and a large formal portrait of the early-18C Whig politician, the Duke
of Wharton, from whose family some of the pictures at Hellens came by
descent to the present owners.

GCT

Kinnersley Castle

4m of Weobley on A4122: Katherine Henning, tel. 0544 327407. Open end
July–early Sept daily except Tues 2–4. Refreshments.

This impressive stone-built house stands in the lush pastoral country of the
Welsh borderland, and incorporates masonry from the fortified medieval
residence of the Kinnersley and de la Bere families—hence the name castle.
In its present form it dates mainly from a rebuilding by Roger Vaughan,
former MP for Radnorshire, who bought the property in 1588 and died in
1607. His widow sold the house the Francis Smallman in 1618, and it was
sold again in 1660 to Sir Thomas Morgan, whose descendants kept it until
1801. Since then it has passed through many hands. There were alterations
at the end of the 18C, and again c 1855 and in 1904–6. The estate was
broken up at the end of the Second World War, but in 1954 the house was
bought by the father of the present owner, and for many years it was a home
for the elderly. It is now used both as a family residence and as a setting for
residential courses, with some rooms let out for bed-and-breakfast accommodation.

The house is an L-shaped building of rubble stone, three-storeys high
with stepped brick gables—a feature more common in East Anglia than the
Welsh borders—and a tall staircase tower at the junction of the two wings;
one of the wings was originally longer than it is now, and the buildings may
once have stretched around a four-sided courtyard. The original entrance
was in the middle of the north range, which still preserves its medieval
masonry, but this range has been shortened and the house is now entered
through a Victorian porch sheltering a late-16C doorway. The Drawing
Room was panelled in wood in the early 18C, but there is some earlier
panelling in the other downstairs rooms, including the Ballroom; this was
the hall of the Elizabethan house, but was turned into kitchens c 1700 and
restored in the early 20C. The most impressive room is the Solar or great
chamber over the hall, with a splendid swirly plaster ceiling and frieze, and
a chimneypiece flanked by Ionic columns and surmounted by a plaster
overmantel showing the English oak rising out of the Tudor rose—a patriotic
allusion to the defeat of the Spanish Armada. There are more early
chimneypieces in the other first-floor rooms, one of them with the date 1618.
Visitors are allowed to climb to the top of the tower to enjoy the view west
to the Black Mountains and Radnor Forest, and they can also descend to
the cellars. They should visit the adjacent parish church with its distinctive
medieval saddleback tower, 16C and 17C carvings and monuments, and
19C embellishments by G.F. Bodley.

GCT

Little Malvern Court

3m south of Great Malvern off A449 Malvern–Ledbury at junction with
A4104: Mr and Mrs T. Berington, tel. 0684 892988. Open late Apr–late July
Wed, Thur 2–5.15. Guided tours.

This picturesque house of timber, brick and stone is attractively situated
against the eastern slopes of the Malvern Hills, next to the 14C and 15C
tower and chancel of Little Malvern Priory, now the parish church. It grew
up after the Reformation around a still extant medieval hall, once the

monks' refectory or part of the Priors' lodgings on the west side of the now-vanished cloisters. The manor was acquired in 1554 by a local man, Henry Russell, and he may have been responsible for building the north range of the present house, at right angles to the Hall, and now forming one of four ranges around a small courtyard. This range was partly clad in brick in the 18C, but some of the original close-studded timber framing survives at the west end.

Like Harvington Hall (qv.), Little Malvern Court was a recusant house, and little was built in the 17C or 18C, when the estate passed to the Berington family. It was subsequently inherited by a distant cousin, William Berington of Hereford, whose son Charles Michael married an heiress from Ireland, and in 1860 commissioned Joseph Aloysius Hansom, a popular architect in Catholic circles (and the inventor of the eponymous cab), to rebuild the south and west ranges. Hansom created the distinctive south elevation facing the gardens, with a conical turret rising above walls of random rubble stone, and the Malvern Hills forming a dramatic backdrop. Since then the exterior has changed little, except for the removal of roughcast from the older timber-framed parts of the house in the 1960s, but the interiors have been considerably altered in recent years.

By far the most interesting of the rooms shown to the public is the medieval Hall which the visitor enters at first-floor level and which still retains its original spere-truss and splendid early-14C open timber roof, revealed when a false plaster ceiling was removed in the 1960s. At the north end, close to the entrance, is a picture by the 19C French artist, Paul Delaroche, of Charles I's minister the Earl of Strafford on his way to execution, and in the roof space at the south end there is a small Catholic chapel recalling one which was there in times of persecution. Visitors then go down a 16C spiral staircase into the tiny courtyard and then to the largely Victorian west range, where the redecorated Dining Room is hung with family portraits. Outside, the present owners have created an attractive garden with lawns and borders sloping down on each side of a series of five lakes formed out of what were once the monastic fish-ponds.

GCT

Lower Brockhampton Manor

1½m north of A44 Worcester–Leominster, 2m east of Bromyard: National Trust, tel. 0885 488099. Open Apr–Oct Wed–Sun, BH Mon 10–5 (Oct 10–4).

This timber-framed late-14C or early-15C house stands hidden away within its moat in deep countryside at the end of a long track leading through the parkland of the Georgian Brockhampton Hall. A comparison of the two houses vividly demonstrates the huge changes in the lives of the landed gentry which took place between the Middle Ages and the 18C. Despite the presence of manorial appurtenances like a detached late-12C chapel (now a ruin) and a miniature gatehouse of c 1530–40, the older house is essentially a large farmhouse, and there are still farm buildings close at hand. It was built, no doubt on the site of an older building, by a member of the Domulton family, and it passed by marriage to the Habingtons and then in the 16C to the Barnebys, who carried out alterations to the east or parlour wing in the 17C. The building of the red-brick Brockhampton Hall (not open to the public) by Bartholomew Barneby on the higher ground to the south (c 1765), probably to the designs of Thomas Pritchard of Shrewsbury, enabled the family to live in the manner expected of the Georgian squirearchy, and the older house was allowed to moulder away in the hands of tenant farmers before being rescued by the National Trust, which took over the whole estate after the Second World War.

Apart from the possible disappearance of a west wing, the old house is an intact example of a small West Midlands manor house of the late Middle Ages. The hall block has the characteristic square timber-framing of the region, but the later gatehouse, with its jettied upper floor, and the surviving cross-wing, have closely set timbers and decorated bargeboards to indicate superior social status; the effect of the modest later additions can be seen by walking round the moat. Inside, the only room of note is the Hall, open to the roof and divided into two bays by a base-cruck truss, with a spere-truss at the east end marking the screens passage. Portraits of the Barneby family hang here, and there are also two 18C estate maps on display.

GCT

Moccas Court

13m west of Hereford off B4352 between Blakemere and Bredwardine: R.T.G. Chester-Master, tel. 09817 381. Open Apr–Sept Sun 2–6.

This plain red-brick house of 1775–81 stands in attractive pastoral country on the banks of the River Wye, celebrated since the late 18C by lovers of picturesque scenery. The builder was Sir George Amyand, a Huguenot who inherited a banking fortune and married Catherine Cornewall, the heiress to the estate, in 1771, subsequently taking her surname. He first approached Robert Adam with a view to replacing the existing house, but settled eventually on a simpler design by Anthony Keck, an architect with a successful practice in the West Midlands, though Adam's decorative schemes were used for at least one of the rooms. The park was laid out by 'Capability' Brown , starting in 1778, and some further improvements were carried out by Humphry Repton in 1793. Repton's partner John Nash designed two lodge cottages (which still exist) in 1804, but since then there have been few changes, apart from the unfortunate sale of the contents in 1946, when the house was let, having been left uninhabited for 30 years. The property later passed to the present owner's father, and when the lease terminated in 1969, the present owner began to refurnish and repair the house, which he has made his home.

The house is a severe though well-proportioned box standing among lawns in the approved late-18C manner, with little external embellishment apart from a Venetian window set in a relieving arch over the unusual semicircular porch (added in 1792). Inside, the rooms are grouped around a central staircase, which is entered through a narrow Hall. As at the almost exactly contemporary Berrington Hall (qv.), built by one of Sir George Cornewall's political rivals, the staircase is dramatically top-lit, but here it is semicircular in shape, with the stairs going up in a single sweep. The tour takes in the main reception rooms, which are, with one exception, sparingly but elegantly decorated; they include the Music Room, with a frieze of musical instruments (but alas without the chamber organ made for it), and the Library, which commands a view over to the River Wye, whose beauties were celebrated by the watercolourist Thomas Hearne in some pictures still hanging in the house. The pièce de résistance is undoubtedly the circular Drawing Room in the centre of the garden front, with a plaster ceiling, chimneypiece and doorcases designed by Adam, and wallpaper with 'grotesque' designs by the Frenchman Jean Reveillon, purchased in London in 1790; this spacious, largely empty room ranks high among the neo-classical ensembles of the late 18C. Equally impressive, though in a very different way, is the small but well-preserved Norman parish church, one of the finest in an area notable for good churches.

GCT

Witley Court

10m north west of Worcester near Great Witley on A443: English Heritage, tel. 0299 896636. Open Apr–Sept daily 10–6; Nov–Mar daily (except Mon and Christmas) 10–4.

This massive house is now a well-cared-for ruin, but in its heyday it was one of the great houses of the Midlands, and its decline and fall in the 20C is a poignant example of the fate of all too many country houses in the modern age. It started life as a Jacobean brick house erected by the Russell family, but was sold after the Civil War to Thomas Foley, a Worcestershire ironmaster. He built two towers on the north side, and his grandson added the wings which project to enclose the entrance courtyard through which the house is approached today. In 1735 the 1st Lord Foley built a new parish church to the west of this courtyard, and in 1747 he employed James Gibbs to incorporate paintings and furnishings bought at the auction of the contents of Cannons House, Middlesex, the spectacular home of the Duke of Chandos. The park was landscaped in the second half of the 18C, involving the removal of the village (which came too close to the south front of the house), and in about 1805 John Nash carried out a major reconstruction of the house for the 3rd Lord Foley, including the addition of giant Ionic porticoes to the north and south fronts, the latter probably the largest in any English country house.

Chronic debt forced the 4th Lord Foley to sell the estate in 1837 to the trustees of William, Lord Ward, who had inherited a vast fortune made by the Dudley family in the coal and iron industries of the Black Country. He was made Earl of Dudley, and, with the help of the local architect Samuel Daukes and the garden designer W.A. Nesfield, set about transforming the house and its setting once again in the 1850s, but in 1920 his son, the 2nd Earl, sold the estate to a Kidderminster carpet manufacturer, Sir Herbert Smith. He, in turn, sold it after a severe fire in 1938, and the estate was subsequently broken up and the house (though fortunately not the church) allowed to fall into ruin. The house and what remained of the garden was 'taken into care' by the Government in 1972, and visitors are now allowed to walk through the shell of the building and explore the sad remnants of Nesfield's magnificent parterres.

The outer walls of the house remain much as they were after Daukes' Italianate remodelling in ashlar stone, and two huge mid-19C fountains survive in dried-up pools in the gardens, but the interior decoration and the paths and flowerbeds shown in early-20C photographs have all gone. Less melancholy is the church, which has one of the finest Baroque interiors in England, the walls and ceiling covered with exuberant decorations copied in papier mâché from those at Cannons (by Bagutti), and enclosing paintings by Antonio Bellucci. The painted-glass windows of 1719–21 also came from Cannons, as did the pulpit and organ case, but the rest of the woodwork dates from the mid 19C. The huge and pompous monument to the 1st Lord Foley, by Rysbrack, somehow epitomises the spirit of a place in which the visitor is unavoidably confronted with the vanity of human aspirations.

GCT

HERTFORDSHIRE

Gorhambury

2m west of St Albans off A4147 St Albans–Hemel Hempstead: the Earl of Verulam, tel. 0727 54051. Open May–Sept Thur 2–5. Guided tours.

The approach to Gorhambury leads past the remains of the theatre of the vanished Roman city of Verulamium, and the bold Corinthian portico of the present house, built to the designs of Sir Robert Taylor in 1777–84, bears witness to the continued allure of classical antiquity in the 18C. The estate belonged to St Albans Abbey in the Middle Ages, but was purchased early in Queen Elizabeth's reign by Sir Nicholas Bacon, Lord Keeper of the Great Seal. He built a new house at Gorhambury in 1563–68, a ruined fragment of which can be seen from a raised terrace in the garden of the present building. It became the home of his younger son, the philosopher and politician Francis Bacon, and John Aubrey later wrote that 'when his lordship was at his country house at Gorhambury, St Albans seemed as if the court were there, so nobly did he live'. His monument can be seen in the parish church of St Michael, close to the remains of the Roman city, but his villa, Verulam House, a mile from Gorhambury, described by Aubrey as 'the most ingeniously contrived little pile that ever I saw', has alas totally vanished.

Bacon left Gorhambury to his former secretary, Sir Thomas Meautys, who married Anne Bacon, great-granddaughter of the Lord Keeper, and the property subsequently passed to her second husband, Sir Harbottle Grimston, Master of the Rolls and Speaker in the Convention parliament of 1659–60. His descendant, the 3rd Viscount Grimston, built the present house, which still contains a notable collection of family portraits transferred from the older building. His son, who inherited in 1806, was made Earl of Verulam, and the family has continued to live at Gorhambury ever since.

The house is a handsome, well-proportioned neo-Palladian building, refaced in Portland stone in the 20C, with a rusticated ground floor and a broad flight of steps leading up to the portico at piano nobile level. The entrance is through a two-storeyed galleried Hall, somewhat altered by William Burn, who carried out work for the 3rd Earl starting in 1847. It contains portraits comprising part of a 'Gallery of the Great' brought together by Sir Harbottle Grimston after the Restoration, a carpet dated 1570, and a remarkable pair of windows with 17C English enamelled glass depicting birds, animals and plants commissioned by Francis Bacon for the gallery of the previous house. The main reception rooms are arranged, as in many of Taylor's houses, around a central top-lit staircase. They contain impressive portraits of Sir Francis Bacon and his contemporaries, including works by his cousin Sir Nathaniel Bacon, 'a great lover of all good arts and learning'. The most attractive room from a decorative point of view is the Drawing Room, with its delicate stucco frieze, eccentric chimneypiece attributed to Piranesi, and some good late-18C and early-19C portraits and furniture (as well as an organ played by Haydn). The Library still houses some of Francis Bacon's books arranged according to his own categories of learning, and there are some unusual late 16C terracotta busts of the Lord Keeper, Sir Nicholas Bacon, his wife and his son Francis as a boy.

GCT

Hatfield House

East of Hatfield, A1(M) exit 4: the Marquess of Salisbury, tel. 0707 262823.
Open end Mar–mid Oct daily except Mon, but open BH Mon 12–4.15
(Sun 1.30–5, BH Mon 11–5). Guided tours. Refreshments.

Hatfield House, the finest and best-known of all Jacobean houses in
England, was built in 1607–12 by Robert Cecil, 1st Earl of Salisbury and
younger son of the great Elizabethan statesman, Lord Burghley
(cf. Burghley House, Cambridgeshire). Cecil not only trod in his father's
footsteps as chief minister both to Queen Elizabeth during her declining
years and to James I at the beginning of his reign; he also inherited his
father's taste for magnificent building. The design of the house was worked
out by the carpenter and surveyor, Robert Lyminge (cf. Blickling Hall,
Norfolk), under the general supervision of Simon Basil, Surveyor of the
King's Works, and of Cecil himself. The west wing was rebuilt after being
gutted by fire in 1835, but otherwise the structure has remained intact in
the hands of the family, several of whom have played an important part in
national and international politics in the last 150 years.

Hatfield came to Robert Cecil from James I, in exchange for the now-
demolished house at Theobalds, not far away. The estate had belonged to
the Bishops of Ely during the Middle Ages, and the hall range of the **old
Bishops' Palace**, a substantial red-brick building of the 1480s with a
spacious hall covered by a high, arch-braced roof, still survives to the west
of the forecourt at the approach to the stark, cliff-like north front of the
house. The new house was planned conventionally, but the main block is
two rooms deep, and the wings are also much wider than usual to allow for
substantial suites of grand rooms at first-floor level, which could be used
as lodgings for both James I and his Queen. The main architectural display
was reserved for the **south front** (the original entrance), an attractive if
somewhat inchoate composition with pairs of ogee-topped towers at the
end of each wing and a stone-clad centre with a loggia, a frontispiece of
the classical orders and clock tower, all of which may show the influence
of the young Inigo Jones, who was paid £10 'for drawing of some architecture' in 1610.

A screens passage leads from the north entrance to the **Hall**, which retains
most of its original Jacobean woodwork, full of fantastic Mannerist
intricacy, with extravagantly carved screens at each end—a most unusual
feature. The already rich effect was heightened in the 19C, when the 17C
Brussels tapestries on the fireplace wall were introduced and the ceiling
painted (by Taldini, 1878). There is an excellent cabinet of c 1600 with two
silver figures of the Apostles, and, close to the fireplace, Nicholas Hilliard's
famous 'Ermine Portrait' of the bejewelled Queen Elizabeth (who spent
much of her childhood at the Old Palace), with an ermine, a symbol of
virginity, by her left hand; a full-length portrait of Mary, Queen of Scots
(possibly by Rowland Lockey) hangs nearby, and there are also anonymous
portraits of Lord Burghley and of Robert Cecil, the builder of the house. A
doorway at the 'upper' end leads to the main Staircase, at the foot of which
hangs another representation of the Virgin Queen, the so-called 'Rainbow
Portrait' of c 1600, attributed to Marcus Gheeraerts, depicting the Queen
holding a rainbow, representing peace, under a Latin inscription translated
as 'No rainbow without the sun'. The **Staircase** itself is an exuberant piece
of wood carving, with highly embellished newel posts surmounted by putti,

some of them playing musical instruments, heraldic beasts, and a pair of gates at the bottom to prevent dogs from going upstairs. There are several family portraits, including the 2nd Earl of Salisbury and his wife by George Geldorp, and one by Wissing of the 4th Earl, painted over the Duke of Monmouth after the failure of his rebellion in 1685.

The first floor was divided, like a royal palace, into a 'King's side' and a 'Queen's side' with a Gallery over the loggia on the south front for communication between the two. The only one of the King's rooms to be seen is the former great chamber, now called the **King James Drawing Room**, which is dominated by a huge marble fireplace and overmantel incorporating a life-sized statue of James I by the French statuary, Maximilian Colt, who also carved the impressive tomb of Robert Cecil in Hatfield parish church. Most of the furniture was introduced in the 18C, and the room was much altered in the 19C, when the intricate ceiling with its stucco pendants was gilded, and full-length portraits of the 3rd Marquis (Prime Minister at the end of Queen Victoria's reign) and his wife, by George Richmond, introduced (there are also earlier portraits by Reynolds and Lawrence). The **Gallery**, one of the most attractive early-17C rooms in England, was furnished comfortably in the 19C, but retains its original texture. It has a ceiling made up of swirling lines of plaster, inlaid wood panelling, two marbled chimneypieces, and contemporary cabinets (a 16C or 17C French ebony cabinet is especially outstanding). It was lengthened in the early 19C by the incorporation of two smaller rooms at each end, the easternmost of which now contains an extremely rare collection of 16C and 17C rock crystal table pieces, exquisitely enamelled with gold and precious stones, some bearing the ownership marks of Lord Burghley and Robert Cecil. The **Winter Dining Room**, on the 'Queen's side', was made out of two smaller rooms in the early 19C, and contains another, rather cruder, Jacobean chimneypiece, brought from elsewhere, along with portraits of James I by Colone and Charles I by Mytens, and a 16C copy of Durer's 'Adam and Eve'.

The **Library** has also been altered since the early 17C, when it served as a second great chamber; the mosaic portrait of Robert Cecil, made in Venice and given by the diplomat Sir Henry Wotton, was moved to its present position over the fireplace in the 1780s. A selection of manuscripts, including letters from Queen Elizabeth, Mary, Queen of Scots, and others, is displayed in cases, and there are portraits on easels of the literary critic and scholar, Lord David Cecil (by Augustus John), and of him and his brothers and sisters by Halliday. A small collection of Old Master paintings, including a Cuyp landscape, is hung on the walls of a room at the west end of the Gallery, where a hat and gloves traditionally said to have belonged to Queen Elizabeth are also preserved in a glass case. From here a subsidiary staircase leads down to the **Armoury**, formed out of the loggia on the south front in 1834; this now houses a chamber organ bought by Robert Cecil in 1609 and a set of tapestries of the Four Seasons made in 1611 at the workshop established by William Sheldon in Warwickshire. The galleried **Chapel** was greatly remodelled in 1869, but still retains the original painted woodwork of the gallery fronts and the early-17C stained glass of Old and New Testament subjects in the east window, by Louis Dauphin and Richard Butler of Southwark and Martin van Bentham. Visitors leave the house through the original Kitchen, which has been restored to its 1832 appearance.

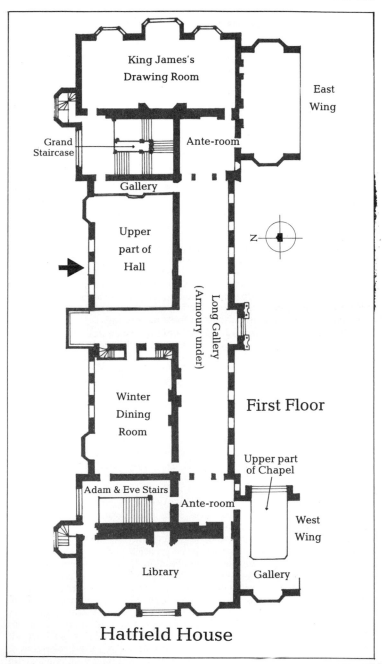

King James's
Drawing Room

East
Wing

Grand
Staircase

Ante-room

Gallery

Upper
part of
Hall

Z

Long Gallery
(Armoury under)

First Floor

Winter
Dining
Room

Upper part
of Chapel

Adam & Eve Stairs

Ante-room

West
Wing

Library

Gallery

Hatfield House

Knebworth House

2m south west of Stevenage, A1(M) exit 7: the Lord Cobbold, tel. 0438
812661. Open Apr–early Oct Sat, Sun, BH Mon (June–early Sept daily
except Mon) 12–5. Refreshments.

In its present form Knebworth is an early-Victorian remodelling of a much
older courtyard house of brick, built by Robert Lytton, a favourite of Henry
VII, soon after he had purchased the estate in 1490. Though much altered
in the 17C and early 18C, this building survived intact until 1814, when it
was drastically reduced in size by Elizabeth Lytton Bulwer, leaving only
the hall range (doubled in width at an earlier date), whose façades were
stuccoed over and remodelled in an uninspired Tudor–Gothic style by John
Biagio Rebecca, son of the late-18C decorative painter of the same name.
The turrets and projections of Rebecca's rebuilding still survive, but in 1844
Mrs Bulwer's son, Sir Edward Bulwer-Lytton, author of *The Last of the
Barons* and other historical novels, friend of Benjamin Disraeli and
subsequently Colonial Secretary, employed H.E. Kendall to heighten the
picturesque effect of the exterior; at the same time the interiors were
sumptuously redecorated by J.G. Crace, a frequent collaborator of A.W.N.
Pugin. Bulwer-Lytton's grandson, the 2nd Earl of Lytton, did his best to
restore a regime of 'good taste' to the interiors, and employed his brother-
in-law Edwin Lutyens to design the formal gardens to the west of the house
in 1907–11 (Lutyens also designed some houses and a church in the village
of Knebworth); Lytton's daughter married the 1st Lord Cobbold, Governor
of the Bank of England, and their son lives here today.

The house stands on its own in a park near the flint church, which contains
an excellent series of family monuments. The interiors reflect a bewildering
series of changes of taste, from the classicism of the 17C and 18C through
the wild extravagance of Victorian Romanticism and back again to neo-
Georgian restraint. The first major room is the Hall, approached through
an ornate screen of c 1630, its medieval walls masked by the highly unusual
wood panelling of c 1700 with giant Corinthian columns and pediments,
attributed to William Talman, embellished by Bulwer-Lytton in the mid 19C
(an inscription by him runs around the frieze) and subsequently stripped
of its varnish; there are portraits of 15C and 16C Lyttons on the walls. The
Drawing Room, on the site of the medieval Parlour, and the Library were
both plainly redecorated in the early 20C; the latter contains Bulwer-
Lytton's collection of books and a fireplace by Lutyens incorporating a
marble roundel with a portrait of his son the 1st Earl of Lytton, Viceroy of
India, by Alfred Gilbert, and a portrait by G.F. Watts hanging above.

The neo-Tudor Staircase has been little altered since Bulwer-Lytton's
time, and still contains the suits of armour and stained glass windows
purchased to enhance the effect of ancient gloom (some of the plaster has
been removed to reveal the genuinely Tudor brickwork behind). At the top
is the novelist's study with a bizarre collection of objects which belonged
to him, including theatre posters, notices of political meetings and even a
crystal ball. His portrait by Daniel Maclise hangs on the landing outside
alongside a bust of 'Flora' by the early Victorian sculptor John Gibson,
whom he 'discovered' in Rome. The finest of the early-Victorian interiors
is the State Drawing Room, which retains its painted heraldic ceiling and
richly carved chimneypiece by Crace, its stained glass figure of Henry VII
by Hardman (another of Pugin's collaborators), and a varied collection of
ornate furniture by Crace. There are paintings by 17C Italian masters, an

early-18C conversation piece attributed to Amigoni (cf. Moor Park), and Maclise's 'Edward IV visiting Caxton's Printing Press at Westminster' (1850), for which Bulwer-Lytton posed as one of the armour-clad figures. The tour ends in a series of bedrooms, one of which has an Elizabethan or neo-Elizabethan plaster ceiling, as well as a bed in the same style supplied by the dealer Pratt of Bond Street, and a series of portraits of 16C personages in frames by Crace. A museum in the service wing commemorates the connection of the 1st and 2nd Earls of Lytton with India, and in particular the Delhi Durbar of 1877 when Lord Lytton as Viceroy proclaimed Queen Victoria Empress of India.

GCT

Moor Park

1m south east of Rickmansworth near A404 Rickmansworth–Harrow: Three Rivers District Council, tel. 0923 776611. Open all year Mon–Fri (not BH Mon) 10–12, 2–4, Sat 10–12.

This four-square classical house stands in the middle of a golf course on the fringe of London's suburbs. It was built in 1720 by Benjamin Styles, a London merchant, on the site of an earlier brick house belonging to Charles II's illegitimate son, the Duke of Monmouth; parts of the structure of this earlier house and some of its internal decoration survive behind the Portland stone façades of the present building, designed by the artist Sir James Thornhill. The exterior, which recalls some of the public buildings of the late 19C and early 20C, is dominated by a huge, free-standing Corinthian portico stretching the full height of the house, but the original appearance was altered for the worse when the wings flanking the forecourt were demolished in 1785 (a later orangery stands on the site of one of them). Styles dismissed Thornhill after a quarrel in 1728, and the interior was subsequently decorated with paintings by the Venetian artists Jacopo Amigoni and Francesco Sleter and plasterwork by Giovanni Bagutti and the two Artari brothers. Styles's son sold the estate in 1754 to the sailor Lord Anson, who commissioned 'Capability' Brown to landscape the park, and his successor, the politician Sir Lawrence Dundas, employed Robert Adam and Cipriani to redecorate the Dining Room in 1767–69. Since then the house has passed through many owners and has been denuded of all its original furniture. It is currently used as a golf club-house.

The main interest of Moor Park lies in its extravagantly painted and plastered interiors of c 1729–32, of which the most lavish is the Entrance Hall. Like the halls at the exactly contemporary Clandon, Surrey (qv.) and Houghton, Norfolk (qv.), it is two storeys high with a gallery at first-floor level; however, it is more richly embellished, with profuse Baroque plasterwork and a trompe l'oeil dome on the ceiling, figures of classical personages in grisaille at first-floor level, and, finest of all, Amigoni's superbly frivolous paintings of the story of Io (who was turned into a cow) from Ovid's *Metamorphoses* on the ground floor walls, between the doorways in their ponderous 'tabernacle frames'. The Saloon retains its ceiling by Verrio from the earlier house, but the wall paintings of the Four Seasons after Veronese in their lavish ornamental surrounds were painted by Sleter, who was also responsible for painting the staircase walls in 1732. The Dining Room, by contrast, has a delicate ceiling 'after the antique' by Cipriani, but its other decorations have alas disappeared.

HUMBERSIDE

Burton Agnes Hall

On A166 Bridlington–Driffield 6m south west of Bridlington: Burton Agnes
Hall Preservation Trust, tel. 0262 490324. Open Apr–Oct daily 11–5.
Refreshments.

This impressive and beautifully maintained early-17C house stands on the
southern fringe of the Yorkshire Wolds, overlooking the flatness of Holderness. It was begun by Sir Henry Griffith, a member of the Council of the
North, and completed c 1610, following a ground-plan which was probably
supplied by the celebrated master-mason, Robert Smythson. Griffith's
ancestors had acquired the estate by marriage in 1355, and the brick-built
medieval manor house with its late-12C vaulted undercroft still survives,
in the care of English Heritage, to the west of the present house, alongside
the parish church in which Griffith is buried. Griffith's son died childless in
1654, and the house passed to his daughter, who married Sir Matthew
Boynton of Barmston, a few miles away. Their grandson, Sir Griffith
Boynton (d 1730), 'improved his seat at Burton Agnes', and the house then
became the family's main residence. Marcus Wickham-Boynton, who
inherited in 1947 and died in 1989, carried out a major restoration and
introduced an excellent collection of furniture, porcelain and late-19C and
20C paintings and sculptures which enhances the already considerable
interest of the house.

The approach is through a detached brick **gatehouse** with corner turrets,
leading into a formal garden with a gravel path on the axis of the Hall. The
south elevation, at the end of this vista, is one of the most impressive pieces
of architecture of its date in the north of England—a long and symmetrical
three-storeyed block of red brick with gabled bow-windowed projections
at the ends and less pronounced projections, topped by strapwork carvings,
on either side of the **Hall**, one of which, to the left (west), contains the porch,
emphasised on its inner face by a 'frontispiece' of superimposed classical
columns. The rooms are grouped around a courtyard, although as at the
contemporary Chastleton House, Oxfordshire (qv.) this is little more than a
light-well. Several of the original mullioned and transomed windows, both
in the south range and in the lower blocks behind, were replaced by sashes
in the early 18C, but otherwise the elevations have been little altered.

The interiors still preserve many of their richly carved and iconographi-
cally complex Jacobean fittings, some of the finest of which are in the Hall,
approached through the usual screens passage. The screen itself is a
prodigious object, its two wooden arches surmounted by a frieze, with
figures representing the Twelve Tribes of Israel, and then by three tiers of
crudely modelled plaster figures stretching up to the flat 18C ceiling and
including the Apostles and Evangelists as well as personages derived from
classical antiquity—a Renaissance version of the carved reredoses of 14C
and 15C churches like New College Chapel, Oxford, and Winchester
Cathedral. The exuberantly carved alabaster overmantel also mixes sacred
subjects (the Wise and Foolish Virgins) with profane (the Five Senses), and
there are figures representing Apollo and Diana on the arch leading out of
the Hall to the east. The vestibule at the former high table end contains a
large portrait by Gheeraerts of Sir Henry Griffiths' three daughters and a
bust entitled 'Sunita' by Sir Jacob Epstein (1930). Beyond is the **Drawing**

Room—the former parlour—with its early-17C panelling intact and a macabre Mannerist version of the 'Dance of Death' carved in wood over the fireplace, flanked by figures of 'Quiet' and 'Liberty'.

The remaining rooms on the ground floor were remodelled in the 18C and rearranged more recently. The **Chinese Room** derives its name from the 18C lacquer panels (formerly screens) on the walls. The **Dining Room**, at the north-east corner of the house, contains a good collection of 18C English pictures, including a fanciful landscape by Gainsborough, a view of the Arno attributed to Richard Wilson, a 'Fishing Party' by the York-based Frenchman Philip Mercier, and a set of four landscapes of the Boynton family's estates painted c 1762–65 by William Marlow, one of which is a splendid panorama showing Flamborough Head and the nearby town of Bridlington. The adjacent vestibule is hung with late-19C and early-20C canvases including Sickert's 'Sheepshanks House, Bath'.

The upstairs reception rooms are reached by a wooden staircase with carved newel posts unusually linked together by arches. The former great chamber (now the **Upper Drawing Room**) was plainly remodelled with bolection-moulded panelling in the early 18C, and now contains a good collection of 18C furniture and some items of *famille verte* porcelain in a cabinet, as well as paintings by Renoir, Boudin, Utrillo and Gauguin ('Tahitian Woman'). To the south are two panelled Jacobean **state bedrooms** with plaster ceilings—that in the Queen's Room is especially elaborate—and early 18C state beds brought from other houses, with their original hangings; the Queen's Room also has an allegorical chimneypiece dated 1610, with figures of the Virtues and their antitheses. These rooms are separated by a dressing room (the Justices' Room), whose early-16C linenfold panelling was originally at Leconfield Castle, near Beverley.

The most impressive interior of all is the **Gallery**, taking up the whole of the top floor of the south front and restored to its present state by Francis Johnson of York in 1974 after being divided into bedrooms in the early 19C. Johnson recreated the Jacobean plastered barrel ceiling, decorated with tendrils of foliage, out of surviving fragments, and incorporated fittings from two vanished Yorkshire houses, Kilnwick Hall and Methley Castle; the Venetian windows at each end were inserted in the 18C. There is a good collection of Chinese porcelain, and on the walls are water-colours by Edward Lear and canvases by Corot, Courbet ('Cliffs at Entretat'), Manet, Matisse and Vlaminck ('The Village, Evening', 1912)—artists rarely encountered in English country-house collections. To the south there are two smaller rooms containing pictures by Duncan Grant and 20C French realist painters.

GCT

Burton Constable

7½m north east of Hull, 1½m north of Sproatley on B1238: the Burton Constable Foundation, tel. 0964 562400. Open Easter–mid Sept Sun–Wed.

The Constables family has been an important landowner in the flat agricultural landscape of Holderness since the 12C, but they did not establish themselves at Burton until the late 16C, when a massive red-brick house flanked by corner towers (one of which incorporates medieval fragments) was constructed by Sir Henry Constable, starting c 1570 and finishing in the early years of the 17C. In its present form, though, Burton Constable is mainly a monument to the tastes and enthusiasms of the family in the 18C and 19C. This is not immediately obvious, because successive owners took care to preserve the structure of the Elizabethan house and to design their additions in a stylistically sympathetic form.

The alterations started in 1736 with the building of a Gallery on the irregular western side of the house by the antiquarian-minded Cuthbert Constable, and continued under his son William, a Catholic who nevertheless admired Rousseau, became a Fellow of the Royal Society and went on three Grand Tours. He began to remodel the east (hall) range in 1757, and over the next 30 years he employed a variety of architects and craftsmen to decorate the interiors and to finish the rebuilding of the west front. He had no children, and after his death in 1791 the house was neglected until 1823, when it passed by descent to Sir Thomas Clifford-Constable of Tixall, Staffordshire (d 1870), another inveterate traveller. He took up residence at Burton Constable and, egged on by his first wife, lavishly refurnished the house in the 1830s, mainly employing Hull craftsmen. He left the estate encumbered with debts, many of them incurred by his second wife, who ordered yet more furniture for her Thames-side villa, much of which subsequently ended up at Burton. Since her death there have been relatively few changes to the house, which remains the home of the family but is now maintained by a Foundation set up to secure the future of the property, including the contents, which now belong to the City of Leeds.

The house stands in open countryside close to the site of a deserted medieval village. To the south there is a vast red brick **stable block** built around a courtyard with corner towers in 1769–71 to the designs of the Lancashire-born Timothy Lightoler, the most important of the architects who worked at Burton. The south end of the house is closed off by a service courtyard added in 1772–73 by 'Capability' Brown, who also landscaped the park. The symmetrical **west front** incorporates genuine 16C work at the south end, but is essentially a pastiche dating from the same time as the stables (note the two-dimensional pediment over the central oriel window); the formal gardens with their decaying statuary date from the 1820s. The original appearance of the east or **entrance front** can be seen from paintings of c 1700 on display in the house; the low two-storeyed wings for lodgings and domestic offices—added to the original house c 1610—remain relatively unaltered, but an extra storey was added to the main block by Lightoler in 1759–60, with William Constable's coat of arms in an open pediment in the centre, and a new central entrance provided on the site of an oriel window at the high table end of the Hall, where Constable revived the ancient practice of dining with his household.

The spacious interiors convey a strange and compelling feeling of faded splendour. The **Hall** still remains much as Lightoler left it, its neo-Elizabethan plaster ceiling resting on coves of almost Gothic character with heraldic corbels. A contrasting classical note is struck by the slightly absurd portrait by the Viennese court painter, Anton Maron, of William Constable and his buxom sister, both of them dressed in togas, and by the statues of Demosthenes and Hercules in niches on either side of the fireplace (by John Cheere); the scagliola-topped tables (originally in the Gallery upstairs) are by Domenico Bartoli, who did a lot of work in the house in the 1760s. The **Dining Room** (1767) occupies the position of the medieval parlour, next to the high-table end of the hall. This is a virtually unaltered and highly original monument to the late-18C enthusiasm for the Antique, the walls painted green and the ceiling by Giuseppe Cortese (cf. Newburgh Priory, North Yorkshire) loosely inspired by Herculaneum, which William Constable had visited. The figure of Bacchus in the apsidal east end is by the plasterer William Collins, who also carved the bas-relief of the same deity abducting Ariadne in an oval plaque over the chimneypiece and the oval relief on the south wall. The furniture, which survives intact, was made by local craftsmen.

The first floor is reached by Lightoler's huge cantilevered main staircase, its walls hung with family portraits (some of them brought from Tixall) and tenebrous neo-classical canvases acquired in the Beckford sale of 1823, and the floor strewn with ponderous 19C furniture acquired by Sir Thomas Clifford-Constable. The **Gallery**, which takes up most of the first floor of the west front, still retains its frieze of the 1730s, but the room was extended to its present 110ft by William Constable, who treated it as his 'Library and Philosophical Room' and carried out experiments here. Sir Thomas turned it into a typically 19C combination of library and living room, and introduced most of the extravagantly ornate furniture, including a pair of marble-topped sphinx tables of c 1815 acquired in Rome on his honeymoon (one of several such tables in the house) and the gilded chairs in the style of the late 17C. From here a doorway leads into William Constable's '**Museum**', one of the most complete 18C scientific collections to survive anywhere in the country, its cabinets crammed with geological specimens, shells and scientific instruments. The **Gold Bedroom** contains more late-18C and 19C gilded furniture—a ubiquitous feature of the house—and from here a passage leads to the so-called **King's Suite** of three rooms, one of the most notable features of which is the set of Chippendale furniture in the Drawing Room.

After taking in more bedrooms, the route leads down via a back staircase to the private Roman Catholic **Chapel** (formerly the Billiard Room), designed by Thomas Atkinson of York in 1774 and repainted in bold colours by Taylor Bulmer in 1844. The **Ballroom**, on the west front, was designed by James Wyatt in 1775–76 and retains his characteristically spindly neo-classical mirrors and ceiling decorations. It was redecorated in 1840 by Sir Thomas Clifford-Constable, who introduced the portraits of his Clifford forbears; the Piranesian chimneypiece is by John Bacon, and the gilded furniture around the walls by Chippendale. The domed **Blue Drawing Room** at the centre of the west front is by Atkinson (1783), and the two remaining rooms to the west are of about the same date, the first (the **Red Drawing Room**) containing a portrait by Liotard of William Constable dressed la Rousseau, with a fur hat, and the other (the **Chinese Room**) with Chinese wallpaper and wildly extravagant chinoiserie furnishings in the style of the Brighton Pavilion brought in later by Sir Thomas and his first wife and made by Hull craftsmen. From here visitors return to the Staircase Hall and proceed to the former Butler's Pantry and a Display Room (part of the original service area), where a selection from the copious family papers is displayed, including designs for some of the rooms in the house.

GCT

Normanby Hall

4m north of Scunthorpe on B1430: Scunthorpe Borough Council, tel. 0724
720588. Open Apr–Oct weekdays 11–5, Sun 1–5. Refreshments in grounds.

This austere classical house was built in 1825–30 for Sir Robert Sheffield to
the designs of Robert Smirke, the architect of the British Museum. The
Sheffields first came to Normanby in 1589, and Robert Smythson built them
a large and impressive new house, but this was replaced in the late 17C by
a dull-looking building which was neglected for most of the 18C, when the
family lived elsewhere. The new house is a more impressive piece of
architecture than its predecessor, but it was not built on a lavish scale, and
in 1906 Sir Robert Sheffield's grandson, a collector of French pictures and
furniture, employed Walter Brierley of York to build a large east extension
and a huge service wing (since demolished). Some of the funds for the new
building came from the growth of nearby Scunthorpe as an industrial town,
but the same development gradually reduced the attractiveness of
Normanby as a residence, and in 1963 Sir Berkeley's son and successor
moved to Sutton Park, near York (qv.), where some of the pictures and
furniture formerly at Normanby can now be seen. The house and grounds
are now leased by Scunthorpe Borough Council, which has gradually
restored the interiors to something approaching their original character.
    The house stands in an unspoiled parkland setting. The façades, of
silvery-grey Ancaster stone, are severe, but are rescued from monotony by
Smirke's skill in varying the elevations and manipulating the surfaces by
means of subtle projections and recessions, thus achieving an effect of pure
architecture without any of the romantic devices which characterise many
of the houses of the period. Brierley's east wing, by contrast, is an exercise
in the 'Edwardian Baroque', and makes no effort to reproduce Smirke's
refined and idiosyncratic brand of classicism.
    Smirke designed the interiors of the main block for comfort rather than
show, with a hall and dining room in the centre, drawing rooms facing south
over the gardens, and a more secluded Library to the north. Brierley made
a new dining room (not shown to the public) in the east wing and inserted
a screen of paired Ionic columns in the Entrance Hall in place of a partition
wall, thus creating an 'Inner Hall' which gives access to Smirke's plain but
impressive staircase with cast-iron balusters. Pictures are scattered through
the rooms, among them two views of London by Samuel Scott on loan from
the Ferens Art Gallery in Hull (in the Entrance Hall); and some excellent
early-19C furniture has also been introduced, including items by Gillow
(note in particular the bookcase in the Library).

GCT

Sledmere House

8m north west of Driffield on B1248 Driffield–Malton: Sir Tatton Sykes, tel.
0377 86028. Open Easter–Sept daily except Mon, Fri (open BH Mon)
1.30–5.30. Refreshments.

Sledmere stands in the high, empty country of the Yorkshire Wolds, where
wolves roamed as late as the 17C. In 1748 the estate came by marriage to
Richard Sykes of Hull, whose forbears had made their fortune in Leeds in

the 16C, and three years later he built a new house on the site of an earlier manor house. This relatively modest building was not grand enough for his nephew, Sir Christopher Sykes, an enthusiastic agricultural improver who inherited the estate in 1783. He came into a fortune through his wife, Elizabeth Tatton of Wythenshawe Hall, Greater Manchester (qv.), and in 1786–90 he doubled the size of this uncle's house, making it a worthy focus to the park already laid out by 'Capability' Brown in his most expansive manner. Several architects were consulted, among them Samuel Wyatt, but Sir Christopher was responsible for the final design, and its was he who employed and supervised the craftsmen, the most important of whom was the plasterer Joseph Rose, one of Robert Adam's collaborators. The house was gutted by fire in 1911, but the pictures and furniture (including items from the Orleans Collection dispersed after the French Revolution) were saved, and Walter Brierley of York was immediately employed to restore the building. He made some internal and external modifications, including the addition of a huge service wing, since demolished, but wisely took care to reproduce Rose's exquisite decoration in the main rooms. In its present form, therefore, Sledmere is a synthesis of late-Georgian and Edwardian classicism.

The activities of the Sykes family are much in evidence in the country around Sledmere, from the spruce estate village to the well-preserved woods, the spectacular Gothic monument to Sir Tatton Sykes (d 1865) beside the Driffield road a few miles away to the south, and the numerous estate churches designed by G.E. Street. The grounds are entered close to the monumental **stable block**, headquarters of a famous stud founded in the early 19C, and the grey ashlar-faced house lies to the south. The central block incorporates the 1751 building, but it was remodelled both internally and externally in the 1780s, when wings were added to the north and south, the latter containing a new entrance overlooking the park, with Temple Moore's estate **church** of 1893 not far away to the west. The engaged portico at the centre of the west front was added by Brierley, but it is the **wings**, with their two layers of windows set in relieving arches—a motif often found in the houses of the Wyatt brothers—which remain in the mind and give the exterior its special quality.

The interiors convey a strong sense of discreet and long-established wealth and comfort. The **Entrance Hall** (formerly the smoking room) owes its present form, with its heavily emphasised surrounds to the fireplace and doorways, to Brierley. His greatest achievement, though, was to open up the centre of the house from the former entrance hall on the south front to the main staircase, thus creating a single space interrupted by scagliola columns: an original effect which ranks high among the achievements of Edwardian country house architecture.

The **Music Room** on the south front takes its name from the organ made for the original house; the room was decorated by Rose in a Hollandesque manner and contains pictures by Luca Giordano ('The Finding of Moses') and others, as well as a pair of elaborate 16C Venetian andirons (by the fireplace) and an unusual early-18C enamel table from Canton. The decoration of the **Drawing Room**, on the opposite side of the Hall, owes more to the influence of Adam, and there is an impressive neo-classical marble fireplace; the original gilt furniture of 1797 by the London cabinet-maker, John Robbins, survives in situ, and there are family portraits by Lawrence and others. The plainer **Boudoir** contains some 17C Italian marquetry furniture and pictures closely hung in the standard 18C manner, including architectural capricci by Viviano Codazzi and Pannini, while in the **Horse Room**, at the opposite side of the Hall there are sporting pictures by J.F. Herring and others. The last room on the ground floor is the **Dining Room**, remodelled in the 1780s but retaining its mid-18C plaster ceiling; the Chinese Chippendale chairs have been in the house since the mid 18C, and there is a superb full-length portrait by Romney of Sir Christopher Sykes and his wife (1793), gliding with effortless superiority out of their rebuilt house into the improved grounds.

The upstairs rooms are reached by Walter Brierley's sleek, top-lit **staircase**, with a copy of the Apollo Belvedere (by Joseph Wilton, 1780) on the landing. The main room on the upper floor is the spectacular **Library**, taking up the whole of the south front and commanding extensive views over Brown's landscape. Inspired by the vaulted baths of ancient Rome, it was conceived by Sir Christopher Sykes, but the decoration was the responsibility of Joseph Rose, whose self-portrait (1799) is hung by the entrance; it alas no longer houses Sir Christopher's collection of books, which were sold off by his spendthrift son to pay for his horses. The luxurious bedrooms on the same floor contain some attractive furniture, including a Chinese Chippendale bed. Downstairs, by the exit, there is a room lined with tiles made in Damascus, created as a **Turkish Bath** by Sir Mark Sykes (d 1919), the architect of the 'Sykes-Picot' agreement for dividing the lands of the Ottoman Empire after the First World War; he also commissioned Walter Brierley to design the small Roman Catholic Chapel just outside the house.

GCT

ISLE OF WIGHT

Appuldurcombe House

½m west of Wroxall: English Heritage, tel. 0983 852484. Open Apr–Sept daily 10–6, Oct–Mar daily (except Christmas/New Year hols) 10–4.

Though now an empty shell, Appuldurcombe in its heyday was the grandest house on the Isle of Wight. It lies in a fold of the chalk downs in the south part of the Island, on or near the site of an alien priory founded in 1090. In the early 16C the ground was leased to Sir James Worsley, who gained outright possession after the Dissolution of the Monasteries. The Worsley family originally came from Lancashire, and Sir James rose to prominence in the court of Henry VIII, becoming Keeper of the Wardrobe and, in effect, the King's deputy on the Isle of Wight. A new house was built by one of his descendants in the late 16C or early 17C, and this in turn was replaced by the present building, which was begun in 1701.

The builder was Sir Robert Worsley, MP for the local rotten borough of Newtown. He had travelled abroad and married a daughter of Viscount Weymouth of Longleat, Wilts (qv.), and he chose as his architect John James, a colleague of Nicholas Hawksmoor and Sir John Vanbrugh in the Office of the King's Works. Work came to a halt, for financial reasons, in 1713, with only the present east and south ranges built, and was not resumed until 1773–82, when the north and west ranges were built and the interior remodelled by Sir Richard Worsley, Comptroller of the Household to George III and subsequently a protagonist in a celebrated divorce case (his wife, who admitted to having 27 lovers, can be seen in one of Reynolds's most masterly female portraits, now at Harewood, Yorkshire, qv.); Sir Richard also employed 'Capability' Brown to lay out the grounds, and filled the house with works of art, including England's first collection of Greek sculpture. He died in 1805, and his daughter and heiress married Lord Yarborough, founder of the Royal Yacht Squadron; he used the house as a *pied à terre* when visiting Cowes and made further alterations, including the addition of a carriage porch on the west side. The estate was sold in 1855, the collection removed to the Yarboroughs' seat in Lincolnshire, and the house was used as a school and then a monastery, before being abandoned in 1909. There was some damage from a land mine in the Second World War, and by 1953 the house had, in Rose Macaulay's words, 'disintegrated beautifully in all the morbid shades of a fading bruise'. Further collapse was prevented by the Ministry of Works, which took over the site in 1952, and in 1986 the building was partially re-roofed.

Appuldurcombe is one of the most idiosyncratic creations of the short-lived 'English Baroque'. It is square in plan, with projecting 'pavilions' at each corner, each of them surmounted by a pediment; these are lower than the main block, producing a somewhat disjointed, though undeniably impressive, effect. The show front faces east, and the walls here, of local limestone with Portland stone dressings, are rusticated and articulated by a giant order of Corinthian pilasters, their capitals beautifully carved by the London masons James and Joseph Clarke; the colonnade on the south front was added in the 19C. Little survives of the interior, and the overwhelming mood is one of vanished glory, tempered by the beauty of the natural setting.

Nunwell House

1m from Brading off A3055 Ryde–Ventnor: Col and Mrs J. A. Aylmer,
tel. 0983 407240. Open early July–Sept Sun–Thur 10–5.

Nunwell is a varied and extensive house of several different dates situated
on high ground overlooking the Solent, which once came up to the edge
of the park. It was constructed piecemeal by the Oglanders, one of the
oldest Island families, who had owned property in the area since the 12C.
They bought the manor of East Nunwell in 1522, together with a small
farmhouse of stone, parts of which survive in an outbuilding behind the
present much larger house, but in the late 16C they lived mainly at Palace
House at Beaulieu, Hampshire (qv.), on the other side of the Solent. Sir John
Oglander, deputy Governor of Portsmouth and the Isle of Wight, returned
to Nunwell in 1609 and greatly extended the house, giving it an H-plan
with a hall range and two cross-wings; his wooden effigy, in the dress of a
medieval crusader, can be seen in the parish church at Brading. He was a
Royalist, and Charles I spent his last night of freedom at Nunwell before
being imprisoned in Carisbrooke Castle, a few miles away, in 1647.

John Oglander's son was made a Baronet by Charles II, and his son
refaced the hall range c 1720, but the most important alteration occurred
in the time of the 5th Baronet, who married an heiress and remodelled the
east range, facing towards the sea, in about 1760. Another major rebuilding
project was conceived by the 6th Baronet and his architect John Nash—an
Island resident—in 1805–7, but it was dropped and Nash was engaged
instead to remodel Parnham, Dorset (qv.), which had been inherited by the
family in the 18C; Nash's only work at Nunwell was the building of a new
stable block (now a separate house). When the 7th Baronet died in 1874,
the Nunwell estate was inherited by John Glynn, who later took the name
Oglander, and he extended the east wing in 1897 and 1905. Since then
there have been few alterations to the house, which was sold, together with
some of the contents, to the present owners in 1982. They have refurnished
the rooms, and now live here with their family.

Much of the appeal of Nunwell derives from its setting on a hillside, with
19C terraces spreading down to the park and views of the Solent and the
Sussex Downs in the distance. Architecturally the house presents an
engaging mixture of styles and materials. In the centre is the 17C hall range,
refronted in the early 18C with red 'mathematical' tiles to look like brick,
and on either side are the 17C stone-built west wing and the taller east
wing rebuilt c 1770 and extended in the late 19C, with a plain grey brick
elevation on the garden side broken by a canted bay in the centre. This
part of the house contains the main reception rooms and bedrooms. The
entrance leads through the Music Room of 1905 (originally the billiard
room), hung with portraits of the Oglander and Glyn families, to the Dining
Room of 1897 and then to the Morning Room, panelled in wood c 1720. The
Drawing Room, enlarged by the addition of the bay window c 1760,
contains a seascape by Thomas Allan (1761) and an early copy of Van
Dyck's self-portrait with a sunflower. The spacious, well-proportioned
Library retains its late-18C neo-classical ceiling and chimneypiece, along
with a pair of bookcases made for the room c 1765; the walls were papered
in 1833.

From here the route passes to the Hall, in the 17C part of the house, with
its original chimneypiece and a neo-Jacobean ceiling of the 1830s. Beyond

is the Staircase, hung with Irish family portraits, and upstairs in the west wing is the much-altered room in which Charles I is reputed to have slept before being imprisoned at Carisbrooke. The rooms over the Hall have been refurnished by the present owner with militaria from his own family collection, and in the cellar is the former local Home Guard headquarters, restored to its condition in 1940–42, when a German invasion of the Isle of Wight was a serious possibility.

GCT

Osborne House

1m south east of East Cowes: English Heritage, tel. 0983 20002. Open Apr–Oct daily 10–6 (Oct 10–5).

'Dear, beautiful Osborne', as Queen Victoria called it, is perhaps the best known of all Victorian country houses open to the public. It was conceived as a seaside villa, overlooking the Solent, by the Queen and her consort Prince Albert, and built in 1845–50. For many years the Isle of Wight had been a favoured spot for villa residences and second homes, and in buying and building on the Osborne estate the Queen and Prince were following a trend which had started in the late 18C. Their aim was primarily to create a holiday home for their large and growing family, free from the stifling formality of court life—the house was built out of the Queen's private income and, like Balmoral and Sandringham , Norfolk (qv.), it was never officially a royal palace. If it seems somewhat large and unwieldy to us today, this is mainly because of the need to provide accommodation for the large numbers of visitors, household staff, officials, and assorted hangers-on who have always attended royalty. The royal family's own apartments were in a compact three-storeyed building no bigger than a modestly-sized gentleman's country house, but attached to this is a building more than twice the size for the household and visitors, and next to it are the kitchens. Osborne is thus a very large building.

Victoria and, even more so, Albert mistrusted architects, so the house was designed by Albert himself with the help of the successful builder Thomas Cubitt, creator of Belgravia in London and, in the words of a contemporary, 'as near an approach to an architect as any man not an architect could be'. Albert was an enthusiast for the art and architecture of early Renaissance Italy, and at Osborne he attempted to create a 19C version of an Italian villa, set among formal gardens sloping down to the Solent, which reminded him of the Bay of Naples: not so much the symmetrical, intellectually disciplined villas of Palladio as the more picturesque villas imaginatively evoked by 17C landscape painters and realised by John Nash (whose own castellated villa at East Cowes was close to Osborne) and Charles Barry. Some of the details at Osborne, notably the two towers with their overhanging roofs, were influenced by Barry's buildings, but in general the Renaissance-style elevations, covered with 'Roman cement' to hide the brick walls, bear a strong resemblance to Cubitt's architecture on the Belgravia estate. The effect is somewhat heavy, and externally the building is curiously depressing, perhaps because of its uncanny resemblance to many 19C hospitals (which it may well have influenced). The house was not to the taste of Edward VII, and in 1902, the year after his mother's death, he gave it to the nation. The household wing then became a convalescent home for officers of the armed services, and the main house was opened to the public. It is now furnished much as it was in the later 19C, and provides a fascinating insight both into Victorian decorative art and into the personality and domestic life of the Queen herself.

The house is approached through an open courtyard and entered through a porch in the household wing to the right; to the left is the **Durbar Wing** of 1890–91 designed by the father of the writer Rudyard Kipling, and in front is the building known as the Pavilion which contains the royal apartments. A spacious corridor or sculpture gallery leads first to the Council and Audience rooms and then, after a right-angled turn, into the main part of the house. After the drab cement-covered exterior, the brightly-coloured decoration of the **corridor** comes as a welcoming surprise. It was devised, like that of the rest of the house, by Prince Albert's artistic adviser the Dresden-born Ludwig Grüner, who also worked at Buckingham Palace in London, and the sculptures are mostly by 19C British artists, including John Gibson's 'Cupid and Psyche' (1845). The ground-floor rooms in the main house are grouped around a central staircase: the **Billiard Room**, dominated by a mammoth porcelain vase donated by the Tsar of Russia; the **Drawing Room**, divided into three sections by pairs of Corinthian columns, and now containing statuettes of the Queen's children (by Mary Thorneycroft); and the **Dining Room**, with a copy of Winterhalter's well-known family group of Victoria, Albert and their children (1849) over the sideboard.

A back staircase leads to the second floor, where three of the nurseries have recently been restored. The **private apartments** of the Queen and Prince were on the first floor, which is reached by the main stairs, at the top of which is a large allegorical fresco of 'Neptune resigning the Empire of the Seas to Britannia' by William Dyce (1847). The rooms on this floor were designed for comfort rather than show. After Prince Albert's untimely death in 1861, his Dressing Room was preserved largely intact, except for the removal of his collection of early Italian pictures, and it now serves as a reminder of the uncluttered, relaxed charm of many early Victorian interiors. Despite the accumulation of family photographs and keepsakes, the Queen's Sitting Room and the Bedroom in which she died have a similarly unpretentious character, unaffected by the 'aesthetic' fads of the late 19C. Upstairs, on the top landing, is a life-sized statue of Albert in Roman armour by Emil Wolff (1842); the rest of this floor was devoted to nurseries.

There is a return to the public face of monarchy in the remaining rooms on the ground floor. The waiting-room known as the **Horn Room** is named after a collection of furniture made out of antlers bought by Prince Albert in 1846, and contains Sir Edwin Landseer's painting entitled 'Sorrow' (1866) showing the Queen in mourning, attended by her servant John Brown. From here a corridor hung with pictures of Indians, including Winterhalter's Maharajah Duleep Singh (1854), leads to the **Durbar Room**, built as a banqueting room for state occasions and profusely embellished with carvings in the Indian style by Bhai Ram Singh. From here a doorway leads to the Italianate terraced gardens designed by the Prince and Grüner. Visitors can also see the Swiss Cottage built for the royal children in 1853–54.

GCT

KENT

Belmont

4m south of Faversham, west from the A251; signposted from Badlesmere:
The Harris (Belmont) Charity, tel. 0795 890202. Open Easter–Sept Sat, Sun
and BH Mon 2–5, last admission 4.30. Refreshments.

Belmont is a neo-classical house of 1789–93, designed by Samuel Wyatt,
with elegant interiors and very complete furnishings, largely of the same
period as the house. The estate was created and the first house built c 1769,
and sold in 1780 to John Montresor, an officer in the Royal Engineers. He
enlarged the estate and built the present house. Alas, he did not enjoy it
for long, being unjustly accused of embezzling army funds in 1799. Belmont
was confiscated and Montresor died in prison soon after, though in 1822
his sons at long last proved his innocence, and received compensation from
the government.

Belmont and its estate were auctioned in 1801, and purchased by General
George Harris, later the 1st Lord Harris. As a general in the army of the
East India Company, he defeated the much-feared Tipoo Sahib, ruler of
Mysore. Tipoo himself was slain, and his city of Seringapatam captured, in
May 1799. General Harris received an eighth of the prize money from the
capture, amounting to £150,000, and this funded the purchase of Belmont,
and established him as a considerable landed gentleman. He died here in
1829, aged 83. The 2nd, 3rd and 4th Lords Harris all held high office, giving
distinguished service in various quarters of the British Empire. The 4th Lord
was also a passionate cricketer, doing much to establish the game in its
modern form. His son, the 5th Lord, followed in the family tradition of
military and public service, while also forming the great collection of clocks
which is one of the glories of Belmont. He established a charitable trust to
secure the preservation of the house, park and collections; his son, the 6th
and present Lord Harris, lives on the estate, and farms a large part of it in
hand.

The house remains almost exactly as designed by Samuel Wyatt; there is
a compact and very handsome main block, with main fronts to north, east
and south. It is actually built of red brick, but the show fronts are faced in
stone-coloured mathematical tiles, which look like very high-quality brickwork, one of several innovative features designed by Wyatt. The south or
entrance front is three wide bays, with an elegant Ionic colonnade; just to
the left of this is a big Orangery. The longer east front has big bow windows
at either end, with low saucer domes on top.

The visitor enters by the Orangery—an early example of such a room
being treated as part of the house, so that it could be used as a summer
living room. Glazed doors at the end lead into the Entrance Hall, from
where you can see a long vista through the Staircase Hall and along a
corridor, the length of the main block. There are souvenirs of the Harris
family's imperial service, including a stuffed lion and tiger, and fine long-
case clocks, the first to be seen of the 5th Lord's great collection. The
Drawing Room is lighter, with curved ends and very elegant neo-classic
decoration; the portraits, pastel drawings and French-style furnishings
make it the most feminine of the main interiors. Going back through the
Entrance Hall, you reach the Staircase Hall, one of the finest produced by
the Wyatt family, rising the full height of the house, with crisp neo-classical

plasterwork. At the foot are more early longcase clocks, and souvenirs of India, including china and bronzes. From here you enter the Dining Room, a long apartment occupying the middle of the east front; the decoration and furnishings form an early-19C ensemble. The large carpet is one of a group made in India in the 1890s for the 4th Lord, while Governor of Bombay. The group portrait at the far end, by Arthur William Devis, is of the 1st Lord Harris and his family. On either side of the fireplace are portraits by Sir Martin Archer Shee, of the 2nd Lord's first wife, and of the 3rd Lord as Governor of Madras.

Passing back through the Staircase Hall, and along the corridor, which is lined with Georgian and Regency furniture, you reach the Library, at the far end of the east front. Like the Drawing Room, it has curved end walls, and Samuel Wyatt's original decoration is complete, with walnut bookcases and grisaille paintings above simulating sculpture. There is Indian, as well as Georgian furniture. The tour returns along the corridor and up the main staircase, which is overlooked by 19C portraits, many of them showing members of the family in uniform. The Blue Bedroom, Blue Dressing Room and the South Bedroom have more Regency furniture. Across the landing, in the nursery, a number of toys and baby clothes are displayed. Finally, two bedrooms have been joined together to form the Clock Museum, where a large selection of the 5th Lord Harris' collection is displayed; concentrating mostly on British and French pieces from the 17C to the 19C, this is one of the best private collections anywhere in the world. The grounds were first laid out, with the house, in the 1790s.

SB

Boughton Monchelsea Place

3m south of Maidstone, off the B2163; leave the A229 at Linton. Tel. 0622 743120. Open Easter–early Oct Sun and BH (also Wed in July and Aug) 2.15–6. Refreshments.

Boughton Monchelsea is an Elizabethan manor house of grey Kentish ragstone, standing on a green hillside and commanding a great view south over the Weald. A house called 'Boltone' is recorded here in Domesday Book, and in the 12C it came into the possession of the Montchensies (a Norman family from Mont Cenis), and the name Boltone Montchensie has gradually evolved into Boughton Monchelsea. In 1551 this manor was bought by Robert Rudston, a member of a Yorkshire family who had made money as drapers. He was involved in the abortive rebellion against Queen Mary led by Thomas Wyatt, and was lucky to escape with his life. The resulting fines meant that Rudston was short of money, so his rebuilding of the house proceeded slowly, but it is nonetheless essentially his work. The medieval house was on the site of the present south wing, facing the church and down the hill. Rudston extended this east, then built the present east (entrance) front c 1575, then added another two wings, so that the house enclosed a small square courtyard.

The Rudston family were succeeded by the Barnhams in 1613, and then the Rider family in 1685. The house's placid history was marked by some internal alterations, including the staircase, c 1700. In the time of Thomas Rider II, the north and west sides of Robert Rudston's courtyard house were demolished, and modest brick outbuildings erected in their place, so that the house proper is now L-shaped. Thomas Rider III carried out a mild 'Gothicisation' of the house, making the Gothic windows and altering some of the main rooms. For much of the 19C, though, the house had no regular occupant, which explains the absence of any major Victorian alterations. In 1903 it was bought by Lt-Colonel G.B. Winch, chairman of a local brewing concern. In 1954 Boughton Monchelsea was inherited by his nephew Michael Winch. Finding it too large, he converted part of it into flats, and on his death in 1990, he bequeathed it to a trust, which maintains it and opens it to the public.

Boughton Monchelsea is approached by a very long, rather rough drive from the B2163: do not be put off by this. At the last moment, the drive turns and descends to the lawn before the east front of the house. To the left there is a tremendous view over the old Deer Park and far across the Kentish Weald. The shape of the façade, with its central porch and four attic windows, is Elizabethan, while the Gothick windows are of c 1810–18. Inside, the square Entrance Hall has Gothick pillars and decoration, and a variety of 18C and 19C furniture. On the right, the Dining Room was also remodelled in Gothick style, and has fine Regency furniture. The large Mortlake tapestry at the far end is one of a set which has always been in the house. Across the Hall is the Yellow Drawing Room, with a mixture of 17C and 18C furniture, including a chinoiserie overmantel mirror and a painting of the Holy Family by Pittoni. The visitor ascends the broad staircase, of c 1685, which is hung with a variety of paintings and another of the tapestries.

Off the landing, the Four Poster Bedroom has old English furniture which has remained here since the time of the Rider family. A further flight of stairs—this time the original Elizabethan stairs—leads to the attic, where you see servants' rooms furnished as in the early part of this century. Back on the first floor, a large bedroom is filled with a fascinating assortment of souvenirs of the Winch family's travels, with 18C and 19C costume, and old toys. Next to this, Mrs Winch's boudoir houses a variety of antique pieces.

Outside, Boughton Monchelsea has an enjoyable walled garden, and in the barn there is a collection of early agricultural implements, wagons and carriages. The adjacent church of St Peter is medieval in origin, but the interior is mostly Victorian, of c 1874; it is worth seeing for the grand Baroque monument to Sir Christopher Parker (d 1742) by Scheemakers.

SB

Chartwell

2m south of Westerham, off B2026: National Trust, tel. 0732 866368. Open, Apr–Oct Tues (except after BH Mon) Wed, Thur, Sat, Sun 12–5; Nov Sat, Sun, Wed 11–4. Refreshments.

Chartwell means Churchill. The house, having been Sir Winston's home for nearly 40 years, is now his principal memorial in Britain. It stands high on the side of a combe, with views over the Weald. The early history of the place is of relatively little moment. Suffice to say that John Campbell Colquhoun extended the old farm-house into a medium-sized mansion in the mid 19C. In November 1922 Churchill, then aged 48, bought it with 80 acres, for £5000; even given its dispiriting condition it was a bargain price. The house was ponderous, dark and infested with dry rot, but Churchill was excited by its dramatic position and views; furthermore, it is only 25 miles from Westminster. He commissioned the architect Philip Tilden (qv. Port Lympne, Kent) to remodel it at a cost of £18,000, and in 1924 the family moved in.

From 1924, Churchill was Chancellor of the Exchequer in the new Baldwin government, and so Chartwell in the 1920s was the setting for great political activity. But in 1929 the Baldwin government fell and Churchill was later out of office, and out of step with his own party on its official policy of appeasement.

Churchill took to writing, painting and building. Chartwell was the object of much of his creative energy. He said later, 'I built with my own hands a large part of the cottages and extensive kitchen-garden walls, and made all kinds of rockeries and waterworks and a large swimming pool...Thus I never had a dull or idle moment from morning to midnight, and with my happy family around me dwelt at peace within my habitation'. On the outbreak of war in 1939, Churchill re-entered the Cabinet as First Lord of the Admiralty. Chartwell was too remote and too easily recognisable from the air, and it was closed for the duration of the war; Churchill maintained a cottage here, and came for a few visits in the war years.

In May 1945, Churchill found himself victorious and celebrated abroad, but stunningly defeated at home in the General Election. As in the 1930s he found solace at Chartwell. In 1951, aged 76, he became Prime Minister again, finally retiring shortly after his 80th birthday. At Chartwell he continued to receive guests and friends, to write and to paint. On January 24 1965 he died in his London house at Hyde Park Gate.

The house Churchill purchased was a long rectangle in shape, with steep gables. Tilden carried out a general reconstruction, adding a short wing at right angles on the east side, where the ground falls away sharply. He simplified and improved the west or entrance side, giving it a mildly 17C air. Tilden's interiors are very simply decorated, following Churchill's own taste. He was not a collector, despite his own activity as a painter. The best of the furniture at Chartwell, good English pieces, was bought by his wife, Clementine. Otherwise, the contents are mainly interesting for their associations. At the end of the narrow Entrance Hall is the Drawing Room, in the wing added by Tilden. It is large and light, with English 18C furniture. There are paintings by Churchill, but pride of place goes to a Monet. Through the Inner Hall is the Library; Churchill was celebrated for the breadth and scale of his reading, and this room contains the overflow from the Study upstairs. The staircase adjoining was built in 1966 to allow for easier visitor circulation, and is hung with political cartoons.

Upstairs is Lady Churchill's bedroom, which conveys her warm but meticulous personality, and houses some good Georgian and Regency furniture. The Ante-Room, next, has china, medals, photographs and other Churchilliana. The Museum Room and the Uniform Room were converted out of guests' bedrooms in 1966. They are filled with official gifts, and with some of the great variety of insignia, uniforms and hats which Churchill wore or received. The Study is the heart of the house; it was used constantly from 1924 to 1964, apart from the war years. There is a high open timbered roof, the big table at which Churchill sat and wrote, and the standing desk given him by his children. Going down the stairs there are several more of his own paintings. Below the Drawing Room in the new wing is the Dining Room, decorated and furnished with great simplicity; in his later years it was also used for film-shows.

The gardens are varied and picturesque. There are lawns on terraces immediately below the house, with views down over the pools in the Combe and beyond to the Weald. The little pavilion is dedicated to the 1st Duke of Marlborough. There are more intimate walled gardens, with elaborate brick walls laid by Churchill himself. There is a cottage and, adjoining this, his Studio, filled with his paintings, and with his painting equipment.

SB

Chiddingstone Castle

Chiddingstone Village, off the B2027 near Edenbridge: The Trustees of the Denys Eyre Bower Bequest, tel. 0892 870347. Open Apr–Oct Wed and Sun only in Apr, May and Oct; June–Sept Wed–Sun, weekdays 2–5.30, weekends and public holidays 11.30–5.30. Please check Saturdays. Refreshments.

Chiddingstone is the creation of two men, Henry Streatfeild, who was responsible for the architecture, and Denis Eyre Bower, a romantic collector and connoisseur, who accumulated its varied and fascinating contents. It is a highly rewarding house to visit, the exotic collections seeming bizarre in the peaceful setting.

The Streatfeild family built a pretty Carolean manor house here, of red brick with a hipped roof, set in about 3000 acres. Henry Streatfeild began the remodelling of the house in Georgian Gothic taste c 1800. William Atkinson added new wings on the north and south sides, with Gothic windows and battlements, but with the Carolean house sandwiched in between. Money ran out, and it was another 30 years before his son completed the re-facing and battlementing. The Streatfeilds sold up in the 1930s, and the house suffered heavily during the war. It was derelict when, in 1955, it was bought by Denys Bower, who came from Derbyshire, with no inherited wealth. From the age of 16, for 20 years, he worked as a bank clerk, all the while developing a deep understanding of art of all kinds. He slowly established a second career as a dealer, and was eventually able to concentrate solely on this. By collecting in what were then unfashionable areas, by developing a tremendous capacity for recognising quality when he saw it, and by his unlimited willingness to forego the comforts and even necessities of ordinary life, Bower achieved the astonishing results one sees now. He died in 1977, leaving the castle and its contents to a charity, the Denys Eyre Bower Bequest.

The castle is faced in smoothly-cut sandstone, with symmetrically placed traceried windows and battlements on top. The South Hall was made as a carriage entrance; from here you enter the east wing, still part of the Caroline house. First seen is a re-creation of Denys Bower's study, with his favourite Regency furniture. Next, the former Billiard Room houses his Buddhist Collection. The several hundred objects on display cannot be summarised easily; there is a wide range of votive images, small shrines, vessels and small carvings. Over a passageway from here, a room looking onto the courtyard houses a collection of views of the house. The Jacobite Room expresses Bower's fascination with the House of Stuart, and contains memorabilia, including early pieces of ceramic and glassware expressing loyalty to the dynasty.

The Great Hall was added by Atkinson at the junction of the north and east wings, in his mild Gothic style. The furniture is 17C oak; on either side of the fireplace are two splendid barrel-organs of the early 19C, operated by hand, and both in working order. Opening from here, in the former Library, is the Stuart Room, with more mementoes—manuscripts, prints, miniatures, medals, coins and personal belongings, relating to that house. Presiding over it all is Lely's nude portrait of Nell Gwynn (posing as Venus, of course).

The White Rose Drawing Room, next door, is a handsome room in conventional Georgian style (not Gothicised). The furniture is all Georgian, and the room is dominated by the array of portraits of nearly every member of the House of Stuart, from James V of Scotland all the way to Cardinal Henry of York, last of the line. The portraits include works by (or from the studios of) Lely, Verelst, Mytens, Van Dyck, Cornelius Johnson and Honthorst. They are variable in quality, but it is fascinating to see the whole of this unfortunate dynasty in one collection.

The next three rooms contain Denys Bower's Japanese Collection. It is the finest private collection of Japanese objects in Britain, probably in Europe, accumulated mostly during the 1920s and 1930s. In what was the Entrance Hall are cases filled with Samurai armour and weapons—a menacing presence. The large room beyond is lined with display cases, with a tremendous wealth of lacquer-work objects, carvings, ceremonial swords and netsuke. At the far end of the room is an immense, gilded shrine of fantastic elaboration. A smaller room opens out of this, with ancient terracotta figures from tombs, with early Japanese ceramics, and a number of figures of animals and insects made from wrought iron—they are jointed to move realistically.

The visitor returns through the Great Hall, up the stairs (noting the portrait of Henry Streatfeild). Two rooms on the first floor house the Egyptian Collection, which includes very many tomb-objects of wood, metal and terracotta, as well as small pieces of sculpture, and papyri. Adjacent rooms are used by the trustees for temporary exhibitions, of objects on loan and of other items from the castle's reserve collections. Back at the South Hall, the Kitchen has been opened, largely restored to its 19C appearance, and nearby are the tearoom and shop.

SB

Cobham Hall

4m west of Rochester, just off the A2: Westwood Educational Trust, tel. 0474 824319/823371. Open on several days in Apr, July and Aug (please check first) 2–5. Refreshments.

Since 1962, this great Elizabethan house has housed an independent public school for girls, and as a result has few historic contents. However, it is well worth visiting for its tremendous architectural interest. There was a house here in the Middle Ages, occupied by the de Cobhams. They are buried in Cobham church, where their memorial brasses form one of the best collections in the country. However, the modern history of the place really begins with William Brooke, 10th Lord Cobham (1558–96). A great figure at Queen Elizabeth's court, he added the two long red-brick wings to the old house. The family's rise was abruptly cut short in the next reign when his son, the 11th Lord, was implicated in the plot to place Lady Arabella Stuart on the throne instead of James VI/James I. He was imprisoned and his estates confiscated. In 1613 King James presented the manor of Cobham to his cousin, Ludovic Stuart, 2nd Duke of Lennox. In 1623 Lennox was created Duke of Richmond in the English peerage, and Cobham remained the principal residence of the Dukes of Richmond and Lennox until 1672. Loyal supporters of the King during the Civil War, they were fortunate to retain their estates. The 6th Duke was the last of his line and after his death in 1672, Cobham passed through the female line three times. In 1713 it passed by marriage to John Bligh, of County Meath, Ireland; in 1721 he was made 1st Earl of Darnley of the second creation (in the Irish peerage). The Bligh Earls of Darnley had Cobham as their principal residence until 1961, when they sold it to the old Ministry of Works, who shortly after sold it to the present owners.

Cobham is a magnificent house, well-maintained inside and out. The main house is built around a west-facing open court. The central block, at the back of the court represents the site of the old medieval and Tudor house. To this the 10th Lord Cobham added the long red-brick wings with octagonal turrets at either end which form the sides of a half H. In 1661 the 6th Duke of Lennox and Richmond demolished the old central block and rebuilt it with the handsome classical façade, with Corinthian pilasters, which forms the centrepiece of the house today. This was probably designed by John Webb, court architect to Charles II. The Earls of Darnley found the house too small, so from 1768 to 1830 they made additions, eventually forming another square courtyard at the back. This was done in the original style, and it is not easy to tell the difference between their work and the old. Most of their additions were to house service accommodation, but they also commissioned James Wyatt to make some alterations to the state rooms.

The house is now entered from the north side, where the 4th Earl of Darnley built the present carriage-entrance and Hall, c 1802, in the Gothic style to Wyatt's designs. The great chimneypiece of coloured marble is dated 1587, and bears the arms of the 10th Lord Cobham. The Inner Hall is also Gothic, and Wyatt's work; the ceiling is of the 1670s and bears the arms of the Dukes of Lennox, but was probably reconstructed by Wyatt. The Granite Staircase is dated 1602, and was the last feature to be added by the Brooke family before their fall. Going up the stairs, the visitor enters the Gallery, which occupies the first floor of the 10th Lord Cobham's north wing. Wyatt blocked the windows on the north side to provide space for the 4th Earl of Darnley's great picture collection, alas dispersed. There are two great marble chimneypieces, dated 1599, by the Flemish craftsman Giles de Witt. At one end of the gallery is the splendid Darnley State Coach, a magnificent Baroque object of c 1715, heavily carved and gilded—a very rare survival. At the far end is Queen Elizabeth's Room, redecorated in 1817 by George Repton (son of the famous landscape designer, Humphry Repton), with another magnificent early Renaissance chimneypiece.

Visitors retrace their steps back along the gallery and down the staircase. The Library is in the east wing, rebuilt by the 6th Duke of Lennox. The room's present neo-classical form was given by George Repton in 1817, with a fine chimneypiece and ceiling. Next, in the centre of the east wing is the Vestibule, the original entrance hall, as remodelled by Wyatt, c 1773. This leads into the Gilt Hall, the climax of the interior. This great room, 50ft by 36ft and two storeys high, is the Hall of the Webb building; its shape and the elaborately plastered ceiling are of the 1670s. The rest of its sumptuous decoration was done in two stages, in 1773–76 by Sir William

Chambers, and 1792–94 by Wyatt. Over the fireplace is a copy of Van Dyck's famous double portrait of Lord John and Lord Bernard Stuart, sons of the 3rd Duke of Lennox, both killed in the Civil War.

From here the visitor enters the ground floor of the Elizabethan north wing. The Large Dining Room was redecorated by Wyatt, and again around 1840, but retains a number of early features. The superb Mannerist classical chimneypiece is of the late 16C. To either side are portraits, of the 2nd Duke of Lennox by Van Somer and of the 4th Duke, after Van Dyck. This room is used as a dining room, as is the next room. The 'Chapel' was decorated in Gothick style by Wyatt, c 1812, with another Elizabethan chimneypiece moved in, as a chapel, but never actually consecrated.

It is well worth walking around the house; the 10th Lord Cobham's long wings, with their tall Elizabethan windows and turrets at either end, and their superb classical doorcases, blend very satisfyingly with Webb's chaste and beautiful façade of the 1670s. At the back, the later wings are lower and picturesque. The park was laid out by Repton for the 4th Earl, and there are laburnums, azaleas and rhododendrons, as well as fine plantations of trees.

SB

Finchcocks

2m west of Goudhurst, signposted off the A262: Mr and Mrs Richard Burnett, tel. 0580 211702. Open Sun from Easter–Sept Wed–Sun and BH Mon in Aug 2–6. Music on all open days. Refreshments.

Finchcocks is a fine and well-preserved early-18C house; thanks to its owners Richard and Katrina Burnett it is also a cultural and musical institution, housing one of Britain's foremost collections of historic keyboard instruments, most of which are maintained in working order. From April to October every year, there are recitals and demonstrations every open day, as well as many larger set-piece events and festivals. Visiting Finchcocks is thus a musical event as much as a visual one.

The house stands in wooded farmland. The property passed to the Bathurst family in 1568 and Edward Bathurst, a barrister and Master of the Bench in the Middle Temple, inherited it in 1718. He married a local heiress, and thus acquired sufficient means to build a new house; it was finished in 1725, the date which appears on the rainwater heads. The house remained in the Bathurst family until its sale in 1797 to the Springett family, who were here until 1860, when it was sold to Edward Hussey of Scotney. The house was let to various tenants, and sold again in 1918. Various different owners held it, including F.M. Lycett Green, a noted art connoisseur; in the 1960s it housed a private ballet school. The house was in rather poor condition by 1971, when it was acquired by its present owner, the pianist, entrepreneur and collector Richard Burnett. For five years, the house underwent restoration, and in 1976 it was opened to the public.

Finchcocks is an important work of provincial Baroque architecture with a tall central block and two lower wings. It was designed to impress; the house has 20 rooms, but much of it is only one room deep. There is little direct evidence of its authorship, but the high proportions, Doric pilasters and some of the detailing have led to Thomas Archer being suggested as the architect. Perhaps the best feature is the brickwork itself, which is a warm orange colour. The rubbed-brick window-surrounds are of very high quality. The house has managed to escape serious alterations at any time and is very well-preserved; much of the original panelling and joinery is intact, including the very handsome oak staircase, and most of the glazing bars and even much of the glass is original.

The Finchcocks collection comprises historic keyboard instruments, mostly from the 18C and 19C. There are about 80 instruments. The largest category is early pianos, but there are also chamber organs, harpsichords, virginals, spinets and clavichords, and most are in working order. The aim of the collection is to enable the works of the classical composers to be played on the sort of instruments they used, producing the kind of sound which they envisaged. The largest piece is the great chamber organ of 1766, from Castle Grant in Moray, made by John Byfield of London. Amongst the harpsichords, that of 1756 by Jacob Kirckman is pre-eminent for its untouched condition. The grand Portuguese instrument by Joachim Antumes, of 1785, is probably the most richly decorated. The oldest instrument is the Italian virginal by Guarracino of 1668. There are 50 pianos, encompassing the whole history of the development of this instrument, with important examples by makers such as Sebastian Erard, Conrad Graf, Clementi, John Broadwood and Sebastian Lengerer. There are also fine paintings on musical themes, from the 17C and 18C.

SB

Godinton Park

1m north west of Ashford, off the A20: Mr Alan Wyndham Green. Open Easter Sat–Mon, then June–Sept Sun, BH Mon 2–5.

Godinton stands in parkland, just to the north west of Ashford. It is a relaxed-looking house in warm orange brick, its façades in the artisan-Mannerist style of the 1630s, with mullioned-and-transomed windows and Dutch gables. Behind, though, its origins go back to the 14C. There was a manor house at Godinton from the 14C; in the reign of Henry VII (1485–1509) it was inherited by John Toke, who served the king as soldier and diplomat; the Toke family owned it until 1896. In 1627 Capt. Nicholas Toke inherited; he married five times and ruled at Godinton until his death in 1680. Soon after his accession he commenced a rebuilding of the house, giving it more or less its present form. An 18C Toke landscaped the park; early in the 19C the direct line came to an end. After 1866 the house was let to various tenants, and in 1896 finally sold to a Mr George Ashley Dodd, with many of its contents. Godinton was bought in 1919 by the Hon. Mrs Bruce Ward; the present owner, Mr Wyndham Green, is her grandson.

There is a long drive through the park, which has magnificent trees, some of them very ancient. The house is roughly square, surrounding a small courtyard. The entrance front faces north with the garden to the south and east; on the west side there are the service ranges. The façades are wide and relatively low, and loosely symmetrical with their shaped gables and big windows; most of what you see dates from Capt. Nicholas Toke's rebuilding in the 1630s. Visitors enter a side door on the north front, and go down a passageway to the Dining Room, occupying the north-west corner of the house. This is a Georgian room—its ceiling was raised, and the fine panelling and doorcases installed in the mid 18C. The fireplace is the first of a number to be seen made of Bethersden marble, a dark, very hard stone with a high fossil content, peculiar to this part of Kent. There is Georgian furniture, some Rockingham china, and portraits of the present owner's ancestors. From here the Great Hall, occupying the centre of the north range, is reached. This is essentially a 15C room, but the panelled ceiling and the elaborate woodwork were added in the 1630s. The richly carved chimneypiece is dated 1574, and probably comes from Flanders; the fireplace itself is of Bethersden marble. There is a wealth of 16C and 17C furniture, and English portraits of the same period; the best is that of the future James II while Duke of York, by Lely. The end of the Hall now opens straight into the Priest's Room, with another elaborately carved chimneypiece.

Steps rise to the Gallery (over the Priest's Room), from where you look down, through a carved, arcaded screen, into the Hall. The room was redecorated with light-painted panelling early this century by Sir Reginald Blomfield, and houses French and English 18C furniture, with an early Aubusson carpet and Sèvres china. It served as an Ante-Room to the Great Chamber, the finest room at Godinton. The very elaborate panelling is of the 1630s; the frieze at the top is filled with figures of militiamen engaging in musket and pike drill. The grand chimneypiece has scenes of Adam and Eve, and figures of men bear-baiting, pig-sticking and hunting. This fireplace was used by R.B. Martineau in his famous painting 'The Last Day in the Old Home' (in the Tate Gallery). The room is filled with extremely fine 17 and 18C English furniture, including some notable Chinese Chippendale pieces, and there is Worcester, Chelsea and Dresden porcelain, and some interesting 17C portraits.

From here you descend the main Staircase, another elaborate display of carved chestnut, with heraldic beasts on the newel posts.

The First Library, looking over the garden, has another carved oak overmantel, this one a veritable inventory of popular symbolism, dated 1631. Here and in the Second Library there is Georgian furniture and cabinet paintings; the latter room has Worcester china of the Dr Wall period (1760–80). Along a passageway is the Garden Hall, on the south front. This was redecorated in the 1920s in a chinoiserie style, to provide a setting for Chinese Chippendale furniture and Chinese porcelain. Opening out of this, the White Drawing Room has light Elizabethan-style decoration from the early 1900s by Blomfield. There are many watercolour and pastel pictures, and 18C furniture and china.

To the east and south of the house there are formal topiary gardens, surrounded by great yew hedges, making a perfect foil to its architecture; this was all laid out in 1904 by Blomfield. Opposite the entrance of the house are the blasted remains of a vast oak tree, the 'Domesday Oak'; it split and collapsed during Neville Chamberlain's broadcast at the outset of the Second World War, at 11am on 3 September 1939.

SB

Great Maytham Hall

Just south of Rolvenden village, about 4m south west of Tenterden, off the A28: The Country Houses Association. Open May–Sept Wed and Thurs 2–4.30.

This big Edwardian house, designed by Sir Edwin Lutyens and built in

1909–10, is today the property of the Country Houses Association; most of it is divided into residential apartments but, as at the Association's other houses, the principal rooms and gardens are open to the public.

Although the owners of Maytham can be traced back as far as the 13C, it always seems to have been subsidiary to other properties, and there does not seem to have been a manor house here until Captain James Monypenny RN built a comfortable brick residence, c 1721. The walled gardens and some outbuildings of this remain. The Moneypenny and Gybbon-Monypenny family held Maytham and Rolvenden, until they were brought down by a series of family disasters in the later 19C. In 1893 Thomas Gybbon-Monypenny died virtually penniless, and the house followed him shortly after by burning down. Enough survived to permit rebuilding, and various tenants lived here, including Frances Hodgson Burnett, authoress of *The Secret Garden* and *Little Lord Fauntleroy*. In 1909 the estate was bought by H.J. Tennant. The Tennants had made a huge fortune as chemical manufacturers in Glasgow, and this had propelled them into the first ranks of society; H.J. Tennant's father, Sir Charles, was a friend of Gladstone, and his sister, Margot, married H.H. Asquith, the Liberal Prime Minister. Lutyens was called in and he demolished the old house except for its cellars, and built the present one; it played host to an opulent way of life until its sale in 1936. The house was requisitioned during the War, and left derelict thereafter. It narrowly avoided partial demolition before its purchase by the Association in 1961; the main conversion work took until 1965.

The main entrance from the lane is through an archway in an impressive building housing lodges and stables; the house stands at the far end of a lime avenue. It is symmetrical, in plum-coloured brick, and very tall. The hipped roof and slightly arched windows give it a vaguely French character. You enter a long Entrance Hall, with white panelling; the staircase rises at one end. Ahead, and running the whole length of the main block, is the Drawing Room. This also has white 17C-style panelling, with fireplaces at either end, and some good Georgian furniture. Down steps at one end is an ante-room, and then the Dining Room, also in Lutyens' 'Wrenaissance' style with a fine marble chimneypiece and Ionic columns. The basement has vaulted 18C cellars from the original house, and a kitchen with Lutyens-designed fittings. Outside, the gardens are spacious and well-maintained. The walled garden is said to have been the inspiration for Frances Hodgson Burnett's *The Secret Garden*.

SB

Hever Castle

Between Sevenoaks and East Grinstead, off the B2026: Broadland Properties Ltd, tel. 0732 865224. Open daily early Mar–early Nov 12–5, gardens open 11–6. Refreshments.

Hever began as a 13C castellated manor house; it is famous as the 16C home of the Boleyn family and thus of Anne Boleyn. The present building, though, owes much to a lavish Edwardian restoration by the Astor family. The shape of the moat and the Gatehouse remain from when it was first built, around 1270; the rectangular courtyard was surrounded by timber-framed buildings and a stone wall. Geoffrey Bullen or Boleyn bought the Castle in the mid 15C. His grandson Thomas and three children survived to adulthood; the youngest, Anne, was born in 1507. Thomas rose steadily in royal favour, becoming Earl of Wiltshire. In 1526 Henry VIII fell suddenly in love with the 18-year-old Anne, making repeated visits to her at Hever; the rest, as they say, is history. Anne and her brother George were both executed in 1536, and their father died two years later, his high ambitions ruined. Henry VIII appropriated the Boleyn estates, eventually giving the castle to his hated fourth wife, Anne of Cleves.

Hever was bought by the Waldegrave family, and periodically occupied in the 17C. Thereafter it declined slowly into picturesque decay, until the arrival in 1903 of an American multi-millionaire, William Waldorf Astor, who had already bought Cliveden in Buckinghamshire (qv.). Hever was too small to contain the armies of guests and servants Astor envisaged. His architect, F.L. Pearson, came up with the solution of building a Tudor 'village'—a huge complex of picturesque buildings—at the back. This was linked by a covered bridge over the moat to the castle proper, which was restored and redecorated at vast expense. Astor went on to have the great lake dug out by hand, and the enormous Italian garden laid out between that and the castle, creating an ultra-luxurious setting for country-house entertainment. Hever belonged to the Astor family until 1983, when it was sold to the present owners.

The castle is small and picturesque, contained within its moat. The **gatehouse** and outer walls are essentially medieval. Behind are the rambling buildings of Pearson's 'village', now used as a conference centre. Inside the courtyard, the half-timbered buildings are a mixture of 16C fabric and Edwardian restoration. The Entrance Hall passageway opens out into the **Inner Hall**, in Tudor times the kitchen. William Astor installed fabulously elaborate panelling, a 'minstrel's gallery' and a rich plaster ceiling. There are numerous portraits of the Tudor court and of continental monarchs; the finest a splendid one of Don John of Austria by Sanchez Coello, and a version of Holbein's portrait of Henry VIII.

To the right, the **Drawing Room** is Edwardian too, with finely inlaid panelling and a low plastered ceiling. Returning through the Inner Hall, the **Dining Hall** is reached. This was the original Hall, but again redecorated with great lavishness by William Astor; the screen, ceiling and a fireplace are covered with elaborate Gothic ornament. The room houses splendid 17C furniture and 16C tapestries; the tapestry over the fireplace bears the arms of Henry VIII. The great Flemish tapestry of a hunting-scene, opposite, is one of the series 'Emperor Maximilian's Hunts', designed by Bernard van Orley (c 1530).

Back through the Entrance Hall, visitors pass through the **Library**, with Edwardian woodwork in Carolean style. The **Morning Room** next door has older woodwork, and some interesting furniture; the triangular chairs are of c 1620. Up a narrow spiral staircase is **Anne Boleyn's Room** with miniatures and portraits of the unfortunate queen. Anne of Cleves' Room is dominated by the long 'Gothic Marriage' tapestry from Tournai, of about 1500. From here, the Staircase Gallery runs over the Entrance Hall, and has 17C furniture and a fine portrait of Elizabeth I. At the end, on the right, are two bedrooms. The Rochford Room has an unusual French Gothic four-post bed; the bed in the Henry VIII Room is English of about 1540. Both rooms are dark-panelled, but the panelling was probably installed early in this century. From here, visitors climb to the top floor; the **Long Gallery** was a 16C addition; the panelling is original, the elaborate ceiling added by Astor. It houses costumed figures of Henry VIII and so on. The Astor Suite, formerly bedrooms, contains memorabilia of the four generations of that family to live here. On the top floor of the Gatehouse is a museum of the local Yeomanry regiments. Finally, on its first floor is the 'Council Chamber', wherein are displayed torture instruments (of somewhat dubious antiquity).

The gardens are magnificent and well-maintained. Astor's Italian Garden has vines climbing over long pergolas, arches and waterfalls. He collected many pieces of ancient Roman sculpture, and these were built into the long border here. The effect—part sculpture gallery and part herbaceous border—is extraordinary, like a millionaire's mansion on Long Island. At the far end, opulent Ionic colonnades look out over the huge artificial lake.

SB

Ightham Mote

South of Ightham village, off the A227 just east of Sevenoaks: National Trust, tel. 0732 810378. Open Apr–Oct Mon, Wed, Thur, Fri 12–5.30, Sun, BH Mon 11–5.30. Refreshments.

Ightham Mote is a suitably medieval-sounding name for this ancient manor house. It is a square, grey building around a courtyard, surrounded by a moat, in a narrow valley deep in the Kent countryside. There has been a house here since c 1340, and it was named 'The Mote' as early as 1370. Although the names of its owners are known reasonably firmly, its building history is very complicated, and has mostly to be deduced from the fabric. It was first built in the 14C with the moat, in its present shape, a square enclosure within, and the stone Hall range on the east side. The west range with the gatehouse was added c 1480, and the rest of the house grew up slowly thereafter. In 1591 it was bought by the Selby family, who owned it until 1880; they made many minor alterations, but none which really disrupted its medieval character. The next owner, Sir Thomas Colyer-Fergusson, carried out conservative restoration work. In 1953 it was bought by an American millionaire, Henry Robinson, who had seen and admired the house while on a cycling holiday decades earlier. He carried out repairs, lived here in the summer months, and eventually bequeathed it to the National Trust in 1985. His ashes are interred in the Crypt.

The house is almost concealed in the well-wooded valley. There are old ponds, above and below it, linked to the moat. The entrance front is symmetrical, with a square gatehouse in the middle; it looks west across broad lawns to a picturesque row of timber-framed Elizabethan cottages. Inside the square courtyard, the hall range is ahead; it was built c 1340, with the large window inserted c 1480. On the right is the south range, with Georgian Gothick windows of the late 18C. The large Tudor-style dog kennel was made for Dido, the Colyer-Fergussons' St Bernard, in 1891.

The shape of the Hall is of the 14C, as is the high roof supported on a great stone arch. The fireplace is 16C and the panelling of the 19C; three large Brussels tapestries hang on the walls. From here, the visitor goes through the Staircase Hall, up a passage, and through a tiny inner courtyard, to the Crypt, the vaulted 14C room under the Chapel. From here the Staircase Hall is re-entered; the present stairs were probably built by Sir William Selby, c 1611, and the large portrait hanging here is of his wife, Dame Dorothy. At the top of the stairs, the Old Chapel opens off the landing. This high, narrow room with its raftered roof part is of the 14C house. It was divided by the insertion of a floor half-way up, but this has been removed.

From here, a suite of four rooms known as the Boys' Rooms are entered; they retain an Edwardian character, decorated and furnished largely as they were during the Colyer-Fergussons' time here. At the far end, the Bathroom retains its Edwardian bath and basin; the other fittings have been brought from elsewhere. This leads into the Oriel Room, the main solar of the 14C house. The crown post roof has mostly the original timber, with some alterations of the 1890s, and 17C chairs and coffers. The Chapel Corridor leads around the north-east side of the courtyard, into the east end of the present Chapel. This was the work of Richard Clement, probably of the 1520s, and probably built as a Gallery, but converted into a chapel at an unknown date. It is a beautiful room, with its barrel-vaulted roof lined with wooden panels painted with royal emblems, the rose, the fleur-de-lis, the portcullis, and the pomegranate (for Catherine of Aragon); the much-faded decoration is original, with hardly a parallel in England (except Loseley House, Surrey, qv.). The fine stained glass is German of the 1520s, and was brought here in the 19C. The chapel furniture is of various dates from the Middle Ages to the 18C, although it now blends into a happy unity.

From here the visitor crosses the head of a staircase to reach the Drawing Room. This long room was remodelled in the 18C when the Venetian window at the north end was added, but retains an elaborate Jacobean chimneypiece from an earlier stage in its history. The frieze, with the Selby family's emblem of a Saracen's head, is also Jacobean. The room has fine hand-painted Chinese wallpaper of the 18C, but this is currently (1993) in store, pending structural repairs. Down the stairs, the Billiard Room under the Drawing Room was fitted up in 1890; the furniture is English of the 17C. It presently houses a display concerning the major restoration programme which is currently in hand, and the Trust's appeal to pay for it. The garden is likewise being restored by the Trust to its late-Victorian or Edwardian appearance. The Selby family had introduced few changes to it in 400 years, and as a result Ightham was seen c 1900 as an ideal 'Olde English' garden.

SB

Knole

Just south east of Sevenoaks, off the A225: National Trust, tel. 0732 450608. Open Apr–Oct Wed–Sat, BH Mon 11–5, Sun 2–5, last admission 4. Refreshments.

Knole is in every respect one of the greatest of English houses. It grew in an organic way over several centuries, so that its grey ragstone ranges now spread around seven courtyards, on the low hill or knoll from which it derives its name. It stands in the middle of a well-wooded deer park, just outside Sevenoaks. It has been aptly likened to a medieval town, and the visitor is well-advised to walk around it, and see how the north side, in particular, merits this description. It is one of the few truly great houses to be mostly of the English vernacular tradition.

There was a substantial manor house here from the 12C. In 1456 it was bought for £266 by Thomas Bourchier, Archbishop of Canterbury. He built much of the present house before his death here in 1486, when he bequeathed it to the archdiocese. It was the residence of four more archbishops, before Henry VIII extorted it from Thomas Cranmer as a rather involuntary 'gift' in 1538. Henry added the big Green Court to house his retinue, but did not spend much time here. After a period of some confusion in its ownership, Elizabeth I gave it to her cousin (on the Boleyn side), Thomas Sackville, in 1566. However, a lease previously given to the Lennard family prevented him from taking up residence until 1603. The Sackvilles were an ancient family, with much property in Kent and London; Thomas's father Sir Richard Sackville was nicknamed 'Fillsack' on account of his wealth. Thomas was at various times Lord High Steward and Lord High Treasurer, and a notable poet. Between 1603 and his death in 1608, he used a good part of his father's fortune in modernising Knole. Changes since then have been relatively minor.

In 1604 Thomas was created 1st Earl of Dorset. The Sackvilles and their house survived the incredibly spendthrift 3rd Earl, and the confiscation of much of their wealth from the royalist 4th Earl. The 5th Earl restored matters somewhat by marrying the heiress of Lionel Cranfield, Earl of Middlesex, James I's financier, and she brought pictures and furniture as well as money. Charles, 6th Earl, proceeded to squander a good deal of this; he was one of the most lavish spenders in Charles II's circle, he was a friend of Dryden, Wycherley and Rochester, as well as lover of Nell Gwynn. However, as Lord Chamberlain to William III, he was able to add to the collections in the house with magnificent pieces from the royal palaces, which make Knole probably the finest repository of 17C furniture in Britain.

His son, Lionel, became 1st Duke of Dorset, and added fine Kentian furniture to the collection. The 3rd Duke, a keen cricketer, ambassador to France and friend of Sir Joshua Reynolds, contributed a whole roomful of that master's works. When his son, the 4th Duke, died in a hunting accident in 1815, the title and the Sackville line came to an end. Knole passed to the West family; the Sackville-West line became Barons Sackville in 1876. The family's conservatism protected their house from any major alterations. The writer Vita Sackville-West grew up here, and her book *Knole and the Sackvilles* is an excellent history of the house and family; her friend Virginia Woolf was inspired by the house to write her novel *Orlando*. In 1946, the 4th Lord Sackville gave Knole and 80 acres of the park to the National Trust. The family still live here.

The house is approached indirectly through the 1000 acre park. The **west front**, the first part seen, is simple and dignified, symmetrical about its central gate-tower. This, with the Green Court behind, is basically the work of Henry VIII, c 1543–48; the shaped gables were added by Thomas Sackville. The **Green Court** is arranged as a series of lodgings, rather like the quadrangle of an Oxford college, to house the royal retinue (the right-hand wing was gutted early in the 19C to make an Orangery). The higher building facing is the original west front of Archbishop Bourchier's 15C palace. Going under the arch in Bourchier's Tower, the visitor is in the smaller **Stone Court**. The buildings here are essentially 15C, although with many alterations (the gables and colonnade on the opposite side are Thomas Sackville's work). Beneath the flagstones is a huge water-cistern, a reservoir for this great household.

Under the colonnade you enter the **Great Hall**. This remains as it was remodelled by Thomas Sackville, 1605–8, and is dominated by the elaborately-carved oak screen, a masterpiece of English art. The immense table is original to the room, and there are fine 17C portraits. The **staircase**, with its painted Renaissance decoration, is also the 1st Earl's work; the luscious reclining nude figure at its foot is said to be of Giannetta Baccelli (known in the house as Madam Shelley), the 3rd Duke's Italian mistress. At the top you enter the first of the house's three long galleries, which introduces the succession of first-floor state rooms. The **Brown Gallery**, 88ft long, is the 1st Earl's work, and is still lined with a great series of portraits, all painted for the room; they represent the Kings of England, important figures of the Elizabethan and Jacobean court, and foreign princes and celebrities. The room also contains the first of the house's sets of late-17C furniture, acquired by the 6th Earl as a perquisite of his post as Lord Chamberlain to William III.

At the end of the Brown Gallery, the visitor normally turns right, into a small and intimate pair of rooms. **Lady Betty Germain's Rooms** are named after a distant relative who lived here in the early 18C, preferring it to her own great house, Drayton in Northamptonshire. The rooms are panelled, with family portraits and smaller Dutch and Flemish pictures, and crowded with the more everyday kind of 17C and 18C furniture. The tour then returns across the head of the Brown Gallery to the **Spangle Bedroom** and Spangle Dressing Room, named for the 17C state bed, whose hangings are embroidered with little metal 'spangles'. These rooms look east over the walled gardens, and are largely of the 1st Earl's time, with 17C furniture and tapestries, and good pictures by Lely. This takes you into the **Leicester Gallery**, a great T-shaped room. This contains much furniture from the courts of James I and Charles I, much of it from Whitehall and Hampton Court, including a very early (17C) billiard table, and (in a museum room leading off it) the original 'Knole settee'; this ancestor of the modern sofa was probably designed as a 'Chair of State', to stand under a canopy. This room, too, is hung with a profusion of 16C and 17C paintings, mostly portraits by Mytens , William Dobson and others, and copies of works by the great masters. From the Leicester Gallery the visitor enters the **Venetian Ambassador's Bedroom**. The decoration here, unusually for the house, is of the early 18C. The magnificent tapestries, representing scenes from *Orlando Furioso*, also came from Whitehall Palace. However, the room is dominated by the great bed with its matching armchairs and stools, made for James II in 1688 and one of the finest sets of 17C furniture in existence.

The tour then proceeds back down the Leicester Gallery and Brown Gallery to the most magnificent rooms of all. They form a long suite down the south front, and were created in their present form by the 1st Earl, as his main set of state rooms. The **Ballroom**, though, originated as the solar of Archbishop Bourchier's house. The 1st Earl installed the elaborate panelling, the ceiling, and the splendid marble and alabaster chimneypiece. There is magnificent French furniture from the reigns of Louis XIV and Louis XVI, and an array of full-length portraits, including one by Van Dyck of the wife of the 5th Earl of Dorset. Next comes the Crimson Drawing Room, or Reynolds Room. It is early 17C in form, but derives its name from the array of portraits by that artist, including likenesses of Dr Johnson, David Garrick, and Wang-y-Tong, a Chinese page of the 3rd Duke of Dorset.

Beyond this is the sumptuous **Cartoon Gallery**, named from the great paintings down one wall, copies by Daniel Mytens of Raphael's famous cartoons (now in the Victoria and Albert Museum, London) of scenes from the Acts of the Apostles. The rest of the decoration is the 1st Earl's, including the beautiful plaster ceiling and another magnificent chimneypiece, but the furniture is from the courts of Louis XIV and William III. At the far end of the gallery, the last major room seen is the **King's Room**. This is a fitting climax to the house. The great bed, chairs and stools were probably made

The staircase at Knole showing some of the painted Renaissance decoration, dating from the early 17C

in France for the marriage of James II to Mary of Modena. The bed retains its original gilding and silvering; the hangings, heavy with gold thread, are among the richest to survive; the whole ensemble is now sealed behind glass. The silver sconces, the silver toilet service, and the silver table, mirror and candlestands are likewise among the finest anywhere.

The walled gardens are not normally open to visitors, although glimpses of them may be had from the first-floor rooms. The park, on the other hand, is open every day of the year.

SB

Leeds Castle

From B2163, near junction 8 of the M20: The Leeds Castle Foundation, tel. 0622 765400. Open Mar–Oct daily 11–5; Nov–Mar Sat, Sun only 11–4. Refreshments.

The view of Leeds Castle, apparently floating in the middle of its lake, its medieval walls reflected in the water, is one of the most famous images of any British house. The castle retains much of its medieval fabric, but the interiors were re-created, in medieval and 18C style, in the 1920s, and now house some very fine items.

After the Norman Conquest, Leeds was given by William the Conqueror to the Crevecoeur family, and they built the first castle on this site. The lake is artificial, and the castle came first. Robert de Crevecoeur built a Keep on a stony outcrop in a marsh c 1119. Outer courtyards were added, and in the 13C his descendants dammed the River Len to create the great lake seen today, as a line of water-defences. In 1278, Leeds came into the ownership of Eleanor of Castille, wife of Edward I, and it remained a royal possession and periodically a royal residence until the time of Henry VIII. Edward I carried out extensive works, and much of the medieval work remaining is of his time. The castle was often held by queens, including Anne of Bohemia, wife of Richard II, and Catherine of Valois, wife of Henry V. She received it in 1422, and carried out many repairs.

Henry VIII, a compulsive spender and builder, also carried out work here. In 1522, though, the castle was granted by the Lord Protector Somerset to Sir Anthony St Leger. The Smythe family, here in the early 17C, built a large new wing on the main island. Leeds later passed to the Culpeper and Fairfax families. It fell into picturesque decay in the 18C, the Gloriette, on the site of the 12C keep, becoming a ruin. The castle was saved by Fiennes Wykeham Martin, who built a large new wing in 1822–24 in a Tudor-castellated style, and renovated the rest. The Wykeham-Martin family remained here until obliged by death duties to sell in 1924, when Leeds was bought by the Hon. Olive, Lady Baillie. Her mother was a member of the American Whitney family and a great heiress, and this provided the wherewithal for Lady Baillie's long and thorough restoration of the Castle. Her architect, Owen Little, and two French decorators, Rateau and Boudin, worked through the 1930s. On her death in 1974, she established the Leeds Castle Foundation, for the purpose of preserving the castle, opening it to the public, and using it for medical seminars and cultural events.

The castle has retained the defensive lake around it, which defines its character. Many castles retain moats, but there is hardly anywhere else where water-defences on this scale remain. The main island is of about three acres; at one end are the medieval gatehouse and Maiden's Tower. At the other end is the main wing—Fiennes Wykeham Martin's smart new house of the 1820s. Behind this, and linked to it by a two-storey gallery carried on arches, is the Gloriette, a separate oval-shaped block rising straight out of the water. It is of 13C and 14C masonry, and occupies the site of the Norman keep.

The visitor is taken by a circuitous route around the side of the castle, and in at basement level through a wine-cellar, then up to a hall in the 1820s building. From here, a gallery leads over the water to the Gloriette, re-roofed in the 1820s. The interior was sympathetically renovated by Lady Baillie in the 1920s. French craftsmen carved the massive beamed ceilings and fittings, and her architect resisted the temptation to make it over-elaborate, so the result is fairly convincing. The first room is furnished to represent Queen Catherine of Valois's bedroom, in the 1420s, with modern recreations of medieval furnishings; her 'bathroom' is next door. The Queen's Gallery, beyond, is a satisfying D-shaped room. There are some fine 16C Brussels tapestries, a 15C English diptych of the Annunciation and a triptych representing the Virgin and Child with Angels, probably German, c 1500. Next door, the Banqueting Hall is a long, handsome room, with a carved ceiling, an ebony floor, and a French fireplace of c 1500. There is some interesting 16C furniture and pictures, and, on either side of the fireplace, 17C tapestries representing equestrian stances made for the 1st Duke of Newcastle. This leads into the little Chapel, which has carved wooden panels from Ulm of the Stations of the Cross, and a splendid tapestry of the Adoration of the Magi, both of c 1500.

The first floor of the Gloriette is reached by a solid oak spiral stair, a medieval French piece brought here by Lady Baillie. The Seminar Room, upstairs, houses some of her collection of Impressionist paintings. The visitor re-crosses the gallery-bridge back to the main building, joining the landing of the main staircase. Here there are magnificent tapestries, including some very unusual hunting and 'verdure' pieces, of the late 15C or early 16C. Downstairs are two large reception rooms from Lady Baillie's time, decorated by Stephane Boudin. The Yellow Drawing Room is a rich Georgian-revival room, with some fine English furniture of the reigns of William and Mary, and Queen Anne. There are flower-paintings by Monnoyer, and 'Pulchinello's Kitchen' by Gian Domenico Tiepolo, a Venetian artist whose work is rarely seen in Britain. Beyond this lies the Thorpe Hall Room, named from the very fine 1650s panelling, taken from the house of that name near Peterborough and installed here in 1927. The Entrance Hall has 15C 'verdure' tapestries from the Chteau d'Enghien. The Front Hall, through which you leave, is dominated by a great full-length Van Dyck portrait of Prince Charles Louis of the Palatinate. A room next to the gatehouse houses a remarkable collection of historic dog-collars from up to four centuries ago—some of them fine works of art.

SB

Lullingstone Castle

Between Eynsford and Sevenoaks, off the A225: Guy Hart Dyke, Esq., tel. 0322 862114. Open Apr–Oct Sat, Sun, BH 2–6. Refreshments.

Lullingstone Castle stands by a large lake in the wooded valley of the Darent. In 1361 the manor passed to John Peche, Alderman of London, and his descendant, Sir John Peche, built the present house in the reign of Henry VII. He was Lord Deputy of Calais in 1509, and accompanied Henry VIII to the Field of the Cloth of Gold in 1520. Sir John's estates went to his nephew, Sir Percyval Hart, who ruled here until his death, aged 84, in 1580. The Hart family held the estate until the death of Percival Hart in 1738; his daughter Anne married Sir Thomas Dyke, a rich Sussex man, and the Hart Dyke family have lived here ever since. Lullingstone has thus passed by descent for over 600 years.

Sir John Peche's new house was moated, and had an elaborate entrance. The traveller coming along the Eynsford road would arrive at the tall turreted brick gatehouse which still stands. Passing through this he would have found himself in a wide grass courtyard, used as a tiltyard, with the little medieval church on the left. Across it was another big brick gatehouse, with the house behind it. In the early 1700s Percival Hart remodelled the front range of the house, and the principal rooms. The impressively feudal entrance remained, but it must have seemed very inconvenient, and in 1738 Sir John Dixon Dyke demolished the inner gatehouse and filled in the moat.

The house now appears across level lawns, covering the site of the inner gatehouse and moat. Percival Hart's early-18C façade is of warm brick with sash windows, three storeys high with hipped roofs. Small alterations were made late in the last century, notably the wide porch in the middle. Behind this façade, the Castle is still basically the quadrangular Tudor manor house built by Sir John Peche.

The Great Hall occupies the centre of the entrance front. The shell is essentially Tudor, and the original timber-roof remains above the plaster ceiling. The room's present appearance, though, is of the early 18C with its big fireplace, white painted panelling and sash windows. There are fine family portraits, in particular a remarkable triptych painted in 1575 and showing Sir Percyval Hart, aged 80, flanked by his sons George and Francis. Over the fireplace, a large painting shows the house before the early-18C alterations, when both gatehouses were still standing.

On the left is the State Dining Room. The panelling, again, is from the reign of Queen Anne, and the furniture is mostly of the 17C. There are portraits of James II, and of knights of the Hart line. Over the fireplace is a jousting helm used by Sir John Peche. The next room, the Library, was likewise panelled in the early 1700s; most of the books are of the 17C and 18C. The principal staircase is also early 18C, the treads very shallow. On the newel posts are wooden lions' heads, the crest of the Peche family. At the top of the stairs, an ante-room opens off the landing, with family relics including an estate map, a 17C travelling trunk, and the family's kettle-drum. Beyond is the State Drawing Room. This is the Great Chamber of the Tudor house, directly over the Dining Room. The splendid barrel-vaulted ceiling has Elizabethan plasterwork, with strapwork, pendants, and medallion portraits of figures from Roman history. The panelling, though, was inserted in the early 1700s, and Queen Anne's portrait dominates the room. There are other fine portraits, in particular that of Sir George Hart, painted c 1600. From here you reach the State Bedroom and Dressing Room, which have more 18C furniture; the latter has fine needlework hangings.

Back outside, the church should not be missed. Although of Norman origins, it was redecorated by Percyval Hart in the early 18C, with a fine plaster ceiling, good woodwork and splendid monuments to the Hart and Dyke families. The monument to the first Sir Percival, of c 1580, is a magnificent columned composition, and the last Percival Hart's monument, of 1738, is a remarkably early and confident exercise in the Gothick style.

SB

Lympne Castle

In Lympne village, 3m north west of Hythe, off the A20/A261 or the B2067: Harry Margary, tel. 0303 267571. Open Easter–Sept daily 10.30–6. Occasionally closed on Sat.

Lympne Castle is a small but well-preserved medieval fortress, restored and extended early in this century to make a country house. It stands on the edge of the chalk downs west of Hythe, looking out over Romney Marsh to the Channel. This is an ancient site on the slope below the castle are extensive remains of the Roman 3C coastal fort of Portus Lemanis. When the castle was built, the sea washed against the foot of the hill. After the Norman Conquest, the Conqueror gave Lympne, or Limne, to his Archbishop of Canterbury, Lanfranc of Bec, who built the first castle here using stones from the long-ruined fort. It became a residence of the Archdeacons of Canterbury, and remained in their possession until 1860. A square tower remains of the Norman castle, but most of the present building dates from the mid 14C during the Hundred Years War, probably to play its part in the coastal defences against the French. The castle was let 1641, and passed through a succession of lay tenants, until in 1860 it was sold altogether. In 1905 it was bought by a member of the Tennant family, who owned a great chemical business in Glasgow (qv. Great Maytham Hall). This paid for a most sensitive restoration by the Scots architect Sir Robert Lorimer, who added a large domestic wing and outbuildings, so that it could function as a spacious Edwardian country house without much altering the plan of the original building. The present owner, Harry Margary, is well known as a publisher of new editions of historic maps.

A lane leads from the main Hythe road through Lympne village, to where the castle and the church stand on the edge of the escarpment, all in grey Kentish ragstone. There is a long row of cottage-like outbuildings by Lorimer, and then a gate to the castle forecourt. The original castle consists of a 14C Great Hall, with a tower at either end; that to the left is basically 13C and that to the right is 14C. On the right are Lorimer's domestic buildings, a model of sensitive Arts and Crafts design, with varied gables and tall chimneys. The castle proper is largely original, with fine 14C windows and porch.

Inside, the Great Hall is well-preserved, with some restoration by Lorimer; it has a 14C Crown Post roof and partly restored linenfold panelling, and the windows on the far side look out over the marsh and sea. Going up the 13C tower, one room has a set of models of English cathedrals, another has an 18C bed. At the top is an 'observatory', added during the last war as a gunnery control centre for the south coast defences. The other, west end was the dais end, with the Archdeacon's apartments. On the first floor, two rooms now house a collection of dolls, dolls'-houses and miniature furniture. In the Solar position is a chamber with another fine crown post roof, and some 16C and 17C furniture. From the top of the tower are fine views over the castle and far beyond.

Next to the castle, the church of St Stephen is of Norman origin. Below is the site of Portus Lemanis; its rectangular shape has been much distorted by landslips, but large sections of the wall remain both visible and accessible.

SB

Penshurst Place

In Penshurst village on the B2176, west of Tunbridge Wells: The Rt Hon. Viscount de l'Isle, tel. 0892 87030. Open Apr–Sept daily 1–5.00, grounds open Mar–Oct 11–dusk. Refreshments.

Penshurst is justly one of the most famous of English houses: it is one of the best pieces of medieval domestic architecture in Europe and it has splendid contents. Its history begins in 1338, when the land was bought by Sir John de Pulteney, a very successful London merchant and banker. Sir John built the core of the present house, including the tremendous Great Hall; he was four times Mayor of London, and died in the Black Death of 1349. Sir John left no children, and Penshurst passed, through a rather complicated series of legacies, to Sir John Devereux. He received licence to crenellate the house in 1392, and enclosed the Pulteney house in a rectangular enclosure of walls with eight defensive towers, which has defined the house's development ever since.

Sir John died in 1394, and the newly-expanded house passed to John Seyntclere, who in 1429 sold it to John, Duke of Bedford, younger brother of Henry V. During his ownership the range now known as the Buckingham Buildings was added; after his death the house passed to his younger brother Humphrey, Duke of Gloucester. On his death in 1447 his estates were given by Henry VI to a favourite, Humphrey Stafford, Duke of Buckingham, who became a leader of the Lancastrian cause in the Wars of the Roses. Five successive generations of the Staffords died by violence, ending with the 3rd Duke of Buckingham, tried for treason by Henry VIII and beheaded in 1521, his estates forfeited to the Crown. Penshurst remained Crown property until 1552, when Edward VI granted it to Sir William Sidney (d 1554). Since then, the house has been indissolubly linked to the name of Sidney.

Sir William was succeeded by his son, Sir Henry. Despite close family links to Lady Jane Grey, he survived the dangerous reign of Queen Mary, to serve Elizabeth I, ruling Wales and Ireland for her at different times. He made great additions to the medieval house at Penshurst before his death in 1586. In the same year his celebrated son, Sir Philip Sidney, the poet, diplomat and warrior, was killed fighting in the Dutch revolt against Spanish rule. Sir Philip's younger brother Robert was made Viscount Lisle, and in 1618, Earl of Leicester, and his descendants maintained Penshurst as their principal seat until the death of Jocelyn, 7th Earl, in 1743. After a struggle over the succession, the estates passed to his niece and her husband, William Perry. Their daughter Elizabeth Perry married Sir Bysshe Shelley of Horsham, Sussex, and the present owners of Penshurst are descended from this marriage. The family reverted to the name of Sidney, and were created Lords de l'Isle and Dudley in 1835; the 2nd Lord carried out a good deal of rebuilding in a Tudor style. The 6th Lord, a distinguished soldier in the Second World War, served twice as a minister under Churchill, and later as Governor General of Australia. He was made a Viscount in 1956, and his son, the 2nd Viscount, now lives at Penshurst with his family.

The house stands just on the edge of its village. Its core is Sir John Pulteney's house, which consisted of a hall, with kitchen wing at one end, and solar wing at the other. What one sees now is a roughly H-shaped group of buildings, the long sides facing north and south. The long **south range**, which is seen first, comprises the original Pulteney house, with the 15C Buckingham Building added to the left. Hidden behind this is the cross-bar of the H, with an open courtyard on either side. The other long range, facing north, was built by Sir Henry Sidney in the reign of Elizabeth, and much altered in the 1830s. Visitors see much of the south range; the north range contains the family's private apartments.

The house is approached through the formal gardens, and under the late-14C Garden Tower. Ahead is a magnificent ensemble of 14C architecture: Sir John's Hall, with its tiled roof and high windows, and battlemented wings on either side. Further to the left is the Buckingham Building, at the far end of which an Elizabethan wing links it to one of the corner towers. The **Great Hall** is entered in the classic manner, under a porch which leads into a screens passage. It is very large—62ft by 39ft and 60ft high—and amazingly well-preserved. The huge open timber roof is a marvel of medieval craftsmanship. No fireplace was ever added, and it is easy to picture the Hall as it was when new, with a fire blazing in the centre of the floor, and the smoke escaping through a louvre in the middle of the roof. The trestle tables are of the 15C, and original to the room. At the upper end of the room is the dais, for the lord's table. The tapestries are French, of the 16C.

Opening from the Hall at the solar end, the vaulted Crypt or undercroft houses a museum devoted to the long and illustrious history of the Sidney family. Next to this room, broad stairs lead up to what would have been Sir John Pulteney's Solar, or family chamber. It is now the **State Dining Room**, and was given its present, austere decoration in the 19C. Along the walls are many fine 16C and 17C portraits, including a group by Marcus Gheeraerts of the 1st Countess of Leicester with her six children.

From here, you enter the first floor of the Buckingham Building, built c 1430, and externally a splendid piece of court architecture in a rather French style. Sir Henry Sidney added an attic storey, and probably divided the upper floor into two rooms, as seen now. The first, **Queen Elizabeth's Room**, has very rare 17C silk appliqu hangings on the end walls, en suite with the magnificent set of furniture here. The elaborate harpsichord at the end of the room belonged to Queen Christina of Sweden. On the north wall hangs a huge group portrait of William Perry and his wife Elizabeth Sidney, who inherited the house in 1743, with their children, all magnificently dressed. The adjacent **Tapestry Room** takes its name from the big Brussels tapestries on two walls, the Page's Room was turned into a china closet in the last century, displaying mostly oriental china. The fine Italian furniture here and elsewhere was bought by William Perry.

Steps take you up from the Buckingham Building into Sir Robert Sidney's **Long Gallery**, added c 1600. It is lined with panelling, and contains a great number of fine 16C and 17C portraits, including good ones of Elizabeth I and Sir Philip Sidney. Stairs in the Record Tower then take you down to the **Panelled Room**. This was created in 1962 with old panelling and furniture from elsewhere in the house, and is furnished as a state bedchamber. The canopied bed with its green velvet hangings is of the 17C, and there is more furniture of the same period. The **Nether Gallery**, beneath the Long Gallery, houses the family collection of armour and weapons. On the centre table is Sir Philip Sidney's funeral helm, surmounted by a porcupine—the family crest; it was carried at his state funeral in Old St Paul's in 1587. There is more fine Italian and French furniture of the 17C and 18C. This leads to the shop, and then back out to the south front terrace.

The gardens date from the 14C, but the present levels and walls were laid out by Sir Henry Sidney in Elizabethan times. The current design, which uses a mile of yew hedges to divide the 11 acres into a series of ten 'rooms' was completed by the 2nd Lord de l'Isle and Dudley in the last century. The different rooms have varied planting, blooming around the year. The current planting is the work of the 1st Viscount de l'Isle, and the gardens provide a perfect setting for the great house.

SB

Port Lympne

3m west of Hythe on the B2067, not far from junction 11 of the M20: John
Aspinall, tel. 0303 264646/7. Open all the year daily 10–5 in summer, 10 to
an hour before dusk in winter. Closed Dec 25. Refreshments.

Port Lympne is a mansion dating from 1911–13, with more than a touch of
the bizarre about it. Thanks to the present owner, John Aspinall, both the
house and the superb gardens are in excellent condition, and form the
centrepiece of an amazing zoo.

House and gardens were the creation of Sir Philip Sassoon (1888–1939).
The Sassoon family were Parsees from Bombay, who made a great fortune
from trading and banking, establishing a branch in England, who converted to Judaism. Sir Philip turned to politics rather than business, serving
as a Conservative MP from 1912 until his death, and holding a number of
government posts in the 1920s and '30s. He remained a bachelor, so had
no need of a great household. Port Lympne, named in reference to the
Roman fort of Portus Lemanis which stood nearby (qv. Lympne Castle), was
designed for lavish weekend house-parties. The architect was Sir Herbert
Baker, who had worked for many years in Cape Colony, where he had
perfected a version of the 17C 'Cape Dutch' style. He adapted this for Port
Lympne, which is of russet-coloured brickwork of very high quality, with
Dutch gables, but also with hints of Roman architecture, a kind of combination which Baker made his speciality. Inside, it was decorated with the
greatest lavishness, even eccentricity, in a variety of styles.

On Sir Philip's death, the house was bought by a Colonel and Mrs Waite,
who simplified some of the interiors slightly; it suffered further damage
from occupying airmen during the war. It stood empty for many years, until
bought by the present owner in 1973. John Aspinall had already established
a wild animal park at Howletts near Canterbury, and his principal aim at
Port Lympne was to build a larger establishment, where endangered
species would have room to breed and live in near-natural surroundings.
He has also restored the house and gardens, after many years of neglect.

The house is roughly H-shaped, with one of the open courts facing south
over Romney Marsh to the Channel; the entrance is on the east side, and
a long white corridor leads across the building from east to west. This is in
Baker's severe Roman manner, as is the staircase. Between the north arms
of the 'H' is a remarkable miniature Moorish patio, based on those in
Granada, with fountains and delicate marble columns. The main reception
rooms have views south; the long room in the middle has 17C-style
panelling, and is used to display wildlife paintings and sculptures. The
Drawing Room, in the east wing, formerly had Baroque murals by the
Catalan artist Sert. These were virtually destroyed during the War, and in
their place Mr Aspinall has commissioned the artist Spencer Roberts to
paint jungle scenes of South-East Asia, with dozens of native species, many
of them 'portraits' of animals in the Port Lympne zoo. In the south west
room, a frieze by Glyn Philpot representing an African procession, formerly
in Sir Philip's Dining Room (dismantled by the Waites) has been re-erected.
But, the pice de rsistance of the interior is the Tent Room, walls and ceiling
of which are lined with murals by Rex Whistler, executed in 1933. The
ceiling is painted like an exotic tent, the walls with lively scenes of a
Baroque city. It is one of the undoubted masterpieces of this fascinating,
and still under-rated artist.

Outside, the 15 acres of gardens were laid out by Baker and Philip Tilden for Sir Philip, with a blend of traditional English planting and Roman grandeur—the great Trojan Staircase could be something out of a Cecil B. de Mille film-set. Much of the planting has now been restored, and the gardens are beautifully maintained. All around is the wooded 300-acre zoo. There is a very wide range of species here, and it has one of the best breeding-records of any zoo in the world.

SB

Quebec House

In Westerham village, at the junction of the A25 and B2026: National Trust, tel. 0959 62206. Open Apr–Oct daily except Thurs and Sat 2–6.

Quebec House was the childhood home of General James Wolfe (1727–59), conqueror of French Quebec and the man with as good a claim as any to be called the founder of modern Canada. It is run by the National Trust as a memorial to Wolfe and a museum of his life. His grandfather and father were both military men; in 1726 Lieutenant-Colonel Edward Wolfe moved from York to Westerham where they rented this house, then known as Spiers. James Wolfe spent his childhood here, until the family moved to Greenwich in 1738. The house is of various dates; it is square, three storeys high, with three gables on each façade. Lower down there is a lot of rubble masonry, probably 16C but most of the walls are later work, of orange brick. The sash windows and door are of the 18C. In 1913 the house was bought by Joseph Bowles Learmont of Montreal, from the Wardes of Squerryes Court (qv.), and in 1918 his widow presented the house to the National Trust, as a memorial to Wolfe.

The Entrance Hall has 17C panelling and furniture; to the left is the Parlour; here there are various depictions of Wolfe's death at Quebec. The corner cabinet contains some of the Wolfe memorabilia, including his snuffbox. The Inner Hall houses a number of portraits of Wolfe. The Bicentenary Room, at the back of the house, has late 17C bolection panelling; the room was restored to its original form in 1959. Further Wolfe memorabilia here include the family bible, his linen dressing-gown and the travelling-canteen he used during the Quebec campaign. The fine staircase is of the 17C, and is lined with views of Quebec; its leads to the Drawing Room. This is furnished with English 18C pieces, and has prints and paintings associated with Wolfe and Canada. At the rear of the garden is the Tudor stable block. This has been renovated to house an exhibition illustrating the life of Wolfe, the capture of Quebec, and his death.

SB

Quex House (The Powell-Cotton Museum)

In Birchington, south west of Margate off A28: Trustees of the Powell-Cotton Museum; tel. 0843 42168. Open Easter–Sept Wed, Thur, Sun 2.15–6, and BH in summer. Refreshments.

Quex House is a square early-19C mansion, with a remarkable museum added to it early in this century, housing the ethnographic and anthropological collections formed by Major Percy Horace Powell-Cotton (1866–1940).

There was a 15C and 16C manor house at Quex. At the end of the 18C, Charles James Fox sold it to John Powell, then Paymaster General. His nephew, John Powell Powell, pulled down the old house, and built the present house between 1808 and 1813. It was a typical Regency gentleman's house, five bays wide, three storeys high and square. In 1849 he left it to his nephew Henry Perry Cotton, a member of a family who made a fortune in the East India Company. His son Henry Horace Powell Cotton enlarged the house in 1883, adding ornamental mouldings and iron verandahs, and the Drawing Room wing. In 1894, his son Percy Horace Powell-Cotton inherited. He was a wealthy man, and devoted most of his life to exploration and the study of ethnography and zoology; between 1887 and 1939 he made 28 journeys in India and Africa. He built the first museum building at Quex in 1896, adding another gallery in 1908. By the time Major Powell-Cotton died in 1940, the house was full to bursting with the accumulated collections. These, and the house, were vested in a charitable trust, which extended the museum buildings in 1955 and 1970. The museum is in itself of great historical interest, as a creation of its time and an evocation of the way in which Edwardian Britain saw Africa, and the natural world. The house now appears as an appendage of the much larger museum.

In the Entrance Hall is a portrait of Major Powell-Cotton, with many items of his safari equipment. Gallery 1 contains dioramas with animals from the African Savannah. The Passage Gallery has large collections of early firearms and hand weapons. Gallery 2 is the original museum building of 1896; the large dioramas may have been the first to display mammals represented in their natural habitat; there are also a great many pieces of tribal art, from the Dodinga people of East Africa, and Christian art from Ethiopia. The enormous Gallery 3 is surrounded by vast glass cases, housing dioramas of stuffed animals (including a bull elephant 11ft 6ins tall). In the middle is a peculiarly savage composition—an immense stuffed lion attacking a buffalo. The lion nearly killed Major Powell-Cotton in 1906, and the buffalo is from a sub-species which the Major discovered, and which is named after him. Gallery 4 contains collections of costumes, weapons, musical instruments, metalwork, etc, from Tibet, Burma and Japan. Galleries 5 and 6 house ethnographical collections from Africa, including costumes, jewellery, metalwork, utensils, weapons, masks, musical instruments and carved heads. Gallery 7 houses local archaeological finds, and a large collection of pottery and china from 17C stoneware to fine Chinese export porcelain and pieces of Meissen, Worcester and Chelsea. Gallery 8 houses an important collection of Chinese porcelain, from the Kang H'si to the Guangzu periods (1662–1908), from the Imperial Summer Palace in Peking.

From here you enter Quex House itself. The Drawing Room is appropriately exotic, being decorated in Indian style, and entirely filled with Indian and Chinese furniture and porcelain. The carved panelling was made for the room in Kashmir walnut, and the embroideries are from Chinese robes. The rest of the house has mostly late-19C or Edwardian decoration, and is furnished in eclectic style. The Hall has 17C-style panelling and English oak furniture; there are marine paintings, and some of the family glassware, miniatures and silver are on display. The Armoury houses no weapons now (they are in the museum), but has a variety of family portraits, furniture and memorabilia. The staircase gallery is lined with 17C portraits. To the right is the Powell Room, furnished as a Regency bedroom, and the Boudoir, furnished with pieces of the same period. Finally, the Library is an evocative period piece, a gentleman's retreat from the Edwardian age.

SB

Sissinghurst Castle

2m north east of Cranbrook, nr A262: National Trust, tel. 0580 712850.
Open Apr–Oct 15 Tues–Fri 1–6.30, Sat, Sun and Good Fri 10–6.30. Visitors may sometimes have to wait for admission. Refreshments.

Sissinghurst is best-known for its beautiful gardens, created by Harold Nicholson and Vita Sackville-West between 1930 and 1962. However, there is also much of architectural and human interest. The manor was a rich one in the Middle Ages; in 1490 the Baker family bought it, and built a great house of brick around a courtyard. The Elizabethan Sir Richard Baker demolished three of the four sides, leaving only the long, low entrance range. He treated it as a kind of gatehouse-wing, building a new quadrangle just to the east in the 1560s. Engravings show that there were three ranges of two-and-a-half storeys in height, with many bay windows, gables, chimneys and doors. The fourth or west side was closed by a wall, and in the middle of this a tall and magnificent gate-tower.

Sissinghurst declined after the Civil War, for the Baker family lost heavily by supporting the Royalist side, and in 1661 they died out. It passed via daughters to other families, who did not regard it as their home, and was left to decay. In the 1750s the house was leased to the Government as a prison for French sailors captured in the Seven Years War (1756–63). As many as 3000 of them were held here at any one time, and conditions were dreadful; guards and prisoners murdered each other, and Sissinghurst became notorious. By the time the war ended Sir Richard Baker's house was a wreck. Sir Horace Mann of Linton, inheriting it, demolished most of it c 1800, leaving only the older entrance range, the tower, a cottage known as the Priest's House, and part of the south wing, now known as the South Cottage. The mansion suffered the final insult of becoming the parish workhouse, until 1855. Thereafter it was a farmhouse. Finally in 1930 it found its rescuers in Harold Nicolson and his wife, Vita Sackville-West. He was a career diplomat; she was a member of the great family who lived at Knole (qv.), and was becoming well-known as a writer. They renovated the buildings and for the next 30 years slowly created the famous gardens. Vita Sackville-West occupied the Tower, Harold Nicholson the South Cottage; the dining room and kitchen were in the Priest's Cottage, and their children lived in the long front building. Their younger son, the writer Nigel Nicolson, gave Sissinghurst to the National Trust.

The long range of Tudor buildings at the entrance were built c 1490, the central arch inserted by Sir John Baker c 1530. Going through the arch, the great Elizabethan tower-gateway is ahead. In the left hand part of the long building is the Library, created by Nicolsons out of a stable; over 4000 books line two walls. At one end is a portrait of Thomas Sackville, 1st Earl of Dorset, Vita's ancestor. Over the fireplace is a portrait of Charles, 6th Earl, and the room has a mixture of English, Italian and French furniture. The Tower was built by Sir Richard Baker, c 1570. The left-hand turret has a spiral staircase leading up to the roof; there are three storeys over the archway. The room on the first floor was Vita Sackville-West's Sitting Room, occupied by her from 1933 until her death in 1962, and remains very largely as she knew it, lined with her books grouped according to her main interests—English literature, history and travel, and gardening. The upper two floors of the tower are unoccupied; from the top there is a fine view over the garden and much of the Kentish Weald.

The wonderful gardens at Sissinghurst are the creation of a marriage of minds, Harold Nicolson providing the linear severity of the formal plan, softened by the rich and romantic planting devised by his wife. Their aim was to combine long axial walks, with enclosed gardens opening like rooms off them, and in all to maintain 'the strictest formality of design, with the maximum informality in planting'.

SB

Squerryes Court

Just west of Westerham off the A25: Mr J. St A. Warde, tel. 0959 562345. Open Mar Sun 2–6; April–Sept Wed, Sat, Sun and BH Mon 2–6.

Squerryes Court exemplifies the sober and dignified gentry houses that were rising in later 17C England, fruits of the stability and prosperity which the reigns of the later Stuarts brought. It has been the home of the Warde family for over 250 years. The manor and site are ancient, but the house was built in 1680 by Sir Nicholas Crisp—a neat central block seven bays wide with a hipped roof, two smaller wings flanking it forming a forecourt, a grand formal garden stretching up the hillside above it, and a formal lake in the hollow below. His son sold the house to the Earl of Jersey, and in 1731 the 3rd Earl sold it to John Warde.

John Warde's great-uncle, Sir Patience Warde, was the eighth son of a Yorkshire gentleman, who went to London at the age of 14 to make his fortune, and did so as a silk and cloth merchant. Sir Patience became an Alderman and, in 1680, the year of the house's building, Lord Mayor. His nephew, Sir John Warde, succeeded him in his business, and was also Lord Mayor. His son was the John Warde who bought Squerryes and his grandson contributed the fine collection of paintings which adorns the house still. The original wings were demolished in the 19C, and their 19C replacements demolished after the war, leaving just the main block. This remains, excellently maintained, in the hands of the Warde family.

The house stands on a terrace looking over a little lake; the gardens rise up the hillside behind. It is perfectly symmetrical, of mellow orange brick, seven bays wide, two storeys high, with an attic in the hipped roof. Inside, the Hall is light and large. It was extended in 1852 to take in what had been a corridor; the two columns mark the line of the wall. The room is lined with imposing family portraits. Over the fireplace is the founder, Sir Patience Warde, by Riley. On either side of him are John Warde and his wife, who came to live here. To left and right are full-lengths by Dahl, Kneller, Vanderbank and Jervas. In the middle of the garden front is the Dining Room. This too was redecorated in the 18C with a fine plaster ceiling. The pictures are all of the Dutch School, mostly of the 17C, and were bought by John Warde c 1747–74. There are some fine pictures here, including two Ruysdaels, a family group by Van der Helst, and a big Hondecoeter over the fireplace. The magnificent gilt-framed mirrors between the windows, and the console tables beneath them, are English of the 1720s, as are the walnut dining chairs. Next is the Drawing Room. Here too the original marble fireplace remains, but the original panelling has gone, replaced by light-painted plasterwork. The room is lined with 18C family portraits. The big painting on the north wall by John Wootton is a group portrait of the Wardes shortly after their arrival at Squerryes, which appears in the background, John Warde gesturing proudly towards it. His son, the collector, appears here and in a portrait by Arthur Devis, just to the left, while in the next painting, by Stubbs, his son appears holding a champion racehorse.

Next the visitor goes up the original Staircase, with portraits by Lely, and some slightly dubious Salvator Rosas. At the top is the Tapestry Room, with fine early-18C panelling framing fine floral panels of Soho tapestry with the arms of Warde impaling Bristow. There is splendid black and gold lacquered furniture, an intriguing Poussin over the chimneypiece, and more portraits by Lely over the doors. The Wolfe Room, next door, commemorates the friendship of the famous general, who came from Westerham, with the Warde family. There are paintings and mementoes of Wolfe, including Pitt the Elder's letter of condolence to his mother after his death in the victory of Quebec (qv. Quebec House).

The first floor Picture Gallery has Old Master 'Grand tour' pictures, and a remarkable group they are, including a fine early Van Dyck of St Sebastian and a magnificent still-life by Peter de Ring. Still more startling are two immense allegorical paintings by Luca Giordano, and a huge equestrian portrait of Philip II of Spain by Rubens (commissioned posthumously by Philip IV—there is another version at Windsor Castle); not what one would expect to find in a Kentish squire's house, and there are more pieces of 18C lacquered furniture.

Back downstairs, teas are served in a pleasant panelled room overlooking the lake. The gardens are well cared-for, with formal beds beneath the east front, and lawns stretching down to the lake to the west.

SB

Stoneacre

In Otham village, 3m south east of Maidstone, signposted from the A20: National Trust. Open Apr–Oct Wed and Sat 2–6, last admission 5.

Stoneacre is one of the National Trust's smaller properties, a timber-framed manor house originally of the 1480s on the side of a narrow wooded valley. It is of especial interest in two ways: as a very fine late medieval hall-house, and for the extremely sensitive restoration carried out early in this century by Aymer Vallance.

John Ellys built the core of the present house in the 1480s, which was extended in the 16C. In 1725 the Ellys family sold out, and for two centuries it suffered the fate of many such manor houses, being let to tenant farmers. In 1920 it was bought by Aymer Vallance, a journalist, architectural writer and Fabian socialist, and an enthusiast for medieval architecture. From 1920–26 he and his wife carried out a careful restoration of the derelict house, inspired by the principles of William Morris and the Arts and Crafts movement. He restored the Hall, and restored the windows to their 15C appearance. At either end of the building he made additions, using old materials from a house in Chiddingstone, North Bore Place, which was being demolished, and the result is very convincing. Aymer Vallance gave the house to the National Trust in 1928, and died in 1943.

Stoneacre is entered from the east, from a narrow lane. In the centre is the big bay window of the Hall, and left of this the Solar wing, both of the 1480s. The wing on the right is of the 16C, and that at the left-hand end is part of Vallance's additions; framed in its cottage-garden setting, it is hgihly picturesque. Entering, you are in the screens passage; Vallance found the oak screen covered up with lath and plaster. He had to remove a floor to restore the Hall to its full height, and he installed the big chimneybreast with its 15C fireplace (from an inn in Sittingbourne). The massive oak framing is visible on all sides, and overhead the roof is supported by a vast tie-beam, with an interesting crown-post. Vallance collected the 16C and 17C oak furniture and the paintings, seen here and elsewhere in the house.

The Parlour is also of the 1480s, with the original oak framing exposed. From here you reach the spiral staircase which was added by Vallance; its treads are solid blocks of oak, brought from North Bore Place. The Solar, over the Parlour, would have been a private living room and bedchamber for John Ellys and his wife; it has a beautiful crown-post roof, like that of the Hall on a smaller scale. The garden is in the old-world style inspired by Gertrude Jekyll and others.

SB

Walmer Castle

In Walmer, 2m south of Deal, on A258: English Heritage, tel. 0304 364288. Open Good Fri–Sept daily 10–6; Oct–Easter Tues–Sun 10–4. Closed 24–26 Dec, 1 Jan–end Feb.

Walmer Castle was built in 1539–42, as one of a series of coastal defence fortresses commissioned by Henry VIII. Early in the 18C, it found a new role as the official residence of the Lord Warden of the Cinque Ports. It is a curious mixture of artillery fort and country house, also housing collections of memorabilia of the younger Pitt and the Duke of Wellington.

By the early 16C it was clear that traditional castles were being rendered obsolete by advances in artillery. A new kind of castle was needed, to serve as a platform for cannon and to resist artillery-fire. Walmer was one of the first of this new generation of fortresses to be built in the British Isles. It was a direct result of Henry VIII's breach with Rome. Having alienated both Francis I of France and the Emperor Charles V, Henry faced a serious risk of invasion, and in 1539 he commissioned a series of fortresses along the south coast. Amongst these, three went up at Deal, Sandown and Walmer (that at Sandown has largely vanished) linked by over two miles of earthworks. As is often the way with elaborate defences, they saw no major military action, and fired few shots in anger. The castles' most notable activity was probably in protecting shipping during the Dutch wars of the 1650s and 1660s. However, by the end of the 17C, they were becoming obsolete. Walmer could have fallen into decay, had it not found a new role.

The Cinque Ports were an ancient confederation, originally of Hastings, Romney, Hythe, Dover and Sandwich, which began in the 11C. In the 13C a Warden, nominated by the King, was placed over this very powerful body, to keep it in order and ensure its loyalty. As the Confederation's power ebbed away, the Wardenship was given to distinguished people, and became a high honour. Lionel, 1st Duke of Dorset became Lord Warden in

1708, and he took over Walmer, adding a number of rooms over the bastions to make it habitable. William Pitt the Younger (Lord Warden 1792–1806) made further alterations; he and his niece Lady Hester Stanhope first laid out the fine gardens. The Duke of Wellington (Lord Warden, 1829–53) was very fond of the Castle, calling it 'his charming marine residence' and often residing here. The most important alterations were made by the Earl Granville, who became Lord Warden in 1865. He had just married, and commissioned the architect George Devey to build extra rooms over the gatehouse, giving the castle a more picturesque and varied skyline. The present incumbent (since 1978) is Her Majesty Queen Elizabeth the Queen Mother, who makes regular use of the castle, and has taken a keen interest in it and its grounds.

The castle was an unlikely candidate for conversion to a residence. At its core there is a massive central circular tower, surrounded by a narrow concentric court. Around this is a very thick wall, with four enormous D-shaped bastions, surrounded in their turn by a broad dry ditch. Originally it would have been almost completely symmetrical, but Devey added an extra storey to one of the bastions (the gatehouse), giving it mullioned windows and pretty battlements. The gatehouse remains grimly military; you follow the narrow courtyard around to the south bastion, filled early in the 18C with a weatherboarded building called the Gunners' Lodging. The rooms here are relatively small and simple. The West Lounge houses furniture which belonged to Pitt the Younger. Upstairs, there are three rooms furnished as a memorial to the Duke of Wellington. The Lucas Room houses a collection of Wellington memorabilia assembled by Wing Commander Thomas Hill Lucas and donated in 1966. Over the landing is the Duke of Wellington's Room, where the great man died on 14 September 1852, sitting in the armchair with the yellow striped cover. The spartan furniture is preserved much as it was then, and to one side is the Duke's campaign bed. The Wellington Museum has more memorabilia, including a pair of 'Wellington boots'. The Pitt Museum, opposite, has more of the simple late-Georgian furniture belonging to that Prime Minister.

From here a print-lined Corridor leads across into the Keep, inside which are Queen Victoria's and the Prince Consort's Rooms, furnished as bedrooms. The Drawing Room, Ante-Room and Dining Room occupy an 18C extension made by the Duke of Dorset. The rooms are now decorated and furnished in a simple Regency style, the Dining Room lined with prints of previous Lord Wardens. From the bastion outside there are wide views over the narrow seas which the castle was built to cover with its cannons. The visitor can descend to the echoing vaults underneath the Keep. Outside, the gardens stretch to the south west. The long Yew Walk, aligned on the south bastion, has magnificent herbaceous borders, and the dry moat too has rich planting, softening the hard grey lines of the castle.

SB

LANCASHIRE

Astley Hall

1m west of Chorley via A581 or B5252: Chorley Borough Council, tel. 0257
262166. Open Apr–Oct daily 11–12, 1–5; Nov–Mar Fri–Sun 11–12, 1–4.
Refreshments.

This curious house stands in a municipal park to the west of Chorley, cut
off from the countryside by a belt of new housing estates. It originated as
a timber-framed courtyard building, of which the oldest surviving portions
seem to date from the end of the 16C, when the estate was leased by the
Charnock family, long-established in the area. The north and west ranges
survive largely intact from this period, but the rest of the house was
subsequently rebuilt, starting in 1616 with the south or hall range. This was
faced in brick and remodelled internally some 50 years later, at about the
time of the marriage of Mary Charnock, the last of the family, to a Cheshire
gentleman, Richard Brooke; it was later rendered, possibly in 1762. The
much plainer east range dates in its present form from 1825, when new
reception rooms were provided, possibly to the designs of Lewis Wyatt, for
Susanna Brooke and her second husband, Sir Philip Hoghton, and since
then there have been no important structural changes. The house was
presented to the Chorley local authority in 1922, since when it has been
used partly as a museum and partly as a furnished 'period' house.

The entrance is through the hall range, which looks out over a lake. It is
a striking but odd piece of architecture, asymmetrical, with two bay
windows projecting on either side of the entrance, and huge mullioned and
transomed windows, those on the upper floor lighting the Long Gallery.
The crudely carved Ionic porch, and the balustrade on the roof-line, reflect
the classicism of the 1660s, but otherwise the design is completely Jacobean
in character—an example of the conservatism of Lancashire architecture of
the time. The elaborate wood panelling in the Hall, which dates from the
early 17C, is further enlivened by paintings of heroic figures from recent
history, including Tamerlane, Christopher Columbus, Sir Francis Drake and
Henry IV of France, apparently introduced by Thomas Charnock (d 1648);
there is also a large chair in which James I is said to have knighted a sirloin
of beef at Hoghton Tower (qv.). But the eye is mainly caught by the
extraordinary stuccoed ceiling of the 1660s, in which the delicate motifs of
the period (flowers, fruit, cherubs, etc.) are perversely magnified and
exaggerated to create a three-dimensional, and strangely disturbing, effect—a result achieved by the use of lead and leather as well as plaster.
There is an even more bizarre ceiling in the adjacent parlour, now called
the Drawing Room, along with two 17C tapestries of Jason and the Golden
Fleece. The other impressive room is the Long Gallery, reached by a
darkened wood staircase of c 1666 leading up from the Hall; most of the
floor space is taken up by an immensely long 'shovel-board table', and other
pieces of locally carved 16C and 17C furniture are arranged around the
walls. The remaining rooms contain more elaborately carved furniture of
the period, and there are also plaster ceilings and overmantels of somewhat
provincial character in the upstairs rooms of the west or kitchen wing.

Browsholme Hall

Bashall Eaves, 5m north west of Clitheroe, signposted from the B6243: Mr and Mrs R. Parker, tel. 0254 826719. Open Good Fri–Easter Mon, Spring Bank Hol, then Sat in July; Sat & Sun in Aug 2–5.

The Parker family have lived at Browsholme (pronounced 'Brusom') since the 14C, and are thus one of the longest-established gentry families in the north of England. Browsholme, as it stands today, is a 16C house with certain 18C and early 19C alterations, in wooded countryside above the beautiful Hodder valley. Until 1975 it was in the West Riding of Yorkshire.

The Parkers trace their descent from Peter de Alcancotes, who lived at Alkincoats near Colne in the mid 13C. His great-grandson, Edmund Parker, became park-keeper of Radholme Laund, one of the two great deer-parks in the Forest of Bowland. From 1380, Edmund's sons Richard and John leased land at Browsholme, and Richard Parker built a house not far from the present one. From then on, succeeding generations of Parkers lived here, through many vicissitudes, marrying into other landed families and holding the office of Bowbearer of the Forest of Bowland. In 1507 Edmund Parker built a new H-shaped house, the basis of the present building. His grandson Thomas purchased the freehold of the estate at last in 1603, and embellished the house, adding the columned frontispeace, and an extra storey with little gables. Edward Parker (d 1721) added the east wing, and carried out other internal modifications. His great-grandson Thomas Lister Parker (1779–1858) was the most original and interesting of the family. A friend of Turner, and many other artists, he spent money lavishly on paintings. At Browsholme he planted trees, landscaped the grounds, and rebuilt the west wing to designs by Jeffrey Wyatt (later Wyattville). Not satisfied with provincial life, he had a household in London, mixing in court society. All of this was beyond the means of a northern squire, and in 1824 he was obliged to sell the estate to his cousin and heir, Thomas Parker of Alkincoats. The present owner, who inherited in 1975, is descended from another line of the Alkincoats branch of the family.

Browsholme is a tall house, facing south over lawns and fields, built in red sandstone. What one sees is essentially of 1507, although much modified. The attic storey was removed in the 18C so the house is three storeys high. In the middle, around and above the front door, is a frontispiece with superimposed columns of the Doric, Ionic and Corinthian orders, a provincial interpretation of Renaissance design, probably derived from the bigger gatehouse at nearby Stonyhurst.

Inside, the Hall is long, with a heavily beamed ceiling. It used to run the full length of the main wing, until the west part was divided off to form the Library in 1754. There is a great wealth of old English furniture, arms and armour, still largely as arranged by Thomas Lister Parker c 1807, as part of a conscious attempt to furnish and arrange his house in a historic, antiquarian manner. He adopted the same approach to the Library; a friend presented him with the fine panelling, dated c 1620, with its very unusual diagonal pattern, and here again he aimed to create a dark, romantically antiquarian atmosphere. The pictures include portraits by Arthur Devis, and the room has more of Browsholme's tremendous accumulation of historic objects, including Jacobite relics, a variety of archaeological finds, and elephant tusks. The Drawing Room is markedly different; this was formed in 1805 when Jeffrey Wyatt rebuilt the west wing. The shape of the room, with its broad segmental arches, is Regency, but the decoration is a very early example of Elizabethan revivalism. It is lined with paintings, mostly bought by its builder, a good illustration of Regency taste, including works by Northcote, Romney, Batoni, and Angelica Kauffmann. The Dining Room, next, was added as a new wing by T.L. Parker in 1807 to house his collection of paintings. Most of these had to be sold, but most of the original decoration survives, and the furniture is mostly of c 1810. The room is still lined with family portraits, including several by Sir James Northcote.

The Ante-Room has dark panelling, a carved overmantel, and more old English furniture. The watercolour view of the house before its Regency alterations is by Turner. At some point, corridors were built behind the long Hall range, doubtless to make a more convenient circulation plan; the ground corridor has armorial stained glass, tapestry, and a variety of furniture. The main staircase is lit by a great window, filled with a jigsaw of medieval stained glass, said to be from Whalley Abbey, and there is more of the house's large collection of 17C furniture. The Yellow Room has 17C-style panelling, actually made by Richard Alston, the estate carpenter early this century, who also made the four-poster bed. The Velvet Room has another bed, reconstructed from 16C pieces by Alston, who also carved the fine chimneypiece. The Oak Drawing Room, also facing south, has fine bolection panelling with vigorous carving, in a provincial version of Grinling Gibbons' style; there are small 16C and 17C portraits, and a variety of furniture. The Oak Bedroom, also shown, also has panelling and a four-post bed restored by Richard Alston. The Back Staircase is of c 1711, contemporary with the east Wing. The house contains large collections of textiles, costume and ceramics, and it is to be hoped that it might be possible to display more of these at some point.

SB

Gawthorpe Hall

2m west of Burnley at Padiham on A671, M65 exit 10: National Trust/
Lancashire County Council, tel. 0282 778511. Open Apr–Oct daily except
Mon (open BH Mon), Fri 1–5; gardens open all year daily 10–6.
Refreshments.

The approach to Gawthorpe, through the built-up suburban sprawl of Burnley, does little to prepare the visitor for the house, which stands alone in its park with Pendle Hill looming impressively to the north. It was built in 1600–5 for the Rev. Lawrence Shuttleworth, a younger son who had just inherited the estate from his elder brother, a successful London lawyer. The strikingly bold and unorthodox design may well have been supplied by Robert Smythson. The family abandoned the house in the 18C, but returned early in the 19C, and in 1850–52 Janet Shuttleworth and her husband, the well-known reforming politician Sir James Kay (later Kay-Shuttleworth), son of a Rochdale cotton manufacturer, brought in Charles Barry to undertake a thorough internal and, to a lesser extent, external, remodelling. Their descendant, the 4th Lord Shuttleworth, moved out after the Second World War, leaving the house in the care of an aunt who established a school of embroidery here, and in 1970, soon after her death, it was given to the National Trust. The most important rooms have recently been restored to their mid-19C state, with furniture lent by the Shuttleworth family and 17C pictures on loan from the National Portrait Gallery.

The house is an interesting synthesis of Elizabethan architecture and the popular 19C taste for 'Old English' internal decoration. It is a tall, compact stone building, of a kind found quite often in Smythson's oeuvre, with three storeys over a basement containing the kitchens and offices—an early example of what was in time to become a near-universal arrangement—and a staircase tower which rises up to a 'prospect room', making the house in essence a reworking of the old idea of the tower house (cf. Levens Hall and Sizergh Castle, Cumbria, not far away to the north), but without any connotations of fortification. Apart from adding a pierced balustrade to the roof-line and heightening the chimneys, Barry left the exterior alone, but he played an important part in creating the formal garden setting and his hand is omnipresent in the interior.

The house is entered through a passage, from which an attractive vista, framed by four-centred stone arches, opens up to the staircase; the detailing here and in the Entrance Hall, created out of the former pantry and buttery, recalls the richly detailed interiors of Barry's most famous building, the Houses of Parliament in London. The original hall, behind the present Entrance Hall, is now called the Dining Room, and was heavily remodelled by Barry with a richly patterned wallpaper by Crace, curtains after a design by A.W.N. Pugin and a new chimneypiece and plaster ceiling; the screen is original, and the portraits include one by William Dobson of the mathematician Sir Thomas Aylesbury. The richest interior is the Drawing Room, with elaborate wood panelling and an intricate, if somewhat crude, frieze and plaster ceiling, but the effect is now even more elaborate than was originally intended because of the profusion of 19C furniture, including pieces designed by Pugin. Barry's wooden staircase leads up to the first floor, devoted entirely to Rachel Kay-Shuttleworth's embroidery collection—one of the best in any country house—and then to the Gallery on the second floor, much restored in the 19C but still retaining its original plaster frieze and ceiling. More of the National Portrait Gallery's pictures are hung here, including two full-length Knellers, and in an adjoining bedroom with more Elizabethan plasterwork (the Huntroyde Room), there are two pictures by the 17C artist, Mary Beale.

GCT

Hoghton Tower

5m east of Preston on the A675: Sir Bernard de Hoghton, tel. 0254 852986. Open Easter–end Oct, Sun, BH; July, Aug Sat; June, July, Aug Tues, Wed, Thur 11–4, but only 2–4 on BHs. Refreshments.

Hoghton Tower is one of the most romantically and spectacularly sited of all English houses. Hoghton Hill rises sharply from the rolling countryside, with woods on all sides, and the chimneys of the house just visible on top. On the west side the drive runs, ruler-straight and nearly a mile long, from the Preston–Blackburn road, all the way up to the battlemented entrance front.

The de Hoghton family have lived here since soon after the Norman Conquest. There may be elements of the medieval house remaining, but the present house was mostly built c 1561–65 by Thomas Hoghton, of granite quarried from lower down the hill. However, he was a Catholic, and in 1569 he went into exile at Douai rather than give up his faith, dying there c 1580. Thomas's descendants compromised and accepted Anglicanism. Under James I they became baronets, and Sir Richard de Hoghton entertained that monarch here with fabled splendour in 1617, almost bankrupting himself. The Civil War saw the family divided, and the Tower besieged by Parliamentarian forces. During the siege the main tower, which stood over the range in between the two courtyards, was blown up; it was never rebuilt. Sir Charles Hoghton, a notable scholar, built a large new wing c 1700 in a traditional style. In the mid 18C the family abandoned the house in favour of Walton Hall, near Preston. They suffered with gambling debts, and much of their furniture and paintings were destroyed in two fires. In the later 19C, they revived their traditions. They resumed the ancient prefix 'de'; they re-embraced Catholicism and from about 1870, Sir Henry de Hoghton began a very slow and careful renovation of Hoghton Tower, under the architects Paley & Austin, which was completed by his son Sir Charles.

The approach up the long avenue is enormously dramatic; the visitor eventually reaches great gatepiers, and the symmetrical entrance front, with castellated gatehouse and towers, looms ahead. Looking back, the Lancastrian coastal plains seem a long way below. The Outer Court is picturesque and irregular; it looks all of a piece, but the big range to the right (where the family now resides) is in fact of c 1700. Going through the archway in the range ahead (above which the great tower used to rise), you are in the Inner Court. This is smaller, enclosed, and feels remote and timeless; the granite buildings are all Thomas Hoghton's, with the big windows of his Great Hall on the left.

You enter a small door to the right, and go up to the first floor; the state rooms run around the courtyard. Most remain as they were redecorated c 1700 for Sir Charles Hoghton, with grand bolection-moulded panelling. The first, the Guinea Room, is named from the 'guineas' painted on the panelling. The Buckingham Room, named for James I's favourite, has good 18C furniture including a fine Hepplewhite-style bed. This leads into the long King's Bedchamber, with more early-18C English furniture. Next comes the Ballroom. The Jacobean-style panelling is by Gillows, and dates from the late-19C renovation, as does the grand fireplace. Next you cross the top of the King's Staircase, to reach the King's Drawing Room and another bedchamber, again with 18C. There are a few de Hoghton portraits here and in the Great Hall, but most were alas lost in the last century.

The visitor descends the King's Staircase, which is again part of the early-18C alterations, to the King's Hall, where the thickness of the walls suggests a medieval origin. From here the Great Hall is reached; it occupies most of the north side of the Inner Court. There are big mullioned and transomed windows to the courtyard, and bay windows to both sides. There is a great Jacobean table, original to the room, and the best of the remaining family portraits, including a small panel of Thomas Hoghton, builder of the house. Finally, up a flight of stairs off the screens passage, you ascend to the Hall's gallery, and to a pretty little Drawing Room opening off this.

There are attractive walled gardens on the south side of the house, and from the walks around it there are fine views across the Irish Sea and to the Pennines.

SB

Leighton Hall

3m north of Carnforth to west of A6 through Yealand Conyers, M6 exit 35: Mr and Mrs R.G. Reynolds, tel. 0524 734474. Open May–Sept Sun, Tues–Fri, BH Mon 2–5 (Aug 11–5). Guided tours. Refreshments.

Leighton Hall stands in an undulating wooded park with the fells of the Lake District as a spectacular backdrop. An asymmetrical house of silver-grey limestone quarried in the grounds, it owes its present appearance entirely to 19C rebuildings. There has been a dwelling on the site since the Middle Ages, but the core of the present structure was built in 1765 by George Townley after he had inherited the estate by marriage. His rather plain house was later sold to Alexander Worswick, a Lancaster banker, but the bank failed in 1822, whereupon the estate was sold again to Richard Gillow, whose grandfather founded the famous Lancaster-based furniture firm. Richard Gillow remodelled the house in the Gothic style in 1822–25, shortly before retiring from the furniture business and settling down as a country squire. His son Richard Thomas Gillow, added the three-storeyed south wing to the designs of Paley & Austin of Lancaster in 1870. This final addition increased the space available for Victorian entertaining, and gave further picturesque irregularity to the exterior, with blocks decreasing in height from the south range to the turreted main block and then down to the stables (disguised by an ecclesiastical-looking window), and finally an iron and glass conservatory.

The interior contains several examples of early-19C Gillow furniture and some good pictures. The most attractive rooms are the Entrance Hall, with its wooden screen of four-centred Gothic arches leading to the sinuous cantilevered staircase, and the panelled neo- Elizabethan Dining Room (originally the billiard room, hence the oval skylight in the roof) containing Gillow furniture and portraits and some large early-18C Flemish landscapes by an unknown artist. The Drawing Room, Victorian rather than Regency in its overall appearance, contains pictures by Jordaens and Guardi and more Gillow furniture, including an attractive and unusual games table. The tour continues upstairs and then down past the Chapel (all the owners of the house have been Roman Catholics) to the Music Room, in the Paley & Austin wing, which houses a large late-17C Italian picture of St Jerome. Outside, on the front lawn, falconry displays are given each afternoon.

GCT

Meols Hall

1m north of Southport, off the A565: R.H. Fleetwood Hesketh. Open mid Jul–mid Aug daily 2–5.

Meols stands in the quiet, flat, countryside between Southport and Preston; it is built of brick with stone dressings, and the handsome seven-bay centre of the main (east) front suggests a date of around 1720, the work of a talented provincial architect, perhaps a follower of the Smiths of Warwick or of Gibbs. In fact, it mostly dates from 1960–64, and is the creation of its present owner, Mr Roger Fleetwood Hesketh and his brother Peter, who converted it out of a rather shapeless 17C and 18C farmhouse. It is one of the most remarkable and successful exercises in Georgian revivalism that post-war England has produced.

The Fleetwood and Hesketh families both go back a long way in Lancashire history. Sir Thomas Hesketh acquired the manor of North Meols by marriage in 1563, and the family lived here and at Tulketh, near Preston. They owned much of the fertile coastal plain of south Lancashire, and in 1733 Roger Hesketh married Margaret Fleetwood, the heiress to another very large but remote and desolate estate, that of Rossall Hall in the Fylde. The combined estates propelled the family into the upper reaches of the gentry, and Rossall and Tulketh Halls were remodelled; the house at Meols was reduced in size as a rectory. However, the family, in the person of the liberal, generous-minded and enterprising Sir Peter Hesketh-Fleetwood, struck disaster. In the 1830s he founded the new town of Fleetwood, and backed a plan for a railway there from Preston. Things went wrong, and the family were almost ruined. Most of the estates were sold to cover the debts, Rossall became a public school, and the house there was demolished in the 1920s.

The Meols estate alone remained, in the hands of Sir Peter's brother Charles, the Rector of Meols. His daughter married a member of the Bibby family, rich Liverpool shipowners, and one of her sons inherited the Meols estate, assuming the name Fleetwood Hesketh. The present owner came into possession of the estate in 1938. He and his brother Peter had both studied at the Architectural Association, developing a keen interest in Georgian architecture, and thought of remodelling the rambling brick house at Meols. This idea received fresh purpose with the inheritance, from a distant cousin in 1938, of the Fleetwood and Hesketh family pictures, but it was not until 1960 that it could take shape. 18C bricks and stone slates came from Tulketh Hall, then being demolished; ornamental stonework came from a service-wing of Lathom Hall, a great Palladian mansion nearby, also being demolished. The plan was driven in part by Mr Fleetwood Hesketh's wish to incorporate the two surviving 17C wings of the old house, and by the need to provide a suitable setting for the family pictures. He not only designed the work, but supervised it all himself, employing direct labour.

The resulting house is a perfect blend of the informal—the remaining elements of the older house—with the new, more formal central block. It has that appearance of 'organic' growth which is the hallmark of so many old English houses. The east front is flanked by handsome gazebos, based on an 18C original surviving at Rossall. The west, or entrance front has three very wide-set bays, with little gables over each, and a large one-storey Regency-style wing on the left. The Entrance Hall is quite narrow, the scale set by the old house. The Yellow Room, to the left, has another low beamed ceiling, with close-hung paintings including works by Raeburn and Cornelius Johnson, and 18C and early 19C furniture. The Library is altogether bigger, with a bow-window, occupying the Regency-style wing, and decorated in the style of c 1810. Its dimensions were dictated by the need to house a very big Regency bookcase and a fine marble chimneypiece from Bold Hall (another of Lancashire's demolished houses), and a great life-size painting by James Ward of Sir Peter Hesketh Fleetwood's Arab stallion; over the chimneypiece is a double portrait by Sir Thomas Lawrence. On the garden front are three reception rooms in early 18C style. The Drawing Room is hung with mostly 18C portraits and landscapes. The beautiful Garden Hall, in the centre of the east front, has a chequered stone floor (from another family house in Cumberland, this one demolished in 1950), furniture based on 18C Austrian originals, and more good 18C portraits.

Beyond it, the Dining Room has Regency furniture, and more family pictures, including a set of oval portraits and a fine 16C full-length. Lancashire's country houses have suffered over a century of loss and destruction, perhaps worse than in any other county, and so it is all the more heartening, at Meols, to see the process reversed, by this work of restoration and creation.

SB

Rufford Old Hall

7m north of Ormskirk on A59 Liverpool–Preston: National Trust, tel. 0704 821254. Open Apr–Oct daily, except Fri 1–5. Refreshments.

The most important feature of this attractive house is the 16C timber-framed Hall, one of the finest of its kind in England. It was built by a member of the long-established Hesketh family, probably Robert, who held the estate from 1523 until his death in 1541. His son Thomas (d 1588) was 'a notable great housekeeper' who kept a company of players at Rufford in which the young William Shakespeare may have spent a few months in 1581–82. The house was originally of the usual hall-and-cross-wings type, but the parlour wing at the 'upper' end of the Hall had disappeared by 1736, and a brick-built range was added on to the north end of the service wing in 1662. The Hesketh family continued to live in the house until the building of Rufford New Hall (not open to the public) in 1760, and for a time the older house played host to the village school, but it was reoccupied in the 1820s by Thomas, eldest son of Sir Thomas Hesketh, 3rd Baronet. He employed the Liverpool architect John Foster to turn the east or former service end into a comfortable gentleman's residence in 1820–25, with neo-Tudor external detailing reflecting the contemporary enthusiasm for houses 'of the olden time'. His son, the 5th Baronet, married the heiress of the last Earl of Pomfret, thus inheriting Easton Neston (Northants), the present family home, and in 1936 the 1st Lord Hesketh gave the Old Hall to the National Trust.

The house stands in flat pastoral country between the village of Rufford and the Leeds–Liverpool Canal. It is entered through the rustic-looking north wing of 1662, but the eye is caught primarily by the black and white timbers of the hall range (close studding with quatrefoils higher up, as at Little Moreton Hall, Cheshire, qv.), resting on a sandstone base, with a roof of heavy sandstone slabs. The louvre and the gabled cross-wing to the left (east) date largely from the restoration of the 1820s, but the main timbers and the bay window to the west, which lit the high table, are original. There is an even more impressive display of 16C timber craftsmanship inside the light and empty Hall, in which the family still dined regularly as late as the 17C. Note especially the hammer beam roof with angels holding shields at the ends of the beams (as at Adlington Hall, Cheshire, qv.); the carvings over the doors leading to the demolished parlour wing; the canopy over the former high table; and, above all, the unique and supposedly movable screen placed between the two 'speres' which demarcate the cross-passage at the 'lower' end, surmounted by fanciful carvings of a barbaric, almost Polynesian, richness. There is a good collection of armour, mostly introduced in the 19C, and carved 17C chairs—a Lancashire speciality.

The rest of the house cannot help seeming rather tame after this exuber-

The Hall, Rufford Old Hall, showing the 16C timber work, looking towards the lower end with the moveable wooden screen

ant display. The main rooms, in the former service wing, date largely from the 19C: the Dining Room, with attractive 17C Brussels tapestries on the walls, and above it the Drawing Room, filled with furniture in typically late-19C fashion, with pictures on loan from the Walker Art Gallery in Liverpool on the walls (the arch-braced roof is of the same date as the Hall, which can be glimpsed through a spy-hole, but was probably brought from a nearby house in 1724). To the east of the house there is a service courtyard containing a stable block with an interesting collection of farm implements and a pigsty complete with pig, and to the south an attractive semi-formal garden laid out in the 19C.

GCT

Samlesbury Hall

5m west of Blackburn on the A677: Samlesbury Hall Trust, tel. 0254 812010/812229. Open all year Tues–Sun 11–5(summer), 11.30–4 (winter; cloosed late Dec–late Jan). Refreshments.

An abundance of oak, and a shortage of building-stone, made Lancashire one of England's chief centres of timber-framed black and white building. 19C industrialisation took a terrible toll of this heritage, but Samlesbury Hall is one of the best examples remaining. In the 13C, the D'Ewyas family lived in a pele-tower down by the Ribble. In 1325 their heiress, Alice, married Gilbert Southworth, and the couple built a new manor house, surrounded by a moat, on the present site. The oldest remaining part of the house is the Great Hall, whose massive cruck frame is of 14C date. The long south wing is partly 15C, partly of c 1545, and has one of the most elaborate surviving black and white façades.

The Southworths were an aggressive and martial family. By a mixture of caution, local feuding and chicanery they amassed large estates, enabling Thomas Southworth (d 1546), to rebuild the house on a square courtyard plan in the 1540s. However, loyalty to the Catholic faith brought persecution and impoverishment to subsequent generations, culminating in the execution of the 72-year-old Father John Southworth at Tyburn in 1654, the last Catholic to suffer death for his faith in England. In 1678 the house and the last Southworth estates were sold to the Braddyll family. Samlesbury was neglected, and let to handloom weavers, and in this period much of it was demolished. In 1821 Thomas Gale Braddyll began work on Conishead Priory, Cumbria (qv.)taking some of the finest woodwork from Samlesbury. The house's humiliation was completed when a major new road from Preston to Blackburn was built, going right past it, and its owner turned it into an inn, the Braddyll Arms, to benefit from the traffic. However, Braddyll had over-reached himself building Conishead, and in 1850 he was declared bankrupt. Samlesbury was sold, becoming a school, and was then sold again in 1862 to a local industrialist, who renovated it as his residence. In 1924 it was narrowly saved from being demolished by a local builder; an appeal was launched to purchase it and vest it in a charitable trust, which still owns and runs it.

The house today is L-shaped. The short west wing is the 15C Hall with some later additions, while the long south wing houses the Chapel and what were the family's apartments. Both are of great architectural interest. The Hall is timber-framed, with low walls and a very high roof. The south wing is brick-faced on its 'outer' side, with big chimney-stacks; this is the earliest dated use of brickwork in Lancashire. The largest traceried windows were taken from Whalley Abbey after its Dissolution. The inner side is black and white, and very heavily timbered, with an all-over pattern of quatrefoils, and fine carving to the windows.

The Entrance Hall, in the south range, has a fine, heavily carved and panelled ceiling. Much of the decoration is Victorian, but it is convincingly done. To the left is the Chapel. This was built c 1420, and was originally a detached building, linked to the Hall by the building of the south wing in the 1540s. It is a grand room rising through both storeys, with some original woodwork. There is some good English furniture on display in the Entrance Hall and Chapel. The other rooms are used as an antiques and exhibition centre, so much of the house is filled with antiques for sale. The Dining Room has elaborate Victorian Jacobean-style decoration, and a fireplace with the date 1545. The first floor of the south range is mostly taken up by the Gallery, where the very fine original roof with trusses and arched braces is to be seen.

The Great Hall has a very impressive 14C roof, with huge trusses of cruck construction, two collar-beams and three tiers of cusped wind braces. The deep bay window is part of the 16C improvements; the broad original fireplace has been restored recently. At the south end of the Hall is a Minstrel's Gallery, added while the house was an inn in the 1830s. Originally there was a wooden canopy here, over the high table (as survives at Ordsall, qv.). The Hall also had a magnificent carved screen, much like the unique surviving example at Rufford (qv.), with the same kind of fantastic rope or shell-like ornament. Alas, this was cut up in the 19C, though most of it may be seen built into the gallery. The melancholy history of the Southworth family is commemorated by the priest hole, concealed in the angle between the two wings.

SB

Towneley Hall

1m south east of Burnley on A671 Burnley–Todmorden: Burnley Borough Council, tel. 0282 24213. Open all year daily except Sat 10–5 (Sun 12–5). Refreshments in grounds (summer).

Towneley Hall, one of the largest and most important Lancashire country houses, stands in a spacious park on the edge of the once-thriving cotton town of Burnley, just to the west of the Pennines. It is a building with a long and complex architectural history, beginning in the 15C with the construction of a courtyard house by John Towneley, whose family were lay deans of the nearby Whalley Abbey. The house was subsequently rebuilt and embellished in a piecemeal manner by his descendants, who, like many of the Lancashire gentry, were Catholic recusants. They lived here until 1902 when, the male line having died out, the house was acquired by the Burnley local authority as a museum. Since then several of the most important items from the family collection have been repurchased, and they are now once again displayed in their original setting along with other pictures and pieces of furniture.

In its present form the stone-built house consists of a hall block, on the site of the medieval hall, with two wings projecting to the east; the gatehouse range which closed the courtyard of the medieval house was demolished c 1700. There is still some medieval masonry in the south wing (to the left of the entrance), but it was remodelled in the 16C, when a Gallery was created on the upper floor. The three-storeyed north wing dates mainly from 1626, and the hall range was totally rebuilt by Richard Towneley, a Jacobite sympathiser, in 1726. His successor William Towneley carried out further alterations to the north wing in 1737, and finally, in 1816–20, Jeffrey Wyatville created new reception rooms for Peregrine Towneley on the ground floor of the south wing. He also remodelled the exterior in a lifeless castellated manner (the previous appearance can be seen in a water-colour of 1799 by J.M.W. Turner occasionally on display in the house), saving only the early-18C rear elevation of the Hall with its heavily enriched architraves to the windows.

The house is entered through the light and spacious Hall, one of the finest and least-known interiors of the 'English Baroque', its effect deriving largely from the plasterwork by Francesco Vassali and his assistant Martino Quadri. The Ionic pilasters lining the walls and the richly embellished ceiling at attic level impart the appropriate architectural scale and dignity, while the plaster reliefs of Roman emperors in the circular surrounds over the doors and windows, the copies of well-known antique marbles (eg, the 'Dancing Faun') over the fireplaces, and the busts on pedestals, lend a note of Roman gravitas and connoisseurship. None of the other rooms is as impressive as this. The two Wyatville rooms in the south wing (originally the dining room and drawing room) are classical in inspiration, contrary to what might be expected from the medievalising exterior; they now contain 19C English paintings, including works by Cox and de Wint, and a set of chairs made in 1823 for Northumberland House, London. The main staircase, next to the Hall, with an iron balustrade by Robert Bakewell and more plasterwork by Vassali, leads up to the wood-panelled Gallery, fundamentally 16C, with a series of bedrooms leading off it, some of them with panelling brought in from elsewhere. There is also an excellent collection of furniture here, including items from the vigorous local school of the 17C and some more sophisticated late-17C pieces in walnut.

The north wing can only be reached by retracing one's steps through the Hall (internal communication can never have been easy at Towneley). The ground floor is given over to kitchens and domestic offices, restored to their 19C state, and to museum rooms. From here a staircase gives access to a former bedroom (the Towneley Room) in which is hung a portrait of c 1600 showing the ardently Roman Catholic John Towneley and his family in prayer before a crucifix, with an inscription recording his trials for the Faith (he was imprisoned nine times). Nearby is the family Dining Room, panelled in wood in 1628 and now containing more good examples of 17C Lancashire furniture and a painting by George Barrett showing the house in its setting in 1777, before the Industrial Revolution made its impact.

Beyond is the Chapel Vestibule, where part of a set of 15C vestments from Whalley Abbey—one of the only two complete pre-Reformation sets to survive in England—is displayed. The Chapel itself, removed to its present position in the 18C, is notable mainly for its panelling of the early 16C and 1601 (removed from the former chapel in the demolished gatehouse range), the late-15C font cover, and the superb early-16C wood-carved altarpiece from Antwerp, bought and installed here in the late 18C by Charles Towneley, best-known for his collection of antique statuary (now in the British Museum). The top floor, originally bedrooms, is now an art gallery and contains some pictures from the family collection, including Zoffany's famous representation of Charles Towneley in the library of his London house, surrounded by Roman marbles (1781–83); there is also a varied collection of 19C English art, including historical and genre pictures by J.W. Waterhouse, Alma-Tadema and others.

GCT

Turton Tower

5m north of Bolton on B6391: Lancashire County Council, tel. 0204
852203. Open May–Sept Mon–Fri 10–12, 1–5, Sat, Sun 1–5; Mar, Apr, Oct
Sat–Wed 2–5; Feb, Nov Sun only 2–5. Refreshments.

Turton Tower stands among trees on the southern slopes of the moors north
of Bolton. There was a rectangular stone pele-tower here from about 1400
to which the Orrell family added cruck-framed wings to the north in the
early 1500s, later adding an extra storey to the Tower, and timber-framed
buildings on the east side of the Tower, housing a new entrance and
staircase, which were clad in stone later in the 16C. In 1628 the Tower was
bought by Humphrey Chetham, a rich Manchester textile manufacturer
and merchant. In the 18C it was let to tenant farmers, until the Kay family,
textile magnates, moved in in 1835. They heightened the north wings,
elaborating and romanticising the half-timbered sections, and they added
the Gothic follies in the gardens. In 1930 the last private owner, Lady Lees
Knowles, left the Tower to trustees, who let it to Turton Urban District
Council; since 1987 it has been run by Lancashire County Council.
   The visitor enters through the Kay family's east wing, where the kitchen
and servant's hall now house the shop and tea room. The principal rooms
are antiquarian Victorian creations in 16C and 17C style. From the Hall you
reach the Dining Room in the base of the pele-tower. It looks convincingly
17C, but is in fact of the 1840s; the 17C oak panelling came from Middleton
Hall near Manchester. There is fine furniture, some 17C, including the big
refectory table, and some 19C. There are good portraits, mostly on loan
from the National Portrait Gallery, including ones of Lord Craven and of
Elizabeth, the 'Winter Queen' of Bohemia (versions of works by Honthorst),
and of Cromwell by Cooper. The Morning Room has more panelling from
Middleton Hall, but is otherwise all Victorian. The staircase is basically 16C,
redecorated in the 19C, hung with 18C and 19C portraits of the Lees
Knowles family and others. On the first floor of the Tower is the Drawing
Room, also lined with 17C panelling and with a splendid Elizabethan-style
plaster ceiling. The furniture is a rich mixture of 17C pieces, 19C pieces in
older styles, and black oriental pieces. Next to this, the Tapestry Room has
lost its tapestries, but gained a magnificent bed, dated 1593, on loan from
the Victoria and Albert Museum. The first floor of the north wing is used to
display work by local craftsmen, and the cruck-framed structure is made
visible. Two little rooms over the Hall, the Chapel Room and Priest's Room,
house some remarkable objects: a fascinating carved 17C bed, a German
carving of the Last Supper, and a death portrait of Charles I, showing him
dead but upright, with a scar around his neck, his execution represented
in the background. On the second floor are rooms furnished in 19C
antiquarian and Arts and Crafts style, and the Chetham Room in the top of
the Tower, housing temporary displays. The gardens are presently under
restoration to their Victorian layout, and visitors should also see the splendid castellated bridge over the railway which runs close by the house.

                                                                    SB

LEICESTERSHIRE

Belvoir Castle

7m south west of Grantham between A52 Grantham–Nottingham and
A607 Grantham–Melton: the Duke of Rutland, tel. 0476 870262. Open
April–Sept daily except Mon (open BH Mon), Fri 11–5 (closes 6 on Sun,
BH Mon). Refreshments.

The name Belvoir (pronounced 'beaver') refers to the beautiful view from
the outcrop of limestone hills in the north-eastern corner of the county, on
which William the Conqueror's standard-bearer, Robert de Todeni, built the
first fortress on this site. In the early 16C the castle passed by marriage to
the Manners family, soon to become Earls and later Dukes of Rutland,
several of whom are commemorated in a series of magnificent tombs in the
nearby church at Bottesford. The Manners family rebuilt the castle, but it
was damaged in the Civil War and replaced in 1655–58 by a new classi-
cally-proportioned house built on the old foundations to the designs of Inigo
Jones's pupil John Webb.

In 1801 the 5th Duke employed James Wyatt to remodel the exterior of
the house in the newly fashionable castellated style. He also designed a
new Gallery as a setting for the lavish entertaining for which Belvoir was
soon to become famous; on the Duke's birthday in 1833, 40 people were
entertained to dinner and 200 dined in the servants' hall. In 1816, three
years after Wyatt's death, the north east and north-west ranges were gutted
by fire, which destroyed most of the pictures and furniture. The rebuilding
was entrusted to the Duke's chaplain the Rev. Sir John Thoroton, a friend
of the artist J.M.W. Turner. He had worked closely with Wyatt on the earlier
remodelling, and he now gave the house a yet more bold exterior, with a
massive tower projecting from the middle of the north-east range. He also
designed the entrance hall, staircase and passages and planned a new
series of state rooms which were decorated after his death in 1820 by James
Wyatt's sons Matthew and Benjamin.

Like Windsor Castle, which was also transformed by the Wyatts, Belvoir
represents the romantic medievalism of the early 19C at its most extrovert.
Visitors approach the house from the bottom of the hill, and are confronted
first by Wyatt's **south-west front** of yellow stone with its round projecting
tower at the west end and flimsily Gothic windows at the east, lighting the
chapel; Thoroton's north west and north-east ranges of grey stone have a
dourer, more intimidating quality and incorporate some neo-Norman detail. The house is entered through a carriage-porch which gives access to
the rib-vaulted entrance hall or **Guardroom** bristling with weapons and
hung with decaying flags; from here there are quasi-Baroque vistas to the
staircases leading up to the important rooms on the second floor. The most
spectacular of these are on the north side of the house, and display the
stylistic variety in which the Regency era revelled. The corridor or **Ballroom**
is decorated in the Early English Gothic style, loosely based on Lincoln
Cathedral; a model of the gaunt 1655–58 house is preserved here, along
with a 12C breviary said to have belonged to Thomas à Becket, and several
medieval charters, including one showing the first castle in stylised form
on the seal. From here the route passes first through a bedroom and
dressing room overlooking the late-17C stable block and furnished in the
mid-18C chinoiserie style, and then into the main drawing room, known as

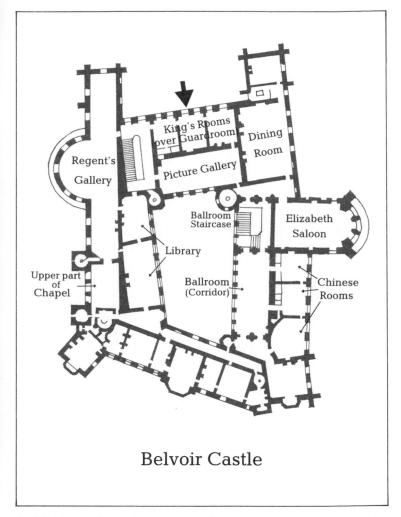

King's Rooms over Guardroom

Regent's Gallery

Dining Room

Picture Gallery

Ballroom Staircase

Elizabeth Saloon

Library

Upper part of Chapel

Ballroom (Corridor)

Chinese Rooms

Belvoir Castle

the **Elizabeth Saloon** after the artistically-minded 5th Duchess, 'the idol of her domestic circle'. Her Francophile taste accounts for the decoration by Matthew Wyatt in the Louis Quinze manner, then almost unknown in England, and her life-size marble statue, carved by Wyatt, still presides over the lavishly gilded room with its furniture, carpet and boiseries imported from France, and its richly painted allegorical ceiling. The severe round-arched **Dining Room** has massive mahogany sideboards, a marble side table by Matthew Wyatt with a white marble 'cloth', and portraits by Reynolds of the 4th Duke—who collected the most important paintings in the house—and his father the Marquess of Granby, a military hero immortalised in the names of many pubs.

The finest works of art are kept in Benjamin Wyatt's top-lit **Picture**

Gallery. They include five of a set of the 'Seven Sacraments', by Nicholas Poussin in his gravest and most austere manner, purchased by the 4th Duke on Reynolds's advice; genre pictures by Jan Steen and Teniers; a portrait of Henry VIII, long ascribed to Holbein; landscapes and 'fancy pictures' by Gainsborough; and an excellent collection of portrait miniatures by Nicholas Hilliard, Isaac Oliver, Samuel Cooper and others. There is also a late-17C state bed with its original hangings and, in a display case in the middle of the room, a superb silver-gilt and agate ewer and basin made in London in 1579–82.

The rooms known as '**King's Rooms**' (after George IV) face out over the entrance front and contain Chinese wallpapers and furniture of the 1820s. They lead via the landing of the main Staircase to the **Regent's Gallery**, the main reception room in James Wyatt's south-west range. This long, spacious bow-windowed room, one of the finest of its date in England, looks out over wooded vistas and is simpler and more relaxing in character than the rooms on the other side of the house. The walls are lined with busts of politicians by Nollekens and hung with faded rose-pink 18C tapestries of the story of Don Quixote, made in the Gobelin factory and bought by the 5th Duke; there is a good collection of French furniture, including several pieces from the Boulle workshop, and a small version of Canova's 'Three Graces' stands on a cabinet to the right of the entrance. To the north are the **libraries**, added by Thoroton and looking inwards to the courtyard; the Small Library is an austere room designed for serious scholarly endeavour, but the large Library next door, with its large Gothic windows and gilded neo-Tudor ceiling, is furnished as a comfortable living room in the usual Regency manner. A staircase from the Regent's Gallery leads down to Wyatt's Gothic **Chapel**, recently redecorated, with the shafts and ribs picked out in grey on a white background. There is a painting of the Holy Family by Murillo over the altar, and three excellently preserved Mortlake tapestries based on the Raphael Cartoons are displayed on the walls, while medieval effigies are preserved in the ante-chapel. From here a passage leads back across the foot of the main Staircase to the entrance, but before leaving it is worth looking at the cavernous, empty Kitchen, left as it was in the early 20C when it catered for the magnificent and already archaic establishment so well evoked by Lady Diana Cooper in her autobiography *The Rainbow Comes and Goes*.

GCT

Donington Manor House

In village of Donington-le-Heath to south west of Coalville, 1m east of A447: Leicestershire County Council. Open Easter–Sept Wed–Sun, BH Mon 2–6. Refreshments.

This late-13C house, hidden away on a side road on the edge of the Leicestershire coalfield, is a virtually complete example of a medieval country gentleman's house of modest size. As such it represents an interesting contrast to the better-known castles of the feudal aristocracy and the courtyard houses of the richer gentry. The name of the builder is not known, and by the end of the 16C the house had become a farmhouse. It then acquired hearths and chimneys, and some of the windows have since been enlarged, although several of the original lancet windows still survive. The house was later all but abandoned, but has been rescued and restored, and is now furnished in an appropriately sparse and rustic fashion.

The house is built of granite from the nearby Charnwood Forest, and is roofed with local Swithland slates. Externally there is no attempt at symmetry or architectural display. The room to the right of the entrance was turned into a farm kitchen in the late 16C, and is furnished as such now. In the Middle Ages the main rooms were on the first floor, and were entered by an external staircase on the south side (since gone). This gave access to the Hall, which still has its open timber roof. Bedchambers project north from each end of this room, on to one of which an extra room was added at a later date, creating a small open-ended courtyard behind the main block. There is also a detached barn which now serves as the tea room.

GCT

Stanford Hall

1m south of B5414 Rugby–Market Harborough, 7½m north west of Rugby: the Lady Braye, tel. 0788 860250. Open Easter–Sept Sat, Sun, BH Mon and Tues following 2.30–6. Guided tours. Refreshments.

Standford Hall stands in open parkland by the banks of the River Avon where it divides Leicestershire from Northamptonshire. The house was built in 1697–1700 for Sir Roger Cave, whose family had lived for many years on the Northamptonshire side of the river, close to the parish church which contains an impressive collection of family monuments. A contract preserved in the library records that the architect and builder was William Smith, elder brother of the more famous Francis Smith of Warwick, who later designed the main staircase and stable block and remodelled the east façade. Francis's son, another William, heightened and redecorated the entrance hall on the south front in 1745 for Sir Thomas Cave, a gentleman 'of a very mechanical turn', who turned the Avon into an ornamental feature by building a dam upstream of the house. The estate passed in 1792 to Sir Thomas's granddaughter Sarah, who inherited a claim to the long-dormant title of Braye through her grandmother Margaret Verney and in 1839 became 3rd Baroness Braye in her own right. The house was neglected for most of the 19C, but was repaired and altered in 1880 and still remains the family home.

In its architecture and general layout, Stanford follows the standard post-Restoration pattern seen in its purest form at Belton, Lincolnshire (qv.). The ashlar-faced south front, first glimpsed at the end of a long, straight avenue, is a particularly satisfying composition, with its hipped roof, sash windows and slightly recessed centre; as in many later Smith houses, the window over the original front door is flanked by carvings of garlands of fruit ending in boldly carved volutes at the base. The other façades are of brick, which was also used in the building of the attractive stable complex of 1737; the stables now house a display of old motor cycles and a replica of a pioneer flying machine tried out in the park in 1899 with fatal results.

The main rooms, raised up over a semi-basement, have an appealingly faded character. They are now entered from the east side of the house, but the finest rooms are in the centre: Francis Smith's main staircase of c 1730, with its delicately carved wooden balusters and restrained plaster ceiling, and his son William's lofty and impressive Ballroom (originally the entrance hall), the most striking feature of which is the coved ceiling decorated by the plasterer John Wright of Worcester; the walls and ceiling were further embellished in 1880 under the direction of a Frenchman, Felix Joubert. The Ballroom contains an important collection of Jacobite portraits and memorabilia formerly belonging to Henry, Cardinal York, the last of the Stuarts, and purchased in Rome by the 3rd Lady Braye in 1842. They include two portraits of the Old Pretender, one of his wife and one of 'Bonnie Prince Charlie' in corpulent middle age (by Laurent Pechaux, 1770); portraits of Cardinal York hang in the entrance corridor and in an upstairs bedroom. The Library and Dining Room, in the east range, were converted out of bedroom suites in the late-18C or 19C, but the Green Drawing Room (the former great parlour) on the opposite side of the house still retains the panelling which was being installed in 1716 (the neo-Rococo ceiling is of 1880). The rooms and passages are now lined with portraits, among them Henry VII's mother Lady Margaret Beaufort (in the Dining Room) and Charles I's standard-bearer Sir Edmund Verney (in the Green Drawing Room); these pictures, together with the miscellaneous collection of old furniture, give the house a strong and pervasive sense of continuity and ancient possession.

GCT

LINCOLNSHIRE

Belton House

3m north east of Grantham on A607 Grantham–Lincoln: National Trust, tel. 0476 66116. Open Apr–Oct Wed–Sun, BH Mon 1–5.30 (gardens open 11–5.30). Refreshments.

Belton is a text-book example of the English post-Restoration house. It was built in 1685–88 for Sir John Brownlow, great-grandson of a successful lawyer who had bought the estate c 1617, and the architect was probably William Winde, a friend of Samuel Pepys and Fellow of the Royal Society. The building operations were entrusted to William Stanton, a leading member of the Masons' Company in London, and some gifted craftsmen were employed in the interiors, including the plasterer Edward Gouge, one of Winde's regular collaborators, and the otherwise unknown wood carver Edmund Carpenter. Brownlow's nephew and successor, Lord Tyrconnel, was an assiduous collector of pictures and books, several of which remain in the house, which, when he died in 1754, went to a nephew, Sir John Cust, who became Speaker of the House of Commons. His son Sir Brownlow Cust (later the 1st Lord Brownlow), married an heiress and employed James Wyatt in 1776 to remodel the main rooms on the upper floor, and Wyatt's son Sir Jeffrey Wyatville did more internal redecoration and designed the Orangery in the grounds c 1811–19 for the 2nd Lord (and 1st Earl) Brownlow. The 3rd Earl restored much of the late-17C character of both house and gardens in the 1870s, and in 1984 the house, park and the most important contents were given to the National Trust by the 7th Lord Brownlow, and the park and contents purchased with the aid of the National Heritage Memorial Fund.

The approach is through the early-19C estate village with its much-rebuilt church—in effect a Brownlow mortuary chapel, with excellent monuments by Stanton, Cheere, Westmacott and Canova—on the north edge of the grounds. Stables and a service courtyard lies to the west of the house, which faces south over lawns laid out over the original formal setting in the 18C; a formal garden was recreated on the north side by the 3rd Earl Brownlow in the late 19C. The **façades**, of local Ancaster limestone ashlar, are meticulously proportioned and convey a sense of dignified grandeur without bombast. The house is H-shaped, with the central block of double width and two main storeys of equal height surmounted by a hipped roof with a balustrade and central cupola (replaced in 1879 after removal by Wyatt). The design owes much to Sir Roger Pratt's short-lived Clarendon House in Piccadilly and embodies many of the refinements advocated by Pratt in his unpublished notes on architecture produced in the 1660s: a basement to keep the 'dirty servants' (Pratt's words) out of the way of their social superiors, a 'stately ascent' to the front door, back stairs and a careful alignment of doorways to allow a view through the house on the central hall/saloon axis.

The slightly gloomy interiors have undergone several changes since the house was first built, but still retain much of their excellent late-17C craftsmanship. The rooms were originally grouped as 'apartments' on either side of the more public rooms in the centre, and some of the downstairs rooms are little altered. They include the **Saloon**, where there is some particularly fine naturalistic wood carving over the fireplaces in the manner of Grinling Gibbons (though some of the authentic-looking wood-work and plasterwork dates from the 19C), as well as a set of late-17C high-backed chairs (re-upholstered in the 19C); and the almost untouched private **Chapel** in the east wing, with its plaster ceiling by Gouge, massive reredos with Corinthian columns supporting a curved pediment, and late-17C silver candle sconces. The **Drawing Room**, next to the Chapel, still retains the two tapestries with exotic oriental scenes supplied by John Vanderbank for Sir John Brownlow in 1691, along with some of the lacquered furniture which formed an important part of the original decoration of the house.

The other downstairs rooms reflect the tastes of later owners. The **Entrance Hall** has some pompous family portraits by Reynolds and others, as well as busts by Chantrey and Nollekens of famous contemporaries of the 1st Earl Brownlow, who employed Wyatt to redecorate the one downstairs bedroom (the **Blue Room**), at the south end of the east wing; this still retains its absurdly tall, re-upholstered early-18C state bed. Wyatville was responsible for the redecoration of the **Red Drawing Room** to the west (left) of the Saloon, which now contains some of the depleted collection of Old Masters; there is also a late-17C Italian lapis lazuli cabinet and some 18C French furniture. The **Tapestry Room** (originally the little parlour), next to the Hall, is a convincing 1890s recreation of a late-17C room, designed to house tapestries of Diogenes and Alexander, possibly from the Mortlake factory.

The upstairs rooms are reached by an impressive wooden **staircase**, altered by Wyatville in 1819, with another rich plaster ceiling by Gouge. The large room over the Hall was originally the main dining room, but was remodelled by Wyatt as a drawing room and turned into a **Library** in 1877, incorporating bookcases by Wyatville designed for two downstairs rooms in the west wing (seen at the end of the tour). Two of the remaining rooms on this floor, the Yellow Bedroom and the Boudoir, are also by Wyatt, but the **Boudoir** was again redecorated in the 1930s by Francis Johnson of York for the 6th Lord Brownlow, a friend of Edward VIII; it now contains an early

Belton House, 1685–88, from the south east, showing the stable block to the left

conversation piece by Philip Mercier of Lord Tyrconnel and his family (1725). The **Chinese Bedroom** contains more late-17C lacquer furniture, and in the **Ante-Library** there is a large collection of Japanese Imari ware and 18C *famille rose* porcelain, acquired in the late 18C and more recently; the marbling of this second room, dated 1884, is an early example of the 'authentic' restoration of a late-17C house. A picture of the house soon after its completion hangs on the west staircase, which leads down to the remaining downstairs rooms, the largest of which was redecorated as a **dining room** in 1877 and hung with large and attractive paintings of garden scenes by the 17C Dutch artist Melchior d'Hondecoeter. An adjoining room contains some of the best items from the lavish collection of silver amassed by Sir John Brownlow and his 18C and 19C successors.

GCT

Doddington Hall

5m west of Lincoln on B1190: A.G. Jarvis, tel. 0522 694308. Open Easter Mon, May–Sept Wed, Sun, BH Mon 2–6.

This large and severe house was begun c 1593 by Thomas Tailor, the Registrar of Lincoln Cathedral, which can be seen from close to the house. Tailor was a self-made man who bought a 9000-acre estate out of the profit he made from managing the bishop's lands, and his house, which may have been designed by Robert Smythson, powerfully asserts his determination to make his mark among the social élite of Elizabethan Lincolnshire. As in several houses of its date, there are few external embellishments apart from the three cupolas on the east (entrance) front and the chimneys, which were lowered in the 18C; otherwise the main visual variety comes from the projections and recessions made necessary by the H-plan, and from the regular placing of large numbers of mullioned and transomed windows across the completely symmetrical red-brick façades. The original setting still survives largely untouched (though the attractive formal west garden dates from 1900), and the house is approached, as it always has been, through a pretty detached gatehouse with curved gables, probably dating from the first half of the 16C, which leads into a walled forecourt.

When Thomas Tailor died in 1606 the house had only 83 pieces of furniture in no fewer than 37 rooms. It remained structurally little altered until the 1760s, by which time it had passed by marriage into the hands of Sir John Hussey Delaval, later Lord Delaval, a younger son from an old Northumberland family (cf. Seaton Delaval). He spent a great deal of time at Doddington, enclosing the surrounding commons and employing the Lincoln master-carpenter Thomas Lumby in 1761–62 to modernise the interiors of the house and subsequently to design the small Gothic Revival church nearby. His younger brother Edward succeeded him in 1808, and carried out further repairs. His daughter and heiress left the house in 1825 to her lover George Jarvis, an army officer who came from a large family of wealthy West Indies planters, and from him it has passed by descent to the present owner. The house escaped the 'Elizabethan revival' treatment meted out to many similar buildings in the 19C, and has remained largely unchanged since the 18C remodelling.

The entrance is through a central porch, which leads directly into the Hall, with panelling of the 1760s recently repainted in the original colours. The

18C craftsmanship throughout the house is plain, serviceable and a little old-fashioned for its date—quite possibly because of a deliberate decision to emphasise the antiquity of the house. The service end (not seen by visitors) is to the left of the Hall, and a doorway on the north side leads to the Parlour, panelled in the early 18C, with an erotic 'Cymon and Iphegenia' by Lely over the fireplace. This was acquired, along with several other pictures, by Edward Delaval, and a portrait by Lawrence of his daughter Sarah Gunman hangs by the door. At the foot of the plain but impressive staircase there is a portrait of the wicked and extrovert Sir Francis Delaval by Reynolds, and on the landing there is a 17C Brussels tapestry, of which there are more examples in an adjacent bedroom, which also contains a bed of c 1680 with its original crewel-work hangings; the early-18C bed in the room at the opposite side of the staircase was originally at Seaton Delaval. The Drawing Room over the Hall—the original great chamber—has Rococo mirrors and other ornaments in *carton pierre*, introduced in 1775, and the furniture includes two Neapolitan 17C ebony cabinets with painted glass panels; the attractive chandeliers of 1720 were originally in the Assembly Room at Lincoln. Some 17C and early-18C nautical pictures hang at the top of the staircase, along with pictures of Seaton Delaval and of the view from the roof of Edward Delaval's London house.

The whole of the top floor is taken up by the Gallery, redecorated by Lumby in the same plain sturdy manner as he employed elsewhere in the house, and now housing a good collection of Chinese porcelain, much of it displayed in specially-constructed alcoves on the south wall, blocking the Elizabethan windows. But the pièce de résistance is the large portrait on the south wall of John Delaval's sister, her husband the Earl of Mexborough and their son, painted by Reynolds at the time of George III's coronation in 1761: a superb example of the artist's grand manner, all the more effective for the fact that it still occupies the place for which it was painted.

GCT

Fulbeck Hall

11m north of Grantham on A607 Grantham–Lincoln: Mrs M. Fry, tel. 0400 72205. Open July daily, also Easter and May, BH Mon 2–5. Refreshments.

Fulbeck Hall stands on a ledge of the limestone hills which extend from Grantham to Lincoln, overlooking the Trent valley to the west. The estate was bought in 1622 by Francis Fane, 1st Earl of Westmorland, whose main house was at Apethorpe (Northants), and was given to his younger son Francis. He built the first known house on a site next to the largely 15C parish church, but the present building with its meticulously squared grey limestone ashlar façade was built by his descendant, another Francis Fane, after a fire in 1733. Like Gunby Hall (qv.), the new Fulbeck Hall looks like a town house set in the country, and features like the pronounced architraves to the first-floor windows (from James Gibbs's 1728 pattern-book) suggest the hand of a Stamford architect, possibly George Portwood. A north extension, containing a new dining room with a rounded end, was added by the Hon. Henry Fane in 1784, and in 1813 his widow extended the rooms on the entrance front forwards, thereby obscuring the bases of the giant Doric pilasters which gave scale and dignity to the façade. The house was put up for sale in 1887, but it was bought, without the contents, by a cousin, William Fane, an enthusiastic antiquarian and great-grandfather of the present owner. He remodelled some of the interiors, and his son created the attractive terraced garden to the north in 1904. The present porch came from Syston Park, a few miles south, in 1934.

The house is approached through splendid early-18C iron gates, which open on to an avenue. Both the exterior and the interior show the effects of successive attempts to enlarge the 1733 building and adapt it for changing patterns of life. The most unaltered parts are the long, narrow Entrance Hall and the wooden staircase which opens out of it beyond an archway flanked by Doric pilasters. To the left are the Drawing Room and Small Dining Room, with pictures by Gerard Dou, Zuccarelli, Samuel Scott and others, originally collected by William Burnside of Gedling (Notts.) in the early 19C, along with good 18C and early 19C porcelain and furniture. The Library (originally a parlour), on the other side of the hall, was created by William Fane in 1894, with neo-Jacobean panelling designed as a framework for a portrait of Francis Fane, the first of the family to live at Fulbeck; the picture can now be seen by appointment, along with other family portraits, at the nearby Fulbeck Manor. The Dining Room of 1784, recently repainted in the original colours, is a spacious room with a neo-classical chimneypiece by James Wallis. Paintings by the younger Teniers and Gaspard Dughet hang on the staircase. The tour ends upstairs, where a Tent Room mentioned in a 19C inventory has recently been recreated.

GCT

Gainsborough Old Hall

In the centre of Gainsborough, south of Gladstone Street: English Heritage/Lincolnshire County Council, tel. 0427 612669. Open all year Mon–Sat 10–5 and Easter–Oct Sun 2–5.30. Refreshments.

This large and important late-medieval house now has a completely urban setting, with the 18C parish church (by Francis Smith of Warwick) to the north and late-Victorian housing in the streets around, but when it was built it was the centre of a substantial rural estate. It consists of a timber-framed north (hall) range, built c 1460, flanked on either side by a brick-built kitchen and an octagonal tower, with two projecting brick and timber ranges of c 1470–80, that to the west containing lodgings and that to the east the grander rooms. The builder was Sir Thomas (later Lord) Burgh, a supporter of the Yorkists, who restored the house after it was damaged by a Lancastrian army in 1470 and entertained Richard III here is 1483. His descendant, the 5th Lord Burgh, sold the house in 1596 to a London merchant, William Hickman, and he carried out some internal and external alterations which are especially noticeable in the east range. Gainsborough became a fairly substantial town in the 18C, and in 1720 the Hickmans moved away, leaving the house to become, inter alia, a linen factory, a theatre, an auction room and a corn exchange. It was restored and opened to the public in the 1950s by Friends of the Old Hall.

Lovers of medieval antiquity should approach the house from the north side, where the Hall with its stone bay window, the embattled brick tower to the east and the massive, almost detached, brick kitchen block to the west can all be clearly seen. The outer face of the west range, with its four massive projections containing chimneystacks and garderobes, has also changed relatively little since the 15C. The most impressive interior is the tall spacious Hall, one of the finest of its date in England; note especially the splendid arch-braced roof and the stone pendant vault of the bay window at the 'upper' end. The screen at the 'lower' end has gone, revealing the usual three doorways (to the buttery, pantry and kitchen) in the west wall, the middle one of which leads via a passage to the vast Kitchen, with its central louvre and huge fireplaces, flanked by larders and bedrooms for the kitchen staff above them; waxwork figures and cooking implements have been introduced recently as aids to interpretation. From here a spiral staircase leads up to two chambers for important members of the household. The rest of the house, reached by the main staircase, south of the Hall, is more mundane. There are some unfurnished 15C lodgings in the north-east tower, and in the east wing there is a set of much-altered 16C or 17C rooms, including what was in Elizabethan times the great chamber.

GCT

Grimsthorpe

On A151 Colsterworth–Bourne, 4m north west of Bourne: Grimsthorpe and Drummond Castle Trust, tel. 077832 205. Open Easter BH Sun/Mon, late May–mid Sept Sun, BH Mon 2–6 (gardens open 12, also Thur 12–6). Refreshments.

This magnificent house in the remote southern uplands of Lincolnshire has one of the finest approaches in England: a long avenue blocked at its south end by the monumental entrance front begun to the designs of Sir John Vanbrugh in 1723. Behind this lies a much older building which has been remodelled several times. There was a house here in the Middle Ages, but according to Leland it was 'no great thing', and only the thickly walled south-east tower still survives. In 1516 the estate came into the possession of William, 10th Lord Willoughby de Eresby. The nucleus of the present house is a courtyard building begun by his daughter Katherine and her first husband Charles Brandon, Duke of Suffolk (d 1545), using stone taken from the suppressed abbey of Vaudey, close to the present ornamental lake in the park. It was probably completed by Katherine's second husband, Richard Bertie, or by their son, Peregrine, Queen Elizabeth's commander in the Netherlands, but during the 1680s the north-facing hall range was rebuilt with a classical hipped-roofed façade by Robert Bertie, 3rd Earl of Lindsey.

This was not grand enough for the 4th Earl, who married an heiress and was created Duke of Ancaster in 1715. He commissioned his cousin and childhood friend Vanbrugh to prepare ambitious plans for rebuilding the whole house in a suitably ducal manner, but his schemes for the south, east and west ranges were soon abandoned, leaving only the north range and forecourt, which rank among his finest surviving works. Work was still progressing in 1730, and over the next 30 or so years the state rooms in the east range were fitted up with great splendour by the 2nd and 3rd Dukes. The 4th Duke died in 1779, and the title passed to his sister, whose husband Lord Gwydyr commissioned an obscure London architect, Samuel Page, and his pupil, Henry Garling, to give a fashionably neo-Tudor facelift to the east and west façades in 1811. This left only the gabled south front as a reminder of the early origins of the house. There were minor alterations by Detmar Blow in 1911–12, and sympathetic restorations of the interiors were carried out by Stephane Boudin in the 1920s and John Fowler in the 1950s.

Vanbrugh's massive **façade** of local limestone is approached through a walled forecourt closed by an iron screen of c 1730, possibly by the Office of Works' blacksmith, Thomas Robinson. The façade is no orthodox piece of text-book classicism. The central portion, corresponding to the hall behind, is flanked by two pairs of giant banded Doric columns, and at each corner there is a balustraded tower with a Venetian window at first-floor level. Despite the classical details, these towers, like the lodges at the corners of the forecourt, should be seen as expressions of the 'castle air' often employed by Vanbrugh to heighten the dramatic impact and historical resonance of a house. The exaggeratedly large keystones further enhance the impression of formidable seigneurial authority.

A staircase at the side of Vanbrugh's Entrance Hall (seen again at the end of the tour) leads up to the state rooms. The **Dining Room**, on the first floor of the north-east tower, has a painted ceiling of the Arts and the Sciences attributed to Francesco Sleter, and is hung with excellent late-17C Brussels tapestries from the workshop of Albert Auwerx. There is much gilded 18C furniture, including royal thrones acquired as perquisites of the hereditary office of Lord Great Chamberlain, and some gilded wall-sconces by William Kent which were originally in the House of Lords. From here there is an *enfilade* through the remaining state rooms in the east range. The first, called the **King James Drawing Room** after the portrait of James I by van Somer over the fireplace, has wood panelling with paired Corinthian pilasters dating from the 1730s, but the delicate plasterwork over the doors is Rococo in character and may have been carried out by William Perritt of York in the 1760s; much of the 18C French furniture, both here and in other rooms, was introduced after a sale of the original furniture in 1829. There is more Rococo decoration in the **State Drawing Room**, which contains some good 18C family portraits, including two striking full-lengths on the south wall, of the 3rd Duke of Ancaster by Reynolds, and his wife in masquerade dress by Thomas Hudson (note also the more intimate portraits of Lord Brownlow Bertie by Reynolds and his wife by Francis Cotes). The adjacent **Tapestry Drawing Room** owes its present character to a superb set of tapestries with arabesque designs woven in the 1720s by Joshua Morris of Soho, and brought to Grimsthorpe from Normanton Park, Rutland, in 1924.

A **Gallery** running along the courtyard side of the Tudor south range is hung with early family portraits, including one of the villainous-looking Charles Brandon, Duke of Suffolk, Henry VIII's brother-in-law. A corridor in the west range leads to the **Chinese Room**, created as a 'tea room' in the mid 18C in the spirit of Rococo fantasy (see for instance the ceiling decorations and the Gothick 'fan vault' of the bow window), enhanced by the introduction of Chinese wallpaper early in the 19C. The last two rooms are graver in character. The **Chapel**, in Vanbrugh's north-west tower, has a richly modelled plaster ceiling dating from the 1680s, but is otherwise a creation of the 1720s, and may have been completed by Nicholas Hawksmoor after Vanbrugh's death in 1726. An arcade screens the west staircase from the **Entrance Hall**, where Vanbrugh used the simple device of an arcade carried around the room on two levels to achieve an effect of calm and austere Roman grandeur. The upper arcade on the south wall is filled with monochrome figures of royal patrons of the Bertie family painted by Sir James Thornhill, who was also responsible for the west staircase ceiling. Otherwise there are few adornments, and the vast room remains a monument to the expressive power of Vanbrugh's architecture.

GCT

Gunby Hall

7m west of Skegness on A158 Skegness–Horncastle: National Trust. Open Apr–Sept Wed 2–6 (garden only Thus 2–6).

This plain red-brick house of 1700 lies in pastoral countryside at the foot of the lonely Lincolnshire Wolds. The builder, Sir William Massingberd, came from a long-established local family with mercantile connections. He married the daughter of a London merchant, and his neat house with its regularly spaced windows, slightly recessed centre and high parapet hiding the roof-line would not look out of place in Chelsea or Hampstead. A stable block was built in 1735 and some internal alterations were carried out by William Meux Massingberd, whose great-granddaughter married a younger son of Dr Johnson's friend Bennet Langton of Langton, not far away. Their grandson sold most of the contents of the house before disappearing on an expedition to the River Amazon, but an uncle, Charles Langton Massingberd, bought many of them back and built a substantial north wing in 1873. Stephen Langton-Massingberd, who inherited in 1897, and his aesthetically-minded wife Margaret, introduced more pictures and furniture, and created the formal garden to the west of the house and the beautiful walled garden (with a square 17C dovecote) to the east (her portrait by Arthur Hughes hangs in the Dining Room). After passing once more through the female line the house, grounds and contents were given to the National Trust in 1944.

The house was originally entered through the west doorway, surmounted by a scrolled pediment, but the present entrance is in the north wing, and the first room to be seen is the Music Room (built as a dining room), an attractively wood-panelled neo-Georgian pastiche; this houses two excellent portraits of Bennet Langton and his wife by Reynolds, a fellow-member of Dr Johnson's literary club, and a set of miniatures of the later Stuarts inherited by Langton's wife. The rooms in the older house were never very large or grand, and they have been much altered, especially in the 1870s, when two rooms on the east side were run together to form a larger drawing room (now the Dining Room). More changes occurred in 1962, when the original entrance hall was similarly opened up into the adjoining Library (formerly the parlour) to the south; this now contains a portrait of James Boswell (one of the only six autographed copies of his *Life of Johnson* is kept in the house). The oak staircase with twisted balusters, lit by a Venetian window in the south wall, is a good specimen of early-18C craftsmanship, and items of 17C, 18C and 19C furniture are scattered around the rooms, along with sketches and water-colours by Arthur Hughes and his pre-Raphaelite-inspired contemporaries.

GCT

GREATER LONDON

Boston Manor

Boston Manor Road (A3002), off the Great West Rd (A4): London Borough of Hounslow, tel. 081 862 5805. Open late May–Sept Sun 2–4.30.

Boston Manor is an architecturally interesting house of the 1620s standing in a small park. It is one of a group of brick houses, built for City merchants in the reign of Charles I; others include Forty Hall in Enfield (qv.). In the 16C Boston belonged to Sir Thomas Gresham, who also owned nearby Osterley Park (qv.). It passed to his stepson, Sir William Reade, and to his widow, Lady Mary, who seems to have built the house in 1622–23; her initials appear on the Great Chamber ceiling. In 1670 it was bought by James Clitherow, an East India merchant. The house remained in the Clitherow family until 1841. After the Second World War it came into the possession of the local authority; in 1963 it was restored, and partly divided into flats.

The house is a neat rectangular block, four bays by six, and three storeys high, with three gables on the long façades and two on the short. It is a notably early example of a double-pile plan, divided lengthways by a spine wall. The gables and the dark red brickwork are in their original condition, but the windows with their heavy classical surrounds are probably of c 1670, as is the entablature above the first floor level. The rainwater heads bear dates 1622 and 1670. The elaborate porch is a Jacobean-revival addition of the 1840s.

The ground floor plan has been much altered. The Entrance Hall may not be in its original form, and its decoration, too, is of the 1840s. The south-west room also has 19C decoration. The staircase is partly authentic, with an arcaded balustrade. On the first floor there are two magnificent original rooms. The Great Chamber, on the east side, has a very rich ceiling dated 1623; the strapwork pattern encloses medallions with symbolic figures, including the five senses, the four elements (from designs by Marcus Gheeraerts), War and Peace, Peace and Plenty, and so on. The chimneypiece has heavy piers and an overmantel with plasterwork of great delicacy, depicting the sacrifice of Isaac. The smaller room to the south west has another original strapwork ceiling, with a medallion of Hope, a frieze and a later (1670) fireplace. The curious point is that the plan of the house should be architecturally advanced, while the splendid decoration is comparatively old-fashioned.

SB

Chiswick House

Off Burlington Lane (A316) just south of the A4: English Heritage, tel. 081 995 0508. Open Apr–Sept daily 10–6, Oct–Mar daily 10–4.

Although it is one of the smallest houses described in this book, Chiswick has an architectural importance out of all proportion to its size. It was built in 1727–29, and was the creation of Richard Boyle, 3rd Earl of Burlington. He inherited immense estates in Yorkshire and Ireland (he was also Earl of Cork) at the age of ten, in 1704. Architecture was his driving passion. He came back from Italy in 1719 having seen the buildings of Andrea Palladio in Venice and Vicenza, and led a revolution in English architectural taste, away from the dominant Baroque of Wren, Vanbrugh and Hawksmoor, to a more strictly mathematical neo-Palladian style in which the design and plan are subordinated to geometrical rules. In 1719 he set the Scots architect Colen Campbell to rebuilding Burlington House on Piccadilly (which survives, much altered, as the Royal Academy). He also inherited a moderate-sized Jacobean house at Chiswick. In 1727–29, he built the present villa next to the old house, with his protégé William Kent designing the interiors and furniture. It was planned as a place in which to entertain friends, to house his collections of pictures and statuary, and as a manifesto for his architectural ideals. In 1732, he added a link to the old house, and began to remodel the gardens.

On Lord Burlington's death in 1753, all his estates passed via his daughter to the Dukes of Devonshire. They had little use for the place until 1788, when the fifth Duke resolved to turn it into a more serviceable out-of-town residence. He had the old Jacobean house demolished, and employed a minor architect, John White, to add large wings to either side of Burlington's villa, radically altering its appearance. It remained with the Cavendish family until 1929, and after the Second World War it was taken into the care of the Ministry of Works in 1956–57. John White's wings were then deemed to be obscuring Burlington's design, and in 1956–57 they were demolished, leaving just Burlington's villa and link building. The grounds have been a local authority public park since 1929, but have undergone some restoration to their 18C state.

The plan of the house, a square with a central domed hall and rooms symmetrically arranged around it, has some resemblance to that of Palladio's Villa Rotonda. The entrance front has a Corinthian portico of the greatest richness; on either side of the façade are weatherbeaten statues, by Rysbrack, of Burlington's architectural heroes—Palladio and Inigo Jones. The visitor now enters the basement storey beneath the portico. On this floor, Lord Burlington kept his library, conducted business, and received visitors; there were also three bedrooms. The first floor is gained by a spiral stair. This has nine rooms arranged around an octagonal saloon under the dome, all having a strangely compressed, miniaturised quality. It is a curious plan, not obviously functional, but intended to recall Roman interiors. The saloon is lit by lunette or 'Diocletian' windows, with splendid gilded coffering on the dome. Around the walls are portrait busts and paintings, the most notable of which is a copy of Guido Reni's Liberality and Modesty. The three rooms to the north have been known as the Gallery since 1761 at least. There are no doors in the arched openings between them; the central space is rectangular with apses at either end, at one end is a circular room, at the other end an octagonal room. The walls are white with gold ornament; they have richly decorated ceilings but little furniture. This is true of the house generally; most of the purpose-made furniture, much of it designed by Kent, has been dispersed (many important objects are now at Chatsworth, Derbyshire, qv.), though some individual pieces have been bought back. The other principal rooms retain their high, coffered and painted ceilings, but are now disappointingly empty, although some of the pictures (eg, four overmantels by Sebastiano Ricci commissioned by Lord Burlington) have been returned. Over the doors of the Blue Velvet Room are portraits of Inigo Jones, and of the poet Alexander Pope.

The garden is large, and marked an important shift away from the geometrical formalism of Baroque gardens. Its appearance in the 18C is known from many paintings, which have been used in recent restoration work. The visitor can still appreciate Burlington's intention, to create a miniature landscape set with 'Roman' monuments, some visible from a distance, some artfully concealed.

SB

Fenton House

On Hampstead Grove, just west off Heath St, about 300yds from Hampstead Underground Stn: National Trust, tel. 071 435 3471. Open Mar Sat & Sun only 2–6; Apr–Oct Sat, Sun, BH Mon 11–6; Mon, Tue, Wed 1–7. Closed Good Fri.

Fenton House is a fine late 17C building at the north end of Hampstead village, and houses important collections of porcelain, furniture and musical instruments. Architecturally, it is a well-preserved representative of a particular type of English house—the substantial, sober, symmetrical brick house, with tall sash windows, a hipped roof over a big white-painted cornice and tall brick chimneys, favoured by merchant and gentry families all over south and east England c 1680–1710. Oddly enough, neither the architect nor the builder of the house is known. The date 1693 is inscribed on one brick, and this seems about right. The only other clue is the fact that it was originally known as Ostend House, suggesting that it was built for a City merchant with interests in Flanders. The house passed through numerous owners in the 18C, and in 1793 was bought by Philip Fenton, a merchant in the Baltic trade. In 1807 his son James carried out some alterations, adding the Doric colonnade between the wings on the entrance front. He also removed some partitions inside, to make fewer and larger rooms. The house passed through several different hands in the 19C, but escaped any major alterations. In 1936 it was bought by Lady Binning who installed a major collection of pictures, furniture, and above all of porcelain, inherited from her uncle, the collector George Salting. In 1952 Lady Binning left the house and its contents to the National Trust, which added a fine collection of keyboard instruments, presented in 1937 by Major George Henry Benton Fletcher.

The house is almost square, apart from the centre of the entrance front, which is slightly inset. When it was built the plan was symmetrical, with four main rooms on each floor. The Hall has original panelling and late 17C furniture. On the left is the present Dining Room, which runs the whole length of the south front. This contains Regency furniture, and early paintings by Sir William Nicholson. The Porcelain Room has interesting 18C bird and flower pictures by Samuel Dixon, and a very early (1610) harpsichord by Hans Ruckers. The alcoves contain some excellent porcelain, including (in the left-hand alcove) figurines from the 18C Bristol and Plymouth factories, Chelsea groups of the gold anchor period (1758–77), and animal-form dishes from the Meissen, Bow, Derby, Chelsea and Worcester factories. The right hand alcove has superb figures from the Meissen and Nymphenburg factories, including several by J.J. Kändler. The Oriental Room has a variety of Chinese porcelain of the Sung, Ming and Ch'ing dynasties.

The staircase remains in its original form, with 17C twisted balusters; the cabinet on the landing has Staffordshire figures. The Rockingham Room mostly contains Staffordshire pottery, some from the factory of that name, and 17C needlework pictures. The Blue Porcelain Room has blue and white Chinese porcelain, most of it from the K'ang H'si period (1662–1722). The Drawing Room probably owes its present appearance to James Fenton; it houses elegant satinwood furniture in the style of Thomas Sheraton, and porcelain from the Worcester, Meissen, Frankenthal and Chelsea factories. The Green Room contains more 17C needlework pictures, and figurines from Staffordshire and from Meissen.

Five more rooms in the attic are given over keyboard instruments including harpsichords, clavichords, virginals and early pianos from many of the most important 17C and 18C makers. The instruments are kept in working order, and made available to students.

SB

Forty Hall

Off Forty Hill (near A10 at Hoe Lane): London Borough of Enfield, tel. 081 363 4046. Open all year Thurs–Sat 11–5.

Forty Hall is a red-brick house of 1629 with later alterations of various periods, standing in extensive grounds. It was built between 1629 and 1636 by a wealthy City merchant, Sir Nicholas Rainton (1569–1646). He was a member of the Haberdasher's Company, Lord Mayor of London in 1632–33 and President of St Bartholomew's Hospital; a fine portrait of him hangs in the Rainton Room. He is buried in St Andrew's Church, Enfield, where he and his family are commemorated by a fine tomb monument. Forty Hall passed to his nephew, Nicholas Rainton, and then experienced several changes of owner. In 1787 it was sold to Edmund Armstrong, and was later occupied by the Meyer and then the Bowles families, until 1951, when it was bought by the local authority, which carried out an extensive programme of restoration 1962–66. The house is now used as a local history museum.

The tall, square shell of the house remains basically as built by Sir Nicholas Rainton, but the original cross-shaped mullions and transoms in the windows have been replaced by sash windows. The hipped roof is one of the earliest of its kind in existence, and the brick chimneys, the quoins and flat window surrounds also seem to be in their original condition. Some alterations were made c 1700, and some internal redecoration was carried out in the mid 18C. James Meyer had the house rendered and more alterations made c 1800, and finally, in the 1890s, Henry Bowles remodelled the staircase and added the elaborate windows with his coats of arms.

The present Entrance Hall has pretty mid 18C Rococo plasterwork and columns; originally there was a screens passage here, leading into the Hall to the left. The screen itself is still visible in the Hall, with fine woodwork carved in the lavish Mannerist style popular with City merchants, and there is strapwork decoration on the ceiling. Behind the Hall is the staircase; the balusters are early 18C, but it is essentially a late 19C rebuilding. Beyond this, another big room has a fine Mannerist chimneypiece. The Rainton Room, next, has more mid 18C decoration, including the screen of pillars across one end. Upstairs, the main rooms were redecorated c 1700, but some of the ceilings retain the original strapwork decoration, and indeed one bears the date 1629.

SB

Gunnersbury Park

Entrance on Popes Lane (B4491) off the North Circular Road (A406):
London Boroughs of Ealing and Hounslow, tel. 081 992 1612. Open
Mar–Oct Mon–Fri 1–5, Sat, Sun, BH 1–6; Nov–Feb Mon–Fri 1–4, Sat,
Sun, BH 1–4. Refreshments.

Gunnersbury is today more a local museum than a country house, but there
is, nevertheless, plenty of architectural interest. A merchant, Sir John
Maynard, commissioned John Webb to build a Palladian villa here in
1658–68. This was later occupied by Princess Amelia, who added ornamental buildings in the grounds. The house was demolished in 1800 and most
of the estate was bought by a successful builder, Alexander Copland. By
1802 he had built a stuccoed house, the present 'Large Mansion' on part of
the site of the Webb house, probably designed by the young Sidney Smirke.
Copland sold a large plot next to this to a retired officer of the East India
Company, Alexander Morison, who built the adjacent 'Small Mansion' by
1805. In 1835 the Large Mansion was bought by Nathan Mayer Rothschild
of the famous banking family, and Sidney Smirke remodelled it for him. In
1925 the two houses and 186 acres were acquired jointly by local authorities. The main rooms are open to the public on summer weekends, and by
appointment to groups at other times.

The Small Mansion was used as an arts centre until 1993. The Large
Mansion is the local history museum for the two boroughs. It is a lush
neo-classical house, stuccoed and white, with low pitched roofs behind
parapets. The interiors are in a rich French-inspired neo-classical style. The
visitor enters a terracotta-painted staircase hall, the staircase with gilded
balustrade rising behind columns. The three main reception rooms are en
suite on the south, garden front. At one end, the former Music Room has a
splendid fireplace and heavy, gilded ceiling, and now houses an interesting
collection of horse-drawn vehicles, including two of the Rothschilds' carriages. The long Drawing Room, in the middle of the façade, has scagliola
columns and a painted ceiling by G.T. Parris. Beyond this, the Dining Room
has an especially splendid fireplace, and a columned alcove for the sideboard. Back on the north front of the house, the former library has been
newly refurbished as a costume gallery.

The kitchen wing, dating from 1835, is substantially intact, with many
interesting features. The Kitchen retains its vast cooking range and many
other historic fittings. The Scullery, Laundry, Chef's Office and Butchery
are also seen.

The grounds are spacious, and the 18C and 19C landscaping and garden
features survive to a considerable degree. South of the Large Mansion is
Sidney Smirke's big stuccoed Orangery. To the south east are Smirke's
stables, with Gothick mock-ruins screening them from the two houses.
North west of the house is a round pond with a little Doric temple built for
Princess Amelia to the designs of Sir William Chambers.

SB

Hall Place

Near the junction of the A2 and A223: London Borough of Bexley, tel. 0322 526574. Open weekdays 10–5, also April–Oct Sun 2–6. Refreshments.

On the south-east edge of London and close to the roaring traffic on the A3, it comes as a surprise to find this picturesque manor house. Hall Place was begun by Sir John Champneis, a City merchant, who bought the property in 1537. He built the stone core of the house, the Great Hall and two wings projecting north on either side; it contains a good deal of medieval carved masonry from dissolved monasteries. His son Justinian extended both wings. In 1649 the estate was bought by another London merchant, Robert Austen, who almost doubled the house in size, adding the red brick ranges which form a courtyard south of the medieval wings, two storeys high with a hipped roof. In the 19C, Hall Place was used as a boarding school. Its last private occupant, the Countess of Limerick, died in 1943; the house had already been purchased by the Borough of Bexley in 1935. It now houses the Bexley Museum, the borough's archives and related offices. The museum has displays concerning the archaeology, geology and natural history of the area, but there are few historic contents.

The house faces north with the great hall framed by the 16C wings. The fine wrought-iron gates were erected by the Austen family in the early 18C. As you approach the house from the east, the right-hand half of the façade is entirely Tudor, of rubble masonry with mullioned windows. To the left is the 17C wing, with a high hipped roof, in warm red brick. The picturesque ground floor corridor of 1653 leads into Sir John Champneis' Great Hall. The ceiling with its carved bosses is 16C, but the room's present symmetrical form is the work of Sir Justinian Champneis, who added a second bay window. The organ is dated 1766 and comes from Danson Park, a nearby 18C house. The staircase, also of 1653, has massive newel posts, treads and balusters of oak and chestnut. You can see the small courtyard enclosed by the 17C ranges; the arches at ground floor level were originally open arcades. Bexley Museum occupies the two big rooms on the first floor of the north-west wing. The first has a very fine coved ceiling, with vigorous grotesque ornament of the 17C. The second room was added as a gallery, c 1560, and has a is simpler 18C ceiling.

SB

Ham House

On the south side of the Thames, off the A307 at Petersham: National Trust, tel. 081 940 1950. Refreshments.

Ham House is perhaps the best surviving example in Britain of the court taste of the reign of Charles II, retaining to a remarkable extent the decoration and the lavish furnishings given to it in the 1670s. The house was first built in 1610 by Sir Thomas Vavasour, Knight Marshal to James I; it was a sumptuous suburban villa rather than a country house at the centre of a large landed estate. It was H-shaped, with the Hall in the cross-bar, and it was bought in 1637 by William Murray, 1st Earl of Dysart, a friend of Charles I and one of the circle of art lovers who adorned his court. He employed many leading craftsmen, notably the painter and tapestry designer Francis Cleyn, to redecorate the old-fashioned Jacobean interior, building the Great Staircase, and redecorating all the main apartments. On Lord Dysart's death, c 1654, his estates and title passed to his daughter, Elizabeth. A beautiful and ambitious woman, she had married Sir Lionel Tollemache, head of an old Suffolk family, but well before his death in 1669 she formed a relationship with the ruthless John Maitland, Earl of Lauderdale, a member of Charles II's CABAL government. In 1672 they were married, and Lauderdale moved into Ham House; soon afterwards, he became Duke of Lauderdale.

Lauderdale was a cultured man who had already been responsible for commissioning the King's new apartments at the Palace of Holyroodhouse, Edinburgh. The architect at Holyroodhouse, Sir William Bruce, was the Duchess's cousin, and he designed new rooms along the south front, filling up the space between the wings. This work was supervised by the gentleman architect William Samwell and was carried out in 1672–74. The exterior was relatively modest, but the interior was redecorated and furnished with the greatest extravagance, 'like a Great Prince's', as John Evelyn put it.

The Duke and Duchess had no children. After the Duke's death in 1682 the Duchess stayed on at Ham, and when she died in 1698, the house and grounds went to her son by her first marriage, Lyonel Tollemache, who became 3rd Earl of Dysart. The family made few major alterations to the house, and, most unusually, preserved the rich original furnishings almost complete. The Earls of Dysart held the house until 1935; in 1948 Sir Lyonel Tollemache presented it to the National Trust.

The house retains enough protected land around it to be insulated from suburbia and looks north to the tree-lined banks of the Thames. The **north front** looks over a walled forecourt, and is largely as Sir Thomas Vavasour built it, apart from the replacement of the original turreted skyline by a hipped roof and the installation of some sash windows. The splendid Doric portal takes you into the **Hall**. As built, this was a big one-storey room, but the Duke and Duchess cut out the centre of the ceiling, and it now appears as a two-storeyed room with a gallery around. It is hung with Dysart portraits at both levels. To the south are the **ground floor state rooms**; in the middle is the Marble Dining Room, and to either side, a suite of rooms in the grand 17C manner, made up of Drawing Room, Bedchamber and Closet. These seven rooms are moderate in size, but they retain many of the original furnishings of the 1670s. The fabrics have been re-woven: black and red hangings in the Duchess's bedchamber, yellow and red in the yellow bedchamber. Over the fireplace in the Marble Dining Room is the famous picture of Charles II being presented with the first pineapple grown in England. The **Chapel**, at the north end of the house is severely plain, a sharp contrast to the opulence of the living rooms.

The 1st Earl of Dysart's splendid **staircase** of c 1637 is hung mostly with 17C copies of Italian paintings, in particular those of Titian. The **Yellow Satin Room** and its Dressing Room, to the left of the landing, are early-19C rooms, decorated in 17C style (although it would take an expert eye to tell the difference). On the other side of the landing is the **Museum Room**, where examples from the rich collection of rare embroideries and other textiles are displayed protected from light and dust. From here visitors pass along the Hall **gallery**, noting Lely's magnificent double portrait of the rather louche-looking Duke and Duchess, to the **North Drawing Room**, with its white and gold panelling designed by Cleyn in the 1630s; the fireplace is flanked by extravagantly twisted columns (the pattern was believed to originate in Solomon's temple). The tiny **Green Closet**, is also of the 1630s, and is hung with miniatures and small, mostly Dutch School paintings. The **Long Gallery** has panelling of the 1630s, and a series of portraits of Charles II's court, mostly from Lely's studio. Over the centre of the South Front is the **Queen's suite**, an ante-chamber, bedchamber and closet prepared for a visit by Catherine of Braganza in 1680; the Bedchamber, now hung with 18C tapestries after Watteau, was converted into a drawing room in the 1790s. The ante-chamber retains its 300-year old damask wall-hangings, exceptionally well-preserved, with lacquered furniture of the 1670s. The **Library** remains lined with the bookcases installed in 1674. From here the visitor returns downstairs, and leaves via the restored 17C Kitchen.

Ham has extensive **gardens**, but the original design had been lost by the time the National Trust took responsibility for the house. It restored the parterres to the east and south of the house in 1975, following surviving plans and views, and using authentic planting. On the south front are grass squares, which in the 17C would have been set out with tubs and pots of plants. Beyond this is the 'Wilderness', an area set out in a symmetrical pattern of paths, divided by hornbeam hedges. The smaller, enclosed garden on the east side has lavender beds lined with box, and arbours of hornbeam.

SB

Hampton Court Palace

15m south west of Central London, (BR Hampton Court from Waterloo); Historic Royal Palaces, tel. 081 977 8441. Open daily 9.30–6 (Mon 10.15–6), closes 4.30 mid Oct–mid March. Gardens open 7–dusk. Refreshments.

Hampton Court is unmatched by any other house in England for historical, artistic and architectural interest. It stands on the north bank of the River Thames on land which belonged in the Middle Ages to the Knights Hospitaller, who leased the site in 1505 to Giles, Lord Daubeny, Henry VII's Chamberlain. He may have done some building before his death in 1508, but the man responsible for establishing the present character of the house was Thomas Wolsey, Archbishop of York and later Cardinal, who leased Hampton Court from the Hospitallers in 1514. Wolsey was the last and most magnificent of the worldly prelates who played so important a part in the management of the medieval English State. He became one of Henry VIII's chief advisers, and, using the revenues of the numerous ecclesiastical offices which he accumulated, lived in a style which provoked the resentment of his aristocratic contemporaries and, eventually, the King himself. In 1515 he began building a vast new house of brick at Hampton Court, where his guests were entertained in surroundings of a splendour parallelled only in the King's own palaces (in the often-quoted words of his contemporary John Skelton, 'The King's court should have the excellence/But Hampton Court hath the preeminence'); according to one contemporary account, 'every place did glitter with innumerable vessels of gold and silver. There were two hundred and fourscore beds, the furniture of most of them being silk, and all for the entertainment of strangers only'. But in 1528 Wolsey fell from favour, and conveyed the house to the King,

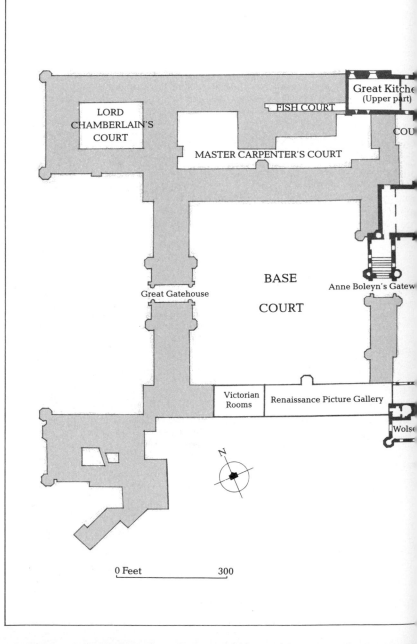

LORD CHAMBERLAIN'S COURT

FISH COURT

Great Kitchen (Upper part)

COU

MASTER CARPENTER'S COURT

BASE COURT

Great Gatehouse

Anne Boleyn's Gatew

Victorian Rooms

Renaissance Picture Gallery

Wolse

N

0 Feet   300

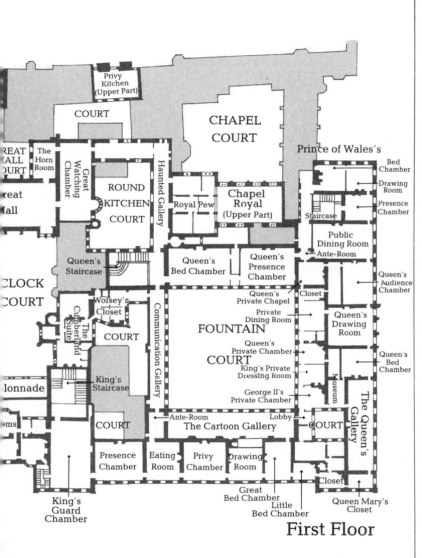

First Floor

Hampton Court Palace

who set about making further improvements, notably the rebuilding of the Hall and the extension of the main royal apartments in 1532–35. For the rest of his life, Henry VIII treated Hampton Court as one of the most important of his sixty or so houses, and it still bears his mark today.

Hampton Court remained one of the main residences of the English monarchy until the mid 18C. The park, to the north and east of the palace, was laid out by Charles II after 1660, but the buildings remained largely untouched until after the accession of William and Mary in 1688. With the example of Louis XIV's Versailles in mind, they asked Sir Christopher Wren, Surveyor of the King's Works, to draw up grandiose plans for a new palace on the site of the 16C buildings, of which only the Hall would be allowed to survive. These plans were set aside, partly on the grounds of cost, and Wren was then asked to plan a large, but architecturally less ambitious, set of state and private apartments for the King and Queen on the site of those built by Henry VIII. Work on the new buildings started in 1689, with the active involvement of Wren's deputy William Talman—who vainly attempted to get Wren dismissed after part of the building collapsed—but was interrupted by the death of Queen Mary in 1694 and was only resumed after the destruction by fire of the Palace of Whitehall in 1698. The interiors of the 'King's side' were completed by the time of William III's death (after falling from his horse in Hampton Court Park) in 1702, those on the 'Queen's side' following during the reigns of Queen Anne and George I; they were turned over to the use of the Prince and Princess of Wales (later George II and Queen Caroline) in 1716. Meanwhile the gardens fronting the new south and east ranges were laid out in the fashionable French-inspired formal style, with a semi-circular parterre probably designed by the Huguenot Daniel Marot, and splendid iron gates by another Huguenot, Jean Tijou. Important changes to the gardens were made by the royal gardeners George London and Henry Wise in the times of Queen Anne, and the last significant alterations to the interior of the palace took place in 1732, when William Kent created a set of apartments for George II's younger son the Duke of Cumberland out of some of the remaining 16C rooms.

George II was the last monarch to live at Hampton Court. In the reign of his grandson and successor, George III, the palace was largely turned over to 'grace and favour' apartments for royal officials, but the state rooms were kept up, and in 1838 they were opened to the public, and filled with Old Master paintings from the royal collection. The 16C parts of the palace were extensively but intelligently restored, starting in 1832, and continuing spasmodically through the 19C, and William III's state apartments were also restored after being partially destroyed by fire in 1986. They were re-opened to the public in 1992, and at the same time the opportunity was taken to re-hang the pictures and re-organise the visitors' route through the palace. At the time of writing (1993) work was beginning on the re-creation of the late-17C Privy Garden on the south front.

Most visitors approach Hampton Court from the west, and from here the early-16C origins of the palace are immediately apparent. Cardinal Wolsey's house consisted of a Base Court, made up of lodgings for guests and household officials, with another courtyard containing the Hall and the main residential apartments beyond it—the present Clock Court—and extensive kitchens and domestic offices arranged around smaller court-yards to the north; a Chapel was begun further to the east shortly before Wolsey fell from grace. The Base Court was entered through a massive five-storeyed **gatehouse**, like the keep of a medieval castle, but the two upper storeys were unfortunately lopped off in 1771–73, and in 1882 the walls were faced in bright red brick as part of a programme of restoration which also included the re-instatement of the stone pinnacles and ornamental brick chimneys which make so striking an impression from the west front. But otherwise Wolsey's **Base Court** remains much as he left it, with its walls of locally-made red brick, embellished with criss-cross patterns in blue brick, and stone-mullioned windows. On the further (east) side there is another turreted gatehouse (Anne Boleyn's Gateway) which remains substantially unaltered from Wolsey's time, save for the addition of an 18C cupola; note especially the terracotta roundels of Roman emperors on either side of the oriel window over the gateway, supplied in 1521 by Giovanni da Maiano—one of the first instances of Renaissance taste in an English house.

On the inner side of the gatehouse is an astronomical clock by Nicholas Oursian, introduced by Henry VIII in 1540. It gives its name to the **Clock Court**, the central courtyard of the palace, which is dominated by the high brick walls and pinnacles of Henry VIII's Hall (1532–34) to the north; this is placed on the first floor, over a vaulted undercroft, and is lit by large windows with Perpendicular Gothic tracery. Facing it, on the south side, is a screen of paired Ionic columns designed by Wren in 1698 to hide the irregular brick wall of Wolsey's south range and to act as a formal approach to William III's state apartments. There is another early-16C gatehouse on the east side of the courtyard, but it was altered and embellished by William Kent in 1732—an early example of the revived Gothic taste in Georgian England.

From the Clock Court visitors have a choice of six clearly defined routes. These encompass all the main interiors, and take about three hours to pursue if justice is to be done to the superb works of art on display. It makes sense to start with the **Tudor state apartments**, which are reached by a staircase in Anne Boleyn's Gateway. This leads into the Hall, high and spacious, with a splendid hammer-beam roof, one of the finest in England, by James Needham, Master Carpenter in the Office of Works; note the armorial devices and Renaissance detailing on the spandrels and pendants. Henry VIII amassed a collection of 2000 tapestries, the largest in Europe, and some of these remarkable works of art are displayed on the walls, with episodes from the Story of Abraham, woven in Brussels c 1540, on the longer walls, and The Triumph of Time over Fame, from the 'Triumphs of Petrarch' series (Brussels c 1510), first acquired by Wolsey, over the place where the high table once stood. This is lit by a bay window surmounted by a delicate stone fan vault. There are more early 16C tapestries, from the 'Triumphs of Petrarch' and other series, in the **Watching Chamber**, which is approached through the Horn Room, formerly the serving-place to the hall. The ceiling of the Watching Chamber was decorated in 1535–36 with a pattern of shallow wooden ribs and pendants, recently re-gilded; the original frieze has gone, and the excellent stained glass in the bay window was made by Thomas Willement in 1846.

A doorway to the south originally led into the rest of Henry VIII's state apartments, on the east side of the Clock Court, but these have been altered out of all recognition, and visitors now proceed through a tapestry-hung **gallery** built by Wolsey to link the house to the Chapel. At the entrance to the Chapel there are three large and impressive pictures commissioned by Henry VIII to commemorate and glorify his reign: one shows the embarkation of the King for the Field of the Cloth of Gold (1520), another the Field of the Cloth of Gold itself, and a third depicts the King, his third wife Jane Seymour, his daughters Mary and Elizabeth, and his son Edward (later Edward VI), with domestic and garden scenes in the background (note the man with a monkey on his shoulder). The vestibule to the **Royal Pew** contains two more excellent early 16C tapestries; the Pew itself was much altered in the early 18C, but still retains some of its early 16C ceiling decoration. From here there is a view down into the **Chapel**, begun by Wolsey and completed by Henry VIII. The wooden ceiling, of 1535–36, is extravagantly embellished with ribs, liernes and pendants, in imitation of earlier stone vaults like that of Christ Church Cathedral, Oxford, though with Renaissance-style putti carved on the pendants. But the woodwork, including the massive reredos by Grinling Gibbons, all dates from a refurbishment carried out for Queen Anne c 1711–12, and so too does the front of the Royal Pew, seen after descending into the body of the Chapel, and uncannily reminiscent of the proscenium arch of a Baroque theatre.

From the Chapel, visitors pass into a shadowy cloister running around two sides of the Round Kitchen Court, and little altered since Wolsey's time. This gives access to the unusually well-preserved, and equally well-displayed, **service quarters** of the 16C palace. Henry VIII's vaulted wine cellar survives intact under the Watching Chamber, and an exhibition on the complicated domestic workings of the Tudor palace can be seen in the former beer cellar under the Hall. The Tudor Kitchens, to the north of the Base Court and Clock Court, are now shown, as far as possible, as they would have been when a feast was in preparation in the time of Henry VIII, with convincing-looking replicas of the food consumed. The **Great Kitchen**, at the heart of the complex, was started by Wolsey, but was extended by Henry VIII in 1529, and still retains the huge original fireplaces in which meat was roasted, although there were alterations in the 17C and the 19C, when the open timber roof was restored to its original form. The Privy Kitchen, further east, dates from c 1570 and has been adapted as a coffee shop.

To appreciate the historical development of the palace, it is best to proceed now to the late-17C **King's Apartments**, created for William III in 1699–1702 under the supervision of William Talman and recently restored to something closely approaching their original state, with careful restorations of the furniture and fabrics where the originals no longer exist. The entrance is through the colonnade on the south side of the Clock Court, and from here the **King's Staircase** leads up to the state rooms, which are arranged in sequence on the south side of the Fountain Court, built by Wren on the site of Henry VIII's Cloister Court. The walls of the Staircase were painted with political allegories by Antonio Verrio in 1701–2; here, along with the usual Baroque cast of naked gods and goddesses perched on clouds, the King can be seen in the guise of Alexander the Great in the company of Hercules, his favourite hero. The excellent ironwork of the balustrade is by Jean Tijou. From the Guard Room, at the top of the stairs, the doors of the main rooms stretch east in *enfilade*, and from the windows there is a view out to the Privy Garden. The rooms are arranged in sequence, with the more public rooms coming first and, the private ones, to which only the most intimate associates of the King would be admitted, at the end. The first rooms are sparsely furnished, as they have always been, but there is good craftsmanship throughout, notably the superb wood carvings of fruit and flowers by Grinling Gibbons, many of them beautifully recarved after fire damage. Blue and white porcelain of the sort collected, and made fashionable, by William and Mary is placed over the fireplaces. The Presence Chamber contains a large and dull equestrian portrait of the King by Kneller, but this is put into the shade by the two huge Brussels tapestries from the 'Grotesque Triumphs' series acquired by Henry VIII in 1542, one of them showing the Triumph of Hercules and both adorned with the delicate Roman ornamental motifs known as *grotteschi*. Next comes the Eating Room, where the King dined in public, with pristine-looking Mortlake tapestries after the Raphael Cartoons on the walls. Next follow the Privy Chamber, with its original glass chandelier, the Withdrawing Room, and finally the King's two Bedchambers—one, with its original bed, for formal *levées*, and the other for sleeping in—and the Closet or study.

A staircase leads down to a group of modestly decorated rooms which formed part of **William III's private apartments**. They contain some of his furniture, in walnut and other woods, arranged as it would have been when he was in residence, and items from his picture collection, including works by Dutch and Italian masters, and, in the West Closet, Van Dyck's portrait of his mistress Margaret Lemon, lasciviously posed with one breast bare. An orangery links these rooms to the Private Drawing Room and Dining Room, the latter set out as for the dessert course of a private dinner party, with Kneller's paintings of statuesque ladies of Queen Mary's Court (the 'Hampton Court Beauties') on the walls.

The **Queen's Apartments** are arranged around the north and east sides of the Fountain Court. They are approached from the Queen's Staircase, painted by William Kent in 1734–35, with Honthorst's large painting of Charles I receiving Apollo and Diana on the west wall. The first rooms—the Guard Chamber and Presence Chamber—were decorated in the time of George I in 1716–18, and the bizarre, ponderous detailing (note especially the burlesque figures of Yeoman of the Guard on either side of the fireplace in the Guard Chamber) has been plausibly attributed to Sir John Vanbrugh. Orazio Gentileschi's 'Joseph and Potiphar's Wife', painted for Henrietta Maria, hangs in the Presence Chamber, which, like the Guard Chamber, looks out into the Fountain Court. The rest of the Queen's state rooms face east, and, like the King's apartments, are arranged in a formal sequence. The **Public Dining Room** has a marble chimneypiece carved by Grinling Gibbons, and on the walls are paintings by Mytens (Charles I and Henrietta Maria, with her resident dwarf, Jeffrey Hudson) and Sebastiano Ricci, including a large 'Christ in the house of Simon' in the manner of Veronese. Next comes the Audience Chamber, with another Mortlake tapestry after the Raphael Cartoons, and then the Drawing Room, with more unmemorable wall-paintings by Verrio (1702–5) and a superb view looking east over the semicircular parterre to the three radiating avenues and the central canal (the Long Water) laid out by Charles II in the 1660s: one of the few surviving examples in England of Baroque gardening on the grand scale. The Bedchamber contains the crimson-hung bed made in 1715 for the Princess of Wales (later Queen Caroline), and the allegorical ceiling painting is by Thornhill, with portraits of the Hanoverian royal family below the cornice. Beyond is a **Gallery** linking the Queen's to the King's apartments, lined with faded 18C Brussels tapestries after Le Brun, and containing large Delftware tulip vases made for William and Mary; the splendid marble chimneypiece is by Van Nost.

Behind the Queen's state apartments is a set of private apartments facing west onto the Fountain Court, and now forming part of the '**Georgian Rooms**' route, which begins at the garden entrance to the Fountain Court.

The private apartments are modest enough from a decorative point of view, save for some excellent wood carving by Gibbons over the fireplace of George II's Private Chamber. But they provide an interesting insight into the domestic life of the Hanoverian Court; note for instance the Queen's Bathing Closet, with its marble basin. There are also some important works of art on display, including de la Tour's 'St. Jerome' in the Private Chapel (completed for Queen Caroline in 1728), a set of panels by Pellegrini in the Dining Room, Terbrugghen's 'Viol Player' and Theophile Bigot's Caraveggesque 'Christ in the Carpenter's Shop' in George II's Private Chamber, and a series of paintings of saints by Domenico Fetti over the doors of all the rooms.

A doorway at the end of the private apartments leads into the **Cartoon Gallery** (1695), flanking the King's state apartments and overlooking the Fountain Court. It was designed to house the Raphael Cartoons bought by Charles I, but the originals (now in the Victoria and Albert Museum) have been replaced by late 17C copies; woodwork is by Gibbons, and there is a delicate marble chimneypiece by Van Nost. The **Communication Gallery**, which follows on the west side of the Fountain Court, is mainly distinguished by Lely's paintings of the sultry 'Windsor Beauties' of Charles II's dissolute Court. It leads to the Queen's Staircase, but visitors are channelled instead into a small room (**Wolsey's Closet**) which originally led off from the vanished presence chamber of Henry VIII's state apartments. The linenfold panelling, though old, was only introduced in the late 19C, but the elaborate ceiling with its Renaissance decoration, and the Mannerist paintings of the Passion and Resurrection of Christ (by an unknown artist) appear to date from the 1530s. Beyond lies the **Cumberland Suite**, on the east side of the Clock Court, decorated by William Kent in 1732. The architectural detailing is distinctly odd, especially in the first of three rooms (the Outer Chamber) with its neo-Gothic ceiling. Paintings in the suite include Annibale Carracci's 'Allegory of Truth and Time', Allori's 'Judith with the Head of Holofernes', Vouet's 'Diana', four panels of the Story of Psyche by Luca Giordano, Ricci's 'Continence of Scipio', and Domenichino's 'St. Agnes' (in the former bed alcove of the last room).

The last route—the Wolsey Rooms and Renaissance Picture Gallery—takes in some first-floor rooms on the south side of the Clock Court and Base Court. The **Wolsey Rooms** date from the 1520s, and became part of the Queen's Lodgings during the reign of Henry VIII. Some of the rooms (under restoration at the time of writing, 1993) have linenfold panelling and plaster ceilings like that of Henry's Watching Chamber; the pictures on display include one by Mytens of Charles I as Prince of Wales, some early views of Hampton Court, including a birds-eye view by Leonard Knyff showing the east parterre as laid out by Daniel Marot, and Robert Streater's view of Boscobel House, Shropshire (qv.), the hiding-place of Charles II after the Battle of Worcester.

The **Renaissance Gallery**, which follows, contains some of the finest pictures in the Royal Collection, and for the lover of art would in itself justify a visit to Hampton Court. They include, in the first room: Gheeraerts 'Portrait of an unknown Woman', Girolamo de Treviso 'Four Evangelists stoning the Pope' (commissioned by Henry VIII), and Holbein's portrait of Johannes Frobenius; second room: Tintoretto 'Venetian Senator' and Jacopo Bassano 'The Good Samaritan'; third room: Lorenzo Lotto's portrait of the collector Andrea Odoni, Giulio Romano's of Isabella d'Este, Bronzino's 'Lady in Green', Correggio's 'St. Catherine', a Virgin and Child by Andrea del Sarto, and Jacopo Bassano's 'Jacob's Journey' and 'Adoration of the Shepherds'; fourth room: Palma Vecchio 'A Sybil', Raphael 'Portrait of a Boy', Correggio 'Holy Family', and Parmigianino's 'Portrait of a Boy' and 'Minerva'; fifth room: Mabuse 'Children of Christian II of Denmark', Quentin Matsys 'Erasmus', Joos van Cleve 'Self Portrait' and 'Portrait of the Artist's Wife', Hans Baldung Grien 'Portrait of a Young Man', Pieter Breughel the Elder 'Massacre of the Innocents' (but with the goriest details painted out in the early 17C), and Cranach's 'Judgement of Paris' and 'Lucretia'. Two rooms beyond are furnished in the manner of a 19C 'grace and favour' apartment.

Having seen the interiors of Hampton Court, visitors should proceed through the Clock Court and Fountain Court to the east front. The **Fountain Court** is built of brick, with Portland stone dressings and a cloister on the ground floor (note the way in which the first floor is held up on segmented arches placed behind its round arches fronting the courtyard). The **east front**, clearly influenced by Versailles, does not quite live up to the grandeur of its surroundings, largely because of the lack of an effective central feature; there are three gaping holes under the engaged temple-front in the middle, and the skyline would have benefited from the addition of some gesticulating figures to add a note of Baroque *brio*. But the craftsmanship is of a very high quality, with excellent brickwork and carved stonework, including Caius Gabriel Cibber's 'Hercules triumphing over Envy' (1694–96) in the pediment. To the north is the indoor Tennis Court, still used for the purpose for which it was first built by Henry VIII, and beyond is the **Maze**, laid out in the 1690s. The Lion Gates give access to Bushy Park, with formal avenues of the same period.

The semicircular **parterre** in front of the east façade has been much altered, but it still retains its formal character, and an iron screen, by Tijou, still divides it from the Home Park to the east. There is even finer ironwork by the same craftsman in the screen dividing the **Privy Garden**, on the south side of the palace, from the terrace along the river Thames; at the west end is a brick **Banqueting House** of c 1700, with wall paintings by Verrio and woodwork by Gibbons, overlooking a 20C recreation of a sunken formal garden. The long south front is of the same restrained character as the east front, but at the west end the regular late 17C elevations give way to the more chaotic appearance of the remaining parts of the Tudor palace. A vine planted in 1768 can be seen in a conservatory here, and in an adjoining **Orangery** are hung perhaps the finest of all the paintings at Hampton Court: Mantegna's nine panels of the 'Triumphs of Caesar', bought by Charles I in 1629, and preserved in the Royal Collection ever since. These superb paintings, recently restored, are among the greatest masterpieces of early Renaissance art, and provide a suitably stately conclusion to a visit to Hampton Court.

GCT

Kenwood House

Hampstead Lane: English Heritage, tel. 081 348 1286. Open Apr–Sept daily 10–6; Oct–Mar daily 10–4. Refreshments.

Kenwood is a white, moderately-sized neo-classical mansion on a wooded hillside, facing south over a beautiful park. There has been a house here at 'Cane Wood' since about 1616, but the present building is essentially the work of Robert Adam and his fellow-Scotsman, William Murray, 1st Earl of Mansfield. When he bought Kenwood, in 1754, Mansfield was already Attorney-General. Two years later, he became Lord Chief Justice, becoming one of the most important figures in the development of English law. In 1764 he commissioned Adam to remodel the early 18C house he had bought. Lord Mansfield spent a peaceful retirement here, dying in 1793. The 2nd Earl added wings to the entrance front and service buildings. The Mansfield family retained the house and about 220 acres until the 1920s. There was then a public outcry at proposals to sell the estate for development, an appeal was launched, and the land bought in stages, for the nation. The house and the last 74 acres were bought from the Mansfield family by Edward Cecil Guinness, 1st Earl of Iveagh, in 1925. He furnished the house, and installed his superb collection of paintings here, and on his death in 1927 he left it to trustees for the nation. It is now run by English Heritage.

A wooded drive leads into the estate from Hampstead Lane, and London is left behind. The **entrance façade** is dominated by Adam's Ionic portico; the white brick wings to either side, housing the Music and Dining Rooms, were added by George Saunders for the 2nd Earl of Mansfield. From the cool **Entrance Hall**, hung with 18C paintings, the visitor goes through the East Staircase Hall and the Marble Hall, the latter containing paintings by Boucher. On the left from here is the **Dining Room**, where Lord Iveagh's greatest Old Masters hang; Vermeer's 'Guitar Player', a fine portrait by Hals (c 1633), Van Dyck's superbly aristocratic portrait of the Earl of Richmond, and above all, one of the greatest of Rembrandt's self-portraits (1665).

Through a pillared ante-room, you enter Lord Mansfield's **Library** (1767–88), which occupies one of two one-storey wings which Adam added to either end of the Garden front (the other houses the Orangery). This is one of the finest Adam rooms in existence. It is a long rectangle in plan, with an apse at either end screened by two columns. The low barrel-vaulted ceiling is a masterpiece of 18C plasterwork, by Joseph Rose. Returning along the south front rooms, you are in the early 18C house. Passing through Lord Mansfield's Dressing Room, you enter the long **Parlour**. Most of the furniture designed by Adam for the house has been dispersed, but a sideboard and wine-coolers have been bought back and are here, together with Dutch and English paintings, amongst them Gainsborough's 'Going to Market' and works by Turner ('Fishermen upon a Lee Shore in Squally Weather', 1802) and Cuyp ('Dordrecht Evening').

Lady Mansfield's Dressing Room and the Housekeeper's Room follows, the latter really a lobby leading into the **Orangery**. This is a plain room, now used for concerts. It houses Van Dyck's full-length portrait of Henrietta of Lorraine, and contrasting works by Gainsborough: a most refined portrait of Countess Howe, one of Lady Brisco (1776), in his later, freer manner, a 'wooded landscape with hounds coursing a fox' (c 1784–85), and one of his rural 'fancy pictures' of boys with fighting dogs. The Lobby and **Music Room**, leading north out of the Orangery, are hung with excellent 18C English portraits. Those of 'Lady Hamilton at a spinning wheel' and 'Anne, Countess of Albemarle with her son' by Romney, 'Mrs Musters as Hebe' (1782), 'Kitty Fisher as Cleopatra' (1759), and 'The Brummell children' by Reynolds, command especial attention.

Kenwood's **park** is part of Hampstead Heath, into which it is now mostly merged. The area around the house was landscaped from designs by

Humphry Repton for Lord Mansfield, with a little lake in the valley below, and views across central London far beyond. English Heritage stage open-air concerts here in the summer, and are in the process of restoring the 18C landscape in a way which is compatible with its enormous popularity as a resort for local people.

SB

Kew Palace ('The Dutch House') and Queen Charlotte's Cottage

Open Mar–Oct daily 11–5.30;. Historic Royal Palace Agency (main office) tel. 081 781 9750. Kew Palace is inside the Royal Botanic Garden and visitors have to pay the general admission fee for these, as well as for the Palace.

The Royal Botanic Gardens at Kew are world-renowned, but most people are probably less well aware that these 300 famous acres began as the grounds of a series of royal residences. There have been royal country houses in the Kew and Sheen area since the 14C, most importantly the great Richmond Palace itself on Richmond Green, most of which was demolished under the Commonwealth. There were several royal parks in the area, and the Old Deer Park had a Keeper's Lodge, with grounds of its own covering roughly the western half of the present Royal Botanic Gardens. Richmond Lodge, as it became known, was rebuilt by the Duke of Ormonde in the early 18C; reverting to the Crown, it was given by George II to his wife, Queen Caroline, as a private retreat. Queen Caroline commissioned William Kent to landscape the grounds. Next, in 1730, her detested son, Frederick, Prince of Wales, bought the neighbouring house and estate, and commissioned Kent to rebuild it, renaming it the White House. The Prince also leased another neighbouring estate with a fine 17C house—the so-called Dutch House—to provide extra accommodation.

The White House and Dutch House were the Prince and Princess's favourite residences; they landscaped the grounds, commissioning Sir William Chambers to design superb garden-buildings. After the Prince's death in 1751 his widow remained here; her son, the future George III, spent a happy childhood at Kew. He later demolished Richmond Lodge and joined the grounds to those of the White House, employing 'Capability' Brown to re-design them. In 1781 he finally bought the freehold of the Dutch House. In 1791 he began building a larger palace, designed by James Wyatt, on the riverside 200 yards from the Dutch House, and in 1802 he pulled down the White House, in anticipation of the new Kew Palace being finished. Alas, he had already been afflicted with the nervous disorder, porphyria, which to his subjects was indistinguishable from lunacy. Work on the castellated palace stopped, never to be resumed. George IV had it demolished in 1827–28, using many of the materials for his works at Buckingham Palace and Windsor. The Dutch House—now known as Kew Palace—is thus the sole survivor of four royal residences here. In 1841 Queen Victoria gave most of the royal grounds at Kew to the Royal Botanic Society.

The Dutch House was built in 1631 by a City merchant, Samuel Fortrey. It is an oblong block of three storeys plus an attic, in fine rubbed brickwork, with shaped Dutch gables from which it probably derived its nickname. It is one of a group of fine houses in the 'artisan mannerist' style of the 1620s and '30s, built on the outskirts of London by rich City men (cf. Boston Manor and Forty Hall). Various internal alterations were made by George III and Queen Charlotte, but externally the house remains very much as first built. It is a perfect exemplar of a comfortable gentry house, and by itself would have been much too small for the royal family. It is now furnished with fine furniture and paintings from the royal collections.

The Dining Room still retains some elements of the original 1631 decoration. The King's Breakfast Room, behind, has fine 17C panelling moved from elsewhere, and furniture and pictures of the same date. Ascending the pretty 18C staircase, visitors tour the first floor. The Queen's Drawing Room has a fine 1631 fireplace, and 18C furniture. Queen Charlotte died in the Queen's Bedchamber in 1818, in the chair seen here. Back on the ground floor, the Library contains personal memorabilia of George III (including his fishing tackle), while the Waiting Room has displays on the history of Kew and the House of Hanover, and a superb architectural model of William Kent's design for yet another (unbuilt) palace at Richmond. The paintings in the house include three very fine views of Florence by Thomas Patch, and good portraits by Ramsay, Zoffany, Benjamin West, Reynolds and the German artist Ziesenis. Behind it is an attractive 17C style formal garden, laid out in 1969.

The Royal Botanic Gardens contain fascinating 18C buildings, such as the famous Pagoda and the Orangery, both built by Chambers for Princess Augusta in 1761. At the far (south west) end of the Gardens is Queen Charlotte's Cottage. This pretty 'cottage ornée' began as the centrepiece of the royal menagerie; it was enlarged to its present size c 1800. It was only ever intended for picnics and garden parties, never as a serious residence. There is a kitchen, an entrance hall, two staircases, and two elegant reception rooms. That on the ground floor is all hung with prints, many of them after Hogarth. That on the first floor is painted with trellis and climbing plants, and has pretty chinoiserie bamboo furniture.

SB

Marble Hill House

Richmond Rd (A305), Twickenham: English Heritage, tel. 081 892 5115.
Open Apr–Sept daily 10–6; Oct–Mar daily 10–4. Refreshments.

Marble Hill is a Palladian villa, a white, cube-shaped building standing in 66 acres of parkland on the Thames, almost opposite Ham House in Richmond (qv.). It was built in 1724–29 by an intelligent and resourceful woman, Henrietta Howard. She was the daughter of Sir Henry Hobart of Blickling Hall, Norfolk (qv.), and, orphaned at the age of 13, was brought up in the household of the Howard Earls of Suffolk. In 1706 she married Charles Howard, later the 9th Earl. They went up in the world by both obtaining positions in the court of the House of Hanover (he in George I's household, she as a Lady of the Bedchamber to the Princess of Wales), but it was not a happy marriage. By 1720 Henrietta had become the Prince of Wales' official mistress. It was not a very passionate relationship, but in 1723 the Prince gave her £11,500, and she began to think about building a house of her own.

She sought the advice of two other members of the Prince's circle, Lord

Ilay (later Duke of Argyll), and the 9th Earl of Pembroke. The design was probably the result of collaboration between Colen Campbell and Pembroke, and the house was executed by Roger Morris, a successful builder and notable architect in his own right. After the death of Lady Suffolk in 1767, the house passed through a variety of private owners, until it was bought by the London County Council in 1902, primarily to protect the park. It was carefully restored in 1965–66.

The house is a compact cube, three storeys high, five bays wide, and with a pyramidal roof; it gains from being quite free-standing, without the extensive outbuildings which country houses usually trail around them. The entrance is on the north side, and behind it, in the centre of the river front, is a square pillared hall, flanked by two smaller rooms one of which, the Breakfast Parlour, houses portraits of Mrs Howard and her circle. The main rooms are on the piano nobile, and the most beautiful of them is the Great Room, facing the river. This is a 24ft cube, with a high coved ceiling,

The north entrance front of Marble Hill House, Lady Suffolk's Thamesside Palladian villa, 1724–27

and carved decoration in the manner of William Kent, all in white and gold. The original contents of the room had been dispersed, but painstaking work by English Heritage has resulted in the purchase of one of the original side-tables, and three splendid views of Roman ruins by Pannini, installed here in the 18C, sold in 1900, and now restored. There are also Van Dyck 'studio' portraits of Charles I and Henrietta Maria. To the left is Lady Suffolk's Bedchamber; the decoration, including the screen of Ionic columns is mostly original. Here, as in Miss Hotham's Bedchamber (named after Lady Suffolk's companion and heiress) and the Damask Bedchamber, efforts are being made to furnish the rooms with furniture and pictures of the period when it was built, including works by Philip Mercier, Hubert Gravelot and Richard Wilson. The Dressing Room (symmetrical to Lady Suffolk's room) houses the Northey suite of chairs and settee with fine petit-point covers.

The rooms on the top floor (not always open) are lower and more intimate in scale; they had to be largely reconstructed after a serious outbreak of dry rot was discovered in the 1950s. The Gallery which runs along one side was a place for displaying pictures and admiring the view; the Plaid Room, Wrought Room and Green Room were named in Lady Suffolk's inventories from the materials with which they were lined. The grounds were laid out for Lady Suffolk, with little temples and buildings and are now a public park.

SB

The Octagon, Orleans House

Near the Thames in Twickenham, off Richmond Road (A305): London Borough of Richmond, tel. 081 982 0221. Open Tues–Sat 1–5.30 (4.30 Oct–Mar); Sun, Easter, Spring and Summer BH 2–5.30 (4.30 Oct–Mar).

The Octagon is the remaining fragment of one of the riverside villas which lined the Thames west of London in the 18C—but what a fragment! A sober brick house was built here by James Johnston, Secretary for Scotland, in 1710. In 1720 he added the magnificent Octagon Room to the designs of James Gibbs. In 1815–17 the house was occupied by Louis Philippe, Duc d'Orleans, and later King of France. It later fell on hard times, and was sold for demolition in 1927, but the Octagon and an adjacent wing were saved by the Hon. Mrs Ionides. She left it to the Borough of Twickenham in 1962, with her collection of views of Richmond and Twickenham. The wing was converted into a gallery and there is a varied programme of exhibitions, including local history displays using Mrs Ionides' collection.

The Octagon itself is of superb brickwork, with Doric pilasters and stone dressings. The interior is a single high, domed space, wonderfully richly decorated and light, with Corinthian pilasters and superb stucco decoration on walls and dome, by the Swiss-Italians Artari and Bagutti. Gesturing women recline on top of the marble chimneypiece, with a great stucco frame above, and other naked figures disport themselves over the pediment of the doorway. This is as rich a Baroque interior as can be seen in Britain, and calls to mind the palaces of Vienna and Rome.

SB

Osterley Park

Access from Thornbury Road, north of the Great West Road (A4) in
Hounslow: National Trust, tel. 081 560 3918. Open Apr–Oct Wed–Sat
1–4.30, Sun, BH Mon 11–5, closed Good Fri. Refreshments.

Osterley stands in majestic isolation in its park, between the M4 and the
Great West Road. It is most famous for the magnificent state rooms designed
by Robert Adam but it was first built c 1575 by Sir Thomas Gresham, banker
and founder of the Royal Exchange. Little but the shape of the house
remains from his time. In the later 17C it belonged to Nicholas Barbon, the
most notorious property developer of his age, who made extensive alterations c 1683–98. In 1711 it was bought by Francis Child, a City banker, and
more remodelling took place for him and his sons. In 1761 Adam presented
designs for the house to Francis Child III's grandson, another Francis, but
they were not accepted, and Francis died in 1763. Adam presented revised
designs to his brother and successor, Robert Child II, and work lasted from
c 1763–80. The house passed by marriage to the 5th Earl of Jersey in 1804;
in 1949 the 9th Earl gave it to the National Trust.

Osterley is a big square building around a courtyard, in warm red brick
with stone dressings. Three of the façades are quite plain and severe, with
rows of sash windows. The east side of the courtyard was taken down by
Adam and a giant 'transparent' **Ionic portico** put in its place, so that the
courtyard is, in effect, open on this side. The one feature which suggests
the house's Elizabethan origins is the square turrets at the four corners, with
little ogee lead caps added by Barbon or by the Child family (it is not known
which) in a conscious reference to the house's Elizabethan origins.

The visitor ascends a broad flight of steps to Adam's tremendous portico
and goes across the courtyard (which is at first-floor level). The **Hall** is in
cool shades of white and grey, with big semicircular recesses at either end,
and fine plasterwork of c 1766. The North Passage leads to the Breakfast
Room, probably of the 1750s, ie, pre-Adam. Next door, the Library of
c 1766–73 has 'architectural' bookcases, with Ionic pilasters, in Adam's
earlier, more structural manner. The walls have inset paintings by Zucchi
and Cipriani. Going back along the corridor, the visitor reaches the North
Staircase, with the original lamps and iron balustrade. The octagonal
ceiling painting is a copy after one by Rubens of the Apotheosis of the Duke
of Buckingham, bought by Sir Francis Child, but destroyed by fire in 1949.

The Child family's apartments are on the second floor, and date from the
mid 18C, before Adam's involvement. **Mrs Child's Dressing Room** has a
particularly elaborate overmantel by John Linnell. The bed in the Taffeta
Bedroom was designed by Adam. Returning to the main floor, the Eating
Room has its original furniture with graceful lyre-back chairs designed by
Adam in 1767, arranged along the walls as they would have been originally.
The walls are filled with panels of plasterwork, and painted scenes of ruins
by Zucchi. The decoration is in white on green and pink, and there are
Bacchic emblems on the ceiling.

The **Long Gallery**, running the whole length of the west front, was
finished in 1759; Sir William Chambers may have had a hand in the design.
The decoration is simple, in yellow and white, as a background for the
collection of paintings, a representative selection of Georgian taste, with
landscapes of English and Italian scenes, and a number of mythological

paintings and portraits. The girandoles (or candle-holders) and pier-glasses here are to Adam's design, as, probably, are the great sofas at either end.

From the far end of the Gallery, the visitor enters the south wing. The **Drawing Room** is the most sumptuous in the house, 'worthy of Eve before the Fall' as Horace Walpole rather oddly put it. It has green silk damask on the walls, and an ornate coffered ceiling, inspired by Wood's *Ruins of Palmyra* (1753). The Moorfields carpet was designed by Adam to match the ceiling, and much of the furniture is by him also, including the magnificent pair of commodes, veneered in harewood. Next comes the **Tapestry Drawing Room**, designed by Adam to house a set of Gobelin tapestries, representing the 'Loves of the Gods', designed by Boucher and Neilson, and dated 1775. The chairs, designed by Adam, have Gobelin covers en suite with the tapestries. The State Bedchamber has a spectacular domed bed, again designed by Adam. The last major room seen is the **Etruscan Dressing Room**, dismissed by Horace Walpole as 'a profound tumble into the Bathos. It is going out of a palace into a potter's field'; the painted decoration by Borgnis is deliberately flat in manner, inspired by Greek vases (a style then believed to be Etruscan), a manner developed by Adam late in his career.

Outside, the brick U-shaped stable block is still largely Elizabethan. The landscaped **gardens** have ornamental buildings of the 18C. Adam's Garden House of c 1780 is semicircular in plan, with five Venetian windows. The Temple of Pan is earlier, probably by Chambers, and has a long low Tuscan portico. South and east of the house, a series of serpentine lakes were made by damming a stream; further upstream, and now cut off from the park by the M4 and inaccessible, in melancholy isolation, is a splendid bridge designed by Adam, with one big segmental arch, and massively rusticated masonry, with great carved heads on the keystones.

SB

Pitshanger Manor

Mattocks Lane, off Uxbridge Road/Ealing Broadway (A4020): London Borough of Ealing, tel. 081 567 1227. Open all year Tues–Sat 10–5, Sun afternoons in July and Aug, closed at Christmas, New Year and Easter.

In the 18C and early 19C, many villages around London were studded with modest villas, rural retreats from the city. Pitshanger Manor is one of the most interesting of these houses, for it was built by Sir John Soane (1753–1837), one of the most original of English architects, for himself. In 1792 he bought 12 Lincoln's Inn Fields in London (now part of Sir John Soane's Museum), and in 1800 he bought Pitshanger from a City merchant, Thomas Gurnell. He knocked down the original house and built a new one, retaining a wing built by Gurnell to the designs of George Dance in 1768. Soane hoped that his two sons would follow him as architects, and that Pitshanger would provide a setting for their training. But by 1810 these hopes were fading, and he sold the house, moving to 12–13 Lincoln's Inn Fields (the latter bought in 1808). For most of the 19C the Manor was the home of the five daughters of Spencer Perceval, the Prime Minister assassinated in 1812. In 1901 it was bought by the local authority for use as a library, and extended in a fairly sensitive way. Since 1985 it has been admirably restored and put to museum use by the Borough of Ealing.

Pitshanger is quite a small house, but Soane made it seem monumental. The main block is of stock brick, three bays wide and two storeys high. On the left is the Dance wing of 1768, and on the right a plain, low 19C wing. The façade has arched windows between engaged Ionic columns, a motif used by Robert Adam at Kedleston (Derbys, qv.) in 1765, and ultimately deriving from the Arch of Constantine in Rome. As at 12–13 Lincoln's Inn Fields, Soane created intimate, domestic rooms, decorated in his own dramatic and original neo-classical style. The original colour schemes have recently been brilliantly restored in a number of rooms. The narrow Entrance Hall is tunnel-vaulted; originally the colour scheme would have been darker, with marbling and bronze-colouring. On the right the Breakfast Room has a shallow dome supported by caryatids in the corners, the walls in characteristically strong colours. This opens into the Library, with a shallow groined vault, bookcases and mirror-lined niches. The Drawing Room is plainer, with incised decoration in the ceiling; it once opened into a Conservatory. In the Dance wing, Soane redecorated the Eating Room in blues and greens, with fluted surrounds to the windows and niche; the extension of the room was tactfully added in 1901. The Drawing Room, upstairs, has delicate arabesque and fan ornament on the ceiling. In the basement of the Soane block, the Monk's Dining Room housed some of his collections of sculpture and architectural fragments, in a consciously eclectic and picturesque setting—hence the curious mixture of decorative styles. In the north wing is a display of Martinware pottery, formerly made in Southall.

The grounds, now Walpole Park, retain considerable elements of the landscaping carried out for Soane in 1800 by John Haverfield of Kew. The lake is now a sunken garden, but Soane's bridge at its north end remains, as does a gateway and a lodge designed by him.

SB

The Queen's House

By the National Maritime Museum, Greenwich, tel. 081 858 4422. Open Mon–Sat 10–6 (10–5 in winter), Sun 12–6 (2–5 in winter), closed Dec 24, 25, 26. Refreshments.

The Queen's House was the first building in the British Isles to be entirely conceived and designed in accordance with the principles of the Italian Renaissance. In the 16C there was a big palace by the riverside at Greenwich, called Plaisance or Placentia. It was first built by Humphrey, Duke of Gloucester in the early 15C. Henry VII made many alterations, and it was much favoured by Henry VIII and Queen Elizabeth I. It was a rambling complex of brick and stone buildings, in appearance rather like St James's Palace, occupying the site of the two lower blocks of the Royal Naval College, and the court between them. To the south there was a tiltyard and gardens, and then Greenwich Park rising up the hill. The Queen's House was built on the south edge of the palace enclosure, between the gardens and the park, so that it looked over the roofs of the Tudor palace. James I's wife, Anne of Denmark, commissioned it from Inigo Jones, who had travelled widely in Italy, and was attached to the household of Henry, Prince of Wales, as a tutor and a designer of costumes and settings for masques. The house seems to have been intended mainly for court entertainments and receptions. The oddest thing about it was its plan; it was H-shaped, with one wing on each side of the main road from Deptford to Woolwich, linked by a bridge-room at first-floor level. Queen Anne died in 1619 when the walls had only reached first-floor level, and King James halted the work. The unfinished walls were thatched to protect them from the weather, and the building remained in this state until 1629, when Charles I decided to complete it for Queen Henrietta Maria, Jones remaining the architect. It was finished c 1638, but may never have been fully fitted out before the Civil War.

In 1661–62, after the Restoration, Charles II had the house adapted and altered for his own use. Two more bridge-rooms were added, giving the house a square plan and forming two suites of state rooms at first floor level—a king's side and a queen's side. The 1660s also saw the demolition of the old Tudor palace, and the start of the long development, of what eventually became the Royal Hospital (now the Royal Naval College). In 1690 the house became the official residence of the Ranger of Greenwich Park, and in 1699 the road through the house was diverted. It continued to be the Ranger's residence until the early 19C, when it was succeeded by Ranger's House, Blackheath (qv.). In 1807 the Queen's House became a school for the sons of naval servicemen; Daniel Asher Alexander added the long colonnades and wings on either side in 1807–16, making it the centre of a large group of buildings. The house was comprehensively restored by the Office of Works after the school closed down in 1933, and in 1937 the whole group was opened to the public as the National Maritime Museum. In 1990, the Queen's House re-opened after another renovation, designed to put an end to its rather neutral, museum-like atmosphere, and to re-create the interiors on the first floor as they were in the 1660s, when Henrietta Maria lived here. New furniture and textiles were made to supplement the Museum's collection of 17C furniture, to match what was here as closely as possible. The ground floor rooms remain a picture gallery, housing the best of the Museum's unrivalled collection of early Dutch and English sea-paintings.

The house is a severely plain block, 160ft by 120ft. On the **north side** (towards the river) is a horseshoe-shaped staircase up to the terrace. The **south or park front** is enlivened by a beautiful Ionic loggia at first floor level; both features may derive from Sangallo's villa for Lorenzo de Medici at Poggio a Caiano near Florence. At the centre of the north block is the **Hall**, a 40ft cube. The original white and gold paint of the balcony has darkened to green and gold, but this does not compromise its perfection. The Italian artist Orazio Gentileschi and his daughter Artemisia were commissioned by Charles I to produce canvases to decorate the ceiling, but they were later removed and are now at Marlborough House, London. The space is now filled with laser-generated copies, with the missing areas of painting sketched in—an inventive but controversial solution. After the Hall, the most dramatic space is the '**Tulip Staircase**', so named from the motif in its wrought-iron handrail—it is a circular cantilevered stair, a brilliant feat of stonework and the first of its kind in England.

The full results of the recent renovation are seen on the first floor. The two sets of apartments are furnished and presented as a King's and a Queen's suite. Starting with the **east ('King's') side**, the Presence Chamber retains its original elaborately carved wooden pilasters, and now has magnificent 17C portraits. The adjoining closet room has a fireplace newly made from one of Jones' drawings. Next comes one of Webb's bridge-rooms added in the 1660s, with a richly decorated plaster ceiling, and Lely's superb set of portraits of the 'Flagmen of Lowestoft', the naval commanders involved in the Battle of Lowestoft (1665), with Prince Rupert of the Rhine over the fireplace. Next comes an Ante-Chamber with restored grained panelling, and then the King's Bedroom, where the balustrade, bed, stools and chairs have all been reproduced to 17C designs. Adjacent to this are the simply furnished Closet and servants' rooms. Here you are on the south side, and Jones's **loggia** gives views over Greenwich Park.

The central Bridge-Room leads back to the Hall gallery, and then to the **Queen's or west side suite**. The Queen's Presence Chamber has a deeply-coved ceiling, with the grotesque paintings in the cove probably by de Critz. The walls are hung with magnificent Brussels tapestries, and at the far end a dais, throne-chair and canopy of state have been set up. The next room has another new fireplace made to a Jones design, and 17C paintings of Greenwich. The West Bridge-Room and the adjacent Ante-Room have striking new textile hangings and furniture; the dazzling colours are disconcertingly strong when you are used to seeing faded antique objects in this kind of setting, but they come as a salutary reminder that all historic interiors were once new. Finally, there is the Queen's Bedroom, again with a balustrade, chairs and a state bed with silver hangings and ostrich plumes. From here you descend the south staircase to the ground-floor gallery rooms.

SB

Ranger's House

On Chesterfield Walk, on the south west side of Greenwich Park: English Heritage, tel. 081 853 0035. Open Good Fri or Apr 1–Sept daily 10–6. Oct–Maundy Thur or Mar 31 daily 10–4, closed Dec 24, 25.

Ranger's House is a handsome brick villa of the early 18C. It was built c 1700–20 by Admiral Francis Hosier on a small plot in between the old royal park at Greenwich and the ancient area of common land known as Blackheath. He was a successful commander in the War of Spanish Succession, and also a keen investor, who made a fortune dealing in cargoes as well as from prize money. After his death in 1727, it was let to the Stanhope family. Philip Stanhope, 4th Earl of Chesterfield and author of the famous Letters to his natural son, lived here 1748–73; he added the big Gallery on the south side to house some of his Old Master paintings. In 1807, the house was leased by the Dowager Duchess of Brunswick, sister of George III. Thereafter, the house became the official residence of the Rangers of Greenwich Park, until 1897, when it was bought by London County Council. It has had a chequered career in this century, but since 1973 it has housed the Suffolk Collection of paintings, originally hung at Charlton Park, Wiltshire (qv.).

The main front faces south west. The seven-bay centre, with its high proportions and warm orange brickwork, is Admiral Hosier's original house. The big one-storey wing on the right is Lord Chesterfield's Gallery, added in 1750 and probably designed by Isaac Ware, who had recently designed Chesterfield House in Mayfair for him (since demolished). The balancing wing on the left, containing servants' rooms, was added in the 1780s. The beautiful wrought-iron gates, of the 1770s, were brought here from Mount Clare, Roehampton, by the LCC. Admiral Hosier's house is simple and compact, with six moderately-sized oblong rooms on each floor. The Stone Hall, named from its flooring, is furnished in spartan style, and has portraits from the studios of Van Dyck and Lely. The Dining Room, ahead, remains as redecorated by Lord Chesterfield c 1749. There are fine 18C portraits from the Suffolk collection, a studio copy of a Titian Madonna and a full-length of Maria Maddalena, Grand Duchess of Tuscany, by Sustermans. The Little Dressing Room, next door to this, retains its original panelling. On the right is the Green Silk Damask Parlour, recently lined with a damask copied from a material of c 1715; it was the Admiral's main sitting room. It now houses portraits of the Stuart court, by Lely and William Wissing, and some fine early 18C furniture.

The Gallery is a complete contrast in its scale, lightness and grandeur. The room is dominated by the Jacobean portraits from the Suffolk Collection, some of the finest of their date to survive anywhere. The most important are the group of nine, all wearing magnificent Court costume, attributed to William Larkin (d 1619). There are portraits of the 3rd and 4th Earls of Dorset (of the Sackville family, of Knole in Kent, qv.). Then there are seven portraits of women connected to the Howard Earls of Berkshire or to the Cecil Earls of Exeter. This group may have been painted together to celebrate the wedding of Thomas, 1st Earl of Berkshire, to Lady Elizabeth Cecil in 1614, although neither bride nor groom is represented here.

The first floor rooms retain most of their original panelling and joinery. Five of the rooms now house historic musical instruments, from the collection of Arnold Dolmetsch, a pioneer in the study of early music and an important maker of instruments on loan from the Horniman Museum, Forest Hill.

SB

Southside House

On the south side of Wimbledon Common, 1m from Wimbledon BR station: the Pennington Mellor Charity Trust, tel. 081 947 7643 (guides) or 081 946 2491 (admin.). Open Oct–May Tues, Thurs, Sat, BH Mon 2–5. Guided tours.

Like Fenton House, Hampstead (qv.), this singular house is not so much a country house as a substantial gentleman's residence built on the edge of what had already by the late 17C become a suburban village, a few miles away from the capital. There was a farmhouse on the site in the 17C, and was expanded and given a new façade by Robert Pennington, a minor civil servant descended from the Penningtons of Muncaster Castle, Cumbria (qv.), after the Great Plague of 1665, when his wife and daughter took refuge there; the date 1687 appears on a fireplace inside. The house later passed through the female line to Nicholas Kemys of Cefn Mably in Wales, and then to a London lawyer, John Lawson, and the main façade was remodelled in its present form in 1776; there were also some 18C alterations to the interior, most notably to the Music Room on the garden side. More female inheritances followed, but in the 19C the house reverted to Catherine Pennington, who married Joseph Mellor, and gave the house to their granddaughter Hilda; she married the Swedish-born writer, collector and philanthropist Axel Munthe. There was substantial bomb damage in the Second World War, but the house was later restored, and it now belongs to a family trust which also administers Hellens, Herefordshire (qv.).

The house is one of a series of large houses strung out close to each other along the southern and western edges of Wimbledon Common. The main façade looks north, and is made up of ten bays, with the main entrance placed somewhat off-centre, next to a canted bay window; the rendered wall-surfaces, the mansard roof and the clock turret may all date from a late-18C remodelling, and the forecourt is enclosed by brick arcades. Visitors enter from the more irregular garden side, and are taken through a series of dark, faded rooms filled with a fascinating and eclectic collection of pictures and objects accumulated by the Penningtons and the numerous families with which they intermarried; they include portraits inherited from the wicked early-18C Duke of Wharton, works by Hogarth, Reynolds, Romney and Burne-Jones, a needlework box belonging to Anne Boleyn and the necklace worn by Marie Antoinette at her execution. There are also items relating to famous visitors, including Frederick, Prince of Wales, and Emma Hamilton. Though not all typical of English country-house taste, the interior of this strangely memorable house nevertheless manages to convey an unusually powerful sense of arrested time.

GCT

Syon House

On the north bank of the Thames between Brentford and Isleworth, off the A310 or A315: the Duke of Northumberland, tel. 081 560 0881/3. Open Apr–Oct daily except Mon, Tues 10–5, last admission 4.15. Refreshments.

Syon was among the greatest of the private palaces of the nobility on the outskirts of London, and is the only one to remain in the hands of the dynasty which built it—the Percy family, Dukes of Northumberland. Its rather dour exterior conceals a suite of rooms by Robert Adam which are one of the great masterpieces of English neo-classical art. The house still stands in over 80 acres of parkland on the Thames, surrounded by Brentford and Isleworth. The first building here was a convent of Brigittine nuns, founded in 1431 by Henry V in expiation of his father's connivance at the murder of Richard II. The nunnery was suppressed in 1534, and the nuns fled to Flanders. King Henry VIII's body lay here on its final journey from Windsor to Westminster in 1547, and in the night his bloated corpse burst its coffin; the convent dogs were found licking the residue from the floor, in gruesome fulfilment of a prophecy made by a Franciscan friar in 1535, that 'the dogs would lick his blood as they had done Ahab's'.

Syon passed in 1547 to the Lord Protector Somerset, who remodelled the convent as a house, probably adding the corner towers. After a complicated succession of owners, in 1594 Elizabeth gave the lease of Syon to Henry, 9th Earl of Northumberland (qv. Alnwick Castle, Northumberland and Petworth House, West Sussex). Syon remained a favourite residence of this powerful but unfortunate family; the 10th Earl was made custodian of Charles I's younger children by Parliament, and they lived here at times from 1646–49. The Percy line died out in 1670, and Syon with the rest of their vast estates passed with Lady Elizabeth Percy to her husband, the 'Proud Duke' of Somerset, rebuilder of Petworth. He planted the avenue of limes which frames the entrance front. When the Duke died in 1748 and his great estates were divided, Syon went with Alnwick Castle to Lady Elizabeth Seymour and her husband, Sir Hugh Smithson. This couple assumed the surname Percy, and Smithson was later made Duke of North-umberland. They were enormously rich, and commissioned Robert Adam to remodel three of their residences, Alnwick, Northumberland House on Trafalgar Square (demolished in 1874) and Syon. The Dukes have lived here regularly ever since.

The approach through the park preserves the illusion of open countryside; the house faces down by broad lime avenue, with two small square lodges of the early 17C framing the entrance façade. It is a quadrangular building, with square towers at the four corners, battlements on its façades and regular rows of sash windows. The square inner court represents the cloister of the 15C nunnery, and there are considerable medieval remains in the basement, although these are not seen by visitors. The upper areas of the house were all rebuilt by Lord Protector Somerset (c 1547–50), and by the Percy family at various dates in the 17C; a late-17C view by Jan Griffier shows the house looking almost exactly as it does now. The major external change since is the smooth, regular facing of Bath stone, added by Thomas Cundy I in 1819. None of this gives any clue of the rich Adam interiors.

Entering under the early-19C porch, the **Hall** rises through two storeys. Adam's decoration is rich, derived directly from ancient Roman models, in cool white and grey colours, and most of the sculptures are ancient, except for the copy of the Apollo Belvedere at one end, and the bronze replica of the Dying Gaul at the other. Adam had to cope with changes of level around the house, and housed the steps up from the Hall into the **Ante-Room** in an apse with Doric columns in front. The Ante-Room is one of the most sumptuous neo-classical interiors in Britain, its tone set by the columns and pilasters of 'verd-antique', dark sea-green marble, some of them antique columns found on the bed of the Tiber in Rome, and bought for Syon in 1765. The floor has an elaborate geometrical design in richly-coloured scagliola, highly polished and very well-preserved, and the rich plaster decoration is by Joseph Rose, one of Adam's favourite craftsmen. The room is furnished with gilded Empire-style pieces.

The visitor follows the processional route through the state rooms. The **Dining Room** is a double cube in shape, with apses at either end, decorated in white and gold, and an especially splendid ceiling. The room is plastered, with no paintings or tapestries, the chief decoration being a series of statues, copied from antique originals to Adam's directions, in maroon-painted niches. Next comes the **Red Drawing Room**, the most splendid interior of all. The walls are hung with the original crimson Spitalfields silk, restored in 1965. The high coved ceiling is divided into octagonal and square panels, set with over 200 circular medallions painted by Cipriani with mythological figures. The great carpet is the original one designed by Adam for the room, woven by Thomas Moore of Moorfields in 1769. The rich doorcases have ivory panels in the pilasters, elaborate filigree decoration of gilded lead. The furniture is of the same period as the room, some of it designed by Adam, such as the fine side tables. The room is mostly hung with royal portraits of the 17C, including a particularly fine double portrait of Charles I and his second son, the Duke of York, by Lely.

At the far end you enter the Long Gallery, last of Adam's state apartments to be seen. Adam did not create the room, which runs the whole length of the east front; it was a 16C creation. His problem was to adapt his style to this very long space, which he did by dividing the long walls by groups of pilasters. This was the ladies' withdrawing room, and the decoration is delicate and intimate in style, the colouring mostly mauve and green. There are bookcases between the pilasters, and over these, medallion portraits of the Earls and Dukes of Northumberland are let into the wall, together with scenes of famous Roman ruins and scenes. Much of the furniture was designed by Adam, and came here from Northumberland House.

From here you enter the north wing, much of it altered by the Italian architect Montiroli for the 4th Duke in 1864. The **Print Room** has a 19C ceiling, and a large collection of Percy family portraits of the 16C to 18C; there are also fine inlaid cabinets and bureaux. From here, the **Oak Passage** leads down by the north side of the house. This too is hung with royal and family portraits. Some of these are less than second rate, but there are interesting things also, such as J.M. Wright's portrait of Thomas Hobbes, and a strange double portrait of Sir Philip Sidney and his sister in Roman armour. At the end of the corridor is a version of John Martin's famous painting of Belshazzar's Feast, painted on glass. The West Corridor leads back into the Hall, and has more portraits. Opening off this is the spacious **Staircase**, of about 1820. This has fine full-length portraits of the 1st Duke and Duchess, and a magnificent great by Rubens, 'Diana Returning from the Hunt'. The sedan chair belonged to the 1st Duke, and the immense Sèvres vase in the middle of the floor was given by Charles X of France to the 3rd Duke.

Outside there is much to see. Syon's gardens are justly renowned. The Great Conservatory was built in 1827–30 for the 3rd Duke by Charles Fowler, and looks over splendid formal gardens.

SB

GREATER MANCHESTER

Bramall Hall

4m south of Stockport on A5102 Stockport–Wilmslow: Metropolitan Borough of Stockport, tel. 061 485 3708. Open Mar–Dec daily 1–5 (Sun 1–4). Refreshments.

Bramall Hall is a large timber-framed house now marooned in a municipal park in the prosperous suburbia south east of Manchester. Its many-gabled exterior has a complex building history which is partly concealed by the thoroughness of a late-19C remodelling carried out by the local silk manufacturer T.H. Neville, who bought the house for his son in 1883. The earliest parts seem to date from the late 14C, when John Davenport was lord of the manor, and the Davenports remained in possession until 1877. The house originally consisted of an open Hall with two cross-wings, but there were later additions, alterations and embellishments, especially in the late 16C, when the Hall was floored over and the external walls adorned with elaborate patterning made up of quatrefoils in squares. A second-floor long gallery was unfortunately removed, along with a gatehouse range to the west, in the late 18C or early 19C. The post-1883 alterations restored some of the picturesque appeal which had been lost by these changes, but most of the old texture was lost in the process, and today, after more than half a century of local authority control, the house is somewhat lacking in charm.

The main approach is from the west, and from here the basic layout is clearly visible; the service wing to the left, the late-medieval chamber or solar wing to the right and the largely Elizabethan hall range in the centre, its first floor made up of an almost continuous wall of glass and the skyline embellished with late-19C gables in conscious imitation of nearby Little Moreton Hall, Cheshire (qv.). Much of the woodwork and most of the brick chimneys were renewed at the same time. The Davenports removed or sold the contents when they moved out in 1877 (some are now at Capesthorne, Cheshire, qv.), and the rooms are now mostly rather bare, with the exception of the miscellany of pseudo-Jacobean objects often found in houses of this sort.

The most interesting room from a decorative point of view is the late-15C great chamber (now called the Ballroom) on the first floor of the south wing, with its original open timber roof exposed to show the elaborately carved tie-beams and cusped wind-braces; in the late 16C the walls were embellished by a series of paintings directly on to the wood (recently exposed and restored) depicting courtly and hunting scenes. The adjacent Plaster Room contains the most important object in the house: a large table carpet of the 1560s, repurchased in 1945, and decorated with the coasts of arms of the Queen and of the Davenports and their marriage alliances. The room over the Hall, now called the Withdrawing Room, has accomplished woodwork of 1592 (the date is carved over a doorway), an attractive plaster ceiling of the same date and a rather cruder chimneypiece; this was all carried out for William Davenport, some of whose relatives are shown in portraits loaned back by the family and displayed on the walls. Other rooms are furnished in the taste of the late 19C, with metalwork of an Arts and Crafts nature by George Faulkner Armitage and paintings by the all-too-appropriately named Herbert Schmalz. One of these rooms, over the much-restored domestic Chapel in the south wing, contains furniture made by A.W.N. Pugin for another Cheshire house, Abney Hall.

GCT

Hall i' th' Wood

On north east side of Bolton, off A58, signposted: Bolton Metropolitan Borough, tel. 0204 51159. Apr–Sept Tues–Sat 11–5; Sun 2–5.

Hall i' th' Wood is a very attractive manor house of the 16C and 17C, run by Bolton's museums department. The wood, however, is long gone, and the house is now stranded amidst Bolton's northern suburbs. The core of the building is a timber-framed range, which may contain late-15C elements, but whose elaborate black and white exterior seems more likely to be Elizabethan. Two stone wings were added to the west of this, one Elizabethan, and the other of the mid 17C. The north-west wing is the simpler, added by Lawrence Brownlow. In the mid 17C the house was bought by Alexander Norris, an ardent Puritan who profited from the confiscated estates of Royalists in the area. He added the more formal south-west wing, with its big porch. In the 18C the house fell on hard times and was divided into tenements. A farming family, the Cromptons, lived in part of it, and here Samuel Crompton invented his 'spinning mule', one of the landmarks of the industrial revolution, in 1779. In 1899 the derelict building was bought by the Bolton-born millionaire philanthropist, Lord Leverhulme. His architects, Simpson and Grayson and Ould (cf. Wightwick Manor, Staffs), carried out a careful restoration, and he presented the house to the town, which has run it ever since.

The visitor enters the Hall, in the timber-framed east wing. It is a big but informal room, with the timber-framing everywhere exposed; there is interesting furniture and a replica of Crompton's original 'spinning mule', and the fireplace has a chimney crane (to hoist a cooking pot over the fire) and a mechanical spit-winder. To the right, the Kitchen is furnished with mostly 18C pieces, and three spinning wheels. The Dairy, at the north-west corner of the house, was built as a withdrawing room, but now houses objects connected with the preparation and cooking of food. Up a steep spiral stair the visitor reaches the Brownlow Bedroom, over the Dairy, with 17C pieces including a bed of 1627. The next rooms, over the Kitchen, house a variety of objects, including miniature furniture (cabinet-makers' samples) and some early musical instruments. The next two rooms, over the Hall, are dedicated to Samuel Crompton, with various possessions including a chamber-organ built by him in 1798.

From here the visitor crosses the front staircase in the more formal part of the house built by Alexander Norris c 1648. Up a few stairs is Norris's Withdrawing Room. The early 17C panelling comes from a house in Kent, while the ceiling is a reproduction of one at Chastleton House (Oxon, qv.), and there is some fine 17C and 18C furniture. Down Norris's staircase the Dining Room is reached, which has late-17C panelling from Hertfordshire and more good furniture, including Restoration dining chairs, and a barrel organ made in 1775, with a Gothick case.

SB

Heaton Hall

In Heaton Park, off the A576, just south of the M66. There are no signs to the Hall (summer 1992); visitors should use the entrance with the Golf Club sign, off the A576 next to traffic-lights: Manchester City Council, tel. 061 236 5244. Open Apr–Sept Wed–Sat 10–1, 2–5.45, Sun 2–5.45.

Heaton Hall was James Wyatt's first major country house; it is (with the possible exception of Tatton Park, Cheshire, qv.) the finest neo-classical mansion in the north-west of England. Since 1902 it has been owned by the city of Manchester, and its grounds are now a large municipal park.

The Holland family had large estates at Heaton and Agecroft; in 1684 they passed by marriage to Sir John Egerton of Wrinehill in Staffordshire, and soon after this a modest brick mansion was built at Heaton. This family was the senior branch of a large clan which included the Egertons of Tatton and the Dukes of Bridgewater. In 1769, Sir John's great-grandson married an heiress, and in 1772 he commissioned James Wyatt to remodel his house. The client was 23, the architect was 26. Sir Thomas' income grew steadily, from his Manchester rents and his new coal mines. In 1784 he was made Lord Grey de Wilton and in 1801, 1st Earl of Wilton. He went on the Grand Tour twice in the 1780s and spent lavishly to furnish Heaton. When he died in 1814, his titles and estates passed to his grandson Thomas Grosvenor, younger brother of the 1st Duke of Westminster, and he and his wife lived in great style, and mixed with the more worldly end of high society. The 2nd Earl laid out a racecourse in the park, and races were held here from 1827 to 1839; this was arguably the origin of the modern Grand National, now held at Aintree. After the death of the Countess in 1858, the family spent little time at Heaton, and in 1902, hall and park were bought by Manchester Corporation for £230,000. The city considered the house to be of no value, and auctioned the contents, including almost all the furniture specially made for it. Latterly, the City Art Gallery has carried out an excellent redecoration after a long period of neglect, and has installed very fine pictures and furniture. Despite this recent redecoration the houses still receives very little publicity.

The house lies deep within its well-wooded park; the visitor comes upon it suddenly. The **north front** is simple and covered in white-painted stucco. The middle seven bays are basically the original house; Wyatt added the stucco and the Tuscan portico, and the long, low wings on either side. The **south front** is much grander, and is entirely Wyatt's work. The centre block has a grand central bow with Ionic semicolumns. On either side are Venetian windows. Flanking this central block are five-bay wings, with rows of Doric columns in front; these end in octagonal end pavilions with more Venetian windows. The bay on the left houses the Kitchen, that on the right is the Library. This beautifully composed façade was very influential, and did much to establish Wyatt as Robert Adam's chief rival. The clerk of works was James Wyatt's brother Samuel, and their nephew Lewis was employed on the later stages of work.

The **Entrance Hall** is simple, with apsidal ends and a stone floor; over the fireplace is a full-length portrait of the 1st Earl of Wilton as an archer, of 1784. The beautiful **staircase** occupies the centre of the main block and is top-lit. It is one of the first examples in Britain of the 'imperial' plan, with one flight going up to a half-landing, then two flights returning to first-floor level. At first floor level are colonnades of scagliola columns. The whole ensemble is superbly executed, including the wrought-iron balustrade by Maurice and Henry Tobin of Leeds.

On the ground floor, in the centre of the south front, is the **Saloon**. The plasterwork is by Joseph Rose the younger to Wyatt's designs; the niches hold copies of famous ancient statues. Gillow's of Lancaster supplied the original furniture, all sold in 1902; instead there are some fine contemporary pieces here. The overdoor paintings are by Biagio Rebecca. On the right is the **Dining Room**, lit by a Venetian window. At the opposite end is a big semicircular niche, housing serving tables; these are some of the very few original pieces to survive the 1902 sale. On the fireplace wall are English portraits of the 17C and 18C, and, on the opposite wall, a huge copy of Guercino's 'Death of Dido' (an appropriate example of Grand Tour taste).

Visitors retrace their steps through the Saloon to the **Billiard Room**. It is dominated by the large oil-paintings set into the walls, by a Pole, Michael Novosielski, who trained in Rome and was brought to England by Wyatt. They depict scenes from the Hunt of the Calydonian Boar, from Ovid's *Metamorphoses*. The long and splendid **Music Room** was decorated by Samuel Wyatt in 1789; the doorcase by which you enter is a triumph of neo-classical design. The 1st and 2nd Earls were music-lovers, and held frequent concerts here. The organ, built by Samuel Green cost £370 5s 0d, with another £40 to Biagio Rebecca for painting the case; it was modernised in the last century, and is still used for recitals. The overmantel mirror by Robert Adam for Derby House, London, and on either side are fine portraits and landscapes, including works by Reynolds, Raeburn, Highmore, Wright of Derby and Romney.

The last room on the south front is the octagonal **Library**, designed by Lewis Wyatt in 1823; it has a heavier character than the previous rooms. There is fine Regency furniture here, but the bookcases were stripped out in 1906; they are now apparently in Manchester's town hall. A long corridor behind the state-rooms leads back to the **Inner Hall**. Both are hung with interesting portraits and landscapes; the 17C portrait of a nobleman by Passarotti is particularly fine. Finally, you ascend the great staircase to see the **Cupola Room**, on the first floor over the Saloon. This is round, with a dome, and delicately painted Pompeian decoration by Biagio Rebecca.

Outside, the large Orangery at the east end of the house is of 1823, by Lewis Wyatt. The Park was landscaped by William Emes, a follower of 'Capability' Brown. North west of the house are the Stables, of 1777 by Samuel Wyatt, and nearby is the Temple, with Tuscan columns and a dome. Further away, at the west end of the lake, is a huge Ionic colonnade. This is not a Wyatt-designed folly; it is part of the old Manchester Town Hall (1819 by Francis Goodwin), re-erected here in 1912, a grand and imaginative gesture.

SB

Ordsall Hall

At the south edge of Salford near the Docks, on Taylorson St, off the A5066 (Ordsall Lane): Borough of Salford, tel. 061 872 0251. Open all year Mon–Fri 10–5, Sun 2–5. Closed Easter Sun, Mon and Dec 24, 25, 26.

Ordsall is an important timber-framed manor house. It is no longer really a country house, deep in the heart of the inner city, but it began life as one. It is now run as a museum by the City of Salford.

Ordsall belonged to the Radclyffe family from around 1335, when there was already a substantial house here. In the 1520s the present Great Hall was built by Sir Alexander Radclyffe, High Sheriff of Lancashire. The brick wing at the west end was added by another Sir Alexander Radclyffe (d 1654). The family suffered hardship by supporting the Royalist cause, and were forced to sell Ordsall in 1662. In the early 18C it declined in status, as such houses often did; in 1756 it was bought by Samuel Hill of Shenstone, Staffordshire, who left it to his nephew, Samuel Egerton of Tatton Park, Cheshire (qv.). The Egertons let it to a succession of tenants, while the fields and woods around it were gradually engulfed by the mills and streets of Salford. In 1875 it was let as a Working Men's Club, and in the 1890s, Lord Egerton established a Clergy Training College here. Unfortunately, he had a Manchester architect, Alfred Darbyshire, carry out a major restoration. He was not a sympathetic architect, and the south front rebuilt by him is rather ugly. The Hall was bought by Salford Corporation in 1959, and after major restoration work, opened as a museum.

The visitor's first sight of the house, amongst terraces of houses, is of Darbyshire's south front; it is of harsh grey brick with red terracotta window-frames, looking like a late-19C school. The north front is highly picturesque and authentic; in the centre is Alexander Radclyffe's black and white timber-framed Hall of 1525–30, with quatrefoil panels, and bay windows at either end. On the right is the brick wing of around 1639, with a high porch. The visitor enters at the right-hand end of the 16C range, where the Kitchen would have been. The undoubted highlight is the Great Hall, in many respects a slightly smaller version of the Hall at Rufford, Lancashire (qv.). As at Rufford, instead of a screens passage, the entrance end is divided off by a huge wooden arch; underneath there would have been a great movable screen, like those which survive at Rufford and at Cheetham's Hospital, Manchester. The roof has cusped wind braces, and the dais end is also framed by carved spere posts, with part of the wooden canopy over the dais remaining. At the dais end is the solar or Star Chamber, named from the little gilt metal stars nailed to the wooden ceiling; there is some early oak furniture here and in the Hall. At the other end, the 17C Kitchen has a variety of fittings and implements of the 18C and 19C. The rest of the house is furnished as a museum of local history.

SB

Smithills Hall

On the north edge of Bolton, off Moss Bank Way (A58), signposted: Bolton Metropolitan Borough, tel. 0204 41265. Open Apr–Sept Tues–Sat 11–5, Sun 2–5.

Smithills stands among trees and parkland on the north edge of Bolton, though suburbia is creeping close. It is a long, rambling and picturesque building; as you approach, the impression is of a large late-19C house in Tudor half-timbered style. This is the big west wing, added in the 1880s for the Ainsworth family by George Devey. Walking past this, the much older core of the house is reached. This consists of ranges built around the north, east and west sides of an open court. The north side is basically a 14C manor house on the traditional plan—a great hall with kitchen wing at one end, and solar wing at the other. This was built by the Radclyffe family. Andrew Barton inherited the house in 1516 and added the east wing, with a Drawing

Room and Chapel. The wing opposite was added later in the 16C, and further buildings west of that were added later. However, the west wing was caught up in Devey's late-19C additions. These were so big as almost to constitute a new house, leaving the older parts of the house as outlying wings, hardly altered. The visitor today sees the 14C hall wing and the early-16C east wing. The later wings are empty, but Bolton has plans to re-furnish them in Victorian style and open them to the public.

The visitor enters the Hall; the end walls are timber-framed, but the outer (north and south) walls were rebuilt in stone in the 16C. The roof is impressive, with boldly quatrefoiled wind braces. It is sparsely furnished with 16C pieces. From here the visitor sees the 'Bower', the ground floor of the solar wing, with a big stone fireplace. From here you ascend into the Solar itself. This is still medieval work, with the massive timber-framing of walls and roof visible. The Solar contains more 16C furniture, including an oak four-post bed, and a small bedroom adjoining it houses another.

From here the route goes back down through the Bower and into Andrew Barton's east wing, which is of stone on the outer side, and timber-framed on the inner, courtyard side. Most of the ground floor is occupied by the Drawing Room, lined with magnificent linenfold panelling, adorned with medallions with heads in profile; the builder's initials and his rebus, a tun with a bar across it, also appear. There is a big square bay window, and some good pieces of English furniture of the 16C and 17C. The passage parallel with this room leads to the Chapel. The original building was Andrew Barton's, but it was largely rebuilt in the 1850s; only the heraldic glass in the east window remains of the original fittings. The first floor passage, leading to the Chapel's Gallery, has a strange carved door with scenes of the Passion carved on it. There are terraces and steps around the house, remaining from Devey's late-Victorian garden layout.

SB

Wythenshawe Hall

On the south side of Manchester. Wythenshawe Park is north of the A560, just west of junction 3 of the M56. No signposts to the Hall, but the entrance is on the north side of the park: Manchester City Council, tel. 061 236 5244. Open Apr–Sept Wed–Sat 10–1, 2–5.45, Sun 2–5.45. Refreshments.

Wythenshawe is a 16C timber-framed house, much altered in the 19C, home of the Tatton family for 600 years and now run by Manchester City Art Galleries. The Tatton family held land here from the mid 14C; the timber-framed centre of the present house was probably built in the early 16C, by John Tatton, Sheriff of Chester and Baron of the Exchequer there. The family rose by obtaining such offices, and by judicious marriages, to being considerable landowners to the south of Manchester. During the Civil War Wythenshawe was stormed by Parliamentarian forces, six of the defenders being killed in the Great Hall. Robert Tatton was heavily fined, but the estates survived; in 1747 his grandson William married Hester, heiress to John Egerton of Tatton Park, Cheshire (qv.). The Egerton estates were much the larger, and so their son, William Tatton, changed his name to Egerton; he inherited both the Tatton Park and the Wythenshawe estates.

On William's death in 1806 the estates were divided again. His eldest son, Wilbraham, succeeded to Tatton Park. His second son, Thomas William, took Wythenshawe and reverted to the surname Tatton. He made extensive alterations to the house, employing Lewis Wyatt (who was working at Tatton Park, too). After the death of Thomas Egerton Tatton in 1924, capital taxation induced the family to sell up. 2500 acres were sold for housing development in 1926. Soon after, Wythenshawe Hall and 250 acres of parkland around it were sold to Sir Ernest Simon, who gave them to Manchester as a public park.

Like its counterpart Heaton Hall (also owned by Manchester City Council) Wythenshawe receives absolutely minimal publicity, to the extent that there are no signposts to it, even at the park gates (summer, 1992). The surroundings, too, are heavily municipalised, but fine belts of trees remain. The house faces east; the west front was reconstructed in the 18C in plain brickwork, much of it restored in the 1950s. The centre of the east front is the original Tudor manor house, with the hall in the centre and gabled wings projecting either side, with a porch and bay window in the angle between hall and wings. The timbers have been returned to a natural wood colour, so the house does not have the usual black and white appearance. It is arguable that staining the timbers black was a Victorian innovation and not the original treatment, but in a house like this, where a large proportion of the timberwork is, in any case, Victorian, this approach seems over-zealous. To the right is the extension of c 1812 by Lewis Wyatt with roughcast walls, and further right are lower, late-Victorian additions. On the left are late-Victorian servant quarters.

The Entrance Hall has very simple early-19C decoration, with equestrian paintings. To the north of this is Wyatt's Library, which has been well redecorated, a big room with the original Gillow bookcases and English 18C portraits. Given that the Hall came to Manchester Corporation largely empty, it has an interesting range of pictures and furniture. The Dining Room is the original Hall, redecorated in rich Jacobean style c 1870. There are old oak court cupboards and a big refectory table, and some fine Dutch and Flemish paintings, including works by Hondecoeter, Hoogstraten, Miereveld and Lely. Back through the entrance hall is Lewis Wyatt's staircase, dominated by large Victorian paintings. Off the landing and over the Dining Room is the Withdrawing Room, the best room in the house. This has splendid early-17C panelling; the fireplace and ceiling are of c 1840, probably by Edward Blore. The north wall has a very good inner porch with strapwork pilasters; the rest of the panelling on this wall has been removed, revealing very interesting painted decoration of c 1539, with Renaissance ornament in the frieze (the heraldry relates to the marriage of a Tatton to one of the Booth family of Dunham Massey, Cheshire, qv.). There is fine early furniture here, including a grand locally-made 16C bed. The Chapel Room is furnished as a bedroom with local 16C and 17C pieces and Dutch cabinet pictures. Another bedroom along the landing is furnished with 19C pieces; the bed is in fact Victorian, using 16C woodwork. The Museum Room, along a short corridor, has early plans and views of the house and documents relating to its history.

SB

MERSEYSIDE

Croxteth Hall

5m north east of Liverpool city centre, in Croxteth Park, signposted from
the A580 and A5088: Liverpool City Council, tel. 051 228 5311. Open
Easter–Sept daily 11–5. Refreshments.

Croxteth, a large quadrangular mansion, stands in what is still an extensive
(500 acre) park, in Liverpool's suburbs. It was the home of the Molyneux
family, who from the 16C were the Catholic rivals to the Stanley Earls of
Derby for the control of Liverpool. They originally lived at Sefton, but Sir
Richard Molyneux built a new house at Croxteth c 1575, part of which
remains, embedded in the south wing. The grandest part of the house, the
west wing, was added in 1702 by Richard, 4th Viscount Molyneux. He
converted to Anglicanism, and in 1771 the 8th Viscount became 1st Earl of
Sefton. In the 19C the family profited hugely from the expansion of
Liverpool over their estates (which included the Aintree racecourse), and
this paid for large additions to Croxteth. In 1874–77 the 4th Earl commissioned T.H. Wyatt to build new south and east wings, incorporating the 16C
house, and in 1902–4, the very large north range was added for the 5th Earl,
by John MacVicar Anderson, closing the courtyard and making Croxteth
a fully-equipped Edwardian mansion. In 1952 a fire broke out in the west
wing, destroying many of the house's most important interiors. In 1972 the
7th and last Earl of Sefton died and the estate was broken up; the house
and half the park were given to Liverpool City Council, which runs them
now. Unfortunately most of the house's contents were sold, and the rooms
on display are now furnished with pieces from the city's Museum and the
Walker Art Gallery.

Croxteth park is level and well-wooded, and the visitor comes upon the
house suddenly. The great architectural set-piece is the west front of 1702,
of red brick with stone dressings painted white. The architect is unknown,
but it is a very grand design, a provincial version of Wren's additions to
Hampton Court. A terrace runs the length of the façade in front of the
basement, with round and oval windows in it. Above this, the windows are
closely spaced, with alternately segmental and triangular pediments. In the
middle is a splendid portal with paired Corinthian columns, and a great
armorial panel over, instead of a window. MacVicar Anderson's north front
takes its cue from this, and is impressive but conventional by comparison.
T.H. Wyatt's work is in a Tudor style, and less successful. On the south front,
just to the left of Wyatt's gatehouse, you can see the remaining part of the
16C house, with two gabled attic windows.

The visitor enters a display area in the north wing, and then crosses the
courtyard to see the kitchens. These are late-Victorian, and are sometimes
staffed by local volunteers giving demonstrations. A back staircase takes
you to the corridor running behind the west wing, then to an Ante-Room
and the big top-lit Staircase Hall. These are in a rich mid-Victorian
Italianate style. The Staircase Hall has Victorian paintings from the Walker
Art Gallery, and Sèvres china in wall-cases. Only two rooms on the west
front are seen, reinstated after the 1952 fire. The Breakfast Room has
modern bolection panelling, and has late-19C paintings and furniture from
the Walker Art Gallery. The Card Room retains its original panelling, and
has early 18C furniture, and a number of Sefton family portraits of the same

period. The Smoking Room is where MacVicar Anderson's north range meets the west wing, and retains its Edwardian decor and panelling, with appropriate furniture and late-Victorian portraits. Next, near the middle of the north front, is a very grand Billiard Room, the most evocative room in the house, with sporting and landscape paintings and Edwardian furniture.

A long vaulted corridor runs behind the north wing with more 19C sporting paintings. Further along are Lady Sefton's rooms, her Sitting Room, Dressing Room and Bedroom. All have Victorian and Edwardian furniture, but only that in the Bedroom was made for the house (for the 4th Earl in 1878). At the end of the north range are Lord Sefton's rooms, with his luxurious fitted bathroom. The visitor returns along the vaulted corridor to the Staircase Hall, and descends to the pillared Entrance Hall in the middle of the north front. The stable block is early 18C, of red brick, and houses 19C carriages and carts; there is a fine pair of gatepiers hidden behind shrubs. Other estate buildings include Kennels designed by John Douglas, and the Laundry and Dairy building by W. Eden Nesfield.

SB

Speke Hall

8m west of Liverpool city centre, on the west side of Speke Airport, off the A561: National Trust, tel. 051 427 7231. Open Apr–Oct daily except Mon (open BH Mon) 1–5.30; Nov–mid Dec Sat, Sun 1–4.30. Refreshments.

Lancashire and Cheshire are famous for elaborate timber-framed houses, and Speke is one of the finest of the survivors. It is a big, quadrangular building, and it is also very authentic, with relatively few later alterations. The Norris family owned the manor of Speke by the late 14C, and most of the present house was built by William Norris (d 1506), Sir William (d 1568) and Edward Norris (d 1606). Its building history is very complicated, and it is not clear who built what. The Norrises were Catholics, and suffered from heavy recusancy fines; in the Civil War they were Royalists, and suffered the confiscation of their estates, which were only restored in 1662. The family staged a recovery in the later 17C but the direct male line died out in 1731, and the estate passed by marriage to Lord Sidney Beauclerk, son of the Duke of St Albans. The Beauclerks paid little attention to the house, and in 1795 sold it to Richard Watt, a Liverpool merchant and plantation-owner in Jamaica. The Watt family occasionally resided here, and in 1855 Richard Watt carried out some restoration work. He died in 1865, leaving the house to his eight-year-old daughter Adelaide, and the house was let to F.R. Leyland, a Liverpool shipping-magnate, patron of the pre-Raphaelites and of Whistler. Leyland carried out minor alterations, but Adelaide Watt came of age in 1878 and came to live at Speke. On her death in 1921 she left the house in trust to the Norris family, with remainder to the National Trust, which became the owner in 1943.

The outer suburbs of Liverpool surround the house, and Speke Airport is close by. However, the house remains insulated by its gardens and the surrounding belts of trees, and by the great earth banks to the south. The house was surrounded by a moat, now dry and grassed over, and it is almost all 'black and white', raised on a red sandstone foundation, and with big stone chimneybreasts. It is highly picturesque, with many gables, irregularly-spaced windows, and quatrefoil ornaments. The oldest parts are the kitchen area in the east wing, and the Hall area in the south wing, probably dating from c 1530–60, but embodying parts of an earlier house. The west side is of the later 16C, and the square was completed by the building of the north (entrance) range, which is dated 1598. The house is entered over a sandstone bridge across the moat. Originally visitors would have passed through the gatehouse and gone straight over the courtyard to the screens passage and the Hall in the south range. The two massive yew trees in the courtyard, known as Adam and Eve, are thought to be 300 years old.

The gatehouse was enclosed as an **entrance hall** in the 19C, and the visitor now turns right, to see the ground floor rooms in the north and west wings. Speke was unusual in being built with corridors along the courtyard side of the north and west wings, and these remain as redecorated by F.R. Leyland, like the first rooms to be seen. The **Small Dining Room** has 18C and 19C furniture, with old views of the house. Leyland turned the next room (previously a kitchen) into a **Billiard Room**; it is furnished with Gothic Revival furniture and sporting pictures. Leyland also turned the small adjacent room into a Library, putting up the William Morris wallpaper.

The **Great Hall** occupies the west part of the south wing, and was built by the first William Norris; the massive fireplace, with its elaborate decoration of battlements, is of unknown, possibly mid-16C, date. On the west wall is very fine carved panelling, installed here in 1564 by Edward Norris, and probably from the Low Countries. The furniture is mostly 17C; the huge portrait in the window depicts John Middleton, the 'Childe of Hale', a local giant who lived in the early 17C. Through the screens passage, visitors reach the **Blue Drawing Room**. This was a parlour for the family, redecorated in the 1850s for Richard Watt in Victorian Louis XV style, with new tulipwood furniture. You now return through the Great Hall to the **Oak Drawing Room**, formerly the Great Parlour. This is the principal reception room, and the most richly decorated room in the house, added by Sir William Norris c 1530. The overmantel has vigorous if crude carvings showing three generations of the family; Sir William with his wife and 19 children in the middle, his parents and their five children on the left, his son Edward, with his wife and two children on the right. The very lavish plasterwork on the ceiling is of c 1610, the panels filled with garlands and flowers. Most of the heavy oak furniture is Victorian, introduced by Richard Watt, but much of it incorporates older carving.

Visitors go upstairs to see several **bedrooms** in the west and north wings. The Blue Bedroom has 19C furniture in Tudor style, and a Mortlake tapestry. The Royal Bedroom has similar furniture, taking its name from the (untrue) legend that Charles I stayed here. Next to the Green Bedroom is a skilfully concealed Priest's Hole; again the bed incorporates much 16C carved work. The Tapestry Room, over the gateway, is hung with Flemish and English tapestries, the adjacent bathroom with a Morris-style wallpaper. From here you descend to the Servants' Hall (possibly the original Chapel), and then to the **Kitchen** in the early-16C east range. It remains largely as equipped by Richard Watt in 1855. Opposite the kitchen door is the Dairy, now the Trust's shop, and the Tea Room is in the old Laundry across the cobbled courtyard.

SB

WEST MIDLANDS

Aston Hall

2½m north of Birmingham city centre, M6 exit 6: Birmingham City
Council, tel. 021 327 0062. Open late Mar–Oct daily 2–5. Refreshments.

An inscription over the entrance to this large and impressive house records
that it was begun by a local squire, Sir Thomas Holte, in 1618 and finished
in 1635. He chose a commanding hilltop site not far from the small but busy
market and manufacturing town of Birmingham, whose phenomenal
spread swallowed up the surrounding farm land in the 19C; today the view
from the house encompasses the Aston Villa football ground and 'Spaghetti
Junction'. The Holte estates were broken up and sold in 1817, and the house
was leased and repaired by the eldest son of the great inventor James Watt,
whose father's Soho foundry, one of the cradles of the Industrial Revolution,
was not far away. He died in 1848, and the house was later acquired by the
Corporation of Birmingham, which has recently carried out a sensitive and
scholarly refurbishment of the interior.

The most striking external feature of Aston Hall is its silhouette made up
of ogee-capped towers, tall chimneys and curved gables. The house is built
of red brick and is laid out according to the conventional 'half H'-plan, with
a hall range two rooms wide and two projecting wings. There are two
lodges on either side of the entrance courtyard, linked to the house by low
walls which were originally carried across the front of the courtyard. The
ground floor of the south front has a round-arched loggia of Italian deriva-
tion, but in general the detailing both inside and outside is a characteristically exuberant if somewhat coarse mixture of motifs culled from
architectural pattern-books. The plans were prepared by the well-known
surveyor John Thorpe, but were executed by an unknown team of craftsmen, no doubt with some creative involvement by Sir Thomas Holte
himself. The main entrance was shifted to a central position after the Civil
War, when the house, a Royalist stronghold, sustained some damage, and
there were further relatively minor internal and external alterations in the
18C. But in general Aston Hall still retains its Jacobean character.

In contrast to many inhabited houses, most of the rooms are open to
visitors. Little of the Holtes' or James Watt's furniture remains, but many
Holte portraits have been re-acquired (including two in the Gallery attributed to Cornelius Johnson, and a Gainsborough and a Romney in the Great
Dining Room on the first floor), and the rooms have been carefully furnished
with objects from the Birmingham museums' and art gallerys' collections
following the evidence of inventories and old illustrations, some of which
are on display in the downstairs rooms. The main rooms occupy the south
and west ranges and are elaborately decorated, with lavish woodwork,
wildly extravagant chimneypieces and inventive plaster ceilings made up
of strapwork, arcane emblems and Italian *grotteschi*. The much-remodelled
Hall contains two fanciful landscapes and an idealised portrait of Sir
Thomas Holte, all of the early 18C, as well as some early-17C shell-backed
wooden chairs and an improving verse over the fireplace which recalls the
fact that Jacobean halls were used as dining rooms for the servants. A stone
archway gives access to the Parlour, which contains a tapestry of c 1590
woven at the Sheldon works in south Warwickshire, and to the richly-
carved oak staircase, which still show signs of Civil War damage. It leads

up to the tall and spacious south-facing Dining Room (so called as early as 1654), with its ornate plaster frieze of the Nine Worthies, and to the superb Gallery which takes up the whole of the west or garden front; it is hung with early-17C French tapestries after the Raphael Cartoons and lined with busts of English worthies introduced by James Watt.

The first-floor rooms on the north side were altered in the 18C and early 19C and now contain furnishings of those dates, while those on the second floor (including a garret now lined with Civil War armour and another furnished as a Victorian housekeeper's room) were used as servants' bedrooms. From here the back stairs descend to the service quarters, with their appropriate contents and cooking implements. The rooms on the garden front on the ground floor were redecorated as living rooms in the 18C and 19C, and now contain contemporary pictures, and furniture by the early-19C cabinet-makers George Bullock and his pupil Richard Bridgens, both of whom were patronised by the Watts and their partners the Boultons.

GCT

Hagley Hall

12m south west of Birmingham on A456 Birmingham–Kidderminster: the Viscount Cobham, tel. 0562 882408. Open Jan, Feb daily except Sat, and Easter, Spring and August BH weekends. Guided tours. Refreshments.

Hagley Hall was built in 1754–60 by the 1st Lord Lyttelton, former secretary to Frederick, Prince of Wales, and for a brief and not very illustrious period Chancellor of the Exchequer; it has remained in the hands of his descendants ever since. It stands close to the site of a timber-framed house erected by Sir John Lyttelton soon after he acquired the estate in 1564, and commands a splendid view over to the hills of the Welsh borders, with the Clee Hills rising up behind to protect the park from the tentacles of Birmingham. The beauties of Hagley made it an almost obligatory place of pilgrimage for travellers in search of the picturesque in the second half of the 18C. In 1747–48, Lyttelton's friend Sanderson Miller designed a ruined castle (not accessible to the public) which the hyper-critical Horace Walpole praised as having 'the true rust of the Barons' wars'. This was followed by numerous ornamental buildings of which the most important was a Doric temple designed by James 'Athenian' Stuart in 1758–59, modelled on the Theseion in Athens and notable as the first building since classical antiquity to employ the Greek Doric order (it stands close to a prominent obelisk in a field on the northern side of the A458).

When it came to his house, Lyttelton played safe by choosing an austere neo-Palladian design with four corner towers, modelled on Houghton, Norfolk (qv.). His architect was again Sanderson Miller, but Miller's designs were somewhat modified by another gentleman amateur, Thomas Prowse, and also by the minor Palladian architect, John Sanderson. The pink sandstone house stands at the extremity of the commuter village, with the rather dull parish church by G.E. Street as a neighbour. But the interest lies less in the architecture than in the luxuriantly Rococo interiors—some of them expertly remodelled after a fire in 1926—which still contain many of their original furnishings and works of art.

The tour takes in all the main rooms on the first floor: a true piano nobile, with the grand state rooms on the south side and the more intimate private

James Lovell's atlantes on either side of the fireplace, with F. Vassali's stucco relief above, in the Entrance Hall of Hagley Hall

rooms to the north, separated by a Hall and Saloon on the central axis. The Entrance Hall has a ceiling of lavish swirling plasterwork, echoed in the gestures of the figures copied from famous classical sculptures arranged in niches around the walls, and also in the massive atlantes on either side of the fireplace, carved by James Lovell (described as 'a countryman of great genius now established in London'), who may have been responsible for the inventive decorative schemes elsewhere in the house. The theme of classical antiquity is sustained in the marble 18C heads of emperors 'after the antique' and in the stucco relief of 'Pan winning the love of Diana' copied by Francesco Vassali from a lost painting by Carlo Maratta, while the claims of the 'moderns' are upheld by the busts of Rubens and Van Dyck by Rysbrack on the opposite wall. The Library, to the north, contains replicas of the original bookcases with busts of literary worthies by Schee-makers in the broken pediments; they originally belonged to Alexander Pope—whose portrait by Jonathan Richardson hangs over the fireplace—and later to Frederick, Prince of Wales, who left them to Lyttelton in his will. The Boudoir and the adjacent Billiard Room or 'Barrel Room' originally formed part of two bedroom suites on the north side of the house, but were remodelled after the fire, the latter in a neo-Elizabethan manner, using panelling preserved from the previous house on the site; pictures here include 'The Misers', by the early-16C artist Marinus van Reymerswaele, and two Van Dycks: an early 'Deposition' and a portrait of Lady Cary.

The sequence of 'public' reception rooms begins with the Saloon, re-painted in 1989 in an attractive lemon yellow and at the same time largely cleared of furniture, thus allowing proper appreciation of the splendid plasterwork (almost certainly by Vassali) on both ceiling and walls. It takes the form of wreaths with festoons hanging down between the pictures, each of them representing one of the interests of Lord Lyttelton, whose gloomy portrait by Benjamin West hangs over one of the doors. Other portraits are by Van Dyck (attd), Allan Ramsay, Henry Wootton and Pompeo Batoni. The adjacent Drawing Room, scarcely altered since its completion, is one of the finest examples of the Rococo taste in England. The walls are hung with arabesque tapestries made in the Soho factory c 1725–30; they serve as the inspiration for the fanciful wreaths of foliage surrounding the portraits of Lyttelton's friends and political cronies. The French-style chairs and ex-travagant pier-glasses were designed as part of the room, and the ceiling paintings are by Cipriani and 'Athenian' Stuart. There is more good plasterwork and furniture in the Gallery, which is divided into three by Corinthian colonnades. Some of the furnishings have been sold, but much still remains, including chairs, chinoiserie pier-glasses, and picture frames carved in a deliberately old-fashioned way to house a collection of portraits bequeathed to the family in 1684. The last room is the Dining Room, recently reinstated to its original purpose—alluded to by the wreaths of vines on the cornice—and containing a 17C Mortlake tapestry taken from a plate in the Duke of Newcastle's treatise on horsemanship. Copies of Old Masters (Poussin, Van Dyck, etc.) hang on the walls of the south staircase, which leads down to the ground floor.

GCT

Wightwick Manor

3m west of Wolverhampton on A454 Wolverhampton–Bridgnorth: National Trust, tel. 0902 761108. Open Mar–Dec Thur, Sat, BH Sun, Mon 2.30–5.30 (possibly subject to change). Guided tours.

Wightwick Manor is not so much a country house as a late-Victorian industrialist's rural retreat. The old manor-house of Wightwick (pronounced 'Wittick') was purchased in 1887 by Theodore Mander, a successful paint manufacturer from Wolverhampton, and he immediately set about replac-ing it with a new house designed—paradoxically—in the 'old English' style by Edward Ould, a former pupil of John Douglas of Chester. A substantial eastward extension was built in 1893, and since then the house has remained largely unaltered. Its interest lies mainly in the interior, which was decorated in the Arts and Crafts taste of the time and has remained substantially unaltered, although several of the pre-Raphaelite pictures and William Morris fabrics which now enhance the rooms were brought in by Sir Geoffrey Mander, who lived in the house after it was given to the National Trust in 1937, and by his wife the late Lady Mander, author of a biography of Dante Gabriel Rossetti.

The house sprawls picturesquely along a south-facing slope, and from the topiary-filled gardens it is easy to distinguish the original, rather Norman Shavian, building of 1887, with its ground floor of harsh red brick and mock-timbered first floor, from the more authentic-looking east wing, rich in decorative timber-framing of impeccable West Midlands pedigree (Ould wrote a book about the vernacular architecture of the area). The entrance, on the north side of the original house, leads first into an Entrance Hall and then to the Drawing Room, largely Elizabethan or Jacobean in its decorative character, with a rich plastered ceiling, wood panelling, Italianate stone chimneypiece, stained-glass windows by C.E. Kempe, and an eclectic but visually satisfying collection of furnishings of different dates, including a late-17C walnut cabinet, a Persian carpet, Chinese porcelain and de Morgan plates and tiles—a vindication of what the architect Ninian Comper called 'unity by inclusion'. The pictures include a water-colour by John Ruskin and a sensitive portrait by G.F. Watts of Ruskin's wife, who later married the painter Millais.

There is another portrait of Effie Ruskin, this time by Millais himself, in the rather gloomy Inner Hall, which occupies the site of the staircase in the original house and leads into the Great Parlour, the most important room in the 1893 extension. This is a romantic recreation of a medieval open hall, with an open timber roof (painted by Kempe, who also designed the plaster frieze, influenced by that at Hardwick Hall, Derbyshire, qv.), a 'minstrels' gallery' and a fireplace with inglenook; there are also comfortable chairs, some of them covered with William Morris chintzes. Chinese porcelain is dotted around the room, and there are excellent pictures by Watts (of Mrs Nassau Senior, the philanthropist sister of the novelist Thomas Hughes) and Burne-Jones ('Love Among the Ruins', 1894, in his most poetic vein). A selection of Morris fabrics is displayed in the Billiard Room, in the furthest part of the east wing, along with portrait drawings by Burne-Jones and Rossetti, and there are more good drawings by Burne-Jones, Holman Hunt and Ford Madox Brown in the wood-panelled Dining Room; note also the neo-Elizabethan plaster ceiling by L.A. Shuffrey and the original electric light fittings (the house was lit by electricity from the beginning). The service corridor (Wightwick had 16 servants in its heyday) leads to the kitchen and scullery. Upstairs, some bedrooms and nurseries are now on show, filled with the usual mixture of period furniture.

GCT

NORFOLK

Beeston Hall

11m north east of Norwich on A1151: Sir Ronald Preston, tel. 0692 630771.
Open Easter–mid Sept Fri, Sun and Wed in Aug and BH Mon 2–5.30.
Refreshments.

Beeston Hall was built in 1785–87 by Jacob Preston, whose family acquired the estate in the mid 17C. He travelled in Italy before settling down as a country squire and taking an interest in poor relief, road improvement and the refashioning of his own house and the moderately sized estate surrounding it. As a Fellow of the Society of Antiquaries (though in his own words 'a very indolent antiquary') he championed the Gothic taste, and his new house was built with symmetrical Gothick façades of knapped flint, a crenellated roof-line, pointed windows and corner turrets surmounted by crocketed pinnacles. These embellishments mask a conventional, two-storeyed, Georgian brick box with light, well-proportioned rooms from which romantic gloom is rigorously excluded. The architect may have been William Wilkins of Norwich, an important figure in local antiquarian circles, whose son was the architect of the National Gallery in London.

The house, which has remained substantially unaltered since the late 18C, stands in rolling country near the Broads. The original late-18C park-like setting has mostly fallen victim to the demands of agriculture, but visitors can still appreciate the contrived view from the house to the round tower of the nearby parish church of Beeston St Lawrence. The unpretentious interiors, Gothic on the entrance front and classic on the garden side, contain no major works of art or outstanding pieces of furniture, but there are good 17C and 18C family portraits in the staircase Hall, where the original architectural pine model of the house—a most unusual survival—is preserved; and in the attractive oval Ante-Room, between the drawing Room and Dining Room on the garden front, there are more family portraits, as well as mementos of the diplomatic career of Sir Thomas Preston, British Consul in Ekaterinburg at the time of the murder of the Tsar in 1918.

GCT

Blickling Hall

On B1354 1½m north west of Aylsham: National Trust, tel. 0263 733084.
Open late Mar–Oct daily, except Mon (open BH Mon), Thur 1–5 (gardens
open 12–5 and daily July, Aug). Refreshments.

Blickling Hall was built in 1619–20 by a rich lawyer, Sir Henry Hobart, Lord Chief Justice of Common Pleas, on the site of an earlier house which had belonged to the Falstofe and Boleyn families. The new house was designed by Robert Lyminge, a carpenter and surveyor who had worked ten years before at Hatfield House, Herts (qv.), and the attractive red-brick façades have certain features in common with Hatfield, notably the distinctive square corner turrets with their exotic-looking ogee-shaped domes, and the clock tower (replaced in 1828) over the entrance front.

The exterior has changed little since the house was first built, but there have been many changes inside the house. Sir John Hobart's great-grand son was raised to the peerage as Earl of Buckinghamshire in 1746, and from 1765 to 1782, the 2nd Earl, a former Ambassador to St Petersburg, employed the Norwich architect Thomas Ivory and his son William to carry out extensive alterations in a spirit sympathetic to the original style of architecture, making Blickling a precocious example of the revival of what Horace Walpole called 'King James's Gothic'. When the 2nd Earl died in 1793 the house and estate passed to his daughter, whose second husband was 6th Marquess of Lothian. Their grandson, the aesthetically-minded 8th Marquis, employed Benjamin Woodward, architect of the University Museum in Oxford, to remodel the rooms in the east wing in 1857–60, with painted decoration by John Hungerford Pollen, but many of these embellishments were removed by the 11th Marquis, a politician who inherited in 1930 and later became British Ambassador to Washington. When he died in 1940 both house and estate were conveyed to the National Trust, of which he was an enthusiastic supporter.

The compact and well-proportioned **entrance front** is one of the most satisfying pieces of Jacobean architecture to survive in England. It is first seen through iron gates at the end of an open outer courtyard flanked by lower service blocks, their roof-lines enlivened by pedimented 'Dutch' gables—one of the first appearances of what was to become a ubiquitous East Anglian architectural feature. The house originally consisted of four ranges around a small courtyard, with a Hall opposite the entrance and two long wings projecting north, in one of which there is a long Gallery overlooking a formal **garden** replanted in the 1930s. The space between the ends of the two wings was later filled in, thus creating a second courtyard, and a new **north range** was built on the site in the 1770s by Thomas Ivory, who had remodelled the west wing a few years earlier. The north range now commands a view of the landscaped park with its lake and woods, in which there is a remarkable **mausoleum** to the 2nd Lord Buckinghamshire designed by Joseph Bonomi in 1794 and modelled on the pyramidal Mausoleum of Caius Cestius in Rome.

The first room to be seen is the **Hall**, which was radically altered in 1767 when the Jacobean screen was destroyed, the entrance shifted to the centre, and the elaborately carved main staircase removed from its original position in the east wing and partially re-erected in the body of the room. At the same time large relief figures of Anne Boleyn and Queen Elizabeth were placed in niches at first-floor level, and a series of full-length figures of local contemporaries of the 1st Lord Buckinghamshire, including Sir Robert Walpole, hung on the walls. A lobby gives access to the **Brown Drawing Room** (originally the chapel), remodelled like its neighbour to the south by the 11th Marquis of Lothian and containing (at the time of writing, 1992) Canaletto's 'Chelsea from the Thames' (1746), a quirky self-portrait by the local artist Goddard Dunning (1678) and an early-15C fireplace with feathered angels, originally at Caister Castle, home of Sir John Falstofe, and brought here in 1732. The adjacent ante-room occupies the original site of the staircase; beyond is the parlour or **Dining Room** with deceptively neo-Jacobean decoration of 1765 and the original oak chimneypiece of 1627. From here a subterranean passageway and staircase lead to the kitchen and a group of **bedrooms** in the west range, the latter reached from a corridor hung with pictures, including a series of Italian water-colours by Goethe's travelling companion C.H. Kniep and a view of Jedburgh Abbey by Girtin; one of the rooms contains pictures collected by the 8th Lord Lothian, including a languid 'Lisa' by his friend Valentine Prinsep.

The Gallery at Blickling Hall with the elaborate Jacobean plaster ceiling, painted frieze by Pollen and bookcases by Woodward

In Jacobean times the main reception rooms were on the first floor of the south and east ranges. The south rooms were all remodelled in the 1760s, among them the attractively wallpapered **Chinese bedroom** and the adjoining dressing room. The former great chamber (the **South Drawing Room**), in the south-east corner of the house, still retains its original Jacobean chimneypiece and plaster ceiling, but was redecorated in the 1930s and now contains a famous picture of George II's mistress Lady Suffolk (cf. Marble Hill, Greater London), sister of the 1st Lord Buckinghamshire, wearing masquerade dress. There is another Jacobean ceiling in the ante-room, made out of the upper part of the staircase hall in 1767, but the most elaborate ceiling is in the **Gallery**, with panels representing the five senses (in the centre) and arcane emblems taken from Henry Peacham's *Minerva Britannica*. The painted frieze is by Pollen and the walls are lined with bookcases designed by Woodward to contain a superb collection of books—one of the best in any English country house—inherited by the 1st Lord Buckinghamshire in the 18C (the Victorian fireplace was unfortunately removed by the 11th Lord Lothian).

The **Peter the Great Room** (1778–82), in the north range, was created in order to display a spectacular tapestry of the Russian Tsar on horseback woven in St Petersburg in 1764 and given by Catherine the Great to the 2nd Lord Buckinghamshire. This impressive 'great room' has an unusual ochre colour scheme, and contains good contemporary furniture as well as full-length portraits of Lord Buckinghamshire and his wife by Gainsborough. After passing through the State Bedroom (possibly by Samuel Wyatt), with an excellent Axminster carpet (one of several in the house) and a portrait by Daniel Mytens of Sir Henry Hobart, the builder of the house, the tour ends in the Document Room (Lord Lothian's bedroom in the 1930s), where some of the books from the library are on display.

NB: some rearrangement of the pictures took place in 1993.

GCT

Felbrigg Hall

2m south west of Cromer, west of B1436: National Trust, tel. 0263 837444.
Open late Mar–Oct daily except Tues, Fri, 1.30–5.30 (BH Sun, Mon
11–5.30). Refreshments.

This attractive 17C house stands in an extensive park, with only the 15C parish church, full of brasses, box pews and family monuments, as a neighbour. The house was built in 1621–24 by a lawyer, Francis Windham, and, like the contemporary Blickling Hall (qv.), has an unusually compact, symmetrical façade with curved gables, tall chimneys and large mullioned and transomed windows. Thomas Windham's son, William, gave it its present L-shaped plan by adding a west wing in 1675–87 to designs provided by the gentleman amateur architect, William Samwell (cf. Ham House, Greater London), and since then the main exteriors have been little altered. But the west wing was transformed internally in 1749–56, when another William Windham, grandson of the builder, employed James Paine to design a new suite of reception rooms; Windham had travelled in Italy, and the rooms still house his largely intact collection of pictures (especially seascapes). Paine also built the service wing to the east of the house, which was Gothicised in 1825 by the local architect W.J. Donthorne, who also designed the castellated stables. The male line of the Windhams died out in 1810, and after an unusually complicated descent, the house and estate were given to the National Trust after the death of the historian and local topographer, Robert Wyndham Ketton-Cremer, in 1969.

The exterior, as seen from the south west, epitomises the revolutionary change that overcame English domestic architecture in the 17C. The flint-built Jacobean south range with its projecting bays is still essentially medieval in character, but the red-brick hipped-roofed wing is an accomplished exercise in the Anglicised classical idiom popular after the Restoration. A porch in the centre of the south range gives access to the Hall, redecorated in a rather crude neo-Jacobean manner in the 1840s, probably by J.C. and G. Buckler (cf. Oxburgh Hall) and containing 15C stained glass panels from St Peter Mancroft, Norwich, and busts of the younger Pitt, Fox, and William Windham, Secretary for War at the beginning of the Napoleonic Wars.

From the west end of the Hall, where the high table originally stood, there is a vista through the main reception rooms, the first of which is the Dining Room, created by Paine on the site of the main staircase and containing excellent Rococo plasterwork by Joseph Rose, the uncle of Robert Adam's plasterer. The Drawing Room still retains its equally accomplished late-17C plaster ceiling in the manner of Edward Gouge, but the walls are hung with paintings introduced by William Windham in the mid 18C, including two large representations of the Battle of the Texel by the elder Van de Velde and two views of London by Samuel Scott (1753). Most of the furniture was introduced in the early 19C. The adjacent cabinet was transformed by Paine into an exquisite receptacle for some of the smaller pictures from William

Windham's collection, including a pretty series of views of Rome and its surroundings by Giovanni Busiri (1739); the equally attractive pair of harbour scenes by the Flemish artist Abraham Storck (1673) were introduced, along with most of the furniture, by Admiral William Lukin, who inherited in 1824. The plaster ceiling dates from the 17C and 18C, but the Rococo overmantel is by Paine, who also built out the canted bay window to the north.

The upstairs rooms are reached by a top-lit staircase in the angle between the two wings; it dates from 1752 and is hung with pictures of William Windham and his tutor and travelling companion Benjamin Stillingfleet. Windham bought many of the books in the Library, created by Paine in the room over the Hall in the Jacobean part of the house. The Gothick bookcases also house some of Dr Johnson's books, brought here after his death by Windham's son, who befriended Johnson in his declining years, and a small adjoining room contains books and pictures (including drawings and water-colours by Cotman and Edward Bawden) collected by R.W. Ketton-Cremer, the last private owner and author of an excellent history of the house. There is a pair of Rococo pier-glasses in the Rose Bedroom in the west wing, and an adjacent room was decorated with Chinese wallpaper and matching furniture in the 1750s.

GCT

Holkham Hall

2m west of Wells-next-the-Sea to south of A149 Hunstanton–Cromer: Viscount Coke, tel. 0328 710227. Open late May–Sept Sun–Thur 1.30–5 (also Easter, May, Spring Aug BH Sun, Mon 11.30–5). Refreshments.

This magnificent neo-Palladian house was begun in 1734 by Thomas Coke (later to become 1st Earl of Leicester), a descendant of Sir Edward Coke, the famous Lord Chief Justice in James I's reign. Leicester was a lavish and discriminating collector who spent six years on the Continent and numbered Lord Burlington among his friends, and in designing Holkham he turned to Burlington's protégé William Kent, entrusting the practicalities of building to a local man, Matthew Brettingham, and calling on his own taste and experience in reaching the final decisions. The main block was still unroofed when Kent died in 1748, and the house was not finished until 1762, by which time Leicester had also died, impoverished by the costs of building the house and laying out the estate. The internal decoration was completed by his widow, since when there have been few major alterations either to the exterior or to the sumptuous interior, which still contains one of the finest 18C collections of art and antiquities in England.

Leicester intended his house to be a 'temple of the arts', with a massive central block containing the grand reception rooms on the piano nobile. But, according to a contemporary, 'conveniency was one of his leading maxims', and smaller free-standing blocks were placed at each corner, one of which served as a self-contained family wing, the others housing kitchens, a guest wing and a private chapel. This unusually expansive plan was derived from Palladio, who like Leicester and his contemporaries had been fascinated by the idea of reviving the domestic architecture of the Romans, and many features at Holkham, like the austere yellow-brick walls, the imposing Corinthian portico on the garden front and the four corner towers of the main block, were intended to convey an impression of Roman gravity. The effect of rigorous abstraction is softened by the surrounding landscape, created by Leicester out of what had formerly been 'an open barren Estate' close to the North Sea.

The house is entered through the **north front**, which faces a column of 1845–50 commemorating Leicester's great-nephew, the agricultural improver 'Coke of Norfolk', whose model farm buildings can still be seen dotted about the surrounding landscape. A low entrance hall, added c 1850, gives access to the spectacular **Marble Hall**, a long rectangular room based on the design of the Roman basilica and flanked by free-standing Ionic columns, but given added richness by the use of Derbyshire alabaster as cladding for the columns and their podium, and by the intricate coffering of the coved ceiling. Busts by Chantrey of the 1st Earl of Leicester and 'Coke of Norfolk' flank the flight of steps, which leads up to the Saloon at the centre of the garden front. At the top, among several relief carvings and pieces of statuary 'after the antique', there is a bas-relief by Chantrey of William IV signing the First Reform Act in the presence of Coke, a fervent Whig; Chantrey also carved the marble relief behind the west colonnade of two woodcocks which he had himself shot (1829).

From here visitors proceed through all the main rooms on the upper floor of the central block, starting in the relatively austere **Dining Room**, a cube-shaped room with a ceiling inspired by Inigo Jones and an apsidal recess in the south wall containing the sideboard; restored busts of emperors rest on brackets supported by consoles on either side of this recess, and there are also antique busts over the two fireplaces. The whole of the west side of the house is taken up by the **Gallery**, which, like the gallery at Lord Burlington's Chiswick House, Greater London (qv.), is divided into three, with a rectangular central section flanked by octagonal 'tribunes'—an arrangement derived from the baths of ancient Rome. These museum-like rooms house the bulk of the antique statuary collected by Leicester and his agent in Rome, the younger Matthew Brettingham, son of the executant architect at Holkham. The statues of Lucius Verus (in the north tribune) and Diana were bought by Leicester himself in 1717, and rank among the most important examples of classical sculpture to survive in an English private collection. The south tribune has been converted into a **library**, in which printed books from the collection are shown.

The main reception rooms are arranged along the south front, overlooking the expansive landscape. These rooms have rich Genoa velvet hangings, ornate gilded ceilings inspired by those of Inigo Jones, and heavy furniture in the style of William Kent. But the main interest lies in the collection of Old Master paintings, many of which, following a recent rearrangement, now hang once again in their original positions. There are landscapes by Claude ('Apollo flaying Marsyas') and Poussin in the **Drawing Room**, along with portraits of the lawyer Sir Edward Coke, the founder of the family fortunes. In the adjoining **Saloon**, with its coved ceiling, there is a Van Dyck (the Duke of Arenburg), a superb Rubens ('Return of the Holy Family'), and, flanking the entrance, two paintings commissioned by Leicester in Rome in 1714: 'Tarquin and Lucretia' by Antonio Procaccini and 'Perseus and Andromeda' by G.B. Chiari. Two of the side tables have mosaic tops from Hadrian's Villa at Tivoli.

Pictures by Guido Reni ('Joseph and Potiphar's Wife') and Pompeo Batoni (a Grand Tour portrait of 'Coke of Norfolk' in fancy dress) hang in the **South Dining Room**. The most memorable pictures in the collection are in the

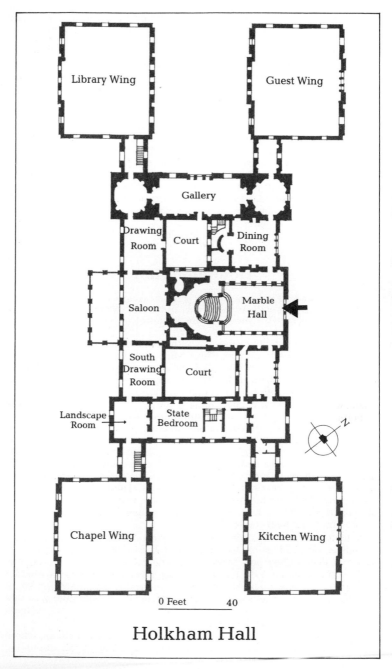

Holkham Hall

Landscape Room (originally the state dressing room), in the south-east corner, notably seven landscapes by Claude purchased by Leicester from Cardinal Albani, one of the leading art dealers of his time; landscapes by Gaspard Dughet hang over the doors, and through the Venetian window on the south side of the room, there is a view of the peaceful Claudian landscape created by Leicester as a setting for the house. The adjoining **State Bedroom** is mainly notable for its upholstered furniture and canopied bed, and for the tapestries of the Four Continents, three of which were designed by Auwerx in Brussels in the 17C and the fourth ('Asia') by Saunders; the pictures of the Seasons over the doors are by Zuccarelli. The **Dressing Room** next door is hung with small pictures, including a 16C copy of Michelangelo's cartoon for an unexecuted fresco for the Hall of the Great Council of Florence and works by Bassano and Luca Giordano. The tour ends in a pair of rather gloomy north-facing rooms, one of which contains Trevisani's Grand Tour portrait of the 1st Earl of Leicester, whose vision of a classical house set in an arcadian landscape and filled with exquisite furnishings and works of art has been so impeccably preserved by his descendants.

GCT

Houghton Hall

10m west of Fakenham, to north of A418 Fakenham–King's Lynn: the Marquess of Cholmondeley, tel. 0485 528569. Open Easter–Sept Sun, Thur and BH Mon 1–5. Refreshments.

Houghton is inseparably connected with the personality and ambitions of its builder, Sir Robert Walpole, Prime Minister to George I and George II. Walpole came from an old Norfolk family, and began planning a magnificent new house while out of office at the time of the South Sea Bubble (from which he escaped with his reputation and fortune intact). The house was intended for large-scale entertaining, and Walpole's biennial 'Norfolk Congresses' at Houghton played an important part in his political success. Until recently it was assumed that the architect was Colen Campbell, who supplied a design in 1723, a year after the first stone was laid, but new research has suggested that the house may have been designed *ab initio* by James Gibbs, who certainly added the corner domes in 1725–28 'in defiance of all the virtuosi'; they give a welcome sense of Baroque movement to the otherwise rather austere façades. The builder was Thomas Ripley, and the lavish interior decoration was carried out c 1726–31 under the supervision of William Kent, who may also have designed the large and impressive brick-built stable block.

Walpole's magnificent collection of Old Master paintings was sold by his grandson, the 3rd Earl of Orford, in 1779, most of them to Catherine the Great of Russia (they now form part of the collection in the Hermitage, St Petersburg), and in 1797 the house passed by inheritance to the 4th Earl of Cholmondeley. For over 100 years until the end of the First World War it was leased out to tenants and escaped unsympathetic alterations, so that today the main state rooms—the only ones to be seen by visitors—remain much as they were in Walpole's time.

The house stands among lawns near the site of a deserted village whose church and village cross still survive, and the hand of the improving landlord is clearly visible in the attractive rows of white-painted 18C cottages near the gate into the park, one of the earliest surviving estate villages. The house is faced with stone brought by sea from Aislaby, near Whitby, Yorkshire and consists of two main storeys: a ground floor, or 'rustick', for everyday use, and a piano nobile which one of Walpole's many visitors called 'the floor of taste, expense and parade'. There are also lower service blocks on each side, joined to the main building by curved colonnades.

The entrance is through a vaulted lower hall on the ground floor, from which a massive wooden **staircase** leads up through the whole height of the building, its walls decorated with monochrome paintings of classical subjects by Kent. The theme of the Antique, which is present throughout the house, is emphasised by the 17C bronze copy (by Le Sueur) of the 'Borghese Gladiator', originally at Wilton, Wiltshire (qv.). The bulk of the first floor is given over to reception rooms, with a Hall and Saloon in the centre flanked by two drawing rooms on the north side and two dining rooms—a major innovation—to the south; bedrooms are confined to the sides of the house. The rooms were decorated in a heavy, masculine style which Kent took to be close to that of the ancient Romans, and the decoration is complemented by the equally solid-looking and beautifully preserved furniture, much of it also designed by him. The first room to be seen is the **Common Parlour** (originally a dining room), which contains a conversation-piece by William Orpen ('The Play Scene from Hamlet') and a portrait by Sargent of the last Marchioness of Cholmondeley, who, together with her husband, restored the house after the First World War. Next comes the monumental two-storeyed **Hall**, inspired by Inigo Jones's hall in the Queen's House at Greenwich, Greater London (qv.) with a gallery at first-floor level supported on consoles. John Wootton's portrait of Sir Robert Walpole in hunting garb rests on an easel, and there is a bust of him by Rysbrack over the fireplace in front of a classical relief of a 'Sacrifice to Diana' by the same sculptor.

From here visitors proceed through the grander (east) side of the piano nobile. The **Marble Parlour** was the main formal dining room, with the serving area placed behind the arches on either side of the massive marble fireplace, over which is a relief carving of a 'Sacrifice to Bacchus' by Rysbrack; Kent's ceiling, like others in the house, features arabesques and other motifs copied from Roman interior decoration, but the richly carved and upholstered gilt chairs, long thought to have been designed by Kent, were probably brought here by the Cholmondeleys. The adjacent **Cabinet Room**, like its namesake at Felbrigg (qv.), was originally hung with small pictures, but was redecorated with Chinese wallpaper and Rococo mirrors complete with ho-ho birds after the picture sale of 1779. Two **bedrooms** in the east wing contain spectacular state beds and Brussels tapestries, with those in the Green Velvet Bedchamber representing legends of Venus, whose shell is represented over the bed itself. The dressing room separating these two rooms is hung with tapestries of the Stuart kings—an odd choice in view of Walpole's Hanoverian sympathies—woven at Mortlake in 1670; the two thrones were designed by A.W.N. Pugin for the House of Lords and acquired by the 5th Marquess of Cholmondeley as perquisites of his office as Lord Chamberlain.

The **White Drawing Room**, on the north side of the house, was rehung with silk in the early 19C after the disappearance of some of Walpole's best pictures, and now contains pastels of Walpole's three sons by Rosalba

Carriera, along with J.-B. Oudry's 'White Duck' and some good 18C French furniture from the collection of the late Lady Cholmondeley's brother, Sir Philip Sassoon (cf. Port Lympne, Kent). The tour ends in the magnificent **Saloon**, with its coved ceiling, enriched cornice, 'tabernacle frame' around the doorway into the Hall, and original wall hangings of deep red damask, complemented by the upholstery of Kent's armchairs, which were originally placed around the walls. All that is missing are Sir Robert Walpole's pictures, and for these, alas, the portrait of a rotund Catherine the Great—a gift to his spendthrift son—is small compensation. Lovers of model soldiers will enjoy the large and well-displayed collection in the north office wing.

GCT

Oxburgh Hall

At Oxborough, 7m south west of Swaffham on Swaffham–Stoke Ferry road: National Trust, tel. 036621 258. Open late Mar–Oct Sat–Wed 1.30-5.30, BH Mon 11–5.30 (gardens open 12). Refreshments.

Sir Edmund Bedingfeld was given licence to crenellate his recently inherited house on the edge of the Fens in 1482, and the red-brick courtyard building, romantically situated in its moat, must date from about that time. The Bedingfelds reached the pinnacle of their power and prestige in the early 16C, when they performed important services for the Tudor monarchs, and they are commemorated in a richly decorated chantry chapel with a terracotta screen in the nearby parish church. But Sir Henry Bedingfeld, Governor of the Tower of London under Mary, refused to conform to the Protestant dispensation restored by Elizabeth, and his successors, who still live in the house as tenants of the National Trust, have remained Catholic. The house was much altered in the 18C, culminating in the destruction of the medieval hall in 1775, but a determined effort was made by later generations, starting in 1830, to restore an 'Old English' character. These alterations were entrusted to J.C. Buckler, an architect much patronised by the Catholic gentry, and today the house is as much a monument to the taste of the 19C as it is to that of the 15C.

Oxburgh Hall is dominated externally by its splendid late-15C gatehouse tower, one of the most impressive of its date in England, with an especially fine use of moulded brick for ornamental effect. The main reception rooms are in the much-restored west wing, approached through a porch and corridor on the site of the medieval hall. With the exception of the 18C Saloon at the south-west corner of the courtyard, they date essentially from the 19C. There is much dark-wood panelling and heavy furniture, some of it made up of old fragments, following the custom of the time. The finest ensemble is the Dining Room, with its elaborate chimneypiece and overmantel enclosing, surprisingly, a portrait of the architect Lord Burlington, whose sister married a Bedingfeld. There is a good late-17C portrait of Sir Henry Arundell Bedingfeld with his sister and a negro servant in the Saloon, and one of Lady Bedingfeld, an amateur artist, by Opie in the Drawing Room.

The north staircase, hung with embossed 17C Spanish leather, leads to a darkened room containing the most important works of art in the house: a set of needlework wall hangings with animal motifs made by Mary, Queen of Scots and 'Bess of Hardwick' (cf. Hardwick Hall, Derbyshire) c 1570 and brought here from the now-ruinous Cowdray House, Sussex (qv.) in the 18C. The tour ends in the two upper rooms of the gate tower, the lower of which (the King's Room) contains a display case with letters from Tudor kings and queens and a pair of scissors belonging to Mary, Queen of Scots: there is also an unusual late-17C votive picture showing Sir Henry Bedingfeld and his eight children sheltering under the skirts of the Virgin Mary. A small room in the adjoining turret has a delicately detailed brick rib vault and a priests' hole into which the intrepid can descend, and a spiral staircase in the corresponding turret—in itself a tour de force of medieval craftsmanship—leads up to the Queen's Room on the top floor, which houses one of the topographical tapestry maps made at the Sheldon works in Warwickshire c 1647. From here it is possible to walk up on to the roof and view the uneventful landscape around, before descending to the National Trust shop in the former billiard room and the tea room in the kitchen. A Roman Catholic chapel ascribed to A.W.N. Pugin stands in the grounds to the north of the house.

GCT

Sandringham

8m north of King's Lynn to east of A149 King's Lynn–Hunstanton: Her Majesty the Queen, tel. 0553 772675. Open early Apr–mid July, early Aug–Sept daily) except when Royal Family is in residence) 11–4.45 (Sun 12–4.45).

The present house at Sandringham has been a royal residence throughout its relatively brief history, but its character is that of a comfortable, well-appointed, late-Victorian and Edwardian country house, not a palace. The estate was bought for the Prince of Wales (later Edward VII) in 1862, partly for its sporting potential, and in 1870 the existing house was replaced by a new building in the neo-Jacobean style designed by A.J. Humbert, the architect of Prince Albert's mausoleum in Windsor Great Park; a ballroom was added by R.W. Edis in 1883, and the second floor was remodelled by the same architect after a fire in 1891. When Edward VII became King he continued to use the house as an occasional residence, and more recent monarchs have all returned to it regularly.

The house stands in a wooded coniferous setting which bears all the marks of careful estate management. A spectacular set of iron gates by Thomas Jekyll of Norwich (1862) marks the main formal entrance, but visitors enter the grounds through a more discreet gateway to the east of the village green and proceed through the spruce, shrub-filled gardens laid out by W.B. Thomas, who like Humbert had worked for Queen Victoria at Windsor. From here the long and rather chaotic red-brick west front can be seen, its skyline enlivened by gables, tall chimneys and ogee-topped turrets (cf. Blickling Hall), with a lower wing overlooking the ornamental lake and incorporating the conservatory from the former house.

The entrance is through a carriage porch on the east side, which gives access to a tall and spacious Saloon modelled on a Jacobean hall, but furnished in the usual late-Victorian manner as a comfortable sitting room. There are portraits here of Queen Victoria and Prince Albert by Winterhalter (1845 and 1850) and of Edward VII as Prince of Wales with his family by Heinrich von Angeli (c 1876). The relatively unpretentious tastes of Edward and his son George V are reflected in the main reception rooms, which stretch along the west front. The ceilings and cream-painted French-inspired panelling of the main Drawing Room were installed c 1900, and the furniture in the style of the French 18C was introduced at about the same time; the portraits of Princess (later Queen) Alexandra and two of her daughters by Edward Hughes were painted for their present positions in 1896. The panelling in the adjacent Dining Room is of about the same date, and surrounds a set of tapestries after paintings by late-18C Spanish artists (including Goya), given to the Prince of Wales by the King of Spain in 1876. From here a lobby and a corridor lined with late-19C paintings and bronzes (including one of Icarus by Alfred Gilbert c 1884) lead to a spacious Ballroom.

GCT

NORTHAMPTONSHIRE

Althorp

6m north west of Northampton on A428 Northampton–Rugby: the Earl
Spencer, tel. 0604 770006/770209. Open Easter weekend, then Aug daily
12.30–5, and some other dates (telephone for details). Refreshments.

The Spencer family has been connected with Althorp since the late 15C,
when John Spencer, a Warwickshire sheep farmer, took a lease of the
manor. The estate was bought by his grandson, who built the house and is
buried in the family mortuary chapel in the nearby church at Great
Brington. The family became very rich, and were raised to a peerage in
1603 and to the earldom of Sunderland 40 years later, but until the Civil
War they lived mainly at Wormleighton (Warwickshire), where part of their
house still survives. The house at Althorp was enlarged into its present
courtyard shape, with projecting wings, in the 1570s, but was completely
remodelled in 1666–68 by the shifty and ambitious 2nd Earl of Sunderland,
later to become a key political figure under James II and William III. His
architect, Anthony Ellis, a pupil of Nicholas Stone, refaced the existing
brick house and adorned it with classical pilasters on both floors; according
to one contemporary visitor, the chambers were 'regularly disposed after
the Italian manner, to which country the earl was indebted for a model of
the design, and it may be said to be the best planned and best arrayed
country seat in the kingdom'.

A new stable block was built in 1729 to the designs of the neo-Palladian
architect Roger Morris, and four years later the entrance hall was redecorated. The 5th Earl, who commissioned this work, inherited the dukedom
of Marlborough in 1734 and went to live at Blenheim Palace, Oxfordshire
(qv.), leaving Althorp to his younger brother, a notable art collector, whose
son was made Earl Spencer and built the magnificent Spencer House on
the edge of Green Park in London. The 2nd Earl, a Foxite Whig, commissioned Henry Holland in 1787–91 to supply a new suite of reception rooms
at ground-floor level and to encase the exterior in grey 'mathematical tiles'
made in Norfolk—an unfortunate choice of material in a county so well-
supplied with good building stone. J. MacVicar Anderson designed a new
dining room and carried out other internal alterations starting in 1877. The
interiors have been changed on several occasions since, notably between
the wars, when chimneypieces, pictures and furniture were brought from
Spencer House, and more recently by the last Earl (father of the Princess
of Wales) and his second wife, whose taste is evident in several parts of the
house.

The house is approached through a monumental stable block of local
brown stone, with four corner towers and a massive Tuscan portico influenced by that of Inigo Jones's St Paul's, Covent Garden, and ultimately
inspired by Palladio and Vitruvius. From here, Holland's south façade can
be seen, with its somewhat awkward engaged portico, through which the
house is entered. The well-proportioned Entrance Hall was created by John
Wootton for the 5th Earl of Sunderland, a keen sportsman, the doorways
are emphasised by Palladian 'tabernacle frames', and the coved ceiling is
decorated with rich plasterwork attributed to John Woolston of Northampton (cf. Lamport Hall). The central doorway leads into the top-lit Saloon,
copiously hung with family portraits; it takes up the whole of the original

16C courtyard and contains a massive oak staircase of 1666–69 leading to the main reception rooms upstairs.

The ground floor rooms date from the late 18C and 19C. The Victorian Dining Room contains paintings by Salvator Rosa ('Diogenes' and 'Cincinnatus Called from the Farm') and Guercino ('King David' and 'The Samian Sybil'), along with furniture by Holland and George Seddon. In the north range is the Marlborough Room, with fireplaces from Spencer House and some of Reynolds's finest portraits, including his sensitive study of the Countess Spencer and her daughter (later the Duchess of Devonshire), painted in 1761. The west range is made up of a suite of three interconnecting rooms created by Holland in the 1780s and described by the then Countess Spencer as 'the image of comfort': the Library, the Rubens Room, with portraits of Philip IV of Spain and his Queen by the Flemish master, and the South Drawing Room (originally the dining room), containing some excellent 18C French furniture, some of it acquired for the house by Holland. These rooms are flanked by a corridor in which Sèvres and Meissen porcelain is displayed, along with several self- portraits of artists, including one by Guercino.

The only important room in the house to survive virtually unaltered from the time of the 2nd Lord Sunderland is the Gallery, which occupies most of the first floor of the west wing. The wood panelling was designed to hold a collection of portraits, which still survive largely intact in the original frames (know as 'Sunderland frames' after the 2nd Earl) made in Spain or Italy. There are works by Van Dyck (eg, his superb double portrait of the Earls of Bristol and Bedford), a series of nubile court beauties by Lely, and several Knellers, including a lively sketch of the astringent Sarah, Duchess of Marlborough. The room is lined with mahogany chairs made for the house by William Vile in the 1750s, and there is a lacquer screen taken on campaign by the 1st Duke of Marlborough. A gallery running alongside the staircase hall at first-floor level leads to a suite of reception rooms on the north side of the house, remodelled in the late 18C and now containing furniture by 'Athenian' Stuart and others, much of it brought from Spencer House. The pictures include two portraits by Carlo Maratta, one of them of the cosmopolitan 2nd Earl of Sunderland in a toga; and, in the Great Room, there are some 16C works including a portrait by Lorenzo Lotto. A view of the house in 1677 by Johannes Vostermans hangs in an adjacent lobby. Visitors also see the well-preserved 17C Chapel, which retains some of its original woodwork.

NB: there have been (1993) some changes to the route through the house, and some pictures and furniture may be moved in future.

GCT

Aynhoe Park

6m south east of Banbury on A41: Country Houses Association. Open May–Sept Weds, Thur 2–5. Guided tours.

Aynhoe Park stands at the southern end of a stone-built village overlooking the Cherwell valley which separates Northamptonshire from Oxfordshire. The estate was bought by a lawyer, John Cartwright, at the beginning of the 17C and remained the home of his descendants until after the Second World War, when it was turned into flats. The main downstairs rooms were preserved as reception rooms for the residents, but when the Cartwrights left they took their pictures and furniture with them. Today, therefore, the main interest lies in the building itself, and particularly in the contributions of two of England's most original architects, Thomas Archer and John Soane.

As seen from the road, Aynhoe Park consists of a pedimented main block with lower service blocks on either side creating a courtyard. This French-inspired arrangement dates from the time of Thomas Cartwright, who employed Archer in 1707–14 to enlarge the existing Jacobean house, which had been rebuilt after the Civil War to the designs of Edward Marshall, master mason in Charles II's Office of Works. Archer had travelled in Italy, and some strange late-Baroque detailing enlivens his work at Aynhoe, eg, the concave surrounds to the central doorways of the office wings and the Borromini-inspired capitals with inturned volutes (like those at Chettle, Dorset, qv.) on the wings at the ends of the garden front. The centre of the garden front still remains largely intact from the 1660s, and the domestic-looking church, to the east, was built in 1723 to the designs of Edward Wing, one of the masons employed on the house.

Archer's interiors, except for the main staircase, have been drastically remodelled, but Aynhoe still retains a sequence of rooms designed by that most creative of English architects, John Soane. He was called in to prepare designs for a thorough internal remodelling in 1795, and coloured perspective drawings in the Soane Museum in London show a series of spectacular monumental interiors which were alas never built. He did, however, redesign the main reception rooms along the garden front in a plainer style in 1800–5, and with one exception (the French Drawing Room) they survive intact to show his ingenious exploitation of curved surfaces; he also designed the top-lit staircase in the south wing, with its iron balustrade uncannily foreshadowing the work of the 1930s, and built the 'triumphal arches' joining the main block to the service wings. Some internal redecoration was carried out in the years before the First World War, and in 1988 the former orangery was turned into a plush dining room.

GCT

Boughton House

3m north east of Kettering off A43 Kettering–Stamford: the Duke of Buccleuch, tel. 0536 515731. Open Aug daily 2–5 (grounds May–Sept daily except Fri 1–5). State rooms by prior booking only. Refreshments.

This magnificent but relatively little-known house lies on land which belonged in the Middle Ages to the Abbey of Bury St Edmunds. The estate was acquired after the Dissolution by Sir Edward Montagu, Lord Chief Justice under Henry VIII, but soon after the Glorious Revolution of 1688 his relatively modest courtyard house was expanded to palatial proportions by his descendant, the 3rd Lord Montagu, four times ambassador to France under Charles II and later Master of the Wardrobe to William III. Montagu married a rich widow, Lady Elizabeth Wriothesley, co-heiress of the Earls of Southampton (cf. Beaulieu, Hants), and was made Duke of Montagu in 1705, but when his son died in 1749 the estate passed through the female line, first to the Brudenells of Deene Park (qv.) and then to the Dukes of Buccleuch, whose main estates were in Scotland. They rarely came to

Boughton, and the house therefore remained virtually unaltered until the early years of the 20C, when the 7th Duke carried out a sensitive restoration. Today the house is chiefly notable for the beautifully preserved block of late-17C state rooms and for the collection of furniture, pictures, tapestries and porcelain amassed by the 1st Duke of Montagu and his successors, notably George Brudenell, 4th Earl of Cardigan and 3rd Duke of Montagu (d 1790), his son Lord Monthermer, and the 5th Duke of Buccleuch (d 1884).

The urbane and sophisticated **north façade**, with its mansard roof and broad bands of rusticated stone, immediately proclaims the Francophile tastes of the 1st Duke of Montagu. The state rooms—perhaps the best-preserved of their date in any English country house—occupy the first floor over an arcade, and two projecting wings. Montagu also remodelled the Hall and built a château-like **stable block** to the east, but otherwise left the Tudor house largely intact. His architect has eluded detection, but there are clear links, especially in the internal layout, to the work of the Huguenot, Daniel Marot.

The house is entered through the **Staircase Hall** in the north range, painted allegorically in monochrome by Louis Chéron, one of several Huguenot artists patronised by Montagu. Visitors are allowed to wander through the main ground-floor rooms, but the state rooms upstairs are only shown in a separate guided tour available by pre-booking. The **Ante-Room** and **Little Hall**, on either side of the staircase, form part of Montagu's remodelling, and his portrait hangs in the Ante-Room beside an elaborate inlaid table attributed to Pierre Gole, possibly a present from Louis XIV. Murillo's 'St John the Baptist' and El Greco's 'Adoration of the Shepherds', in the Ante-Room, were both acquired by the 4th Earl of Cardigan, along with the head of a youth by Annibale Carracci in the Little Hall. Other paintings here include a Kneller portrait of Charles II's first-born son, the Duke of Monmouth, who married Anne Scott, ancestress of the Scotts of Buccleuch, and flower pictures by Monnoyer, another artist patronised by Montagu.

The **Drawing Room** on the west side of the Tudor courtyard contains a set of oil sketches by Van Dyck, two carpets of 1583–85, outstanding 18C French furniture by Martin Carlin and others, and a pair of Meissen swans (1745). Next door, in the **Morning Room**, there are tapestries from the 'Playing Boys' series made c 1640 in the Mortlake factory, which was bought by Montagu, and in the **Rainbow Room** there are more Mortlake tapestries, as well as some excellent late-17C and early-18C English and French furniture, including a Boulle writing table given to the 1st Duke of Montagu by Louis XIV.

The Tudor exterior of the Hall can be seen from a **corridor** running along the south side of the courtyard, hung with Dutch and English paintings, including works by Cuyp and van de Velde and two views by Samuel Scott of the unembanked Thames at Westminster, one of them showing the long-vanished Montagu House. Sèvres and Meissen porcelain is displayed in the **Audit Room** on the east side of the courtyard, which leads to a former dining room now known as the **Egyptian Hall**, with a painting by Chéron of the Triumph of Bacchus on the ceiling; 16C and 17C paintings are hung here, including a cornucopian market scene by Beuckelaer, and there is also a model of a Gothic bridge by the antiquary William Stukeley, a friend of the 2nd Duke of Montagu. Next door is the **Hall**, whose 16C timber roof is hidden by the present plaster barrel vault, painted by Chéron in the 1690s, when the walls were also panelled; the silver sconces were given as

One of the State Rooms at Boughton House, showing the Mortlake tapestries after Raphael, 1636, and late 17C furniture

a wedding gift to the Duke of Monmouth by Charles II, whose royal cipher they bear. Above the panelling is a superb series of Mortlake tapestries of the Elements (c 1676) and a large equestrian portrait of the Duke of Monmouth. Other paintings include a portrait by John de Critz of Shakespeare's friend, the long-haired Earl of Southampton and his cat, painted while he was in the Tower of London in 1600–3; there are also three sensitive portraits by Gainsborough and one by Batoni of the collector, Lord Monthermer. This part of the tour ends in the **Armoury**, with the extensive collection of ornate weapons belonging to the 1st Duke of Marlborough, father-in-law of the 2nd Duke of Montagu, and a strange series of imaginary portraits of medieval Montagus painted in the 17C.

The high, wood-panelled **state rooms** in the north wing convey a strong feeling of time arrested. Designed to be used only by important visitors, they comprise an apartment made up of an ante-room, bedroom and closet (now a bathroom) in the west wing and a grander 'great apartment' in the central block; the east wing was never finished internally and remains an empty shell. The apartment in the west wing contains tapestries, French late-17C and 18C furniture and paintings by Frans Pourbus, Sébastien Bourdon and van Dyck, but it is overshadowed in decorative splendour by the five rooms of the 'great apartment'. The late-17C furniture by James Moore and Thomas Roberts has been supplemented by later pieces, and the state bed is now in the Victoria and Albert Museum in London, but otherwise there have been few changes since the 1st Duke of Montagu entertained William III here in the 1690s. There are well-preserved tapestries, including four after the Raphael cartoons from the Mortlake factory (1636) and others of rural scenes from the early-17C Frenchmen, Gombaut and Maçée; there is also a pair of early-16C cartoons for tapestries attributed to the Italian master, Penni, and there are paintings by Solimena, Carlo Dolci and others. But the overriding impression is not so much of the individual items as of an ensemble preserved intact for 300 years regardless of necessity or changing fashion.

GCT

Canons Ashby

On unclassified road off B4525, half-way between Banbury and Northampton: National Trust, tel. 0327 860044. Open Apr–Oct Wed–Sun, BH Mon 1–5.30. Refreshments.

Canons Ashby stands in remote country in the still deeply rural southern part of this most squirearchical of counties. The house is named after a small Augustinian priory founded in the mid 12C, and the two west bays of the monastic church, with the massive west tower, still survive close to the house, having been used as a family chapel for the past 450 years. The village was depopulated as result of the Black Death and sheep-farming enclosures, and c 1551 part of the monastic estate was acquired by John Dryden, who built the oldest parts of the present house, including the hall range, on a virgin site away from the church. His son Sir Erasmus Dryden, a zealous puritan, extended the building to form a courtyard shape in the 1590s, and internal alterations were carried out in the 1630s and again, more extensively, in 1708–10 by Edward Dryden, cousin of the poet John Dryden. The Drydens never became as grand as some Northamptonshire families, and now Canons Ashby is one of the best surviving examples of a 16C gentleman's house altered in accordance with the taste of the early 18C, but left unaffected by subsequent changes in fashion and still retaining many of its original furnishings. The house sank into neglect after the Second World War when it passed to Louisa Dryden, who lived abroad, but it was rescued by the National Trust, which carried out an exemplary programme of restoration, including the remarkably intact early-18C formal garden setting, in 1980–84.

The house is plainly built of the local brown stone, and, apart from the stuccoed tower which marks the original limit of the south front of the 1550s, there are no especially striking external features. Sash windows were introduced on the south front in 1708–10, as was the central doorcase on the west front, surmounted by a segmental pediment. This was intended to be the formal entrance, as is apparent from the arrangement of the garden outside (note especially the statue of a shepherd boy by van Nost), but now the house is entered less impressively through the east or service wing. A flight of steps leads up from the cobbled courtyard to the spacious Hall, with its flat, early-18C plaster ceiling hiding the original open timber roof; above the fireplace is a large painted overmantel discovered during the restoration work, dating from c 1708–10. A doorway leads from the north side into the Kitchen, little changed since the 19C, and from here stairs lead up to the Winter Parlour, in which late-16C armorial paintings have recently been discovered on the wood panelling.

The main reception rooms, arranged on either side of a solid oak stair case introduced by Sir John Dryden in the 1630s, face south over the attractive walled gardens and the pastoral landscape beyond. The finest rooms are the ground-floor Dining Room (formerly the best parlour), and the upstairs Drawing Room (the former great chamber). The Dining Room is an untouched interior of 1710, with good plain panelling, furniture and family portraits, including one by Kneller of the poet John Dryden; two unusual features are the landscape mirror and a recently restored speaking-tube, enabling servants to be summoned. The Painted Parlour (formerly the withdrawing room), on the other side of the largely early-19C Book Room, is notable for its unusual (but visually not altogether successful) cut-out Corinthian pilasters introduced in the early 18C. The Drawing Room upstairs, by contrast, dates from the 1590s, and contains an excellent chimneypiece and overmantel of that date, with much of its original painting as well as some good, late-17C walnut furniture; the most impressive feature is the extraordinarily fanciful domed plaster ceiling of the 1630s, with a central pendant from which a chandelier originally hung. Next door is the Spencer Room, named after the poet John Spencer, a cousin of Sir Erasmus Dryden, and notable mainly for some crude but unusual late-16C grisaille decorations on one of the walls depicting the story of Jeroboam from the First Book of Kings; there is also a portrait of Sir Edward Turner and his wife by Allan Ramsay hanging over the fireplace. The Tapestry Room, on the other side of the Drawing Room and staircase, contains good early-18C furnishings, among them gilt gesso pier glasses of c 1710 and a set of embroidered chairs supplied for the house in 1714–16.

GCT

Cottesbrooke Hall

10m north of Northampton to east of A50 Northampton–Leicester at Creaton: Capt. & Mrs J. MacDonald Buchanan, tel. 060124 808515. Open mid Apr–Sept Thur, BH Mon 2–5.30. Guided tours. Refreshments.

One of several Midland houses with claims to be the original of Jane Austen's *Mansfield Park*, Cottesbrooke Hall is a moderately sized red-brick house standing in remote squirearchical country and built in 1703–13 for Sir John Langham, the grandson of a successful London merchant trading with Turkey. The main body of the house is a rectangular block of two storeys over a basement articulated by Composite pilasters, with a balustrade hiding the roof. What gives Cottesbrooke its architectural distinction, however, is the visually very satisfying arrangement of the south front (originally the entrance), with detached service pavilions joined to the main house by curved walls, enfolding an open courtyard looking out onto a vista terminated in the distance by the spire of the largely 7C parish church at Brixworth—one of the most important buildings of its date to survive in Europe. The architect was probably Francis Smith of Warwick, who had already worked with his brother William for Sir John Langham's cousin Sir Roger Cave at Stanford Hall, Leicestershire (qv.), not far away.

The exterior has altered relatively little since the early 18C, but there have been many changes to the interior and to the garden setting. There was some internal redecoration in the mid 18C, and in the 1780s most of the remaining interiors were remodelled in an Adamesque manner by the little-known architect Robert Mitchell, a process which also involved adding bow windows to the rooms on the north front (now the entrance front); Mitchell also designed the impressive new stone bridge in the newly-landscaped park with its carefully contrived vistas from the house. The estate remained in the hands of the Langhams until 1911, when it was sold. In 1937 there was a second sale, and in that year the new owner, Sir Reginald MacDonald-Buchanan, made further alterations to the interior, with Gerald Wellesley (later the 7th Duke of Wellington) and Trenwith Wells as his architects. He also created an outstandingly beautiful Italianate garden in the south courtyard and to the west of the house, incorporating statuary from Stowe, Buckinghamshire (qv.) and elsewhere, and introduced an excellent collection of 18C and 19C English sporting pictures, one of the finest of its kind in any English country house.

The tour starts in the west wing and takes in all the main reception rooms, which are reached by a corridor redecorated in 1937 and hung with 18C tapestries and pictures by Ben Marshall, John Ferneley, James Ward and others; there is also some good 18C English and Chinese export porcelain, and 18C embroidered chairs are arranged along the walls. The Library, with portraits by Allan Ramsay, Zoffany and Arthur Devis, as well as a self-portrait by Wright of Derby, was also remodelled in 1937, but the adjacent Pine Room (the original entrance hall) is the one room to retain its original early-18C wood panelling, though now stripped of its paint. Beyond lies the Staircase Hall, the finest interior at Cottesbrooke, with an iron balustrade to the cantilevered stairs by William Marshall, one of the craftsmen at Chatsworth, Derbyshire (qv.), and delicate Rococo decorations in papier-mâché by the Northampton craftsman John Woolston, who also worked at Althorp (qv.). The north front is taken up by a Dining Room and Drawing Room, both part of the 1780's alterations, on either side of the saloon (now the Entrance Hall), which has a mid-18C Rococo ceiling.

The Dining Room contains some good 18C furniture, including two tables by Giles Grendey, and excellent pictures, among them George Stubbs's 'Gimcrack on Newmarket Heath' (c 1765) and works by Ben Marshall, while in the Hall there are two marble-topped tables in the manner of William Kent and four more canvases by Marshall. There is another Stubbs in the Drawing Room, along with pictures by Zoffany and a family group by Devis and more good furniture, including late-17C cabinets and late-18C mirrors on either side of the fireplace. From here a passage with a 'vault' of saucer-domes leads to a staircase which gives access to the ground floor; here more sporting pictures are displayed, including works by Ferneley and Sir Alfred Munnings, several of them celebrating the exploits of the famous Pytchley Hunt, in the heart of whose country Cottesbrooke lies.

GCT

Deene Park

6m north east of Corby on A43 Kettering–Stamford: Edmund Brudenell,
tel. 078085 223, 278 or 361. Open June–Aug Sun and all BH Sun/Mon 2–5.

The origins of Deene Park go back to the Middle Ages, but its present appearance derives from a series of rebuildings and extensions carried out by the descendents of Sir Robert Brudenell, a lawyer who acquired the estate in 1514 and later became Chief Justice of Common Pleas. He or his son built the south east part of the present house as a parlour wing, and in 1571–72 his grandson Edmund rebuilt the earlier hall on the south side of the courtyard. The east range dates in its present form mostly from the early 17C, when extensive work was carried out by Sir Thomas Brudenell, who was made Earl of Cardigan after the Restoration in return for services to Charles I during his imprisonment after the Civil War. He also rebuilt the west or service range, added the crenellated tower at the north-east corner—a striking example of neo-medievalism, adorned with the coats of arms of his family and kinsmen—and, after the Restoration, rebuilt the two-storeyed north range which closes the courtyard and now forms the entrance to the house. The next major alteration occurred in the early 19C, when the 5th or 6th Lord Cardigan built a new staircase to the west of the hall and extended the early Tudor south range to the west to accommodate the large reception rooms and comfortable bedrooms demanded by the contemporary style of entertaining. The effect of these changes was to shift the centre of gravity of the house from the east to the west. A ballroom was added in the time of the 7th Earl, famous for his part in the Crimean War, but this has been demolished. When he died the estate passed to a cousin, Lord Robert Brudenell-Bruce, whose grandson lives here now.

The first impression of the house is of a sprawling pile of local silver-grey limestone surmounted by a forest of tall chimneys. Before entering, it is worth noting the curious blind bay window on the outside of the east range, probably dating from the mid 16C, with mullions in the form of Ionic columns and strapwork panels below—an early example of classical detailing applied to a country house. The courtyard, entered from the north, has something of the atmosphere of one of the smaller Cambridge colleges, with its prominent hall and two-storeyed porch embellished with classical pilasters and a carving of mermaids and cupids on the frieze over the entrance; this is balanced by a tall bay window at the high table end. The visitors' route starts in the east range, with an early-16C bay window, and continues into the present Great Hall, tall and narrow, with a magnificent double-hammerbeam roof and armorial chimneypiece. Some of the original wood panelling survives on the east wall, and there are several portraits, including Sir Robert Brudenell, founder of the family fortunes, in his lawyer's robes; Sir Edmund Brudenell, the builder of the hall; his melancholy-looking nephew, the 1st Earl of Cardigan (by John Michael Wright, 1658); and the Countess of Oxford by the Jacobean painter William Larkin (best seen at the end of the tour).

An early-17C staircase gives access to the upper floor of the early Tudor south-east range, where one of the rooms has linenfold panelling. The former great chamber in the east range (now called the Tapestry Room) has a striking plaster ceiling with pendants and mythical beasts and a portrait over the fireplace of two Princesses of Orange by Gerard Honthorst; the bedroom in the tower beyond also has a good plaster ceiling of c 1610 and an armorial overmantel. The Oak Parlour, on the ground floor of the south-east range, with early-17C panelling from another house, leads to the main reception rooms in the early-19C wing, starting with the Bow Room, built as a library and still containing many of the books acquired by the 1st Earl of Cardigan, some of them with good bindings—note also the portrait by Reynolds of Lady Mary Montagu, wife of the 4th Earl (her portrait by Gainsborough can be seen at Boughton, qv.). The Drawing Room contains more family portraits, including a series on wood, in identical frames, dating from c 1620, and two inlaid tables by Gerrit Jensen (c 1680). The Dining Room, by contrast, is notable mainly for a series of equestrian pictures by John Ferneley, one of them showing Deene Park in the background (1844); the swashbuckling portrait over the fireplace is of the 7th Earl leading the Charge of the Light Brigade. This memorable event also figures in a group portrait in the Staircase Hall showing the Earl explaining the Charge to the Royal Family (1855); among the other memorabilia, overlooked by whiskery 19C portraits, is the head of Lord Cardigan's charger in a glass case. The Ante-Hall, next door, contains an excellent portrait of Sir Thomas Salusbury and his family by an unknown artist (c 1640) and a bust of the 1st Earl of Elgin, attributed to Edward Pierce; it leads back into the great Hall, from which the courtyard is regained.

GCT

Kirby Hall

2m north east of Corby off Rockingham–Deene road: English Heritage, tel. 0536 203230. Open Oct–Mar (not Christmas) Tues–Sun 10–4; Apr–Sept daily 10–6.

Kirby Hall was begun in 1570 by a local country gentleman, Sir Humphrey Stafford of Blatherwyke. It stands alone in a hollow, and from a distance it presents as impressive a vision of gabled magnificence as can be found in any English house of its date. Closer inspection reveals that the house is largely ruinous, as indeed it has been since it was abandoned at the beginning of the 19C. Yet because of the superb quality of the local limestone and the lack of obtrusive later additions, it still evokes the half-medieval, half-classical world of Elizabethan architecture in an unusually vivid way.

Kirby was laid out after the medieval fashion around a spacious courtyard. The master mason, at least in the early stages, was Thomas Thorpe of Kings Cliffe, the father of the famous Elizabethan surveyor John Thorpe, who as a boy of seven laid the foundation stone. When Sir Humphrey Stafford died in 1575, the house was sold to one of Queen Elizabeth's courtiers, Sir Christopher Hatton. He or his son, who succeeded him in 1591, added a new range of bow-fronted reception rooms at the 'upper' end of the hall range, and was probably also responsible for the impressive array of obelisk-capped gables around the outside. Then in 1638–40 the north (entrance) range was remodelled by Sir Christopher's grandson to the designs of Nicholas Stone, master- mason in the royal Office of Works; this has a towering centrepiece and classically proportioned windows, but the presence of pedimented gables betray the fact that it is the work of a skilled master-mason and not of an architect who had absorbed the principles of Renaissance classicism. A rather more Italian effect is achieved in the courtyard facing this block, where the round-arched gateway is surmounted by a pediment containing the name of the Hatton family and flanked by heavily rusticated blocks of stone, like decaying fungi—a highly sculptural and Mannerist piece of design. The house remained in the hands of the Hattons and their descendants until 1930, when the empty shell was acquired by the Office of Works as an Ancient Monument.

Kirby is famous for its courtyard façades, which are articulated by giant classical pilasters, among the first to appear in English architecture. The capitals are of a curious hybrid form and support a frieze- like moulding; pilasters also frame the doorways which originally gave access to individual lodgings. The entrance range takes the form of a round-arched loggia, with rooms over it lit by windows inserted by Stone in 1638; the pilasters on either side of the entrance are carved with pretty quattrocento reliefs probably taken from the title page of John Shute's *First and Complete Grounds of Architecture* (1563), the first architectural pattern-book published in England. Elsewhere around the courtyard the Renaissance features co-exist in a characteristically Elizabethan manner, with large mullioned and transomed windows designed to let the maximum light into the rooms. These reach prodigious size in the hall range, which is entered through a very elaborately decorated porch. The large open Hall—one of the last of its kind to be built in this region—is still roofed, and gives access to a spacious stone staircase of French character leading to the grand but now deserted and empty rooms on the first floor. These look out on a 20C re-creation of the late-17C formal gardens.

GCT

Lamport Hall

8m north of Northampton on A508 Northampton–Market Harborough: Lamport Hall Trust, tel. 060128 272. Open Easter–Sept Sun and BH Mon, and Thur in July, Aug 2.15–5.15. Refreshments.

From an architectural point of view the most important part of Lamport Hall is the five-bay section at the centre of the long garden front. This refined exercise in Renaissance-inspired classicism started life in 1655, as an extension built on to the parlour-end of a house begun nearly a century earlier by John Isham, a younger son from an old Northamptonshire family. He purchased the estate after making his fortune as a merchant, and is shown in a furred gown, with his hand on a skull and a clock, in a portrait in the present Entrance Hall.

The 1655 building was designed by Inigo Jones's pupil John Webb for John Isham's great-grandson Justinian, whose world-weary royalism is expressed in the inscription on the frieze: 'IN THINGS TRANSITORY RESTETH NO GLORY' (he was arrested by the Cromwellian regime only a year after the new building was completed). His Italianate tastes were shared by his son Thomas, who went on a Grand Tour in 1676–77 and interrupted his dissolute progress by purchasing pictures, many of which still survive in the house. Wings were added on each side of the Webb building by Francis

Smith of Warwick in 1732–40, and the final remnants of the Tudor house were cleared away in 1819–21, when a new dining room was built on the site of the old hall to the designs of Henry Hakewill. There were minor alterations in 1842, and in 1861 William Burn remodelled the entrance front. The last of the Ishams to occupy the house was Sir Gyles, a distinguished actor and local historian, who left the house to a charitable trust designed 'to promote historic and aesthetic education'.

The external proportions of the present house are largely determined by those of Webb's building, which is enriched with motifs borrowed from Inigo Jones's Banqueting House in London, eg, the rusticated stonework, the alternating semicircular and triangular pediments over the windows and the balustrade at roof level (the pediment and pitched roof are later additions). The rooms, with one exception, are mainly interesting for their pictures and furniture. They include the Grand Tour purchases of Sir Thomas Isham, who is seen posing languidly in a portrait by Carlo Maratta painted in Rome in 1677 and now hanging in the Library; other items on display here include a Bible formerly belonging to Charles I, and what is claimed to be the oldest garden gnome in the country, brought here in the mid 19C. Next door is the Oak Room, with canvases by Salvator Rosa, while the Staircase Hall, with its ceiling of 1740 and armorial glass taken from the demolished Pytchley Hall (another Isham house), has a Bacchus after Pietro da Cortona.

The finest room is the former entrance hall (now called the High Room), which takes up most of the Webb building. It still retains its elaborate chimneypiece carved by Caius Gabriel Cibber, with a copy of a Titian over the fireplace; there are also copies of famous Stuart portraits acquired by Sir Justinian Isham, who refused to remove them during the Interregnum. The panelling was introduced in 1686 and the splendid, almost Rococo, plasterwork on the ceiling was added in 1738–40 by John Woolston of Northampton (cf. Althorp) under the general supervision of Francis Smith's son William. Beyond, in the other Smith wing, is the Cabinet Room, which now houses some of the finest pictures in the house, including Van Dyck's 'Christ and St John', bought by Sir Justinian on the recommendation of John Webb, a copy of Guido Reni's 'Adoration of the Shepherds' and two pictures by Sebastiano Ricci bought in the 1770s. The room takes its name from four spectacular late-17C Flemish and Neapolitan cabinets bought at the same time. Some first-floor rooms have recently been opened to the public, containing exhibitions, a childrens' nursery, and various important pictures and items of furniture which have not been on display before.

GCT

Lyveden New Bield

3m east of Brigstock via A6116, 4m south west of Oundle via A427: National Trust, tel. 08325 358. Open all year daily.

This extraordinary, unfinished house was begun in 1594 by Sir Thomas Tresham, a Roman Catholic recusant who was imprisoned for the faith in 1600 and died in 1605. It stands isolated on a hilltop, some distance away from the manor house (the 'Old Bield'—not open to the public), and was intended to serve both as a 'garden lodge' for contemplative retirement, and as a symbolic statement of Sir Thomas's religious beliefs. Like the famous Triangular Lodge near his other Northamptonshire house at Rushton, a few miles away (under the management of English Heritage and also open to the public), the New Bield conveys a mood of intense, almost obsessional, religious introspection, as intense in some respects as the music of Sir Thomas's Catholic contemporaries William Byrd and John Dowland. It is planned in the form of a cross, and the carved inscriptions and the decoration of the Doric frieze which runs around the building at first-floor level refer to the Passion of Christ and the Sorrows of the Virgin Mary. Sir Thomas clearly played a large part in working out the design—he had more than 20 architectural books in his library—but he also enlisted the help of John Stickells, a mason from the Office of Works who was later described as 'the excellent architect of our time'. The silver-grey local limestone was supplied by the Grumbolds of Weldon, who built many of the colleges of Cambridge.

The building, which is approached across two fields, stands to the height of the second floor, and, though a roofless shell, is remarkably well preserved, despite some damage at the hands of a Cromwellian army officer after the Civil War. The architecture is highly sophisticated for its date—the plan may owe something to one in Sebastiano Serlio's *Architettura*, the most influential architectural book of its time—and the workmanship is of the highest quality. Inside, there were to be four main rooms on each floor, including a kitchen, hall, parlour and great chamber, and formal gardens were also planned, the ghostly earthworks and moats of which are still visible. The building passed out of the hands of the Tresham family in the early 18C, and it was acquired and repaired by the National Trust in 1922.

GCT

Rockingham Castle

2m north of Corby on A6003 Kettering–Oakham: Michael Saunders Watson, tel. 0536 770240. Open Easter–Sept Sun, Thur and BH Mon/Tues and Tues in Aug 1.30–5.30. Refreshments.

The castle at Rockingham was first built by William the Conqueror, who also enclosed a large tract of the surrounding countryside as a royal forest. The motte of his castle still survives, overlooking the Welland valley separating Northamptonshire from Rutland. The oldest extant buildings are the south curtain wall with its gateway of c 1200 and rounded flanking towers of the 1280s, and some of the hall range, including the 13C doorway leading into the screens passage. The late-medieval kings lost interest in the castle, and in 1538 the traveller John Leland reported that the residential quarters had fallen into ruin.

In 1544 the decrepit building was leased to Edward Watson of Lyddington, Rutland, who married one of the daughters of the eminent lawyer Sir Edward Montagu of Boughton (qv.) and became Constable of Sandgate Castle, Kent. He rebuilt the hall range in 1579 and added a long cross-wing at the west end with a Gallery on the upper floor, but left it unfinished; the service end at the other side of the Hall was remodelled in 1584, the year of his death. His grandson Lewis, later to become the 1st Lord Rockingham, purchased the castle outright and completed the gallery range just before the Civil War, in the course of which the keep and most of the outer walls were demolished. The hipped-roofed steward's house

('Walker's House', now the tea room), to the north of the gatehouse, was added in 1655 by the 2nd Lord Rockingham, who married the daughter of Charles I's minister Strafford. The vast estates she inherited in Yorkshire went to the descendants of their younger son, but Rockingham was inherited by the elder son, and has since passed, by a complicated line of descent, to the present owner. The castle was used as a hunting lodge for much of the 18C, but was restored in 1838–40 by the Hon. Richard Watson, a friend of Charles Dickens, who stayed here and drew on his experiences in writing *Bleak House*; the architect was Anthony Salvin and the alterations included the building of new staircases and an embattled tower beside the gallery wing.

Entering through the medieval gatehouse, the visitor finds a pleasingly varied collection of relatively unpretentious gabled buildings of local limestone with Collyweston slate roofs. The tour of the house starts at the service end and takes in the servants' hall and kitchen, as well as a vista along 'the Street', a picturesque assemblage of outbuildings of various dates culminating in the gabled Laundry of 1669, with its clock and bell-turret. The main reception rooms were extensively remodelled in the 19C and early 20C. The Hall retains its medieval hearth and roof timbers of 1579, but the panelling and screen were removed in 1840 and restored in 1905. It is now chiefly of interest for its contents, which include an iron chest said to have been left here by King John, and 16C portraits of Francis I of France (attributed to Joos van Cleve), Queen Elizabeth and of Edward Watson (1567), who presumably composed the pious inscription on the ceiling beams.

The other downstairs rooms are the former parlour (now called the Panelled Room), decorated in the 1680s and restored by Thomas Willement in 1839, and the Library, created out of smaller rooms in the south wing and decorated in a neo-Adam fashion in 1905. They contain an interesting collection of 20C British paintings amassed by the present owner's uncle, Sir Michael Culme-Seymour, including works by Sickert (a study for 'Ennui'), Matthew Smith, Josef Herman and Stanley Spencer; there is also an oil sketch of Hampstead Heath by Constable in the Library, and a sensitive portrait by William Dobson of the 1st Lord Rockingham, looking careworn after the Civil War. The Gallery, upstairs, owes its present form largely to Salvin. There are three Venetian glass chandeliers and some good pieces of 18C French furniture, and the walls are hung with portraits, including Zoffany's conversation piece of the children of the 1st Lord Sondes, a lively portrait of the 2nd Lady Sondes by Reynolds, and sporting pictures by the Leicestershire-born Ben Marshall. From the former billiard room below (now the gift shop) a staircase leads to the roof of the tower, which commands good views of the well-maintained gardens and surrounding landscape.

GCT

Southwick Hall

3m north of Oundle. Christopher Capron, tel. 0832 274064. Open May–Aug Wed, all BH Sun/Mon 2–5. Refreshments.

Southwick Hall is a stone-built house begun in the 14C and successively altered and added to down to the 19C. It stands in the valley of the River

Nene on the edge of what was once the royal forest of Rockingham, and its origins go back to some time after 1320, when the manor was acquired by the Knyvett family. Richard Knyvett was probably responsible for building a hall block and chamber wing on the site of the main body of the present house, and the low tower which stands to the south may also date from his time; it was enlarged in the second half of the 14C, probably by his son Sir John Knyvett, Lord Chancellor in the 1370s, who may also have built the adjacent parish church with its typically Northamptonshire spire. In 1442 the property was sold to John Lynn, a London merchant, and his descendant George Lynn rebuilt the hall range and the adjoining chamber wing in their present form in 1571–80. Some alterations were carried out in the mid 18C by another George Lynn, who inherited in 1742; he is commemorated by a monument by Roubiliac in the church, which was remodelled internally in 1760. The house later went through the female line, and in 1841 it was sold to a London solicitor, George Capron, whose descendants have lived here ever since.

From the south or entrance side it is easy to distinguish the 14C tower, which survives largely intact, from the body of the house, which was rebuilt in the 1570s. The tower is built of rubble-stone, and consisted originally of a vaulted undercroft, converted into an Entrance Hall in 1909 (note the expressive 14C carved heads supporting the vault), and a room which may have served as an occasional chapel above, lit by two-light windows; the extension to the west, with a staircase turret, is clearly a little later in date. The main house is faced in ashlar and, like many Northamptonshire houses of the late 16C, has little external embellishment apart from the spikes on the gables; behind it is a courtyard with some more evidence of medieval work, including a semicircular turret. Some of the rooms, including the Hall and the Study, were remodelled internally in the mid 18C, and they are hung with portraits of the Capron family; the Parlour, with its Gothick bay window, forms part of an 18C extension. Visitors also see the main rooms in the medieval tower and a barrel-vaulted room over the Hall dating from 1571–80, with its contemporary wood panelling.

GCT

Sulgrave Manor

7m north east of Banbury in village of Sulgrave to west of B4525 Banbury–Northampton: Sulgrave Manor Board, tel. 0295 760205. Open Mar–Dec daily, except Wed, 10.30–1, 2–4 (5.30 Apr–Sept). Guided tours.

This modest stone-built house is visited today partly because of its associations with the Washington family, ancestors of the first President of the United States. The first Washington to live at Sulgrave was Lawrence, a wool merchant from Northampton, who bought the manor in 1539 and was probably responsible for building the core of the building—represented by the two- storeyed hall block—in the 1560s. The estate was sold to a cousin, Lawrence Makepeace, in 1610, and finally left the family in 1659, three years after Col John Washington, the President's great-grandfather, had emigrated to Virginia. A kitchen and parlour wing were added at right-angles to the hall block in about 1700, but the house was later occupied by farmers and reduced in size. It was acquired just before the First World War by an Anglo–American charitable trust which employed Sir Reginald Blomfield to carry out a tactful restoration of the surviving portions, and to rebuild the original service end as a caretaker's house. Furniture and Washington memorabilia were introduced into the rooms, and the house was opened to the public in 1921.

Sulgrave Manor is a good, though not outstanding, example of the vernacular architecture of the area. It stands in a well-kept walled garden in the heart of the village, and the main façade, with its projecting porch, faces south, but the approach today is from the north, alongside the still completely vernacular early-18C wing. All the older rooms are shown on the tours, which naturally emphasise the Washington associations while at the same time pointing out the contents which have gradually been brought in since the First World War. The finest work of art is perhaps the portrait of George Washington by Gilbert Stuart in the Hall, but attractive pieces of furniture of various dates are scattered through the house and there is a good collection of culinary implements in the Kitchen. The rooms have been carefully arranged and the house, quite apart from the American connection, conveys an accurate—if inevitably somewhat anaesthetised—sense of the surroundings in which the lesser squirearchy lived in the 16C, 17C and 18C.

GCT

NORTHUMBERLAND

Alnwick Castle

In Alnwick off A1, 30m north of Newcastle: the Duke of Northumberland, tel. 0665 510777. Open Maundy Thur–mid Oct daily 11–5.

Alnwick Castle has belonged to the Percy family since 1309, when it was bought by Henry, 1st Lord Percy, one of Edwards I's commanders in the wars against Scotland. It then consisted of a stone shell-keep constructed by Eustace FitzJohn in the mid 12C around an earlier motte and standing between two walled enclosures—the Outer Bailey and the Middle Bailey—on a promontory overlooking the River Aln, strategically close to the main route to the border. Lord Percy rebuilt the castle in accordance with the latest ideas on fortification which he had perhaps learnt from his association with the King. The potentially vulnerable west entrance from the town of Alnwick was protected by a new gatehouse and barbican, circular bastions were built around the keep, and the curtain wall running around the Middle and Outer Baileys was strengthened by new towers. Henry Percy died in 1315, and his son, another warrior against the Scots, further strengthened the keep (c 1350) by adding a pair of polygonal towers to flank the entrance gateway. By this time the Percys had become the most powerful of all the border families, and in 1377 they were made Earls of Northumberland.

For the next 200 years Alnwick Castle served mainly as a fortress in the interminable wars and raids which dominated the history of the disputed borderlands between England and Scotland. For much of this time the family chose to live at the now largely ruined Warkworth Castle, a few miles to the south, and by the 1560s Alnwick was in disrepair, 'utterly unfurnished and not so much as one bed in it'. During Elizabeth's reign the Percys fell foul of the Crown because of their Catholic sympathies, and in the early 17C they abandoned both Alnwick and Warkworth in favour of Syon House, Greater London (qv.) and Petworth, Sussex (qv.). The male line died out on the death of the 11th Earl in 1670, and Alnwick Castle, along with the extensive family estates in Northumberland, was inherited by his daughter; she married the 6th Duke of Somerset (the 'Proud Duke'), from whom it passed to their son, whose daughter married a Yorkshire squire, Sir Hugh Smithson. He was created Duke of Northumberland in recognition of his political services to George III, and set about turning Alnwick once more into a suitably ducal residence, with the help first of James Paine and then of Robert Adam (who also worked for him at Syon and at Northumberland House in London). The alterations, which lasted from c 1754–80, involved creating a suite of reception rooms and bedrooms on the first floor of the keep, most of them decorated in an extravagantly frothy Gothic style, which the Duke apparently disliked but adopted 'out of complaisance to the Duchess his lady'. At the same time 'Capability' Brown was employed to landscape the extensive park, where Adam designed the impressive Lion Bridge over the Aln—from which the best distant view of the castle can be obtained—as well as 'eyecatchers' like the Brizlee Tower of 1777–83.

The 4th Duke, who inherited in 1847, 'found a great absence of domestic comfort and a deficiency of those modern conveniences requisite in a residence of a nobleman of His Grace's rank', and carried out a second reconstruction of the interior in 1854–65, also taking the opportunity to remove the 'tameness and insipidity' of the exterior by the addition of a new tower (the Prudhoe Tower). His architect was Anthony Salvin, but he placed the decoration of the interiors in the hands of Luigi Canina, the Director of the Capitoline Museum in Rome, who died in 1856 and was succeeded by Giovanni Montiroli. They employed a team of Italian and local craftsmen to create a sequence of rich neo-Renaissance rooms which still serve as a suitably splendid setting for the superb collection of Italian 16C and 17C pictures acquired by the Duke in 1856.

The castle is approached from the attractive stone-built town through the formidable and little-altered early-14C **gatehouse**, with its barbican built out in front to trap foolhardy attackers; the statues on the battlements date from the 18C. It leads into the **Outer Bailey**, surrounded by a curtain wall punctuated by towers—most of which show signs of Salvin's restoration—with the keep rising in front, protected by its own circuit of towers: a castle within a castle. Here too Salvin is much in evidence, especially in the tall Prudhoe Tower on the left of the keep and the adjoining chapel (not open to the public) which replaced one in the **Middle Bailey**. A gateway to the right leads into the Middle Bailey, and from here the less-altered east side of the castle can be seen (the north curtain wall was demolished by Salvin to improve the view).

The keep (or **Inner Bailey**) is entered through the tall gateway built by the 2nd Lord Percy and enclosing a round arch, enriched by zigzag carvings, which has survived from the original 12C building. The medieval hall stood on the first floor to the right of the entrance, but almost all traces of the original masonry inside the circular courtyard disappeared in the 18C and 19C restorations, and today what we see is Salvin's heavy, hard-edged, but in its way convincing, neo-Gothic hand. The 4th Duke's reconstruction of the interior involved building corridors corbelled out from the walls to ease access to the main reception rooms. Salvin also replaced James Paine's staircase by a new library and built a block on to the north-west side of the courtyard with a carriage porch leading to a new staircase, and it is through this that the house is entered.

The reception rooms, arranged around the north and east sides of the courtyard, come as a surprise after the gauntness of the exterior, with their lavish cinquecento-style craftsmanship—massive marble chimneypieces, gilded plaster ceilings and painted friezes—and their abundance of richly carved and gilt furniture, some of it brought to Alnwick after Northumberland House was demolished to make way for Northumberland Avenue in the 1870s. At the top of the staircase is the **Guard Chamber**, with a frieze containing paintings (by Francis Gotzenberg) of the ballad of Chevy Chase. Lower down on the walls there are paintings by Van Dyck (the 10th Earl as Lord High Admiral), Claude (a characteristic Harbour Scene) and Canaletto (views of Syon House and Windsor Castle); there is also furniture by John Linnell and Robert Adam. More superb pictures can be seen in the adjacent **Ante-Room**, notably three Titians (a poetic triple portrait, a portrait of the Bishop of Armagnac and his Secretary, and an 'Ecce Homo'), three parts of a monumental fresco by Sebastiano de Piombo, and Palma Vecchio's 'Lady with a Lute' (c 1520).

To the left of the Ante-Room is the **Library**, occupying the first floor of Salvin's Prudhoe Tower, and to the right the **Music Room**, with portraits of the 10th Earl and Queen Henrietta Maria by (or after) Van Dyck, an excellent triple portrait by William Dobson showing him with Sir Charles Cotterell and another man (possibly the musician Nicholas Lanier), and

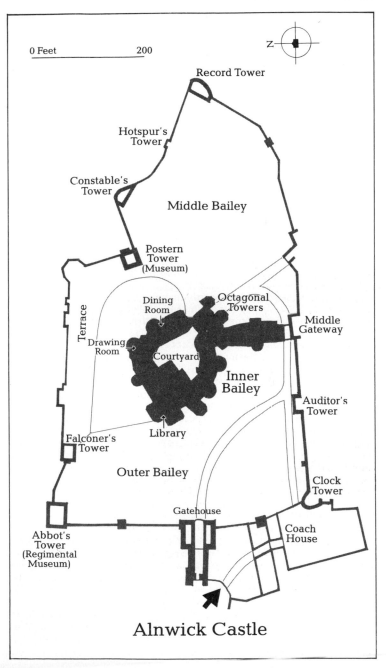

0 Feet   200

Z

Record Tower

Hotspur's
Tower

Constable's
Tower

Middle Bailey

Postern
Tower
(Museum)

Dining
Room

Octagonal
Towers

Middle
Gateway

Terrace

Drawing
Room

Courtyard

Inner
Bailey

Auditor's
Tower

Falconer's
Tower

Library

Outer Bailey

Clock
Tower

Gatehouse

Coach
House

Abbot's
Tower
(Regimental
Museum)

Alnwick Castle

views by Canaletto of Northumberland House and of Alnwick Castle before its 18C restoration; there is also some good French 17C and 18C furniture. Two more rooms follow: the **Drawing Room**, with a self-portrait by Andrea del Sarto, Turner's 'Temple of Jupiter Panhellenois, Aegina' and Guido Reni's 'Crucifixion' (c 1625–26), and two splendidly ornate *pietra dura* cabinets of 1683 on either side of the chimneypiece; and the Dining Room, which occupies the site of the medieval hall and contains portraits of the 1st Duke and his wife in a specially carved frame over the chimneypiece, and an excellent Meissen porcelain service of c 1745 which the Duke may have won in a raffle. From here a corridor hung with family portraits leads back to the main staircase.

GCT

Bamburgh Castle

On the coast 16m north of Alnwick, B1340 and B1342: the Lady Armstrong, tel. 06684 214208. Open Easter–late Oct daily 1–5; July–Aug 12–6. Refreshments.

Bamburgh is one of the largest and most spectacularly-sited fortresses in Britain. It sits on a long rocky outcrop hard by the sea, commanding a tremendous sweep of wild, low-lying coastline; the dramatic silhouette of towers and battlements is visible for miles. The rock was inhabited before the Roman conquest, and Bamburgh's history can be first traced from the 7C, when the area was conquered by King Edwin of Northumbria, and a royal fortress established here. Bamburgh never fell to the Viking invasions, even when Lindisfarne itself was sacked. However, the Kingdom of Northumbria waned, and thus in the 10C Bamburgh emerged as the seat of an Earl, no longer as the fortress of an independent king.

After the Norman Conquest the castle was captured by William Rufus; henceforth it was a royal fortress. Henry I gave the church of St Oswald, within its walls, to the Augustinian canons, and they rebuilt it in masonry. The Keep was probably built in the mid 12C for Henry II. Henry III remodelled the defences, and added extensive residential buildings, the origin of the present main range, and more work was carried out in the reigns of Edward II and Richard II. The castle was assaulted by Scots armies on a number of occasions, but never surrendered, having a copious supply of water (from the well beneath the Keep). Eventually, it was besieged and captured by Yorkist forces, after the Lancastrians were defeated in the Battle of Hexham (1464)—the first castle in England to succumb to artillery. Although remaining a royal fortress governed by a Constable, it fell into disrepair, and was never again a seriously defensible fortress.

The Forster family became hereditary Constables of the castle, and in the 16C and 17C it decayed slowly under their stewardship, most of it becoming ruinous. In 1700, Sir John Forster's daughter Dorothy married Nathaniel Crewe, Bishop of Durham, who later bought the castle. In 1721 Bishop Crewe left his estate to a charity, for public welfare and education. In the later 18C Dr John Sharp, Archdeacon of Northumberland, restored the residential buildings, mostly at his own expense. He set up a dispensary, a surgery and hospital, a free school for two or three hundred children, opened his library to the public, and set up a pioneering coast-guard station. He died in 1792, and for another century the Crewe Trustees ran Bamburgh as a prototype of the welfare state.

In 1894 the Crewe Trustees sold the castle to the 1st Lord Armstrong, celebrated inventor and industrialist. This magnate was then 84 years old and had already built an extraordinary house, Cragside near Rothbury (qv.). Nonetheless, he immediately set about a major programme of rebuilding and renovation at Bamburgh. His architect was the little-known Charles Ferguson. He restored the Keep and the defences, and replaced Dr Sharp's plain 18C buildings with a tremendous new range in a mixed medieval-Tudor style, along the Inner Ward. Lord Armstrong died in 1900, before work was completed. Bamburgh had become an Edwardian country house on the grand scale, but it was only fully occupied until the First World War. The Castle still belongs to an Armstrong family trust and the Dowager Lady Armstrong resides.

The Castle is all of red sandstone; from a distance it presents a convincingly warlike and defensible appearance. Visitors enter by the medieval gate at the east end; the road climbs between battlements, with great views over the sea. At the top you turn left into the Inner Ward. The 12C Keep follows the classic Norman pattern, a massive square block with a square turret at each corner. Along the landward side of the Inner Ward is Ferguson's immense main range of buildings. They still contain a lot of medieval masonry, but nearly everything that you can see is of 1894–1904; it is picturesquely composed, all of beautifully-cut dark sandstone, with a variety of detailing, in 14C–16C styles.

The first room seen is the Museum, probably the medieval Kitchen; Dr Sharp used it as a schoolroom. It has a variety of objects, including archaeological finds, Asian armour, paintings and old furniture. The next two rooms are medieval in origin, and were probably the buttery and pantry area, housing a variety of furniture and china. The Lobby, next, was designed by Ferguson as the principal entrance. Next comes the magnificent King's Hall. When Lord Armstrong demolished the Crewe Trustees' buildings, clear evidence of the medieval hall was revealed, and Ferguson followed its outline. The panelling and the great false-hammerbeam roof are of teak, the walls of exposed sandstone, with a row of 18C and 19C portraits. There is much 16C and 17C arms and armour on display, together with insignia, snuff boxes and other works of art. Above the dais are superb tapestries, depicting the life of the Emperor Justinian, and over the fireplace a fine painting by Honthorst.

The Porch, opening off the dais, has stone vaulting carved in imitation of knotted rope. West of the Hall and up stairs is the Faire Chamber, a drawing room with Louis XV and XVI furniture and decorative china, and portraits by Kneller. A passageway hung with Flemish tapestry leads to the Keep, which is entered at first-floor level. The arms and armour are from the 15C–19C, some of it on loan from the Royal Armoury and the Joicey Museum in Newcastle. The adjacent Court Room has English and continental furniture, and portraits of the Armstrong family. Visitors descend to the ground floor of the Keep; the walls here are 9–12ft thick, and here is the great Saxon well, bored 140ft down through sandstone and basalt.

To the west of the Keep, the East Ward has buildings along its landward side; they are mostly 18C, but with much Norman masonry. An arch in the Neville Tower at the far end leads into the West Ward, which slopes down to the end of the rock. The round mill-house is 18C. The walls here remain ruinous, as they have been since the 15C; at the far end is St Oswald's Gate, the west entrance to this great fortress.

Belsay

14m north west of Newcastle on A696 Newcastle–Jedburgh: English
Heritage, tel. 066181 636. Open all year daily 10–5 (Apr–Sept 10–6).

There are two houses at Belsay: a well-preserved late-14C tower house
extended in the early 17C, and a new house built about half a mile away
in 1807–15 which ranks as one of the most impressive monuments of the
Greek Revival in Europe. The two houses are linked by a picturesque
sunken garden contemporary with the 'new' house, and the well-cared-for
ensemble is a strikingly successful example of the marriage of art, nature
and history to which the Romantic era aspired.

The man responsible for the creation of Belsay in its present form was Sir
Charles Monck, representative of the Middletons who had held the estate
ever since the 13C (he took the name Monck on inheriting a Lincolnshire
estate from his maternal grandfather). Soon after his marriage in 1804 he
went on what was then a relatively unconventional Continental tour, which
lasted until 1806 and took him to Berlin (already an important centre for
neo-classical architecture) and Greece. The influence of this tour can be
clearly seen in the new house, which he designed himself, though he was
helped in the preparation of the meticulous drawings by the gifted local
architect John Dobson. Nowhere in English domestic architecture is the
stark majesty of Grecian architecture more powerfully and cleverly adapted
to the needs of the 19C. The house is built on a square plan, and the
proportions are mathematically worked out, apparently to three decimal
places. There is very little ornament, and the plainness of the meticulously
cut limestone throws into greater relief the giant Doric portico *in antis* (the
details are taken from the Theseion in Athens) and the Doric frieze which
runs around the building. Internally the now-empty rooms are arranged,
like those of a Greek or Roman house, around a top-lit central space
recalling the *atria* of antiquity, surrounded by superimposed colonnades of
the Ionic and Roman Doric orders. Visitors are allowed to wander freely
through the interior and even to descend to the extensive wine cellars, but
the Middletons abandoned the house after the Second World War, and in
the absence of any furnishings it now has a slightly depressing, desolate
feeling.

The stone for the new house came from a quarry a short distance away
to the west. This was transformed by Sir Charles Monck into an extension
of the gardens, with a serpentine path leading through an abundantly
planted ravine to the old tower house, which was allowed to survive as a
visual surprise at the end of the tour of the grounds. The 'castle', as it is
now usually called, is a typical compact fortified dwelling of a late-medieval
border lord, with massive stone walls, small windows and a crenellated and
turreted skyline. There are three storeys, each with one large and two
smaller rooms. The kitchen was on the ground floor, the hall above it and
the great chamber at the top, reached by a spiral staircase; there are
fireplaces in the upper rooms and garderobes in the thickness of the walls.
This arrangement represented the acme of comfort in the robber-infested
wilds of 14C Northumberland. In the more peaceful conditions which
followed the accession of James I, the Middletons expanded into a new hall
range and wing with up-to- date mullioned and transomed windows, dated
1614–29. When the early-19C house was built the Jacobean wing was
pulled down, the hall range unroofed and the village of Belsay relocated

near the park gates, leaving the medieval tower almost isolated in the empty landscape.

GCT

Chillingham Castle

12m north west of Alnwick between A1 and A697: Sir Humphry
Wakefield, Bt, tel. 06685 359. Open Easter BH weekend, then
May–Sept daily except Tues 1.30–5. Refreshments.

There was a tower-house at Chillingham, in the wild country near the
Scottish border, in the 13C, but the present formidable pile dates back in
essence to 1344, when Sir Thomas Grey de Heton obtained licence to
crenellate a larger courtyard building with four corner towers (still visible),
the area having recently been ravaged by the Scots. The castle remained
in the hands of the Greys, one of the leading Northumberland families, and
in the early 16C it was said to be capable of accommodating 100 horsemen.
It was attacked by the Percys during the Pilgrimage of Grace rebellion in
1536, but it was subsequently repaired, and there was a substantial reconstruction of the north or entrance range in the early 17C by Sir William, the
1st Lord Grey of Wark, or by his father, who negotiated with James VI of
Scotland over his succession to the English throne (some of his correspon-
dence with Lord Burghley has recently been found concealed in the
masonry of the castle).

The 3rd Lord Grey, a zealous Whig who became Lord Privy Seal under
William III, was given the old family earldom of Tankerville in 1695, and
he may have been responsible for alterations inside the courtyard (he also
built Uppark, Sussex, qv.). When he died the castle passed via his daughter
to the 2nd Lord Ossulston, who was made Earl of Tankerville. The 2nd Earl
(d 1753) sold the Uppark estate and remodelled the south range at Chillingham, at the same time carrying out improvements to the landscape.
Further changes took place in 1803, when the upper part of the east range
was rebuilt after a fire to the designs of the Edinburgh architect John
Paterson (whose designs for the stables are on view in the castle), and in
1828, when the 5th Earl—who married the daughter of the French Duc de
Gramant—employed Sir Jeffrey Wyatville to make alterations inside the
south range; Wyatville also embellished the grounds with avenues and a
formal garden near the house, and built new gates and entrance lodges.
Decline set in after the death of the 7th Earl in 1931, when the castle was
abandoned and the contents sold. During the Second World War it became
a barracks, and the north range was burnt down (it was subsequently
rebuilt by Sir Albert Richardson). Most of the 18C and early 19C interior
decoration perished through wet and dry rot when the house lay empty
after the war, but the building was rescued in the 1980s by the present
owner and his wife, both of them descendants of the Greys. They have
energetically embarked on a restoration of the interior and gardens, which
is still in progress.

The castle stands on the western edge of the medieval park, famous for
its wild cattle, and close to the estate village (mostly by Edward Blore,
1830s) and the medieval parish church, which contains a superb monument
to Sir Edward Grey (d 1443). From the outside the late-medieval origins of
the house are still obvious, with the four corner towers rising above the

residential ranges built within the original curtain walls. The north or entrance range was remodelled in the early 17C with a 'frontispiece' of superimposed columns—a favourite Jacobean motif also found in the Schools Quadrangle in Oxford—at the centre and a long gallery on the top floor. The medieval hall was on the south side of the courtyard, but it has been much remodelled, and is now hidden behind a curious arcade, probably dating from the late 17C, with a central staircase leading up to a first-floor corridor and figures of the 'Seven Worthies' resting on niches over the spandrels of the arches. Some early-17C craftsmanship survives inside the house, including two carved chimneypieces in a room in the east range (one of them originally in the long gallery) and a plaster ceiling in the room over the hall; the 18C and 19C interior decoration has mostly disappeared, and the recent restoration has revealed the older masonry underneath. Much of the interest of the interior derives from the objects brought in by the present owner, including armour, tapestries, paintings, documents relating to the castle and to the Grey family, and an excellent collection of prehistoric stone artefacts from the neighbourhood. Outside, there are lawns coming up to the largely mid-18C south front, and a formal garden to the west—possibly on the site of a medieval tilt yard—has been expertly reinstated.

GCT

Cragside

1m north east of Rothbury on B6341: National Trust, tel. 0669 20333/20266. Open Apr–Oct daily, except Mon (but open BH Mon) 1–5.30 (grounds 10.30–7, and Tues, Sat, Sun in Nov 10.30–4). Refreshments.

Cragside represents the triumph of human ingenuity over nature. Until 1863, when the site was bought by the 53-year-old Newcastle armaments manufacturer Sir William (later Lord) Armstrong, there was nothing here but bare moors overlooking the upper reaches of the River Coquet. In 1864–66 Armstrong built a modest hunting lodge on the slopes above the river to the designs of an unknown architect, and in subsequent years he expanded the original 20-acre gardens into an estate of 1729 acres. Much of this he covered with lakes and trees—seven million in all, mostly coniferous—thus transforming the landscape for miles around. Starting in 1870, the original house was also enlarged to become one of the most spectacular new country houses of late-Victorian England. The architect was Richard Norman Shaw, whose skill in planning, combined with his deft handling of the nostalgic 'Old English' idiom, made him the most successful domestic architect of his time. His additions were carried out piecemeal over a period of 14 years, and by the time they were completed the house was large enough and grand enough to play host to the Prince of Wales, the Shah of Persia and the King of Siam. It remained the home of the Armstrong family until 1977, when the 3rd Lord Armstrong retreated to Bamburgh Castle (qv.), and Cragside with its grounds was acquired by the National Trust.

The various additions to the original core of the house have given it a disjointed but undeniably picturesque appearance, especially when seen from the river below. The main visual elements, as in the old houses which Shaw and his contemporaries assiduously sought out and sketched, are the chimneystacks, the turrets and the gable roofs, some of them adorned with mock half-timbering more appropriate to the Home Counties, where Shaw had built most of his previous houses, than to the north of England; the overall effect, though, is strangely Germanic. The house is approached through the service courtyard and entered from the south; from here the original building can be seen to the left, much remodelled externally by Shaw, who also designed the gabled tower, while to the right is a later tower and wing, completed in 1884.

The tour encompasses most of the rooms (and even Lord Armstrong's Turkish Bath), but since the departure of the family the effect is, perhaps inevitably, a little lifeless. Lord Armstrong was less interested in aesthetics than in comfort and applied the latest technology to the house (it was the first in the world to be lit by electricity derived from water power), and the earlier rooms, at least, were designed for use rather than show. The most attractive interior is that of the Dining Room, solidly panelled and ceiled in oak, with a massive hearth and inglenook, surmounted by the sentimental inscription 'East or West, Hame's best'; next to this is a portrait by the local artist, Henry Emmerson, of Lord Armstrong in his carpet slippers reading a newspaper in front of the fire—a perfect illustration of the essentially bourgeois spirit in which the house was conceived. The adjacent Library contains the usual late-19C clutter of spindly, often ebonised, furniture, some of it designed by Shaw himself. There is some glass by the William Morris firm in the bay window, and loaned paintings by minor pre-Raphaelites hang on the walls (most of Lord Armstrong's own collection was sold by his son in 1910). The other impressive interior is that of the top-lit Drawing Room at the opposite end of the house. This room was an afterthought, designed to cater for large house parties, and the decoration demonstrates the shift to classicism which marked Shaw's later career; the dominant feature is an overpowering alabaster chimneypiece with neo-Renaissance detailing, designed by Shaw's pupil W.R. Lethaby. After this display of frigid grandeur it is something of a relief to escape into the spacious grounds and the empty moors which surround them. The formal pleasure grounds and Orchard House can be explored, and the Power House with hydro- electric machinery can also be seen on a circular walk.

GCT

Lindisfarne Castle

On Holy Island 5m east of Beal off A1 Newcastle–Berwick: National Trust, tel. 0289 89244. Open Apr–Oct daily except Fri (open Good Fri) 1–5.

Perched on an outcrop of rock on an island linked tenuously to the Northumberland coast by a causeway, Lindisfarne Castle in its present form is a romantic 20C recreation of a Tudor fortress. The Castle was first built in 1550 to defend the harbour of Holy Island from raids by the Scots, but it was never a family home and it fell into disrepair in the 18C, later becoming a coastguard station. In 1902 it was bought by Edward Hudson, the owner of *Country Life* magazine, and in 1903 it was deftly turned into a house by Edwin Lutyens. Lutyens owed much of his early success to the championship of Hudson and his magazine, and he had already built Hudson a house in Sonning, Berkshire, employing the idiom of the Home Counties vernacular in which he had been brought up; Lindisfarne, with its stark, rugged stone walls, celebrated in drawings by the Scottish architect Charles Rennie

Mackintosh in 1901, gave him the opportunity to design in a very different style which he was later to employ again to dramatic effect at Castle Drogo, Devon (qv.). The castle, which was finished in 1912, was never intended to be other than a temporary residence, and in 1921 Hudson sold it to a banker, Oswald Falk. It was later sold again before being given to the National Trust, along with some of Hudson's original furniture, in 1944.

From a distance the castle appears to grow out of the rock, and Lutyens left it with a plain, bald outline, wisely refraining from adding battlements, turrets and other paraphenalia. The original fortress was on different levels, and Lutyens made use of these in constructing a sequence of contrasting fairly small rooms linked together by staircases with ample opportunity for vistas and visual surprises (eg, the staircase leading to the Gallery, framed between two massive arches). The decoration is appropriately rough and rugged, especially in the low, barrel-vaulted Ship Room, and the furniture consists mostly of simple items in the manner of the 17C, some of them, like the tables in the Kitchen and Dining Room, designed by Lutyens himself. Never a very comfortable house—Lytton Strachey complained that it was 'very dark, with nowhere to sit, and nothing but stone under, over and round you'—Lindisfarne Castle is nevertheless a remarkable *jeu d'esprit* by one of England's most talented domestic architects and a vivid reminder of the continued vigour of the country-house building tradition in the early 20C.

GCT

Seaton Delaval Hall

Off the A190 between Blyth and Whitley Bay: the Lord Hastings, tel. 091 237 3040. Open 1 May–30 Sept Wed, Sun and BH 2–6.

The Delaval family lived here from Norman times, but the house is one of the great masterpieces of that remarkable playwright-turned-architect, Sir John Vanbrugh. Vanbrugh had made his name with Castle Howard and Blenheim Palace, and had a number of other commissions for great houses in hand, when Admiral George Delaval commissioned plans for a new house from him in 1718. Work began in 1720, and was supervised by William Etty, a very able builder and architect from York who was also supervising matters at Castle Howard.

Whether the Admiral expected anything quite so astonishing is not clear. He was killed, thrown from a horse, before the house was finished, and the rest of the Delavals, a singularly boisterous family, suffered misfortunes. Francis Blake Delaval completed the house before falling down dead under the portico, in 1752. He was succeeded by Sir Francis, the 'most accomplished Lothario of his age', who staged dazzling parties in a house which must have been a perfect setting for them. The heir to the family died of a kick delivered to his groin by a laundrymaid in 1775, and his father, Lord Delaval, died at the breakfast table in 1808.

The house and property passed, via Lord Delaval's sister, to the Astley family, for whom Queen Victoria revived the ancient title of Lord Hastings. Alas, in 1822 the house almost followed the Delaval family into extinction, when the whole central block was gutted by fire. After some 40 years, the roof was replaced, so that it survived into the 20C century as a shell. The present owner, the 22nd Lord Hastings, has undertaken major restoration work, which has saved the main block from dereliction; the roof and

The north, entrance, front of Seaton Delaval Hall, designed by Sir John Vanbrugh, 1718

windows have all been renewed, the massive entablature of the south portico rebuilt, the floors repaved, the interior made safe, and the original ironwork copied by local craftsmen.

Seaton Delaval stands on a windswept site close to the North Sea, facing due north. This house alone would confirm Vanbrugh as one of the greatest masters of the Baroque. The central block rises at the end of a long courtyard which is flanked by lower ranges. That to the left houses the stables. That to the right was the kitchen and service wing, and is now the family's residence. The flanking wings are relatively austere, with long rusticated arcades running along the ground floors, but the central block is utterly original; almost overpowering with its massive ringed columns and turrets rising to either side, like the architectural fantasies dreamed up by the opera designers of the age. Inside, the Entrance Hall is now open to the rafters, the stone arcades on either side still blackened from the 1822 fire. Damaged statues by Bagutti still posture in the niches high up. There are gaunt state rooms on either side, and dramatic cantilevered oval staircases in the flanking towers. The whole of the garden side is taken up by one vast Saloon in three sections, rising through both storeys; some of the architectural stonework here has been restored.

The stable block survived intact; the centre is a huge arched hall, all of stone, the fine wooden stalls still having boards painted with horses' names over them. The west wing is now the family's residence, but some rooms are open by special appointment, notably the former Kitchen, with a groined vault and a great Venetian window. On the south, garden side,

Vanbrugh was in lighter mood. The central block here has an Ionic portico of a feminine elegance, to contrast with the Doric masculinity of the entrance front. There are formal gardens on this side and to the west, with some fine lead figures by John van Nost, and immense statues on stone pedestals after the Florentine sculptor Giambologna. Further afield, in a wood, is the Delaval mausoleum built in 1766, with a dark seven-bay façade and a ruined dome rising above, but this is not yet accessible to the public.

SB

Wallington

On B6342 at Cambo, 2m north of A696: National Trust, tel. 067074 283.
Open Apr–Oct daily except Tues 1–5.30 (grounds daily all year).
Refreshments.

This large and well cared-for house stands in squirearchical country some 20 miles north west of Newcastle. It was built by Sir William Blackett, a successful Newcastle merchant, in about 1688, following the then old-fashioned courtyard plan. In 1738–41 Sir Walter Blackett, MP for Newcastle and five times mayor of the city, employed Daniel Garrett, a member of Lord Burlington's circle, to create a new suite of state rooms on the south front; he also remodelled the exterior and shifted the main entrance from the south to the east. These alterations were part of an ambitious programme of improvement which took in the gardens, the park, the estate village of Cambo and the surrounding farms. When Sir Walter Blackett died in 1777, the estate passed to a nephew, Sir John Trevelyan. He lived in Somerset, but his grandson Sir Walter Trevelyan established the main family residence at Wallington soon after he inherited in 1846, and in 1853–54 the central courtyard was roofed over to the designs of the Newcastle architect John Dobson. Sir Walter's wife Pauline was a friend of John Ruskin and a follower of the pre-Raphaelites, and the walls of the new central hall were decorated with historical and naturalistic paintings under the direction of the local artist William Bell Scott. Sir Walter Trevelyan was succeeded by his cousin Charles, perhaps the most influential of all Victorian civil servants. He married the sister of the historian Thomas Babington Macaulay, and his successors at Wallington followed him into public life. None of them made any major alterations to the house, and in 1941 it was given to the National Trust.

The best approach to Wallington is from the south. From here the plain façades of local sandstone can be seen across the park and ornamental lake, made by damming a stream and crossed by James Paine's bridge of 1755 ('Capability' Brown was born very close by, but seems to have had little to do with the layout). The public road separates the park from the ornamental gardens to the east, and the house is entered through the service courtyard to the north. This is approached through the monumental **coach-house** block of 1751–54 (by Garrett and Paine), surmounted by a cupola in the form of a circular domed temple. The grassy courtyard is surrounded by mid-18C stables and estate-workers' cottages, and the service range of the house lies to the south. Grisly stone heads from London's Aldersgate stand on the lawn to the east, guarding the entrance.

Wallington is famous for its collection of porcelain, some of which can be seen in the **Entrance Hall**. Some of the English porcelain, which includes

Bow figures dating from 1750–54, may have been in the house since the 18C, but most of the oriental pieces here and in the other rooms were introduced by the Trevelyans during the 19C. The main reception rooms are arranged in an *enfilade* along the south front, looking over the park to the hills beyond. The **Dining Room** and the adjoining Saloon were decorated in 1740–41 with stucco-work of the highest quality by Pietro Lafrancini, a member of a family which did most of its work in Ireland but which worked with Garrett on several occasions. Both rooms contain marble chimneypieces by Henry Cheere and attractive displays of oriental porcelain, some of it housed in oval recesses surrounded by stucco ornament. The **Saloon** is one of the best rooms of its date in England, its Palladian shape softened by the delicate, Rococo garlands and cornucopias on the walls and coved ceiling (the striking grey colour scheme was worked out by John Fowler); on the walls are good full-length portraits by Reynolds of Sir Walter Blackett and by Romney of Sir John Trevelyan. The third of the state rooms was originally a drawing-room and was turned into a **library** in the 1850s. It contains some of Macaulay's books, a few of which have been left open in a showcase to display his acerbic pencilled comments.

Three smaller rooms in the west range contain more Macaulay and Trevelyan memorabilia. In one of them, the **Parlour**, there are watercolours by Ruskin, Turner and others collected by Pauline, Lady Trevelyan, whose portrait by William Bell Scott hangs here; this room also contains some Continental porcelain, including maiolica and some Meissen pieces of c 1745. The main monument to the taste of the mid-Victorian Trevelyans, though, is the top-lit central **Hall**. This was intended partly to ease communications within the spread-out house, partly as a 'living-hall' for house parties (today concerts are occasionally held here). The design is classically inspired, as would be expected from the architect of the superbly monumental Grey Street and railway station in Newcastle, but the naturalistic paintings on the piers and spandrels of the surrounding arcade betray Lady Trevelyan's pre-Raphaelite sympathies (one of the piers was painted by Ruskin himself). The north and south arcades are filled with large paintings of Northumbrian history by William Bell Scott, installed in 1861. These are of varying artistic quality, but the finest, with the title 'The Northumbrian shows the world what can be done with Iron and Coal', has earned itself a place in the annals of Victorian art as an example of the 'historical' treatment of a subject taken from England's Industrial Revolution.

The staircase on the south side of the Hall, originally created in 1743, leads to the **bedroom floor**. Two rooms here are of particular note. An east-facing room is decorated with needlework panels made by Sir Walter Blackett's mother in 1717 and hung in Rococo frames of 1755 (a needlework screen in the corridor outside dated 1727 is decorated with scenes taken from Virgil). Upstairs, in an attic on the south front, there is a **museum** created in the 1820s to house a motley collection of objects of scientific and antiquarian interest inherited by the Trevelyans. With its Grecian-inspired decoration by an unknown architect, this room is an interesting and little-known monument to the scholarly interests of the family.

GCT

NOTTINGHAMSHIRE

Holme Pierrepont Hall

5m east of Nottingham to north of A52, 1½m beyond National Water
Sports Centre: Mr and Mrs Robin Brackenbury, tel. 0602 332371. Open
June–Aug Sun, also Thur July and Aug, Tues, Fri Aug, and Easter, Spring
BH Mon, Tues 2–5.30. Refreshments.

The village of Holme Pierrepont has long ceased to exist, and the Hall and
grey sandstone parish church are now hidden away from the outside world
by the lakes of the National Water Sports Centre. In the early Middle Ages
the estate belonged to the Manvers family, and it has remained with their
descendants ever since, passing by marriage to the Pierreponts in 1288.
The house was probably built by Sir William Pierrepont, who inherited in
1499 and married the daughter of Henry VII's financier Sir Richard Empson.
The family flourished in the 16C, and was raised to the earldom of Kingston
under Charles I. The 1st Earl enlarged and beautified the house in 1628,
but in 1680 the family shifted their main residence to Thoresby in the
'Dukeries', leaving Holme Pierrepont to moulder gently away as a dower
house. The hall and state rooms were demolished in the 1730s, and what
was left of the house was repaired and stuccoed over by the 1st Earl
Manvers in about 1800. The building was virtually abandoned between the
wars, but was rescued by the present owner and his wife, who purchased
it in 1969 to prevent it leaving the family. They restored the courtyard
garden including the attractive late-Victorian formal parterre, refurnished
the rooms and stripped the exterior of its stucco. These alterations have
been carried out with great sensitivity.

The house is built of brick, that most fashionable of early-Tudor building
materials. The rooms were originally arranged around a courtyard, which
was entered through a gateway flanked by projecting turrets. This still
survives today, along with the adjoining range to the east, and is substantially unaltered externally apart from the replacement of the original
pointed-arched windows by larger mullioned and transomed windows
early in the 17C. The entrance range originally contained lodgings for
members of the Pierrepont household, and two of these rooms are seen first,
with their wooden partitions and plain brick walls. The furniture and
pictures both here and in the rest of the house are family possessions of the
present owners, and include Pierrepont portraits formerly housed at Thoresby.

Most of the rooms shown to the public are upstairs. In one, at the east end
of the entrance range, there is an open medieval timber roof with cusped
wind-braces, and in the Long Gallery in the east range there are two Tudor
fireplaces. The main item of decorative interest, though, is the very grand
carved wooden staircase of c 1660–80; it was resited at the north end of the
east range after the demolition of the state rooms in the west in the 18C,
and is now hung with portraits of Mrs Brackenbury's ancestors.

GCT

Newstead Abbey

6m south of Mansfield on A60 Mansfield–Nottingham: Nottingham City
Council, tel. 0623 793557. Open Easter–Oct daily 12–6 (gardens open all
year daily 10–dusk). Refreshments.

Newstead Abbey is best-known today as the home of the poet Lord Byron,
but even without its literary associations it is a house of considerable
interest. It lies in the heart of the ancient Sherwood Forest, and incorporates
the remains of an Augustinian priory founded in the 12C and bought after
the Dissolution by the poet's ancestor, Sir John Byron of Colwick, near
Nottingham. Sir John built his house around the old cloister garth, incorporating many of the old monastic buildings and also sparing the superb
late-13C west front of the church. None of the later Byrons seem to have
had the money to make substantial alterations to the house, although in the
18C they created a spectacular landscape setting, complete with a lake in
front of the entrance guarded by 'forts' where mock naval battles were held
in the time of the 5th Lord Byron (the 'Wicked Lord') and his sailor brother,
'Foul Weather Jack', the poet's grandfather. When the 'Wicked Lord' died
in 1798 the estate was encumbered with huge debts, and his successor, the
poet, was forced to sell it in 1817, having done little to restore the by-then
severely dilapidated house.

The new owner, Col Thomas Wildman, was a school-fellow of the poet
and an admirer of his work. He spent large sums of money—much of it
derived from West Indies sugar plantations—on restoring the house in
1818–29 to the designs of the London architect John Shaw, an able practi-
tioner of the 'Old English' style. After Wildman's death in 1859 the house
was sold to an explorer, William Frederick Webb, who introduced much of
the furniture now on show, and carried out some internal alterations. He

*The late 13C west front of Newstead Abbey, with the façade of the church
to the left and monastic buildings to the right, converted into a house after
the Reformation, remodelled 1818–29*

left Newstead to his daughter, who created the famous Japanese Garden to the south, but the house and grounds were sold in 1925, and six years later they were given to the City of Nottingham. Since then more furniture has been introduced, along with large quantities of manuscript and other material relating to the life and works of the poet.

The west-facing entrance front summarises the history of Newstead, with the façade of the priory church on the left, Sir John Byron's hall range in the centre, and Shaw's office wing to the right, separated from the main house by a neo-Norman tower. The house was originally entered by a flight of stairs leading up to the Hall, which was formed out of the monastic guest quarters on the first floor. Shaw created the present ground-floor entrance, which leads through the vaulted undercroft, containing some tombs of the Byron family removed from Colwich church, to the medieval cloister, where an impressive early-16C fountain survives in the centre of the garth. A well-preserved mid-13C doorway on the east side gives access to the former chapter-house, converted into a family chapel in the 1860s after the poet had reputedly used it to house his menagerie; it is rich in high-Victorian stencilled decoration by C.A. Buckler and stained glass by Hardman.

The main rooms, on the first floor, still preserve much of the atmosphere of a large country house in the 19C. They are flanked by galleries over the cloister walks dating from the mid 16C and now filled with Byron memorabilia. Starting in the east range, formerly the monks' dormitory, there is a group of former bedrooms, one of which, the Charles II Room, has a good ceiling with 'grotesque' decoration of c 1720. Two rooms in the same range contain barbarously carved and painted mid-16C overmantels brought, probably in the 18C, from Colwick Hall, and a fourth room was decorated by the Webbs at the end of the 19C, in the Japanese taste. The rooms in the family wing, at the south-east corner of the house, have good woodwork of the mid 19C, and the Salon, which occupies the site of the monastic refectory in the south range, has a roof with plaster panels dating from 1631–33; there is also a miscellaneous collection of 17C and 18C furniture, a good mid-18C marble chimneypiece, possibly by Thomas Carter, and a picture by Peter Tillemans showing the house c 1730. The Hall, on the west front, where the poet practised pistol-shooting, was totally remodelled by Shaw with excellent wood panelling and doorcases in the French Flamboyant manner. The poet's bedroom on the second floor, occupying part of the former priors' lodgings, is the only room in the house to have remained much as he left it. It contains his four- poster bed with exact reproductions of the original hangings, and from here it is possible to look down on to the grassy site of the priory church, where his dog was buried near the high altar.

GCT

Wollaton Hall

In Wollaton Park, 2m west of centre of Nottingham; City of Nottingham, tel. 0602 281333 or 281130. Open daily all year weekdays 10–7 (Oct–Mar 10–dusk), Sundays 2–5 (Oct–Mar 1.30–4.30).

This most prodigious of all Elizabethan 'prodigy houses' was built by Sir Francis Willoughby in 1580–88. Like other houses of its type and date (eg, Hardwick Hall, Derbyshire), it is a highly personal and sophisticated exercise in the fusion of medieval and Renaissance architectural ideas. Sir Francis, a choleric, obsessive man, paid for the building in part out of the profits of coal-mining on his estates. But he was no parvenu (the family traced its origins back to the 13C), and he wanted his house to convey a sense of pride of lineage and ancient possession. The unconventional ground-plan was taken from Italy via du Cerceau's *Premier Livre d'Architecture* (1559), a copy of which Sir Francis had in his extensive library, but the architectural treatment was worked out by Robert Smythson, who was described on his tomb in Wollaton church as 'architector and surveyor' of the house. Smythson, one of the most able and inventive of all Elizabethan mason-architects, had already designed the very influential façades of Longleat, Wiltshire (qv.), and at Wollaton he adapted the classical manner employed there to produce an exterior of improbable richness, evoking the dream world of *The Faerie Queene*.

Wollaton Hall was deliberately placed on a prominent hilltop site, some distance away from the old manor-house in the village below. A sense of isolation lingers in the park, which still has a herd of deer, even though it is now encircled by the suburban sprawl of Nottingham. From a distance the house, which is faced with limestone from Ancaster in Lincolnshire, resembles a fantasy castle, with a central 'keep' flanked by lower corner towers. The central feature, with its French-looking corner turrets, was intended as a prospect-room from which Sir Francis could muse on his extensive possessions; it has no fireplace, and can only be reached by a narrow spiral staircase. It stands above the Hall, which was placed in the centre of the house over the kitchens, with the service rooms to the west (the right of the entrance) and the main living accommodation to the east. The rooms are lit by large mullioned and transomed windows, and the completely symmetrical façades and corner towers are adorned with exuberant Mannerist motifs taken from contemporary Flemish pattern-books. This profusion of carved ornament creates a very north-European effect of *horror vacui* which verges on the visually indigestible.

The vision of courtly romance is unfortunately not sustained inside the house. The interior was remodelled by Wyatville in 1801–7 and, since its abandonment by Sir Francis's descendants soon after the First World War, has been stripped of all its furnishings and turned into a natural history musuem. The only room to convey anything of the former splendour is the Hall, a vertiginously tall room, lit from above by round-arched windows and covered by a mock hammerbeam roof; Smythson's stone screen also survives, articulated by Doric columns and adorned with strapwork and figures holding globes and compasses, apparently alluding to the exploits of the explorer, Sir Henry Willoughby (d 1554). The main staircase, on the north side of the house, has wall paintings, by Laguerre, of c 1699 which were subsequently altered by Thornhill, but none of the rooms to which it leads retain anything of historic or artistic interest. More satisfying are the buildings around the house, notably the red-brick stables of 1794, which now house an industrial museum, and the early-19C glass and iron Camellia House, designed by Wyatville.

GCT

OXFORDSHIRE

Ardington House

2½m east of Wantage to south of A417: Mrs Desmond Baring, tel. 0235
833244. Open May–Sept Mon, BH 2.30–4.30. Guided tours.

This plain but dignified brick house stands on the edge of an unspoiled
village to the north of the Berkshire Downs. It was built in 1719–20 by
Edward Clarke, whose forbears had been lords of the manor since the early
17C, and it remained the home of the Clarke family until it was sold in 1831
to Robert Vernon, a successful horse dealer and art collector. It was later
purchased on behalf of Robert Loyd-Lindsay (later Lord Wantage), the
inheritor of a substantial banking fortune, and was incorporated into the
large and notably well-run estates centred on his house at Lockinge, a mile
or two away (since demolished). But while the land and the village have
remained part of the still-flourishing Loyd estate, the house was sold in
1939 to the present owner and her late husband, a member of another
banking family. Since then it has been maintained as an unpretentious and
unobtrusively comfortable family home.

Except for some minor embellishments made by Robert Vernon, the house
has changed little externally since it was first built. It is a tall three-storeyed
building, recalling some of the larger early Georgian town houses, and
notable more for its satisfying proportions and for the pleasing contrast
between the grey brick of the walls and the red of the window surrounds
than for any particular felicities of design or ornament. The architect was
almost certainly Thomas Strong, son of one of the most important of
Sir Christopher Wren's master masons, and some of the details (eg, the
emphasised keystones and the circular and round-headed windows on the
side elevations) are clearly derived from the style developed by Wren and
his team in the Office of the King's Works in the early 18C. Internally, the
most remarkable feature is the wooden staircase, situated on the central
axis, with two flights leading up to a landing, and a single flight proceeding
from there to the first floor. Though wasteful of space, this arrangement
imparts an unexpected note of drama, and the effect is enhanced by the
delicate carving of the twisted balusters. The original bolection-moulded
oak panelling survives in the Dining Room on the ground floor, and in the
Drawing Room there are some pictures by 19C landscape painters.

GCT

Ashdown House

2m south of Ashbury on B4000 Lambourn–Highworth: National Trust,
tel. 0494 528051. Open April–Oct Wed, Sat 2.15–5.15. Guided tours.

This unusual house was built in the 1660s as a hunting lodge by William,
1st Earl of Craven, an ardent Royalist and protector of Charles I's sister, the
'Winter Queen', widow of the Elector Palatine, during her long exile in
Holland and England. Craven's main country seats were Combe Abbey
(Warwickshire) and Hampstead Marshall (Berkshire), at both of which he
employed the Dutch-born gentleman architect William Winde, and Winde
seems the most probable designer of the strikingly Dutch-looking

Ashdown. The house originally stood mysteriously in the middle of a dense plantation at the top of the Berkshire Downs (Ashdown was in Berkshire until 1974), but, except to the north, the trees have long been felled and there is now a formal garden setting. The exaggeratedly tall dolls'-house-like proportions derive from the need to treat the house as a viewing stand for the chase—hence the balustraded platform and glazed cupola at the top of the typically 1660s hipped roof. The walls are of chalk, often used as a building material in the nearby villages and farms, and the quoins and window architraves are picked out in a darker limestone; the two massive chimneystacks are typical of the more 'advanced' country house architecture of the post-Restoration period, as is the overhanging wooden eaves cornice. Lower service blocks stand on either side of the entrance front, to the east.

Because the house was intended as a retreat from the formality of Lord Craven's main houses there are relatively few rooms, and none of any great architectural or decorative distinction, although there is a good sturdy doorcase leading from the entrance lobby to the main rooms beyond. The main interest of the interior, of which only the entrance lobby and staircase are accessible to visitors, lies in the collection of Craven portraits, purchased from the family by the National Trust in 1968 and arranged on the walls of the massive oak staircase which extends to the top of the house. With the exception of an unfinished group portrait attributed to William Dobson (c 1644) at the top of the stairs, they are all by, or after, the Dutch artists Michael Miereveldt and Gerard Honthorst; note especially Honthorst's portraits of Lord Craven and the 'Winter Queen' (1650) at the foot of the stairs, those of Prince Rupert and his sister Sophia of Hanover (1650), mother of George I, higher up, and Miereveldt's portrait of the soldier Sir Horace Vere (1629)—perhaps the finest in the collection from an artistic point of view. The tour ends on the roof platform, from which visitors can enjoy the view over the empty downs.

GCT

Blenheim Palace

8m north west of Oxford at Woodstock on A44 Oxford–Evesham: the Duke of Marlborough, tel. 0993 811325/811091. Open mid Mar–Oct daily 10.30–5.30. Guided tours. Refreshments.

Blenheim is the most magnificent of all early-18C English country houses. Its great size and splendour derive from its having been conceived as a gift by the English government to John Churchill, 1st Duke of Marlborough, the allied commander in the Battle of Blenheim during the War of the Spanish Succession. It was thus, in the words of the architect Sir John Vanbrugh, not only a private residence but also 'a Royall and a National Monument', imbued with 'the qualitys proper to such a monument, viz., Beauty, Magnificence and Duration'.

The site was in the former royal park of Woodstock, and the distinctive ochre-coloured stone came mainly from quarries at Burford and Taynton owned by the chief mason-contractor Edward Strong, who had worked with Sir Christopher Wren on St Paul's Cathedral. As at Castle Howard, Yorkshire (qv.), which anticipates Blenheim in many respects, Wren's right-hand man Nicholas Hawksmoor collaborated with Vanbrugh on the design, though in a subordinate capacity. Building began in 1705, and was attended with many problems. Marlborough's political opponents castigated the house as a waste of public funds—the final cost was three times the original estimate—and work came to a halt after the formidable Duchess of Marlborough was displaced in the favour of Queen Anne and dismissed from office as Mistress of the Robes and Keeper of the Privy Purse, along with her husband, in 1711. Treasury payments stopped in 1712, but work resumed at the Duke's own expense in 1716. But the Duchess, enraged at Vanbrugh's alterations and extensions to the original plan, succeeded in dismissing him as architect, even refusing him permission to enter the grounds. The house was completed under Hawksmoor's supervision, and Vanbrugh never saw it in its finished state. Structurally it has changed very little since the completion of the chapel in 1732, but the park and gardens were transformed by 'Capability' Brown for the 4th Duke in the 1760s, and the same Duke employed William Chambers to remodel some of the interiors. Further internal alterations were carried out by the 9th Duke in the 1890s after a series of sales of furniture and works of art by his immediate predecessors; he also brought in a Frenchman, Achille Duchêne, to restore formality to the east and west gardens adjoining the house, whose early-18C parterres were landscaped away by Brown.

Blenheim's arcadian landscape setting is best appreciated by visitors on foot, who enter from the town of Woodstock through a **triumphal arch** designed by Hawksmoor; the entrance for vehicles, through the extraordinary Hensington Gate, also by Hawksmoor, leads straight to the house. The distant view of the house, with its extravagantly turreted outline, conjures up, especially in misty weather, an improbable vision of medieval romance, to which Vanbrugh was very susceptible (he argued vainly for the preservation of the existing medieval house). It overlooks the River Glyme, which was first channelled into a formal canal and subsequently dammed by Brown to create the present lake, crossed by a gargantuan **bridge** designed by Vanbrugh; Brown was also responsible for the plantations which spread up to the **Victory Column** (designed by the 9th Earl of Pembroke) on the northern horizon. The house itself, for all its proliferation of strange 'eminencys' (Hawksmoor's word) on the skyline, was designed as a great Baroque palace: an English answer to Versailles. The focal point is the porticoed **central block**, behind which rises a pedimented attic with windows lighting the Hall from above and a gilded copper ball on the apex of the pediment. Curved walls link the main block to wings stretching forward, that to the east (left) containing the private apartments (sometimes open to visitors on payment of an extra charge) and that to the west housing the chapel. Huge rusticated towers, unlike anything else in the architecture of early-18C Europe, appear to anchor the vast mass of masonry down at the corners. An open courtyard spreads out in front, with a service courtyard on either side linked to the main house by a colonnade, and it is through the overpoweringly heavy **gateway** to the east (kitchen) courtyard that visitors enter (note the cannonballs at the foot of the pilasters on either side of the entrance and the chauvinistic carvings of the English lion strangling the French cockerel over the entrance to the courtyard in front of the house—an eloquent testimony to the triumphalist spirit in which Blenheim was conceived).

The first room to be seen is the Hall, 67ft high, with a fine ceiling by Sir James Thornhill showing the 1st Duke, in Roman costume, presenting Britannia with the plan of the Battle of Blenheim. The architecture evokes

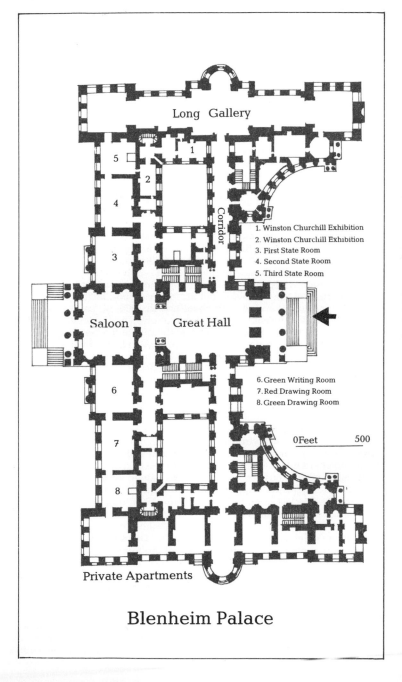

Long Gallery

5

1

2

4

3

Corridor

1. Winston Churchill Exhibition
2. Winston Churchill Exhibition
3. First State Room
4. Second State Room
5. Third State Room

Saloon   Great Hall

6

7

8

6. Green Writing Room
7. Red Drawing Room
8. Green Drawing Room

0 Feet   500

Private Apartments

Blenheim Palace

the solemn grandeur of the public buildings of the Romans, especially the tiers of plain rounded arches screening the intended staircases to the east and west, and the massive proscenium-like segmental arch, flanked by giant Corinthian columns, which frames the doorway into the Saloon at the centre of the state apartments on the garden front. The impression of Roman dignity is further reinforced by the bronze copies by Maximilano Soldini, of the Dancing Faun and the Medici Venus, two of the most famous of all antique sculptures, commissioned by the 1st Duke. From the Hall visitors proceed along a dome-vaulted **corridor** to the west, reminiscent of the aisles of St Paul's Cathedral, to the room in which Sir Winston Churchill, nephew of the 8th Duke, was born in 1874; this looks out on to an internal courtyard, and it and the surrounding rooms are given over to a display of **mementoes** of the statesman's life and a selection of his oil paintings.

The state rooms were originally made up of two 'apartments' (ante-room, drawing room and bedroom), on either side of the central Saloon. By the end of the 18C this arrangement had gone out of fashion and the rooms were turned into drawing rooms. The first three rooms retain their original ceilings designed by Hawksmoor, but the decoration is otherwise relatively plain, presumably reflecting the taste of the 1st Duchess, who wrote that she 'always liked to have things plain and clean, from a piece of wainscot to a lady's face'. There are paintings by Kneller (of the 1st Duchess) and Reynolds (the 4th Duchess, holding her child on her knee) in the **Green Drawing Room**, while the **Red Drawing Room** contains Reynolds's spectacular portrait of the 4th Duke and his family (1788), facing John Singer Sargent's portrait, executed with equal brio in 1905, of the 9th Duke, his wife Consuelo Vanderbilt (whose autobiography *The Glitter and the Gold* gives a vivid picture of life at Blenheim at the turn of the century) and their children; there are also portraits by, and after, Van Dyck, including one of his wife. Kneller's portrait of the 1st Duke hangs in the **Green Writing Room**, along with two of the superb set of Brussels tapestries (by Judocus de Vos) commissioned to commemorate his military victories.

The majestic **Saloon** is largely unaltered except for the intrusion of a permanent dining-table (the room was originally largely free of furniture); the trompe-l'oeil wall paintings are by Louis Laguerre, who included his self-portrait, and the marble doorcases are by Grinling Gibbons. Three more tapestry-hung **drawing rooms** follow, all of them embellished in the French taste by unknown decorators brought in by the 9th Duke in the 1890s (he later said that the work was 'quite out of scale...and leaves a very unpleasant impression to those who possess trained eyes'); he also acquired most of the original and reproduction 18C French furniture seen in all the state rooms. The last room to be seen is the 180ft long **Library**, originally intended as a picture gallery. It was the last room in the house to be finished (by Hawksmoor), and has a superb plaster ceiling by Isaac Mansfield, and a statue of Queen Anne and a bust of the 1st Duke by Rysbrack. For 150 years this magnificent room housed one of the finest collections of books in the country, brought here by Charles Spencer, Earl of Sunderland, when he became 3rd Duke of Marlborough in 1733, but it was sold (for £30,000) by the 7th Duke. In 1891 the 8th Duke introduced the organ by 'Father' Willis on which a resident organist entertained house party guests until the First World War.

The most striking feature of the **Chapel** is the massive marble monument to the 1st Duke by Rysbrack and William Kent. From here visitors descend through Duchêne's west parterre *all' Italiana* to the terrace below, with a preliminary model, given to the 1st Duke, of Bernini's fountain in the Piazza Navona in Rome. Visitors should not leave Blenheim without seeing the monumental south or **garden front**, less busy than the north front, with a bust of Louis XIV captured at the siege of Tournai in 1709 placed trophy-like over the centre; this originally overlooked another parterre, which was alas swept away by Brown.

GCT

Broughton Castle

2m west of Banbury off B4035 Banbury–Shipston-on-Stour: Lord Saye and Sele, tel. 0295 262624. Open mid May–mid Sept Wed, Sun and Thur in July, Aug and all BH Sun/Mon 2–5. Refreshments.

This large moated house dates back at least to the early 14C, when it belonged to Sir John de Broughton (d 1315). He rebuilt the adjacent church with its broach spire, and built the core of the present building, using the distinctive dark brown iron-tinged stone quarried in the Banbury region. The manor was purchased in 1377 by William of Wykeham, Bishop of Winchester and Chancellor to Edward III, probably as a base for supervising the building of New College, Oxford, and in 1406 his great-nephew and heir, Sir Thomas Wykeham, obtained licence to crenellate the house and to build the gatehouse which still commands the entrance over the moat. In 1448 the estate passed by marriage to the 2nd Lord Saye and Sele, and in 1551–54 his descendant Richard Fiennes, *de jure* 6th Lord Saye, carried out an ambitious remodelling of the house, as a result of which it obtained its present unmistakably 16C appearance; further alterations followed in 1599. In 1624 the 8th Lord Saye was made a viscount; he subsequently played an important part in the opposition to Charles I's personal rule and became, in Clarendon's admittedly biased words, 'the pilot that steered all those vessels freighted with sedition to destroy the government'.

Broughton passed by marriage to the Twisleton family in 1710, but although they successfully claimed the title in 1761 they were never very wealthy and some of their members were notably extravagant; in 1837 the 14th Lord Saye was forced by the excesses of his son—'the greatest epicure of his day', according to Captain Gronow—to sell almost all the contents of the house and even the swans in the moat. Lack of money proved the saving of the old building, and apart from some internal redecoration in the late 1760s, it remained remarkably untouched. There was a sensitive restoration by the younger George Gilbert Scott in 1865–80, and today it exudes a comforting sense of age and ancient possession.

Broughton was always a semi-fortified manor house rather than a true castle, and until the mid 16C it consisted of the usual hall range, with a turreted and crenellated chamber block at the east or upper end and a service range to the west. In 1551–54 the hall range was heightened and refenestrated, with large mullioned windows and a roof-line made up of gables surmounted by tall chimneystacks in the most up-to-date style. At about the same time a new chamber block was constructed at the west end, and the medieval chamber block was downgraded to become the new service end, thus ensuring its survival (note the two-light early-14C window on the left of the north or entrance front). There are more indications of the medieval origins of the house on the south front, including a crenellated garderobe turret on the extreme right; the two gabled projections overlooking the attractive early-20C walled knot garden contain staircases leading to and from the rooms built over the Hall in the mid 16C.

Most of the phases in the architectural evolution of the house are visible inside the Hall. The rubble-stone walls are fundamentally medieval, and the original doorways on the west wall were uncovered when the plaster was scraped off the walls in 1900. The windows which flood the room with light were inserted in the 1550s, but the flat 16C ceiling was replaced by the present plaster ceiling with its globular pendants in the 1760s, posiibly in the designs of Sanderson Miller, who lived only a few miles away.

The tour begins in the medieval part of the house, where an intriguing network of vaulted early-14C passageways (note the carved corbels in the form of human faces) is wrapped around the family Dining Room, originally an undercroft to the medieval great chamber; the linenfold panelling was inserted in the 16C. Upstairs the influence of the Renaissance is immediately apparent in the crudely carved mid-16C chimneypiece in Queen Anne's Room, built within the walls of the medieval great chamber; it encloses an anonymous portrait of James I's queen, Anne of Denmark, who stayed in the house in 1604. The largely unaltered early-14C Chapel can be seen through a squint in the wall.

Most of the space above the Hall is occupied by a Gallery, remodelled in the 1760s with vestigially Gothic 'pilasters' and Gothick doorways, and containing oval reliefs of Inigo Jones and Ben Jonson by Rysbrack (c 1737). To the left, in the King's Chamber, there is a chimneypiece of the 1550s, possibly designed for Dudley Castle (Worcestershire) in imitation of one at the Palace of Fontainebleau in France, and reflecting the sophisticated Mannerist taste of the Somerset/Dudley circle; the stuccoed overmantel contains a scene of dryads dancing round an oak tree, with lines from Ovid's *Metamorphoses* underneath. The plaster ceiling with its shallow ribs is of the same date, but the walls are covered with 18C Chinese wallpaper. A staircase at the west end of the Gallery leads up to a room in which the 1st Viscount Saye and his friends are said to have plotted against Charles I, and from here it is sometimes possible to walk up on to the roof and survey the attractive pastoral country around—a favourite 16C and 17C pastime.

The Great Parlour, at the west end of the house, was the main dining and reception room after the 16C remodelling; it retains its severe classical chimneypiece and delicate arabesque frieze of the 1550s, but a much more ornate ceiling was inserted in 1599, and the doorcases and wallpaper (possibly by Thomas Willement) are of c 1840. The last room to be seen is the Oak Room on the ground floor below, with late-16C wood panelling and a profusely carved internal porch of the same date.

GCT

Buscot Park

3m north west of Faringdon on A417 Faringdon–Lechlade: National Trust/Lord Faringdon, tel. 0367 242094. Open Apr–Sept Wed–Fri and 2nd and 4th Sat, Sun 2–6. Refreshments.

The main interest of this late-18C house lies in its varied and impressive collection of furniture, pictures and porcelain. The house itself was built c 1780, to the designs of an unknown architect, by Edward Loveden Townsend, representative of a family which had owned the estate since the mid 16C, but the collection was largely brought together by two later owners: the financier Alexander Henderson, chairman of the Great Central Railway, who bought the estate in 1880 and was ennobled as Lord Faringdon in 1916; and his grandson, the 2nd Lord Faringdon, a keen supporter of the Labour Party, who inherited in 1934 and lived at Buscot until his death, having conveyed the house and grounds to the National Trust in 1949 and established a separate trust to protect and add to the collection.

The excessively austere house, of grey limestone, stands isolated on a ridge overlooking the valley of the upper Thames. The low pedimented pavilions on either side were added by the 2nd Lord Faringdon's architect, Geddes Hyslop, in the 1930s, and Hyslop also made extensive changes to the house itself, removing sundry Victorian additions and remodelling some of the interiors in the neo-Georgian manner. A broad flight of steps leads up to the uncompromisingly neo-classical **Hall**, furnished with spectacular black and gold painted chairs and sofas designed by Thomas Hope for the Egyptian Room in his London house c 1800–4, and acquired by the 1st Lord Faringdon; the room is divided by scagliola columns dating from the 1780s, but the trompe-l'oeil trophies on the walls were painted in 1950. From here visitors proceed through the main rooms on the piano nobile, starting with the **Music Room**, to the west of the Hall. This contains some of the best of the pictures in the house, notably a Rembrandt portrait, probably of Pieter Six, and Rubens's gorgeous portrait of the Marchesa Veronica Spinola-Doria (1608); there are also works by Jacob Jordaens and other 17C Flemish and Dutch artists. From here a passage containing Roman and Egyptian antiquities gives access to the **Dining Room**, the first of three reception rooms on the north side of the piano nobile (note the Italian landscape by Richard Wilson). The finest of these rooms is the **Saloon**, dominated by Burne-Jones's exquisite series of paintings of the Legend of the Briar Rose (the Sleeping Beauty), completed in 1890 and displayed in ornate gilded frames designed by the artist himself; the verses underneath were contributed by William Morris, whose house at Kelmscott (qv.) is on the opposite bank of the Thames. The almost overpoweringly rich effect of the room is enhanced by the 18C and 19C furniture, much of it gilded, and some of the family's excellent collection of Chinese porcelain (including dishes of the Sung period and other items of the K'ang Hsi and Chien Ch'ing eras) is on display. The **Drawing Room** retains its original late-18C furniture. The paintings are Italian, with works by Sodoma (a 'Sacra Conversazione' of c 1518), Palma Vecchio (a somewhat truncated 'Mystic Marriage of St Catherine'), a charming 'Rest of the Flight into Egypt' by Andrea Previtali, and a 'St Jerome' by the little-known 17C artist Giovanni Pace, in the manner of Salvator Rosa; there is also a display of Italian ceramics, including some 16C maiolica items.

Beyond is the **Staircase Hall**, remodelled in the 1930s, with a painted ceiling rescued from James Wyatt's demolished Badger Hall (Shropshire); Old Master drawings, including some by Rembrandt and others attributed to Guercino and Ludovico Carracci, hang at the foot of the stairs, and on the walls there are 16C and 17C paintings, including Palma Giovane's 'St Jerome' (c 1580) and Murillo's outstanding 'Triumph of the Eucharist', painted c 1662–65 for a church in Seville and removed during the Napoleonic Wars.

A detour upstairs takes in three rooms hung with 18C and 20C English pictures. The **Pre-Raphaelite Room** contains a Rossetti (a soulful-looking

Jane Morris as Pandora) and three canvases by George Frederick Watts, including his 'Wife of Pygmalion', based on an antique sculpture which can still be seen among the Arundel Marbles in the Ashmolean Museum, Oxford. Lord Leighton's colourful if somewhat vapid 'Daedalus and Icarus' hangs over the fireplace in the adjacent dressing room, and there is an 'Entombment' by Ford Madox Brown on the wall opposite. The **Normanton Room**, named after the early-18C state bed formerly at Normanton Park (Rutland), commands extensive views over the Thames valley; the pictures here include works by 20C English painters, including Graham Sutherland. The last room to be seen is the neo-Georgian **Sitting Room** downstairs. It contains early 19C furniture, some of it possibly by Gillow, and is hung with English 18C paintings, including two 'fancy pictures' by Reynolds ('Mercury as Cut-Purse' 1777 and a 'Beggar Boy' of c 1775) on either side of a picturesque landscape in monochrome by Gainsborough (c 1772).

On leaving the house, visitors should make sure not to miss the **east pavilion**, decorated in the 1930s with murals by Lord Hastings, a pupil of Diego Rivera, celebrating the high-minded dinner parties frequently held at Buscot by the 2nd Lord Faringdon. Beyond this is the beautiful Italianate **Water Garden**, laid out in the early 20C by Harold Peto, partner of the architect Sir Ernest George, who designed the Arts and Crafts estate cottages in the nearby villages of Buscot and Eaton Hastings. The garden leads down to the 18C lake, and on the west side of the house another garden has been created by the present Lord Faringdon within the red-brick walls of the old kitchen garden.

GCT

Chastleton House

5m north west of Chipping Norton off A44 Oxford–Evesham: National Trust. Closed for repairs.

Chestleton is perhaps the best-preserved early-17C gentleman's house in England. The builder, Walter Jones, was a lawyer and MP for Worcester who claimed descent from King Priam of Troy, although his father was, more prosaically, a wool merchant from Witney. He bought the Chastleton estate from the Catesbys, soon to be notorious for their involvement in the Gunpowder Plot, in 1603, and began building the house soon afterwards. It never had much land to support it, and apart from some internal remodelling by John Jones in the late 18C it underwent remarkably few alterations, retaining much of the original 17C furniture in situ. In 1828 the house passed to a branch of the Whitmores of Dudmaston, Shropshire (qv.), and from them by descent to Alan Clutton-Brock, art critic of *The Times*, whose widow maintained it until 1991, when it was acquired by the National Trust with the help of the National Heritage Memorial Fund.

The approach from the main road leads up a steep hill, and the walls of lichened local limestone present a gaunt face to the outside world. The house is entered through a gateway which leads into a walled courtyard, where the former farm buildings can be seen to the left and the medieval church to the right. Castellated staircase towers stand on each side of the gabled main block, which is built round a small internal courtyard or light-well; the ground-plan and tall proportions recall the work of Robert Smythson, but there is no definite evidence of his involvement. The south or entrance range is completely symmetrical, with the porch, as at the earlier Broughton Castle (qv.), placed in one of two bays projecting from the façade. This leads via a screens passage into the Hall, very little changed since the early 17C, with the original dais at the 'upper' end, lit by a large window, a carved frieze over the wood panelling, and a portrait of Walter Jones hanging between suits of armour over the fireplace. The screen itself is a good piece of Jacobean wood carving, with profuse strapwork like that in the contemporary chapel at Wadham College, Oxford, and the long table is one of several pieces of furniture mentioned in an inventory of 1633 which is still in the house. Beyond are two parlours, one of which contains a mid-17C Flemish tapestry, along with the high table originally in the Hall.

The grandest rooms are on the first floor, reached by a carved wooden staircase with spiky newel posts and faded family portraits on the walls. A panelled bedroom at the top of the stairs called Mr Fettiplace's Chamber has changed hardly at all since the time of Walter Jones, when it was hung with the three pieces of 16C Flemish tapestry of Jacob and Esau still in the room, and the adjoining closet still has its original 17C needlework hangings. The most sumptuous decoration is in the great chamber (now called the Drawing Room); there is an elaborate plaster ceiling with pendants, a carved stone chimneypiece displaying the arms of Walter Jones and his wife, and richly carved wood panelling with 24 small contemporary paintings of the Prophets and Sibyls on the frieze. The Middle Chamber, next door, also contains its Jacobean chimneypiece and plaster frieze, but the room was redecorated in the late 18C, when the adjacent Library (which contains the bible taken to the scaffold by Charles I) was created out of another bedchamber. A room opening out of a bedroom redecorated in the 19C is said to have served as the hiding-place for the Royalist Arthur Jones, grandson of the builder of the house, when Cromwellian troops paid a visit after the Battle of Worcester. From here the west staircase—less elaborate than its counterpart on the other side of the house—mounts up to the empty Gallery on the second floor with its barrel-vaulted ceiling enriched with rustic designs of flowers and tendrils. A topiary garden to the east of the house, possibly dating from the 17C, reinforces the haunting effect of time stopped in its tracks.

NB: please note this house was undergoing restoration at the time of writing (1993), and there may be some changes when it is opened to the public again.

GCT

Greys Court

3m north west of Henley-on-Thames on Henley–Rotherfield Peppard road: National Trust, tel. 0491 628529. Open Apr–Sept Mon, Wed, Fri 2–6 (gardens open daily except Thur, Sun 2–6). Refreshments.

The origins of this picturesque, rambling set of buildings go back to at least 1347, when the first Lord Grey of Rotherfield was granted the right to crenellate the walls surrounding his manor house. Some of the walls and four defensive towers survive from this once-formidable house, which stands in unspoilt wooded country at the head of a dry valley in the least suburbanised part of the Chilterns. The house later fell into disrepair and, having passed into the hands of the Crown, was granted in 1518 to a courtier, Robert Knollys. He or his son Francis, who became Lord Treasurer of the Household under Queen Elizabeth, built a new but much smaller house of brick within the courtyard, and this was rebuilt in the early 17C as a secondary residence by William, Lord Knollys (the family's main house, now totally disappeared, was at Caversham, near Reading). The estate later passed to the Stapleton family, whose wealth derived from the West Indies, and c 1750 Sir Thomas Stapleton modernised the interior of the house, since when there have been few major structural changes. The Stapletons removed the contents when they left in 1935, but a later owner, Sir Felix Brunner, refurnished the house, and in 1969 he gave it to the National Trust, the family continuing to live here as tenants.

The buildings are scattered haphazardly around a grassy courtyard, with the tallest of the 14C towers to the east, from the top of which there are excellent views over the pretty walled gardens and a recently constructed maze. A 16C red-brick block known as the 'Cromwellian Stables' lies to the south, next to a lower tower, and opposite is the main house, a compact 'double-pile' structure with a three-gabled façade of flint, brick and stone, and an earlier 16C brick portion to the south. Successive remodellings have removed most of the original interior decoration, and the most interesting of the three rooms open to the public is now the comfortable bow-windowed Drawing Room of c 1750; its walls and ceiling are embellished with floral cornucopias attributed to Thomas Roberts of Oxford on the basis of their similarity to his work in Christ Church Library. Outside, to the west, there is an early-16C wheel-house containing the largest surviving donkey-wheel in the country, used until 1914 to raise water for the house from a well, and in the nearby church of Rotherfield Greys there is a superb monument to Sir William Knollys (d 1596).

GCT

Kelmscott Manor

2½m east of Lechlade off Lechlade–Clanfield road: the Society of Antiquaries, tel. 0367 252486. Open Apr–Sept Wed 11–12.30, 2–4.30.

This gabled grey stone house is inseparably connected with the personality of the poet, craftsman and pioneer socialist William Morris, whose occasional residence it was from 1871 until his death in 1896. It was first built c 1570, probably by Richard Turner, a prosperous farmer, and was enlarged about a century later by one of his descendants to provide more spacious reception rooms. Since then it has been little altered. Until Morris's time the house was always the centre of a working farm (it was called Lower Farm until the mid 19C), and the Turner family, who are probably best described as gentleman farmers, remained in possession until the late 19C. Morris leased the house from them and their successors, but his widow Jane bought it, together with the immediate surroundings, in 1913. When their daughter May died in 1938, it passed first to the University of Oxford and then, in 1962, to the Society of Antiquaries, under whose aegis it has been successfully refurnished with pictures, hangings and furniture belonging to Morris, many of them originally in his London house, Kelmscott House, Hammersmith. The interior now evokes the world of Morris and his circle with compelling intensity.

Morris was attracted to Kelmscott by its situation in the remote meadow-

Kelmscott Manor, late 16C with 17C alterations

land of the upper Thames valley, but the house also has many of the characteristics which he thought were essential in good domestic architecture. Like so many of the farmhouses and smaller manor houses of the area, it is the product of a craft-based tradition which stretched back to the Middle Ages and lasted into the 18C. As seen from the walled garden which separates it from the muddy track leading from the village to the River Thames—a view immortalised in the frontispiece to the Utopian romance *News from Nowhere* (1892)—it consists of a gabled two-storeyed hall block with a slightly taller gabled extension of c 1670 to the right; wings extend back from the main block on the west side, where a conical-roofed outbuilding also survives. Apart from the pediments over the top-floor windows of the 17C extension, all the detailing is taken from the local vernacular tradition, and lovers of rural architecture can derive much pleasure from the interplay of stone walls, mullioned windows, stone-tiled roofs, tall chimneys and plain triangular gables.

The entrance is through a screens passage which bisects the main block and gives access to the Old Hall and the North or Garden Hall beyond it. They retain their old stone floors, and several Morris fabrics and hangings are displayed, including the 'Cabbage and Vine' tapestry (1879) and embroideries made for the Red House at Bexleyheath (Kent), Morris's former country home, in 1860–65. There are also charcoal drawings of the Signs of the Zodiac by Morris's friend Edward Burne-Jones, probably studies for the painted figures in the dining room (now called the William Morris Room) in the Victoria and Albert Museum in London. The Panelled Room, in the late-17C wing, has white-painted wood panelling and a stone chimneypiece with carved swags of fruit. Above it there is a painting of 'Spring' by the younger Pieter Breughel (1632) and the walls are hung with pictures of Morris's wife Jane and their two daughters, by Dante Gabriel Rossetti, whose desultory affair with Jane was carried on in part at Kelmscott. The first of many paintings of her by Rossetti, entitled 'The Blue Silk Dress' (1866–68) hangs in the adjoining closet; she appears gorgeously dressed, with a characteristically withdrawn and enigmatic expression on her face. A good collection of the blue and white porcelain admired by Rossetti and his fellow-aesthetes is shown opposite on shelves designed by the architect Philip Webb. On the other side of the Garden Hall is the Green Room, originally one of the parlours of the 16C house but now containing several Morris chintzes on the chairs and walls.

The first floor is reached by a 16C carved wooden staircase. The bed in Jane Morris's bedroom is the one in which William was born in his father's house in Walthamstow, London (now the William Morris Gallery), and on the chest nearby is Jane's jewel casket painted with Arthurian figures by Rossetti. William's bedroom is on the opposite side of the landing, and contains his bed, a 17C four-poster hung with embroideries by his daughter May, while on the walls are prints by Mantegna and Dürer. Next comes the Tapestry Room, in the late-17C part of the house, with a chimneypiece displaying the arms of the Turners and a set of mid-17C Brussels or Antwerp tapestries of the Life of Samson completely covering the walls in the fashion of the period. In the middle of the room, which was used by Rossetti as a studio from 1871–74, is a heavy wooden table made by Philip Webb for the Red House c 1860. Upstairs in the attics there are some pieces of green-painted furniture made by Ford Madox Brown for William Morris's firm in 1862–63. Before leaving Kelmscott, it is worth exploring the village, which contains cottages in the vernacular style by Philip Webb and Ernest Gimson, and also the medieval village church in whose shadow Morris was buried in 1896 (a stone designed by Webb marks the spot).

GCT

Kingston Bagpuize House

10m south west of Oxford near junction of A415 & A420 Oxford–Swindon: Lady Tweedsmuir, tel. 0865 820259. Open Apr–Sept Sun, BH Mon 2.30–5.30. Guided tours. Refreshments.

This little-altered early-18C house stands in an attractive garden setting on the edge of the village, which derives its unusual name from Ralf de Bachpuise, lord of the manor after the Norman Conquest. The builder was probably Edmund Fettiplace, a member of an important local family who bought the estate in 1670 and died in 1710. The house is an impressive structure of red brick, with dressings of Burford stone. There are two main storeys over a basement, as in most of gentlemens' country houses of the time, but here the three central bays project slightly, and are raised to incorporate a third storey and a pediment; there are also pediments over the shorter side elevations. Some of the details, like the round- and segmental-headed windows, the prominent keystones and quoins, the rusticated door surrounds, the carved urns of the roof-line and the massive arched chimneystacks, are reminiscent of contemporary work in Oxford, and the Oxford mason William Townesend has been suggested as a possible designer, though there is no documentary evidence to support the attribution. When John Fettiplace died, the house went to his daughter, who married John Blandy, and it remained in the possession of the Blandy family and their descendants until 1917, when it was sold. There were two more sales in the 1930s, the second of which was to Miss Marlie Raphael, whose niece and her husband Lord Tweedsmuir (son of the novelist John Buchan) live here now.

The house was originally entered from the east, where a sadly denuded avenue stretches into the distance, but it is now approached from the north, through re-sited 18C wrought-iron gates next to the small classical parish church built by a member of the Blandy family in 1799. Traces of the original formal garden layout survive near the house, including an iron gateway facing the north front and a gazebo standing over a former ice-house, approached by a raised walkway flanking the former east or entrance courtyard; from here the excellent craftsmanship of the house can be appreciated, down to the original glass and glazing bars in the windows. The tour takes in all the main rooms, which are comfortably and appropriately furnished with 18C and later items brought in by Miss Raphael and the present owners. The entrance, from the west, leads into the Staircase Hall, with a cantilevered wooden staircase making a 'stately ascent' around the four sides of the room (the original paint was unfortunately removed from the stairs and from the woodwork elsewhere in the house in the 1920s). The Saloon (the original entrance hall), contains two impressive stone fireplaces in the Vanbrugh manner, and on either side are smaller, wood-panelled rooms now used as the Library and Dining Room. The tour also includes some of the bedrooms on the first floor.

GCT

Mapledurham House

4m north west of Reading off A4074 Reading–Oxford: J.J. Eyston, Esq, tel. 0743 723350. Open Easter–Sept Sat–Sun, BH 2.30–5. Refreshments.

Though virtually within sight of the suburbs of Reading, Mapledurham is still a manorial enclave, scarcely touched, at least on the surface, by the 20C. The red-brick Elizabethan house rises at the end of the village street, close to the River Thames, with the medieval church, restored by William Butterfield, and late-15C wooden watermill (open to the public) as near neighbours. In the later Middle Ages the estate passed from the Bardolf family, some of whom are buried in the church, to the Lyndes, and a substantial fragment of their timber-framed house was allowed to remain when the present, much larger, house was begun c 1588 by Sir Michael Blount, Lieutenant of the Tower of London and grandson of the Richard Blount who purchased the estate in 1490. The house appears at first to be an unaltered example of late-16C domestic architecture, but closer inspection, especially of the interior, reveals many later modifications. The Blounts were Catholic recusants and the estate fell on hard times in the 17C and early 18C. As at Stonor (qv.), another Catholic house not far away, much of the original detailing was lost in a drastic 18C face-lift, but at Mapledurham the exterior was 'restored' in the Elizabethan manner and new interiors created by Michael Henry Blount c 1828–31. The direct line of the Blounts died out in the early 20C, and in 1943 the house passed by descent to the present owner, who comes from one of Oxfordshire's oldest Catholic families.

There is a striking contrast between the picturesque remains of the rambling late-medieval house of the Lyndes, now containing the tea room, and the cliff-like walls of its austere Elizabethan replacement. The house stands among lawns stretching backward and forward to provide an H-plan; tall chimneys break the skyline and the overall plainness is alleviated by the attractive texture of the brickwork, with criss-cross patterns of blue on a red background. The chimneys were rearranged, the original gables removed from the roof-line and the long gallery destroyed in the 18C, and in the 1820s the brickwork of the east or entrance front was restored, the neo-Tudor porch added and mullioned and transomed windows re-introduced; the short ends of the hall block are much less altered, as is the west front (best seen from the churchyard through a handsome 18C gateway).

The 18C alterations included moving the Hall to the centre of the main block, with a new dining room and library on either side. The 'Old English' decoration of the Hall dates from 1863, but the attention is caught mainly by William Dobson's swashbuckling portrait of Sir Charles Blount, who died in the siege of Oxford in the Civil War, and by the carved animal heads and life-size wooden deer dating from the 17C and 18C. The plainly decorated Library contains books bequeathed by the poet Alexander Pope, who visited Mapledurham often in the early 18C in the vain hope of marrying one of the Blount daughters; there are also portraits by Romney and the 18C Italian artist Andrea Soldi. A Catholic chapel was built onto the west side of the Hall in 1797, and still retains its engagingly frivolous Gothic decoration in plaster. From it a passage leads to the Staircase Hall, with the wooden staircase dating from the mid 17C, and the walls hung with early family portraits, including representations of Sir Michael Blount—the builder of the house—by (or attributed to) George Gower, and his son Robert by Peake. On the ceiling there are plaster medallions of assorted worthies (from Venus to Julius Caesar) dated 1612.

The main first-floor rooms were drastically altered in the late 18C, but the Saloon—the original great chamber—still retains its early-17C plaster ceiling with roundels of figures from Roman history; there is some attractive 18C furniture, and the portraits include one by Charles Jervas of Pope's friends Martha and Teresa Blount (1716). Pope's own portrait, by Kneller, hangs in the adjacent Boudoir, along with a mirror and a landscape by John Wootton once belonging to him; there are also some pieces of 18C French furniture. After passing through the State Bedroom, visitors descend a staircase with a posthumous portrait by Paul van Somer of Sir Michael Blount's cousin Lord Mountjoy and reach the Dining Room, on the south side of the Hall, decorated in a restrained neo-classical style by the little-known Thomas Martin in 1828, and containing its original furniture. This room contains the finest picture in the house: a full-length portrait attributed to William Larkin of Lady St John (c 1615) dressed in black with a skull to her right and standing, unusually for a picture of this type and date, in a recognisably English landscape.

GCT

Milton Manor

3m south of Abingdon off A34 Oxford–Newbury at junction with A4130: Anthony Mockler-Barrett, tel. 0235 831287 or 831871. Open Easter, Spring and Aug BH weekends also June–Aug Tues–Fri 2–5. Guided tours. Refreshments.

Milton Manor is a good example of the compact, classically-inspired red-brick houses which became popular in the Home Counties in the mid 17C. It was almost certainly built by Paul Calton, descendant of a London goldsmith who had bought the estate in the mid 16C, probably soon after his marriage in 1659. The architect is not known, but the tall box-like proportions and the rather 'incorrect' use of classical detailing point to the involvement of a London builder, conceivably John Jackson (d 1663), who moved to Oxford to superintend the construction of the Canterbury Quadrangle at St John's College in the 1630s. In 1764 the estate was sold to Bryant Barrett, lace maker to King George III, and in the following year he employed Stephen Wright, master-mason in the Office of Works, to add wings which contained a new Roman Catholic chapel and library, and new service accommodation in lower outbuildings to the north. Since Catholicism was still officially proscribed the wings were deliberately given plain exteriors. Internally, however, the chapel and library were fitted up in the attractive Gothick manner later employed by some of the older Catholic families of the area (eg, the Stonors of Stonor and the Blounts of Mapledurham, qv.), presumably to stress the antiquity of the Faith. The landscape setting dates from the same time, and since then there have been few major alterations to either house or grounds. The house has passed by descent to the present owner, although some of the furniture and pictures have been sold.

The house stands on the edge of the village, with the A34 an unwelcome neighbour to the west. The original 17C house, seen first from across a lake, is only five bays wide, with three storeys over a basement and a hipped roof; the main decorative features are the elongated Ionic pilasters on the main façades and the white-painted eaves cornice. There are four rooms on each floor, with the Hall and Drawing Room on the ground floor of the east (entrance) front, the former reached through a screen opening off from a passage bisecting the house, and the Dining Room on the garden side, next to a staircase stretching the full height of the house. Many of the rooms were altered by Bryant Barratt in the 18C, but there is a good if somewhat crudely carved wooden chimneypiece in the Hall. Contemporary with the original house it is surmounted by an overmantel with a pair of scantily clad women holding cornucopias enclosing a late-17C Dutch painting of game birds. The Drawing Room has a more sophisticated 18C chimneypiece apparently brought from Gunnersbury Park, Greater London, but the plaster ceiling of oak and laurel wreaths, modelled on the type introduced by Inigo Jones in the Banqueting House of Whitehall Palace, is contemporary with the original house. Behind the Hall is the Dining Room, dating from the 1760s, with a pretty overmantel enclosing a late 17C Dutch marine picture.

The Library in the south wing is more spacious than the other rooms, befitting the larger scale of late-18C country-house entertaining. It has a delicate plaster frieze and cornice, and the Gothick windows and bookcases, carved by Richard Lawrence of London, are surmounted by ogee arches. The bookcases now contain items from the family's collection of late-18C and 19C English porcelain including a tea service with views of the newly-enlarged house made by the Pinxton factory c 1796. Other objects on display include a Viking sword and Admiral Benbow's telescope, and over the fireplace there is a conversation piece by Joseph Highmore showing Bryant Barrett with his wife and brother-in-law. The wooden staircase, of the 1680s, leads via an east-facing bedroom with hand-painted Chinese wallpaper and a good chimneypiece to the pretty Gothick Chapel, dedicated in 1773; this contains medieval English and 17C Flemish stained glass in the windows, a painting of the Assumption after or by Murillo, and some Mass vestments of 1760.

GCT

Rousham House

12m north of Oxford on A423 Oxford–Banbury: C. Cottrell-Dormer, Esq, tel. 0869 47110 or 0860 360407. Open Apr–Sept Wed, Sun, BH 2–4.30 (gardens open daily all year 10–4.30). Guided tours.

Rousham is best known for its gardens. They were laid out in the 1730s by William Kent for General James Dormer, a friend of Alexander Pope and Jonathan Swift, and a descendant of the Sir John Dormer who purchased the manor and built the house of grey limestone c 1635. It was a conventional enough H-planned building, but Kent remodelled it both internally and externally in 1738–40, adding single-storeyed projections on either side of the main block and replacing the gabled roof-line with the present crenellation. When General Dormer died in 1742 the estate was left to his cousin Sir Clement Cottrell, who married an heiress and carried out internal alterations. In 1876 Clement Cottrell-Dormer called in the architect William St Aubyn to enlarge the house, sweeping away Kent's garden front in the process and replacing his delicate glazing bars on the entrance front with the present unsympathetic plate-glass windows. Otherwise, though, both house and grounds remain much as Kent left them.

Visitors approach through the noble classical stable block, probably by Kent, and enter through the Hall, placed centrally in the new fashion of the mid 17C and lined with pictures hung on the plain early-18C panelling. They include portraits of Sir Robert Dormer—the builder of the house—and his wife, by Cornelius Johnson, and works by Lely, Kneller and Michael Wright; sketches by Kent of his improvements in the gardens are also on show. There are more good portraits on the walls of the plain mid-17C staircase, which leads up to a bedroom retaining its original 17C panelling, and then to the Drawing Room, originally the great chamber; this is comfortably furnished in the fashion of the early 19C, and contains miniatures by Samuel Cooper and portraits by William Dobson, painted during the siege of Oxford in 1645, of the Royalist Sir Charles Dormer (later to be Charles II's Master of Ceremonies) and Lady Dormer.

The Parlour, on the east side of the Hall downstairs, is one of the finest and best-preserved of all Kent's interiors. His intention was to impart Roman grandeur to what had formerly been a small and relatively insignificant room, and the result is almost overpoweringly rich and heavy. There is an abundance of carved woodwork (the green paint is not original) with three false doors and, above the marble chimneypiece, an overmantel by John Marden under an open swan-necked pediment; this is flanked by brackets supporting Italian bronzes. The pictures, most of them copies of works by Italian masters, were chosen by Kent, who also designed the tables against the walls and painted the ceiling with 'grotesques' in imitation of the ancient Roman decorative painting which he had seen in Italy. The Dining Room, part of the 19C additions, contains more family portraits and a painting by William Dobson of 'The Four Kings of France'; from here there are views across the valley of the River Cherwell to the 'eyecatcher' designed by Kent to terminate the vista from the house. A corridor, containing a late-17C view of Greenwich by Henry Danckerts, leads finally to the Great Parlour in the westernmost of the pavilions added by Kent to the original house. This was designed as a library to house the books collected by General Dormer (whose portrait, by Van Loo, hangs over the fireplace), and Kent's chimneypiece survives, as does his eccentrically ribbed, quasi-Gothic ceiling. But Dormer's successor did not share his literary interests, and in 1764 the room was remodelled as a 'great room' for entertaining guests, with new doorcases and exuberantly moulded Rococo picture frames by the plasterer Thomas Roberts of Oxford.

On the outside, visible en route to the gardens, are Kent's whimsical Gothick niches enclosing lead copies (by Henry Cheere) of classical statuary, and at the end of the lawn there is a sculpted group by Scheemakers. The main interest of the gardens themselves lies in the miniature classical Arcadia contrived by Kent on the slopes of the Cherwell, with winding paths and glades. A monumental arcade known as Praeneste—the Latin name of Palestrina in Italy—appears as a carefully managed surprise near the beginning of the route and again half-way round the circuit, which also encompasses Venus's Vale; a glade with cascades and statuary by van Nost. Together with the house, the garden well merits the verdict of the often critical Horace Walpole that Rousham is 'the most engaging of Kent's works. It is Kentissimo'.

GCT

Stanton Harcourt Manor

9m west of Oxford on B4449 Eynsham–Standlake: Crispin & the Hon. Mrs Gascoigne. Open selected but irregular dates Apr–Sept (see relevant publications for details) 2–6. Refreshments.

Ever since the 12C the Harcourts have been one of the most important families in Oxfordshire. The Stanton estate, situated among the water meadows of the upper Thames, came to them by marriage in 1191, and the oldest part of the present house probably dates from the time of Sir Thomas Harcourt (d 1417), who was custodian of Oxford Castle. His grandson Robert carried out major alterations in the 1460s, including the building of the chapel tower and possibly also the spectacular wooden roof of the kitchen; they now constitute the main architectural interest of the house. Sir Simon Harcourt added a gatehouse c 1540, but after the death of Sir Philip in 1688 the family abandoned Stanton as their main residence, settling first at Cokethorpe, not far away, and eventually at Nuneham Courtenay, a few miles south of Oxford. Here, starting in 1757, Simon, 1st Earl Harcourt, a politician, courtier and governor to George III as Prince of Wales, built a substantial neo-Palladian villa in a carefully contrived landscape setting overlooking the Thames. The house at Stanton had already fallen into disrepair by 1718, when the poet Alexander Pope stayed here for a short time, describing it as 'the true picture of a genuine Ancient Country Seat' and 'an excellent place for retirement and study', and by 1760 the hall and most of the main rooms had been pulled down. But the Tudor gatehouse survived and was incorporated into a house built by Col Edward Harcourt c 1866. It was to this relatively modest building that the family retreated, with much of their art collection, after Nuneham Courtenay was conveyed to the University of Oxford in 1948. A drawing room was added by the 2nd and last Viscount Harcourt in 1953, and when he died in 1979 the house passed to his daughter and her husband, who live here now.

The surviving fragments of the medieval house form part of an interesting complex of buildings on the edge of the stone-built village, next to the parish church, one of the finest in Oxfordshire, in which generations of Harcourts are commemorated by a series of impressive monuments. The house itself was built around an irregular courtyard with the hall on the north side, but all that now survives is the domestic chapel and its tower, which stood to the east of the hall, and the kitchen, with various ancillary buildings attached. The chapel is a modest enough building inside, but the crenellated tower over the chancel is an unusual and impressive feature, possibly built by the Oxford mason William Orchard. It was in the top room that Pope finished his translation of the *Iliad* in 1718. The vast, shadowy kitchen is an even more striking piece of late-medieval architecture, square in plan but with an octagonal wooden roof rising to a point high above the ground; there were originally no chimneys, and the smoke escaped through shutters where the windows now are.

The present house stands to the north of these buildings. Traces of the 16C gatehouse can be discerned in the Hall, but the chief interest lies in the rich and varied collection of pictures and objects brought from Nuneham Courtenay, many of them acquired by the art-loving 1st and 2nd Earls Harcourt. They include a portrait by Gentile Bellini, landscapes by Salomon and Jacob van Ruisdael, a large seascape of 1661 by Willem and Adrien van de Velde, Chardin's 'Maker of Card Houses' (1735) and several landscapes by Paul Sandby, an artist much patronised by George III. There are also excellent family portraits, including some by Gheeraerts and Mytens, and three of the 1st Earl, his countess and his brother by Reynolds, originally placed in the Eating Room at Nuneham and now in the Dining Room here; Reynolds's own pencil self- portrait is in the Library, as is a portrait of Pope by Kneller. Some of the family's collection of porcelain is also displayed, as are items of 18C furniture, a fireplace from Nuneham (in the Drawing Room), and presents given to the 1st Earl by George III. To the south and east of the original house an attractive garden was created by the last Viscount and Viscountess Harcourt, incorporating a series of medieval fish-ponds, and punctuated by urns and other garden ornaments from Nuneham, including one commemorating the poet Whitehead 'who made discretion punctuate his lyre'.

GCT

Stonor Park

5m north of Henley on B480 Henley–Watlington: Lord Camoys, tel. 0491
638587. Open Sun in Apr, also Wed in May–Sept, Thur in July–Aug and
Sat in Aug and all BH Mon 2–5.30. Refreshments.

The unusually elongated 18C red-brick façade of this beautifully situated
house conceals an ancient building which has been remodelled many times
over the last eight centuries. The Stonor family were already living in their
secluded Chiltern valley in the 12C, and in the late 13C, or possibly even
earlier, an aisled hall was built of stone, with an attached chamber block
and a detached flint chapel; this latter survives in much-rebuilt form, with
its brick tower of 1416–17, at the east (right) extremity of the house.

In the mid 14C the house was more than doubled in size when Sir John
Stonor built a new hall, chambers and service rooms to the west of the older
building, which may then have been turned into a residence for chantry
priests. His descendant, Sir Walter Stonor, a soldier and courtier, enlarged
the house to roughly the present dimensions in the 1530s, and a painting,
of c 1690 on view inside, shows it with a regular gabled roof-line, possibly
dating from the second half of the 16C. The family's adherence to the
Catholic faith meant that many of their estates had to be sold off to pay
recusancy fines, and very little work was done to the fabric of the house
until 1753–60, when Thomas Stonor inserted the present eaves cornice and
sash windows and replaced the gables by a hipped roof. He also employed
an otherwise unknown architect, John Aitkins, to remodel the hall, and
there were further internal alterations in 1834 (by another obscure architect, George Masters), for his great-grandson, who successfully claimed the
ancient title of Lord Camoys. Many of the original contents were sold after
the death of the 6th Lord Camoys in 1976, but the house has since been
successfully refurnished with the help of gifts and loans, including pictures
formerly at Bisham Abbey, Berkshire (now the National Sports Centre).

The house looks out over open lawns—the 16C walled forecourt was
swept away when the grounds were landscaped in the later 18C—and is
entered through a porch flanked by mid-16C stone figures in classical
draperies. It leads, via the screens passage, into the passage-like Hall, all
that remains of the 14C hall after it had been given a Gothick face-lift in
1757 and then reduced in size by the building of the Drawing Room within
the old walls in 1834; when this happened the garishly coloured ogee-
arched fireplace was resited. The striking Jacobean portrait in a mid-18C
Gothick frame is of Lady Abergavenny and her stepdaughter, and on either
side of it are early-17C bronzes of Jupiter and Juno by Alessandro Algardi
which form part of a collection amassed by Francis Stonor (d 1968). The
Drawing Room, by contrast, was designed in the Grecian manner, with an
Ionic colonnade at the west end to give it dignity; there are more bronzes
of different dates, portraits by Kneller and others, and some furniture by
Gillow which has always been in the house. The next two rooms, at the
parlour end of the medieval house, were also redecorated in 1834. The walls
of the Dining Room are hung with an unusual wallpaper of 1816 showing
the buildings of Paris, and the Study contains two paintings of boys and
womens' heads by Antonio Carracci and drawings by Tintoretto and
Tiepolo; there are also two Venetian globes of 1699 with richly carved
stands.

A back staircase leads up to a bedroom containing more of Francis

Stonor's collection, of which the most spectacular item is a sybaritic shell-shaped bed made in France in the early 19C. Next comes the Library, occupying the site of the medieval great chamber and now housing an excellent collection of recusant books, along with a painting by Agostino Carracci of his two painter brothers and a pair of mid-18C German wooden statues of gesticulating saints. There are Stonor family portraits, some of them by Michael Wright, and a late-17C bed with embroidered hangings in Lady Camoys' Bedroom, created when the hall was divided up in 1834. In a room at the top of the house over the porch there is an exhibition of the life of the Catholic martyr Edmund Campion, who set up a printing press here not long before his execution in 1581 (he was subsequently canonised). The last room to be seen is the Gallery, built behind the hall in the late 16C on the level of the ground which slopes up steeply behind the house, and now hung with 16C and 17C tapestries. On the walls of the main staircase, of 1790, there is another, Flemish, tapestry of Tobias and the angel, bought for Bisham Abbey in 1538, and there is also a good painting of Sir Edward Hoby of Bisham (1573).

Having passed through the hall of the 13C house, the pointed arcade of which has been uncovered, visitors emerge close to the Chapel, which was Gothicised internally by James Thorp in 1796–97 (the startling colours are supposedly original), with an east window of painted glass by Francis Egington after Carlo Dolci. Here, where Mass has been celebrated according to the Roman rite since at least 1349, the enduring Catholicism of the Stonor family is particularly vividly felt. At the rear of the house is a walled garden which preserves some of the original 16C layout and contains some ornate 18C Italian features.

GCT

SHROPSHIRE

Acton Round Hall

6m north west of Bridgnorth, to the west of A458 Bridgnorth–Shrewsbury: H.L. Kennedy. Open May–Aug Thur 2.30–5.30.

From the outside, this early-18C gentleman's house seems conventional enough, though hard to find among the winding lanes of rural Shropshire. But inside it contains an extraordinary collection of objects accumulated by the present owner, who farms the surrounding land. The house was built, perhaps as a dower house, on land belonging to the Actons of Aldenham Park nearby (not open to the public), either by Richard Acton (d 1703) or his son Sir Whitmore Acton (d 1731), both of whom are buried in the nearby church. The architect is unknown, but there are resemblances to houses designed by Francis Smith of Warwick, and the house is certainly an accomplished, well-proportioned building, with a hipped roof, tall chimneys and grey stone dressings against the red brick of the walls.

The Actons seem to have tired of the house soon after it was built, and for most of the 18C and all of the 19C it was little used. The interior is conventionally laid out, with the Hall (now no longer the entrance) and saloon (now the Drawing Room) in the centre, parlours on either side, and bedrooms on the first floor reached by an impressive wooden staircase of the kind often found in Smith houses, with twisted balusters. Some of the rooms retain their original plain bolection-moulded panelling, but far more memorable are the objects introduced by the present owner: big game trophies from Africa, Chinese porcelain figures, ceremonial halberds from the Habsburg Empire, a splendid Rococo mirror, Gothick bookcases in the Library and a late-17C state bed. These combine to create an interior which is full of interest and free from the deadening hand of 'good taste'.

GCT

Adcote

7m north west of Shrewsbury at Little Ness to east of A5 Shrewsbury–Llangollen: Adcote School Educational Trust, tel. 0939 260202. Open mid Apr–mid July; mid Sept–mid Oct daily 2–5.

Adcote is one of the finest houses built by Norman Shaw, perhaps the most creative and certainly most successful of all late-19C English domestic architects. It was built in 1876–81 for Mrs Rebecca Darby, the widow of one of the descendants of Abraham Darby, who had pioneered modern iron manufacture at Coalbrookdale, to the east of Shrewsbury. Rebecca Darby's husband, a great-nephew of the builder of the celebrated iron bridge at Coalbrookdale, had relinquished his direct association with the family business, and the building of Adcote reinforced the family's move into the ranks of the landed gentry. The style of the house deliberately emphasises continuity with the past and with the building traditions of the area. It is built of local sandstone, beautifully cut and laid, and from the outside there is a reassuring array of pointed gables, tall chimneys and mullioned and transomed windows, all borrowed from the architecture of the late 16C and early 17C and piquantly reassembled with carefully contrived irregularities which the Elizabethans would never have tolerated.

The house stands in flat parkland and is surrounded by well-maintained gardens. Inside, Shaw showed his customary skill in planning, and in creating memorable architectural spaces. The plan is not at all like that of a typical Elizabethan or Jacobean house, but follows instead the common Victorian arrangement of a thick main block containing the reception rooms, family rooms and bedrooms, with a substantial service wing to the side. The deliberately understated Entrance Hall leads via a short flight of steps to a screens passage at the end of the Great Hall, one of Shaw's finest rooms, with massive stone arches spanning the open timber roof, a hooded medieval-style stone fireplace and a huge mullioned and transomed window; this was designed as a 'living hall' for entertaining large numbers of house-party guests, and now very effectively serves the different purposes of the school which occupies the building. The other dramatic interior is the Staircase Hall which opens off from the screens passage, from the top of which it is possible to look down into the Hall. The remaining rooms are now bereft of the Darbys' furniture and porcelain (some of which can now be seen at Dudmaston, qv.), and inevitably seem a little empty. But there is still much to see in the way of good woodwork and plasterwork, stone fireplaces (eg, in the former Dining Room), inglenooks, stained glass by the William Morris firm, and tiles by William de Morgan, of which there is a particularly good collection in the library (the former Drawing Room).

GCT

Attingham Park

4m south east of Shrewsbury on A5 Shrewsbury–Telford: National Trust, tel. 074377 203. Open Apr–Sept Sat–Wed and Sat, Sun in Oct 1.30–5 (grounds open daily all year). Refreshments.

This austere-looking neo-classical house was built in 1783–85 to the designs of a little-known Scottish architect, George Steuart, who was also responsible for the impressive circular church of St Chad, Shrewsbury. The client was Noel Hill, a member of an old Shropshire family, who went into politics and was raised to the peerage as Lord Berwick in return for political services to the younger Pitt, and the scale and grandeur of the house reflects the family's new sense of dignity. It stands in an attractive landscaped park in flat country, with the Wrekin in the distance and a bridge carrying Watling Street (the A5) over the River Tern in the middle distance; the park was later improved by Humphry Repton. The house is three storeys high over a basement and is built of smooth ashlar; the proportions are most peculiar, with floors of diminishing height and a tall portico of attenuated Ionic columns. Behind lies a service courtyard, on either side of which are two pavilions joined to the main house by colonnades.

The 2nd Lord Berwick, a Grand Tourist, collector and bon viveur, employed John Nash to alter the interior in 1805 by creating a picture gallery on the site of Steuart's staircase. But he had to sell the bulk of his collection, including over 300 pictures and much of the furniture, in 1827, and he retired to Italy, leaving the estate to his brother, 'a middle-aged sybarite' and former ambassador to Naples, whose furnishings and collections can still be seen in the house today. His successors lived not at Attingham but at Cronkhill, an Italianate villa on the estate designed by Nash (and open to the public on application), and as a result the house was little changed when it was reoccupied by the 8th Lord Berwick and his wife after the First World War. They gave it to the National Trust in 1947.

The plan of Attingham is as unusual as the architecture, with two suites of reception rooms stretching back from the Dining Room and Drawing Room at the front of the house, one of them designated for Lord Berwick and his guests and the other for Lady Berwick and her guests—an arrangement which derives, like some aspects of the architecture and interior decoration, from France. The entrance is through the Hall, lined with elongated Ionic columns and pilasters in scagliola. From here the tour proceeds in an anti-clockwise direction, encompassing all the rooms on the main floor. The Drawing Room has a plaster ceiling reminiscent, like some of the other interior decoration, of the work of Henry Holland, and over the fireplace there is a portrait by Angelica Kauffmann of the 2nd Lord Berwick in Van Dyck costume, painted while he was in Italy in 1793; the early-19C Empire- style furniture was introduced by the 3rd Lord Berwick, who also bought the Neapolitan landscapes by the German artist Jacob Philipp Hackert. The other 'female' rooms are the Sultana Room, named after the early-19C Turkish-style sofa in an arched recess, an Ante-Room containing a portrait by Sickert of the wife of the 8th Lord Berwick (1933), and a circular Boudoir, perhaps the most attractive room in the house, with a domed roof supported on Corinthian columns and arabesque paintings on the walls attributed to the French artist Louis-André Delabrière.

The Picture Gallery of 1805–7 is lit from above by a glazed iron roof (Coalbrookdale is only a few miles away) and is screened at the ends by Corinthian columns in scagliola, anticipating Nash's later interiors at Buckingham Palace. The pictures, most of them by minor 17C and 18C masters, give a good indication of conventional early-19C taste, with the two large views by Hackert of Pompeii and the Lake of Avernus (1799–1800) making the strongest impression. There is an organ of 1788, and from a door in the north wall it is possible to see Nash's theatrical though strangely tawdry-looking staircase curving up to the bedroom floor.

The 'male' side of the house includes an octagonal Study, an Ante-Room hung with water-colours by Nash showing picturesque improvements to the village of Atcham, just outside the park gate, and the Inner Library. The last room to be seen in the main house is the Dining Room, painted in the early 19C in a startling Pompeian red and upholstered by the Gillow firm, who probably also made the chairs; the most important of the pictures is Salvator Rosa's 'Christ Expelling the Money Changers from the Temple'. Downstairs, in the vaulted basement, there is an excellent collection of silver amassed by the 3rd Lord Berwick, including his set of silver-gilt ambassadorial plate made by Paul Storr and others in 1805–18, and outside, in the west pavilion, is the splendid Outer Library or Museum Room, which still retains its original late-18C appearance; it originally contained sculpture, vases and other Grand Tour memorabilia, and has recently been refurnished with books and sculpture lent by the Walker Art Gallery in Liverpool, including a version of Canova's self-portrait.

GCT

Benthall Hall

1m north west of Broseley on B4375: National Trust,
tel. 0952 882159. Open Apr–Sept Wed, Sun, BH Mon 1.30–5.30.

This attractive manor house of weathered, local grey-brown sandstone
occupies an isolated position next to a rustic church of 1667, not far from
the Severn gorge at Ironbridge, celebrated in England's industrial history.
It was built, probably towards the end of the 16C (the date 1583 is
mentioned, though there seems to be no firm evidence), by a member of
the Benthall family, which had lived here since the 11C. Internal, and
possibly external, alterations were carried out by Lawrence Benthall, who
inherited in 1623 and left his initials on the porch, but the direct male line
died out in the early 18C and the house passed through several hands
before being sold in 1844 and subsequently leased to tenants. In 1934 it
was purchased by a descendant of the Benthalls and refurnished with their
possessions. The family still lives here today as tenants of the National
Trust.

The approach leads past the church (which contains an extraordinary
painting of the Coronation of the Virgin by Edward Burra) and through an
attractive 'Old English' garden laid out in the late 19C by George Maw, a
local tile manufacturer, and improved by the Birmingham architect Robert
Bateman, who succeeded him as tenant. The house is three- storeyed, with
mullioned and transomed windows, a gabled roof-line and massive brick
chimneystacks. A note of pleasing irregularity is imparted by the two
canted bay windows projecting from the main façade, one of them lighting
the 'upper' end of the Hall and the Great Chamber above it; the rectangular
porch shows signs of being an afterthought (the arcane symbols over the
door may relate to the fact that the family were Catholic recusants in
Elizabethan times). The comfortable-looking interiors contain some good
craftsmanship in wood and plaster, most of it dating probably from the
1620s, but the furnishings and pictures, of various date, have all been
introduced in the 20C. There are elaborate chimneypieces in the Dining
Room and Drawing Room, on either side of the Hall, and the Drawing Room
also has an intricately moulded plaster frieze and ceiling full of strapwork,
arabesques and weird animals; the fireplace surrounds are characteristic
Gothick confections by the Shrewsbury architect Thomas Pritchard (cf.
Croft Castle, Herefordshire). The heavy wooden staircase bears a strong
resemblance to that in Aston Hall, West Midlands (qv.), and must also date
from the 1620s or thereabouts. It leads to the Great Chamber, placed as in
many late-16C houses directly over the Hall, but less richly decorated than
the Drawing Room; it contains a neo-romantic *capriccio* by Felix Kelly
showing the house and the Ironbridge gorge.

GCT

Boscobel House

8m north west of Wolverhampton: English Heritage, tel. 0902 850244.
Open Apr–Sept daily 10–6; Oct–Mar Tues–Sun 10–4 (except
Christmas/New Year hols). Refrshments.

The main interest of this modest timber-framed house lies in the fact that for two nights in September 1651 it sheltered the future Charles II, in flight from the disastrous Battle of Worcester. The oldest part of the building is the two-storeyed north range, probably dating from the 16C. A taller wing was added to the south in about 1630, when the house was used as a woodland lodge—the *bosco bello* of the name Boscobel—by Edward Giffard of White Ladies, a house (now demolished) on a monastic site half a mile away which belonged to a branch of the Giffards of Chillington, Staffordshire (qv.), a leading local Catholic family. By 1651 Boscobel had passed by marriage from the Giffards to the Fitzherbert family, who lived in Derbyshire and leased the house to William Penderel and his wife; they helped protect the future King from capture, and guided him to his next destination, Moseley Old Hall, Staffordshire (qv.). After this moment of glory, Boscobel settled down to a mundane existence as a farmhouse before being bought in 1812 by Walter Evans, who came from Derbyshire. Fired by a sense of romance, he attempted to re-create the house, which had long attracted historically-minded tourists, as a shrine to Charles II, filling it with dark oak panelling and 'period' furniture, and making a formal garden. His descendants sold it in 1918 to Lord Bradford of Weston Park, Staffordshire (qv.), and in 1954 it was taken over by the Ministry of Works. By this time the house had been denuded of its 19C furnishings, but it has recently been carefully restored to something closely approaching its 19C state.

The house is approached through the former farmyard, and is entered through a 19C brick-built farmhouse, deceptively painted outside to resemble black and white timber framing. The house itself, which is genuinely built of timber, was stuccoed over in the 18C, and, as at Moseley, the framing is now no longer visible. The 16C north wing contains a display of dairying equipment, and gives access to the extension of c 1630, in which Charles II stayed. This originally consisted of just one room on each floor, with a polygonal projection to the south, probably for the staircase; the rooms are heated by hearths which are grouped together in a tall brick chimneystack, externally the most prominent feature. The dark, panelled interiors offer an interesting insight into the way in which the past was perceived by the romantic sensibility of the 19C, and there are the inevitable hiding-places which may or may not have been occupied by the King.

The formal garden outside, with its raised viewing-mound, has also been expertly restored by English Heritage. A short distance away to the south is an oak tree which may be the one in which Charles hid before taking refuge in the house, and which has given its name to countless pubs.

GCT

Dudmaston

4m south east of Bridgnorth on A442 Bridgnorth–Kidderminster: National Trust, tel. 0746 780866. Open Apr–Sept Wed, Sun 2.30–6. Refreshments.

This plain red-brick house was built c 1695–1701, probably to the designs of Francis Smith of Warwick, for Sir Thomas Wolryche, a member of a long-established local family. The male line of the Wolryches died out in 1723 and the estate was inherited in 1775 by a cousin, William Whitmore, who formed an attractive landscape garden with a picturesquely wooded 'Dingle' influenced by the poet William Shenstone's now- obscured garden at the Leasowes at Halesowen, not far away. His son William Wolryche Whitmore employed a local builder, John Smalman, to carry out alterations in the 1820s, and in 1833 he added a new bay-windowed dining room on the garden front; these changes did not improve the external appearance of the house, but the creation of a lake in the 1850s enhanced the view from the gardens to the Clee Hills in the distance. The interior was much altered after 1952, when the house was inherited by Rachel, Lady Labouchere, wife of a diplomat and descendant of the Darbys of Coalbrookdale, pioneers of the early Industrial Revolution. Lady Labouchere and her husband have implanted their taste firmly on the house, filling it with their varied collections, including an unusually large number of post-Second World War paintings and sculptures. These were transferred, with the house itself, to the National Trust in 1978, but the family still lives here as tenants.

The house is approached past an earlier service wing, and the entrance front, with its typically late-17C proportions, has changed little since it was first built, apart from the remodelling of the roof and the addition of low pediments over the slightly projecting wings in the 1820s. A doorway with moulded architraves and a segmental pediment of the local red sandstone leads into the Entrance Hall, the finest room in the house, with its original stone floor and dark wood panelling on which are displayed portraits of the family and, more unusually, their servants, including the gamekeeper and the fool or jester (1719) holding a large glass; another picture shows the Wolrych Hunt, spending on which is said to have accelerated a disastrous decline in the family's fortunes in the 18C—hence the lack of original furniture (the late-17C high-backed chairs and settees were bought by Sir George Labouchere from Burley-on-the-Hill, Rutland). The Oak Room, beyond the early-19C Staircase Hall, also has its original panelling, but the Library, the other room shown to visitors in the Smith part of the house, was created out of two smaller rooms in the early 19C; it contains 18C chairs, Chinese porcelain, and 18C Dutch flower pictures inherited by Lady Labouchere from her Darby forebears and formerly housed at Adcote, near Shrewsbury (qv.). The rest of the house, including the Dining Room and much of the service wing, is now arranged museum-fashion to display other items from the collection. The ex-dining room is a gallery of 20C painting and sculpture, with works by Jean Dubuffet, Ben Nicholson, Henry Moore, Barbara Hepworth and other representatives of the avant-garde taste of the 1950s and 1960s; there are also two cabinets with Chinese porcelain of the Ming and Sung periods. Other galleries contain works by 20C Spanish artists of an abstract expressionist tendency and, perhaps more attractive to most visitors, British topographical water-colours (but none by the major masters), botanical pictures, and Darby memorabilia.

GCT

Shipton Hall

6m south west of Much Wenlock on B4368: J.N.R.N. Bishop, tel. 074636 225. Open Easter–Sept Thur, BH Sun, Mon 2.30–5.30. Guided tours.

Shipton Hall is a late-16C manor house of rough grey limestone lying in remote pastoral country in Corve Dale, to the south of Wenlock Edge. The estate belonged to Much Wenlock Priory in the Middle Ages and the house is traditionally said to have been built c 1587 by Richard Lutwyche, whose son certainly remodelled the adjoining church. The entrance front is an unusually satisfying piece of Elizabethan architecture in its more restrained mood. There are two storeys, with mullioned and transomed windows, gables over the centre and wings, and tall brick chimneystacks at each end, like those at the nearby Benthall Hall (qv.), but the symmetry is broken by a stark tower placed off-centre, which contains the porch and rises to what was presumably once a 'prospect room' at the top. The effect is enhanced by the formal walled garden in front of the house and by the group of estate buildings to the east, consisting of a circular dovecote and a massive pedimented stable block at the entrance to a farm courtyard. The stables were built in the mid 18C, possibly to the designs of Thomas Pritchard of Shrewsbury, who certainly remodelled the interior of the house for Henry or Thomas Mytton in 1762. The Myttons inherited Shipton in the early 17C and remained here until 1795, when the house passed by marriage to Thomas More, representative of another local family; his grandson sold it at the end of the 19C to the present owner's great-grandfather.

The predominant atmosphere inside the house is of the 18C. The tour starts in the light and cheerful Hall, with a plaster ceiling of 1762 displaying a sunburst motif, and an elaborate Rococo overmantel, also of plaster, incorporating a coat of arms; the Palladian-style doorcases have broken pediments housing busts of Homer and Shakespeare. To the right, at the former service end, is the Dining Room, with panelling brought in from a house in Bridgnorth, and to the left is the Drawing Room, little altered since the late 18C. Pritchard's alterations in 1762 included the addition of a new staircase to the north of the Hall, lit by a Gothic window, next to which is a two-storeyed extension (this can be clearly seen from the garden at the back of the house). The first floor of the extension houses the Library, an attractive room with a pretty Rococo overmantel flanked by Ionic pilasters incorporating devices representing music and letters and surmounted by a swan-necked pediment (the iron fire grate was made in Coalbrookdale nearby). Some of the bedrooms in the older part of the house have retained their original Elizabethan panelling.

GCT

Stokesay Castle

8m north west of Ludlow off A49 Ludlow–Shrewsbury, to the south of Craven Arms: English Heritage, tel. 0588 672544. Open Apr–Sept daily 10–6; Oct–Mar Wed–Sun (not Christmas) 10–4.

As the most complete surviving example of a 13C fortified manor-house in the southern part of England, Stokesay Castle has an important place in the early history of the country house. It occupies an attractive and strate-gically important site not far from the Welsh border, commanding the valley through which an important north–south road (and, since the 19C, the main Hereford–Shrewsbury railway) runs. The locally powerful Say family built a small castle here in the 12C, but most of the buildings to be seen now were erected by a prosperous wool merchant, Lawrence Ludlow, who bought the estate c 1280 and lived here until his death in 1296. His rise to riches and eminence is an example of the social mobility possible in late-medieval England, and his descendants lived as country gentry at Stokesay until the late 16C, the estate passing c 1500 through the female line to a younger branch of the Vernons of Haddon Hall, Derbyshire (qv.). The castle was sold in 1620 to Elizabeth Craven, the widow of a phenome-nally rich London merchant. During the Civil War it was garrisoned on behalf of the King on the orders of her son, the devotedly Royalist Lord Craven, but it fortunately escaped significant damage from its Parliamentarian captors, and in 1648 it was leased out to a local family, the Baldwins. On his return from exile after the Restoration, Lord Craven settled on his Berkshire estates, where he built Ashdown House (now in Oxon, qv.). Stokesay Castle became a farmhouse in the 18C, ensuring that it escaped 'improvement', but by 1814 it had been abandoned as a residence and was 'rapidly advancing to ruin'. The Earls of Craven (as they had then become) carried out repairs to the fabric in the mid 19C, but sold it in 1896 to J.D. Allcroft, whose descendants cared for the building until it was taken over by English Heritage.

As seen from a distance the castle presents an idyllic picture of old stone walls and towers blending in with the surrounding pastoral countryside. The approach leads past the parish church, remodelled in 1654–64 and little altered since, and through a late-16C or early-17C timber-framed gatehouse adorned with the vigorous decorative carving common on the Welsh borders. In the Middle Ages there was a stone gatehouse and a high curtain wall around the courtyard, giving the building a more castle-like appearance than it has today, but now the only obviously fortified part is the south tower (licence to crenellate was granted in 1291), with small arrow-slit windows lighting large rooms arranged on two floors over a basement; though bare and inhospitable now, these must have been important lodging chambers when first built (note the window seats and fireplaces) and the crenellation was no doubt intended as much to proclaim Lawrence Ludlow's status as to protect him from marauding Welshmen. To the right (north) is the main hall and chamber block, with three large curvilinear-traceried windows lighting the Hall, and an external staircase (originally roofed) leading up to the Solar or great chamber at the south end, which is placed over a storage basement. The Solar has late-16C or early-17C panelling and a carved wooden chimneypiece of the same date; note the peepholes in the north wall enabling the lord to look down into the Hall. The Hall itself, entered from the north, may originally have been aisled, but there is now an arch-braced roof of the usual late-medieval type covering the whole wide expanse of the room; the original stone hearth survives in the centre of the floor, and from the lower end a staircase leads up into the lodgings in the north tower (there is no screen and there may never have been one). The north tower was begun c 1240, before Lawrence Ludlow's time, and the top floor has a timber-framed projection corbelled out from the stone walls below; a medieval fireplace survives here, without its original hood. The kitchens stood in a separate block to the east, but this has long disappeared.

GCT

Upton Cressett Hall

4m west of Bridgnorth, to the west of A458 Bridgnorth–Shrewsbury: William Cash, tel. 074631 307. Open May–Sept Thur 2–6. Guided tours.

This largely 16C but fragmentary house is romantically situated in a moat (now dry) at the end of a long narrow lane in deep countryside, with only the redundant medieval parish church as a neighbour. It started life as a late-medieval timber-framed hall house probably built by Thomas Cressett, who married the heiress of the Upton family. This was rebuilt in red diapered brick by Richard Cressett in the second half of the 16C (there is a date 1580 on an outside wall), and at about the same time the hall was floored over and an impressive brick gatehouse constructed at the entrance to the courtyard. This is still medieval in feeling, with large mullioned and transomed windows lighting what was clearly an important room over the gate, reached by spiral staircases with conical tops, and with a plaster ceiling, like one at Wilderhope Manor (qv.), incorporating heart-shaped motifs with the name 'JESU'. The house later fell upon hard times and was greatly reduced in size, but was rescued from almost total dereliction by the present owner. It now consists of part of the medieval hall range encased in a farmhouse-like exterior and part of the parlour wing with its late-16C brick exterior and an impressive chimneystack. Inside, one of the roof trusses of the original hall, can be seen in an upstairs bedroom.

GCT

Walcot Hall

3m south east of Bishops Castle, off B4385 near Lydbury North: C.R.W. Parish. Open BH Sun, Mon; May Sun, Wed Fri; June Wed, Fri; July, Aug Sun; Sept Wed 2.15–4.30.

This handsome red-brick house occupies a splendid site in the remote, hilly country of the Welsh borders. The estate was acquired in the 12C by the Walcot family, but in 1763 it was sold by Charles Walcot to the Shropshire-born Lord Clive, Governor of Bengal (Clive of India). He was in the process of building up a substantial landed estate—and the resulting political influence—in his native county, and in 1764–69 he brought in William Chambers to remodel completely the house; it is his low, plain but well-proportioned elevations which we see today. The 2nd Lord Clive married the heiress of the last Earl of Powis, thus inheriting Powis Castle near Welshpool in Wales, and in 1804 the earldom of Powis was revived on his behalf. He made certain alterations to Walcot in the early 19C, including the addition of a ballroom wing, and he also improved the grounds. The house remained in the family's hands as a secondary residence until 1933, when the contents were removed to Powis Castle and the house and grounds sold to Ronald and Noel Stevens. They created a private zoo and bird sanctuary in the grounds (since dispersed) and employed the Wolverhampton architect A.T. Butler to demolish some of the early-19C additions to the house and to remodel the interiors in a restrained neo-Georgian manner; the house still remains much as they left it. It was sold to Michael Woodbine Parish in 1957, and is now partly used for holiday flats.

The house stands in a landscaped park complete with lakes (dug by French prisoners in the Napoleonic Wars) and a backdrop of woodland. Its layout and proportions were in large part determined by those of the previous house, with a long 11-bay entrance front facing east and a nine-bay wing stretching back from the south end; the recently-restored ballroom is further to the west, but the block connecting it to the main house was demolished in the 1930s, and it now stands detached. The entrance to the house is through a Tuscan colonnade and leads into a Hall, beyond which is the Staircase Hall, created in the 1930s with a wooden staircase in the early-18C manner. The main reception rooms were also altered in the 1930s, but some of Chambers's refined plaster ceilings and marble chimneypieces survive. There is a handsome stable courtyard some distance away from the house, and in the arboretum started by the 1st Lord Powis close to the ballroom is the first Douglas Fir to have been planted in Europe (in 1842).

GCT

Wilderhope Manor

7m east of Church Stretton, south of B4371 at Longville-in-the-Dale: National Trust, tel. 06943 363. Open all year Sat, and Wed in Apr–Sept 2–4.30.

This late-16C manor-house occupies an isolated position in the depths of rural Shropshire, overlooking Corve Dale. It was solidly built of the local limestone for Francis Smallman, a member of a family which had farmed in the area for 300 years; his initials, along with the dates 1583 and 1593, appear on the plaster ceilings inside. The façade has four large gables and the usual display of mullioned and transomed windows, with a projecting porch at the 'lower' end of the hall, a large bay window at the 'upper' end, and another projection for the parlour; there are tall brick chimneystacks at each end of the house, and another at the back, which is more irregular, with a semicircular projection housing the original spiral staircase leading up to the great chamber over the hall. The structure has been little altered and gives the impression of having grown out of the limestone hills; its good preservation derives in part from the fact that it became a farmhouse in the 18C and was rescued from dilapidation in the 20C by the National Trust, which leases it out as a youth hostel. The large, light rooms are now entirely adapted to this purpose and contain little of historical interest apart from some plaster ceilings, of which that in the former parlour is the most elaborate, with shallow ribs incorporating religious and other motifs.

GCT

SOMERSET

Barrington Court

5m north east of Ilminster off B3168 Ilminster–Langport: National Trust, tel. 0985 847777. Open Apr–Sept Wed 1.30–5.30 (gardens Sat–Wed 11–5.30). Refreshments.

From the outside, Barrington Court is one of the best surviving examples of a large mid-16C country house. It stands near the site of the medieval house of the Daubeney family, and the builder seems to have been a London merchant, William Clifton, who bought the estate in 1552 and died in 1564. His grandson sold the estate to Sir Thomas Phelips of Montacute (qv.), and in 1625 it was sold again to William Strode, a merchant from Shepton Mallet who had married an heiress; he carried out some internal alterations, and his son built a new stable block in 1674. The house was sold in 1755 and was later used as a farmhouse, falling into a state of dilapidation by the early 20C, by which time some of the floors had been removed and part of the house had become a cider cellar. In 1907 it was presented to the National Trust as their first country house, and in 1920 the Trust leased it to Col A.A. Lyle, of the Tate and Lyle sugar firm. He employed the architect J.E. Forbes in 1921–25 to restore it and reconstruct the interior, using 16C wood panelling brought from elsewhere. An elaborate new garden was also created after a design by Gertrude Jekyll, the stables were restored as an extension of the main house, and a model farm was constructed with attendant cottages, thus creating a complete manorial ensemble geared to the needs of the 1920s. The Lyle family has since moved away, and the house is now let to Stuart Interiors, a firm which specialises in making reproduction furniture.

The house lies at the east end of the attractive village, and the approach leads past a surprisingly spacious and formal arrangement of stone-built Arts and Crafts-influenced cottages and farm buildings, visually linked by long, straight avenues. The north front, which now contains the main entrance, is an irregular composition, with massive chimneys and mullioned windows disposed haphazardly across the flat wall surface. But the main façade is to the south, and is nearly symmetrical, with lower wings projecting from the hall block, a central porch, and projections at the angles for a staircase and bay window at the upper end of the Hall: an early appearance of the E-plan found in so many late-16C country houses. The visual effect is unusually satisfying, due in part to the materials—brown Ham Hill ashlar stone for the walls and stone tiles for the roofs—and in part to the accomplished detailing, still medieval in its fundamental character, but with twisted chimneystacks and finials above the gables to give an air of exotic richness to the roofline; these French-influenced features were first taken up by the Tudor court and enjoyed a special vogue in mid-16C Somerset and Dorset (cf. Sandford Orcas Manor, Dorset). To the west is the impressive red-brick stable block (now called the Strode House) of 1674, laid out around a courtyard and surmounted by a hipped roof and tall chimneys; it was much altered internally in the 1920s, and an excellent restaurant and tea room has recently been created in a room with Italian Renaissance-style chimneypieces. Beyond, to complete the idyll, lie the main formal gardens, divided into three walled 'outdoor rooms'.

Those who expect to find an authentic series of 16C rooms at Barrington to complement the exterior will be disappointed, for by the early 20C the house had been stripped of almost all its original panelling and furnishings. The interior can nevertheless be enjoyed as a set of 1920s Tudor-revival rooms, with much excellent craftsmanship in wood taken from houses in Hereford, King's Lynn and elsewhere, and reproduction furniture to add to the somewhat sanitised old-world atmosphere. The Hall, with linenfold panelling of the 1920s, is to the left of the north entrance, and beyond it is the Jacobean-style wooden Staircase with an elaborate ribbed wooden ceiling—an insertion of the 1920s but with some old timbers. There are two early-17C chimneypieces in the first-floor rooms of the east (parlour) wing, one of them of stone with the arms of the Strode family, and the other of plaster with a representation of the Judgment of Solomon.

GCT

Dunster Castle

In Dunster, 3m south east of Minehead off A39 Bridgwater–Minehead: National Trust, tel. 0643 821314. Open Apr–Oct Sat–Wed 11–5 (11–4 in Oct); gardens also open Feb, Mar, Nov, Dec 11–4.

The origins of this large and impressive house go back to soon after the Norman Conquest, when William de Mohun built a fortified dwelling on a naturally defensible hilltop site overlooking the coastal plain and designed to dominate the part of West Somerset lying between the Quantocks and Exmoor. Very little survives of the Mohuns' castle, and the oldest building of any size to be seen today is a tall gatehouse built in 1420–24 by Sir Hugh Luttrell, whose mother had bought the castle and estate some 50 years earlier. The Luttrells were already an important local family, with a house at East Quantoxhead (where their descendants still live), and the purchase of the castle further enhanced their prestige. When Leland visited Dunster in the early 16C the buildings at the top of the motte (actually a hill with the top shaved off to provide a platform) were in poor repair, but the residential quarters in the bailey or lower ward—the 'fairest part of the castle'—were 'well maintained', and they were rebuilt by George Luttrell at the end of the 16C (the date 1589 appears in the present hall). They were given a mock-castellated façade in a gesture of self-conscious medievalism c 1617, when William Arnold (cf. Montacute), the master-mason responsible for the design, was taken to court for making unauthorised changes to the plan. The castle was seized and slighted by the Royalists during the Civil War, but the residential part, which was used to shelter the well-known agitator William Prynne, survived, and was lavishly remodelled inside in the 1680s by George Luttrell's grandson Francis, who married the heiress of Milton Abbey, Dorset (qv.) but died in debt.

The direct male line of the Luttrells died out in 1737, and the castle then passed by marriage to Henry Fownes, a distant descendant of the Mohuns. He changed his name to Luttrell, planted the park, created the lawn in front of the house in 1764 and built the prominent folly tower on Conygar Hill to the north in 1775. The last major changes were made by his great-grandson, George Fownes Luttrell, who employed Anthony Salvin, the doyen of castle-restorers, to extend and rebuild the main house in 1868–72, demolishing an early-18C chapel designed by the painter Sir James Thornhill in the process (the altarpiece is now in the parish church, where several of the Luttrells are buried). The Luttrells continued living at Dunster until 1974, and the castle and surrounding land were given to the National Trust in 1976.

The castle rises above the pretty, and much visited, small town of Dunster, with its famous octagonal yarn market built by George Luttrell c 1589. The first building to be seen after the attractive early-17C stable block is the oldest: the tall early-15C **Gatehouse** of local red sandstone, with the remains of an earlier 13C gatehouse at right angles to it, through which a flight of steps leads to the courtyard in front of the house. The west side is occupied by the Norman **motte**, turned into a bowling-green in 1727 (the summer house of that date still survives). To the south is the house, built within the original curtain wall, with the ground sloping steeply away beyond. Here Salvin reigns supreme. It is a matter for historical regret that the early-17C façade was swept away (it is illustrated in a drawing by Buckler of 1839), but the present Victorian front is undoubtedly picturesque, especially when seen from a distance, and the craftsmanship and detailing carry conviction. Salvin added the keep-like tower housing the service quarters to the left, but the rest of the façade follows the general lines of its predecessor, albeit with the addition of some calculated irregularities.

The entrance is through a porch displaying the Luttrells' coat of arms, and leads into the **Outer Hall**, created by Salvin on the site of two former rooms, but retaining part of the original plaster ceiling; the furniture includes three elaborate 16C or 17C 'thrown' chairs. The **Inner Hall** is the hall of the late-16C house, and retains its original plaster ceiling with pendants hanging down in the popular west-country manner, but the heavy stone chimneypiece is by Salvin, who also swept away the 18C panelling recorded in early photographs; among the family portraits hanging here is a version of Hans Eworth's famous allegorical portrait of Sir John Luttrell (1550), showing him up to his waist in water, with a nude figure of Peace touching his arm. Beyond is the bolection-panelled **Dining Room** (formerly the great parlour), with a sumptuous plaster ceiling of 1681, possibly by Edward Gouge; this was part of the alterations undertaken by Francis Luttrell, whose portrait hangs, with that of his wife, over the marble fireplace. The decoration of the small adjacent room (originally the withdrawing room) dates from the same time (note the Cupid in the plaster ceiling), as does the magnificently carved wooden **Staircase**, possibly by Edward Pierce, reached from the Inner Hall and with another splendid late-17C plaster ceiling displaying hunting motifs. The portrait of the elaborately dressed young man against an architectural background is by the little-known Edward Bower (1638).

The largely late-18C **Morning Room** contains a picture showing the east front of the castle in the 18C before Salvin added the present towers, and from here a corridor leads first to a bedroom furnished in late-Victorian fashion and then to the **Gallery**, the formal dining room of the 17C house, but now mainly notable for an unusual set of mid-17C Flemish leather wall hangings of the story of Anthony and Cleopatra brought to Dunster in the early 18C. The **King Charles Room** next door has a rather crude plaster overmantel of the Judgement of Paris, dated 1620, and not unlike some at Montacute, where the mason William Arnold also worked. From here a secondary staircase leads down to a group of rooms created by Salvin: the Billiard Room (on the site of the old kitchen); the Justice Room; the Library, with a neo-Jacobean ceiling; the Conservatory; and the Drawing Room, on the ground floor of the tower which replaced Thornhill's chapel, and now furnished with items mostly dating from the 18C.

GCT

Gaulden Manor

1½m west of Lydeard St Lawrence, to west of A358 Taunton–Watchet: Mr and Mrs J. LeGendre Starkie, tel. 09847 213. Open May–early Sept Sun, Thur, all BH 2–5. Guided tours. Refreshments.

From the outside, this modest-looking building has little to differentiate it from the many stone-built late-16C or early-17C farmhouses dotted about the attractive, hilly countryside of west Somerset, but inside it contains some remarkable plasterwork introduced by the Turberville family in the mid 17C. It now survives as a good example of a home of successive families of gentleman-farmers of a type more common in the West Country than in most other parts of England.

The manor belonged to Taunton Priory in the Middle Ages, and it passed through several families before being acquired in 1615 by John Turberville on behalf of his son, also called John, who moved to Gaulden after his marriage in 1639. The Turbervilles came from Dorset, and their name was immortalised by Thomas Hardy in *Tess of the D'Urbervilles*. They moved away in the 18C, and structurally the house has changed little since. It is simply built of the rough local stone, with later slate roofs, and consists of a late-16C hall block extended at the back at an unknown date, with a porch and a lower service wing. The most impressive room is the Hall, with its lavish plaster overmantel, frieze and ceiling, the latter containing three roundels, the central one encircling a massive pendant and the other two with representations of King David and the Angel of Judgment; there are more religious motifs on the frieze. To the right of the fireplace is a wooden screen dating from the mid 17C, with the initials of John Turberville, and beyond it is a room known as the Chapel with more 17C plasterwork. There is another heraldic plaster overmantel dated 1640 in the bedroom over the Hall, and outside there are attractive gardens formed by the present owners. They farm the surrounding land, and have introduced portraits and items of furniture inherited from their Lancashire forbears into the house, which they bought in 1966.

GCT

Lytes Cary Manor

2½m north east of Ilchester to west of A37 Yeovil–Bristol: National Trust, tel. 0985 847777. Open Apr–Oct Mon, Wed, Sat 2–6.

Lytes Cary derives its name from the Lyte family, who were lords of the manor from the late 13C to the mid 18C, and their picturesque irregular house of grey lias stone is one of the finest of the late-medieval houses in south-west England which have lasted to the present day. The earliest surviving part of the building is a small domestic chapel, probably built by Peter Lyte (d 1348), and originally free-standing, like that at Sheldon Manor, Wilts (qv.). It now abuts onto the main house, which was built in the mid 15C and was expanded in the early 16C by John Lyte, who, according to one of his descendants, 'new built the hall oriel, the 2 great porches'—one of which has gone—'the closets, the kitchen, and divers other places'; he was also responsible for remodelling and extending the south or parlour range. The heyday of the house was in the 16C and early 17C, when it belonged to a succession of wealthy and scholarly owners, among them Henry Lyte, the author of *Lyte's Herbal* (1578). But, like many other houses of its kind, it fell on hard times in the 18C. The Lytes sold the estate in 1748, and by 1810 the service range to the north of the hall had been demolished and replaced by a two-storeyed building which served as a residence for the local farmer; the range on the west side of the small courtyard, facing the hall, was also demolished and the remaining rooms denuded of their furnishings. Deliverance came from Sir Walter Jenner, son of a leading Victorian physician, who bought the run-down property in 1907 and, with the help of the architect C.E. Ponting, laid out new gardens, built a new west range (not open to the public) and sensitively restored the rest of the house, filling it with a well-chosen collection of late-16C, 17C and early-18C English furniture which admirably complements the beautifully textured old rooms. When Sir Walter died in 1948, the house and many of the contents were conveyed to the National Trust.

The house is approached from the north, past farm buildings and the plain but not unattractive early-19C north range. The east or entrance front makes a pleasing composition, with the Hall in the centre, flanked by the later porch and the oriel at the 'upper' end, and the Chapel projecting from the south end. Around the corner to the south is the early-16C parlour wing, the most notable external feature of which is a canted bay window carrying the date 1533 and embellished with elaborate carving of a type found in several other local houses of the period (eg, Forde Abbey, Dorset). The visual appeal of the old stone walls is complemented by the gardens, laid out as a series of 'outdoor rooms' in the first half of the 20C.

The interiors remain largely as Sir Walter Jenner left them. The 15C Hall, entered through a carved wooden screen, retains its original arch-braced roof with carved angels at the foot of each of the beams, and there is a good collection of furniture and fittings, including a landscape by Jan Wyck and pair of late-17C Delft tulip vases on the table at the 'upper' end. A small room leads off from this end of the Hall through a four-centred early-16C arch embellished with late-Gothic panelling; it contains a curious 18C bird-cage shaped like a house, and a portrait of Lady Catherine Neville by Robert Peake (1590) hangs over the fireplace. The Parlour, the most important room on the ground floor of the south range, was panelled in wood in the early 17C, and now contains excellent items of late-17C and early-18C furniture. But the most impressive room in this part of the house is the Great Chamber upstairs, with its barrel-vaulted ceiling of c 1533 embellished with plaster 'ribs'—an early example of this form of decoration—tapestry-hung walls and excellent walnut furniture, more examples of which can be found in the Little Chamber next door, along with an 18C bed originally at Burton Pynsent, the Somerset home of the elder William Pitt. The Chapel, entered through its own door outside the house, contains furnishings and coats of arms introduced by the antiquarian-minded Thomas Lyte in 1631, reinforcing the sense of mellow age which pervades the house.

GCT

Midelney Manor

South of Drayton, to south east of A378 Taunton–Langport at Curry Rivel:
John Cely Trevilian. Open late Apr–late Sept Thur, BH Mon 2.30–5.30.
Guided tours.

Midelney means 'middle island', and in the Middle Ages the monks of the
nearby abbey at Muchelney (the 'great island') had a summer retreat here,
linked to the village of Drayton by a mile-long causeway across the fenny,
and often flooded, agricultural land of the Somerset levels. After the
monastery was dissolved the land was leased by its new absentee owners
to John Trevilian of Kingsbury Episcopi, a village some two miles away, and
the present house was built by his two sons, Richard and Thomas, towards
the end of the 16C. Architecturally it resembles a large farmhouse rather
than a full-scale gentleman's country house and although Richard Trevilian's son, Ralph, became lord of the manor in 1603, the house has retained
an agreeably rustic character down to the present day. A new formal
entrance was created on the present garden side by John Trevilian in the
early 18C, and at about the same time there was some internal remodelling.
The building fell into disrepair in the later 18C, by which time it had passed
by inheritance to the Cely family and had been let out to tenants. The
Cely-Trevilians (as they had by now become) built a new house at Drayton
in 1860, but in 1926 Major M.F. Cely-Trevilian moved back to the older
building, and his grandson lives and farms here now.

The house, of local lias stone with brown Ham Hill dressings, is romantically isolated at the end of the causeway linking it to the outside world. It
consists of a long, low two-storeyed hall range, with projecting wings at
each end linked by a low wall with a gate in the middle. There are, most
unusually, two entrances, one in each wing, a relic of the arrangement
whereby the house was built by two brothers, each of whom insisted on
retaining his own privacy. There was originally a dividing wall down the
middle of the house, but this was later removed and today the building is
occupied as a single unit. The garden side has been much altered, especially in the early 19C, when the original wings fell down, but the brick
walls and stone gate-piers of the 18C formal entrance have survived, with
a vista through to a plantation of trees and the marshy land beyond; to the
west there is a 17C red-brick mews for falcons.

The tour takes in the two halls of the original house, the further of which
is now the Dining Room, some wood-panelled early-18C reception rooms
in the right-hand wing, and some of the main bedrooms; they are reached
by a small-scale version of the wooden staircases found in so many Georgian country houses. The rooms are comfortably and unpretentiously
furnished, and the walls are hung with family portraits and other pictures
accumulated over many generations to give an atmosphere of timelessness
and ancient possession often absent from houses of this kind.

GCT

Montacute House

4m west of Yeovil to south of A3088: National Trust, tel. 0935 823289.
Open Apr–Oct daily (not Tues) 12–5.30 (gardens open all year daily except
Tues 11.30–5.30 or dusk if earlier). Refreshments.

Montacute, one of the finest of all Elizabethan country houses, stands in
the shadow of a sharply pointed hill—the *mons acutus* of the name. It was
built in the 1590s by Sir Edward Phelips, a successful lawyer whose family
had lived in the area since the early 16C, and was finished in 1601. Phelips
later acquired the lands of the dissolved priory of Montacute and went on
to become Speaker of the House of Commons and Master of the Rolls. His
son was an important member of the Parliamentary opposition to Charles
I in the 1620s, but his descendants were ordinary country squires who
lacked the means to rebuild the vast house, and it remained largely
unaltered until 1785–86, when Edward Phelips built a corridor range
flanking the hall, using materials from a demolished mid-16C wing at
Clifton Maybank House, six miles away over the Dorset border. His great-
grandson William Phelips carried some internal remodelling in 1847–52,
but agricultural depression forced his son and successor, another William
Phelips, to sell most of the contents in 1895. The house was then let, and
from 1915 until his death in 1925 it was the home of Lord Curzon, the former
Viceroy of India (cf. Kedleston Hall, Derbyshire) and an aficionado of old
houses. It was sold, unfurnished except for the family portraits, to the
Society for the Protection of Ancient Buildings, which, thanks to the
generosity of Ernest Cook, presented it to the National Trust in 1931. It has
subsequently been refurnished with items donated and loaned to the Trust,
and they were joined in 1975 by an excellent collection of 16C and 17C
portraits from the National Portrait Gallery in London.

Much of the appeal of Montacute derives from its setting, and from the
beautiful yellow limestone from the Ham Hill quarries, not far away, of
which it is built. The house was originally approached from the east,
through a gatehouse (since demolished) and walled forecourt; the corner
pavilions with their ogee-shaped roofs have happily survived. The designer
was almost certainly the Somerset-born mason William Arnold, who later
went on to build Wadham College, Oxford, and to work at Dunster Castle
(qv.). His **entrance front** is a superb composition, three storeys high and
completely symmetrical, with wings surmounted by Dutch gables at either
end, a projecting porch in the middle and huge mullioned and transomed
windows spread across the façade. As in most of the larger late-Elizabethan
houses, the architecture is a synthesis of medieval ideas with others of
classical origin, like the Doric frieze at first-floor level, the segmental
pediments over some of the first-floor windows, the figures of the Nine
Worthies in the niches on the top floor and the balustrade punctuated by
obelisks on the roof-line. The **west front** was originally plainer, but it was
drastically altered in 1786 by the addition of the mid-16C porch from Clifton
Maybank, with its spiral-shaped pinnacles, similar to those at Barrington
Court (qv.); the lozenge over the entrance contains an armorial achievement of the builder John Horsey (d 1564) and his wife Edith Phelips,
surrounded by swirling Renaissance arabesques and supported by cherubs.

The house is laid out in the conventional Elizabethan manner, with the
service quarters to the south of a screens passage bisecting the building
and the reception rooms to the north and on the upper floors. Sir Edward

Phelips's visitors would have turned immediately right into the hall, but the first room to be seen now is the **Dining Room** to the left, originally the buttery but turned into a 'common parlour' in the late 18C. It contains a selection of Elizabethan portraits, but the finest work of art is the splendid 'millefleurs' tapestry with a figure of a knight on horseback, made in Tournai (Belgium) in 1481–82 for the Governor of the Dauphiné in France and presented to the National Trust by the industrialist Sir Malcolm Stewart, along with other tapestries, in 1960. The **Hall** was originally used mainly as a vestibule and dining room for the servants. It is only one storey high and is entered through an impressive stone screen with Corinthian columns and strapwork at the top. Phelips family portraits hang on the walls, and on the north wall, over a Gothic-arched doorway, there is a crude plaster panel depicting the 'skimmington ride' referred to in Thomas Hardy's *Mayor of Casterbridge*. The **Parlour**, in the north wing, retains its original stone chimneypiece, plaster frieze and wooden panelling, together with a Gobelin tapestry entitled 'The Hunter' (c 1731). The **Drawing Room**, by contrast, is decorated in 18C fashion and contains furniture and pictures of that period, along with a mid-17C chimneypiece brought from Coleshill House (Berks), gutted by fire in 1952 and since razed to the ground.

A stone **staircase**, hung with late-15C and early-16C Brussels tapestries from the Stewart collection, leads up to a spacious and brightly lit great chamber, used originally as the main formal dining room but subsequently turned into the **Library**. It still contains its original chimneypiece of Portland stone, plaster frieze, wooden internal porch (brought from downstairs) and, more unusually, the original heraldic stained glass, but the ceiling and much of the panelling date from the mid 19C. The adjacent **Crimson Bedroom**, created out of the original withdrawing room, contains an elaborately carved four-poster bed of 1612, given to the National Trust, and a good collection of contemporary portraits including two by Cornelius Johnson. The original plaster frieze survives here too, as does the overmantel, but the chimneypiece has gone. In the next room, the **Hall Chamber**, there are some 18C needlework hangings depicting the formal gardens of the demolished Stoke Edith House, Herefordshire. From here the 18C corridor leads back to **Lord Curzon's Bedroom**, with his bath cunningly hidden in a cupboard, and then to the staircase, which leads up to the **Gallery** on the second floor, the longest in any surviving country house. It has lost its original decoration (if indeed it ever had any) and now contains the bulk of the pictures on loan from the National Portrait Gallery. They are grouped chronologically, starting in the north west wing (to the left on entering). The pictures are chosen primarily for their historical interest, and are of very varied artistic quality, but among those which should be singled out are a version of George Gower's 'Armada' portrait of Queen Elizabeth I, a meticulously detailed likeness of Lady Scudamore by Marcus Gheeraerts (1615), an anonymous portrait of Sir John Backhouse, a shareholder in the New River in London (1637) and works by, or attributed to, Rowland Lockey, Daniel Mytens, Gerard Honthorst, William Dobson and Michael van Miereveldt. Taken together, they represent the whole panoply of English history in the 16C and early 17C, and greatly enhance the evocative appeal of the house.

GCT

STAFFORDSHIRE

Chillington Hall

8m north west of Wolverhampton via A449 Wolverhampton–Stafford, M54
junction 2, M6 junction 12: Mr and Mrs Peter Giffard, tel. 0902 850236.
Open May–mid Sept Thur, and Sun in Aug and all BH Sun 2.30–5.30.
Guided tours.

Though only a few miles from the Black Country, Chillington is still isolated
in its remote hilltop site in the former Forest of Brewood. The estate has
remained in the hands of one family, the Giffards, since the late 12C, but
the present house at Chillington dates entirely from the 18C, when the
property passed to a junior branch of the family, who were Catholics. It was
built in two stages, as can be clearly seen from the outside. The three-
storeyed south wing, to the left of the entrance range, was built in 1724 by
Peter Giffard, probably to the designs of Francis Smith of Warwick or his
brother William, and represented a rebuilding of one side of the existing
16C courtyard house. The rest of the older house remained standing until
1786–89, when Giffard's grandson Thomas called in John Soane to build
the present entrance range and north wing, proposals to build a completely
new house having been dropped. There have been few changes since then,
and the house now represents one of Soane's most important excursions
into country house design.

The entrance, approached by a long, straight avenue, is dominated by a
giant Ionic portico of local sandstone. Soane's façade is of plain red brick
(originally intended to be stuccoed), but the front of the 1724 south wing is
more elaborately treated, with decorative mannerisms found in several
Smith houses. The entrance is through a bare Ionic-columned Hall, which
leads through to the finest room in the house, a cavernous top-lit Saloon
contrived by Soane within the walls of the hall of the previous house, and
originally intended as a chapel. With its high, bare walls, and lantern rising
out of a dome resting on pendentives, this is one of the most impressive
rooms in any late-18C English house, and clearly served as a trial run for
the even more spectacular interiors which Soane was to create in the Bank
of England. There is little to deflect attention from the architecture, apart
from the strange and rather clumsy-looking chimneypiece allegedly made
up, or copied, from armorial fragments in the previous house. The other
Soane rooms—the Drawing Room and Dining Room in the main block and
the Library in the north wing—show none of the architect's genius in
organising internal spaces, largely because funds were drastically reduced
when Thomas Giffard married in 1788, and most of the exiguous decoration
looks as if it was applied after his death in 1827; the most interesting of the
contents are a pair of Grand Tour portraits of Thomas Giffard and his father
by Pompeo Batoni and a bust by Christopher Hewetson, in the Dining
Room.

The tour of the house also encompasses the Morning Room in the south
wing, more cosy and comfortable than the forbiddingly spacious Soane
rooms, with a swirly plaster ceiling of c 1730–40, and the Staircase Hall of
1724, with more exuberant plasterwork and a well-crafted wooden staircase of a kind found in other houses associated with the Smith brothers.
Outside, though invisible from the house, is the lake, part of a programme

of landscape improvements carried out by 'Capability' Brown in the 1760s, with a sham bridge to impound the waters and a real bridge built later byJames Paine. There are also three temples, one of which (the Grecian Temple) may be by Soane.

GCT

Moseley Old Hall

4m north of Wolverhampton between A449 W'hampton–Stafford & A460 W'hampton–Cannock: National Trust, tel. 0902 782808. Open Apr–Oct Wed, Sat, Sun, BH Mon, Tues in July, Aug, 2–5.30 (BH Mon 11–5). Refreshments.

The plain red brick exterior of this modest-looking gabled house hides an exuberantly timber-framed building of a type which was once very common in the West Midlands. The house was built in about 1600 by Henry Pitt (d 1602), a merchant of the Staple, but its main claim to fame derives from the fact that it sheltered Charles II on his flight from the Battle of Worcester in 1651. By then it had passed to the builder's grandson Thomas Whitgreave, a Roman Catholic, and he and his resident priest, John Huddleston (who was later to receive the dying King into the Church), provided temporary accommodation for the King after he had left Boscobel, Shropshire (qv.), protecting him from the attentions of a party of Cromwellian troops who came to arrest Whitgreave. The house remained in the hands of the Whitgreaves and their descendants until 1925, but, while the interior remained relatively unspoiled, the outside was unfortunately encased in brick c 1870. By this time the building had become a farmhouse, and, with the tentacles of the Black Country spreading uncomfortably close, it was all but abandoned between the two world wars. It was rescued by the National Trust in 1962 and refurnished with mainly 17C items. Recently a walled garden has also been intelligently replanted in 17C style, using only plants known to have existed in England at that period, and incorporating a formal knot garden.

The remodelling of the exterior in the 19C—which seems to have been occasioned by the decay of some of the timbers—preserved the general outline of the house, and the gabled roof-lines and tall brick chimneys of the original building can still be seen. What has vanished is the attractive texture of the old oak framing, shown in early photographs, and the original windows, which have been replaced by others of a type found in countless Midland farmhouses. Inside, more has been preserved. The house, which has two main storeys, consists of the usual hall block, with a projecting porch extending the full height of the building, and a slightly higher parlour wing. Some of the rooms, like the Parlour to the left of the Hall, are panelled in wood, and the introduction of appropriate furniture, porcelain and pictures of the Whitgreaves and the Stuart royal family helps convey the intended sense of the past. Up the back stairs is a room containing the bed in which the King is said to have rested in 1651. Father Huddleston's oratory, in the attic, can also be visited and some priest-holes seen, all of which reinforces the atmosphere of a house which James Lees-Milne described in 1944 as being 'redolent of papistry, monarchy and sanctity'.

GCT

Shugborough

6m east of Stafford at Milford on A513: National Trust/Staffordshire
County Council, tel. 0889 881388. Open late Mar–Oct daily 11–5.
Refreshments.

This large and impressive 18C house is a monument to the aesthetic and
antiquarian enthusiasms of two generations of the Anson family. The
Ansons first came to Shugborough in the early 17C, and in 1693 a compact
three-storeyed house was built on a site close to the confluence of the rivers
Trent and Sow, north of Cannock Chase. This was enlarged in the late 1740s
and early 1750s by Thomas Anson, an enthusiastic virtuoso and founder-
member of the Society of Dilettante. He also laid out the grounds in the
manner of a *ferme ornée*, with the help of the eccentric architect and
amateur astronomer, Thomas Wright. In 1762 Anson inherited the fortune
of his younger brother Admiral Lord Anson (cf. Moor Park, Hertfordshire),
and extended the grounds, which were embellished with buildings
designed by James 'Athenian' Stuart; they are among the earliest monuments of the Greek Revival in Europe. His great-nephew Thomas, Viscount
Anson, a Whig politician and improving landlord, employed the Stafford-
shire-born Samuel Wyatt, elder brother of the more famous James, to carry
out a thorough internal and external remodelling of the house in 1790–1806,
and Wyatt also designed new lodges, estate cottages and a model farm, all
of which still survive. Anson's son, the 1st Earl of Lichfield, squandered
much of the family fortune on sport and the turf, resulting in the sale of most
of the splendid art collection in 1842. There were minor changes to the
interior in 1899 and 1911, and in 1960 the house was conveyed to Staffordshire County Council. But the 5th Earl of Lichfield, a well-known photographer, lives here as tenant.

Shugborough lies at the end of a long drive, from which Stuart's **Triumphal Arch** and **Temple of the Winds** can be seen, both of them inspired by
buildings in Athens. At the end is an impressive grey-brick mid-18C **stable
block** (possibly by the local builder Charles Trubshaw), part of which now
houses the Staffordshire County Museum. Next to it is the house, with
Samuel Wyatt's massive Ionic **portico** extending the whole width of the
original late-17C building, flanked by wings added in the 1740s; the stucco
rendering replaces the covering of painted slate applied by Wyatt in the
1790s.

The antiquarian interests of the 18C Ansons are immediately apparent in
the low **Entrance Hall**, which is encircled by a ring of Doric columns in
scagliola introduced by Wyatt as a setting for a pair of Roman tablets and
casts of centaurs 'after the antique'. From here two smaller rooms lead into
the spacious **Dining Room** (originally the drawing room) in the north-
ernmost wing. The decoration here is in the Rococo manner fashionable in
the 1740s, and includes a version of Guido Reni's 'Aurora' on the ceiling by
the stuccoist Vassali; over the chimneypiece (by Scheemakers) there is a
portrait by Thomas Hudson of Admiral Lord Anson, but it is his older
brother's tastes which are reflected in the huge ruin pictures, painted in
Bologna and and attributed to Nicholas Dall, which take up most of the wall
space. The room was adapted to its present purpose when Samuel Wyatt
built the adjacent **Red Drawing Room** in 1794, with an excellent plaster
ceiling by the younger Joseph Rose in a delicate Adamesque neo-classic
manner. Some pictures which escaped in the 1842 sale are hung on the

walls, among them Gerard Honthorst's 'Angel Appearing to St Peter', and an 'Immaculate Conception', by Miguel Melendez, a follower of Murillo; the French furniture of the Louis XV and XVI periods, including pieces by J.H. Riesener, was introduced by the 2nd Earl in the 19C, but the sofas and armchairs were designed for the room. This room is approached through the smaller **Blue Drawing Room**, which now houses some of the superb collection of porcelain and chinoiseries amassed by Admiral Anson, many of which were originally housed in the Chinese House which still survives in the grounds; some of the items are shown in a mahogany cabinet designed after a plate in Chippendale's *Director* (1755).

From here a passage leads to the **Saloon**, in the centre of the garden front, enlarged to its present rather disproportionate length by Samuel Wyatt in 1803–6 and given a pompous decorative treatment out of keeping with the intimate scale of the neighbouring rooms (the external appearance is even more clumsy). Next door is the **Verandah Room**, dating in its present form from 1911 and containing a service of armorial porcelain given to Admiral Lord Anson by the European merchants of Canton c 1743, and a Wedgwood sauce tureen of c 1774 adorned with a view of Shugborough Park; the paintings (eg, James Ward's 'Longhorn Cow and Farm Labourer' and Francis Grant's 'Sporting Party at Ranton Abbey') reflect the agricultural and sporting interests of Viscount Anson and the 1st Lord Lichfield. A passageway lined with views of the house and grounds in the 18C by Nicholas Dall and Moses Griffith leads from here to the Library, the most attractive room in the house, created in 1745–48 by knocking a hole through the south wall of the old house and taking in the wing leading to the new south pavilion; it is divided into two by a low segmental arch resting on Ionic columns, and further variety is imparted by the excellent Rococo plasterwork (by Vassali).

Following the usual late-18C fashion, the first floor is largely given over to bedrooms, with the exception of the light and cheerful Bird Room (not always open to the public), behind the portico, recently redecorated as a sitting room for the present Lord Lichfield. On leaving the house visitors should take care not to miss the gardens and 18C **garden buildings**, notably the Chinese House of 1747, the mock-elegiac Shepherd's Monument of c 1748–58 (probably by Thomas Wright) and Stuart's slightly later Doric Temple, which originally served as the entrance to the vanished kitchen garden. The service courtyard can also be explored, and so too can the impressive Home Farm of 1805.

GCT

Tamworth Castle

In Tamworth 15m north east of Birmingham: Tamworth Borough Council, tel. 0827 65363. Open all year (except Christmas, Boxing Day), weekdays 10–4.30, Sun 2–4.30.

The history of Tamworth goes back at least to the 8C, when Offa, King of Mercia, built a 'palace' on or near the site of the present town. A fortified *burg* was founded in 913, and following the Norman Conquest Robert 'Dispentator' built a timber castle next to the Anglo-Saxon town. A shell-keep was built of red sandstone on top of the motte during the 12C, and lean-to structures were constructed within the high walls and then replaced by the present apartments in the late 16C or early 17C. By this time the castle had passed by descent to the Marmions, the Frevilles and then, in 1423, to a branch of the Ferrers family, whose ancestors came over to England with William the Conqueror. They fixed their main residence in the castle, entertaining James I here on three occasions in the early 17C. They took the Royalist side in the Civil War, but the shell-keep surprisingly escaped being slighted, the upper section of the walls may represent a post-war reconstruction.

The direct male line of the Ferrers died out in 1688, and in 1751 the castle passed to the 1st Marquess Townshend, of Raynham (Norfolk). In 1807–11 the 2nd Marquess, a former President of the Society of Antiquaries, remodelled some of the exterior, removing in the process most of the Elizabethan gables and bay windows shown in Samuel Buck's view of 1729. He also carried out some internal alterations, including the creation of a new suite of rooms at second-floor level. In 1869 the castle was leased to a local clothing manufacturer, Thomas Cooke, whose family lived here until 1897, when it was bought by Tamworth Corporation. Since then it has been a museum, but in the last few years the interiors have been sympathetically restored and refurnished, and the castle can now be enjoyed both as a medieval fortress and as a country house of a most unusual kind.

The castle stands on the edge of the historic town centre—which has yet to recover from the ravages of 1960s planning—overlooking the flood-plain of the Rivers Tame and Anker. The buildings around the medieval Bailey have all gone, and the area now serves as a public park, but the **shell-keep** is remarkably intact. Work of several different periods can be clearly distinguished from the outside: the crenellated walls and tall tower built by the Marmions in the 12C; a gabled bay (the Warder's Lodge) with mullioned windows of the late 16C; and the plain surfaces of the 2nd Marquess Townshend's work of the early 19C. Inside the keep, the extent of the rebuilding carried out by the Ferrers family is clearer, for on entering the small entrance courtyard the visitor is immediately confronted by what looks like a substantial Elizabethan or Jacobean country house squeezed inside the old castle walls. Facing the entrance is the rebuilt medieval **Great Hall**, flanked on one side by an early-17C classical porch with the Ferrers' coat of arms over the arch, and on the other by a staircase tower leading up to the main reception rooms at the 'upper' end; the Hall is open to the roof, and its front wall is made up almost entirely of glass, dating from the 17C.

The tour starts in the wing to the right of the Hall, where the **State Dining Room** occupies the site of the medieval great chamber on the first floor; the doorcases and chimneypiece date from the mid 17C, and the room, like the ante-chamber and bedroom on either side, is well furnished with 17C pieces on loan from the Victoria and Albert Museum. Upstairs is the much-altered **Long Gallery**, and from here a doorway leads onto the ramparts, from which it is possible to look down into the tiny courtyard behind the Hall. The route then passes through the upper storey of the 12C tower, containing a 'Haunted Bedroom' (complete with ghost), and then, via the private chapel made by the Ferrers on the upper floor of the Warder's Lodge, to another section of ramparts; these give access to the part of the house rebuilt by Lord Townshend in the early 19C. The top-floor **bedrooms** are now furnished in Victorian fashion, and from them stairs lead down to the first floor, where Townshend created a **Breakfast Parlour** and **Drawing Room** in the neo-Jacobean fashion, incorporating soft-wood panelling and coats of arms of the Ferrers family. The Parlour contains a superb carved oak chimneypiece which may date from the early 17C, though not necessarily original to the castle. These rooms have also been recently refurnished, this time with 19C pieces, including some from Drayton Manor, the vanished house of the Victorian Prime Minister, Sir Robert Peel, just south of the town. The last room to be seen is the Great Hall, with its much-restored medieval roof and 17C doorcases and windows.

GCT

Weston Park

9m east of Telford on A5, M54 junction 3, M6 junction 12: Weston Park Foundation, tel. 095276 207. Open Easter–mid Sept—please enquire for dates and times. Refreshments.

This large red-brick house was built in 1671 by Elizabeth, Lady Wilbraham, who inherited the estate from her father Edward Mytton, a member of an old Shropshire family. Lady Wilbraham owned a 1663 edition of Palladio in which she wrote down the costs of building, and she seems to have acted as her own architect, making Weston one of the earliest English buildings known to have been designed by a woman. When her husband died the estate went to their youngest daughter, who had married Richard Newport, 2nd Earl of Bradford, and his son, the 3rd Earl, purchased the nucleus of the collection of Old Master paintings which constitutes the main artistic interest of Weston. The male line of the Newports died out in 1762, and the property then passed to Sir Henry Bridgeman of Castle Bromwich (Warwickshire), descendant of Orlando Bridgeman, a successful lawyer who became Lord Keeper of the Great Seal under Charles II. Bridgeman refurbished the interior and spent large sums of money on the grounds, which were landscaped by 'Capability' Brown and contain notable buildings by James Paine. He was also a keen agricultural improver, evidence of which can be seen in the splendid farm buildings to the north of the house.

The title of Earl of Bradford was revived for Bridgeman's son, a friend of the Prince Regent, and he employed John White, author of the first plan for Regent's Park in London, to carry out alterations to the house in 1802–8. Further changes were made in 1830–31 for the 2nd Earl, another discriminating art collector, this time with Thomas Rickman as architect. William Burn made yet more alterations for the 3rd Earl in 1866, building a new guest wing and orangery and shifting the entrance to its present position on the east side; the attractive formal gardens to the south and west were created at about the same time. More internal changes were made by the 4th Earl, who inherited in 1898, and, more recently, in the 1960s, by the wife of the 6th Earl.

These piecemeal alterations have robbed the house of most of its original interiors, and today the prevailing impression is one of 20C comfort. The outside has changed much less, and would still be recognisable to Lady Wilbraham. As first seen by visitors, from the south, it consists of a solid three-storeyed red-brick block with grey sandstone dressings, a balustrade hiding the roof, and segmental pediments of the two end bays on either side—a French-inspired feature—from which wings go back to enclose what must originally have been the entrance courtyard facing the village (largely relocated along the A5 in the late 18C). To the east is a pedimented stable block of 1688.

The house is entered through a carriage-porch in the east wing, and there are pictures by Stubbs and Ferneley in the **Entrance Hall**, which was much altered by Lady Bradford in 1961–68. Beyond it lies the **Marble Hall**, hung with portraits of the daughters of Lady Wilbraham by John Michael Wright. Some of the family's excellent collection of Chinese porcelain is displayed in a wall cabinet. The **Tapestry Room** derives its name from a superb set of Gobelin tapestries dated 1766 and acquired by Sir Henry Bridgeman for an upstairs bedroom, with mythological scenes after Boucher set against a deep red background (cf. Osterley Park, Greater London); the room also contains French 18C furniture, more Chinese porcelain and Sir Orlando Bridgeman's official bag for the Great Seal. The **Drawing Room**, originally the entrance hall of the 1671 house but dating in its present form from the early 19C, is hung with family portraits by Lely and others; it is mainly notable now for its French furniture and for the pretty Bow china groups on the mantelpiece. The **Library** (originally the dining room) takes up the rest of the front of the original house and contains more portraits, by Reynolds and Constable inter alia, as well as a good collection of books, including several 18C architectural works. Since 1866 the **Dining Room** has been in the west wing, where Burn created a lofty room (redecorated and embellished by Lady Bradford in 1968). It is now hung with Old Master paintings, including one of the best collections of Van Dyck portraits to be found in any English house (eg, Sir Thomas Hanmer c 1637, praised by John Evelyn when he saw it in the family collection in 1685), though pride of place over the fireplace is given to a 'Homage to Handel' by R.E. Pine, in which Sir Henry Bridgeman and his family are shown making music.

More Old Master paintings are shown in two top-lit **galleries** created out of the 19C billiard and smoking rooms on the site of the former entrance courtyard; they are reached by a corridor hung with two works by the Mannerist painter Amiconi. The first gallery contains works by Jacopo Bassano (an Annunciation and a Winter Scene) and Joseph Vernet, as well as a pair of Aubusson tapestries and, in a display case, letters written by Benjamin Disraeli to Lady Bradford, wife of the 3rd Earl and one of the politician's main confidantes. In the second gallery there are pictures by Guido Reni, Salvator Rosa and some smaller Dutch and Flemish 17C low-life paintings. The last room to be shown is the **Breakfast Room**, in the east wing, hung with what are, apart from the Van Dycks, the finest pictures in the house, including Holbein's portrait of Sir George Carew, who was drowned in the 'Mary Rose', and portraits of Protector Somerset by François Clouet and of an unknown woman by Antonio Moro. There are also portraits by Paul van Somer and Gainsborough. On leaving the house it is worth seeing the adjacent church, with its family monuments, and James Paine's **Temple of Diana** of c 1765, one of the largest and most ambitious garden buildings of its date; from here there is a good view of the undulating landscape which complements the house so effectively.

GCT

Whitmore Hall

4m south west of Newcastle-under-Lyme, on the A53: Mr R. Cavenagh-Mainwaring, tel. 0782 680478. Open May–Aug Tues, Wed 2–5.30, last admission 5.

Whitmore Hall is a medium-sized Carolean manor house of the 1670s. The manor of Whitmore has been held by just five families since the Norman Conquest. It has always passed by descent, never by sale. In 1546, the heiress Alice de Boghay married Edward Mainwaring of Peover in Cheshire (qv.). Their son Edward died in 1604, and his grandson, another Edward, rebuilt the house (which was up till then a timber-framed building) in the artisan Mannerist style of the age, in red brick, completing the work in 1676. In 1891, the estate again passed to an heiress, Ellen Jane Mainwaring, who married Wentworth Cavenagh. From 1863 to 1928, the Hall was let to the Hollins and Twyford families, who remodelled the main interiors; unfortunately, much of the Cavenagh-Mainwaring's furniture was dispersed at this time. The present owner is Ellen Jane Mainwaring's grandson.

The house stands at the end of a fine avenue of lime trees. The main, south front is essentially of the 1670s, nine bays wide with a hipped roof, and big symmetrically placed chimneystacks; the elaborate porch is a 19C embellishment. The other façades are asymmetrical, with a number of 19C alterations. Inside, none of the main interiors is from the 1670s; all was redecorated early this century, in a fairly plain Edwardian taste. The Hall has some good pieces of English furniture, including a fine cabinet on a stand, and 18C portraits of the Mainwaring family. At the back of the Hall is the staircase, now quite plain; on the landing are the oldest pictures, a group of four 16C and 17C Mainwaring family portraits. To the right is the big Drawing Room, created out of two rooms. There is Georgian furniture and 18C portraits, the best a big double portrait by Enoch Seeman. Across the Hall is the Dining Room, with mahogany dado-height panelling and 19C furniture. There are family portraits and two large funeral hatchments. Next to this is the Admiral's Room, named for Adm. Rowland Mainwaring. He fought on HMS *Majestic* at the Battle of the Nile, and a painting of this battle hangs here, together with a portrait of the Admiral himself.

Outside, there is a pleasant park with a large lake. The early-17C stables are of considerable interest, retaining their original stalls, divided by Tuscan pillars with ornamental arches above.

SB

SUFFOLK

Christchurch Mansion

In Christchurch Park, Ipswich: Ipswich Museums and Galleries, tel. 0473
253246/213761. Open all year Tues–Sat, BH Mon 10–5 (dusk in winter),
Sun 2.30–4.30 (dusk in winter).

The Augustinian priory of Holy Trinity or Christ Church was founded in the
mid 12C on a site on the northern edge of Ipswich, one of the most important
coastal towns in England during the Middle Ages. After the Dissolution of
the Monasteries, the buildings and the adjoining estate were sold to Paul
Withypoll, a merchant tailor from London who had married a Suffolk
woman and had lent money to Henry VIII. In 1548–50 his son, Edmund,
began to build a new house on the site of the monastic buildings, which
were razed to the ground, along with the church. Like Kentwell Hall (qv.)
and Melford Hall (qv.), 20 miles away to the west, his house was a
two-storeyed brick building with a central hall block flanked by two
projecting wings. The kitchen wing to the west was enlarged and remodelled c 1564, but otherwise the house seems to have remained largely
unaltered until after the estate passed by marriage in 1645 to Leicester
Devereux, later 6th Viscount Hereford. He was responsible for rebuilding
the exterior in its present form, with its distinctive array of pedimented
'Dutch' gables—a popular East Anglian motif—and a sequence of upright
windows, each of them with a single mullion and transom. The character
of the work would suggest a date in the mid 17C, and the house as it is
shown today is almost the same as it appears in a drawing of 1674; rainwater
heads dated 1675 refer to further internal remodelling after a fire.

In 1732 the 10th Lord Hereford sold the house, together with the estate,
by now reduced to only 70 acres, to Charles Fonnereau, a London merchant
of Huguenot origin. He or his son, an MP, who inherited in 1740, redecorated most of the interiors in the east or parlour wing, and added an
extension at the north-east corner for a new Drawing Room and State
Bedroom. The Fonnereaus remained at Christchurch until 1892, by which
time Ipswich had greatly expanded. The house and the park—which had
long been thrown open to the public—were then put up for sale, and were
purchased by a property syndicate, one of whose members, the banker
Felix Cobbold, offered the house to the town council on condition that it
purchased those parts of the park which had not been sold for building.
The gift was accepted in 1895, and the house was subsequently opened as
a museum. In 1909 Cobbold presented an endowment fund enabling the
town to buy works of art for the house, and today it contains an excellent
collection of paintings, with important works by East Anglian artists including Thomas Gainsborough (eg, 'A View near the Coast'), and John Constable (eg, 'Golding Constable's Flower Garden', 1815), as well as furniture
from the 16C to the 19C, and panelling and other features rescued from
demolished timber houses in Ipswich between the two world wars. A wing
for temporary exhibitions was added in 1931–32.

The house is entered through a porch with disproportionately tall Doric
columns, part of the mid-17C alterations. It leads into the Hall, two-storeyed
like the hall of the Tudor house, but with bolection panelling, and a black
and white marble floor which may date either from the mid 17C or from
1675; the superimposed arcades at the west end mark the position of the

former screens passage. To the left of the Hall are the former service quarters, and to the north is a re-erected early-16C merchant's house, moved here in 1924. Here and elsewhere there are excellent pieces of 16C and early-17C carved oak furniture, chimneypieces and panelling, and in a small room over the porch there is a fascinating set of early-17C painted panels originally at Hawstead Place, near Bury St Edmunds, with subjects taken from contemporary emblem books.

The main reception rooms, to the east of the Hall, were redecorated in the late 17C and mid 18C, and have been refurnished in the style of those periods, with walnut and mahogany pieces, some of which originally belonged to the Fonnereau family. The Dining Room, on the ground floor, has plain wood panelling and a good collection of 18C portraits of members of Suffolk families. Upstairs is a suite of more elaborate rooms comprising the Saloon (later the library), with a rich plaster overmantel of c 1740, the State Drawing Room, with another chimneypiece of about the same date, and the State Bedroom. The most sumptuous 18C room in the house, it still retains its original flock wallpaper, and there is some exuberant Rococo plasterwork, by an unknown craftsman, around the bed alcove (the bed itself comes from the demolished Belhus, Essex). Downstairs, a collection of pottery and porcelain is displayed in the former Billiard Room to the north of the Hall, and beyond this, in a small room by the entrance to the exhibition wing, there is some outstanding early-Renaissance wood panelling of c 1535–40, brought from a demolished house (later an inn) in the town built by Sir Anthony Wingfield, Comptroller of the Household to Henry VIII.

GCT

Euston Hall

3m south east of Thetford on A1088 Thetford–Bury St Edmunds: the Duke of Grafton, tel. 0842 766366. Open June–Sept Thur 2.30–5.

This surprisingly modest ducal house lies on the south edge of the pine-covered wastes of Breckland. The estate, part of the huge holdings of Bury St Edmunds Abbey in the Middle Ages, was acquired in 1666 by Henry Bennet, Earl of Arlington, a member of Charles II's CABAL ministry, doubtless because of its suitability for hunting and the relative proximity of Newmarket. He built a magnificent, French-inspired house of brick round three sides of a courtyard, with four domed corner towers, and, with the aid of the diarist John Evelyn, laid out the surrounding park with extensive woods and long avenues. He also built a new church in the grounds, begun in 1676, which survives largely intact with its original plasterwork and wood carving. His daughter and heiress married Charles II's natural son (by the Duchess of Cleveland) Henry FitzRoy, 1st Duke of Grafton, and their son, the 2nd Duke, employed William Kent to lay out the park in its present form. Kent's impressively rusticated domed Banqueting House of 1746 can still be seen from the grounds, but his plans for rebuilding the house in the fashionable neo-Palladian manner were shelved; instead Matthew Brettingham, the executant architect at Holkham, Norfolk (qv.), was asked to carry out more modest alterations in 1750–56, including the introduction of the sash windows and pyramid tops to the towers, visible on the garden front. A disastrous fire in 1902 swept away the sumptuous late-17C interior decoration described in Evelyn's diary, and in 1952 most of the rebuilt west (entrance) range and the whole of the south range of the house were demolished, leaving only the north range standing.

The main interest of Euston Hall today lies in the beautifully maintained gardens created by the present Duke, and in the excellent set of portraits collected in the 17C by Lord Arlington, added to in the 18C, and still surviving intact. The house is approached through Brettingham's austere but well-proportioned stable block, and, entered by the Outer Hall in the old north range, hung with copies of Van Dyck portraits of Charles I and his family. Full-length portraits by Van Dyck (Lord Grandison, father of the Duchess of Cleveland), Lely (Charles II and the Duchess of Cleveland) and Reynolds (the 3rd Duchess of Grafton) hang in the Inner Hall; and in the adjacent Small Dining Room there is a view of the house and grounds in the late 17C by Thomas Wyck and a Stubbs painting showing the 3rd Duke's mares and foals grazing by the river. The walls of the Large Dining Room—the most impressive of the rooms shown to the public—are hung with more portraits, by Van Dyck (Queen Henrietta Maria, 1636), Lely (of Lord Arlington), Philippe de Champaigne (Charles II) and other 17C artists. A staircase next to the Inner Hall leads to the first floor, where more of Arlington's portraits hang in a top-lit Gallery. They include the 1st Duke of Buckingham by Mytens (1626), a double portrait of James II and his first wife, Ann Hyde, by Lely in his less formal manner, and another Lely of the Duchess of Cleveland with her baby son (later 1st Duke of Grafton)—a parody of a Renaissance Madonna and Child.

GCT

Haughley Park

4m north west of Stowmarket near Wetherden (not Haughley), signposted from the A45: Mr A.J. Williams. Open May–Sept Tues only 3–6.

Haughley Park is a symmetrical Jacobean house of red brick; its present owner has filled it with some fine furniture and paintings. For most of its history, this was the home of the Sulyard family, who were long-established in Suffolk. A Sir John Sulyard was Lord Chief Justice to Henry VII, and added a chantry chapel to Wetherden church. In 1538, Andrew Sulyard was granted the manor of Haughley. The family remained Catholics, and suffered for it in Elizabeth's reign, but the third Sir John nonetheless found the means to build the present house, c 1620. In 1799, the last male Sulyard died, and in 1811 Haughley was sold to a family called Crawford, who remodelled the north wing. The house passed through a number of owners before being bought by Mr Williams in 1957. In 1961, while the house was undergoing renovation, the north half was gutted by fire; many interiors were destroyed, including the original Jacobean staircase. Mr Williams carried out a full restoration over three years, work being completed in 1964.

The main façade faces east; it is of red brick, and symmetrical, with crow-stepped gables, and triangular pediments over the mullioned and transomed windows. The north front has sash windows, inserted c 1820. A number of historic fittings were brought in after the fire in 1961; the Dining Room fireplace is from Hungerford Park in Berkshire, and the Drawing Room fireplace from one of the Nash houses in Regent's Park. The fireplace in the Hall was carved new, in 1964. In the south part of the house, which escaped the fire, the Justice Room retains its original panelling. The staircase was replaced with as close a facsimile of the old one as possible, with massive treads of solid oak, 6ft wide. The rooms on display have a variety of antique furniture, and c 40 paintings, mostly Dutch School pieces of the 16C and 17C. Outside are 12 acres of varied gardens, with flowering shrubs and herbaceous plants, a giant magnolia 40ft wide, and an oak tree with a trunk over 30ft in girth, believed to be 1000 years old.

SB

Ickworth

3m south west of Bury St Edmunds at Horringer on A143: National Trust, tel. 0284 735270. Open Apr, Oct Sat, Sun, BH Mon; May–Sept daily except Mon (open BH Mon), Thur 1.30–5.30. Refreshments.

The Ickworth estate was acquired by the Hervey family in the 15C, and they were raised to the peerage as Earls of Bristol at the beginning of the 18C. But despite the fact that they played an important part in both local and national politics, their house was for a long time surprisingly unpretentious for a family of their rank. This defect was remedied in a spectacular fashion by Frederick Hervey, Bishop of Derry, who became 4th Earl of Bristol on the death of his elder brother in 1779. He was an inveterate collector and traveller, as the numerous Hotels Bristol on the Continent bear witness, and his new house was intended to impress, both by its neo-classical purity and by its stupendous size—the façade is 600ft long—as well as to house his sizable art collection. He had already built two houses in Ireland, one of which anticipated Ickworth in its unusual shape and layout: an oval domed rotunda with curved wings leading to pavilions at the ends. The design came from Mario Asprucci, son of the curator of the Borghese collection in Rome, but it was an Irishman, Francis Sandys, who carried it out, with some modifications, work starting in 1796.

The Earl-Bishop died in Italy in 1803 without ever having seen the new building, and it was made habitable by his son, the 1st Marquess of Bristol, in 1824–29, employing local craftsmen. The Earl-Bishop had intended to live in the rotunda and to use the wings as sculpture and picture galleries, but much of his art collection was captured by Napoleon and never recovered, and in the end the east wing became a sizable family residence—its present function—while the west wing was never finished. The rotunda was given over to reception rooms of unusual height with guest bedrooms above, but the interior of the dome remains incomplete to the present day, its bare walls an impressive memorial to the Earl-Bishop's megalomaniac ambitions.

The house is built of brick, but, following antique precedent, it was covered with stucco, and the classical theme is further underlined by the terracotta plaques over the windows and in the frieze by the Carabelli brothers from Italy, after Flaxman's exquisite illustrations to Homer. A marble group by Flaxman (the 'Fury of Athamas'), commissioned by the Earl-Bishop in Rome in 1790, is the central object in the dramatically top-lit **Staircase Hall**, intelligently remodelled by Sir Reginald Blomfield in 1908–11; it is framed by Ionic columns supporting a landing, above which hang portraits of the 1st Earl and Countess and a copy of Domenichino's famous 'Last Communion of St Jerome' in the Vatican collection.

The main reception rooms were decorated and furnished in an opulent Regency manner by the 1st Marquess, whose portrait by Lawrence hangs in the Dining Room. The most impressive of the rooms is the **Library**, facing the gardens, its ends screened off by Ionic columns of scagliola. The 1st Marquess collected 18C French furniture, several items of which are displayed here; he also introduced the extravagantly ornate Portuguese pier-tables and glasses incorporating landscapes after Vernet. The taste of earlier Herveys is represented by two conversation pieces, one of them, of the future 3rd Earl and his family, by Gainsborough's teacher Gravelot, with some of the figures by other artists, and the other by Hogarth (c 1737), of Lord Hervey, author of the *Memoirs* of George II's reign, dining al fresco with a group of friends, including a parson about to fall off a chair. The 3rd Earl is depicted in admiral's uniform in a superb full-length portrait by the Suffolk-born Gainsborough in the **Drawing Room**, and the same artist was responsible for the equally suave portrait of his nephew, another sailor. Other excellent portraits in this room include a Reynolds (Sir Charles Davers), two Romneys, a Lawrence (Lord Liverpool), Angelica Kauffmann's representation of the Earl-Bishop's daughter Lady Elizabeth Foster (1785), and Elisabeth Vigée-LeBrun's of the Earl–Bishop himself (1790), enigmatically smiling, with Vesuvius—which he climbed regularly—smoking in the background.

More items from the family collection are shown in the **East Corridor**, including early Hervey portraits and some Meissen porcelain in the Chinese style (c 1720). The Smoking Room, mid-way along the corridor, contains Old Master paintings, including a Titian portrait, a landscape by Gaspard Dughet, and Velasquez' portrait of the son of Philip IV of Spain in hunting clothes (1635); the lively self-portrait by Louise Vigée-LeBrun was commissioned by the Earl-Bishop in 1791.

The **West Corridor** was not decorated until the second half of the 19C. The main interest here lies in the miniatures displayed in cases and in the unusually fine collection of silver, including Rococo items acquired by the 2nd Earl—a former ambassador to Madrid and Turin—and early-19C pieces collected by the 1st Marquess. The Pompeian Room, which punctuates this corridor, was decorated by J.D. Crace to the designs of F.C. Penrose in 1879, recreating the decoration of the Villa Negroni on the Esquiline Hill in Rome. Fragments of the painted decoration had been acquired by the Earl-Bishop, and the room serves as a tribute to his adventurous taste. The tour concludes on the upper floor of the rotunda, where a model of the house c 1796 can be seen.

GCT

Kentwell Hall

On north edge of Long Melford, entrance from A134 Sudbury–Bury St Edmunds: J. P. Phillips. Open late Mar–early June Sun and BH weekends; mid July–late Sept daily; late Sept–Oct Sun 12–5. Refreshments.

Kentwell is an early-Elizabethan house standing in a moat and approached by a long avenue. The builder, William Clopton, was the representative of an important local family which had held the estate since the late 14C and had been largely responsible for the building of the superb 15C parish church at Long Melford, one of the finest of its date in England. The house was completed at about the time of Clopton's death in 1562, and the family continued living here until 1618, when the male line died out. It subsequently passed through several hands, including those of the Civil War diarist, Sir Simonds d'Ewes, and extensive internal alterations were carried out by successive owners, starting with the construction of a new staircase in the east (parlour) wing, probably by the lawyer Sir Thomas Robinson, who purchased the estate in 1676. But the present interiors date mainly from a thorough remodelling in the neo-Tudor style by the versatile Thomas Hopper (cf. Melford Hall) in 1826, for another new owner, Robert Hart Logan, who had made a fortune from Canadian timber. The estate was sold yet again in 1838, and in 1969 the by-now very dilapidated house was bought by the present owner, who has energetically restored it and organises 'historical recreations of everyday Tudor life' here for a month early each summer (separate opening arrangements).

The impressive red-brick house has the usual Elizabethan plan of a main hall block flanked by projecting wings enclosing an open courtyard, which now contains a brick maze created in 1985. The symmetrical entrance front is a sophisticated piece of design, with large mullioned and transomed windows and a skyline made up of gables, tall chimneystacks and two ogee-topped staircase turrets at the ends of the wings. The north front, facing the romantically derelict walled garden was refenestrated in the 18C, and close to the west (service) wing, with its projecting garderobe turrets to the former lodgings, there is a detached 15C building called the Moat House with some of its timber framing still visible.

When Kentwell was bought by the present owner, it was empty, and although some of the furniture is old, none of it has been in the house for very long. Visitors wander freely through the rooms, starting in the west wing and proceeding to the main block, where Hopper created a large and draughty Dining Room, panelled in the 'Jacobethan' manner, out of the former buttery and pantry; the huge table was made in China and brought in recently. Hopper was also responsible for the roof and panelling of the Hall—as large as that of one of the smaller Oxford or Cambridge colleges—with 15C stained glass introduced as part of the ensemble. The Drawing Room, Billiard Room and Library are also Hopper's, but the staircase with its turned balusters is of the late 17C. The tour encompasses some of the bedrooms upstairs, and concludes in an attic in the west wing, where old tools and other rural objects are displayed.

GCT

Melford Hall

To east of A134 Sudbury–Bury St Edmunds in Long Melford: National Trust, tel. 0787 880286. Open Apr–Oct Sat, Sun (also May–Sept Wed, Thurs) and BH Mon 2–5.30.

There was a country retreat of the Abbots of Bury St Edmunds on the site of this attractive red-brick house in the Middle Ages, and some of the cellars still survive under the hall range. Soon after the Reformation the estate was purchased by a local man, Sir William Cordell, who had prospered through the law and became Master of the Rolls. He built the bulk of the present house which probably dates, like its neighbour Kentwell Hall (qv.), from the late 1550s or 1560s, and he entertained Queen Elizabeth here in 1578. After his death the estate passed to the descendants of his sister, and the east (entrance) range was demolished at an unknown date, leaving the house in its present form with a main block and two projecting wings. The house was sold to another branch of the family in 1649, and there was a substantial internal remodelling in the late 1730s or 1740s by Sir Cordell Firebrace, a descendant of the purchaser, when many of the windows were sashed. He died without children, and the house was sold again in 1787—though with the pictures and furnishings in situ—to Sir Harry Parker, the son of an admiral and cousin of the Parkers of Saltram in Devon (qv.). His son, Sir William Parker, employed Thomas Hopper in 1813 to add new reception rooms and bedrooms on the west side of the house and to build a new staircase on the site of the original service end of the hall range. The house was given to the National Trust in 1960, the Parkers staying on as tenants.

The house stands a little to the south of the triangular green of Long Melford, with its almshouses founded by Sir William Cordell and its splendid 15C church in which he is buried. The most striking feature of the exterior is the array of ogee-topped staircase turrets, two of them flanking the wings on the entrance front and four more on the west side facing the village street. The entrance is through a stone porch leading into the Hall, with a pair of Tuscan columns standing in place of the Elizabethan screen, through which there is a vista to the staircase of 1813. The fireplace is by Hopper, and the panelling, armorial glass and grisaille wall panels were introduced in the mid and late 19C, but some of the portraits, including that of the builder of the house, survive from the 16C. The Rococo plasterwork of the Hyde Parker Room at the former 'upper' end was destroyed in a fire in 1942, but the Drawing Room in the north-west corner—formerly the dining room—still contains its panelling and fireplace of c 1740.

The most attractive room is the long Library of 1813, divided into two by scagliola columns, with most of the books kept in attractive rosewood cases in the octagonal south portion. There is good early-19C furniture, and the walls are hung with naval pictures (by Dominic Serres and others), mostly of incidents from the career of Vice-Admiral Hyde Parker, whose ship was lost at sea in 1783. There are also portraits of the Admiral and his son by Romney, and Chinese porcelain and ivory figures from Goa captured from a Spanish ship during the Seven Years War. The first floor is reached by Hopper's impressive staircase, with its barrel-vaulted ceiling and Ionic colonnades; and in one of the bedrooms there are pictures by the childrens' writer Beatrix Potter, a frequent visitor to the house. Remains of Elizabethan terraces can be seen in the grounds, along with a pretty red-brick gabled gazebo.

GCT

Somerleyton Hall

5m north west of Lowestoft on the B1118, between the A143 and A12: The Lord Somerleyton, tel. 0502 730224. Open Easter–Sept Thur, Sun; July–Aug Tues, Wed, Thur, Sun and BH Mon 2–4.30. Refreshments.

Somerleyton is a grand Victorian mansion, in magnificent grounds, at the north-east corner of Suffolk. The site is an ancient one; old Somerleyton was rebuilt c 1610 by John Wentworth, passing to the Allin family, who changed their name to Anguish. This family died out in 1843, and the 4500 acre estate was bought by Sir Morton Peto, a most remarkable man and a prime example of the heroic Victorian engineer. He started work in his uncle's modest building business at the age of 14, inheriting a share in it at the age of 21, and built it up to become the largest contractor in Britain. Grissell & Peto built much of the Houses of Parliament, Nelson's Column, and railways in Britain, Denmark, Canada, Argentina and Russia. Sir Morton developed Lowestoft harbour and esplanade, and used the former to import the Caen stone for his rebuilding of the house. His architect was John Thomas, better known as a sculptor; it was a very thorough remodelling, and the visitor might never know that there was anything of an older house here. Work was finished in 1851, but in 1863 Sir Morton sold the Somerleyton estate to Sir Francis Crossley, and in 1866 he was dragged down in the great Overend and Gurney bank crash, with debts of over £4 million.

The new owner represented another strand of the Victorian entrepreneurial spirit. John Crossley, a Yorkshire weaver, worked his way up to be a mill-owner. His three sons, Joseph, John and Francis, succeeded him, building the world's largest carpet business and becoming the uncrowned kings of their native Halifax. Francis was a Nonconformist, and a radical Liberal MP; nonetheless he accepted a baronetcy in 1863, the same year he established himself as a country landowner by buying Somerleyton. His son, Sir Savile, became the 1st Lord Somerleyton, and the family have since devoted themselves to military and public service.

The house is approached by a long drive through the park. The visitors' entrance is through the kitchen garden and hot-houses, then across the broad lawns. Somerleyton has a massive, symmetrical main block, of red brick and stone, in an eclectic style mostly based on Jacobean architecture. The house is entered, rather unexpectedly, at the north-west corner. The Oak Parlour is the one main room to retain features of the earlier house, most notably its 17C panelling with the finely carved chimneypiece. There is a mixture of English and French furniture, and a Flemish tapestry on the south wall. Next is the Library. The area was originally Sir Morton Peto's Banqueting Hall, a grand two-storey room. In 1920, a ceiling was inserted to create more bedroom accommodation above; the woodwork is all of the later period. At the far end visitors cross the Vestibule in the middle of the garden front of the house, hung with more Flemish tapestry. Beyond this is the Dining Room, with Adamesque decoration also of the 1920s. The furniture is mostly Georgian, and the finest paintings hang here. Flanking the fireplace are a great pair by the mid-Victorian artist Clarkson Stanfield, depicting scenes from the Napoleonic wars. At one end of the room is a grand double portrait by Ferdinand Bol, a pupil of Rembrandt, believed to be of the great artist with his wife, Saskia; at the other end is a fine work by Wright of Derby. Through the Vestibule is the Staircase Hall, which retains its original Victorian decorative scheme; the windows have the coats of arms of the successive owners of the estate, and the walls are hung with portraits of the Crossley family. Beyond, the Entrance Hall also retains its rich original decoration, with elaborate dark panelling and a dome of coloured glass. There is white marble sculpture, but the room is dominated by two immense stuffed polar bears (both about 9ft high), trophies of an expedition to the Arctic by the 1st Lord in 1896.

Down a passageway is the Ballroom; the heavy white and gold plaster-work and crimson damask hangings are the original decorative scheme; originally the room looked into a huge Winter Garden, mostly dismantled in 1914. Here is the dolls' house, made by the estate carpenter in 1931 as a model of the house before its Victorian renovation. The Green Room Passage houses a fine Landseer, 'Stag, Hind and Calf', and leads to the former Billiard Room, which houses paintings of the house. From here visitors leave the house, through the loggia which once enclosed the Winter Garden and which now houses the tea room.

The gardens at Somerleyton are grand and very well maintained. There is a great formal parterre before the west front, and around this are groups of specimen trees, with rhododendrons and other flowering shrubs. A popular feature is the Maze, one of the largest in Britain, laid out in 1846 by W.A. Nesfield.

SB

Wingfield College

In Wingfield village, 7m east of Diss, off the B1118: Mr Ian Chance, tel. 0379 384505. Open Easter–Sept Sat, Sun, BH Mon 2–6. Refreshments.

Wingfield College is on the south side of the sprawling village of Wingfield, next to the great 14C church. From the road it looks like a provincial Georgian manor house, with a curiously low and wide façade. In fact, it is the surviving part of a College founded in 1362 by Sir John de Wingfield. He fought at the Battle of Poitiers in 1356, making a fortune out of ransom money. He died in 1361 and left the manor house at Wingfield for the establishment of a College. The Hall of the manor was retained, and adjoining this a quadrangle of timber-framed buildings went up. There was a Master and nine Secular Chaplains, and three choral scholarships for boys. These men were to live here, and say prayers for Sir John, the Black Prince and King Edward III; they were also to minister to the parish and run a boarding school.

Sir John's daughter and heiress married Michael de la Pole, a member of a very rich merchant family from Hull; he was shortly made the 1st Earl of Suffolk. The family suffered heavily in the Wars of the Roses, and the 5th and last Earl was beheaded by Henry VIII. The College was dissolved in 1542 and given to the Bishops of Norwich. A series of tenants lived here, and much of the building was demolished. In the later 18C a Squire Buck remodelled the remaining wings in a provincial Palladian style. The college's medieval origins were largely forgotten until the property was bought by the present owner in 1971. He has carried out a sympathetic restoration, revealing the 14C structure. Since 1981, a season of concerts, recitals, lectures and exhibitions has been held regularly.

What remains of the College is the west range of the quadrangle with the Great Hall. The façade to the road is broad with low proportions, and covered in white rendering. There is a five-bay centre with a broad pediment, and further bays on either side, including Venetian windows; many of the windows are in fact dummies. The Entrance Hall is a narrow passageway with Georgian joinery; to the right is the Green Panelled Room, with mid-Georgian panelling. The Library to the left is furnished in Regency style, with prints by Piranesi and Norwich School artists. The passageway running behind the west range is the original 14C cloister. To the left is the Press Room, where the timber-framing is visible. To the right, the Old Kitchen is now used as a tea room. Opening out of this is the Hall, dating from about 1300. It had been so much subdivided that its true identity was forgotten until the 1970s, when Mr Chance removed the floors and partitions, and restored it. The roof has one tremendous queen-post truss, with a cambered tie-beam. The upper floor of the west range originally consisted of large chambers with open roofs; it was subdivided and ceilings inserted in the 16C.

Outside, Mr Chance has planted a Topiary Garden in the area of the College quadrangle, and laid out gardens around the remaining Fish Pond. Immediately north of the College is the great 14C church with its fine tomb-monuments of Sir John de Wingfield and of the ill-fated de la Pole family. A little to the north, in the village, is Wingfield Castle, residence of the de la Poles. This is intact, and its very fine 15C façade is visible from the road, but it is not open to the public

GCT

SURREY

Albury Park

Off the A25 between Guildford and Dorking: Country Houses Association.
Open May–Sept Wed and Thur 2–4.30.

Albury stands in splendid grounds, on the south side of a small wooded valley; not much of the house is open, but the gardens, church and setting are themselves well worth seeing. The manor is of ancient origin; by the 16C there was a rambling timber-framed house here. In 1641 house and estate passed into the possession of Thomas Howard, 14th Earl of Arundel; he fled abroad from the Civil War, and Albury remained unoccupied until 1653, when it passed to Henry Howard, a grandson of the 14th Earl, who rebuilt the house to designs by a near-neighbour George Evelyn, who had travelled in Italy. George's brother John, the famous diarist and horticulturalist, designed a great garden layout in the Italian manner, covering a slope opposite the house. Henry Howard became the 6th Duke of Norfolk, and died in 1684, by which time most of this work was complete. Albury was sold to Sir Heneage Finch, who rebuilt it after a fire (1697). Later owners had alterations carried out by Sir John Soane, c 1800 and by Henry Hakewill, c 1815.

In 1819 Albury was bought by Henry Drummond, member of a banking family and co-founder (one of twelve 'Apostles') of the 'Catholic Apostolic Church', which believed in the urgent imminence of the Second Coming. He remodelled the house to designs by A.W.N. Pugin. He also carried out a good deal of building on the estate, and much of Albury village's picturesque appearance, with its red tiled roofs and tall Tudor-style chimneys, dates from this period. Drummond wanted to fulfil his obligations to the Anglican parishioners, even after his new sect broke away, so he built a new Anglican church in Albury village, as well as a magnificent Catholic Apostolic Church, which still survives.

On Drummond's death in 1860, the estate passed to his daughter, who married the heir to the Duke of Northumberland. Albury remained in the Northumberland family until 1965. The house and part of the garden was bought by the Country Houses Association, which converted it into 45 apartments for retired people, preserving the principal rooms. The rest of the estate, including the park and half the garden, still belongs to the Duke of Northumberland.

The house is as Pugin and Drummond left it, more Tudor than Gothic in style, of soft red brick, with battlements and picturesque chimneys; it is much quieter and more low-key than most of Pugin's work. On the left of the forecourt are magnificent 18C Baroque wrought-iron gates and railings, brought from a Hungarian convent. Only four rooms are open to visitors. The Entrance Hall is long and low, with simple Pugin decoration; the carved overmantel with military trophies is Scottish work of the 17C. The Staircase occupies a long oblong hall; it was designed by Soane, and has a simple wrought-iron balustrade. The large Library, looking north over the gardens, is of 17C shape, and its wide chimneypiece is of this period. A few fine pictures remain in the house, including full-length portraits of Charles I and Henrietta Maria, from Van Dyck's studio. Next door is the Drawing Room, with simple Regency decoration from the Soane period and long French windows leading into the garden. There is a fine marble chimneypiece, and portraits including a version of Lely's picture of the young Lady Elizabeth Percy.

The house stands on a terrace looking north over a little valley. When John Evelyn remodelled the gardens, the stream was widened into a canal a quarter of a mile long. The slope on the far side was made into vineyards, and above this Evelyn created a great pair of terraces, also a quarter of a mile long. The canal has now been reduced to a lushly overgrown stream, and the vineyards are orchards. Above, however, Evelyn's terraces remain intact. In the centre there is a summer house and steps, and above this a great semicircular recess or exedra, framing a pool. At the back of the recess an arch leads into a tunnel cut from the rock, going for over 200 yards through the hill. This layout was inspired by the ancient grotto of Posillipo, near Naples, close to the site of Virgil's tomb. The ancient lines of yews, the great terraces with their lawns a quarter-mile long, the exedra and tunnel, are all indescribably noble and serene, one of the earliest surviving masterpieces of English garden design.

The old parish church, next to the house, should not be missed. The nave is essentially Saxon and the tower is Norman, though both are much altered. The south transept was redecorated by Pugin for Henry Drummond c 1839 as a mausoleum for his family, and it retains the richly patterned walls and ceiling and glass added at this time. Near the end of the drive is Drummond's magnificent Catholic Apostolic Church, in the richest English Perpendicular style.

SB

Clandon Park

3m east of Guildford on the A247: National Trust, tel. 0483 222482. Open Apr–Oct daily except Thur and Fri 1.30–5.30, last admission 5. Refreshments.

Clandon has been the home of the Onslow family since 1641, when Sir Richard Onslow moved here from Shropshire. The Elizabethan house he bought was demolished by his great-grandson, the 2nd Baron Onslow, c 1729, and replaced with the present mansion. The Onslows were always a political family and three have been Speakers of the House of Commons; in 1801 they were made Earls of Onslow. The house was renovated and the porch added by the 4th Earl in the 1870s. The family sold the house and garden to Lady Iveagh, the 6th Earl's aunt, who gave Clandon to the National Trust in 1956; the 7th Earl and his family live in a house in the park.

Clandon is a massive rectangle, 140ft by 80ft, in perfect red brickwork, the roof quite hidden by a stone balustrade; the centre of the west front is faced in smooth white stone. The severe and restrained façades, with a high ratio of wall to window, are not quite English in character, and are the work of a Venetian architect, Giacomo Leoni, who first came to Britain in 1714, to produce an English edition of Palladio's *Four Books of Architecture* (cf. Lyme Park, Cheshire). The dating of the house is not clear, but the rainwater heads, dated 1733, suggest that it was largely complete by then. The design of the west (entrance) front has rather been compromised by the enormous porch added in the 1870s.

Through this, the visitor immediately enters the Marble Hall, a 40ft cube and one of the grandest of all English 18C interiors. In dramatic contrast to

The Palladian Marble Hall at Clandon Park, completed in the 1730s

the hot red brick of the façade, it is white, relieved only by the yellowish marbling of the lower columns. The walls are treated architecturally with two storeys of columns, with magnificent entablatures, and Classical surrounds or 'aedicules' in between, some housing doorways and openings, some blank. Much of the room's dramatic quality comes from the tension between the Palladian orderliness and straight lines of the wall-decoration, and the magnificent Baroque plasterwork by Artari and Bagutti on the ceiling, all curves, drapery, and angels dangling their legs over the cornice. The carved chimneypieces are by Rysbrack.

On the right, you cross the foot of the Oak Staircase and reach the Morning Room. Here you will see the first pieces of the important Gubbay

Collection of Georgian furniture, porcelain and decorative arts, left by Mrs David Gubbay to the Trust in 1968. Clandon, having lost most of its own contents, was the ideal setting. Here also you see the results of the comprehensive restoration and redecoration of 1968–70 by John Fowler, whose work for the Trust has greatly influenced the ways in which country houses are decorated and presented. The Palladio Room, on the south side of the house, has another splendid ceiling by Artari, and dramatic floral flock wallpaper of the 1780s; the portraits are by Dahl and Kneller.

The Hunting Room, a small room on the corner of the house, is named from its Soho tapestries and hunting scenes. It contains Chinese porcelain birds and English furniture. The Green Drawing Room is named for its dramatically vivid wallpaper, probably the original one of c 1735. The ceiling and chimneypiece are in a more sober Palladian mode, white and gold, with grand English and French furniture. The huge Rococo mirror is by Matthias Lock. This brings you to the Saloon, in the centre of the garden front. The elaborate colour scheme, with the black and white marble chimneypiece and three shades of blue on the walls, is startling. The State Bedroom, beyond, has a grand bed and chairs of c 1700, with its original hangings, in very good condition. Through the Library, with more 1730s plasterwork, the Speaker's Parlour is reached; it is in fact furnished as a dining room, and is hung with portraits of the three members of the Onslow family to serve as Speakers of the House of Commons.

Next the visitor ascends the Stone Staircase, with paintings of racehorses by Ferneley. On the bedroom floor, the Blue China Room has been adapted to show much of Mrs Gubbay's porcelain and pottery; the Bow porcelain figures, 18C Derby, and K'ang Hsi and Ch'ien Lung porcelain are especially good. Over the Saloon is the State Dining Room; the placing of this room on the first floor is unusual but not unique, but it was understandably inconvenient, even for the 18C, and by 1778 it was a billiard room, then subdivided. The National Trust restored the room in 1968. It has early Georgian furniture with original needlework. The Prince Regent's Room houses more fine furniture and oriental porcelain. From here the visitor descends the Oak Staircase to the Basement, which houses the Queen's Royal Surrey Regimental Museum, as well as the shop and restaurant.

SB

Claremont

South west of Esher on the Esher–Cobham Road (A307): The Claremont Fan Court Foundation, tel. 0372 467841. Open Feb–Nov on the 1st complete weekend in each month 2–5. Guided tours. Also Claremont Landscape Garden, off the A307: National Trust: tel. 0372 469421. Open daily Nov–Mar 9–5; Apr–Oct 9–7. Refreshments.

Claremont is best known for its garden, one of the finest to survive from the early 18C, but it is important to note that house and garden are now in separate ownership and are separately run. Since 1931, the great neo-classical mansion has housed an independent school. The interiors are well-preserved, but are furnished and used as schoolrooms.

The first house here was built by Sir John Vanbrugh for himself in 1708. In 1714 he sold the estate to his friend Thomas Pelham, Earl of Clare, later Duke of Newcastle, who named it Claremont. Newcastle, an immensely wealthy man, had Vanbrugh add huge wings to the existing house, and lay out magnificent formal grounds, which were to go through many stages of development. On the Duke's death in 1768 the estate was bought by Robert Clive, celebrated general of the East India Company's army and conqueror of Bengal, who had retired to England with a great fortune. He found Vanbrugh's mansion old-fashioned and damp, and replaced it with the present house. This was designed by Lancelot 'Capability' Brown, the great landscape gardener, and built with the help of his son-in-law, Henry Holland. The shell was complete by 1772. Clive spent over £100,000 on the house and grounds, but died in 1774, possibly by suicide, ill and depressed by the constant attacks of critics.

Claremont then passed through several owners, most notably Princess Charlotte, the daughter of George IV, and her husband Prince Leopold. The Princess died in childbirth in 1817; her husband went on to become King of Belgium, and owned the house until his death in 1865. His niece, Queen Victoria, often stayed here during her childhood, and from 1848 to 1871 it was the home of the exiled King Louis Philippe, his widow, and some of their numerous family. Queen Victoria bought the estate thereafter, and settled it on her youngest son, the Duke of Albany, whose widow lived here until the First World War. The house was finally sold in 1922, and since 1930 it has housed a school for the children of Christian Scientists.

Claremont stands on a high basement, on a high ridge, commanding tremendous views. It consists of a massive, square free-standing block, with the service areas fitted into the basement, linked to outbuildings by tunnels. The entrance front is nine bays wide, and has an august Corinthian portico, at the top of a flight of 22 steps. Due to the shortage of local stone, the house is built of light-coloured brick.

The Hall has Doric columns in purple scagliola and was designed by Holland with the assistance of the young John Soane, then working in his office. The guided tour proceeds around all the state rooms on the main floor, and then down into the remarkably high and light basement. Highlights are the Great Room, now the school library, the beautiful little tunnel-vaulted State Dressing Room, now the headmaster's study, and, in the basement, Clive's marble-lined cold plunge bath. The ceilings, early works by Holland, should be seen by anyone interested in neo-classical design, and there are magnificent chimneypieces, in particular that in the Great Room, for which Clive chose the theme of the 'Continence of Scipio'. The interiors are remarkably complete given the house's history and present use; even details like the original doorhandles mostly survive.

The house lost most of its grounds when the estate was sold, but in 1949 the National Trust acquired the 50 most important acres including the lake and amphitheatre, and has slowly restored many of the features by Vanbrugh, Kent, Bridgeman and others, which made this one of the greatest of English landscape gardens. However, the school grounds contain the most important surviving Vanbrugh building, the Belvedere, a battlemented lookout tower on top of a hill next to the house, seen also from the Bowling Green in the National Trust part of the grounds.

SB

Farnham Castle

Just north of Farnham town centre, on the A287. The Castle: the Church
Commissioners. Open all year Wed only 2–4. The Keep: English Heritage,
tel. 0252 713393. Open Easter–end Sept daily 10–6.

Farnham Castle looms over the market-town from its wooded hillside
immediately to the north. It was an episcopal fortress, built by the Bishops
of Winchester in an age when bishops had tremendous secular power. It is
architecturally a complicated group of buildings with many interesting
features, but apart from a number of episcopal portraits there are very few
historic contents. The great shell-keep, which is ruinous, is in the care of
English Heritage and is separately administered.

The Bishop of Winchester's estates stretched from Taunton to Southwark,
and Farnham was conveniently placed on the main road from London to
Winchester. The first castle was built by Henry of Blois, bishop 1129–71 and
younger brother of King Stephen. It would have been lined with wooden
palisades, with a stone tower on an artificial mound in the middle. In the
late 12C the mound was expanded on all sides, and a retaining wall built
around it and carried upwards, forming a shell-keep. In the later 12C,
residential buildings were added south of the Keep, around a triangular
courtyard, with a Great Hall and Chapel on the south side; the Kitchen and
the Bishop's Camera (great chamber) were probably added early in the
13C. In the 14C an outer circuit of walls was built on the line of the Norman
defences. In 1470–75, Bishop William Waynflete, energetic builder and
founder of Magdalen College, Oxford, added the brick tower on the south
side of the main range, to provide a grand new entrance and more living
accommodation;

The castle was in regular use as an episcopal residence throughout Tudor
times; for a while it was let to King James I for the hunting. In 1642 it was
stormed by Parliamentarian forces and in 1648 it was slighted; the residential buildings escaped relatively lightly, but the upper walls of the shell
keep were largely destroyed. After the Restoration Bishop Morley (1662–
84) carried out an ambitious programme of alterations, completely recon-
structing the Great Hall and modernising the rest of the residential
buildings. Bishops of Winchester continued to reside at Farnham until 1927,
when it was transferred to the new see of Guildford. Since 1955 the castle
has been leased to the Centre for International Briefing as a residential
training and conference centre.

The entrance is from the west. The west range is timber-framed and 16C;
to the south and east there are massive older buildings, of Norman origin
but much altered by Bishop Morley in the later 17C. On the north side is
the cliff-like face of the shell-keep. The Hall is a great rectangular room,
its present appearance mostly 17C, the fireplace, doorcases, galleries and
ceiling all being Bishop Morley's work. The original Norman Hall would
have been much lower, with aisles on either side, and a pitched roof in the
middle, supported on massive wooden pillars. Around the Hall are portraits
of Bishops of Winchester, most of them copies. The massive oak staircase,
at the far end of the Hall, is also of the 1670s. At the top is the Drawing
Room, now used as a lecture room. It was built as the Bishop's Camera in
the 12C but its present appearance dates from the mid 18C, when the
ceiling, fireplace and door were inserted. Next to this is the Bishop's Chapel,
another of Bishop Morley's creations, with fine carved pews and panelling,

with heavy carved garlands of fruit and flowers. Visitors return along the gallery which runs above the Great Hall. A series of corridors and stairs takes you down to the Norman Chapel, the least altered 12C building. The roof is a single barrel-vault of rubble-masonry. The Norman Kitchen is now the Centre's refectory; its shape, and the massive fireplace, seem to be original. The ruins of the keep are well worth seeing, in particular for the cavernous vault which was the base of the original Norman donjon, and for the fine views.

SB

Greathed Manor

South east of Lingfield on the B2028 (Edenbridge) road; turn off at the Plough Inn, Dormansland: Country Houses Association. Open May–Sept Wed and Thur 2–5.

Greathed Manor, formerly Ford Manor, is a rambling Victorian house in well-wooded countryside. Since 1958 it has been owned by the Country Houses Association, which has divided it into residential apartments. A few of the principal rooms and the garden are on view.

The manor of Ford was in existence by 1430, and passed through a great many hands, ending with Joseph Spender Clay, a wealthy banker from Burton-on-Trent. He commissioned Robert Kerr to design him a new house; Kerr had little architectural experience, and probably got the job on the strength of his influential book *The Gentleman's House*, published in 1864. The new house was finished by 1868; Kerr was simultaneously building a vast house for John Walter, owner of *The Times*, Bear Wood in Berkshire, and Ford, or Greathed, is like a smaller version of it. Kerr's design was angular and uncompromising, but with a certain power. Unfortunately, it did not appeal to Joseph Spender Clay's son, Herbert, who c 1913 had the house enlarged, greatly simplifying Kerr's design. The house's heyday ended with the Second World War; thereafter it was occupied by the London College of Divinity, and from 1958 leased by the Mutual House-holds Association, now the Country Houses Association. They renamed the house Greathed Manor, in honour of their founder, Rear-Admiral Bernard Greathed.

Greathed stands at the top of a slope looking over the Eden valley. It is a big, rambling house with many gables. The tower at the north-west corner with its decoration in different coloured stones is Kerr's, but the rest of his design has been greatly reduced in its impact by the Edwardian alterations. Inside, the plain Entrance Hall is Edwardian. It leads into the large, panelled Library-Hall; the staircase opens off this to the left. Straight ahead is the Drawing Room, with an elaborate Jacobean-style ceiling and panel-ling by Kerr, extended west in 1913. The best internal feature is the fine carved fireplace in the Dining Room, originally the Billiard Room; the rest of the decoration has been much watered-down and there are few contents of note. Outside, there is an attractive, very architectural oval garden designed by the architect Harold Peto, and there are pleasant lawns under the long south front.

SB

Hatchlands

North of the Leatherhead–Guildford road (A246) at East Clandon:
National Trust, tel. 0483 222787. Open Apr–early Oct Tues, Wed,
Thur, Sun and BH Mon, also Fri in Aug 2–5.30. Refreshments.

Hatchlands, a compact red-brick mansion in a park by Repton, has the
distinction of being the first house where Robert Adam is known to have
worked. The Hatchlands estate was bought c 1750 by Adm. Edward
Boscawen, one of the great naval commanders of the Seven Years War. The
old house (a little to the west of the present one) was demolished, and by
1754 Mrs Boscawen was considering plans for the new one. The Boscawens
seem to have commissioned a design from the Berkshire architect, Stiff
Leadbetter, and the building was 'ready for the roof' in 1757, when work
began on fitting out the interior. In the winter of 1758–59, Adm. and Mrs
Boscawen commissioned the 30-year-old Robert Adam, who had recently
returned from Italy, to produce designs, and the house was ready for
occupation in 1760. The Admiral, died the following year, aged 49, and Mrs
Boscawen sold the estate in 1770 to William Sumner, a director of the East
India Company. Joseph Bonomi made some fairly minor alterations for
Sumner's son c 1797.

In 1889 the house and estate were bought by Stuart Rendel MP, who in
1895 was created Lord Rendel. He made a number of additions, employing
his nephew-by-marriage, Halsey Ricardo, and also Reginald Blomfield, as
architects, and Gertrude Jekyll to lay out part of the garden. In 1913 he
bequeathed Hatchlands to his grandson, the architect Harry Goodhart-
Rendel and later became President of the Royal Institute of British Architects. He renovated Hatchlands in a careful and conservative way, and built
some fine new houses on the estate. He presented the house to the National
Trust in 1945, living there until his death in 1959. The house had few historic
contents, and so was let to a girls' school for many years. In 1988 a new and
more satisfying period in the house's history was ushered in by Alec Cobbe,
who has taken a lease on the house and introduced fine paintings and
furniture from his family's house in Ireland, along with an important
collection of early keyboard instruments.

Adm. and Mrs Boscawen built a neat block of hot red brick; it is ingeniously planned, some of it two and some three storeys in height. The main
fronts face south, east and west, and to the north there are lower, mostly
later buildings around two service courts. The façades are quite severe, but
all different, in a move away from the absolute regularity of Palladian
design. The house is entered from the west; this was the original entrance
front, until Lord Rendel constructed a new porch on the east side. The
Garden Hall was part of Bonomi's alterations of c 1800, the ceiling is
Adam's, the benches in the recesses by Bonomi. To the right is a square
Drawing Room, in the south-west corner of the house, originally the 'Lesser
Dining Room'. The frieze here is by Adam, but his ceiling collapsed and
was replaced in the mid 19C. The room has been furnished with late 18C
and Regency pieces by Mr Cobbe, and there are numerous fine 18C
portraits of his family. The silk pelmets were supplied by Ince and Mayhew
for Blenheim Palace c 1760.

The next room, the Saloon, was designed as the main Dining Room, and
Adam's splendid decoration survives complete. The ceiling is in a richer,
more fully moulded style, than his later designs, and has dolphins, sea-

horses and seashells in tribute to the owner. The fireplace is flanked by caryatids (cf. Harewood, West Yorkshire). The room has been hung with red silk, as a background for old master paintings, mostly of the Italian school of the 17C and 18C, including an altarpiece by Allori. The gilt console tables with eagle supports were acquired with the house, and may have belonged to the Boscawens. The Library has another richly decorated ceiling, based on one at the Villa Pamphili in Rome, with more references to the Admiral's naval career. The bookcases, of an appropriately neo-Classical design, were installed by Lord Rendel. The East Entrance Hall, and the Dining Room beyond it, were originally the Admiral's bedroom and dressing room, but were converted to their present shapes by Lord Rendel c 1890. Mr Cobbe is (1993) decorating the Dining Room walls with panels of arabesque painting based on 18C French designs.

The Staircase Hall is in the centre of the block. Much of the decorative plasterwork may already have been executed, perhaps to Leadbetter's designs, when Adam was called in, but the ceiling may well be by Adam. The very unusual chinoiserie-style balustrade of gilt metal seems to be original. The Music Room was added for Lord Rendel to designs by Reginald Blomfield in 1902–3, and the interior is in his favourite Queen Anne style. The result is, nonetheless, impressive with two columns at either end and a dome over.

Dispersed throughout the house is Mr Cobbe's collection of keyboard instruments, notably harpsichords and fortepianos of 1750–1840. There is a notable series of fortepianos by makers like Johann Andreas Stein, Conrad Graf and Sebastian Erard. There are also very important early harpsichords, in particular one by Girolamo Zenti, made in Florence in 1622, and one by Andreas Ruckers dated 1636, both in the Saloon. The collection is kept in working order, and recitals and other musical events are held here regularly during the open season.

SB

Loseley Park

3m south west of Guildford, off the B3000 between the A3 and A3100: Mr and Mrs James More-Molyneux and Michael More-Molyneux, tel. 0483 304440. Open early May–early Oct Wed–Sat 2–5. Refreshments.

The More and More-Molyneux families have lived at Loseley continuously since 1508. Sir Christopher More was an official in the Exchequer under Henry VII. He came from Derbyshire, but made his fortune at Court, and in that year he bought the manor of Loseley. His son, Sir William More, was a trusted adviser to Queen Elizabeth I, and held many high offices. He inherited in 1549, and built the present house between 1562 and 1568, using stone from the demolished Cistercian abbey of Waverley. He supervised the work, acting as his own Clerk of Works, and the house cost £1640 19s 7d. Queen Elizabeth came to stay four times.

Sir William was knighted in 1576, and died in 1600. His son, Sir George, was a member of parliament, Lieutenant of the Tower of London, and Treasurer to Henry, Prince of Wales. He added another wing to the house, with a picture gallery, a chapel and a riding school; this was all pulled down in 1820. The male line of the More family died out in 1689, the estate passing to Sir George's great-granddaughter Margaret More and her husband Sir

Thomas Molyneux. He was a member of a Lancastrian family, later Earls of Sefton (qv. Croxteth Hall), and subsequently the family were called More-Molyneux. In most generations they have held local offices, and many have given distinguished military service. The present owner inherited in 1946, and has developed the estate vigorously to ensure its survival.

The house has a big main block, facing north and south, with a lower service wing projecting to the south. The main (north) front is loosely symmetrical, with seven gables; the big windows in the middle light the Hall. It was a fairly traditional design, with the familiar pattern of the Great Hall in the middle, the family's rooms at one end and the kitchen at the other. On the other hand, the use of classical ornament in various places represented a concession to fashion. A screens passage leads into the Hall, which occupies the whole centre of the house. It has a flat ceiling (there are rooms above); the panelling with pilasters is said to have come from Nonsuch Palace, Henry VIII's enormous hunting lodge, demolished in the late 17C. The great group portrait on the far wall is of Sir More-Molyneux and his family; it was painted by Somers in 1739. The fine full-length portraits of James I and Anne of Denmark are by de Critz, and there are several other 16C and 17C portraits. Up in the gallery are a series of canvas panels painted with very delicate Renaissance ornament, once used as decorations for Henry VIII's banqueting-tents.

The visitor now sees the state rooms to the west of the Hall, starting with the Library, which is lined with elaborately-carved bookcases; Sir William More was one of the first non-clerical English gentlemen to collect books seriously. At the west end of the house is the Drawing Room. It has an elaborate ceiling with pendants, and a superb chimneypiece carved from chalk; the very elaborate overmantel panel is flanked by smiling caryatids and atlantes. The room has a variety of family portraits including one of the builder, Sir William More, with a skull for a memento mori. The dramatic sea-scene is by Van de Velde (1696).

The staircase is early 18C and is hung with numerous paintings of the life of Christ. A very fine 16C triptych by de Bles shows the adoration of the Shepherds and of the Magi, and there are modern religious paintings. On the first floor, the first bedroom to be seen is Sir More's Room, with a geometrical ceiling and large 18C bed. The King's Room (occupied by James I) has another geometrical ceiling, and is lined with verdure tapestries from Oudenarde. The unusual carpet has royal emblems, and the bed is mid-Georgian. Finally, Queen Elizabeth's Room, adjoining this, is hung with a Mortlake tapestry and an Antwerp tapestry; the overmantel carving shows the story of the Good Samaritan. The wooden curtain-pelmet, original to the room, shows a boar hunt. The bedcover is of very fine needlework, of the late 17C.

The house has fine gardens, in particular the border created along part of the old moat. The barn has been made from two old barns, and houses the restaurant and farm shop.

SB

Polesden Lacey

North of Dorking, reached from the A246 at Great Bookham: National
Trust, tel. 0372 458203. Open Mar and Nov Sat and Sun 1.30–4.30;
Apr–Oct Wed–Sun 1.30–5.30; BH mon and previous Sun 11–5. Last
admission ½ hour before closing. Refreshments.

Polesden Lacey is a mansion of the 1820s, set on high ground in beautiful
wooded countryside; however, its atmosphere and style are those of an
opulent Edwardian country house, the creation of Mrs Ronald Greville, an
eminent society hostess.

The first house here was built in 1632 by Anthony Rous, and from 1797
this was the home of the playwright Richard Brinsley Sheridan. After
Sheridan's death in 1816 it was demolished, and the present mansion, two
storeys high and faced in yellow roughcast, was built by Thomas Cubitt for
Joseph Bonsor between 1821 and 1824. In 1906 it was bought by Capt. the
Hon. Ronald Greville, who died in 1908. His wife, Margaret Helen Anderson Greville, was the daughter and heiress of a very wealthy Scots brewer,
William McEwen. Introduced into Edward VII's circle by her husband, she
became one of the principal society hostesses of Edwardian England,
entertaining on a lavish scale here and at her London house in Charles St.
Edward VII stayed here in 1909, and the Duke and Duchess of York, the
future George VI and Queen Elizabeth, spent part of their honeymoon here
in 1923. When Mrs Greville died in 1942 she left the house, its contents and
1000 acres to the National Trust.

The house is a large two-storeyed building arranged around a square
courtyard. It has a simple but symmetrical exterior, clad in honey-coloured
rendering, by Mèwes & Davis, the architects of the Ritz, for Capt. and Mrs
Greville. Most of the interior, too, dates from their time, and is a good
illustration of grand Edwardian life and taste. Mrs Greville inherited a small
collection of pictures of the Dutch school from her father. To this she added
16C Flemish and Italian pictures, and a small group of English portraits,
French furniture, continental and oriental porcelain. It is not the collection
of an art lover; rather, Mrs Greville was buying the necessary furnishings
for a grand society house.

The double-height Hall is dominated by the elaborate panelling taken
from a Wren City church, St Matthew, Friday St, which had been demolished in the 1880s. There are Flemish and English tapestries of the 16C–
18C, and fine Chinese porcelain. The showcase on the stairs contains some
good 16C Italian maiolica. The Dining Room on the right houses Mrs
Greville's English portraits, including four by Raeburn and a fine Lawrence
double portrait. The furniture includes both English and French pieces of
the late 18C. The Corridor, running around the central courtyard, has a
'Jacobean' plaster ceiling and dark panelling. Most of the paintings are
hung here. Mrs Greville's taste was somewhat hit and miss, but there are
some fine pictures, such as the little panel portraits by Corneille de Lyon
and Matsys. The Library is decorated in a neo-classic style, with some good
early 18C English furniture and fine Italian bronzes of the 16C and 17C. In
the Study, the main feature is the collection of Furstenberg and Meissen
china, housed in large cupboards and display cases.

Back down the Corridor is the Drawing Room. It is long and sumptuously
decorated in white, gold and crimson. The panelling, installed by Mrs
Greville, is thought to be early 18C Italian. The room is certainly dazzling,

though some visitors may be reminded more of Las Vegas than Italy. There is 18C French furniture, particularly esteemed by the Edwardian upper classes, Louis XV commodes and bureaux, and settees in the neo-classical Louis XVI style. The showcases house porcelain; there are biscuit and *famille verte* figures of the K'ang Hsi period, and rare figurines from the Derby, Meissen and Nymphenburg factories.

The Tea Room is lined with Louis XVI-style panelling, with 18C paintings of pastoral scenes set into it. The furniture here is Louis XV and Louis XVI again. Back at this end of the corridor there are some of the best pictures, notably a portrait by Bernardo Strozzi, a sea scene by Jacob van Ruisdael, Terborch's 'Dancing Couple', and a Madonna and Child by Bernard van Orley. On the west side of the house are the Billiard Room and Smoking Room, the only rooms not redecorated by Mrs Greville, with memorabilia of the weekend parties with which she regularly filled the house.

The house has a magnificent site, facing south over a deep wooded valley, and the gardens, excellently maintained by the National Trust, are at least as well worth seeing as the house; there are enclosed gardens devoted to roses, peonies, irises and lavender, and wide lawns with great views. Mrs Greville left over 1000 acres to the Trust, and there are many walks to the woods on Ranmore Common over the valley.

SB

EAST SUSSEX

Bateman's

½m south of Burwash on the A265: National Trust, tel. 0435 882302.
Open Apr–Oct daily except Thur and Fri 11–5, last admission 4.30.
Refreshments.

Bateman's is a handsome small manor house, built in 1634 by an unknown Wealden iron-master. Its fame derives from the fact that in 1902 it was bought by Rudyard Kipling, who lived here until his death in 1936, and wrote some of his greatest works here. It was built on the traditional E-plan, in the local yellow-brown ironstone, with mullioned windows with drip-moulds above. As the Sussex iron industry declined in the 18C, the house sank in status, and by the time Kipling found it, it had lost one of the side-wings, or bars of the E.He installed his own electric generator worked by a turbine, carried out conservative repairs to the house, and laid out the garden. Here he wrote *Traffics and Discoveries* and *Puck of Pook's Hill*, and the poems *If* and *The Glory of the Garden*, as well as his memoirs, *Something of Myself*. He died in 1936, and his widow Caroline in 1939, bequeathing the house to the National Trust.

Apart from the loss of the right-hand wing, and the addition of the oast-houses in 1770, the exterior of the house remains largely as built. On the left of the archway in the porch are the initials of Kipling and his family, cut into the stone. The main rooms remain largely as they were furnished by Kipling. The Hall has simple panelling; the Kiplings bought 17C and 18C furniture for the house. The watercolours are by Sir Edward Poynter, Kipling's uncle. On the right is the Dining Room; the Kiplings bought the painted Cordoba leather which covers the walls. On the left at the foot of the stairs is the Parlour, with a 17C Flemish tapestry, and more good furniture. Upstairs is Kipling's Study, exactly as he left it. It is lined with books on two sides; the Indian rugs were woven to his order. The portrait over the fireplace of Mrs Kipling is by Sir Philip Burne-Jones, the writer's cousin. Kipling's desk looks out through the window. His huge waste-paper basket, the pewter ink-pot on which he carved the names of his books, and other accoutrements of his literary career, are here. In the exhibition room next door are some of the sculpted plaques by the author's father, John Lockwood Kipling, illustrating *Kim*, and various of the short stories.

Kipling and his wife laid out the garden, planting the yew hedges in the formal area, and the flowering shrubs and trees in the natural garden. Close by is the mill-pond, and Park Mill. This dates from about 1750, and is a white weatherboarded, traditional building. Restored to full working order in the 1960s, it still houses much of the 18C mill machinery, as well as Kipling's turbine and generator.

SB

Bentley House

7m north east of Lewes, off the A26 and A22: Bentley House, Wildfowl and Motor Museum, tel. 0825 840573. Open mid Mar–Oct 10.30–4.30 (July & Aug 10.30–5). House opens at 12 noon daily. Refreshments.

Bentley is a new country house, although formed around the nucleus of a

Tudor farmhouse. It was created by Gerald and Mary Askew, who bought Bentley in 1937 and ran it as a farm and stud. The original brick farmhouse had been rather unsympathetically altered, and they commissioned Raymond Erith, an architect who worked in the Georgian style and in traditional materials, to remodel it. After the war, Erith proposed that a large reception room be added at either end, and these went up in the 1960s. At the same time, the Askews developed an important wildfowl sanctuary in the grounds, and laid out the gardens. Gerald Askew died in 1970, and in 1978 his widow gave the house, the wildfowl sanctuary and the nucleus of the estate to East Sussex County Council, for the enjoyment of the public.

The house is a long low range of orange brick with a hipped tile roof. The centre is the original house, of two storeys plus an attic, and to either side of this are the big rooms added by Erith, lit by Venetian windows. The Bird Room has Palladian proportions, with a high coved ceiling and Palladian-style fittings, and a fine marble floor. The room is lined with a series of paintings of wildfowl by the artist Philip Rickman, commissioned by Mr Askew. The Dining Room, in the old house, has decorative painted furniture, including a fine painted screen. The Hall is another intimate room, with English antique furniture. The Sitting Room has a corner fireplace, and a wave-topped bookcase designed by Erith. Next is an oval anteroom, leading into the Chinese Drawing Room. This is identical in shape to the Bird Room, with another high coved ceiling and green mid 18C Chinese wallpaper. There are Louis XV chairs, English Rococo wall-sconces, and elaborate gilt side-tables, the whole being a grand 20C evocation of a mid Georgian interior.

The gardens, behind the house, are in the 'Sissinghurst' style, divided into compartments by hedges, with a mixture of formal and informal planting. Beyond is the large wildfowl reserve, supporting almost 100 species. The farmyard also houses a motor museum with cars ranging from early veteran vehicles to modern sports cars.

SB

Brickwall House

On the south side of Northiam village, at the junction of the A28 and the B2088, entrance from the B2088: The Frewen Educational Trust, tel. 0797 252494/223329. Open Apr–Sept Sat, BH Mon, 2–5.

The first sight of Brickwall belies its name, for the handsome, symmetrical entrance front looking down the straight driveway is entirely timber-framed, with three big equal-sized gables. There has been a substantial house here at least since the 15C. The White family rebuilt it early in the 17C; the left-hand gable is dated 1617, the central one 1633. In 1666 the house and estate were bought by a rich London furrier, Stephen Frewen, Alderman and at one time Master of the Skinners Company. His father, 'Puritan John' Frewen, came to Northiam as its Rector. Puritan John had 11 sons, of whom one, Accepted Frewen, became Archbishop of York, Thankful became Keeper of the Seal, and John succeeded as Rector of Northiam. Alderman Stephen's descendants owned Brickwall until 1974. His grandson, Sir Edward, modernised the house in the 1680s. He rebuilt the side-façades in brickwork, built a new staircase, and built the Drawing Room in the courtyard between the wings on the garden side, with the magnificent plaster ceilings which are the house's chief glory. Around 1832 Sydney Smirke carried out further alterations, building the stables and the splendid gatepiers for Thomas Frewen Turner. Later in the 19C a picturesque gabled wing was added to the garden front, apparently by George Devey. Admiral Sir John Frewen gave the house to an educational trust in 1974, and it has since housed a school for dyslexic boys. It retains a fine collection of family portraits and other pictures.

The house makes a powerful impact from the road, the black and white façade framed between Smirke's elaborate gatepiers. The bay windows are 19C replacements, but the close-studded timbering is Jacobean. The Entrance Hall is lined with panelling of the late 17C; at either end are big 'sea pieces' of the two great naval victories of 1 June 1794, while on the far wall are portraits of 'Puritan John' and Alderman Stephen. Ahead is the Drawing Room, added in the mid 1680s by Sir Edward Frewen. Larger in scale than the Jacobean rooms, it is the grandest kind of post-Restoration period state room, with fine panelling and a superbly elaborate ceiling. It is lined with family portraits, mostly of the 17C and 18C, including works by Lely, Kneller and Verelst. The main staircase, to the right of the Hall, is also late 17C, with an octagonal dome over it, and more remarkable plasterwork, the garlands and fruit being fully modelled. The portraits here include a remarkable likeness of Henry VIII with Prince Edward. Outside there is a pleasant arboretum, and formal walled gardens extending to the south of the house, also laid out in the 1680s. The topiary work has recently been added to, with a remarkable 'chess garden', the different sides represented by dark green and golden yew.

SB

Charleston

6m east of Lewes, off the A27: The Charleston Trust, tel. 0323 811626.
Open Apr–Oct Wed–Sun and BH Mon 2–6 (mid July–early Sept 11–6),
last admission 5.

Charleston is a shrine to the Bloomsbury Group, if the word 'shrine' can be used of this demure 18C farmhouse. In 1916 the artist Vanessa Bell, her fellow-artist and sometime lover Duncan Grant, and the writer David Garnett came to live here and do farm-work (the men being conscientious objectors). The house had been found by Leonard and Virginia Woolf, who had left London to live in Asheham, a few miles away (they later moved to Monks House at Rodmell, now a property of the National Trust). Virginia Woolf wrote to Vanessa Bell—her sister—saying, 'if you lived here you could make it absolutely divine'. Conditions were primitive, with basic plumbing and no gas or electricity. The three, however, gradually filled the house with their murals and paintings and painted furniture, giving it a unique ambience which remains perfectly preserved. They also filled it with guests; John Maynard Keynes, T.S. Eliot, E.M. Forster, Desmond MacCarthy, the Woolfs, Lytton Strachey and Roger Fry were close friends and regular visitors. In 1939 Vanessa's husband, the writer Clive Bell moved in, bringing more furniture, books and paintings. Vanessa and Clive Bell, Duncan Grant, and their children made Charleston their home until their respective deaths; the era came to an end with Duncan Grant's death in 1978, aged 93. Since then the house has been vested in a charitable trust and opened to the public.

Charleston is a medium-sized farmhouse and most of its rooms are quite small; visitors see almost the whole of the house, but numbers are sometimes restricted. Although the contents were accumulated over half a century by several people, it has a strong and very homogeneous character. Most of the rooms have painted decoration by Duncan Grant and Vanessa Bell, in strong colours now a little faded, often of witty and allusive subjects; flowers, clowns, nudes and animals abound. Charleston is crammed with works of art, with paintings and lithographs by Grant, Bell, Derain, Picasso, Roger Fry, Walter Sickert, Keith Baynes and Nina Hamnett, amongst others. Bell and Grant were also very fond of decorating ordinary furniture, in the same kind of bright, breezily drawn style as their murals. There are many pieces of their painted furniture, as well as much good English antique furniture, most of it inherited.

The Dining Room has strong stencilled patterns on the walls, done in the 1940s. The fireplace was decorated by Duncan Grant, and the circular table by Vanessa Bell; the chairs were designed by Roger Fry and made in his Omega Workshop. On the first floor is the Library. This was Vanessa Bell's bedroom until 1939; Duncan Grant decorated the window for her, with a dog to protect her and a cockerel to wake her up. Clive Bell's bedroom has painted furniture, and many small paintings. The next room is known as Maynard Keynes Bedroom; it was here that the great economist began writing 'The Economic Consequences of the Peace'. Duncan Grant's Bedroom, and the little Dressing Room opening out of it, were decorated early on. The patterned window-opening, hearth and firescreen are by Vanessa, the curtain-fabric and carpet were designed by Duncan Grant. The Spare Bedroom has decoration in lavender and salmon pink, by Vanessa.

The tour now returns to the Ground Floor; the Garden Room, the main sitting room, was a setting for entertainment, talk and argument, and some of the most important pictures hang here, including Vanessa Bell's self portrait (c 1958). Along a passageway is Vanessa Bell's Bedroom, again with many smaller paintings, and then the big Studio. This was added in the summer of 1925 and was Duncan Grant's main place of work. The mural decoration was carried out gradually, and is dominated by the magnificent fire-surround, with its buxom caryatids. There is an array of ceramics and objets d'art of all cultures and kinds. The cottage-style gardens are beautifully maintained, and house sculptures by Duncan Grant and Quentin Bell.

SB

Firle Place

5m south east of Lewes off the Lewes–Eastbourne road (A22): The Viscount Gage, tel. 0273 858335. Open Jun–Sept Wed, Thur and Sun 2–5, also Easter, May, Spring and Summer BH Sun and Mon 2–5. Refreshments.

Firle Place stands in an ancient park at the foot of the South Downs, and has been the home of the Gage family continuously since 1472; its contents vie with those of almost any house in England. The Gages were a Gloucestershire family, but in 1472 William Gage married Agnes Bolney, heiress to West Firle. His son, Sir John Gage, built a house here, making it his principal home. He held a great number of high offices in succession, including those of Constable of the Tower and Comptroller of the Household, and Henry VIII made him an executor of his will. He died at Firle in 1556, and he and his wife are buried in Firle church, where their monuments (by the Flemish sculptor Gerrit Janssen) may still be seen.

From the reign of Elizabeth, the family were recusant Catholics, and they did not make any major alterations to the house. John Gage bought a baronetcy from James I, but on the death of the 7th baronet in 1744 the title became extinct, and the estates passed to his cousin, Thomas Gage. He was a sober figure, who embraced Protestantism and had been rewarded with an Irish Viscountcy in 1720. He married a Gloucestershire heiress, and could thus afford to remodel Firle, in a rather piecemeal way, c 1744–54. The 2nd Viscount married the daughter of a Jewish banker, Sampson Gideon, and in 1780 he became a Baron in the peerage of the United Kingdom. His younger brother, General Thomas Gage, was Governor of Massachusetts and Commander-in-Chief in North America on the outbreak of the American Revolution, and was defeated at the Battle of Bunker Hill. The 6th Viscount married Imogen Grenfell, daughter of Lord Desborough, who inherited important paintings from her mother, formerly in the collection of the Earls Cowper, of Panshanger near Hertford (now demolished). The 7th Viscount Gage is the present owner of Firle.

Firle is a large, informal-looking house, which preserves the approximate shape of Sir John Gage's Tudor building. The main rooms are around a square outer courtyard; at the back (west) of this is the Hall. Behind is a smaller inner courtyard, with kitchens and family rooms around it. Beyond this there are two more office wings; the whole house is about 350ft long. A lot of Tudor masonry is visible, but the façades were comprehensively remodelled in the 18C for the 1st Viscount. Little is known about this work, and indeed the façades, with their hipped roofs and tall sash windows, were old-fashioned for the 1740s, which has led to speculation that some of the remodelling had in fact been carried out earlier. The grandest feature is the **east front**, which is a re-building of the gatehouse range; its broad, rather Baroque proportions are reminiscent of the work of James Gibbs. The visitor goes under the arch into the outer courtyard, which is all Tudor in origin, reclad or remodelled in the 18C.

Ahead is the **Hall**. This is a Tudor room, turned into a light and cool Georgian entrance hall; the hammerbeam roof remains intact above the plaster ceiling. There is Georgian furniture, and 17C Beauvais tapestries, and the first of the house's superb portraits. At the south end is Van Dyck's enormous group portrait of John, Count of Nassau with his family, one of the pictures inherited by the 6th Viscountess Gage. The **Staircase Hall** has grand Palladian decoration, the staircase having a closed string and square newel posts. One Tudor doorcase has been left exposed, to testify to the house's origin. The **Drawing Room**, to the east, was planned as a dining room, with pairs of pillars dividing it into three sections. The joinery and furniture are all mid-Georgian, and the room is lined with full-length portraits, including works by Reynolds and Gainsborough. The **Library** at the far end has a fine Rococo ceiling.

Visitors return to the Staircase Hall. The portraits are of Lady Penelope Darcy and her three husbands, including the first Gage baronet. The full-length portrait shows the Tudor Sir John, in Garter robes. The **Upstairs Drawing Room** has Louis XV-style decoration of the 1890s, and houses more paintings from the Panshanger collection. The 2nd Earl Cowper collected Dutch School pictures in the mid 18C; his son the 3rd Earl lived in Florence for 30 years, and was a famous collector of Italian art. The Holy

Family by Fra Bartolommeo, a head of Christ by Correggio, and portraits by Rubens, Moroni, Puligo and others were his, and are set off by the 18C French furniture. The little Ante-Room is furnished in the style of the 1840s with its bordered wallpaper, and display of blue and white china hung on the wall.

This leads into the **Gallery**, running the length of the east wing and entirely of the 18C. It is a magnificent room, and has much of the finest furniture and some excellent paintings. They include delightful paintings of children and the Melbourne family by Reynolds, fine Dutch and Flemish pictures by Teniers, Koninck and van Goyen, and a remarkable pair of portraits, of the 3rd Earl and Countess Cowper, painted in Florence by Johann Zoffany (1772). There are 18C French commodes, cupboards and tables, and Sèvres porcelain in the display cabinets. Going along a corridor, two bedrooms furnished with Regency and Victorian pieces are sometimes on view. The tour ends in the Billiard Room, in the middle of the north front, which has more portraits and landscape paintings.

The balustrades and **terraces** to the north of the house, laid out with rose-beds, were added late in the 19C. To the south of the house, wooded slopes rise to Firle Beacon. A short distance to the west is the village, where Firle church has Gage family monuments, and a fine stained-glass window designed by the late John Piper.

SB

Glynde Place

4m south east of Lewes, signposted off the A27 and the B2192: Viscount Hampden: tel. 0273 858337. Open Jun–Sept Wed, Thur and last Sun of each month 2.15–5. Refreshments.

Glynde is a handsome Elizabethan courtyard-house, of knapped flint and Caen stone. For over 800 years the Manor of Glynde (the next village up the valley is Glyndebourne), has passed by descent through four families, the Waleys, the Morleys, the Trevors and the Brands. William Morley (1531–1632) built Glynde Place c 1579. His grandson, Harbert Morley, was the leading figure in the Parliamentary cause in Sussex. He married Mary Trevor, a member of a North Wales family, who were linked by marriage to John 'Patriot' Hampden, the Parliamentarian leader. On the death of their son William Morley in 1679, the estate passed to the Trevors. They were a shrewd family, heavily involved in politics, and in 1712 they became Lords Trevor. The 4th Lord was Minister to the Hague, and became 1st Viscount Hampden. With the death of his younger son, the 3rd Viscount in 1824, this line died out and Glynde passed to a distant cousin, Henry Otway Brand, the 20th Baron Dacre. His younger son, Henry Bouverie Brand, was Speaker of the House of Commons and received a Viscountcy, reviving the title of Hampden. From him, Glynde has passed by descent to his great-great-grandson, the 6th Viscount, who lives here now.

The house is quadrangular, and from the outside it remains largely as it was when new. William Morley built the house to face west, ie, facing the main road, and his main entrance is clearly visible. In the mid 18C, the house was turned around, so that the front door was on the east side. The fine gatepiers, bearing the Trevor wyverns, and the flint and brick stable-block are both of this period. The east front is symmetrical; the main alteration has been the substitution of the shaped Dutch gables (in brick) for the original straight-sided gables. The porch in the middle leads to the long, white Entrance Hall, redecorated in the 18C. The pictures include an impressive family group of Sir John Trevor (1596–1673) by Cornelis de Vos. The fine bronze reliefs over the fireplaces showing Old Testament scenes are Italian of the 1760s, by Francesco Bertos. North of the Hall is the Library, created by the present Viscount Hampden in 1980; the wallpaper depicts the family crest, and a rare contemporary description of the defeat of the Armada is among the books on view. In the Hall between the Library and the Drawing Room are portraits of the Brand family, mostly that of Speaker Brand in his robes. The Drawing Room has fine furniture, including a 17C Florentine cabinet, and 18C paintings.

The impressive staircase is one of a number of late 17C alterations paid for by Elizabeth Clarke, an heiress who married the last Morley owner and then the first Trevor owner of the house. Numerous paintings, mostly copies from old masters like Titian, are set into the dark panelling: an unusual form of decoration. The landing looks over the inner courtyard; the painted glass medallions in the window are Flemish. There is early 18C needlework and early Derby china on display. The Gallery, next, is the largest room in the house, running over half the length of the east front. It is Elizabethan in origin, but was grandly redecorated in the Restoration period too, and altered again c 1760. It now has fine bolection-moulded panelling, a coved ceiling and elaborate carving on the doorcases and overmantel. The room is surrounded by 17C and 18C portraits by artists including Kneller, Cornelius Johnson, John Singleton Copley and Lely. The broad mid 18C armchairs covered in crewel- work are called Mendlesham chairs, and over the fireplace is the third of the bronze reliefs by Francesco Bertos.

The Dining Room was also redecorated in the late 17C and has furniture of the same period; the room is hung with Flemish still-life paintings showing an abundance of foodstuffs, two by Frans Snyders, two by Jan Fris and one by Jan Weenix. The visitor descends the Elizabethan oak staircase to the Bottom Hall, with a large portrait of the 22nd Baron Dacre. The house is surrounded by picturesquely planted gardens. The estate is well-wooded, but suffered heavily in the 1987 storms; re-planting and renovation are in hand.

SB

Great Dixter

Just north of Northiam, about 10m north of Hastings, off the A28: Mr Quentin Lloyd, tel. 0797 253160. Open Apr–mid Oct daily except Mon 2–5. The gardens open at 11 on Sun in July and Aug. Refreshments.

Great Dixter is a moderately-sized 15C timber-framed manor house set in one of the most beautiful gardens in England. The manor of Dixter existed in the 13C, but the core of the present house—the hall, solar wing and porch—was built by the Etchingham family c 1464. This, like so many others like it, was in a sorry state by this century. It was saved by Nathaniel Lloyd, who bought it in 1910, and for whom Sir Edwin Lutyens carried out a deeply sympathetic renovation and enlargement, 1910–14. The estate is managed by Quentin Lloyd and the gardens by Christopher Lloyd, sons of Nathaniel Lloyd.

By the time Mr Lloyd bought the house it had lost its former Kitchen wing, and he needed rather more accommodation. He and Lutyens found a derelict 'Wealden House' at nearby Benenden, which was due to be demolished. Mr Lloyd bought it, had the timbers numbered and brought to Great Dixter, and it was re-erected at the back, with a new tile-hung wing linking it to the old house. Lutyens deployed his great compositional skill to produce a deeply satisfying house from these three elements. The 15C house has a close-studded frame, the woodwork very well preserved. In the middle is the big porch, with unglazed openings at ground floor level, and a projecting upper storey. To the right is the Great Hall, with its tall bay window, and at the right-hand end, the Solar Wing, with old windows and curly barge-boards. To the left of this is Lutyens' russet-coloured tile-hung extension, blending in gently.

The Hall is large and very well preserved. The massive oak frame and the great crown post roof are fully visible, and have fine original carved decoration. The roof has great carved shields, two with the diamond-pattern of the Etchingham family. As built there would have been a central hearth rather than a chimney, so Lutyens added the fireplace at one end. There are a number of small portraits, and a Dutch tapestry of a forest scene over the fireplace, and a variety of good 16C to 18C furniture collected by the Lloyd family. The great refectory table at the dais end is Jacobean; the other long table was made by Mr Lloyd and his son Patrick in 1932. Opening off the dais end of the Hall, the Parlour has a long mullioned window and a closely beamed ceiling; on one of the beams is an Elizabethan inscription. The fireplace again was created by Lutyens; there is 18C furniture. Back through the Hall, you ascend the stairs, added by Lutyens, to the Solar. This has a high open roof, supported by crown posts. The carved stone fireplace is original, the oriel windows are careful restorations. A little window enabled the lord of the manor or his family to view what was going on in the Hall. There is some fine Georgian furniture, including a rare draughtsman's table and a wing spinet (1688).

The garden, laid out by Lutyens and the Lloyd family, is divided into a number of little gardens or compartments by great yew hedges and by several timber-framed outbuildings with red-tile roofs. It is notable for its wide variety of unusual plants.

SB

Michelham Priory

10m north of Eastbourne, near Upper Dicker, signposted off the A22: The Sussex Archaeological Society, tel. 0323 844224. Open late Mar–Oct daily 11–5.30; Nov, Feb and Mar Sun only 11–4. Refreshments.

Michelham Priory, a picturesque house of many periods, was created out of the remains of an Augustinian house founded in 1229; it is today run as a museum. The Priory of the Holy Trinity was founded by Gilbert d'Aquila, with canons from Hastings. A cruciform, aisleless church was built (of which only foundations survive), with a cloister to the south, the Chapter House on the east side of the cloister, the Refectory and Kitchen to the south, and cellars with dormitories over them, on the west side. In 1388 Prior Leem had a moat dug, surrounding the Priory and its immediate grounds, to protect it from the threatened French raids, building the gatehouse at the same time.

The Priory was dissolved in March 1537 without resistance. The church and the east cloister range were immediately demolished for their materials, and in 1556 the Priory was bought by John Foote, who adapted the south and west cloister ranges as a house. In 1587 the Priory was bought by a richer gentleman, Herbert Pelham, an ironfounder and landowner, and he replaced Foote's alterations with a new stone wing. Pelham overreached himself financially, and was obliged to sell in 1599, to Thomas Sackville, later 1st Earl of Dorset (qv. Knole). The Sackvilles owned the freehold for three centuries, letting Michelham to a succession of tenant farmers. Barns and farm buildings went up around the house, and in the late 19C a corn-mill was built. The house itself sank into a state of picturesque decay but in 1896 it was bought by James Eglington Gwynne, who began restoration of the medieval buildings. Walter Godfrey, a well-known conservationist architect, carried out further restoration after 1924, and in 1959 the house was given to the Sussex Archaeological Society. The Society has since carried out more repairs and restored the mill to working order.

The bridge and the fine Gatehouse were built c 1388–90; the Gatehouse is over 60ft high, faced with greensand stone. The church and cloister stood directly to the north of the present house; the lines of the walls are marked out in the grass. The long range of the house represents the south side of the medieval cloister, plus the taller building added at the west end by Herbert Pelham. The short wing projecting to the north is of 13C masonry, and contains a vaulted Undercroft, with the Prior's Chamber over. The Undercroft has a fine tripartite vault supported by a central pillar. The Slype (a vaulted passageway, part of the 13C building) leads into the Hallway, part of Herbert Pelham's additions of the 1590s. To the left are the Kitchen and Picture Gallery. Originally this area was the Priory's Refectory, and would have had an open timber roof; the shape of its big windows is still visible from the south. Herbert Pelham inserted floors, walls, chimneys and new windows, creating the Kitchen, which is now furnished with 18C pieces. Returning to the Hallway, two reception rooms in Pelham's new wing contain panelling is of the 1920s, the original work having been destroyed by fire; the furniture is English of the 17C and 18C. In the first room are two large 17C Flemish tapestry cartoons of mythological subjects.

On the first floor, the Michelham Priory Room has displays illustrating the history of the place; the walls here are left exposed, showing some of the house's complex building history. The Child's Room is furnished as an 18C children's bedroom. The Music Room, on the first floor of Pelham's wing, houses an interesting collection of historic musical instruments. Over the Undercroft is the Prior's Chamber, a 13C room. The hooded fireplace is medieval, the beamed ceiling was restored c 1896–97 by Mr Gwynne. The room has 17C Brussels tapestries and old oak furniture.

Within the moat and a short distance from the house is the Great Barn, a great ten-bay oak-framed structure, built around 1600. A group of low 19C farm-buildings forms a little yard next to the barn; in the yard is a collection of Suffolk farm carts and wagons. There is also a Forge and Wheelwright's Shop fitted out with 19C and early 20C equipment. The Rope Museum illustrates the history of this local industry, with more historic machinery.

SB

Preston Manor

Just off the A23 London–Brighton road, in Preston Park, 1m north of town centre: Brighton Borough Council, tel. 0273 603005. Open all year Tues–Sat 10–5, Mon 1–5, Sun 2–5, closed Good Fri, Christmas, Boxing Day.

Preston Manor is of medieval origin, long pre-dating the development of Brighton. The town, though, has grown up around it, and today the house stands at one end of a fine municipal park (formerly its grounds), surrounded by pleasant suburbs. Elements of the 13C and 16C house remain in the basement, but the present house is largely of the 18C, as remodelled in 1738 by the then owner, Thomas Western. He left it with a rectangular main block five bays wide, of two storeys over a basement, with lower wings to either side each containing one big reception room. The Western family left the house for Rivenhall in Essex in 1771, and in 1794 it was sold to William Stanford of Horsham. In 1867 his grand-daughter and heiress married Vere Fane Benett (d 1894), of Pythouse in Wiltshire (qv.), and they had one son, John Benett-Stanford. She had a lavish lifestyle, and building-leases on the Preston Estate were sold to finance it, enabling Brighton and Hove to grow apace. She did not get on well with her son, who lived at Pythouse, and in 1897 she was re-married, to Charles Thomas, a member of a rich shipping family and an associate of Cecil Rhodes. In 1905 they settled at Preston, refurbishing the house, which enjoyed an Edwardian 'belle epoque'. Charles Thomas served as Mayor of Brighton in 1910–13, and the house was the scene of lavish entertainment. When they died in 1932 it was left to Brighton Corporation, which had already purchased a large area of the estate around to form Preston Park.

Preston is an informal-looking house, the walls covered with grey rendering, the windows altered early this century. Unfortunately, the walls, lodge and stables which formerly stood between the house and the main roads have all been demolished, leaving it looking somewhat exposed. The house is shown as it was in its Edwardian heyday under Ellen and Charles Thomas-Stanford. It is furnished with a great variety of furniture and pictures, representing the lavish, eclectic taste of the period. The Hall remains as remodelled for Ellen Thomas-Stanford in 1905; it stretches the width of the main 18C house, with a screen of Ionic columns dividing it in two. It is furnished as a 'living hall' with the best of the Stanford's 17C and 18C English furniture, and a variety of family portraits. In the left-hand wing is the Macquoid Room. In the 18C this was the dining room, then from 1905 it was Sir Charles Stanford's library. It is now named after the artist and designer Percy Macquoid (1852–1925) whose widow Theresa left a part of his collection of early furniture, paintings and silver to Brighton Corporation. The fine 17C-style panelling and chimneypiece, designed by Macquoid, formed part of the bequest, and there is splendid 16C and 17C inlaid furniture, silverware, maiolica, and early Flemish paintings. Next to this is the Morning Room, very much as it was when Ellen Thomas-Stanford used it, with watercolour paintings and family memorabilia. The Cleves Room has 17C-style panelling, and a fine set of embossed gilt-leather hangings, 17C Netherlandish work, and 18C furniture. The Drawing Room, the biggest in the house, occupies the other wing. It dates from the 1738 rebuilding, but is essentially Edwardian in character, with its mixture of 18C, and 19C furniture, landscape paintings and crowds of photographs and objets d'art. Next door is the Dining Room, added in 1905 in a simple classical style. It is furnished in a sober, masculine taste, and dominated by a great display cabinet filled with Chinese porcelain 'Dogs of Fo'—124 of them.

The staircase is also of 1738, and visitors are shown five rooms on the first floor, one housing a small library, the others bedrooms, furnished and equipped with the blend of comfort and austerity characteristic of Edwardian country houses. The spartan aspect of life is most apparent in Ellen Stanford-Thomas' bathroom, and in the adjacent servants' bedrooms. In the attic, one room is furnished as a nursery with a collection of historic toys. Finally, visitors are shown several rooms in the basement, where the Kitchen, Scullery, Servants' Hall and Butler's Pantry retain much of the furnishings and the atmosphere of the Edwardian age. Two fine moulded 16C doorways down here serve as a reminder of the house's early origins.

SB

WEST SUSSEX

Arundel Castle

In Arundel: Arundel Castle Trustees, tel. 0903 883136. Open Apr–end Oct daily except Sat 11–5. Refreshments.

Arundel is the principal seat of England's premier Duke and Earl Marshal, the Duke of Norfolk. Both family and castle are very grand indeed. Arundel's story begins with Roger de Montgomery, who governed Normandy for William the Conqueror while the latter was engaged in the conquest of England. Roger received a third of Sussex as his reward, and probably built the great motte, or mound, which remains the heart of the castle. Henry I gave Arundel to the d'Aubigny family, and they rebuilt the castle in stone. On the death of Hugh d'Aubigny in 1243, it passed to John Fitzalan, lord of Clun in Shropshire. The Fitzalans became Earls of Arundel, and held it until 1556.

The 12th and last Earl left an heiress, Lady Mary Fitzalan, who married Thomas Howard, 4th Duke of Norfolk. The Howards were a family of Norfolk gentry, who rose to power during the Wars of the Roses. They have a larger place in the history of England than any other non-royal family. The first four dukes all had prominent, and often tragic, roles in the turbulent history of Tudor England. The 1st Duke was killed at Bosworth. Two of the 3rd Duke's nieces, Anne Boleyn and Catherine Howard, were married to, and subsequently beheaded by, Henry VIII. The 3rd Duke's son, the poet Earl of Surrey, was beheaded by the same monarch, and the duke himself only escaped the same fate because King Henry died a day before he, too, was due for execution. The 4th Duke married the heiress Mary Fitzalan; he, too, was executed in 1572 for plotting to marry Mary, Queen of Scots, and the dukedom was attainted. His son Philip became 13th Earl of Arundel, inheriting the castle and the Fitzalan estates. He was a Catholic recusant, was imprisoned in the Tower of London and died there, possibly poisoned. He was canonised in 1970.

Thomas Howard, 14th Earl of Arundel, accepted Anglicanism and was one of the great collectors of Charles I's circle. He died in exile, and Arundel was besieged and sacked in the Civil War. At the Restoration, the family were restored as Dukes; since then their history has been less dramatic. The 8th Duke carried out a modest rebuilding of the south end of the castle, c 1716. In 1777, the extrovert 11th Duke inherited. In 1787 he began the reconstruction of the residential buildings around the south bailey in a romantic Gothic style of his own invention, and laid out the park. The 14th Duke began a second rebuilding of the castle. He died in 1860 before much had been done. His son, the 15th Duke, reigned until 1917, and rebuilt the castle in its present spectacular form with the architect C.A. Buckler, 1875–1900. The present Duke is the 17th; his heir, the Earl of Arundel, has recently moved back into the Percy Lodgings in the east wing of the castle.

The castle occupies a low ridge on the east side of the picturesque town. It is set in extensive grounds, surrounded by castellated walls. Although there is much medieval work in the building, its spectacular silhouette and much of its present character comes from the 15th Duke's great rebuilding. In the middle rises the motte, with the stone Keep on top, first built by William d'Aubigny c 1138; north and south of this are large walled baileys, the whole castle having something like an hour-glass shape, a little like that of Windsor. The north bailey, or tiltyard, retains its full circuit of medieval walls and towers, but there are no longer any buildings inside. The south bailey has immense ranges of buildings on its south, west and east sides, all rebuilt by the 15th Duke and Buckler.

The **south bailey** is entered through the great Barbican. Buckler's ranges spread out in a U-shape to the right; the design is scholarly and sober, the craftsmanship is the finest that late-Victorian Britain could produce. Entering the right-hand (west) range, you enter the **Chapel**, a magnificent exercise in 13C Gothic style, the detail based on Salisbury Cathedral. The Stone Hall was built by Buckler as the main entrance. Ascending the Stone Staircase you reach the **Armoury**; the collection of arms and armour was mostly assembled by the 15th Duke to furnish his rebuilt fortress, but the great English longsword named 'Mongley' has always been at Arundel. Across the screens passage is the 15th Duke's huge **Barons' Hall**. Buckler based the design on the Hall at Penshurst, Kent (qv.) and the Guesten Hall at Worcester Cathedral. In the great hammerbeam roof, the superb late 19C craftsmanship appears at its best. The Hall is furnished with fine pieces of 16C furniture bought by the 15th Duke, and hung with family portraits. Next comes the **Picture Gallery**, which runs the length of the south range. Along this are family portraits of the Fitzalan-Howards, in chronological order, some of them being important works of art. On the right is the **Dining Room**; this immensely high room was built in the 18C as the Chapel, and rebuilt by Buckler in his severest Gothic style, with three huge lancet windows at the south end and a tremendous ceiling supported on stone arches. There is very fine 18C furniture here; the door is flanked by portraits of the 14th Earl and of the 'Winter Queen', daughter to James I.

The **Grand Staircase**, opening north off the gallery, is in stone and marble, dramatically vaulted as if this were a cathedral. In the gallery opposite this is a famous posthumous portrait of Henry Howard, the Earl of Surrey, beheaded by Henry VIII, shown in a 'triumphal arch' setting perhaps designed by Inigo Jones. Nearby, the **Victoria Rooms** are still furnished as they were for a visit by Queen Victoria in 1846. The **Drawing Room**, back on the south side, is another of Buckler's rooms, with grand English and French 18C furniture. The superb portraits include a famous pair of the 14th Earl and Countess of Arundel by Daniel Mytens (c 1618), showing the picture gallery and sculpture gallery of their London house in the backgrounds. The visitor then heads north, up the east wing. The **Ante Library** is dominated by Van Dyck's 'Madagascar Portrait' of the 14th Earl and Countess, so named from an ill-fated attempt to colonise that island by the Earl. The **Library** itself is the one room remaining from the 11th Duke's work, and is one of the most extraordinary Regency interiors in Britain. It is a gallery, 122ft long, entirely panelled in mahogany in the Gothic style, with little galleries running all the way around it. The library itself is a great collection, and the carpet has recently been re-woven to the original design. At the end of this is the **Billiard Room**, and from here, the visitor returns to the courtyard.

Finally, visitors should not miss the **Fitzalan Chapel**, or Collegiate Church, dating from c 1380, attached to the town's parish church but entered from the Castle grounds. It is a Catholic Chapel, and Mass is still occasionally celebrated here. It houses magnificent tomb monuments of the Fitzalan and Howard families, dating from the 15C–20C. There is a particularly splendid view of the Castle from the Chapel steps.

Cowdray House

Just north east of Midhurst, off the A272: The Viscount Cowdray.

Cowdray House is the picturesque ruin of a great Tudor courtyard-house. The manors of Midhurst and Easebourne were held from the 1180s by the de Bohun family. In 1492 the last of the line died, and his heiress married Sir David Owen, illegitimate son of Owen Tudor, the grandfather of Henry VII. Sir David pulled down the old Bohun house and built the Great Hall, the Chapel and kitchen tower. Before it was complete, the house was sold to Sir William Fitzwilliam, later Earl of Southampton. He completed the courtyard, with the south range, the porch and perhaps the great Gatehouse. Cowdray went to his half-brother, Sir Anthony Browne, 1st Viscount Montague. The Brownes held fast to their Catholic faith through 250 years of intermittent persecution, and the resulting fines may provide some explanation as to why they never undertook a general rebuilding of their house, restricting themselves to some internal redecoration. Family and house both came to a dramatic end. In 1793 the young 8th Viscount Montague attempted to 'shoot' a waterfall at Laufenburg in Switzerland, and drowned in the attempt; a few weeks before, the house burnt to the ground. A distant cousin became the 9th Viscount, but died in 1797.

During the 19C the house fell into picturesque decay; no attempt was made to renovate it, and the north and south sides of the courtyard had to be demolished. The Earls of Egmont, now owners of the estate, built a big Victorian mansion a short distance away. In 1908, the estate was sold to Sir Weetman Pearson, later 1st Viscount Cowdray, a highly successful engineer and businessman. He had Sir Aston Webb carry out a careful consolidation of the ruins, to which we owe their survival today. The estate now belongs to the 3rd Viscount Cowdray.

From the town of Midhurst, a long straight causeway leads over water-meadows to the ruins. Most of the east and west sides of the courtyard stand to their full height. The west range has a big, grand gatehouse with octagonal turrets, but the large mullion-and-transom windows to either side give the building a strongly domestic character. This would have been accommodation for the large household. The east range housed most of the principal rooms; the Hall has particularly fine tall windows, and the porch retains its lovely fan vault. To the left was the Parlour, Great Chamber, and other state apartments. Behind the Hall is the shell of the Chapel; high on the walls there are considerable remains of the rich Baroque plasterwork added late in the 17C. On the right were the servants' rooms. The one part of the building to remain roofed is the hexagonal kitchen tower. The tall kitchen retains its great hearths. A spiral stair gives access to an upstairs room which has a little museum dedicated to the site; from the roof there is a fine view of the ruins, and the great park around.

SB

Danny

South of Hurstpierpoint, off New Way Lane, approached via B2116: Country Houses Association. Open May–Sept Wed, Thur 2–5, last admission 4.30.

Danny is a late Elizabethan E-plan house of dark orange brick, though its architectural history is rather more complex than the grandly uniform entrance front would lead you to believe. At the time of the Domesday Survey (1086), the manor of Hurst was held by Robert de Pierpoint. In the 13C William de Warenne gave Simone de Pierpoint licence to enclose 'the wood at Danye and the demesne lands bounding the wood'. From the Pierpoints it passed in the 14C to the Dacres and in 1582 Sir Gregory Dacre sold the property to George Goring. There was an L-shaped house surrounded by a moat here, roughly represented by the main block and the north wing of the present house. Goring carried out a thoroughgoing reconstruction, rebuilding and raising much of the house. He created the Hall, added the porch and built the whole south wing from scratch, making the house E-shaped. Work was still in progress on his death in 1594, and a year later a valuation referred to '...a house at Danny not fullye finished built of brick which cost as may appear £4000'.

The Goring family sold Danny to a Parliamentarian squire, Peter Courthope, in 1652. His grandson, another Peter Courthope, died in 1725, and the estate passed to his daughter Barbara and her husband, Henry Campion of Combwell in Kent. They modernised the house, rebuilding the south wing, which bears the date 1728 on the rain-water heads. In 1918 Lord Riddell leased the house for the summer from Sir William Campion, and Lloyd George's Imperial War Cabinet retreated here periodically from June to October of that year. Many of their deliberations, settling British policy for the Treaty of Versailles, took place in the house. In 1956 the Campion family leased Danny to the newly-formed Mutual Households Association, which turned it into flats. In 1984 the Association (now the Country Houses Association) bought the freehold and also managed to buy a large number of the Campion family portraits.

The house is approached by a long and winding drive from Hurstpierpoint. The E-shaped east front remains almost exactly as George Goring built it, with the immensely tall bay windows of his Hall to the left of the porch; one would never guess that it embodies much of the medieval house. The north front is more asymmetrical, with the earlier fabric more visible. The south front is in strong contrast; it was rebuilt c 1725–28 by Henry and Barbara Campion as a brick nine-bay façade with giant Doric pilasters. It is in the Baroque manner of Queen Anne's reign; one more bay was added at the left-hand end in the late 19C. The rear, or west front, is irregular, with more of the pre-1590s house visible.

Entering by the front porch you are in the screens passage. To the right is the main staircase, a late Victorian replacement. The Hall, created by George Goring in the 1590s, was one of the last great halls of the old style. It was remodelled by Henry Campion in the early 18C; he opened the arches in the far (south) wall, and inserted the plaster ceiling. The magnificent open timber roof remains above, and is visible from a second-floor passageway. The tall bay windows have heraldic glass, showing the arms of the Campions and families with whom they intermarried. Many 17C and 18C Campion portraits hang around the room and there is a remarkable posthumous portrait of King Charles I, showing him in Coronation robes and attended by cherubs. Through the arches at the far end is the fine main staircase, of 1728. On the left is the White Drawing Room, with 1728 panelling. There are more Campion portraits, and over the fireplace is another one of Charles I, a version of the painting made by Edmund Bower during his trial. The Library, at the east end of the wing, has mostly Victorian bookcases and panelling, but the overmantel is an Italian coffer-panel of the 16C. On the other side of the staircase hall is the Billiard Room, used by the Campions as their Dining Room, hung with many more 17C and 18C portraits. Visitors now re-cross the Hall and screens passage. The Spice Room, next to the main stairs, has 16C panelling. The Association has recently (1989) created a new Dining Room on the ground floor of the north wing, with panelling based on that in the Parish Library at Langley Marish in Berkshire (of c 1630). To the south of the house is a formal garden surrounded by topiary yew hedges, and beyond is a ha-ha.

SB

Goodwood House

3m north east of Chichester, off the A27, A283 or A286: the Duke of Richmond and Gordon, tel. 0243 774107. Open Easter Sun and Mon, then early May–late Sept Sun and Mon 2–5. Open Sun–Thur Aug only 2–5. The house may be closed during equestrian and other special events. Refreshments.

Goodwood House, the seat of the Duke of Richmond and Gordon, is a great Georgian mansion, standing in magnificent wooded parkland at the foot of the South Downs near Chichester. The Dukes of Richmond are one of the four ducal houses to be descended from illegitimate children of Charles II (the others being Buccleuch, St Albans and Grafton). The 1st Duke was born in 1672, son of the king and his French mistress Louis de la Kérouaille, Duchess of Portsmouth (a Catholic and a spy for Louis XIV). The child was named Charles for his father, and created Duke of Richmond and Lennox in 1675. The name and title, and the surname Lennox, were given in commemoration of a previous family, the Stuart Dukes of Richmond and Lennox, closely linked to the royal house, who had become extinct in 1672 (see Cobham Hall, Kent: Charles II was their collateral heir). In 1697 the 1st Duke bought the 1000 acre estate of Goodwood, with an early 17C house built by Henry, 9th Earl of Northumberland (qv. Petworth). The 3rd Duke of Richmond, succeeding in 1750, was a soldier and diplomat, serving as ambassador to Versailles. Enormously rich, he spent enormously, increasing the Goodwood estate to 17,000 acres. He built the great stable block designed by Sir William Chambers, and then remodelled the 17C house. He brought back pictures, furniture and china from France to furnish it, and it was he who started horse-racing at Goodwood; the flourishing modern estate is to a large degree his creation.

This enormous expenditure took its toll and the 3rd Duke died in 1806 leaving an incomplete house and his estate burdened with debts of £180,000. The interior was not completed until the 1820s. The family fortunes were much restored by the 5th Duke's inheritance, through his mother, of the enormous Highland estates of the Gordon dukes of Gordon. Subsequently the 6th Duke of Richmond was created 1st Duke of Gordon (of the second creation) by Queen Victoria, and the family have been doubly titled since then.

The house bought by the 1st Duke was H-shaped and moderately-sized, certainly not ducal in scale. In the 1760s the 3rd Duke commissioned Chambers to make some alterations, but in the 1790s he adopted an altogether grander plan by James Wyatt for an enormous octagonal house around a central courtyard. One end of the old house was to be incorporated in this, and the rest, apparently, would have been demolished on completion of the new work. However, by the Duke's death in 1806 only the three southern sides of the octagon had been built, with the older house now hidden at the back. Sussex has little building-stone, so the house is of knapped flint, with dressings of a grey-white stone. The long entrance front has a two-storeyed portico in the middle, and at the angles there are round towers with low copper domes.

The visitor enters at the right-hand, or east end of the Wyatt house, through a modern foyer. The **Round Reception Room** occupies one of Wyatt's angle-towers, and has the first of the house's large collection of superb 17C portraits. Here there are full-lengths of Frances, last Duchess of Richmond of the old Stuart line and of Barbara Villiers, Countess of Castlemaine (a rival mistress of Charles II). From here the **Ballroom** is entered. This is a spectacular room, running the length of one of the shorter sides of the Wyatt building. It was intended as a picture gallery, and a sketch in the 3rd Duke's hand survives, showing which paintings he intended to hang here. Like most of the house, the Ballroom was not decorated until after the 3rd Duke's death, and is in the sumptuous, gilded style of the 1820s. It is dominated by a magnificent set of portraits of the Stuart court. In the centre is a great group of Charles I and his family by Van Dyck. There are several other Van Dycks, including two of Charles I's children, and works by Lely, Wissing, Kneller and Gascar. At the near end of the room is one of the 1st Duke as a little boy, in Garter robes.

The **Yellow Drawing Room**, facing south, is furnished with the finest of the furniture and porcelain brought from Paris by the 3rd Duke. There are portraits by Reynolds and Romney, and coronation portraits of George III and Queen Charlotte by Allan Ramsay. Opening off one end is the **Card Room**, in another of the round towers. The Axminster carpet was woven for the room early in the 19C, and there is more fine Louis XVI furniture. Here and in the Yellow Room there is much Sèvres porcelain, part of a huge service commissioned by the 3rd Duke. At the back of the Yellow Drawing Room is the **Blue Hall**, essentially a grand corridor, which should have looked over the inner courtyard if the house had been completed. It now houses a variety of pictures, some of them Italian of the 17C. Most notable is the strange 'Monument of Lord Darnley', a late 16C painting, showing the tomb of Lord Darnley, murdered husband of Mary, Queen of Scots, with his family praying for the punishment of his murderers (amongst whom they numbered the Queen).

To the west is the **Entrance Hall**, in the centre of the Wyatt building. This is divided by a screen of beautiful columns of Guernsey granite. There are two fine 18C fireplaces, pre-dating the Wyatt house; over them are portraits of the last Duke of Gordon, in Highland dress, and of Cardinal Fleury by Rigaud. On the rear wall are paintings by Canaletto; there are familiar views of Venice, and also stunning views of London from old Richmond House on Whitehall. Across the Hall, symmetrical with the Yellow Drawing Room, is the **Dining Room**. This too was decorated for the 5th Duke, and a great portrait of his duchess by Lawrence dominates the room. There are portraits of the 1st Duke and Duchess by Kneller, amongst others, and another beautiful early 18C chimneypiece. Behind this the **Green Hall** houses a rather eclectic group of furnishings and pictures, with mostly 19C portraits of the family and some very fine Dutch and French cabinets.

Finally, from the Entrance Hall the visitor crosses the rear court, under a covered walkway, to the remaining part of the old 17C house. The **Long Hall** is the core of the original house, although redecorated with its beautiful screens of Ionic columns by Chambers. It is hung with equestrian paintings, by Stubbs and Wootton, commemorating the Lennox family's long association with the turf. Opening from here is the **Tapestry Drawing Room**, so named from the magnificent Gobelin tapestries, dated 1762–63 and representing stories from *Don Quixote*. These, and the fine French furniture in the room, were also brought from Paris by the 3rd Duke.

SB

Hammerwood Park

3m east of East Grinstead, on the Tunbridge Wells road (A264): Mr David Pinnegar, tel. 0342 850594. Open Easter–end Sept Wed, Sat, BH Mon 2–5.30. Refreshments.

Hammerwood dates from 1792, and is an important landmark in the history of neo-classical architecture. The house stands in a well-wooded valley; the name 'Hammerwood' probably derives from the iron industry which once flourished hereabouts. In 1792 the estate was bought by John Sperling, an Essex landowner, and he almost immediately set about building a new house. His architect was 28-year old Benjamin Henry Latrobe, who had studied engineering under John Smeaton, and worked for the architect Samuel Cockerell. The house is in Latrobe's highly personal Greek Revival style, showing the influence of Soane and of the French architects Ledoux and Boullee. But for all Latrobe's talent and originality, he only built one other house in England, and in 1795 he emigrated to the United States, where he became one of the leading architects and surveyors, designing the Catholic cathedral of Baltimore, and rebuilding the White House and the Capitol in Washington after their destruction in 1812.

John Sperling did not enjoy his new house for long; in 1795 his mother died, and he returned to Essex to look after his father. Hammerwood was sold to the oddly-named Magen Dorrien Magens, a banker and bullion dealer and it subsequently passed through several hands. After the Second World War it was divided into eleven apartments, but as these fell vacant its condition began to decline. The house was struck by vandalism, wet rot and dry rot; by 1982 it was on the verge of collapse. The house was then bought by David Pinnegar. For the last ten years he and his family have carried out a careful and devoted restoration, which is still in progress.

The house has a stark and dramatic character, belying its relatively small scale, and reminiscent of the work of Vanbrugh and Hawksmoor. The centre is square, five bays wide and three storeys high, built of a dark yellow stone. The main front, towards the garden (also facing the original drive through the park) is a taut and dense composition, the Doric pilasters deliberately closely spaced. To either side, set back somewhat, there are wings. Each has a little Doric temple front at the outer end, with the exaggerated entasis (bulging of the columns) that the Greek revivalists took from the temples of Paestum. The capitals are of Coade stone, and set into the doorways are Coade friezes based on the Borghese Vase. The entrance front is asymmetrical, with a big Doric porch. There was clearly alteration at some point in the mid 19C, probably including the library bay window, the service buildings and a rebuilding of the main staircase. Tours of the house are led by members of the family, who vividly convey the long and painstaking process of renovation. The east end of the house has been re-roofed, but otherwise it has not yet been renovated (1993). A small Drawing Room leads through to the central block. The Drawing Room has mirror-covered pilasters. These and the mutule cornice seem original, but the strapwork ornament on the ceiling is presumably mid-Victorian; it is at present used as a dining room. The Fleur-dy-Lys Room is a smaller Drawing Room, named for the Victorian ceiling plasterwork. Behind these is the big staircase hall. The stairs themselves look mid-Victorian; the walls have been covered with trompe l'oeil murals commissioned by Mr Pinnegar to commemorate the house's bicentenary. A number of bedrooms are shown, one furnished in Victorian style, one in French 'Louis' style, one with a magnificent carved Italian bed. Back on the ground floor, the Library occupies the whole ground floor of the west wing, and has fine original bookcases and joinery. Teas are served in the galleried 'Elgin Room', so named from the full set of casts of the Parthenon frieze, housed here.

SB

Parham

7m north west of Worthing, between Pulborough and Storrington on the A283: Parham Park Ltd, tel. 0903 742021. Open from Easter–1st Sun Oct Wed, Thur, Sun and BH Mon 2–6, last admission 5. Refreshments.

Parham (pronounced 'Parrum') is a very beautiful Elizabethan house in a fine setting just north of the South Downs, with magnificent contents. In the Middle Ages the manor was owned by Westminster Abbey, and in 1540 Henry VIII gave it to Robert Palmer, a mercer of London. At first he lived in the old manor house, as did his son Sir Thomas. Eventually, it would no longer suffice, and on 28 January 1577, the foundation-stone of a new house (incorporating elements of the old one) was laid by his two and a half-year-old son, also Thomas. In its essential form, the house remains as it was built then. In 1601 Thomas Palmer sold the estate to Thomas Bysshop of Henfield, and it was owned by 11 generations of his descendants until the present century. In 1816 Sir Cecil Bysshop established a claim to the dormant Barony of Zouche of Haryngworth, becoming the 12th Lord Zouche. In 1922 the 17th Baroness Zouche sold the estate to the Hon. Clive Pearson, second son of the 1st Viscount Cowdray (qv. Cowdray Park). Mr Pearson bought many of the Bysshop family paintings with the house, and added greatly to these, collecting portraits, English furniture, and objets d'art of all kinds. He died in 1965; the house is now vested in a charitable trust, and is the home of his eldest daughter, Mrs P.A. Tritton.

Parham is approached from the east; a long drive leads through the deer-park, which is well-wooded, and unexpectedly wild-looking. The house comes into view quite suddenly, standing on broad level lawns, with magnificent parkland on every side, looking south to the Downs, half a mile away. It is of grey stone and at first seems quite irregular and picturesque, with varied gables and chimneys. The **principal (south) front** is more symmetrical, on the Elizabethan E-plan, with the big Hall windows to the left of centre. In the early 18C the entrance was moved to the north front, and in the late 1700s the large stable, estate and laundry buildings were added north of the house. In the early 19C a new porch and entrance hall were built on the north front, in a Tudor Revival style, by the 12th Lord Zouche, and this is the present entrance.

The **Entrance Hall** is hung with equestrian paintings by Seymour and Wootton, and with 18C portraits. A flight of stairs (needed because the north side of the house is lower-lying than the south side) takes you to the **Upper Hall**; this low room is dominated by a view of Venice by Bernardo Bellotto, Canaletto's nephew. This takes you into the **Great Hall**, one of the most beautiful Elizabethan rooms in Britain. It rises through two storeys, and has a flat plaster ceiling with fine geometrical rib-ornament. The room is light, from its very high windows, and the light-coloured walls and stone floor. There is much old English oak furniture here, and a tremendous array of 16C portraits. There are especially fine pictures of Elizabeth I, Essex, Burghley, Leicester and the poet-Earl of Surrey. The most remarkable is the great allegorical equestrian portrait of Henry, Prince of Wales, attributed to Robert Peake. A landscape background was added, probably late in the 17C to make it look more Van Dyckian, but this was recently cleaned off (1894–85) to reveal a winged figure of Father Time, whom the Prince is leading by his forelock; it is one of the most remarkable allegorical portraits of its age to survive.

At the west end of the house is the **Great Parlour**. In the 16C this was a private sitting-room, with the more formal Great Chamber above. The Bysshop family removed the ceiling, making another very high room. Mr Pearson restored the ceiling in 1924, creating three rooms on the first floor; Esmond Burton was commissioned to make the plaster ceiling-decorations, in Elizabethan style, in 1935. The many 17C chairs and settees are covered in original needlework, the Kouba and Shirvan carpets are also of the 17C. Much of the panelling is covered by splendid early 17C portraits, including ones by Pourbus of Louis XIII and Anne of Austria, by Mytens of Charles I, and one of the countess of Denbigh by William Larkin. The **Saloon**, next, was decorated and fitted out c 1790 by the 12th Lord Zouche, in cream and gold, and has Georgian furniture to match, including chairs by Sheraton and a harp by Sebastian Erard. The two views of London and the Thames are by William James. The set of five portraits of John Fawcett and his family, rather in the manner of Sir Thomas Lawrence, are by G.H. Harlow.

Visitors now ascend the stairs, which rise around the square core of chalk masonry. The walls are, again, covered with very fine English portraits. The first floor lobby has a variety of interesting furniture, and a big walnut cabinet is filled with an 18C Derby dinner service. The **Great Chamber** is over the Great Parlour, and was re-formed in 1924 (see above) and redecorated with Elizabethan-style plasterwork. The room has fine 16C and 17C furniture and portraits, but is dominated by the great bed, with its very well-preserved 16C needlework bedspread and hangings. The Tapestry Ante-Room is named from its 16C Flemish tapestry. The **West Room** has more very rare early needlework—a set of late 16C Italian wool hangings with abstract patterning in a kind of early Flame stitch. The furniture is mostly English of the early 18C, and above the hangings are late 17C portraits mostly in the style of Kneller or Lely; the most striking is a great double portrait of Sir Ralph and Lady Assheton by Lely, which is far more eloquent of the sitter's personalities than most of that artists' works. The **Ante-Room**, next, has more very fine embroidery; there is a very early needlework carpet in gros-point, and one wall is hung with Hungarian point needlework curtains of silk and wool. There are highly revealing portraits of Charles II (looking positively disreputable, painted by Simon Verelst), of his long-suffering queen Catherine of Braganza, and of two of his mistresses. The **Green Room** was redecorated around 1770, in a simple

The Elizabethan Entrance Hall at Parham, showing the splendid wood-work, the paster ceiling and the collection of portraits

Verelst), of his long-suffering queen Catherine of Braganza, and of two of his mistresses. The **Green Room** was redecorated around 1770, in a simple but elegant way, and has 18C English furniture, and a collection of objects relating to Sir Joseph Banks, the naturalist, explorer and President of the Royal Society. There are several of his possessions and objects relating to his work, such as Stubbs' paintings of a kangaroo and a dingo-dog. The grandest object in the room is Reynolds's full-length portrait of the Tahitian chief Omiah (or Omai), who was brought to London by Captain Cook after

Visitors return to the stairs and ascend again; there are many more 18C portraits. The Top Floor Lobby has 16C and 17C needlework pictures, and leads into the **Long Gallery**, the climax of the tour of the house. It runs the length of the house, 160ft, just under the roof, with views in all directions. For all its great length it is low and intimate. The original ceiling was long lost when the Pearsons bought the house; they added the excellent panelled ceiling one sees, designed by Oliver Messel, who also executed the paintings of leaf-patterns, c 1960. The panelling and the floor-boards are original. The Gallery is like a very superior country-house museum; there is a great variety of furniture, embroideries, smaller pictures, antiquities and objets d'art of all kinds. The White Room, leading off the Gallery, has the main collection of 17C stumpwork embroidered pictures.

This ends the tour, and visitors proceed down the stairs to the Entrance Hall again. The walled gardens, to the north of the house, are very fine, with long mixed borders in the tradition of Jekyll and Robinson. To the south of the house are great lawns with wide views over the romantic parkland, and the little 16C church of St Peter, all that remains of the old village.

SB

Petworth House

In Petworth, 5m east of Midhurst (A272): National Trust, tel. 0798 42207.
Open Apr–Oct daily, except Mon, Fri 1–5.30. Refreshments.

Petworth is a great Baroque house with contents worthy of a national museum, on the edge of one of 'Capability' Brown's finest parks. However, it does not trumpet its presence like other Baroque houses; its outbuildings come right up to the streets of the little town of Petworth, but everything is concealed behind high grey walls. The house turns its back on the town with something like aristocratic aloofness; for the visitor, this makes the revelation of the great park front, and the vast park itself, all the more remarkable.

The manor of Petworth was given to the Percy family in 1150, and they held it until 1670. They became Earls of Northumberland in 1377, and although they are perhaps better remembered as a Border family (qv. Alnwick Castle, Northumberland and Syon House, Greater London), they were often here. Of the eleven earls, seven were killed in battle, executed, murdered or imprisoned. The last Earl of the original Percy line died in 1670, leaving an only daughter, Elizabeth. This unfortunate girl was married three times before her sixteenth birthday, the third time to Charles Seymour, 6th Duke of Somerset in 1682, nicknamed the 'Proud Duke' for his arrogance and pride in his aristocratic descent. In 1688 his wife came of age and he gained control of her fortune; his response was the magnificent rebuilding of the medieval house at Petworth in its present form, in 1688–93.

The Proud Duke died in 1748, and his son the 7th Duke in 1750. The estates were divided, with Petworth and great possessions in Cumberland going, via the Proud Duke's daughter, to the Wyndham family, who became Earls of Egremont. They were great collectors, notably the 3rd Earl, a friend and patron of many painters, especially J.M.W. Turner. The 3rd Earl's natural son was made Lord Leconfield in 1859; in 1869–72 the 2nd Lord employed Anthony Salvin to make the house more convenient for a Victorian household, and to add a new entrance. In 1947 the 3rd Lord gave the house and park to the National Trust. His great-nephew, the present Lord Egremont and his family still live here.

Little is known about the appearance of the medieval house at Petworth, but it was remodelled by the Proud Duke, not demolished, hence the rather strange plan. The house is a very long free-standing rectangular block, the long sides facing east and west. The **east (entrance) front** is surprisingly informal, in rubble masonry, with buttresses and irregularly spaced sash-windows. Much of the masonry is medieval and to the right a great traceried window marks the place of the early 14C Chapel, retained by the Proud Duke. To the left, part of the façade has been re-fronted in smooth ashlar, with a new entrance. This represents the mid 19C work of Salvin, and is the part now occupied by Lord Egremont.

Walking around the north end of the house the visitor suddenly sees the scale of the park, and the superb **west front,** 21 bays long and three storeys high, as rebuilt for the Proud Duke. It is a most restrained design, without columns or pilasters, but with the most refined masonry and carving. It is very French in style, and has been tentatively attributed to Daniel Marot, a French Huguenot who became court architect to William of Orange.

Although the Proud Duke would have entered his house from the middle of the west front, the entrance-court here was swept away by Brown in the 1750s, and the visitor enters by a modest door in the east front, into the Oak Staircase Hall. In 1992–93, the National Trust began extensive repairs and refurbishment of the principal rooms. At the time of writing (1993) these were still in train, and the pictures and the visitor route will probably be subject to further changes.

The **Oak Staircase Hall** is hung with portraits of the 16C and 17C, notably Lely's 'Children of Charles I'. On Wednesdays and Thursdays, two **bedrooms** and two dressing rooms upstairs are shown, one with an excellent bed of the 1750s originally in the downstairs state bedroom, the other with a Chippendale bed of c 1770 with original hangings. Back on the ground floor, a large room to the left of the Oak Stairs, on the site of the medieval Hall, was divided in 1794. In the **Somerset Room**, the magnificent quality of the collection becomes clear, with works by Bellotto, Cuyp, and Teniers, eight small Elsheimers, a characteristically bizarre 'Adoration of the Magi' by Hieronymus Bosch, and above all, one of Claude's greatest works, the 'Landscape with Jacob and Laban'. The **Square Dining Room** is closed for repairs (1993), but normally contains some of the finest of the Van Dyck portraits currently dispersed through the other rooms. Visitors currently turn into the **Little Dining Room**, in the late 17C west front, with some of the earliest pictures in the collection, including works by Matsys and Van Cleve, and two panels attributed to Van der Weyden. Turning to the left, you are in the **Marble Hall**, the original entrance hall in the centre of the west front. It retains its full decor from the Proud Duke's time, with black and white marble flooring, and grand white and grey panelling. The robustly Baroque carving is by John Selden, the estate carpenter. The ancient Roman sculpture is part of the collection brought from Italy by the 2nd Earl of Egremont, and Titian's portrait 'A Man in a Plumed Hat' currently hangs here.

Further along the west front is the **Beauty Room**, named for the portraits of ladies of Queen Anne's court by Kneller and Dahl. Here too is the 'Leconfield Aphrodite', from the 4C BC and probably by Praxiteles, and at the moment, Van Dyck's wonderful portrait of the 9th 'Wizard' Earl of Northumberland, in melancholy pose. An arch gives into the **Grand Staircase**, a Baroque tour-de-force, its walls and ceiling frescoed by Louis Laguerre, c 1715, with gods and goddesses in architectural settings; on the landing two figures hold aloft a plan of the remodelled house.

On Tuesdays another two rooms, the **White and Gold Room** and **White Library**, are shown. Both have very fine Rococo panelling, and the former has three more portraits by Van Dyck. Visitors return through the Beauty Room, Marble Hall, and Little Dining Room to the **Carved Room**, named from Grinling Gibbons' celebrated carved decoration on the panelling, carried out c 1692, for the Proud Duke. The 3rd Earl of Egremont had the present long room made out of two rooms in 1794–95, re-organised the woodwork, and employed his estate carpenter Jonathan Ritson to make more carvings in Gibbons' style. The carvings are in light-coloured lime-wood, against a darker background. Ritson's carved panels on the end wall are brilliantly accomplished, but Gibbons steals the show. He carved the huge garlands and wreaths around the four big portraits on the east wall. Classical vases, musical instruments, cherubs blowing trumpets, songbirds, baskets of flowers, all seem to spill out of the great garlands; it is hard to believe that one is looking at carved wood. The portraits (including one by Reynolds of the courtesan, Kitty Fisher) and the Louis XIV furniture are almost overwhelmed by it all.

Next comes the **Red Room**, currently lined with more superb Old Master paintings, pre-eminent among them Van Dyck's remarkable pair of portraits of Sir Robert Shirley and his Circassian wife. There are also several superb paintings by Turner, including two of the park at Petworth, painted c 1828–29, and two others of Chichester Canal and the Old Chain Pier at Brighton, both of them enterprises in which the 3rd Earl Egremont had a financial interest; they were originally hung in the Carved Room, and may be returned there as part of the current programme of restoration. A short corridor takes you into the **North Gallery**, added in various stages in the mid 18C and early 19C as a setting for sculpture and pictures. The National Trust has recently completed a comprehensive redecoration and re-hanging, and it is one of the best expressions anywhere of British art and taste of the Regency period. The 3rd Lord Egremont was one of the greatest patrons of the British artists of his day, reacting against the tendency of his class to prefer the work of Continental masters. He was a close friend of J.M.W. Turner, and most of the Turners in the house are now in the North Gallery, including the famous 'Egremont Sea Piece', two studies of the Thames at Windsor, the atmospheric 'Hulks on the Tamar' and 'Teignmouth Harbour', and a view of the house and park at Tabley in Cheshire (qv.). The densely-hung pictures also include major works by Gainsborough, Reynolds, Wilson, Zoffany, Fuseli and Northcote. The Gallery also contains ancient sculptures bought by the 2nd Lord Egremont; few English houses retain such collections, and this is one of the best, with many excellent Roman portrait heads. There is also British sculpture of the 3rd Earl's time, the greatest piece being Flaxman's 'St Michael overcoming the Devil', ten feet high and carved from a single block of marble in 1826, the last year of the sculptor's life.

The visitor goes along the Chapel corridor, with its three paintings by William Blake, to the last major room on the tour, the **Chapel**. This is the only part of the Percy's medieval house to remain intact, dating from c 1309. It has its original east window. The windows remain along the sides as well, but are now blocked up. The chapel was lavishly re-fitted around 1690 for the Proud Duke with fine Baroque pews, altar-rail and altar, like a Wren City church. At the west end over the entrance is the ducal pew, like the royal box in an opera house, with carved and painted wooden 'curtains' being drawn back, and the Duke's arms and coronet borne aloft by angels.

Petworth does not have a **garden** in the conventional sense; north of the house is the Pleasure Ground, a woodland garden, with winding paths and two little temples. Otherwise, a great smooth lawn extends from the west front of the house to the lake. Brown worked here over many years from 1751, and it is one of his greatest achievements. He created the serpentine lake, framed by great clumps and stands of trees. Thanks to careful management over two centuries, the park is still largely as Brown designed it and Turner painted it, vast and idyllic.

SB

St Mary's

In Bramber village, off the A283, 10m north east of Brighton: Mr Peter Thorogood, tel. 0903 816205. Open Easter Sun–end Sept Sun, Thurs 2–6, also Mon in July, Aug, Sept, BH Mon 2–6. Refreshments.

St Mary's is a picturesque, basically 15C timber-framed house, which originated as a hostel for travellers. In the 12C, the river Adur had a broad navigable estuary, and there was a bridge at Bramber; next to it, on the site of St Mary's, was a house belonging to the Knights Templar. Around 1230 the bridge and its tolls were given to the Benedictine monks of Sele Priory, and by 1350 they had acquired the Templar's house also. In the mid 15C, the Priory was given to the newly-founded Magdalen College, Oxford, and c 1470 the College's founder, William Waynflete, Bishop of Winchester, rebuilt St Mary's as a hostel for travellers; the present building represents about half of his work. On the suppression of the monasteries, St Mary's passed to Francis Shirley of West Grinstead, and then to the Gough family. They seem to have used the house as an occasional residence, making a number of alterations in the late 16C. St Mary's declined in status in the 18C and 19C, but in 1896 it was bought by the Hon. Algernon Bourke, a younger son of the Earl of Mayo, who renovated it, adding two new wings to the west. The house suffered another decline, requisition by the army in the war, and used as guest-house thereafter; one of the Victorian wings was demolished, and the house deteriorated. Latterly, it has been renovated, and is once more a family home.

The main 15C part of the house is a long rectangle, the first floor jettied out, with close-studded timber framing. The massive roof is covered in great stone slates, not tiles. The house represents the eastern half of William Waynflete's building; there was originally a narrow, galleried courtyard and a very similar building to the west. The ground-floor interiors are low and picturesque, with panelling and fittings partly from the 16C and partly from the late 19C, and there is a variety of English furniture from the 16C to 18C. The Drawing Room at the south end has good panelling and a chimneypiece with fine ebony columns and marquetry-work. The staircase is Elizabethan, and stands in what would have been the courtyard. On the landing is a remarkable shuttered window—now blocked, but retaining its original shutters and ironwork of the 16C. The Painted Room has interesting architectural decoration on its panelling, said to have been done for a visit by Elizabeth I. The Charles II Room is said to have sheltered that monarch while fleeing to safety in 1651 after the Battle of Worcester. The Library has good 19C fittings, and a fine 16C chimneypiece, and a collection of books relating to the poet Thomas Hood. The Music Room, added by Algernon Bourke, has elaborate Gothic fireplaces, and is now the tea room, also used for concerts. Outside, the pleasant gardens have topiary animals.

SB

Standen

1½m south of East Grinstead, signposted from the B2110: National Trust, tel. 0342 23029. Open Apr–Oct Wed–Sun, also BHs and Good Fri 1.30–5.30, last admission 5. Refreshments.

Standen is one of the few Victorian houses owned by the National Trust. It is, inside and out, a masterpiece of the Arts and Crafts movement, with few surviving parallels. The house was designed in 1891–92 and finished in 1894, for a successful solicitor, James Beale. His wife, Margaret, had artistic interests, and was probably the main influence behind the building of the house. They bought three small farms near East Grinstead in 1890, intending to build a holiday house big enough for their seven children. James Beale died in 1912, and his widow in 1936. Her youngest daughter, Helen, bought the house from a family trust and left it to the National Trust in 1972.

What makes the house remarkable is its completeness as a work of the Arts and Crafts movement. Its architect, Philip Webb, was a lifelong friend of William Morris, and Standen is the only building of his mature period to remain intact and unaltered. A founder-member (with Morris) of the Society for the Protection of Ancient Buildings, Webb persuaded Beale not to demolish the medieval farmhouse here, but to place his new house to one side, forming a village-like group.

The visitor passes under an arch into a little courtyard. In front is the big rectangular main block. The lower kitchen range is on the left. The house is asymmetrical, its informality disguising the great subtlety of Webb's design. Various materials are used, including brick, rubble masonry, tile-hanging and weather-boarding. The roofline all around is enlivened with dormers, little gables and big brick chimneys. The entrance side looks onto an enclosed courtyard, but the garden sides are more boldly composed, and stand on terraces with magnificent views south and east over the Medway valley.

Inside, Webb left his interiors deliberately plain, relying on Morris' wallpapers and textiles for decoration. Most of the joinery is white-painted deal, a little of it of oak. The house had electricity from the outset, and a number of the original electrical fittings remain. In the Hall is a piano designed by C.R. Ashbee, pottery by de Morgan, and Morris & Co. furniture. There are Morris textiles in the adjacent Billiard Room. The Drawing Room has Morris' famous 'Sunflower' wallpaper, wall-lights designed by Webb, Morris curtains and carpet. The oriental porcelain was especially fashionable at the time. Going up the staircase are larger works of art, not all original to the house, but including pictures by Ford Madox Brown, Frampton and Burne-Jones. All 12 bedrooms in the house had Morris wallpapers and curtains, beds from Heal & Co., other furniture from a variety of sources. There were four dressing rooms but only one bathroom. Three bedrooms and two dressing rooms are now shown.

Back downstairs, the Dining Room has muted green-painted panelling, contrasting with blue and white Chinese porcelain, a combination dear to the Arts and Crafts movement. Down the corridor is the Morning Room. The wall-hangings are in Morris's 'Daffodil' chintz. The light fittings are original, and some of the furniture was designed by Webb for the house. The visitor goes through the Business Room to the Kitchen, where the ranges and table are original; the dressers were designed by Webb. From here, the exit leads through the shop into the picturesque Kitchen Court. The garden makes the most of its fine, sloping site and wide views, and remains largely as laid out by Margaret Beale.

SB

Stansted Park

Near Rowlands Castle, north east of Havant, off the B2148 or B2147: The Stansted Park Foundation, tel. 0705 412265. Easter Sun and Mon, then May–endSept Sun, Mon, Tues 2–5.30, last admission 5. Refreshments.

Stansted Park is a grand Edwardian house, built of red brick and white stone in the William and Mary style, with elements remaining of the previous houses on the site. It stands in broad and splendid parkland on the Sussex–Hampshire border on an ancient site. Earl Godwin, father of King Harold, had a house here, and in the Middle Ages there was a hunting lodge surrounded by great forests, belonging to the Earls of Arundel. Early in the 16C it passed by marriage to John, Lord Lumley, who did a lot more building work, a little of which remains. This house was largely destroyed by Parliamentary forces in the Civil War, and in the 1680s the Lumley family built a new house, possibly designed by Robert Hooke. It was in brick and stone with a hipped roof, rather similar to the nearby house at Uppark (qv.). The Lumley family also did a lot of planting on the estate, which is the basis of the present park, with its long avenues. In 1778 the estate was bought by Richard Barwell, a nabob who had made a fortune in India. 'Capability' Brown redesigned the parkland, and James Wyatt and Joseph Bonomi remodelled the house, encasing it in white stucco and adding porticos. On Barwell's death in 1804, the estate was sold to Lewis Way, who tried to establish a college for the conversion of Jews to Christianity here; he added the remarkable Chapel to designs by Thomas Hopper as part of this scheme. Late in the 19C, Stansted belonged to the Wilder family, but in 1900 the main house was destroyed by fire, and they commissioned Sir Reginald Blomfield to rebuild it.

The next important date is 1924, when the estate was sold again. The Ponsonby family, Earls of Bessborough, had lived at Bessborough House in County Kilkenny, Ireland but in 1924 this house was burnt down by Irish nationalists. The 9th Earl of Bessborough saved most of his family's pictures and furniture from the fire, and bought Stansted as his new seat, to house them. In the 1930s he served as Governor General of Canada; on his death in 1956 he was succeeded by his son the 10th Earl, who continues to live at Stansted.

The Lumley family's park, as altered by Brown, forms a magnificent setting for the house; its great trees seem to have suffered little from the hurricane of 1987. The house stands on broad lawns, looking down a great avenue. The main block as rebuilt c 1900–4 by Blomfield, bears a strong resemblance to the Lumley house as built in the 1680s. To the left, the yellow brick buildings of the stable court are earlier, by Wyatt and Hopper.

The visitor enters by a side door from the stable court, leading into the Staircase Hall. The broad staircase is in 17C style. There are fine Dutch paintings of birds, and 17C furniture. High up on the walls are Flemish tapestries depicting scenes from Marlborough's campaigns, in which Richard Lumley, 1st Earl of Scarborough was a general. The tapestries were woven for Stansted, and were bought back for the house by Lord Bessborough in 1961. The Main Hall is in the centre of the entrance front. There are portraits by Lawrence Phillips, Holbein, Kauffmann and others, a fine Flemish tapestry, and Irish Chippendale furniture. The Blue Drawing Room on the garden front was redecorated in Louis XIV style in 1924, to house the fine French furniture brought by the 9th Countess of Bessborough, who was herself French. There are fine Louis XIV and XV pieces, and the walls are dominated by the four Arcadian landscapes by the 17C Dutch artist, Dirk Dalens. There are portraits by Lely and Van Loo, and a storm scene by Claude Vernet (1770). Next, in the centre of the garden front, is the Music Room. This has more modern family paintings, including a group portrait of the 9th Countess with her children by Sir Oswald Birley (1932), and an interesting mixture of 17C, 18C and 19C furniture. The Dining Room, next, has fine portraits by Hoppner, Zucchero and Liotard, and an appropriate Flemish painting of the 'Feeding of the Five Thousand'. There are Irish Chippendale sideboards, and a Chinese export dinner service.

Beneath the Dining Room, are a number of servants' rooms in their Edwardian state. Finally, the Kitchen, which was in regular use until 1956, is essentially in its Edwardian state, with original fittings and a large collection of copperware.

Visitors should not miss the fascinating Chapel, a short distance to the south west. The west façade is a surviving fragment of the Tudor house, the rest was built by Thomas Hopper in a pretty Gothick style. Inside, the nave is white and simple, but the sanctuary is a blaze of blue and gold. The east window, most unusually, represents the sanctuary of Solomon's Temple in Jerusalem, with the Ark of the Covenant and the seven-branched candelabrum, installed by Way as part of his scheme to found a college for the conversion of Jews.

SB

Uppark

Off the B2147 just south of South Harting, 4m south west of Petersfield. National Trust.

Uppark, a famously beautiful and atmospheric house standing high on the South Downs, was tragically damaged by fire in 1989. At the time of writing it is still undergoing the most detailed and complete restoration for the National Trust. It will re-open to the public in 1995.

The site is spectacular, isolated on the highest point of the Downs, with woods to the north, looking south over the rolling countryside to the Channel, 12 miles away. There was a house at 'Up Park' in the 16C, belonging to the Ford family. In 1674 it passed by marriage to Ralph, Lord

Grey of Wark, a Northumbrian landowner; he died the following year and was succeeded by his son, Forde, Lord Grey. He became Earl of Tankerville and c 1690–94 he built Uppark, to the designs of William Talman.

In 1746 Sir Henry Featherstonhaugh, a Newcastle merchant, died, leaving his immense fortune (over £400,000) to a young nephew, Matthew Featherstonhaugh. The bequest came with two curious conditions; Matthew was to buy a baronetcy and an estate in the south of England. He lost little time in doing either, and in 1747 purchased Uppark and its estate for £19,000. He married Sarah Lethieullier, and in 1749 the couple set out for an extended Grand Tour. In Italy, Sir Matthew bought and commissioned paintings on a grand scale, and on their return in 1751 Uppark was thoroughly modernised and redecorated. His son, Sir Harry, commissioned Humphry Repton to modernise the house and park, 1810–13. The house remained largely unaltered for most of the 19C, and it made a deep impression on the writer H. G. Wells, whose mother was housekeeper here for 13 years.

The house was given to the National Trust in 1954, but members of the Featherstonhaugh family continued to live here until the time of the fire in 1989. The roof was almost entirely destroyed but fortunately the most important of its contents along with much of the woodwork and plasterwork were saved. A number of writers argued in the press that the house should be left as a shell, suggesting that any renovation would be a 'fake'. The National Trust quite rightly ignored this barbarous and destructive viewpoint, and a superb restoration is well under way under the architects, The Conservation Practice. It is not yet possible, though, to produce a full description of the house as it will be shown to visitors.

Uppark is one of the best examples of the classic type of Restoration mansion, with brick-and-stone façades and a high hipped roof, of nine bays by seven. The **north or entrance side** was built with projecting wings framing a forecourt. In 1810–13, Humphry Repton remodelled this front, adding a Doric colonnade as the new entrance. Visitors enter here, and proceed down an arcaded corridor lined with Georgian hall-chairs, to the original **Staircase Hall**. This remained largely as it was built, with the stairs, panelling and doors all of the 1690s. Two large views of Uppark by Pieter Tillemans show the house as it was when new; the set of eight little portraits is by Arthur Devis. The **Dining Room** also retained its original panelled decoration from Lord Tankerville's time. Otherwise, the state rooms were all redecorated by Sir Matthew and Lady Sarah, c 1751–52, with beautiful Rococo plaster ceilings, damask wall-coverings and the finest joinery. The grandest room is the great **Saloon**, of the transitional period between the Palladian, Rococo and neo-classical styles; the designer may have been Henry Keene. Its brilliant ivory, grey and gold decoration was complete and intact up to the time of the fire, and it is to be hoped that the restoration can recapture its haunting beauty.

The redecoration was intended to provide a suitable setting for the paintings purchased in Italy. Uppark has one of the best examples of a 'Grand Tour' collection of any country house. Sir Matthew commissioned nine portraits from Pompeo Batoni, of himself, his wife, their friends and relations. He bought a splendid set of six paintings 'The Parable of the Prodigal Son' by the 17C Neapolitan artist, Luca Giordano, and landscapes by Orizonte and Claude Vernet. There are 'veduti' of the Bay of Naples, copies of works by Vernet and Canaletto, and a group of fine Dutch and Flemish pictures. Sir Matthew bought the best English furniture for the remodelled house, and Sir Harry added splendid French furniture. The house also has an important collection of porcelain, especially English, French and Chinese. There is also a dolls' house, made in the early 18C for Sarah Lethieullier, with every piece of miniature furniture, down to the hallmarked silver, every doll fully dressed, a microcosm of the house itself.

The two original service wings were replaced by Repton; they are linked to the main house by tunnels. They stand back from the house, allowing it to command its wide grassy shelf and the superb views below. At the highest point in the park is the 'Vandalian Tower', a great Gothic folly designed by Henry Keene for Sir Matthew c 1770 to commemorate his investment in a New American colony, to be called Vandalia but interrupted by the American Revolution.

SB

TYNE AND WEAR

Washington Old Hall

In Washington Old Village, New Town District 4, 5m west of Sunderland, 2m from A1: National Trust, tel. 091 4166879. Open Apr–Oct daily except Fri, Sat (open Good Fri) 11–4.30.

Washington Old Hall, a Jacobean manor house incorporating parts of a 12C house, was the medieval home of the Washington family, ancestors of George Washington. The first of this line to live here, William de Hertburn, came to Washington in c 1183. Soon after, the family adopted the name of the village. They owned village and house until 1613, when it was sold to the Bishop of Durham. The first President's actual ancestors left Durham for Lancashire and Westmorland in the late 13C, subsequently living at Sulgrave Manor in Northamptonshire (qv.). Washington Old Hall was narrowly saved from demolition in 1936, and with donations from both sides of the Atlantic it was restored and vested in the National Trust; the house opened to the public as a memorial to the Washington family in 1955.

The house is a sober two-storey building of rugged stonework, with small mullioned windows and big gables. In its present form it is mostly of c 1613. The entrance is on the south side, where the boldly projecting wing houses the staircase. The middle wing contains, on the ground floor, the Great Hall, with a flagged floor and heavily beamed ceiling. The stone arches at the west end, uncovered during renovation, are from the medieval building. The Hall, like the other rooms, contains good north-country vernacular furniture. Through the arches, in the west wing, is the Kitchen, with an early spit and roasting-jack. At the east end, in the more private wing, is the Panelled Room, with fine Jacobean panelling from the Old Manor House, Abbots Langley, given to the house with more early furniture by Miss Mabel Choate, to commemorate her father, US Ambassador to Britain. Three rooms on the first floor are used as a Community Centre.

SB

WARWICKSHIRE

Arbury Hall

2m south west of Nuneaton on B4102 Nuneaton–Solihull: the Viscount
Daventry, tel. 0203 382804. Open Easter–Sept Sun and BH Mon 2–5.30.
Guided tours. Refreshments.

Hidden away in its wooded grounds not far from the depressing suburbs
of Nuneaton, Arbury Hall is the finest 18C Gothic house in England. It owes
its present form to Sir Roger Newdigate, a scholarly country gentleman of
artistic and antiquarian tastes and Tory sympathies. He inherited the estate
in 1734 at the age of 14, went on a Grand Tour, and, starting in 1750, began
to remodel the existing house. This was built around a courtyard out of the
ruins of a small Augustinian priory by a lawyer, Edmund Anderson, early
in the reign of Queen Elizabeth, and was purchased in 1586 by John
Newdigate of Harefield (Middlesex), and altered in the 1670s by his
grandson, Sir Richard Newdigate. The 18C rebuilding was carried out
piecemeal over a period of 50 years, during which time Sir Roger took
advice from several different people, notably his fellow Warwickshire
squire, Sanderson Miller and, in the 1760s, Henry Keene, the Surveyor of
Westminster Abbey. The practical details were entrusted to William Hiorn
of Warwick, and subsequently to Thomas Couchman, but throughout the
long-drawn- out rebuilding, Sir Roger remained in overall control, and the
house embodies his taste and personality to a marked degree. Since 1800
there have been virtually no alterations, and his collection of paintings and
furniture remains largely intact.

The first building seen by visitors is the prodigious brick stable block,
which now houses a collection of vintage bicycles. This mammoth building
with its three 'Dutch' gables dates from the 1670s and was probably
designed by a Leicester builder and statuary, William Wilson, who was later
knighted after marrying the daughter of a Warwickshire landowner; Sir
Christopher Wren sent Sir Richard Newdigate a design for the doorcase,
but it is impossible to say whether or not the present chastely classical
entrance was designed by him.

The low grey sandstone house lies to the south, isolated among mani-
cured lawns and overlooking a lake created in the mid 18C out of earlier
formal canals and ponds. The main entrance is in the gaunt, turreted, north
front of c 1782, but before entering it is worth examining the nearby 'exedra'
of classical statuary—an indication of that merging of the classic and Gothic
sensibilities which seemed more natural to the 18C than it does to us—and
also the delicate south façade. It was created out of the original hall range
in 1750–70, with bay windows designed by Miller lighting each wing, and
a richly carved three-bay projection (designed by Sir Roger Newdigate
himself with the help of Henry Keene) in the centre.

Arthur Devis's portrait of Sir Roger lounging in his newly Gothicised
Library c 1756 greets the visitor in the low Entrance Hall, the walls of which
are hung with Grand Tour views of Italy. From here a corridor, on the site
of the monastic cloister walk, extends around the courtyard. There is
Flemish stained glass in the windows and pictures by Italian and Flemish
masters hang on the walls, among them Jacopo Bassano's 'Noah's Ark',
Joachim Beuckelaer's 'Christ in the House of Martha and Mary', Jordaens's
'Julius Caesar', an architectural capriccio by Jan Vredemann de Vries, and

The Saloon at Arbury Hall showing the intricate plaster Gothic ceiling, 1760s

a 'Nativity' by Luca Giordano, easy to miss in a corner. The Chapel of 1678 has an excellent plaster ceiling by Edward Martin, who also worked at Burghley House, Cambridgeshire (qv.), and from here the tour proceeds in a clockwise direction.

The first of the rooms redecorated by Sir Roger is the Schoolroom, with its plaster fan vault and ogee-arched chimneypiece inset with neo-classical relief carvings. The Gothic motifs are applied with increasing profusion in the remaining rooms, starting with the Saloon, whose amazingly complex plaster ceiling (modelled on the vault of Henry VII's Chapel in Westminster Abbey) was likened by George Eliot, daughter of the agent of the Arbury estate in the early 19C, to 'petrified lace-work'. A highly carved cabinet of the 1630s, formerly owned by Archbishop Laud, and a good collection of Chinese porcelain are displayed here, along with a small 15C Flemish panel of the Madonna and Child, a version of Reynolds's 'St John the Baptist as a oy' and a full-length portrait by Romney of Sir Roger Newdigate dressed in the robes of a Doctor of Civil Law at Oxford University; he holds the plans for the Oxford Canal, which linked the university city to the burgeoning industrial Midlands, whose development he promoted by sinking coal mines on the Arbury estate. The Drawing Room, on the south front, contains the most elaborate chimneypiece in the house, modelled on the late-13C tomb of Aymer de Vallance in Westminster Abbey; the walls and ceiling are completely covered with Gothic 'panelling' in plaster, set into which are large family portraits.

The adjacent Dining Room, on the site of the Elizabethan hall, is one of the most beautiful interiors of the Gothic Revival, with its plaster fan vault and its arcade on the south wall partially screening the body of the room from the light coming in through three huge windows. Copies of classical statuary rest happily in intricate Gothic niches, and on the walls there are some excellent Elizabethan portraits, including John Newdigate and his wife, and pictures of Queen Elizabeth's maid of honour Mary Fitton and of the Queen herself (by John Bettes), their lavish clothing matching the rich architectural setting. The last room to be seen is the Gallery on the upper floor of the north range; though given a shallow plaster vault and Gothic chairs by Sir Roger, this wood-panelled room still retains its ornate Elizabethan chimneypiece.

GCT

Baddesley Clinton

¾m west of A4141 Warwick–Birmingham at Chadwick End: National Trust, tel. 0564 783294. Open Mar–Sept Wed–Sun and BH Mon 2–6 (grounds open 12.30); Oct Wed–Sun 12.30–4. Refreshments.

Baddesley Clinton is a moated manor house of grey sandstone hidden away in wooded country in the heart of what was once the Forest of Arden. Its origins go back to the 15C, when Nicholas Brome, the son of a Warwick lawyer, built the east or entrance range and the west range which faces it across a small courtyard; he also built the tower of the parish church a short distance away. Since then there have been several alterations. The estate came by marriage in the early 16C to Sir Edward Ferrers, a member of an important Midlands family whose lineage can be traced back to the Norman Conquest (cf. Tamworth Castle, Staffs). His descendants were Catholic recusants, the estate relatively small and the family often in-debted; the house therefore never became very large or grand. Henry Ferrers (d 1633), an enthusiast for local and genealogical history, built the timber-framed south range, the south side of which was encased in brick in the early 18C, but the north or hall range was pulled down c 1750. The last of the family to inherit in direct male succession was Marmion Edward Ferrers (d 1884), who lived at Baddesley with his wife Rebecca, her aunt Georgiana, Lady Chatterton, and her husband Edward Heneage Dering.

Dering continued to live in the house after Ferrers's death and carried out alterations which enhanced its picturesque appeal. He also married Ferrer's widow, his own wife having died a few years earlier, and brought in a good collection of furniture and tapestries, much of which was dispersed between the Wars after the house had passed to a great-nephew of Marmion Ferrers; some items found their way to Packwood House (qv.), only a short distance away. The house was sold to a distant kinsman in 1940, and was acquired by the National Trust in 1980.

Baddesley Clinton is approached through a collection of red-brick farm buildings dating from the early 18C. The entrance front epitomises the complex and puzzling architectural history of the house, with its medieval gatehouse (heightened in the early 17C), its mixture of 15C, 17C and (on the left) 18C windows, and its tall brick chimneystacks introduced when the house was remodelled by Henry Ferrers. A stroll around the outer rim of the moat reveals the west range, with its array of three-light 15C windows and a projecting privy block added later, and the plain farmhouse-like brick façade of the south range, dating from the early 18C. The west range seems originally to have contained the main residential accommodation leading off from the hall, but by the 18C, if not earlier, the main focus of the house had shifted to the south range, and the west range became the service wing; this was widened and given a gabled frontage to the courtyard by Edward Heneage Dering in 1890. Medieval fish ponds survive to the west and north.

The house is entered through the south range, and after a detour to the kitchen the tour starts in the room which now serves as the Hall. The most striking feature here is a massive stone chimneypiece adorned with Mannerist motifs taken from North European pattern-books; this is the largest of a number of chimneypieces commissioned by Henry Ferrers when he refurbished the house in the 1620s, and may originally have been in the medieval hall, demolished in the 18C. There is a great deal of heraldic stained glass both here and elsewhere in the house, some of it dating from the late 16C and 17C, and several items of furniture of the same date are arranged in the attractively wood-panelled rooms. Early-17C wooden chimneypieces can be seen in the Dining and Drawing Rooms downstairs, and there is another good chimneypiece in the upstairs room known as Henry Ferrers's Bedroom, with some of its original painted decoration.

Several of the rooms contain paintings by Rebecca Ferrers, immortalising the self-consciously neo-feudal and fervently Catholic life of the house in the late 19C, and this is also vividly brought to mind in the rather claustrophobic Chapel upstairs. The light and airy Great Parlour over the gatehouse, with its large 17C mullioned window and barrel-vaulted ceiling, presents a sharp contrast. Here, more than in any of the other rooms, the original character of the house can be experienced. But in many ways, the appeal of Baddesley Clinton derives not so much from authenticity to any one period as from the romantic sense of its having stood outside the main currents of history and having been sympathetically altered over many generations.

GCT

Charlecote Park

5m east of Stratford to the north of B4056: National Trust, tel. 0789 470277.
Open Apr–Oct daily except Mon (but open BH Mon), Thur, 11–1, 2–5.30.
Refreshments.

The Lucy family has lived at Charlecote since the 12C, but the present house is primarily a monument to the building enthusiasm of two men: Sir Thomas Lucy, who built a new house of brick in 1551–59, and his descendant, George Hammond Lucy, and his wife, who remodelled and extended it, starting in the 1820s. From the outside, Charlecote is still in many ways a text-book example of an Elizabethan country gentleman's residence. A detached gatehouse flanked by angle turrets leads into a forecourt in front of the gabled house, which consists, like many others of its date, of a hall range with wings projecting at right-angles. It is entered through a porch embellished, like those at Deene Park and Kirby Hall, Northants (qv.), by classical pilasters and columns of the Ionic and Corinthian orders; this was probably added as an afterthought shortly before a visit by Queen Elizabeth in 1572. To the left of the forecourt there is a 16C service block containing a brewhouse.

Like many Elizabethan houses, Charlecote was greatly altered in the mid 18C. The present landscaped grounds, by 'Capability' Brown replaced the more formal gardens shown in a late-17C painting on display in the Hall, and sashes took the place of mullioned windows, as at Canons Ashby, Northants (qv.). Then, in the 1820s, George Hammond Lucy, fired by a romantic enthusiasm for the history of the house (Shakespeare was said to have been caught poaching deer in the park by Sir Thomas Lucy), employed the local architect C.S. Smith, a pupil of Wyatville, to reinstate the mullioned windows and to double the width of the hall range by the addition of a new block with a Dining Room and Library overlooking the River Avon. The decoration of the new rooms, and the redecoration of the Hall, was entrusted to Thomas Willement, best-known for his heraldic stained glass, of which there are some good specimens in the house. A new family wing (not shown) and stable block followed, and the forecourt and gardens by the Avon were laid out more formally. Finally, in 1852–56, after George Hammond Lucy's death, his widow employed John Gibson, a pupil of Sir Charles Barry, to remodel the north wing, containing the other main reception rooms (he also designed the parish church a short distance away to the north). In its rebuilt form the house is a splendid example of the 19C revival of interest in Elizabethan art and architecture.

Charlecote is also notable for its collections, and in particular for its furniture, most of which was brought into the house by George Hammond Lucy. He was an enthusiastic traveller and haunter of auction rooms, and in 1823 bought 64 items from the collection of the eccentric recluse William Beckford, some of which can be seen in the Hall, including a late-16C *pietra dura* table formerly in the Villa Borghese in Rome. The Hall owes its present appearance largely to Willement, who was responsible for the ceiling and panelling, the fireplace and the heraldic stained glass in the oriel window (the marble floor was brought from Venice in 1843); there are Lucy family portraits on the walls, including two by William Larkin, and busts of Shakespeare, Queen Elizabeth and George Hammond Lucy and his wife are placed elsewhere in the room. The Dining Room is an equally effective ensemble of the 1830s, with attractive wallpaper, a good plaster ceiling and a set of reproduction late-17C chairs supplied in 1837; the most prominent object (though not perhaps the most beautiful) is the 'Charlecote Buffet' by the Warwick carvers J.M. Willcox, introduced in 1858. The Library is similar in style and is furnished in the usual 19C fashion as a comfortable drawing room, with items supplied by the London cabinet-maker and antiques dealer, E.H. Baldock. Of these the most notable are a set of ebony and ivory chairs made in India in the late 17C, but thought by Lucy to date from the time of Queen Elizabeth. The room also houses an outstanding collection of Greek vases dating from the 6C BC and bought by George Hammond Lucy in Naples in 1829 and 1841; they can easily be missed since they are placed, as they always have been, on the tops of the bookcases.

The rooms in the north wing were decorated by the London upholsterers, George Troloppe & Sons, under the general supervision of John Gibson in the mid 1850s. The room now called the Ebony Bedroom was originally the billiard room, but has been rearranged to house a bed from one of the upstairs rooms made up from a late-17C settee, and purchased at the Beckford sale; a portrait of an earlier George Lucy painted in Rome by Pompeo Batoni in 1758 hangs over the fireplace. More of George Hammond Lucy's furniture is on view in the Drawing Room, including a *pietra dura* cabinet of c 1620, a casket of c 1740, and two ebony cabinets formerly at Fonthill Abbey, Beckford's wildly extravagant Gothic house in Wiltshire. After leaving the house, it is possible to visit the kitchens, brewhouse and coachhouse which, taken together, give a good indication of the life of a comfortable squirearchical establishment in its Victorian heyday.

GCT

Coughton Court

2m north of Alcester on A435 Birmingham–Evesham: National Trust/the Throckmorton family, tel. 0789 762435. Open April and Oct Sat, Sun and BH Mon, also May–Sept daily except Thur, Fri 1.30–5.30 (grounds open noon). Refrshments.

The most impressive feature of Coughton Court is the spectacular stone gatehouse, built by Sir George Throckmorton, who succeeded to the estate in 1518. With its turrets and oriel windows commanding a view over the surrounding flat meadow-land, this is a major monument of early Tudor architecture, and it was no doubt intended as a prelude to even greater glories within. Today this is no longer the case. The Throckmortons of Coughton were Catholic recusants (other branches of the family adopted the reformed religion), and although Sir George intended to make the rest of the house match the gatehouse, the funds were never available. By the end of the 16C two of the sides of the courtyard behind the gatehouse had been built in a homely mixture of brick and timber framing. Little is known about the east range, which was damaged by a Protestant mob enflamed by the Glorious Revolution of 1688, and later demolished. The house had meanwhile suffered from the attention of Parliamentary troops in 1643, but was rebuilt in 1663–65, and the south range, which contains the main rooms, was widened, with the external brick elevations crowned by curved 'Dutch' gables. There was a Gothick face-lift in 1783–95, when the front of the house was stuccoed and the moat filled in, and there were further alterations in the early 1830s and again in 1910.

The Throckmortons still live at Coughton in the north (private) wing as tenants of the National Trust, and the parts of the house which are shown to the public convey a sense of long and continuous possession by a Catholic family conscious of its ancient lineage. The Entrance Hall in the gatehouse, with its 18C plaster fan vault, gives access to a staircase of 1784–85 lined with portraits, including a Grand Tour portrait by Pompeo Batoni of Thomas Giffard (cf. Chillington Hall, Staffordshire). This leads to the Drawing Room on the first floor of the gatehouse, remodelled in the late 18C with a delicate Gothic frieze in plaster and containing two portraits by Nicholas de Largillière showing Sir Robert Throckmorton wearing armour (over the fireplace, 1729, with an ornate contemporary frame) and his aunt Anna, the abbess of a Parisian nunnery patronised by the family. The heraldic glass in the southernmost oriel window contains the arms of the Throckmortons and other local Catholic gentry, and in the display cases there is an attractive collection of 19C portrait miniatures of the Throckmortons and the Actons with whom they intermarried. A good collection of Worcester and Rockingham porcelain is displayed on the walls of the adjacent Little Drawing Room.

The upper levels of the gatehouse can be reached by a spiral staircase. The room above the Drawing Room, in which a priest-hole is visible, is mainly given over to a display of the copious family archives, and there is also an unusual memento of 16C Catholicism in the form of the 'Tabula Eliensis' (1596): a painting depicting the sufferings of the faithful in the years of persecution. After a detour to the roof, from which the timbered courtyard elevations can be seen, visitors descend to the Dining Room on the first floor of the south range; it is lined with unusually attractive wood panelling, including a frieze in the Renaissance taste of the early 16C. The adjacent dressing room has a collection of gouache drawings of Naples by the late-18C artist A.L. Ducros, and the room called the Tribune has panelling like that in the Dining Room; it contains several items of historical interest, including a cope said to have been embroidered by Catherine of Aragon and the garment in which Mary, Queen of Scots, was executed. From here a 17C staircase brought from Harvington Hall, Worcestershire (qv.) leads down into a room which may have been the medieval hall but was fitted up as a Catholic chapel in the 18C (the painted heavenly clouds on the ceiling are by a post-World War II scenery painter) and converted into a Drawing Room in 1910. Some early printed books are shown in a case under the staircase, along with the famous 'Throckmorton Coat', made in a day to win a bet in 1811.

GCT

Farnborough Hall

6m north of Banbury, to the west of A423, M40 exits 11 and 12: National Trust/Mr & Mrs Holbech, tel. 0788 535555. Open Apr–Sept Wed, Sat 2–6 (terrace walk only Thur, Fri 2–6).

Farnborough Hall has been the home of the Holbech family since 1684, when the estate was purchased by Ambrose Holbech of Mollington, just over the Oxfordshire boundary. His son added a classically proportioned west wing of the local brown Hornton stone to the existing manor house in the 1690s, but in its present form the house is largely the creation of Ambrose Holbech's grandson, William. He travelled extensively in Italy between 1730 and 1745, and soon afterwards began to transform what must have been a relatively modest building into one which would act as a suitable receptacle for his collection of antique busts and views of Italy by Canaletto and Pannini. At the same time he transformed the grounds into a classically inspired Elysium whose most striking feature is a gently curving terrace walk rising up the slope of the hillside on which the house stands; the walk is punctuated by two temples and an obelisk, and commands pastoral views over to the Edge Hills (now somewhat spoiled by the M40). Holbech's architect and garden designer have not been recorded, but his neighbour Sanderson Miller of Radway, the guiding spirit behind many of the building and gardening projects in the south Midlands in the mid 18C, may have been involved. The house came to the National Trust in 1960, and the Holbech family still lives here.

Farnborough is one of those houses, quite common in the mid 18C, in which the plain exterior gives no inkling of the decorative richness within. The north and south façades, both remodelled by William Holbech soon after his final return from Italy in 1745, are very restrained, but the Entrance Hall and the Saloon which faces the garden are adorned with superb plasterwork of a Rococo character; some, at least, of this work was designed and executed by William Perritt of York, who received a payment of £434 in 1750. The Hall was chosen by Holbech as the place to display the bulk of his collection of busts of Roman emperors and other worthies of the ancient world (some are 18C copies) in oval niches high on the walls. The decoration was carefully designed to complement these valuable objects; the ceiling pattern is echoed in the marble floor, and there is an impressive marble fireplace with a wooden overmantel of Palladian character, probably by Benjamin King of Warwick, framing a copy of a Pannini view of the piazza of St Peter's, Rome (the original was sold in 1928). The Dining Room, on the garden front, occupies the space between the wings of the original manor house. The plasterwork here is more exuberant than that of the Hall, and celebrates Holbech's musical and sporting interests. The room was designed to show off Holbech's Grand Tour views to good advantage, and although these have been replaced by copies, the ensemble, especially after recent repainting in the original light blue and pink colouring, remains a largely untouched example of mid-18C taste at its most engaging.

There is more plasterwork of the same date in the Staircase Hall, but the staircase itself, with its turned wooden balusters, and the oval wreath of plaster flowers and fruit on the ceiling, dates from the 1690s; the glazed dome was introduced in the mid 18C to light the stairs after the Saloon was built against the former outer wall, and at the same time William Holbech placed some of his finest Roman busts (eg, the emperor Lucius Verus) on the walls. The Library, the final room to be shown, dates from an internal remodelling of the west range by Henry Hakewill in the early 19C.

GCT

Honington Hall

1m north of Shipston-on-Stour, approached by a lane leading east from A3400: tel. 0608 661434. Open June–Aug Wed and BH Mon 2.30–5.

This attractive red-brick house was built in 1682 by Henry Parker, MP for Evesham, who subsequently inherited a baronetcy and fortune from his uncle, a London merchant. The house stands in parkland adjoining the parish church, in which Sir Henry and his son are commemorated by a massive marble monument. The unknown architect of both buildings was obviously familiar with metropolitan fashions, and the neat, well-proportioned house with its hipped roof would not look at all out of place in the Home Counties. The entrance front has changed little since it was first built, apart from the substitution of sash for casement windows. The main doorway is marked by a wooden doorcase surmounted by a broken pediment enclosing an achievement of arms (there is an even finer doorcase on the north or service side of the house, with a shell-hood of a type often seen in London), and busts of Roman emperors sit in niches over the ground-floor windows.

The estate was acquired in 1737 by Joseph Townsend, the son of a London brewer, who married an heiress and sat as an MP for various rotten boroughs from 1741 to 1754. He remodelled the main interiors, starting with the Entrance Hall in the 1740s and culminating in 1751 in the creation of an impressive octagonal Saloon on the site of the original staircase, lit by a canted bay window built out from the west front and designed by a talented amateur, John Freeman of Fawley Court, Bucks (qv.). These rooms were decorated with ornamental plasterwork of the highest quality. At the same time Townsend landscaped the gardens with the advice of his neighbour, Sanderson Miller of Radway, and some of the ornamental buildings still survive. The house descended through Townsend's family until 1922, when it was bought by the grandfather of the present owner. Though denuded of its original furniture, it has been little altered since the mid 18C, and today it is still occupied as a comfortable family home.

The main interest of the interior lies in the plasterwork, which is first seen in the profusely decorated Entrance Hall. Figurative panels of 'Venus Appearing to Aeneas' and 'Hector Bidding Farwell to Andromache' over the chimneypieces have been attributed on stylistic grounds to the Danish plasterer Charles Stanley, but the decorative surrounds, the panels of the Arts over the doors, and the ceiling with its representations of the Elements, may be by Thomas Roberts of Oxford. The Drawing Room retains its dark wood panelling of the early 18C, but Townsend introduced the Kentian mirror on the east wall and the massive Palladian doorcase with cherubs sprawling on the pediment. This leads into the Boudoir, where there is a plaster representation of Flora on the ceiling. The adjacent Saloon is a *tour de force* of mid-18C craftsmanship. The basic architectural framework is again Palladian, but much of the plaster decoration, especially the exuberant festoons tumbling down the walls at the corners, is Rococo in character, as are the splendidly extravagant mirror frames; these features were introduced against the wishes of the architect, probably at the suggestion of the builder, William Jones, surveyor to the East India Company. The Staircase Hall, cunningly contrived in the space to the east of the Saloon, has more good plasterwork, and the staircase itself has a curly wrought-iron balustrade of the kind which was soon to become common in English domestic interiors.

GCT

Packwood House

2m east of A3400 Stratford–Birmingham at Hockley Heath: National Trust, tel. 0564 782024. Open Apr–Sept Wed–Sun and BH Mon 2–6; Oct Wed–Sun 12.30–4.30.

Packwood House started life as one of the many large timber-framed farmhouses built in the former Forest of Arden in the second half of the 16C. The builder, William Fetherston, described himself as a yeoman, but his grandson, John, was trained as a lawyer and led the life of a country gentleman. He proclaimed his new-found status in the 1670s by laying out a walled forecourt flanked by a red-brick office wing, and a walled garden with gazebos at the corners; this now contains an impressive display of topiary begun c 1650–70 but greatly expanded in the late 19C. The house lost much of its external character when sash windows were introduced and the ornamental timber-framing was rendered over at some stage in the late 18C or early 19C, and today, despite the reinstatement of mullioned windows, the timber-framing of the main building is still concealed.

Like many other English manor houses of its type, Packwood was 'discovered' at the end of the 19C. In 1904 the property was bought by Alfred Ash, a Birmingham industrialist, and his son Graham Baron Ash, restored and extended the house in 1925–32 as a setting for his collection of furniture, tapestries and pictures of the 16C, 17C and 18C. House, contents and grounds were presented to the National Trust in 1941, and although Packwood is now best-known for its gardens, the house, with its carefully chosen contents, can be appreciated as an interesting example of the 'Old English' taste of the inter-war period.

The original 16C house was a square two-storeyed 'double-pile' building with only four rooms on each floor. It is entered through the Hall, which like the other rooms was totally refashioned by Ash and his architect, Edwin Reynolds of Birmingham, to contain furniture, hangings and even floorboards brought from other houses. Close by is the Parlour, overlooking the entrance courtyard and containing tapestries and some small 17C pictures (eg, Jan van Kessel's 'Peasants Carousing'). This leads into a corridor (the Long Gallery) built behind the service wing in 1931–32 to connect the original house with a 'Great Hall' formed out of an old barn. The outside of this extension was designed in a bland neo-Tudor style employed in countless inter-war public houses and schools, but inside the rooms come to life through the use of old panelling and chimneypieces. The Gallery is hung with tapestries, including 16C and 17C Flemish, Aubusson and Mortlake pieces, and there are some interesting items of furniture, including a 16C 'Nonesuch' chest, a late-17C chest inlaid with mother-of-pearl (there is another in the Dining Room) and a set of early-18C chairs with needlework covers of the same date. The Great Hall still has its rustic raised-cruck roof dating from its days as a barn. The huge early-17C chimneypiece with its plaster overmantel was taken from an inn in Stratford-upon-Avon, but the long refectory table with a medieval top and early-16C supports came from Baddesley Clinton (qv.), as did the three very attractive tapestries: a late-17C Brussels scene of the Muses in a terraced Italian garden, and Soho pair dating from c 1733 of the Continents of Africa and America (stolen and not, alas, recovered at the time of writing).

The original house is regained through the Gallery, from which a staircase leads up to the bedroom floor, where, among other rooms, there is a bathroom fitted out with Delft tiles in the 1920s. The remaining rooms on the ground floor are reached by another staircase; they contain 17C Flemish stained glass from Culham House (Oxfordshire), some early pictures, including an anonymous early-16C French Virgin and Child (in the Inner Hall), and furniture appropriate to the calculatedly picturesque character of the house.

GCT

Ragley Hall

2m south of Alcester on A435 Birmingham–Evesham: the Earl of Yarmouth, tel. 0789 762090. Open Easter–Sept daily except Mon, Fri and BH Mon 12–5. Refreshments.

Ragley Hall was built in 1680 on a commanding hilltop site near the small town of Alcester by the 3rd Viscount (and 1st Earl of) Conway, one of Charles II's courtiers and a former governor of three counties in Ulster. The design was worked out by Conway in consultation with his friends, who included the scientist and amateur architect Robert Hooke, with the Hurlbut brothers (cf. Warwick Castle) acting as builders. With its vast central hall and saloon on the first floor, flanked by 'apartments' for family and guests, the house was conceived in the spirit of a contemporary French château, but it was left unfinished after Lord Conway's death (childless) in 1683; it remained an empty shell until 1750, when it became the main residence of Francis Seymour, Earl (and later Marquess) of Hertford, whose father had inherited the estate from his cousin, Lord Conway.

Lord Hertford commissioned James Gibbs to complete and embellish the Hall and some of the adjoining rooms, which now served as living rooms for the family and guests. Work stopped in 1760, and a break of some 20 years ensued before the remaining rooms were decorated in 1780–83 by James Wyatt, who also designed the stable block. There have been few major architectural changes since then, thanks largely to the virtual desertion of Ragley by some of the 19C owners, notably the 3rd and 4th Marquesses, the second of whom lived in Paris and built up what is now the Wallace Collection in London. The house was rescued from near-dereliction after the Second World War by the present Marquess, who has enterprisingly commissioned good works of art by living artists—an all too rare occurrence in houses of this kind. Ragley is now occupied by his son, the Earl of Yarmouth.

The massive house is built of the local blue lias stone, and presents a somewhat bland face to the outside world, enlivened mainly by Wyatt's Ionic portico on the entrance front. The house is entered underneath the portico, and the piano nobile is reached by the **South Staircase**, the walls of which are covered with highly original trompe-l'oeil mural paintings of 'The Temptation' carried out in 1969–81 by Graham Rust. These paintings, which include portraits of the present Marquess, his family and friends, take their stylistic cue from the Rococo mirrors on either side of the doorway into the Hall (seen at the end of the tour), and in their exuberant vitality pay a fitting tribute to the *genius loci*. The tour starts in the **Prince Regent's Bedroom**, at the southern extremity of the long garden front; it contains the canopied bed from which the Prince (a crony of the 2nd Marquess) was roused to be told of the death of this daughter Princess Charlotte. The **Green**

Drawing Room has a plaster ceiling of the 1750s, two large mirrors in the Chinese taste of the time and several Reynolds family portraits of varying quality. Next comes the **Red Saloon**, sumptuously decorated in the style of the early 19C, with heavily draped curtains and upholstered furniture. There is a good collection of porcelain, including Sèvres, Meissen and Chinese items, and Old Master paintings collected by the 1st Marquess hang on the walls, including a Poussinesque 'Christ Entering Jerusalem' by Sébastien Bourdon (1670) and a 'Raising of Lazarus' by Cornelius van Haarlem (1602). The ceiling is by Wyatt, with neo-classical motifs, some of them in grisaille, set among delicate linear patterns, and there are more Wyatt ceilings in the next two rooms, the first of which (the Mauve Drawing Room) also contains landscapes by Vernet and Richard Wilson.

A large canvas by the 20C artist Ceri Richards ('The Defeat of the Spanish Armada') hangs in the **North Staircase Hall**; the staircase itself is part of a remodelling by the obscure architect William Tasker for the 5th Marquess, who inherited in 1870. He was Lord Chamberlain to Queen Victoria, and her portrait occupies the place of honour over the fireplace in the adjacent **Dining Room**, which was redecorated by Wyatt, but owes much of its present appearance to a further remodelling in the 1870s. There are several other portraits of royal personages here, and a superb collection of silver is also on display, including some pieces of 1772 and a cruet set by Paul Storr dated 1804.

The remaining rooms are decorated in the exuberant Rococo taste of the 1750s. There is some good plasterwork in the **Breakfast Room**, including a representation of Leda and the Swan on the ceiling, and also in the **Music Room** (originally a dining room, as can be seen from the Bacchic decorations over the fireplace); note also the carved overmantel in the Breakfast Room and the attractive Regency furniture. But these rooms are eclipsed in splendour by what Horace Walpole called the 'leviathan **Hall**', the last major work of James Gibbs. This palatial room may appear excessively large, but such mundane considerations pale in the face of the overwhelming sense of space and the quality of the plasterwork (by Giuseppe Artari 1756–60). To the south of the Hall (and open only on request) is the Library, with Reynolds's well-known portrait of Horace Walpole over the fireplace, and the Study, with more delicate plasterwork on the ceiling. Outside, the grounds were landscaped in the usual way in the late 18C, but a **formal garden** was created in the west (garden) front by Robert Marnock in the 1870s.

GCT

Upton House

7m north west of Banbury on A422 Banbury–Stratford: National Trust, tel. 029587 266. Open Apr, Oct Sat, Sun and BH Mon; May–Sept Sat–Wed 2–6 (possibly subject to change). Refreshments.

Upton House is mainly visited today for its gardens and its outstanding collection of pictures and porcelain. The house was first built in 1695 by Sir Rushout Cullen, the inheritor of a mercantile fortune, using the local brown stone still quarried at Hornton, just over the Oxfordshire border. It was sold twice in the early 18C, latterly to the Child family, subsequently Earls of Jersey, and for most of the 19C it was used as a hunting box and let out for long periods of time. The original house was extended in 1735 and again after 1757, but in its present form it is largely the creation of Walter Samuel, the 2nd Viscount Bearstead, who bought the estate in 1927. He used the fortune accumulated by his father, one of the founders of the Shell oil company, to build up one of the most important private art collections in 20C England, and, under the direction of the architect Percy Morley Horder, the house was expanded and modernised in a tactful neo-Georgian manner in 1927–29. It was given to the National Trust in 1948.

The excessively elongated house faces south over a lawn, with luxuriant terraced **gardens** created by Lady Bearstead with the help of Morley Horder sloping down towards a lake; to the west there is a 'bog garden' overlooked by a late-17C brick banqueting house. The entrance is through the late-17C north front, the central three bays of which are surmounted by a broken segmental pediment. The discreetly comfortable interiors date almost entirely from the inter-war period. The **Entrance Hall**, hung with mid-17C Brussels tapestries, contains one of the few surviving 18C chimneypieces in the house, and the staircase which leads up to the first floor (not shown to visitors) makes use of the original balusters; a Canaletto view of Venice can be glimpsed on the first-floor landing. A Lobby, containing a view of the house and grounds by Anthony Devis (c 1803), leads into the **Dining Room**, dating from c 1775 and lit by a canted bay window; the furniture is Georgian, and the walls are hung with 18C English sporting pictures, together with three large canvases of rural occupations by George Stubbs (1783), which rank among the finest of his works. The rooms in the centre of the garden front were run together into a single **Long Gallery** or drawing room by Morley Horder; it now contains French and English 18C furniture and 17C Dutch pictures (note especially Saenredam's 'St Catherine's Church, Utrecht', Saloman van Ruisdael's 'Country Road' and a set of small allegorical pictures of the Senses by Jan Steen). There is also a superb collection of porcelain, including Chelsea 'gold anchor' figures of the 1760s (eg, a group based on Boucher's 'l'Agréable Leçon') and Bow figures (eg, of the actress Kitty Clive and the actor Henry Woodward) from the early 1750s.

The **French Room**, on the north front of the house next to the Entrance Hall, contains pictures by Greuze and a view of the quay at Olaveaga by the late-18C Spanish artist Luis Paret y Alcazar, rarely represented in English collections; in the lobby outside is a portrait by Romney of an arrogant-looking William Beckford, the builder of Fonthill Abbey. The adjacent **Staircase Lobby** contains two family groups by Arthur Devis, a portrait by Raeburn, and a small oil sketch by Constable. From here visitors can descend to the **Porcelain Lobby**; where excellent Sèvres items are displayed, including a tea service of 1764 with scenes after Boucher on a yellow background, part of a tea and coffee service made for Catherine the Great of Russia in 1778, and a pair of ice pails made for Louis XVI of France in 1792. Nearby is the **Sports Room**, decorated in a restrained Arts and Crafts manner with a comfortable inglenook by the fireplace. English 18C paintings are hung here, among them Hogarth's 'Morning' and 'Night' from his 'Times of Day' series (better-known as engravings), and there are more English paintings in the adjacent **Billiard Room** (eg, John'Opie's 'Country Girl', 1795).

The cream of the Upton picture collection—one of the richest and most varied in any English country house—is to be found in the Gallery, created out of a former racquets court in the 1930s. It is approached through a

corridor hung with several important Italian and Dutch pictures, among them Tintoretto's 'Wise and Foolish Virgins' (c 1548), Giandomenico Tiepolo's 'Madonna and two Saints', Guardi's 'Pope Pius VI Blessing the Venetians', Gabriel Metsu's 'The Duet' and an atmospheric view towards Haarlem by Jacob van Ruisdael; there is also a Holbein 'Portrait of a Young Man' and a powerful El Greco of 'The Disrobing of Jesus'. The Italian and early Flemish schools are especially well-represented in the Gallery proper, with pictures by Giovanni di Paulo ('Presentation of the Virgin') and Carlo Crivelli ('Two Apostles'), portraits by Memling and Roger van der Weyden, a triptych by Hieronymus Bosch (the 'Adoration of the Magi'), two panels by Jan Provoost ('Nativity at Night' and 'Virgin Mary and Joseph at Bethlehem'), a Madonna and Child by Gerard David, Joachim Patenir's 'Temptation of Christ', and the elder Pieter Breughel's grisaille 'Dormition of the Virgin' (c 1564); note also the portraits of Francis I and Henry II of France from the studio of François Clouet. A display case contains illuminated late-medieval manuscripts, including some by the French artist Jean Fouquet.

SB

Warwick Castle

In Warwick, approached from the west, M40 exit 15: tel. 0926 495421.
Open daily, except Christmas Day, all year 10–5.30 (Oct–Feb 4.30).
Refreshments.

This magnificent feudal fortress stands on the southern edge of the county town on an escarpment overlooking the River Avon. It started life as a Norman motte-and-bailey structure, but in a large-scale rebuilding programme undertaken by the Beauchamp Earls of Warwick in the 14C, it acquired new residential accommodation and a splendid array of towers interrupting the high curtain walls along the vulnerable approaches from the north and east. The castle became Crown property after the death of the notorious 'Warwick the Kingmaker' in 1471, and fell into a decline, but was rescued in 1604 when James I granted it to the poet and courtier Sir Fulke Greville, 1st Lord Brooke. He began to refurbish the state rooms, a process which was impressively completed after the Restoration by the 4th Lord Brooke. The 8th Lord Brooke (1st Earl of Warwick of the new creation) carried out further alterations starting in the 1750s, and employed 'Capability' Brown to landscape the grounds, which were further embellished in the late 18C and 19C. The 2nd and 3rd Earls acquired an impressive collection of furniture, armour and Old Master paintings, and Anthony Salvin did some extensive restoration work in 1863–66, but the Hall and private apartments had to be remodelled again following a fire in 1871. The Greville ownership came to an end in 1978, and under its present enterprising owners the castle is now visited by more people than any other English house in private hands.

No English castle can match Warwick for late-medieval splendour. Rebuilt at a time when the great magnates vied with each other for local and national dominance, it was designed more as an exuberant display of the power of the Beauchamp family than as a functional fighting machine. The **east range**, seen immediately on entering the grounds through the former stable block, is made up of a curtain wall flanked by three towers: the impressively machicolated Caesar's Tower of the 1370s at the south end, the main **Gatehouse** with its barbican in the centre, and the polygonal Guy's Tower finished in 1393 closest to the viewer. These towers, built of the local grey sandstone, all contained 'lodgings' for visitors and members of the household of the medieval Earls, and some of the rooms can be seen inside the Gatehouse, which also preserves its portcullises and the 'murder holes' through which unpleasant objects and liquids could be poured on to attackers. Caesar's Tower, entered from inside the courtyard, now contains a grisly but popular collection of torture instruments on the ground floor. Beyond this, in the former brewhouse, there is an exhibition of **armour** which includes the massive 14C sword long believed to have belonged to 'Guy of Warwick', the legendary founder of the castle, as well as other items of both English and foreign armour acquired in the late 18C and early 19C. The south side of the courtyard is occupied by the much-rebuilt domestic apartments, centred on the Hall and resting on massive stone foundations which can be seen to very good effect from the opposite side of the Avon (reached by a path through the grounds). To the west of the courtyard is the Norman motte, and to the north a curtain wall with the lower part of what was to be a huge keep-like gatehouse planned in the late 15C in the centre. Stairs lead from here to **Guy's Tower**, from which there is an exhilerating walk along the eastern ramparts.

The residential quarters are shown in three sections: a small group of early-17C lodgings centred on the **Watergate Tower**, next to the motte; the state rooms, to the west of the Hall behind the early-16C Spy Tower; and the largely Victorian private apartments on the site of the original service range. The **state rooms** are reached through an inconspicuous doorway which leads first into the private **Chapel**, remodelled in the 19C, and containing a Flemish wood carving of c 1740 based on Rubens's 'Battle of the Amazons'. A corridor with a ribbed plaster ceiling in the Gothick taste gives access to the **Great Hall**, whose present rather gloomy appearance is the result of rebuilding by Salvin after the fire of 1871. The vast room is filled with armour, including some important 16C German and Italian pieces as well as objects of mainly associational value like Oliver Cromwell's death mask; they are complemented by the gargantuan 'Kenilworth Buffet', a tour de force of the mid-Victorian 'Warwick school' of wood carvers. The **Dining Room**, to the left of the Hall, was designed by the Liverpool architect, Timothy Lightoler, in 1763, and with its intricate plaster ceiling by the local craftsman, Robert Moore, presents an early example of the revival of interest in Elizabethan architecture and decoration; the picture of two lions on the fireplace wall is by Rubens's pupil, Frans Snyders.

The remaining state rooms stretch in an *enfilade* to the west of the Hall. After their 17C remodelling they formed a 'great apartment', consisting of a public ante-room, a great chamber (or formal dining room) and withdrawing room, followed by a private bedroom and closet. New furniture and pictures were introduced in the second half of the 18C, but most of the sumptuous post-Restoration panelling and plasterwork remains. The highlight of the ante-chamber (now called the **Red Drawing Room**) is a portrait of Joanna of Aragon, long attributed to Raphael but now thought to be a copy, possibly by Giulio Romano; there is also a portrait by William Dobson of the Civil War commander Montrose. The great chamber (the **Cedar Drawing Room**) is the most magnificent room in the suite, and one of the finest of its date in England. It takes its name from the superb wood panelling by two local carpenters, Roger and William Hurlbut, who also designed the Market House in the centre of Warwick and worked at the

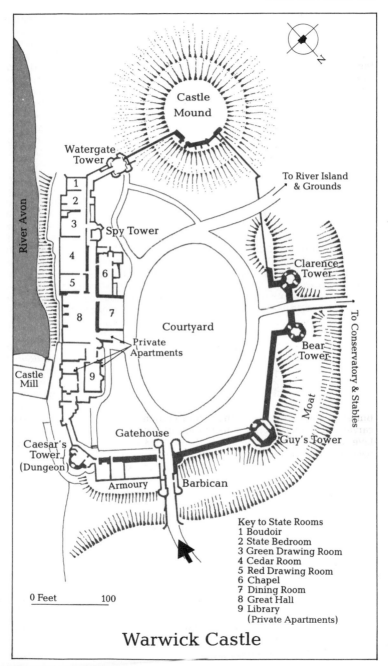

Castle Mound

Watergate Tower

To River Island & Grounds

River Avon

1
2
3
Spy Tower
4
6
5
Clarence Tower
8
7
Bear Tower
Courtyard
Private Apartments
9
Moat
To Conservatory & Stables
Castle Mill

Gatehouse
Guy's Tower

Caesar's Tower (Dungeon)

Armoury
Barbican

Key to State Rooms
1 Boudoir
2 State Bedroom
3 Green Drawing Room
4 Cedar Room
5 Red Drawing Room
6 Chapel
7 Dining Room
8 Great Hall
9 Library
 (Private Apartments)

0 Feet   100

Warwick Castle

castle from 1669 to 1681; the equally fine plaster ceiling is possibly by James Pettifer (cf. Sudbury Hall, Derbyshire), and the portraits include Van Dyck's 'Princess Beatrice de Cousance'. The adjacent **Green Drawing Room** has late-17C panelling and a ceiling of the 1760s modelled on one in the Temple of the Sun at Palmyra; the *pietra dura* table was acquired by the 3rd Earl of Warwick in the mid 19C. The **Queen Anne Bedroom** has a plaster ceiling of the 1670s, and early-18C state bed given to the 1st Earl by George III, and a very fine collection of tapestries made in Delft in 1604 showing people and animals disporting themselves in formal garden settings; of all the state rooms, this remains closest to its original appearance. The final room in the suite was once the closet, but is now known as the **Blue Boudoir**; the ceiling is again of the 1670s and there is a portrait of Henry VIII, from the studio of Holbein, over the fireplace.

The **private apartments**, approached through the main entrance to the Hall, are now peopled with waxwork figures representing visitors at a house party in 1898; the displays have been carefully contrived and provide an excellent insight into the life of a large late-Victorian country house. The rooms themselves date mostly from after the fire of 1871 and exhibit a wide variety of decorative styles; the most attractive are the neo-Renaissance Library by Anthony Salvin and C.E. Fox and the Boudoir, in the French Rococo taste of c 1900. A staircase leads up to the bedroom floor, and from here a passage along the upper south wall of the Hall gives access to some older rooms, including one by Salvin containing Elizabethan panelling said to have been brought from Kenilworth Castle, not far away, and another in the Gothick style of the 1760s, with a bed in the Chinese taste.

Peacocks roam freely in the grounds, where there is a **conservatory** designed by a local architect, William Eborall, in 1786, to house the famous late-Roman 'Warwick Vase' dug up in pieces at Hadrian's Villa at Tivoli and subsequently acquired and restored by the 2nd Earl (the original is now in the Burrell Collection in Glasgow, but a replica has recently been installed). The parterre in front was created in 1868 by the Victorian garden designer, Robert Marnock, who also designed the recently restored rose garden in the east part of the grounds. A path close to the Norman motte leads down to the Avon, where there is a splendid view, painted by Canaletto, of the formidable south front of the castle (the picture is now in the Paul Mellon Collection in the USA), and from the top of the motte there is an extensive vista over 'Capability' Brown's park.

GCT

WILTSHIRE

Bowood

2½m west of Calne on A4 Calne–Chippenham at Derry Hill: the Earl of Shelburne, tel. 0249 812102. Open Apr–Oct daily 11–6. Refreshments.

The Bowood seen by visitors today is a substantial fragment of the largely 18C house of the Marquesses of Lansdowne, set in one of the most beautiful country-house landscapes in the south of England. The fortunes of the Fitzmaurice-Petty family, Earls of Shelburne and later Marquesses of Lansdowne, go back to the Interregnum, when Sir William Petty, former Professor of Anatomy in Oxford and a friend of the philosopher Thomas Hobbes, built up a large and profitable estate in Ireland. His grandson, the 2nd Earl, bought the Bowood estate with its plain early-18C house in 1753, and two years later he set about rebuilding it to the designs of Henry Keene. He died in 1761, and his son turned to 'Capability' Brown to landscape the grounds and to Robert Adam to complete the interior. Adam also designed the noble classical mausoleum near the edge of the park (1761–64) to commemorate the 1st Earl (only accessible mid May to mid June), and in 1768–70 he added the range now known as the Diocletian Wing to mask the office courtyard next to the house; this included a new Sculpture Gallery.

Lord Shelburne, a friend of Benjamin Franklin and Jeremy Bentham, was made Marquess of Lansdowne in 1784 after a long and controversial political career during which he served briefly as Prime Minister. He died in debt and his books and works of art were sold, leaving only his collection of antique statuary in the house. The 3rd Marquess, who also became a leading Whig politician, established the nucleus of the present collection of pictures, and made important alterations to the house and grounds, starting c 1813, when the library was altered by Sir Robert Smirke. Smirke also designed the upper terrace in front of the Diocletian Wing in 1818, and in 1822–24 C.R. Cockerell built a new chapel behind the wing. Later alterations were entrusted to Charles Barry, including the impressive Italianate 'Golden Gates' lodge at the north-west corner of the park (1834–57). In 1956 the 8th Marquess demolished the main house and took up residence in the former private wing or 'little house' (not open to the public) on the east side of the service courtyard; the library, chapel and orangery were retained, and they are now open to the public.

The present house faces east towards Brown's expansive, arcadian landscape, with the terraces laid out by the 3rd Marquess in 1818 and 1851 to the south: a telling juxtaposition of the 18C and 19C styles of gardening. With the demolition of the main house, which stood to the east of the terraces, the architectural focus shifted to the monumental Diocletian Wing, with its long, low façade of Doric columns interrupted by higher pavilions in which Adam made use of a variant of the Corinthian order which he had discovered in Diocletian's palace at Split in Croatia (the tower over the chapel, of 1860, is by Barry). The entrance leads into a vestibule between paired Ionic columns, with the austere Grecian Chapel beyond—one of the few interiors by Cockerell to be seen in a country house—and picture galleries stretching out on either side. They house changing displays relating to the history of the family, and a selection from their art collection, which is also changed from time to time. Pictures on display at the time of writing (1992) included a portrait of Baldessare Castiglione by Girolamo de Treviso, Thomas Gainsborough's poetic 'Landscape with cattle coming home' (early 1770s), and a number of works by early-19C British artists patronised by the 3rd Marquess, who was one of the first Trustees of the National Gallery; they include Sir Augustus Calcott's 'Pool of London' (1815) and some of the canvases painted by Clarkson Stanfield for the dining room in the main house (eg, 'Citara in the Gulf of Salerno', and 'Venice from the Dogana').

At the east end of the gallery is an ante-room known as the Laboratory, where Joseph Priestley, 'the father of modern chemistry' and a protégé of the 1st Marquess, discovered oxygen gas. Beyond is the Library, by Cockerell, like a room in a London club, with a coved ceiling embellished with roundels of ancient philosophers; there are antique vases on the tops of the bookcases, and a 'Portrait of a Woman' by Gerard Terborch hangs next to the fireplace. At the opposite end of the picture gallery is a sculpture gallery containing some of the antique sculptures bought by the 1st Marquess, and beyond, at the west extremity of the house, there are more pictures displayed in a series of smaller rooms and corridors created out of the former grooms' quarters in 1979–80. They include an excellent collection of 19C British watercolours, many of them acquired by the present Lord Shelburne, including works by Varley, Cox, Turner, David Roberts and Edward Lear, and an important collection of drawings by Bonington bought by the 3rd Marquis after the artist's death in 1829. There are also Indian items collected by the 5th Marquess, Viceroy from 1888 to 1894. Outside, 'Capability' Brown's lawns beckon visitors down to the lake with a Doric temple on the further shore and a picturesque cascade designed in 1785–87 by the Hon. Charles Hamilton of Painshill (Surrey) hidden away on the north side.

GCT

Charlton Park

½m north of Malmesbury on A429 Malmesbury–Cirencester: the Earl of Suffolk and Berkshire. Open May–Oct Mon, Thur 2–4. Guided tours.

Though relatively little known, Charlton Park is one of the major Jacobean houses in England, and there is the added bonus of a fine late-18C interior. The house stands in an extensive park on land formerly belonging to the Benedictine Abbey of Malmesbury, which was bought after the Reformation by a wealthy clothier, James Stumpe. His daughter married Sir Henry Knyvett, who built what he called a 'poor cottage' on the site of the present house, and when he died in 1598 it went to this daughter and her second husband, Thomas Howard, Earl of Suffolk, later Lord Treasurer to James I and builder of the phenomenally grand Audley End, Essex (qv.). They greatly enlarged Knyvett's house in the early 17C, adding the west range— through which the house is now entered—as a new show front and raising the height of the existing building to match.

On the death of Lord Suffolk in 1626 Charlton went to his younger son, who was created Earl of Berkshire, but since 1745, when the 10th Earl of Suffolk died without heirs, the titles have been united. In 1772–76 the 12th Earl of Suffolk (and Berkshire), brought in the younger Matthew Brettingham to create a magnificent domed hall out of the former courtyard and to remodel the north and east fronts and some of the interiors. He died in 1779, and the work remained unfinished for over a century. The family moved to a smaller house after the Second World War, and the main house lay empty for 25 years before being restored and converted into flats. This involved dividing up the long gallery on the first floor of the west range—the only surviving Jacobean interior—which may once have housed the superb set of portraits by William Larkin now in the Ranger's House at Greenwich, Greater London (qv.). The only important interiors to survive now are Brettingham's Hall, Dining Room and Staircase, and these are the rooms which are shown to the public.

The west front is perhaps the most fanciful surviving piece of Jacobean country-house architecture; an outstandingly inventive composition with a classical loggia on the ground floor—originally open and leading to the courtyard—and the long gallery above, flanked by ogee-capped turrets and low projecting wings surmounted by exotic cresting, matching the almost decadent display of contemporary costume and the complexities of metaphysical poetry. The other façades are much less exciting, and are in any case not visible to visitors. By far the most impressive of the interiors is the Hall, Adamesque in its decorative detail and vying in architectural grandeur with all but the very best of Adam's rooms. The inspiration derives from ancient Rome, which Brettingham had visited in 1747 to 1754, when he was also collecting sculpture for the Earl of Leicester's Holkham Hall, Norfolk (qv.), and the spacious top-lit room admirably recreates the nobility of the Roman public buildings on which it was modelled. It is not easy to see how much of the stucco decoration is original, but the 'grotesque' panels and medallions are certainly in keeping with the overall style. The Dining Room and Staircase are plainer, but the grandeur of the Hall and the exuberance of the west front in themselves justify a visit to Charlton.

GCT

Corsham Court

In Corsham, 4m west of Chippenham on A4 Bath–Chippenham: the Lord Methuen, tel. 0249 712214. Open Jan–Nov daily, except Mon (open BH Mon), Fri (open Good Fri) 2–4.30 (Good Fri–Sept 2–6).

The main interest of Corsham Court lies in its superb collection of Old Master paintings amassed by Sir Paul Methuen in the 18C. The Methuen fortune originated in the flourishing Wiltshire cloth industry of the 17C, but Sir Paul's father followed a legal and political career and in 1703 he became ambassador to Portugal, in which capacity he negotiated an important trade treaty for the import of wine and export of cloth. His son also went into politics, but he resigned in 1730 and focused his energies on building up his art collection, which he kept in his London house. When he died in 1757 he left the pictures to his godson, another Paul Methuen, heir to the cloth business, who had purchased the Corsham estate 12 years earlier. He employed 'Capability' Brown to landscape the grounds and to build a new picture gallery on to the existing, mainly Elizabethan, house in 1761–64; this has survived intact, along with its furnishings, although the rest of the house has been much rebuilt.

The somewhat forbidding stone house is approached directly from the small town, a former centre of the domestic cloth industry; stables and a former riding school flank the entrance, rather as in a French château. The original builder was Thomas Smyth, a local man who made a fortune from farming the London customs, and the core of his house of 1582 survives on the south (entrance) front, with its three-gabled hall range in the centre and wings projecting forward. Brown doubled their width in order to accommodate the new picture gallery and a new library, but, unusually for that date, he maintained the Elizabethan character externally. In 1797 Paul Cobb Methuen called in John Nash to remodel the Elizabethan hall internally and to build a new range in a flimsy Tudor-Gothic style on the garden side to the north, but his work turned out to be badly built and it was all swept away in 1844–49 by the 1st Lord Methuen and his architect, Thomas Bellamy, who was responsible for the heavy, pinnacled staircase tower at the centre of the north front which still casts a blight over the rest of the building. More pictures, including several by 15C Italian masters, came into the house in 1849 when the 2nd Lord Methuen inherited the collection of his father-in-law, the Rev. John Sanford, a long-standing resident of Florence. Both the house and the collections have remained in the family, but from 1946 until recently the present Lord Methuen shared the building with the Bath College of Higher Education.

The house is entered through the Hall, by Bellamy, but the tour starts in the **Picture Gallery**, begun in 1761. This is one of the finest rooms of its type in any English country house. Brown's craftsmen—notably the plasterer Thomas Stocking of Bristol and the carpenter John Hobcraft—created a lavish setting for Paul Methuen's pictures, and the effect is enhanced by the furnishings, including the red silk damask wall coverings, the marble chimneypiece by Scheemakers, the chairs and settees by Chippendale and the neo-classical tables and pier-glasses by the Adam brothers. The pictures themselves, still hung much as they were in the 18C, many of them in their original frames, offer an almost unparalleled insight into 18C artistic taste. A version of Van Dyck's famous portrait of Charles I on horseback hangs on the north wall (to the left on entering), while the long west wall is dominated by three more large canvases: Guido Reni's 'Baptism of Christ' (to the left of the fireplace), Rubens's 'Wolf and Fox Hunt', in a frame by Adam (over the fireplace), and Van Dyck's splendidly painted 'Betrayal of Christ' of c 1629 (to the right). Other pictures worth noting are Caravaggio's 'Tobias and the Angel' (west wall), Guercino's 'Christ and the Woman of Samaria' and 'Christ Visited by Nicodemus', two landscapes by Salvator Rosa and two religious pictures by Bernado Strozzi (north wall), Tintoretto's 'Adoration of the Shepherds', an Annunciation by Veronese, Ribera's 'Mathematician' and 'Physician's Consultation', a charming group of children by Sofanisba Anguisciola and a portrait by William Dobson (west wall).

The **Cabinet Room**, next door, with another ceiling by Stocking, was also designed for the display of pictures, and now contains Filippo Lippi's 'Annunciation', painted for the cathedral at Pistoia, along with works by Jacopo Bassano and Murillo, and a plaque of the Madonna by Andrea della Robbia. The commode of inlaid wood, flanked by similar candle stands carrying marble vases, was supplied by John Cobb in 1772, and there are three *pietra dura* cabinets of c 1650 and three 17C Italian bronzes, including a copy of the 'Laocoön'—one of the canonic pieces of antique sculpture. Next comes the **State Bedroom**, created within the Elizabethan east wing, with the original mid-18C bed in situ; pictures here include Guercino's 'Infant Christ' from the Sanford collection, and there are two beautifully carved Rococo mirrors attributed to Thomas Johnson (c 1761). More important pictures hang in the **Octagon Room** (no longer octagonal since remodelling in the 1840s), including one of Queen Elizabeth I in a melancholy posture with a skeleton looking over her shoulder, and works by Claude ('Landscape with St John in the Wilderness'), Jan Breughel and Teniers. There is also a marble sculpture of a 'Sleeping Cupid' (1494), attributed to Michelangelo, and more Rococo furnishings, including a splendidly crazy console table attributed to Johnson.

The main corridor, lined with cases of Chinese porcelain, joins the state rooms to the west or private wing. The **Music Room**, dating largely from the 1840s, contains an early piano by Clementi and an unusual Regency drinking table, along with large canvases by the 17C painter Francesco Albani; and in the **Dining Room**, of the same date, there are portraits by Reynolds of Paul Methuen, the builder of the Picture Gallery, and of his three children (1758–59), and by Romney. 'Capability' Brown's landscape spreads out to the north and east of the house, and visitors should not leave Corsham without seeing his whimsical Rococo-Gothic Bath House to the north, with a cold bath at ground level, a changing room above, and a mysterious passage leading through the building to a walled garden beyond.

GCT

Great Chalfield Manor

2½m north east of Bradford-on-Avon to the north of B3109 Bradford–Melksham at Holt: National Trust. Open Apr–Oct Tues–Thur 12.15 & 2.15–4.30. Guided tours.

Great Chalfield is one of the finest late-medieval country houses in England. The builder, Thomas Tropnell, was a local man who gained possession of the manor in 1467, and it is assumed that the house was built soon afterwards. It stands on its own within an earlier moat next to the parish church, which Tropnell enlarged, and the ensemble of house, church and ancillary buildings has remained remarkably intact since the late 15C, as has the deeply rustic setting. The Tropnells died out in the 16C, and the house then passed through several families before being sold to a local clothier in 1769. Like many smaller medieval houses (eg, Sheldon Manor) it served for some time as a farmhouse, and in 1838 it was partially demolished. But 40 years later it was bought by a local squire, G.P. Fuller, and his younger son Robert, the managing director of a rubber firm in nearby Melksham, employed Harold Brakspear to carry out a thorough and sensitive restoration on 'conservative' principles in 1905–12. Fuller gave the house to the National Trust in 1943, and his family live here still.

Thomas Tropnell was clearly a wealthy and ambitious man, and the north or entrance front of his house is an example of late-medieval domestic design at its best: harmonious in the careful balancing of the various components, though not pedantically symmetrical. It is built of grey local limestone rubble, and is made up of a high-roofed hall range flanked by gabled wings, each of them with an elaborately carved oriel window on the first floor. There are lower gabled projections on each side of the hall itself, that on the right containing the porch, and there are carved stone figures on each of the gables. A lower and slightly later wing—possibly built to house the members of the Tropnells' household—stretches forward from the west end, with former farm buildings to the west, and on the other side of the entrance forecourt is the church with its pretty bell turret and chantry chapel built on by Tropnell to the earlier building (note the medieval screens and also the 17C 'three-decker' pulpit). There was originally another range of buildings on the other side of a small courtyard behind the hall, but these have long disappeared.

The house is entered through a porch, which leads via the expected screens passage into the Hall, restored by Harold Brakspear to something closely approaching its original state after being divided up in the 19C, the wooden screen is a replica (the original was fortunately recorded in a drawing of 1823) but the three peculiar stone masks concealing peepholes from the upstairs rooms have remained untouched since the 15C, and the beams of the flat roof retain some of their original colouring. Robert Fuller furnished the room as a comfortable 'living hall' of the type popular in the Edwardian era, and it was he who introduced the 17C Antwerp tapestries and the mainly 16C and 17C furniture (some interesting medieval or early-16C furniture can also be seen elsewhere in the house). Thomas Tropnell's house contained several features which were somewhat 'advanced' in the late 15C. Not only does the Hall have a hearth on the front (north) wall and two vaulted recesses at the east or 'upper' end, which may have served as private dining areas, but there is also what seems to have been a full-blown parlour (the present Dining Room) at the 'lower' end where one would normally expect to find the buttery and pantry; this was panelled in wood in the 16C, but in the 20C restoration an earlier mural painting of a man was uncovered.

The Bedroom above was clearly one of the most important rooms in the house, and still retains its impressive open arch-braced roof (note also the bathroom cunningly contrived in the early 20C out of the adjoining room over the porch). But the corresponding room on the other side of the Hall (now called the Solar) is a successful reconstruction by Harold Brakspear, the original east wing having been demolished in 1838, save only for the north wall with its splendid semicircular oriel window (detailed drawings were fortunately made by a pupil of A.W.N. Pugin just before demolition); underneath there is a vaulted room probably used for storage in medieval times. The gardens to the south and east were laid out in 1907–11, and admirably complement the weathered walls of the house.

GCT

Hamptworth Lodge

10m south east of Salisbury, near Landford to the south of A36 Salisbury–Southampton: N. Anderson, tel. 0794 390215. Open end Mar–end Apr daily except Sun 2.30–3.45. Guided tours.

This attractive gabled house was built in 1912 to the designs of Guy Dawber, a member of the Art Workers' Guild, a founder of the Council for the Preservation of Rural England, and author of books on farmhouses and cottages in the Cotswolds and the Home Counties. The Hamptworth estate lies close to the northern edge of the New Forest, near the Hampshire border, and was bought in 1870 by George Morrison, who left it on his death in 1884 to his nephew, Harold Charles Moffatt, the grandfather of the present owner. He was a skilled craftsman who had inherited a substantial commercial fortune from his parents, and soon after the death of Morrison's widow in 1907 he decided to demolish the existing house, a building of no great architectural distinction, and replace it with one which in a sense reproduced the 16C house known to have stood on the site. The new house embodied the philosophy of the Arts and Crafts movement, in which both Moffatt and the architect fervently believed, and it represents a highly successful marriage of old techniques with modern comfort and convenience. It is less quirky than the better-known country houses of Dawber's contemporary, Sir Edwin Lutyens, and therefore more representative of the best of English domestic architecture in its Indian summer before the First World War.

The house stands in a wooded setting, and is built of timber, with an infill of red brick. It is modelled on the early-16C timber-framed country houses of south-east England, but it is in no sense a copy, and everywhere there are signs of the creative imagination of the patron and architect at work: in the bargeboarded gables, in the chimneystacks with their patterned brickwork, and even in the lead-work of the rainwater heads. The plan is satisfyingly lucid, with the main rooms facing south and west onto well-maintained formal gardens, and reached by a broad corridor or gallery; to the north there is a substantial service wing (not open to the public).

The tour of the interior takes in the main ground-floor rooms, including an impressive Great Hall with a hammerbeam roof and an organ by Willis (now no longer playable), and two of the bedrooms upstairs. Most of the rooms contain furniture carved by Moffatt himself in a great variety of different woods and styles, and there are also earlier items including a splendid late-16C four-poster bed in which the conspirator Anthony Babington is said to have slept. There are some excellent plaster ceilings and wooden chimneypieces, two of which are clearly Elizabethan or Jacobean work and may have come from the now-demolished Goodrich Court (Herefordshire), which Moffatt also owned. Outside, the gardens with their formal flower-beds and Italianate terraces effectively complement this very appealing house.

GCT

Lacock Abbey

In Lacock, 3m south of Chippenham to the east of A350 Chippenham–Melksham: National Trust, tel. 0249 730227. Open Apr–Oct daily (except Tues) 1–5.30 (grounds and cloister open daily 12–5.30).

Lacock Abbey is one of the best-surviving examples of the conversion of a set of monastic buildings into a country house. The Augustinian nunnery of Lacock was founded in 1232 by Ela, Countess of Salisbury, among the meadows close to the village, which later became a flourishing centre for the manufacture of cloth. The nunnery regularly supported some 15 to 25 women, but it was dissolved in 1539 and the lands and buildings were sold to an ambitious and rapacious courtier, Sir William Sharington, a follower of Thomas, Lord Seymour of Sudeley Castle, Gloucestershire (qv.). Over the next ten years or so he demolished the church and converted the rest of the monastic complex into a house, retaining the cloister and many of the ancillary buildings intact. He was succeeded by his brother and then by his niece, who married a Warwickshire squire, John Talbot, and since then the house and estate have remained in the family, although they have passed through the female line on several occasions. John Ivory Talbot made major alterations to both house and grounds in the mid 18C, employing Sanderson Miller to build a new Hall in the newly fashionable Gothic style in 1754–55. This alluded to the venerable origins of the house, and in 1827–30, with a similar aim in mind, William Henry Fox Talbot, best-known as one of the pioneers of photography, remodelled the south range in the Tudor-Gothic manner. Since then there have been few changes. The house and village were given to the National Trust in 1944, but the house is still occupied by members of the family, and it retains the slightly faded charm of a long- established family home.

The approach from the singularly attractive village leads past a former barn adapted by the National Trust as a **museum of photography**, and from the driveway there is an attractive vista of the long, low entrance front, little changed since the mid 18C. To the north (left) of the house is a mid-16C **service courtyard**, in which two Renaissance doorways can be seen—evidence of Sir William Sharington's interest in classical architecture, which he shared with John Thynne of Longleat (qv.), not far away; there is also a brewery which still retains much of its original equipment. The house itself is reached through an ogee-arched gateway, through which Miller's façade to the Hall can be seen, flanked by turrets obviously deriving from the early-Tudor royal chapels and lit by ogee-arched windows placed symmetrically on either side of the doorway. But before entering visitors should walk round to the south front, at the east end of which is an octagonal **tower** built by Sharington to house a muniment room, with a balustraded roof up to which he could climb to 'command the prospect'. A doorway in the south wall leads into the **cloister**, and from here it is immediately evident how much of the medieval structure Sharington retained. The cloisters themselves, with their intricate 15C lierne vaults, survive intact, as do the Sacristy, Chapter House and Warming Room, reached from the east walk and dating back to the original foundation of the nunnery in the 13C; they have fine vaulted roofs, but the east walls were rebuilt in a restoration by Sir Harold Brakspear in 1894, having been demolished in the 18C.

Sharington and his successors have all lived, like the nuns before them, in first-floor rooms arranged around the cloister garth. The house is entered through Sanderson Miller's **Hall**, which replaced an earlier hall recorded in a 17C drawing; this has remained virtually unaltered since the mid 18C. John Ivory Talbot, like many of his antiquarian-minded contemporaries, was obsessed with heraldry, and liberally spattered the high curved ceiling with coats of arms, but the attention is mainly captured by the extraordinary terracotta figures of personages connected with the early history of the Abbey bursting out of the Gothic niches on the walls in a frenzy of Baroque gesticulation; they were made by an Austrian, Viktor Sederbach, in 1756. A passage (the Brown Gallery) leads past small rooms made out of the monastic Refectory (note John Piper's atmospheric view of the Abbey, 1942) to the **Stone Gallery** in the east range, made out of the nuns' dormitory. It contains an austere but well-proportioned classical chimneypiece made for Sharington by the stonemason John Chapman, who had worked for Henry VIII; there is also an unusual set of shell-backed chairs made c 1630, probably by Francis Cleyn.

Visitors now pass through some smaller rooms to the **Muniment Room** in the mid-16C tower at the south-east corner of the house, with its extraordinary vault and massive stone table of c 1550, supported by Mannerist satyrs; here it is easy to imagine Sharington counting his money—he was vice-treasurer of the Bristol mint—and poring over the title deeds of the estate. The **Blue Parlour**, panelled in the early 18C (note the portrait of Sanderson Miller), leads into the **South Gallery**, redecorated in the neo-Tudor taste in 1828–30 and containing several family portraits, including one of Sharington; the central oriel window, overlooking the gardens, was photographed by Fox Talbot in 1835, and the negative is the earliest in existence. The last room to be seen is the **Dining Room**, created in its present form by John Ivory Talbot in the mid 18C and little altered since. This is a complete classical ensemble, with a Doric frieze, pediments over the doors (some of which are false) and moulded frames around the pictures, of which the most important is Cornelis van Harlem's 'Peace and the Arts' (1605) over the fireplace; there are also copies of well-known canvases by Van Dyck. A doorway in the north wall leads back into the Hall, thus completing the circuit of the house.

GCT

Littlecote

2m west of Hungerford near Chilton Foliat: Peter de Savary, tel. 0488 684000. Open daily July–Sept 10.30–5. Refreshments.

There has been human habitation on the banks of the River Kennett at Littlecote since at least the 2C AD, when a Romano-British villa was built not far to the west of the present house. A splendid mosaic pavement of c 360 AD, showing Orpheus surrounded by representations of the Four Seasons, was discovered in 1827, and can now be seen by visitors. A village grew up on and near the site in the Middle Ages, but had become depopulated by the 15C, when the manor came by marriage to the Darrell family. They made a park on the site of the village, and lived in a flint-built house, part of which survives, albeit with considerable modification, at the west end of the present large, sprawling building. 'Wild William' Darrell, who inherited in 1549, built a large extension, also of flint, to the east of the medieval house, but was accused by his enemies of throwing his wife's illegitimate child onto a fire at Littlecote. His kinsman John Popham (d 1607), who successfully defended him when the case was tried, later became Attorney General and Lord Chief Justice, and when Darrell died in 1589 without male heirs he inherited the estate and built the present south (entrance) range of brick in front of Darrell's extension, thus making a second and larger courtyard next to the medieval one.

There were important alterations to the interior in the time of the Lord Chief Justice's grandson Col Alexander Popham, a leading Parliamentarian soldier who played an important part in the Battle of Newbury and later became a member of Oliver Cromwell's Council of State. The west end of the medieval house was also rebuilt in brick, but otherwise the house remained largely unchanged until c 1810, when Col Edward Leybourne-Popham demolished much of the medieval portion, leaving the site of the west range open, and replacing the south range with a new Gothic-windowed conservatory. There was some internal redecoration by a tenant c 1900, and in 1929 the house was bought from the last of the Leybourne-Pophams by the then tenant Sir Ernest Wills, inheritor of a tobacco fortune. The present owner came into possession in 1985, since when Littlecote has played host to numerous 'historical' activities—medieval jousting, falconry, mock Civil War battles and the like—as well as supporting a traditional farm, craft workshops, a collection of old cars, and similar attractions.

The house stands among walled gardens—there was no major 18C landscaping—and is entered through Sir John Popham's austere south range: an accomplished example of Elizabethan design, completely symmetrical, with unusually large mullioned and transomed windows, and a stone-tiled roof. The mullioned windows in the wings are an early 19C replacement of sash windows shown in 1700 painting, by Thomas Wijk, on view in the house. To the left is the early 19C conservatory (now a swimming pool). Brick gives way to flint on the long N side of the house, essentially two buildings placed next to each other. The late-medieval house of the Darrells is to the W (right), with a central block flanked by projecting wings, and is separated from the long, gabled late 16C extension to the east, by a brick portion of indeterminate date.

The porch at the centre of the south front gives access to the Hall, flooded with light from the huge windows, and still retaining its late 16C or early 17C panelling and plaster ceiling enlivened by globular pendants. On and along the walls is displayed what is probably the best collection of Civil War armour, coats and firearms in an English country house, arranged in its present form by Col Leybourne-Popham at the beginning of the 19C, and virtually untouched since it was drawn by Joseph Nash for his *Mansions of England* (1839); note also the long shuffle-board table and the portraits of the portly Sir John Popham, the lawyer, and his grandson, the Parliamentary soldier, on horseback. The Drawing Room and Library, reached from the former high-table end, were remodelled c 1810 and again c 1900, the former with a Chinese hand-painted wallpaper. Beyond, in the older part of the house, is the Dutch Parlour, completely covered with wooden panels painted, allegedly by Dutch prisoners-of-war in 1712, with scenes from *Don Quixote* and Samuel Butler's *Hudibras*.

The Long Gallery, which takes up most of the upper floor of the north range, is embellished with a late 16C plaster frieze of arabesques interrupted by the Darrell crest of the rampant lion. To the west are bedrooms, one of them with a plaster overmantel of Queen Elizabeth's coat of arms—she visited the house in 1601—and another dated 1592. Downstairs, the Brick Hall—so named from its brick floor—contains well-preserved panelling of the mid 17C. It leads into the chapel, probably on the site of the hall of the medieval house, but dating in its present form from the mid 17C, with plain, sturdy woodwork, a raised pulpit in the place where an Anglican would expect to find the altar, and a notable lack of carved or painted decoration: a vivid reminder of the spirit of Puritanism which gives the house much of its interest.

GCT

Longleat

3m south east of Frome off A362 Frome–Warminster: the Marquess of Bath, tel. 0985 844551. Open all year daily (except Christmas Day) 10–4 (Easter–Sept 10–6). Guided tours. Refreshments.

The history of English architecture cannot be written without making reference to Longleat, for in no other 16C house are Renaissance-inspired ideas assimilated more convincingly into the native tradition of domestic building. As seen first, from the long drive snaking down through the park past the viewpoint known as 'Heaven's Gate', the large windows and busy skyline seen in most Elizabethan country houses are clearly evident. But closer inspection reveals that the huge building is visually held together by classical friezes and a balustrade on the roof-line. Each of the serene façades is symmetrical, and the windows do not look into the courtyards in the semi-defensive medieval way, but out on to the surrounding landscape. By the time it was finished c 1580, Longleat was the most 'advanced' country house in England.

Longleat in its present form took shape after 40 years of experiment by the builder, Sir John Thynne, ancestor of the present owner. A keen Protestant, he was steward to 'Protector' Somerset, the most powerful man in England at the beginning of Edward VI's reign and a major patron of Renaissance architecture; like other members of Somerset's circle, he built up a large estate with the spoils of the dissolved monasteries. They included the small Augustinian house at Longleat, which he purchased in 1541 and soon afterwards adapted to residential use. This house was later expanded, but in 1567 there was a serious fire, after which Thynne immediately began a new and much larger house on the same site. The internal structure of the present building dates from the first stage of this remodelling, as do the domed turrets or 'banqueting houses' (for post-prandial desserts) on the roof. But in 1572 Thynne decided to wrap new façades of Bath stone around the whole house, and these are the façades which we see now. As in most Elizabethan houses it is impossible to point to a single architect, but it is clear that two men played a major creative role, along with Thynne himself: the Frenchman Allen Maynard, and the Englishman Robert Smythson (cf. Wollaton Hall, Notts, etc), whose first identifiable work this is.

If Thynne were to return to Longleat now he would find the outside of his house relatively unaltered, but the interior and the gardens would be unrecognisable. Sir Thomas Thynne, 1st Viscount Weymouth, created some new rooms in the south (entrance) range soon after inheriting in 1682 from his notorious cousin 'Tom of Ten Thousand (Pounds)'; he also laid out new formal gardens, which were altered in the 1730s and swept away by 'Capability' Brown in 1757–62 (there were later improvements by Repton). The 3rd Viscount, who was thus responsible for the present landscape setting, was made Marquess of Bath in 1789 after a long political career, and in 1806–18 the 2nd Marquess brought in Jeffrey Wyatville to make more alterations. They included the completion of the north range—left unfinished in the 16C—the construction of a new staircase and the building of a new stable block; further internal alterations took place in 1829–31. Finally in 1874–82 the 4th Marquess, who had travelled extensively in Italy and was described as 'the very exemplar of an immaculate, unemotional, self-possessed British aristocrat', employed the decorator J.D. Crace to transform the main reception rooms in the east range in a sumptuous yet sophisticated Italian Renaissance manner which acts as a splendid back-drop to a varied collection of furniture and Old Master pictures, many of which he acquired himself.

The house is built round two courtyards (created out of the original three), with three storeys of rooms over a basement—a very innovative feature for the 1570s—and a flat roof for fashionable promenading 'on the leads'. The façades are all uniform in character, itself an innovation, with ranks of huge mullioned and transomed windows, and projecting bay windows to break the monotony and allow more light into the rooms; they are articulated by classical pilasters—Doric at ground-floor level, then Ionic and Corinthian—and there are busts of Roman personages in the roundels underneath the first-floor windows. The house is entered through a doorway of 1705 in the south range, and from here a screens passage leads into the **Hall**, the only room shown to visitors to retain anything of its Elizabethan appearance. The richly carved screen (attributed to Adrian Gaunt, a Frenchman), the stone chimneypiece, possibly by his compatriot Allen Maynard, and the hammerbeam roof, all date from the 1570s, but the flat ceiling was put in in the 1680s, when a library (not open to visitors) was made on the top floor to house the books of the 1st Viscount; the huge equestrian paintings of c 1736, by John Wootton, were commissioned by the 2nd Lord Weymouth, and the waistcoat worn by Charles I at his execution is also shown.

The tour of the state rooms starts in the **Ante-Library**, reached through one of the corridors introduced by Wyatville into the east courtyard to improve communication through the house. Longleat has one of the best country house libraries in England, and many of the books (though not the oldest) are kept in the Ante-Library and the adjacent Red Library. Both rooms were redecorated by Crace in the Italian (more specifically, Venetian) cinquecento taste, with ceilings, wall hangings, woodwork and marble door surrounds of the highest quality, and the deep, rich colour schemes favoured by many Victorians; the portrait of the late Marquess of Bath by Graham Sutherland (1971) in the Ante-Library strikes an unexpected but not unpleasing 20C note. The **Breakfast Room** contains a Venetian 16C painting in the manner of Veronese in the ceiling roundel and a selection of 18C and 19C family portraits on the walls, including the 4th Marquess (who commissioned Crace) by Richmond, and his wife, by Watts. Next door is the **Lower Dining Room**, with an even more ornate Crace ceiling and a collection of earlier portraits, among them the grim-visaged Sir John Thynne, builder of the house. 17C silver-gilt items are displayed on the table, and on the early-19C ebony sideboard, made to match some 17C Portuguese ebony chairs, is a tortoiseshell punch-bowl on a silver mount, made by Pierre Crespin for the 2nd Marquess in 1750 (the tortoise is said to have come from an island in the West Indies which he owned).

From here a back staircase leads, via a largely unaltered 19C bedroom and bathroom installed in 1840, to the **State Dining Room**, the first of three rooms by Crace which rank among the richest of all Victorian country house interiors. 16C Venetian paintings are inset into the ceiling, inspired, like the frieze, by the Council Chamber of the Doge's Palace, while the walls are hung with 17C Spanish leather, against which are placed early-17C full-length portraits, including one of Catherine Thynne attributed to William Larkin (c 1610). The **Saloon**, on the site of the 17C long gallery, has a ceiling of 1873 designed by George Fox (cf. Eastnor Castle, Herefordshire) but embellished by Crace, with pretty arabesque paintings by Henry Scholz; the massive chimneypiece, flanked by straining Michelangelesque figures, was copied from one in the Doge's Palace, and there are 17C Flemish tapestries of the story of Cyrus, King of Persia, on the walls. The **State Drawing Room**, the most expensive of Crace's rooms, was designed to display the 4th Marquess's collection of Italian Renaissance paintings, of which the most important are Titian's early 'Rest on the Flight into Egypt' and Tintoretto's erotic 'Ascalaphus and Proserpine' of c 1578–80; more Venetian paintings are inset into the ceiling, designed by Fox but embellished by Crace, and the frieze is attributed to the 17C Italian artist Pietro Liberi, while the walls are hung with red 17C Genoa velvet. There is also some good, later-18C French furniture, including a desk which once belonged to Talleyrand.

From here a passage leads past the Hall and across the top of Wyatville's staircase to a pair of **bedrooms** with a connecting sitting room on the south-west side of the house. They contain more good furnishings, including mid-18C Rococo mirrors, and some notable pictures, including a portrait of James I's eldest son, Prince Henry, possibly by Robert Peake, and a view of Haarlem by Saloman van Ruisdael. There are more pictures by 17C Dutch masters, including Steen, Terborch, Van Goyen and de Keyser, in the adjacent **corridor**, along with a view of the house painted by Jan Siberechts in 1675. The ground floor is regained by the gloomy, ponderous **staircase**, built between the two courtyards and hung with yet more pictures, including several 16C and early-17C portraits, of which the most interesting is an engagingly naïve one of Lord Cobham and his family (1567) and a 'Lion Hunt' after Rubens. Real lions can be encountered in the Safari Park, which for many visitors constitutes the main attraction of Longleat.

GCT

Lydiard Park

5m west of Swindon to the north of M4 junction 16: Borough of Thamesdown, tel. 0793 770401. Open weekdays 10–1, 2–5.30, Sun 2–5.30 (closes 4 Nov–Feb).

This impressive but relatively little-known neo-Palladian house stands in a country park on the edge of Swindon's sprawling high-tech factory belt. It dates in its present form from 1743, when John, 2nd Viscount St John, half-brother of the famous Tory politician and philosopher Lord Bolingbroke, drastically rebuilt an older H-plan house, some of whose walls survive behind the present classical elevations. The St Johns first came to live at Lydiard Tregoze (pronounced 'Tregooz') in the 15C, and the estate remained in the family until after the First World War, but there were frequent financial crises and both house and park were finally sold to Swindon Corporation in 1943. Since then the local authority has restored and refurnished the house, which was empty when first acquired, bringing back much of the original furniture and all the portraits, and turning the service wing into a management centre.

The house now stands among tree-studded lawns of the usual late-18C kind. Externally it has changed very little since the 1743 remodelling. The plain two-storeyed façades, possibly designed by Roger Morris, are of meticulously cut limestone ashlar, with a central pedimented feature on the south or entrance front and four Italianate towers after the manner of Holkham, Norfolk (qv.) and Wilton (qv.) at the corners. Because much of the old structure was retained, there was no opportunity of raising the main rooms on to a piano nobile, and the building consequently seems to hug the ground in a rather homelier manner than is usual in houses of this kind.

Internally there have been relatively few major changes since the 18C. The rooms, many of them created within pre-existing walls, are strung out on either side of the Hall in what was by the 1740s a distinctly old-fashioned way. The Hall itself is an excellent example of Palladian decoration in the Kentian manner, by unknown craftsmen, with a coved ceiling, enriched frieze and cornice, dignified chimneypiece and busts on wall-brackets to lend an air of classical seriousness. To the left is the Library, with a ribbed ceiling of unusual design, and bookcases with busts in open pediments lining the walls; another bust, by Rysbrack, of the politician Lord Boling-broke in Roman garb (1737), is one of the few items to have escaped a sale of the contents of the house in 1824, and the portraits include two by the 17C artist, Mary Beale.

On the other side of the Hall is the Dining Room, more richly decorated, with a screen of Ionic columns at the service end and a collection of 17C and early-18C family portraits on the walls. Next comes the Drawing Room, with flock wallpaper of the late 18C (much restored) and an excellent marble chimneypiece. Beyond, in the east wing, the State Bedchamber with its adjacent Dressing Room, both of them with delicate plaster ceilings in the Rococo taste. The bedroom has lost its original bed, but the Corinthian colonnade screening off the alcove is still there, and there is an excellent Rococo mirror contemporary with the room, complete with ho-ho birds. The Dressing Room is notable chiefly for a 17C painted-glass window by the Dutchman Abraham van Linge, presumably preserved from the old house and now lighting a semicircular apse-like projection with an embellished plaster ceiling of the same first-rate craftsmanship as can be found every-where in the house; the room now contains some panels painted in the 18C by Diana Spencer (later Lady Diana Beauclerk), a member of Horace Walpole's circle, for her long-demolished house, Little Marble Hill, at Twickenham (Middlesex).

Visitors should not leave Lydiard without seeing the church, situated just to the north (key obtainable in the house) and famous for 17C fittings and for its superb monuments, most of them erected by Sir John St John, Bt (1648); these monuments to a family which seems to have specialised in lost causes evoke the doomed world of the Cavaliers with particular poignancy.

GCT

Newhouse

9m south east of Salisbury, 3m east of Downton off B3080: Mr and Mrs George Jeffreys, tel. 0725 20055. Open Aug daily except Sun 2–5.30. Refreshments.

The novelty of Newhouse lies in its most unusual Y-shaped plan, formed by a hexagonal centre and three projecting wings. It began life as a hunting lodge, and was described as 'lately erected' in 1619; the builder was probably William Stockman, from whom it passed to Sir Edward Gorges, whose father had built the triangular Longford Castle nearby (not open to the public). Newhouse, like many other lodges, stands isolated on a hilltop, and is now surrounded by woods; the original gardens, if there ever were any, have gone. As in many Elizabethan and Jacobean houses, the plan may express some arcane hidden meaning, but if so that meaning has long been forgotten and the simple gabled brick elevations do nothing to solve the mystery. The house was acquired in 1633 by Giles Eyre, and it remained in the family until the late 18C; it then went through the female line, and has since passed by descent to the present owners. The two wings on the entrance side were lengthened in the mid 18C (between 1742 and 1764 according to the dates on the rainwater pipes), but externally the extensions were made to match the existing building, and today the house still retains its highly individualistic Jacobean character.

Inside, there have been more changes. There is a late-17C staircase with twisted balusters in the older part of the house and an early-17C fireplace in the Library, while some mid-18C Rococo plasterwork survives in one of the wings. But most of the original decoration has been swamped or removed by later alterations, some of them carried out (eg, the Drawing Room) in 1906. There are numerous family portraits on display, showing successive generations of the Eyres and the Nelsons, with whom they intermarried in the 19C (the admiral's country estate was not far away). But they are eclipsed in interest by a picture called 'The Triumph of the Hares', possibly painted in England in the mid 17C, and uncannily resembling a set of mural paintings in the castle at Bucovice in the Czech Replublic which also shows hares lording it over human beings; the oddity of the picture, which may have been acquired as a pun on the family name Eyre, admirably complements the character of this singular house.

GCT

Pythouse

2½m west of Tisbury: Country Houses Association. Open May–Sept Wed, Thur 2–5.

Pythouse derives its name from the Pytt family, who acquired the land on which the present house stands in 1225. They later changed their name to Bennett, and in about 1725 Thomas Bennett built a new house on the site of the present building, together with a detached orangery, which still survives. But in its present form the house is the creation of his grandson John Bennett, who married the heiress of a Bengal 'nabob' and subsequently enlarged the estate, making a name for himself as a local MP and agricultural improver. Acting as his own architect, he encased the early-18C house in new façades of meticulously cut Chilmark stone, remodelled the main interiors, and added an entrance range facing south towards Cranborne Chase; this carries the date 1805 on the rainwater heads. After his death in 1852 the estate passed through the female line to his grandson Vere Fane-Bennett, who married the heiress of the Preston Manor estate outside Brighton, East Sussex (qv), and in 1891 he added wings to the back (north) of the house which blend discreetly in with the rest of the building. His daughter-in-law left the estate to a distant cousin, Sir Anthony Rumbold, son of the diplomat Sir Horace Rumbold, and in 1958 he sold the house and its immediate surroundings to the Mutual Households Association (now the Country Houses Association). It has converted the building into flats for the elderly, leaving the main reception rooms (the only ones seen by the visitors) intact.

The house is superbly situated high on the slope of a hillside, with a backdrop of woods. It is a handsome and well-proportioned building with a basically Palladian south or entrance front dominated by a giant Ionic portico, and marred only by the insertion of plate glass into the windows in the late 19C. The east and west façades have recessed Ionic porticos *in antis* in the manner of several early-19C neo-classical buildings; to the west, and detached from the main house, is the attractive pedimented orangery which is now the only recognisable part of the early-18C house to survive. The interiors have lost their original furniture, but a comprehensive collection of portraits and busts of the Bennetts and Rumbolds is on loan to the present occupiers. Most of the rooms are decorated with restrained Grecian ornament, and in the two rooms on either side of the Entrance Hall (originally the drawing room and dining room) there are 16C Italian marble chimneypieces which may have come from the nearby Fonthill Abbey, sold by the notorious William Beckford in 1826. The most impressive part of the interior, though, is the Staircase, in the centre of the house and lit from above by a glazed dome; it is of the 'Imperial' type, with one flight dividing into two, and on ascending it there are exciting vistas to the upper floors of the house.

GCT

Sheldon Manor

1½m west of Chippenham to south of A420 Chippenham–Bristol, M4 exit 17: Major Martin Gibbs, tel. 0249 653120. Open Easter–early Oct Sun, Thur, BH Mon 2–6; garden 12.30–6. Refreshments.

Hidden away in unspoiled countryside, Sheldon is an unusually attractive example of a medieval stone-built house altered and remodelled over several generations. The house is now isolated, with only farm buildings for company, but when the oldest part of the present building was constructed in the mid 13C there was a village to the west, now only discernible by a series of humps and bumps in an adjoining field where the houses once stood. On approaching through the early-18C walled courtyard to the south, the different phases of building can be clearly seen. In the centre, behind three yew trees, is the porch of a house built by Sir Geoffrey Gascelin, who inherited the manor through his wife in 1250. The lower gabled block to the right was built in 1431 for Sir Walter Hungerford, who had purchased the manor seven years earlier, and the small free-standing chapel to its right must, judging from the small square-headed Perpendicular windows, date from about the same time. To the left of the porch, on the site of the medieval hall, is a taller three-storeyed block of 1659 built on inadequate foundations (hence the sagging walls) by William Forster, then tenant of the Hungerfords. The manor subsequently passed through the hands of several absentee owners, and the house became a farmhouse until 1911, when it was bought and restored by Captain F. Bailey, who sold it in 1917 to Henry Martin Gibbs, younger son of William Gibbs, a successful merchant and fervent Anglo-Catholic who had financed the building of Keble College chapel in Oxford. His grandson, the present owner, moved to Sheldon in 1952 and introduced an interesting and idiosyncratic collection of pictures, furniture and other objects, most of them brought from his former home (Barrow Court, Somerset); he also created the present garden with its sequence of 'outdoor rooms' and enticing vistas.

The appeal of Sheldon Manor derives chiefly from its atmosphere of great age, and from the picturesque grouping of rubble-stone walls, steep stone-tiled roofs and tall chimneys. A similar air of irregularity pervades the interior. The rooms are filled with an assortment of 17C and later furniture, porcelain of different dates (including some good 19C items from the de Morgan firm), as well as curiosities like narwhals' tusks. The Hall, entered through the former screens passage, has been much remodelled, but the wooden staircase, dating from the 1660s rebuilding, still has its original dog gate at the foot, and a bedroom over the Hall retains its 18C wood panelling. The most impressive rooms are the Priest's Room over the porch, with its 13C timber roof, and the adjacent Library in the 15C part of the house, with a much-restored open timber roof and a portrait by John Callcott Horsley of William Gibbs, father of the present owner, as a boy (1886), his pose taken from Reynolds's well-known portrait of Master Crewe as Henry VIII—itself a parody of Holbein. The Dining Room, underneath, may occupy the site of the medieval buttery and pantry, but now has linenfold panelling introduced in 1911, on which are displayed more 19C and earlier pictures, including James Tissot's historical costume-piece 'Marguerite a l'Eglise' (1860), from Goethe's *Faust*. The refreshments in the nearby stables, built in 1723, are particularly good.

GCT

Stourhead

At Stourton, 3m north west of Mere off NB3092 Mere–Frome: National Trust, tel. 0747 840348. House open Apr–Oct Sat–Wed 12–5.30 (gardens open all year 8–7, dusk if earlier). Refreshments in Stourton village.

The gardens at Stourhead are perhaps the most beautiful of all surviving 18C English landscapes. They were largely created by Henry Hoare, son of a wealthy London banker of the same name, who bought the estate from the Stourton family in 1717 and two years later set about building the core of the present house to the designs of Colen Campbell, the apostle of neo-Palladianism; this was completed a year before his death in 1725. The transformation of the grounds began some 20 years later, when the second Henry Hoare decided to create a classical landscape in the village to the west of the house, with a lake formed by damming the River Stour and temples designed by Lord Burlington's former draughtsman Henry Flitcroft. Drawing for inspiration on recently-designed gardens by William Kent (eg, Stowe, Bucks; Rousham, Oxon) and, more distantly, on the paintings of Claude Lorrain and on literary accounts of the gardens of the ancients, he thus paid quasi-pagan homage to the 'genius of the place' and evoked a Virgilian Golden Age of perfect harmony between man and nature.

When Hoare died in 1785 Stourhead passed to his grandson, Richard Colt Hoare, an enthusiastic collector, amateur artist and antiquarian who had spent some time in Italy and later wrote histories of ancient and modern Wiltshire (the latter left unfinished at his death) which were models of scholarly topographical research. To accommodate his growing collection of books and pictures, he added wings to the house in 1793–95; he also enriched his grandfather's landscape by large-scale planting of exotic trees and shrubs. His half-brother, who succeeded him, added a portico in 1841, thus fulfilling Campbell's original intention, but in 1902 the central portion of the building was gutted by fire, destroying the original interiors but fortunately not the contents. The rooms were refurbished by Sir Aston Webb, architect of the west front of Buckingham Palace, since when there have been few major changes. The house and gardens were given to the National Trust in 1946.

When the house was first built the gardens were not yet conceived, and the building faces east towards the western edge of the Wiltshire Downs. Stourhead was one of the first houses in England to be modelled on one of Palladio's villas—the Villa Emo at Fanzolo—and in its original form it was a plain compact box, with the centre emphasised by a temple-like portico of the Composite order (originally engaged), the main rooms on a piano nobile and the roof hidden by a balustrade. Inside, the rooms were grouped villa-fashion around a central staircase, an arrangement destined to become very popular in English domestic architecture. The addition of the wings gave the house a much more elongated appearance, but the work was tactfully done and the original house still stands out in the centre of the present east or **entrance façade**.

The house is entered through a cube-shaped **Hall**, with an enriched frieze and heavy architectural embellishments of the kind found in many neo-Palladian houses; these were reproduced after the 1902 fire, and the walls re-hung with family portraits, including one (by Michael Dahl) of the first Henry Hoare holding Campbell's front elevation of the house, another of his son, the creator of the gardens, out hunting and a third (by Samuel Woodforde) of Sir Richard Colt Hoare with his son, holding a portfolio of drawings. The bronze bust of Charles I, by Hubert le Sueur, was made c 1635 and displayed in Whitehall Palace, but was later bought by the second Henry Hoare, and there are also two Greco-Roman statuettes, of the 1C or 2C AD, probably acquired by Colt Hoare. The **Music Room** and **Ante-Room**, to the south (left), contain pictures painted and acquired by Richard Colt Hoare, including watercolours of Italian scenes by his teacher John 'Warwick' Smith and by J.R. Cozens. Beyond lies Colt Hoare's **Library**, which survives largely untouched with its furniture by the younger Thomas Chippendale and its collection of topographical books. The architectural setting is simple and spacious, with the green-painted walls, barrel-vaulted ceiling and French windows flooding the room with light (the lunettes at each end have copies of paintings by Raphael in the Vatican, one of them done in painted glass by Samuel Eginton); the furniture, of c 1802–5, is appropriately solid and sturdy, some of it showing the influence of the newly- fashionable Egyptian taste, and the carpet (a copy of the original) is based on a Roman mosaic pavement. There are busts of Milton in youth and old age by Rysbrack over the doors, and a terracotta model by the same sculptor of his 'Hercules' (1744), in the Pantheon in the gardens, is placed on the desk.

From here visitors return to the original house through the **Little Dining Room**, reconstructed much as it had been before the 1902 fire, with its serving alcove. The **Inner Hall** and **Saloon** are largely the work of Aston Webb, the latter containing a bust of King Alfred by Rysbrack (1764), and there is more furniture by the younger Chippendale in the **Italian Room**, originally a bedroom but now named after the Italian views on the walls, some of them by A.L. Ducros, an artist much admired by Colt Hoare. The **Cabinet Room** (originally the library) derives its name from the spectacular cabinet made for Pope Sixtus V c 1585–90, and bought by the younger Henry Hoare, who had the stand made, probably by John Bossom, c 1742–43; the pictures include a storm scene by Joseph Vernet, and there is more Chippendale furniture. Finally comes the **Picture Gallery**, reached through an ante-room. This was another of Colt Hoare's additions to the house, and, like the Library, it contains excellent Chippendale furniture of 1793–1802, this time in a delicate neo-classical taste. The pictures themselves, most of them collected by the younger Henry Hoare, include works by Poussin (the 'Choice of Hercules'), his nephew Gaspard Dughet, Carlo Maratta and Anton Raphael Mengs ('Octavian and Cleopatra', 1759), and in the ante-room there is an altarpiece by the 16C Flemish artist Jan Prevoost.

The house and the gardens share the common aim of recreating the glories of classical Rome in an English setting. When approached from the house, as they ideally should be, the **gardens** are first seen from below, with the finest of Flitcroft's temples, the Pantheon (1754–56), on the opposite shore of the lake, framed by trees in the manner of a Claude landscape. The circuit of the lake takes in not only the Pantheon (also known as the Temple of Hercules), with the full-scale version of Rysbrack's Hercules in the domed interior, but also the Temple of Flora (1744–45), a rustic cottage, and a Grotto which alludes allegorically to Aeneas's journey into the underworld before the founding of Rome; it contains a statue of the River God by John Cheere (1751) and a cast of the Nymph of the Grot, after the antique, with lines by Alexander Pope inscribed on the marble pavement in front, and only the trickle of water to interrupt the moist stillness. On the hillside on the south side of the lake is Flitcroft's Temple of the Sun (c 1755), based on a temple at Baalbek in the Lebanon, and to the east, by way of contrast, is the 14C Bristol High Cross, demolished for road- widening and placed at the entrance to the garden from the village in 1765. A more awe-inspiring monument to the growing fascination with the Middle Ages is the triangular **Alfred's Tower**, designed by Flitcroft in 1765 some three miles away on the edge of the estate, near the site in the Forest of Selwood where King Alfred was supposed to have rallied his troops before defeating the Danes; this stark landmark, which can be seen for miles around, formed part of an 'outer circuit' of the grounds.

GCT

Westwood Manor

1½m south west of Bradford-on-Avon in Westwood to the west of B3109 Bradford–Frome: National Trust, tel. 0225 863374. Open Apr–Sept Sun, Tues, Wed 2–5.

Westwood Manor is one of several smaller National Trust houses which owe their survival to the timely intervention of an early-20C purchaser sensitive to the character and texture of a neglected old building and discerning enough to refurnish it in a pleasing fashion. The manor of Westwood belonged to Winchester Cathedral from medieval times to 1861, and the hall block which forms the core of the present stone-built house—by no means the first on the site—was built in 1480 by Thomas Culverhouse, whose family leased the manor for much of the 15C. Additions were made after 1515 by a wealthy local clothier, Thomas Horton; they include most of the west wing which stretches forward from the hall block and incorpo- rates part of an earlier building (the east wing which once faced it across the entrance forecourt has long vanished). The Hortons stayed at Westwood for about a century, but the lease was sold c 1616, and the new occupant, John Farewell, brother-in-law of the last Horton, carried out a thorough reconstruction of the 15C hall block. For most of the 18C and 19C the house was sub-let to tenant farmers (it was called 'the farm house of the manor of Westwood' in 1649), but it was bought and rescued in 1911 by Edgar Lister, a diplomat and Fellow of the Society of Antiquaries. He restored and refurnished the house, created the present garden, and left house, garden and collection to the National Trust in 1956; since then the building has been let to tenants, with Lister's furniture and embroidery still in situ.

The house stands on the edge of the rather nondescript village, and forms part of an attractive manorial complex along with a 15C stone barn (not open to the public) and the parish church, whose impressive west tower was built by Thomas Horton (note also the east window with excellent 15C or early-16C stained glass). An early-17C archway leads into the forecourt, with the hall range in front. Like Great Chalfield Manor (qv.), not far away, this originally had a central hall open to the roof, but it was 'floored over' by John Farewell in the early 17C and at about the same time the exterior was reconstructed in a plain, workmanlike manner, with a projecting porch, simple mullioned windows and a rounded staircase turret at the junction with the west wing. To the right is the garden, laid out in the early 20C as a series of 'outdoor rooms' divided from each other by tall clipped yew hedges.

The interior has a mellow, timeless quality. There is a great deal of 17C and early-18C oak furniture, its effect enhanced by needlework of 'Florentine stitch' done by Lister himself, and added warmth and colour is supplied by the oriental carpets on the floors. The entrance leads into the Hall through a screens passage blocked off by a 17C staircase. It has plain plastered walls enlivened by 17C Flemish 'verdure' tapestries, but the small room known as the King's Room on the opposite side of the passage contains exuberant early-17C plasterwork on the overmantel and ceiling, and wood panelling introduced by Lister, along with the series of rather crude 17C portraits of English monarchs brought from Keevil Manor, only a few miles away. The Dining Room, on the other side of the Hall, must have been the main parlour of the house in the 16C and 17C, and is lit by an early-16C bay window; there is more panelling introduced by Lister here, together with an early-17C internal porch surmounted by strapwork ornament. Upstairs, visitors see two bedrooms, but the most impressive room is the Music Room over the Hall—the great chamber formed by John Farewell— with two more internal porches and a splendidly elaborate plaster ceiling enriched with shallow ribs, hanging pendants and stylised foliage patterns; there are 17C Dutch and Flemish pictures by minor masters, and visitors may be lucky enough to hear recordings of the spinet and virginals acquired by Lister and still in playing order.

GCT

Wilton House

At Wilton 2½m west of Salisbury on A30: the Earl of Pembroke, tel. 0722 743115. Open Apr–mid Oct daily 11–6 (Sun 12–6). Refreshments.

The Herbert family have lived at Wilton since 1544, when the dissolved Benedictine nunnery which stood on the site of the present house was granted to William Herbert, later 1st Earl of Pembroke. He married the sister of Catherine Parr, Henry VIII's sixth wife, and became a major power in the land during Edward VI's reign, finally acquiring the Wiltshire estates of the disgraced 'Protector' Somerset, along with extensive property in Wales. Like other beneficiaries of the Reformation in Wiltshire (eg, Sir William

Sharington at Lacock and Sir John Thynne at Longleat), he lost little time in converting his newly-acquired monastic buildings into a house, and recent research has shown that some of the thick walls survive within the present building, which was constructed around the four sides of the former cloister, with four corner towers and a gateway on the east side.

But the man mainly responsible for creating Wilton in its present form was his grandson the 4th Earl, a leading courtier and politician in the reigns of James I and Charles I, who, according to John Aubrey, 'did love Wilton above all places, and came thither every summer'. The Earl 'exceedingly loved painting and building, in which he had singular judgement', and soon after inheriting the title and estates in 1630 he set about laying out a new garden and building 'that side of the house that fronts the garden, with two stately pavilions at each end, all *al Italiano*'. The layout of the garden was entrusted, on the recommendation of the King's Surveyor of Works, Inigo Jones, to a Frenchman, Isaac de Caus, and de Caus also designed the new south range of 1636, with its suite of lavishly decorated state rooms. The designs were prepared with the 'advice and approbation' of Jones, and when the new range was gutted by fire it was Jones's gifted pupil John Webb who was given the task of repairing the exterior and remodelling the interior in 1648–50. Pembroke supported Parliament during the Civil War, and emerged with his fortune and political credit intact; this enabled him to fund the rebuilding of what has ever since been regarded as one of the key buildings in the history of English domestic architecture.

The art collections of the 4th Earl of Pembroke were augmented in the early 18C by the 8th Earl, a keen traveller and virtuoso whose collection of antique sculpture and Old Master paintings still survives relatively intact. His son, the 9th Earl, was one of the main aristocratic backers of neo-Palladian architecture in the 1720s and '30s, designing a number of major buildings himself, including Marble Hill, Greater London (qv.); his Palladian bridge of 1736–37 formed part of a programme of landscape 'improvements' which had the unfortunate effect of obliterating the magnificent 17C garden layout, and he also carried out some redecoration of the state rooms. His son brought in William Chambers to rebuild the west (private) range, and in 1801–11 the 11th Earl employed James Wyatt to remodel the north range (the original hall range) once more, and to construct a Gothic cloister around the inside of the courtyard, thus both improving internal communications and alluding to the medieval origins of the building. Much of Wyatt's work was altered again by the little-known Edmund Warre in 1913, but since then the building has remained largely unchanged, and John Webb's state rooms have recently been successfully restored.

The approach from the small town of Wilton leads through a **triumphal arch** designed by Chambers and surmounted by a copy of the equestrian statue of Marcus Aurelius on the Capitol in Rome; the arch was originally placed on the hill facing the south front, but was moved by Wyatt. To the right is the former **Riding School** built by the horsey 10th Earl, and now containing an excellent set of antique marble sarcophagi, as well as a small cinema in which a film about the history of the house is shown. Since the early 19C the main entrance has been through the **Front Hall** in the north range, the centre of which is taken up by a large statue of Shakespeare by Scheemakers (1743); there are portraits of the 1st and 4th Earls (the latter by Mytens), paintings by Pietro da Cortona and others, and copies of well-known antique statuary, as well as a genuine Greek marble relief carving of the 5C BC and a Hellenistic statue of Hercules. The Hall leads into the **Upper Cloister**, at first-floor level, where it is worth examining the classical busts acquired by the 8th Earl on their specially-made pedestals of Carrara marble, the porphyry and marble relief of Pyrrhus made in Italy in the late 16C (and once belonging to Cardinal Mazarin), and the series of Claudian paintings by Richard Wilson of the Wilton landscape after it had been 'improved' by the 9th Earl; there are also paintings on the west wall by members of the Breughel dynasty, and views of Covent Garden and Lincoln's Inn Fields in London by the 'English Canaletto', Samuel Scott.

A doorway leads from here into the **state rooms** on the south front. They constitute the finest set of domestic interiors to survive in England from the mid 17C, with a Great Room or dining room (now called the Double Cube Room) and Withdrawing Room (the Single Cube Room) at the west end and a bedroom suite to the east. The rooms conform to the mathematical proportions propounded in Renaissance architectural theory, but any effect of severity is banished by the lavish decoration in wood, paint and plaster (note especially the figures of Bacchus and Ceres on the overmantel of the Double Cube), scarcely altered since the 1650s. There are also some outstanding portraits, including Van Dyck's 'Lady Morton and Mrs Killigrew' and his tender study of the 5th Earl and Countess of Bedford in the **Single Cube** (note also Lely's 7th Countess, sister of Charles II's mistress Louise de Quérouaille, en déshabille, over the fireplace), and the superb set of royal and family portraits by Van Dyck in the **Double Cube**, culminating in the huge canvas of the 4th Earl and his family on the west wall; the floor of this magnificent room was almost certainly originally bare of furniture, but is now occupied by massive gilded chairs and settees by Kent, and later ones in the same style by Chippendale, designed to complement the opulent decoration of the walls and ceiling.

Until the 19C visitors approached the state rooms by a staircase leading out of the courtyard, but this was removed by Wyatt, and there are now more pictures to be seen in the **Ante-Room** created out of the upper level, including two by Van Dyck and one of an old lady attributed to Rembrandt. Next comes the **Colonnade Room** (so called from the Ionic colonnade which once screened off the state bed), with a chimneypiece by Webb and a set of 18C family portraits, including several by Reynolds of varying quality; the heavy, gilded furniture was probably made to the designs of William Kent for the 9th Earl, who also commissioned the ceiling painting by Clermont with its 'grotesques' *all' antica*. The **Corner Room** has another good chimneypiece and overmantel by John Webb enclosing a portrait of Prince Rupert by Honthorst , while on the ceiling, painted in the 1730s by Clermont, there is a histrionic picture by Luca Giordano of the Conversion of St Paul; but the main attraction is the collection of 'cabinet pictures' on the walls, including works by Andrea del Sarto ('Virgin and Child with St John' and 'Christ Carrying the Cross'), Lorenzo Lotto ('Temptation of St Anthony' and 'The Assumption'), Parmigianino, Rubens and Claude (note also the view of a picture gallery by the early-17C Flemish artist Frans Francken). There are more small pictures of equally high quality in the **Little Ante-Room**, originally the closet of the bedroom suite, including works by Hugo van der Goes ('The Nativity'), Jan Gossaert ('Children of Christian II of Denmark') and Lucas van Leiden ('The Card Players'; on the ceiling is a 'Birth of Venus' by the 16C Mannerist painter Lorenzo Sabbattini.

A plain **staircase** by Wyatt leads down past Ribera's masterly 'Democritus' (c 1635–37) to the lower cloister and thence to the **Large and Small Smoking**

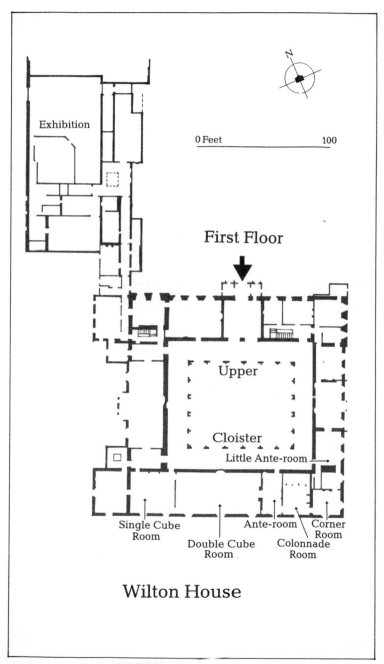

Exhibition

N

0 Feet   100

First Floor

Upper

Cloister

Little Ante-room

Single Cube Room

Double Cube Room

Ante-room

Colonnade Room

Corner Room

Wilton House

Rooms, the first of which contains a collection of paintings of horsemanship brought together by the 10th Earl, whose portrait by Pompeo Batoni is also on display; note also the Chippendale bookcase with carvings of musical instruments. The last room to be seen is the **Garden Hall** in the east range. This was originally the main entrance to the house, but Wyatt inserted a flimsy-looking Gothic vault in plaster over the space where the carriages drove formerly into the courtyard; 18C and 19C busts are now arranged around the walls, including one by Roubiliac of the pugnacious-looking 9th Earl.

Visitors leave the house through the mid-16C gate tower in the centre of the east front; at each end of this range are the towers of the 16C house, classicised in the 1630s and '40s. But the most important **façade** at Wilton is that to the south. This range was originally intended to be twice as long as it is now, but even in its truncated form it ranks among the most innovative pieces of domestic architecture of its date in England. Built of the locally-quarried Chilmark limestone, the proportions echo those of the Italian houses admired by Inigo Jones, Pembroke and other members of Charles I's rarified court, with a balustrade hiding the roof and the centre emphasised by a Venetian window. The only slightly jarring note comes from the towers on either side, retained from the old house and given their present pedimented tops by Webb after the fire of 1647. The south range was originally designed to be seen as a backdrop to the richly patterned Italianate garden, but it now overlooks a lawn stretching to the River Nadder, which is crossed by the 9th Earl of Pembroke's exquisite **Palladian bridge**.

GCT

NORTH YORKSHIRE

Allerton Park

Just east of the A1, at the junction with the A59 (York–Knaresborough):
the Gerald Arthur Rolph Foundation for Historic Preservation and
Education, tel. 0423 330927. Open Easter–Sept Sun, BH 1–6, last
admission 5. Refreshments.

This Victorian Gothic colossus rears above its wooded park just off the A1,
plainly visible from the road. From the time of the Norman Conquest,
Allerton belonged to the Mauleverer family, and the now-isolated church
of St Martin nearby houses several fine tomb-monuments to them. In 1692
Richard Mauleverer died without an heir, and his widow remarried, leaving
the estate to her son by her second marriage, Richard Arundell. In the 1740s
he rebuilt the house at Allerton and in 1745 he rebuilt the church in a curious
'Norman revival' style, probably to the design of John Vardy; its mid-18C
interior is still virtually intact. He died in 1758, and the estate passed to a
relation, Viscount Galway, who added more features in the park.

In 1786 Galway's son sold Allerton to Frederick Augustus, the second son
of George III and the future 'Grand Old' Duke of York. He rebuilt the house
to designs by Henry Holland, and carried out more landscaping around it.
However, the estate was sold in 1789, and again in 1805 to the 17th Baron
Stourton. He was the premier baron in England, a wealthy Catholic peer
and head of a branch of the Howard family. He added a chapel in Gothic
style, but in 1843 his son razed the Georgian house to the ground, and built
the present house to designs by a little-known London architect, George
Martin. Work stopped in 1856; money ran out before all the interiors were
completed. During the Second World War the house was occupied by the
Canadian Royal Air Force; the family ceased to live here after the death of
the 22nd Baron Stourton in 1965, and the contents were sold. Allerton's
future seemed very bleak, until in 1983 it found its saviour in an American
entrepreneur, Dr Gerald Rolph, who purchased the house and part of the
park. For the last ten years Dr Rolph has been renovating the house to the
highest standards, and collecting pictures and furniture of an appropriate
scale and grandeur.

The village of Allerton Mauleverer has long disappeared, and the house
is isolated in parkland. A short drive leads up from the lane; a fine late 18C
stable-block, in the style of Henry Holland, comes into view. The house
appears quite suddenly around a corner; it is a deliberately dramatic and
spectacular building, in a Tudor-Gothic style; the skyline bristles with
pinnacles, chimneys and gables. The main block is almost symmetrical,
with a high tower rising over the entrance porch, built of a dark-coloured
stone. On the right is a lower, plainer range of brick; this is the Chapel of
c 1805. Behind are the lower buildings of the service courtyard, partly 18C
work.

The scale of the interior is enormous. The regular, symmetrical planning
is still in the Georgian tradition, but the rich decoration is in an English
late-Gothic style, very similar to Pugin's work at the Houses of Parliament.
The quality of the early Victorian workmanship, and of the recent restoration-work, is everywhere apparent. The galleried Great Hall, 80ft high, is
lit from a great lantern which rises, like that of Wollaton, Notts, from the
centre of the main block, and the walls are hung with full-length portraits,

including works by William Dobson and Michael Dahl. The Hall is rendered the more dramatic in that the principal Staircase opens off it, under another very high vaulted ceiling. The full-length portraits here are of members of the Mowbray and Stourton family. The Drawing Room, the room on the left of the entrance, has a splendid plaster ceiling. The immense Rococo mirrors were made for Melton Constable in Norfolk c 1750, the Louis XV style furniture is French of the late 19C, and there are suitably large portraits by Charles Jervas and Michael Dahl. The great Ballroom, occupying the west end of the house, was never finished by Lord Mowbray and Stourton. Dr Rolph found it with walls left as bare masonry, and has decorated it, with a magnificent plaster vaulted ceiling based on William Porden's Saloon at Eaton Hall in Cheshire (of 1803–12, and long-demolished).

On the north side of the Hall are the Library and Dining Room. The Library retains its original rosewood bookcases, the wallpaper is copied from one of Pugin's designs for the Palace of Westminster; over the fireplace is a full-length portrait by Lely of James II as Duke of York. The elaborate ceiling has been repainted in the original colours, and the chairs bear the Stourton crest. The panelled Dining Room is huge and dark. The great table is original to the house, and the chairs, a good match for the room, came from a Scottish castle. The ormolu candelabra are of c 1848, and the windows are filled with stained glass with the arms of the Mowbray and Stourton families. Back on the entrance-side are the Billiard Room, the Music Room, housing Dr Rolph's very unusual collection of automatic musical instruments of the late 19C and early 20C, and the Morning Room, with some early-Victorian furniture, and fine portraits.

The restoration-work continues, and it is hoped to open more rooms in due course. Outside, in the service yard, a large garage contains Dr Rolph's collection of luxury veteran and vintage cars. Away to one side is the great Kitchen Garden, surrounded by high red brick walls, with a long 'rustic' loggia of timberwork built against them. Away to the west, on a prominent knoll is an octagonal temple, a fine piece of Palladian design, currently being restored.

SB

Beningborough Hall

8m north west of York, to the west of A19 near Newton-on-Ouse: National Trust, tel. 0904 470666. Open Easter–Oct Sat–Mon, Tues, Wed, also Fri in July, Aug 12–5 (grounds open 11–5.30). Refreshments.

This large early-18C house stands alone in the flat, rather featureless countryside of the Vale of York. It was built c 1714–16 by John Bourchier, representative of an old family which had acquired the estate by marriage at the end of the 15C. The architect is not known for certain, but William Thornton, a York carpenter and joiner, was involved in the design of the interiors and may have designed the whole house, which is notable for its eccentric Baroque external detailing and its sequence of dramatic internal spaces, as well as for its well-preserved woodwork.

The house passed through the female line after 1767 and remained relatively little altered until it was sold to Lord Chesterfield in 1917. He carried out some internal redecoration, including the removal of varnish from much of the woodwork, and also introduced pictures and furniture from his Herefordshire house, Holme Lacy, to replace the original contents removed at the time of the sale. Most of these items were in turn removed when the house came to the National Trust after the Countess's death in 1957. Since then the Trust has refurnished the most important rooms and restored much of the original 18C colouring on the advice of the decorator David Mlinaric, so that now Beningborough is one of the best places in which to experience how early-18C country houses were decorated and used. In 1976 the National Portrait Gallery chose Beningborough as a provincial outpost for some of its reserve collection of 18C portraits, and the walls of the main rooms are now hung with a much more distinguished array of portraits than would normally be seen in a country house of this type. At the same time the whole of the empty top floor was turned into a series of galleries for yet more portraits, many of them of great artistic and historical interest.

The house stands foursquare at the end of a formal avenue, with low ancillary buildings on either side of an entrance courtyard and a large stable block away to the east, through which visitors enter. The detailing on the **entrance front** shows an acquaintance with some of the more zany minutiae of the late Italian Baroque (note especially the strongly emphasised cornice resting on brackets and the 'eared' frame of the window over the main doorway); these features were all culled from pattern-books, possibly on the advice of John Bourchier's neighbour Lord Bingley of Bramham Park (qv.), although the involvement of the Italian-trained Thomas Archer cannot be ruled out. The two-storeyed **Entrance Hall** is one of the most architecturally impressive rooms of its date in England. Corinthian pilasters appear to support a quasi-medieval 'vault', and arches at first-floor level allow vistas through to the spacious corridors that bisect the house and give the interior much of its grandeur. Over the fireplace is a bust of the art-loving Pope Clement XIV by the Irish sculptor Christopher Hewetson, acquired in Rome in 1771.

The layout of the rooms on the two main floors follows the usual early-18C pattern of public reception rooms in the centre with 'apartments' on either side. The east apartment on the ground floor was probably John Bourchier's own, and now contains a magnificent bed of c 1710 from Holme Lacy and a good collection of blue and white porcelain of the K'ang Hsi and Ch'ien Lung periods in the closet and dressing room, acquired by a 19C diplomat in Peking and bequeathed to the National Trust. The rooms on the garden front are arranged in *enfilade*. They include the **Dining Room**, hung with some of Kneller's Kit Cat Club portraits, and the **Drawing Room**, created in the 19C out of the two main rooms of the main guest apartment, with elaborate wood carving by Thornton and his team, good contemporary furniture (including an early-18C walnut bureau-bookcase bequeathed to the Trust along with other objects in the house by Lady Megaw), and portraits of Alexander Pope (by Simon Jervas) and of the builder, John Bourchier. The adjoining **Dressing Room** now contains a collection of early-18C lacquered furniture, and the circuit of the ground-floor rooms concludes with the main **Staircase** with its superbly carved wooden balustrade.

The first floor is reached by the secondary staircase, from the top of which there are exciting vistas down into the hall. The Saloon, in the centre of the garden front, has Corinthian pilasters against the white-painted panelling, and contains portraits by Johann Closterman (of the aesthetically minded 3rd Earl of Shaftesbury and his brother dressed as Greek philosophers),

Gainsborough and Pompeo Batoni. Lady Chesterfield's Room next door was originally part of the first-floor guest apartment and now contains another bed from Holme Lacy and a sensitive portrait by Reynolds of Georgina, later Duchess of Devonshire, as a child; the adjacent Closet has more blue and white porcelain piled onto the corner chimneypiece in the fashionable early-18C manner. Another staircase leads to the top floor, where the best of the portraits from the National Portrait Gallery collection are displayed, including works by all the main 18C English artists arranged thematically and accompanied by helpful descriptions. This splendid collection in itself makes a visit to Beningborough immensely valuable and enjoyable for anyone interested in English 18C life and culture.

GCT

Castle Howard

15m north east of York, 3m north of A64 York–Scarborough: the Hon Simon Howard, tel. 065384 333. Open mid Mar–Oct daily 10–4.30. Refreshments.

Castle Howard derives its name from the medieval Henderskelfe Castle, which came with other vast estates to Lord William Howard, younger son of the 4th Duke of Norfolk, when he married the heiress of Lord Dacre of the North in 1571. Howard's great-grandson was made Earl of Carlisle, and the 1st Earl's grandson built the present house after the older one had been burnt down in 1693. He played a minor part in national politics, serving twice as First Lord of the Treasury—then not as important an office as it later became—but his chief claim to fame lies in the building of Castle Howard and the creation of its superb landscape setting. His first choice as architect was William Talman, the designer of the impressive south front of Chatsworth, Derbyshire (qv.), but, as often happened, Talman quarrelled with his patron and in 1699 Carlisle turned to the as yet completely untried John Vanbrugh, writer of bawdy plays and fellow member of the convivial Kit Cat Club. It soon became apparent that Vanbrugh had a genius for bold architectural composition, but at both Castle Howard and later at Blenheim, Oxfordshire (qv.) his magnificent effects could not have been achieved without the help of the equally inventive Nicholas Hawksmoor, who was involved in the preparation of the final designs in 1700 and took over as architect when Vanbrugh died in 1726. By then the house was finished apart from the west wing, and Hawksmoor's main independent contribution was the design of the awe-inspiring domed mausoleum in the grounds, one of the great monuments of classical architecture in England.

Carlisle's son, the 4th Earl, visited Rome twice and brought together an important collection of antique statuary, which still survives in the house; he also employed his brother-in-law, the Palladian enthusiast Sir Thomas Robinson of Rokeby, Durham (qv.), to build the west wing to a new and more 'correct' design in 1753–59. The 5th Earl, who went on the Grand Tour with Charles James Fox, assembled an important collection of Old Masters, many of them purchased at the Orléans sale in 1798 (some have since been sold), and turned much of the west wing into a Gallery, designed by Charles Tatham in 1800. The Chapel, also in the west wing, was redecorated in 1875–78 by the 9th Earl, a friend of Burne-Jones and William Morris; the 9th Earl and his wife disapproved of primogeniture, and when she died the

The Hall at Castle Howard by Sir John Vanbrugh, one of the crowning achievements of the 'grand manner'

eldest son inherited the title and the old Dacre border stronghold Naworth Castle, Cumbria (qv.), while Castle Howard went to their younger son, whose grandson lives here today. The central range suffered from a disastrous fire in 1940 in which most of the early-18C state rooms were gutted, and although the building has been reconstructed some of the rooms remain empty and unused.

The house is approached by long avenues, the south one interrupted by massive cyclopean **gateways** conveying a mood of primitive power. The grounds are entered through the **stable block**, designed by Carr of York in 1774–82 and now containing a costume museum. This restrained but impressive building stands some distance away from the house, whose **entrance front** faces north over a lake. Vanbrugh had spent some time in

France (much of it in prison as a spy), and the general layout of the house, with a central *corps de logis* and lower wings joined to it by colonnades— only one of which was built—owes much to French precedent. But the overall character is less restrained than anything in contemporary France, and in its dramatic massing and sculptural treatment of the wall surfaces the huge building comes as close as anything in England to the theatrical display associated with the Baroque. To gain the maximum visual impact, Vanbrugh introduced a dome over the centre of the main block, and this feature dominates both the entrance front and the more exuberant south or **garden front**, where the central block is flanked by lower wings which originally contained the main formal 'apartments'; in designing these façades he flouted the rules of classical architecture by changing the order from the sombre Doric on the north front to the festive Corinthian on the south. Another aspect of Vanbrugh's architecture can be seen in the turreted quasi-medieval kitchen courtyard to the east of the east wing, and yet another in the **Temple of the Four Winds**, built in 1725–28 at the east end of a gently rising path leading from the garden front along the line of the main street of the former village of Henderskelfe, erased by Carlisle when he planned the grounds. From this building, loosely modelled on Palladio's Villa Rotonda near Vicenza, the vista encompasses a rugged ornamental bridge and Hawksmoor's brooding **mausoleum**.

The house is entered through Robinson's neo-Palladian **west wing**. A chilly staircase leads, via a landing with a cabinet filled with 18C English and German porcelain, to some **bedrooms**, one of which contains furniture by John Linnell, and then to a groin-vaulted passage lined with some of the 4th Earl's collection of antiquities. They include a particularly impressive collection of Roman and imitation-Roman portrait busts on 18C plinths, separated from each other by massive tables in the manner of William Kent, some of them with Roman mosaic tops. Vanbrugh's soaring **Hall**, at the end of this corridor, is one of the crowning achievements of the 'grand manner' in England, with its dome resting on pendentives—painted by the Venetian artist Antonio Pellegrini—and supported by tall, squared, Corinthian columns; the side walls open out to reveal vistas of the flanking staircases, partly hidden by the chimneypiece on one side and a massive scagliola niche housing a figure of Bacchus on the other. The former saloon—now called the **Garden Hall**—was gutted, like most of the east range, in 1940, but has recently been redecorated with evocatively neo- romantic frescoes by the artist and illustrator, Felix Kelly, out of the profits of the television adaptation of Evelyn Waugh's *Brideshead Revisited*, much of which was filmed here.

The rooms in the west part of the garden front were remodelled in the mid 18C, and now contain the finest pictures and furniture in the house. There are works by Gainsborough and Reynolds in the **Music Room** and **Tapestry Room**, including portraits by Reynolds of the 5th Earl and of the Tahitian 'noble savage' Omai, and Old Masters acquired by the 5th Earl in the Orléans Room, notably portraits by Annibale Carracci and Domenico Fetti (a man holding a sheet of music) and Rubens's vigorous and colourful 'Salome'. In the **Museum Room**, at the corner of the west range, there are pictures by the pre-Raphaelite-inspired 9th Earl, and also a massive and unique late-17C Delft 'flower pagoda'.

Most of the west range is taken up by the spacious early-19C **Gallery**, which serves as a setting for a collection of Renaissance bronzes, 18C furniture (including neo-classical items by the Swedish cabinet-maker

Christopher Fuhrlong), early family portraits—notably the famous early-16C portrait of the poet Earl of Surrey and portraits of Henry VIII and of the 3rd Duke of Norfolk by or after Holbein—and 17C and 18C Italian works. Among the latter are Guercino's 'Tancred and Erminia' (1650), Orazio Gentileschi's 'Finding of Moses', small panels attributed to Giovanni Bellini, Parmigianino and others, and four large ruin capricci by Pannini (1740), bought by the 4th Earl in Rome. The tour ends in the richly coloured **Chapel**, with an altarpiece by C.E. Kempe (whose pupils were responsible for the painted decoration) and stained-glass windows by Burne-Jones.

GCT

Duncombe Park

At Helmsley, 14m east of Thirsk on A170 Thirsk–Scarborough:
Lord Feversham, tel. 0439 70213. Open Apr Sun, Easter weekend;
May–Oct Sun–Thur and Sat before BH 11–6. Refreshments.

This formidably impressive house was built out of the proceeds of a fortune accumulated in the late 17C by a prodigiously wealthy London banker, Sir Charles Duncombe, reputedly the richest commoner in England. In 1695 he bought the Helmsley estate, with its medieval castle on the edge of the small market town, from the 2nd Duke of Buckingham (cf. Cliveden, Bucks), thus occasioning Alexander Pope's cynical couplet: 'Helmsley once proud Buckingham's delight/Slides to a scrivener or a City Knight'. In 1713, two years after his death, his nephew and co-heir Thomas Browne, having changed his name to Duncombe, began to build a magnificent new house on a new site some distance away from the castle, to the designs of the local amateur architect William Wakefield of Huby Hall, Easingwold. The site was chosen for its scenic potential, and to the east of the house a spectacular grass terrace was laid out, probably by Charles Bridgeman, overlooking the River Rye and the country beyond, and punctuated by circular classical temples of c 1730 at each end, Ionic to the north and Doric to the south. The terrace ranks high among the achievements of English landscaping, and in 1758 Thomas Duncombe's grandson formed a second terrace a couple of miles away to the north, overlooking Rievaulx Abbey, which then formed part of the estate. Two more temples were built here, probably to the designs of Sir Thomas Robinson, one of them with excellent contemporary furniture and frescoes by Giuseppe Borgnis. In 1770 Arthur Young wrote that the Duncombe landscape 'cannot be viewed without the most exquisite enjoyment' (the Rievaulx terrace now belongs to the National Trust, and there are separate opening arrangements).

While the setting of Duncombe has been well preserved, there have been many changes to the house. Charles Duncombe, great-grandson of the original builder, was raised to the peerage as Lord Feversham in 1826, and in 1843 his son the 2nd Lord, whose monument stands in Helmsley market place, employed Charles Barry to add the detached service blocks which flank the entrance forecourt to the west of the house and to close it off with an impressive screen. At the same time a formal parterre was created by W.A. Nesfield to the east of the house, and a conservatory built in the woodland to the south. There was a disastrous fire in 1879, but in 1891–94 the house was rebuilt with some modifications by the Scottish architect William Young, only to be abandoned by the family for a second time in 1924, when it was leased out as a girls' school. It has recently been reoccupied by the 6th Lord Feversham, who has reintroduced some of the pictures originally in the house and has bought and commissioned new items of furniture to augment those few which survived from before it became a school.

As first seen from the west, Duncombe Park appears like a smaller and plainer Castle Howard (qv.), albeit with a pedimented attic rather than a dome in the centre, and there seems little doubt that both the nouveau riche Thomas Duncombe and his architect were strongly influenced by the example of Vanbrugh and Lord Carlisle in conceiving the house. It is built of local limestone, and the architectural features, from the sturdy Doric pilasters on the entrance front to the round-headed windows and Doric portico on the east or garden front, convey an impression of masculine strength of a kind often found in Vanbrugh's own buildings, though without their enlivening eccentricities. As originally planned, the house consisted of a central block containing a hall and saloon flanked by staircases and 'apartments' which extended into the projecting wings. These arrangements have been greatly modified, and now the only room to survive relatively unchanged from the early 18C is the Hall, reached by an external flight of stairs and extending the full height of the two main storeys, with giant Corinthian half-columns to add the appropriate note of solemn grandeur. The Baroque plasterwork on the walls and ceiling (possibly by Artari and Vassali) was copied in the 1890s by the London firm of George Jackson & Sons from the pre-fire original, and there are portraits of Sir Charles Duncombe and some of his famous customers on the walls.

The remaining rooms date in essence from the late 19C, though all bear signs of the recent sensitive redecoration by Lord and Lady Feversham. The centre of the garden front is occupied by a long Saloon, divided at each end by Ionic colonnades and panelled in wood, with a late-17C-style plaster ceiling; this is flanked to the north by a rather portly Dining Room and to the south by the more cheerful Withdrawing Room, with neo-Rococo plasterwork on the ceiling, furniture in the Louis XV manner, and family portraits by Mercier, Reynolds and Andrea Soldi ('Thomas Duncombe and his family', 1741) on the walls. To the north of the Hall are smaller rooms, including the Library, and from here an impressive staircase leads up to a group of bedrooms, one of which (the Italian Bedroom) contains some early Italian paintings. Downstairs, on the ground floor or 'rustic', are the late-19C servants' quarters which can be explored by those interested in the domestic life of great Victorian country houses, and from here there is an exit leading to the gardens and terrace.

GCT

Ebberston Hall

6m east of Pickering on A170 Pickering–Scarborough: W. de Wend Fenton. Open Easter–Sept daily 10–6.

This miniature villa, or 'small rustick edifice', as it was called by its architect, Colen Campbell, is one of the most original houses of its date in England. The builder was William Thompson, bachelor MP for the nearby seaport borough of Scarborough, Warden of the Royal Mint, and grandson of an East Riding country gentleman who had acquired the estate in 1674. The house, which dates from 1718, is small by country house standards—more a hunting lodge than a 'seat'—but its architecture is monumental and far more original than might be expected from the bland monotony of Campbell's better-known designs. The entrance façade is of only three bays, but as in the villas of Palladio and his contemporaries the main rooms are placed upstairs on a piano nobile, reached after the fashion of a Roman temple by a broad flight of steps flanked at the bottom by obelisks. The walls are rusticated and the doorway enclosed in a massive Doric aedicule, while the roof is hidden behind a balustrade; an 18C painting (not in the house) shows a cupola and a pair of one-storeyed lodges joined to the main house by curved walls, but these embellishments were removed later, after the house had been sold in 1814 to the notorious 'Squire Osbaldiston', a well- known Regency rider to hounds. The house has since been sold twice, most recently in 1941 to the present owner's father.

The interior is made up of a sequence of spacious, well-proportioned rooms panelled in wood and enriched with pilasters and highly carved cornices, but now gently sinking into a state of faded elegance. There is some attractive late-17C and 18C furniture, including some marquetry chairs. The central room on the front opposite the entrance—originally an open loggia with Ionic columns, deriving from Inigo Jones's Queen's House at Greenwich, Greater London (qv.)—overlooks a now somewhat overgrown rectangular 'canal', fed by waterfalls, from which the water was originally channelled underneath the house. The gardens at Ebberston marked an important step away from the clipped trees and gravelled paths of the previous era; and as seen from the end of the canal, with the Yorkshire Wolds on the horizon to the south, the house in its landscape setting can still evoke the contrived harmony of man and nature which was one of the main legacies of the Italian Renaissance to Britain.

GCT

Markenfield Hall

3m south of Ripon to west of A61 Ripon–Harrogate: the Lord Grantley.
Open Apr–Oct Mon, 10–12.30, 2.15–5 (exterior only other days on May).

Difficult to find, and virtually unsignposted, Markenfield Hall is a surprisingly intact example of a medieval country gentleman's house. It was begun by Sir John Markenfield, who obtained licence to crenellate in 1310, and was probably completed by his son Thomas; the family estates were confiscated after the Rising of the North in 1569, and subsequently came into the hands of a lawyer and politician, Fletcher Norton (nicknamed Sir Bull-face Double Fee), who was made Lord Grantley of Markenfield in 1782, and whose descendants live here today. For most of the time since the 16C the house was not the main residence of the family which owned it, hence the fortunate survival of the 14C buildings.

The house stands in a moat, and is approached through an attractive complex of farm buildings dating largely from the 18C. The L-shaped main block, of white magnesian limestone, occupies the north side of an irregular courtyard entered through a 16C gatehouse. The main rooms are on the upper floor, and were originally entered by an external staircase (since demolished) leading into the Hall, which is lit by large windows with Decorated Gothic tracery. It is now empty and rarely used, as is the only other room open to visitors, the former chapel in the cross-wing to the east (note the traceried east window and piscina); the medieval solar or great chamber was to the north of this, but has been much altered and is not shown. An original spiral staircase leads up from the chapel to the roof, where visitors are allowed to wander freely.

GCT

Newburgh Priory

South of Coxwold, 3m east of A19 Thirsk–Easingwold: Sir George Wombwell, tel. 03476 435. Open Apr–June Wed, Sun and BH Mon 2.30–4.45 (grounds opne 2–6, also early July–Aug). Guided tours. Refreshments.

This large and impressive house stands on the site of an Augustinian priory acquired in 1540 by one of Henry VIII's chaplains, Anthony Belassis, a member of a Durham family which became rich through the plentiful spoils available in this part of the country after the Dissolution. Unlike some of the neighbouring monasteries, Newburgh was soon turned into a house, and today there is no obvious visible evidence of the church or monastic buildings. Sir Henry Belassis enlarged and embellished the house in the early 17C, but most of these alterations were masked by a series of piecemeal improvements carried out, over a period of nearly 50 years starting in the mid 1720s, by his descendant, the 4th Viscount (and 1st Earl) of Fauconberg, who possibly acted as his own architect. In 1825 the estate passed to Lord Fauconberg's granddaughter, who had married a member of another Yorkshire family, Sir George Wombwell, and since then it has remained in the same family, having been reoccupied in 1969 after a long period of use as a school.

The house is approached through delicate iron gates, part of a formal vista terminated by the monumental stable block of c 1725—perhaps the most impressive piece of architecture at Newburgh. The house itself has the typically 16C plan of a hall block with projecting wings, and faces north over a pastoral, almost Claudian, landscape with a lake and distant hills. Two late-17C paintings in the house show the usual gables and mullioned windows, but they were replaced in the Georgian face-lift, and today the long entrance façade has a somewhat denuded air, enhanced by the ruinous state of the east wing, which until after the Second World War contained the Long Gallery. The unusually disparate south front still retains its three-storeyed early-17C 'frontispiece' displaying the classical orders; it is squeezed up against a bow-windowed projection added in the early 17C but remodelled in the 1760s, and there is a long, plain, 16C rubble-stone range to the west.

The house is entered through the former screens passage, but the tour starts upstairs, where three rooms are shown; one of them contains a 1755 conversation piece of the 4th Viscount Fauconberg and his six children by the Florentine artist Andrea Soldi, several of whose portraits hang in the house. A gloomy bare room over the porch may contain the remains of Oliver Cromwell, said to have been brought here by his daughter, who married the 2nd Viscount; the eerie effect increases as the tour proceeds to the main staircase, which became derelict at the time of the Second World War, and to an adjacent room whose decoration has never been completed on account, it is said, of a curse.

The ground floor is reached by a secondary staircase hung with good 17C portraits, including one of James I's daughter, the 'Winter Queen' aged 14; there is also a view of Windsor Castle by Danckerts. The Dining Room (formerly the library) occupies the site of the Elizabethan hall, and contains the finest work of art in the house: a massive chimneypiece and overmantel with a sophisticated relief carving of a reclining Venus flanked by figures of Mars and Diana, almost certainly the work of Nicholas Stone, who received a payment from Sir Henry Belassis in 1615 and subsequently carved the monument to Sir Henry's daughter-in-law in Coxwold church. There are more Soldi portraits here, along with earlier pictures of Cromwell's daughter and her husband, the Ambassador to France under the Protectorate (in the next generation the family reverted to Catholicism and produced two nuns, before settling back into Anglicanism in the time of the 4th Lord Fauconberg). A passage leads to two Drawing Rooms (one of them originally a dining room) on the south front, both dating in their present form from the 4th Lord Fauconberg's time. The delicate ceilings by Giuseppe Cortese date from 1765–67, but are still Rococo in their frothy exuberance, and there are marble chimneypieces of the same date by the London carver, Thomas Moore; the smaller room has a screen of columns which might have been designed by Sir William Chambers in 1774. There are good items of 18C furniture and porcelain, and pictures by Philip Mercier, Soldi (two of them in unusual contemporary frames which incorporate mirrors) and Romney, as well as a picture of Lord Fauconberg himself dressed as a painter.

GCT

Newby Hall

4m south east of Ripon on B6265 Ripon–Boroughbridge: R.E.J. Compton, tel. 0423 322583. Open Apr–Sept daily except Mon (but open BH Mon) 12–5. Refreshments.

The nucleus of this externally restrained but internally lavish red-brick house was built in the 1690s by Sir Edward Blackett, MP for Ripon. He came from a family of Newcastle coal-owners (cf. Wallington, Northumberland) and spent some of the money left over from purchasing the estate in erecting a square-profiled house which Celia Fiennes in 1697 called 'the finest…in Yorkshire', set in extensive formal gardens; the architect is unknown, but William Etty of York was the carpenter. The estate was sold in 1748 to Richard Weddell, whose son William went to Italy in 1765–66, where he met Piranesi and collected 19 chests full of classical statuary. Soon after his return he was elected to the Society of Dilettante and set about remodelling and extending the house to accommodate his collection. His first architect was John Carr of York, but he was superseded c 1767 by Robert Adam, who with the assistance of a local man, William Belwood (who designed the stables), transformed the interior into one of the finest neo-classical ensembles in England, a process which took some ten years.

Weddell died childless in 1792, and the house was inherited by his cousin Thomas Robinson, 3rd Lord Grantham. He added a wing containing a new dining room on the north side of the house in 1807 and introduced some of the French furniture which can be seen elsewhere in the house, but in 1833 he inherited Wrest Park, Bedfordshire (qv.), and conveyed Newby to his daughter and her husband Henry Vyner, descendant of a leading late-17C London goldsmith. In 1870 she employed William Burges to build the magnificent estate church of Skelton, which stands just inside the park walls, and a few years later her son Robert Vyner enlarged the north wing of the house to include a billiard room and other paraphernalia of 19C country house life. His daughter and heiress married a younger son of the Marquess of Northampton, and their son (the present owner's father) created the superb gardens to the south of the house between the wars.

The original character of Newby can be best appreciated today by looking at the **south (garden) front** with its slightly emphasised central bay and curved pediments over the central doorway and first-floor window. When William Weddell remodelled the house he shifted the main entrance from the west front (not accessible to visitors) to the east, and employed Carr to build the lower projecting wings, thus creating a forecourt. But it is Adam's hand which is immediately apparent in the design of the **Entrance Hall**, whose walls are adorned with martial trophies (cf. Osterley Park, Greater London) by the plasterer Joseph Rose, and with paintings by Annibale Carracci and Rosa di Tivoli; the organ may have been designed by 'Athenian' Stuart, one of Weddell's associates in the Society of Dilettante, and the side tables are by Chippendale, who visited the house in 1772 and 1776. Doorways in the west wall lead into Adam's drawing room, but this is not seen until near the end of the tour and visitors are channelled first into a corridor which allows glimpses into two less important rooms, one of which (originally the library but now called the Drawing Room) has a vivacious portrait of Lady Theodosia Vyner by Lawrence (1791) hanging over the fireplace. The **Dining Room** of 1807, sparser in its decoration than the Adam rooms, contains neo-classical satinwood side tables designed by Adam and executed by Chippendale, alabaster urns made by Adam for the former dining room, and portraits of the family of the Empress Maria Theresa by Van Loo, given to the 1st Lord Grantham, Ambassador to Vienna.

A neo-Jacobean staircase leads to the **Billiard Room**, an unaltered late-Victorian interior, and from here a passage leads to a series of comfortable bedrooms and finally to a circular room possibly designed by William Belwood, with light green walls inset with panels of 'grotesque' designs inspired by Roman interior decoration, which may have been painted by Weddell's wife; a small painting of Weddell by Pompeo Batoni hangs between two of these panels. On the walls of the **staircase**, with its iron balustrade of anthemion ornament, there are portraits of the Earls of Kent, originally at Wrest Park, and at the bottom there is another, larger, portrait of Weddell by Batoni, facing one of his aesthetic mentor, the 2nd Lord Grantham, by Anton Raphael Mengs.

The finest rooms at Newby form a sequence, starting with Adam's drawing room (the Tapestry Room) in the centre of the west front, and ending in his Sculpture Gallery in the south wing. Nowhere is Adam's genius as a designer of interiors seen to more satisfying effect. The rooms are contrasted in colour, furnishing and in architectural treatment, and they have been remarkably little altered. The character of the **Tapestry Room** is determined by the set of Gobelin tapestries ordered by Weddell on his Grand Tour, with erotic scenes after Boucher on an ochre-coloured ground; and the plaster ceiling with paintings by Zucchi, the carpet, the tapestry-covered Chippendale chairs and the gilded pier-glasses all enhance the sumptuous effect. The **Library**—originally the dining room—is a long room with apsidal ends closed off by Corinthian colonnades—a device employed in several Adam houses (eg, Kenwood, Greater London)—and plasterwork by Rose. This leads into the **Gallery**, designed as a monumental framework for Weddell's collection of Roman and Greco-Roman statuary, which still survives intact. At the centre is a top-lit domed rotunda, with niches containing some of the most prized items including the celebrated 'Barberini Venus', and on either side there are lower rectangular rooms—a masterly stroke of planning which creates dramatic contrasts of light and shade. Thanks to Adam, there are few places in England in which the allure of the Antique for the 18C mind is more vividly and sympathetically expressed.

GCT

Norton Conyers

3m north of Ripon, south of Wath: Sir James Graham, Bt, tel. 076584 333. Open late May–early Sept Sun and all BH Sun/Mon, also last week of July 2–5 (garden open all year Mon–Fri 9–5, also Mar–Aug Sat Sun 2–5.30). Guided tours.

The essential structure of this attractive house as it now stands was built by a member of the Norton family c 1500, but in 1569 Sir Richard Norton, the then head of the family, joined the Rising of the North, and the estate was confiscated by the Crown. In 1624 it was bought by Richard Graham, a member of a Border family which had entered the service of James I's favourite, the Duke of Buckingham, and had gone in the previous year on the abortive expedition to marry the future Charles I to the Spanish Infanta. Graham carried out some internal alterations, possibly including the addition of the present main staircase. His eldest son inherited Nunnington Hall (qv.), not far away, and Norton Conyers went to his second son, another Richard, who was given a baronetcy by Charles II. He added the 'Dutch' gables which adorn the roof- line. Sir Bellingham Graham, the 5th Baronet, introduced sash windows in the 1770s, and in 1780–86 he employed William Belwood, Robert Adam's clerk of the works at Newby Hall (qv.), to improve the Dining Room and Parlour, and to build an impressive stable block. The house was sold by his extravagant, fox-hunting grandson, but it was later bought back and sensitively refurnished.

The house stands in a park, with the stables and an attractive early-18C walled garden some distance away. A pedimented late-17C doorway framed by paired Corinthian columns leads into the spacious, well-lit Hall, altered in the 18C and hung with pictures, including a portrait of Charles V and his son, Philip II of Spain, brought back, it is said, from the ill-fated marriage expedition of 1623, and a large picture of the Quorn hunt by John Ferneley, won at dice by the profligate 7th Baronet. There is also a late-16C German inlaid table which may have been in the house since the early 17C. A conversation piece of the 5th Baronet and his family, probably by Zoffany's pupil Henry Walton, hangs in the adjacent Parlour, and in the plain but attractive Dining Room on the other side of the hall there are two Romneys and Pompeo Batoni's excellent Grand Tour portrait of a nonchalantly lounging Sir Humphrey Morice (1763). More family and sporting pictures hang on the walls of the main staircase, reached from the Hall through a wooden archway; it leads to a panelled early-17C bedroom and to another formed in the 18C out of the former great chamber. Above are the attics (not shown), in which a mad woman is believed to have been incarcerated in the 18C, a legend which so impressed the Yorkshire-born Charlotte Brontë when she visited the house in 1839 that she incorporated it into *Jane Eyre*. The walled 18C garden, in full cultivation, is about 100 yards from the house. Inside the main gate, a gravel path flanked by herbaceous borders leads to a late-18C orangery flanked by contemporary greenhouses.

GCT

Nunnington Hall

1m north of B1257 Helmsley–Malton: National Trust, tel. 04395 283. Open Apr–Oct daily except Mon, Fri, but open Good Fri and BH Mon, also July and Aug Fri 2–6. Refreshments.

Nunnington Hall stands by the River Rye on the edge of an attractive stone-built village in the quiet countryside to the south of the Vale of Pickering. In the early 16C the estate belonged to the Parr family, but it came into the hands of the Crown after the Lady Jane Grey rebellion and was leased out in 1567 to Queen Elizabeth's doctor, Robert Huickes. He built some of the west wing of the present H-shaped house, but the building was enlarged to its present size by his successor Thomas Norcliffe, who took over the lease in 1583. The estate was sold by Charles I and acquired in 1655 by Ronald Graham, a younger son from a Cumberland family which had already settled not far away at Norton Conyers (qv.). His nephew and successor was made Viscount Preston by Charles II and later became a leading supporter of James II, during the last year of whose reign (1687–88) he carried out important alterations to the house. He was imprisoned by the new regime and subsequently retired to Nunnington, where, according to his monument in the parish church, he 'dedicated the remainder of his days to a pious retirement and the service of the King of Heaven'.

The house fell into disrepair after Viscount Preston's descendants sold it in 1839 (some of the portraits are now at Norton Conyers), but it was rescued in 1921 by Mrs Ronald Fife, who employed the York architect Walter Brierley—inheritor of John Carr's practice—to restore it. Her daughter and son-in-law continued to live here after she bequeathed it to the National Trust in 1952, but they left in 1978, and the Trust has augmented the furniture and pictures they left behind with items brought from elsewhere.

The house is built of the attractive silver-grey local stone, and consists of a two-storeyed hall block flanked by gabled wings, looking south on to a formal walled garden with Mannerist gateways in some of the walls. These date from the time of Viscount Preston, who also heightened the central block, replaced the Elizabethan mullioned windows with the present sash windows, and introduced the pedimented window with its iron balcony over the central doorway; this window lit the formal dining room or great chamber (now a Drawing Room) over the Hall, which was also redecorated with large bolection-moulded panels and given an elaborate, if somewhat crudely carved, French-inspired chimneypiece taken from a contemporary pattern-book. At the same time a solid oak staircase was built next to the Hall to provide a stately ascent to the upstairs rooms. Lord Preston's architect is unknown, but the York master-carpenter William Etty has been suggested as a possible candidate.

The house is now entered through the west wing and most of the rooms are shown. The downstairs Dining Room and the adjoining closet (now called Lord Preston's Room) originally comprised a late-17C 'apartment', and the closet has a contemporary heraldic ceiling. The Hall contains three sporting pictures of 1820 by John Ferneley, and there is an 18C Soho chinoiserie tapestry. Flemish 17C tapestries, probably acquired by Lord Preston, hang on the walls of the staircase, which is approached through wooden arches, and there are more tapestries, together with 17C Dutch pictures and 18C English furniture, on loan from various sources, in the Drawing Room over the Hall. Several appropriately furnished bedrooms occupy the west wing, one of them containing a pastel drawing attributed to Boucher. From here a staircase leads to the attics where the roof timbers can be seen, along with a refurnished nursery and servant's bedroom and the Carlisle collection of model rooms given to the National Trust and brought here in 1981. A back staircase in the east wing leads down to two late-17C panelled rooms on the ground floor in which teas are served.

GCT

Ripley Castle

3½m north of Harrogate on A61 Harrogate–Ripon: Sir Thomas Ingilby, tel. 0423 770152. Open Apr, Oct Sat, Sun; May–Sept daily except Mon, Fri (but open Good Fri, BH Mon) 11.30–4.30 (closes 3.30 weekdays in May). Guided tours. Refreshments.

The Ingilby family have been lords of the manor of Ripley since about 1320, when Sir Thomas Ingilby married the heiress of the estate, which lay along the banks of the River Nidd. He obtained permission from the King to hold a weekly market in the village which had grown up beside what was to become Ripley Castle, and in the mid 15C his descendant Sir John Ingilby built the oldest surviving part of the present complex of buildings: a crenellated stone gatehouse standing a little to the west of the market place. But the house itself dates mainly from two later building campaigns, the first in 1548–55, when Sir William Ingilby built a three-storeyed tower of the semi-fortified type still popular at that time in the north of England, and the second in 1783–86, when another Sir John Ingilby, who owned (and later sold) the site of Harrogate town centre, employed John Carr of York and his assistant William Belwood to build what was in effect a new house next to the tower on the site of the dilapidated medieval hall and its associated buildings. The house has since remained remarkably unchanged, but Sir John's eccentric son William, an enthusiastic Continental traveller, improved the gardens, and in the 1820s he rebuilt the estate village at the gates of the house in a picturesque style which was supposedly influenced by memories of a village he had seen and admired in Alsace (the splendidly ornate village hall or 'Hotel de Ville' followed in 1854). This picturesque ensemble also survives intact, and today the sense of family continuity and ancient possession is still very apparent at Ripley.

The house is approached through the village and entered opposite the largely 15C parish church in which many of the Ingilbys are buried. In a letter of 1784 Sir John Ingilby wrote that he 'was determined upon preserving as much as possible of the old place and by that means have spoiled my plan (sic) in the opinion of some people, but notwithstanding the inconveniences of our ancestors' buildings I prefer them to the modern structures'. This must account for the plain castellated appearance of Carr's house, which from the outside complements the architecture of the 16C tower, to the left of the entrance, with its gritstone walls and crenellated roofline. The garden side of the house betrays Carr's classical training, but even here no attempt was made to compete with the earlier building.

The interior was a different matter, and here Carr employed the neo-classical idiom with which he is more usually associated. The house he built is a square block with the older tower projecting to the south and a service wing to the east, and is entered through a deep Entrance Hall with a Doric colonnade screening off a smaller Inner Hall, oval in shape. The family portraits, in which the house is rich, include one of Sir John Ingilby holding plans of the house, and there are also four pictures commissioned by him showing the old house before it was demolished. The north front is taken up by three rooms overlooking the gardens: the Dining Room and two drawing rooms, the first of which, the Round Drawing Room, contains a set of chairs and settees by Thomas Chippendale, whose father had been a joiner on the estate and whose brother made a survey of it in 1752. The Large Drawing Room has an Adamesque plaster ceiling and more good 18C furniture, including a French Louis XV bureau and two Kentian mirrors on either side of the chaste neo-classical chimneypiece; there are also portraits by Kneller and Gainsborough, but pride of place among the works of art must be given to Canova's sculpture of 'Venus emerging from her bath', modelled on Pauline Bonaparte and bought by Sir William Ingilby in 1817. To the south is the semicircular Staircase Hall, lit by a Venetian window filled with painted armorial glass by William Peckitt of York (1784–85). Beyond lies the dark, wood-panelled Library, on the ground floor of the 16C tower, containing early printed books, family portraits, and various memorabilia including a lead ingot mined by the Romans in the 1C AD, the foundation charter of Mount Grace Priory (1396) near Northallerton, a chalice cover of c 1600, and some Civil War armour (Cromwell is said to have been refused permission to enter the castle after the Battle of Marston Moor in 1644 by the sister of the owner).

The tour concludes in the two upper floors of the tower, but before entering them it is worth looking at some of the paintings at the top of the staircase, notably a 'Mystic Marriage of St Catherine' by a follower of Parmigianino, 'Meleager presenting Atlanta with the head of the Calydonian boar' by Jacob Jordaens, and a remarkable picture of Constantinople by Jean van Mour (c 1730). The room on the first floor of the tower has a plaster ceiling said to have been made for a visit by James I on his way from Edinburgh to London in 1603, and the tour concludes in the so-called Knight's Chamber above, which retains its original mid-16C wooden roof, panelling and carved inscription asserting that poverty with mirth and gladness is preferable to riches with sorrow and sadness. These rooms, filled with portraits and objects accumulated by the Ingilbys over many centuries, retain the feeling of the past to an unusual degree.

GCT

Stockeld Park

2m north west of Wetherby off A661 Wetherby–Harrogate: Mr and Mrs P. Grant, tel. 0937 586101. Open Apr–early Oct Thur 2–5.

This impressive stone-built house was designed in 1758–63 by James Paine, one of the leading country-house architects of the mid 18C, and is the only complete house by him regularly open to the public. It was built for William

Middleton, representative of a Roman Catholic family who had been lords of the manor since 1318; according to Paine, the work was 'carried on with great spirit, as the worthy proprietor spared no expense to make it permanent and beautiful'. Middleton died just after the house was finished, and a proposed new office wing was never built. In 1893 the house and estate were sold to Robert John Foster, owner of the Black Dyke Mills in Bradford, and he employed the architect Detmar Blow to make certain changes. These involved moving the entrance from the south to the north, adding a large east wing, and creating a new detached chapel out of a former orangery adjoining the stable yard. The house is still a family home, but the main rooms are let out on occasion for conferences and receptions.

The present entrance front was much altered at the end of the 19C, and to see the house as Paine left it, it is best to proceed to the south-facing garden front (originally the entrance), one of the most original reinterpretations of Palladian architecture of its period. The façade is divided into three contrasting portions, with a three-storeyed block surmounted by a pediment in the centre, flanked on either side by lower wings, each of them with an open pediment over a bold semicircular relieving arch. The ground floor is rusticated, and there are canted bay windows in each of the wings, creating a sense of variety and 'movement' of a kind which Vanbrugh had earlier achieved, and which Robert Adam was later to champion.

Inside, the house is laid out after the fashion of a villa, with the main rooms, all of which are on the ground floor, grouped around a central top-lit Staircase Hall. This is the most impressive interior in the house, the stairs with their distinctive curvy iron balustrades stretching up through the full height of the house. Much of the original plaster decoration survives in the large and well-proportioned reception rooms, which contain furniture and pictures brought in by the Foster family; the Morning Room (originally the entrance hall) and the Library (the upper part of what was originally a two-storeyed chapel) are especially notable.

GCT

Sutton Park

At Sutton-on-the-Forest 8m north of York on B1363 York–Helmsley: Mrs Sheffield, tel. 0367 810249. Open Easter weekend and early May–late Sept Sun, Wed, BH Mon 1.30–5.30. Gardens open Easter–Oct daily 11–5.30. Refreshments.

The village of Sutton grew up in the ancient Forest of Galtres, to the north of York, in the Middle Ages, but the present house, which stands on the edge of the village, was not built until the mid 18C. By this time the ownership of the manor had passed from the Crown to the Harland family, and Philip Harland demolished the existing house soon after inheriting in 1750, replacing it with the present structure, which was finished before his death in 1764. The design has been attributed to the York architect Thomas Atkinson, but in its restrained Palladianism it probably owes something to the influence of James Paine, who had a large and fashionable country-house practice in the north of England. There were some internal alterations at the end of the 18C, but otherwise the house remained relatively unchanged until the 20C, passing through a complicated series of female inheritances before being sold in 1926. There was another sale in 1944, and in 1963 the house was bought by the present owner and her late husband.

They introduced pictures, furniture and even chimneypieces from the old Sheffield country seat, Normanby Park, Humberside (qv.), some of which had formerly been in Buckingham House, the family's town house built on the site of the present Buckingham Palace by John Sheffield, Duke of Buckingham, in the early 18C. The Sheffields and their immediate predecessors were also largely responsible for the layout of the terraced gardens overlooking the flat parkland to the south. They add greatly to the visual appeal of the house.

The house is a plain though well-proportioned brick building designed in the fashion of a villa, with a five-bay central block under a huge pediment, and lower pavilions (possibly an afterthought) lit on the garden side by Venetian windows and joined to the main building by colonnades which have subsequently been filled in. There is remarkably little external ornament, and the house shares the solid, dignified character of many of York's 18C public buildings. Inside, though, there is a richer effect, due partly to the excellent Rococo plasterwork by the local specialist Giuseppe Cortese and partly to more recent embellishments. Some of the best of the plasterwork is in the Entrance Hall, which contains an early drawing of Buckingham House and is screened off from the Staircase by a pair of Corinthian columns. The main reception rooms, which face south over the gardens, contain a rich collection of family portraits going back to the 16C, there is also English, French and Dutch furniture, and porcelain from the Meissen, Chelsea, Bow and Worcester factories, as well as early blanc de Chine and Japanese 'Imari' items. The Library has an excellent plaster ceiling with motifs of fruit and hops, but the chimneypiece and bookcases (by Sir Robert Smirke) came from Normanby, while the early-18C wood panelling in the Morning Room was brought from Potternewton Hall, near Leeds, by the predecessor of the present owner. Some of the best porcelain is displayed in the Tea Room, strikingly painted to imitate tortoiseshell, and the adjacent Porcelain Room, and in the Boudoir, beyond there are pictures of 18C London by the 'English Canaletto' Samuel Scott. Next to this is the Chinese Room, hung with hand-painted wallpaper of c 1750–70.

The upstairs rooms are reached by the main staircase, delicately carved in wood, with another ceiling by Cortese; the portraits include one of Edmund, Earl of Mulgrave, who commanded a ship in the Spanish Armada (shown in the background), and others by Kneller and Wissing. After seeing some bedrooms and enjoying the view over the park, visitors descend by a secondary staircase to the neo-Georgian Dining Room, created by Mrs Sheffield and her late husband to the designs of Francis Johnson; there are more good pictures here, including one of Windsor Castle by Paul Sandby and another by Felix Kelly of Normanby Park, painted in an elegiac neo-Romantic vein.

GCT

SOUTH YORKSHIRE

Cannon Hall

1m west of Cawthorne on A635 Barnsley–Manchester: Barnsley
Metropolitan Borough Council, tel. 0226 790270. Open all year
Tues–Sat 10.30–12, 2–5, Sun 2.30–5.

Cannon Hall is an unpretentious 18C house standing in an attractive
country park, much enjoyed by the citizens of nearby Barnsley. It started
life as a plain stone box of c 1710, built by a member of the Spencer family,
whose wealth derived from the local iron industry, and this survives as the
central block of the present house. John Spencer employed John Carr of
York in 1764–68 to modernise the interior and add wings, which were
subsequently heightened by his nephew and heir, and he also brought in
the landscape gardener, Richard Woods, to improve the grounds, starting
in 1761. His descendant, Sir Walter Spencer-Stanhope, added a Ballroom
in 1890–91, but in 1951 the family sold the house to the Barnsley local
authority, having removed the furniture and pictures. The main rooms were
subsequently refurnished with appropriate 18C objects and pictures, and
the rest of the house is now used to display an unexpectedly rich and varied
collection of pictures, glass—a major local industry—ceramics and Art
Nouveau objects.

Visitors proceed clockwise through the house from the Tuscan-columned
Entrance Hall, taking in the late-19C Ballroom, decorated in the neo-Tudor
taste, and a former outbuilding now used to display glass. The most
important rooms are on the ground floor of the south front, commanding
the view of the park and containing good furniture, of the second half of
the 18C, intelligently arranged, and well-chosen pictures, including works
by Joseph Highmore, Philip Mercier and John Constable (one of his best
portraits, of Mrs Tuder). The sequence starts in the Dining Room, with a
Rococo-style ceiling of 1767 by the York plasterer, James Henderson, and
proceeds through two drawing rooms in the older part of the house—redecorated in the neo-classic manner towards the end of the 18C—to the
Library, which has an attractive Rococo chimneypiece by York craftsmen
of the 1760s and some particularly good furniture, including a bookcase of
c 1780 formerly in the offices of The Times in London. Another downstairs
room contains a selection of late-19C Arts and Crafts furniture. Upstairs
there is a display of ceramics, with work by Walter Crane and others, and
another room houses a collection of local views, including industrial scenes,
by the topographical artist, J.C. Nattes. The remaining rooms are used to
show Dutch and Flemish pictures, including works by Metsu and the
younger van de Velde, collected by a Barnsley man in the 19C and now
constituting the National Loan Collection.

GCT

WEST YORKSHIRE

Bolling Hall

1m south of Bradford city centre, in Bowling Hall Road: Bradford
Metropolitan Council, tel. 0274 723057. Open all year daily except Mon
(but open BH Mon) 10–5 (Apr–Sept 10–6).

The approach to this large, rambling stone house is not very promising, but
visitors prepared to venture through the streets of inner Bradford will find
that it is a well-maintained building with an interesting and complex
architectural history. The oldest portion is a late-medieval tower, which now
contains the entrance, at the south extremity of the garden front. This was
built by a member of the Bolling family, from which the then-completely
rural estate passed at the end of the 15C to the Tempests. They subsequently built the hall (or 'housebody' in the local dialect), probably on
the site of an earlier house; this is easily recognisable from the large
mullioned and transomed window on the garden front which contains
contemporary heraldic glass removed in the 19C and later reinstated.
Further alterations were carried out in the late 16C and early 17C, including
the rebuilding of the present kitchen block against the original tower, the
construction of new bay-windowed rooms between the tower and the hall
(c 1600–40), and the addition of a second tower to the north of the hall. The
hall range was subsequently widened and a symmetrical façade built to
the west (the present street front).

The house served as the Royalist headquarters during the siege of
Bradford in the Civil War, and was sold by the Tempests in 1649, after which
it passed through several ownerships before ending up in the hands of
Charles Wood of Barnsley, a naval officer and ancestor of the Marquesses
of Halifax. In 1779–80 he employed John Carr of York to create new
reception rooms lit by canted bay windows at the north or 'upper' end of
the hall, one of which (the Drawing Room) has a good Adamesque ceiling.
But, as on earlier occasions, no attempt was made to make the additions
harmonise with the earlier work, and today the house, especially as seen
from the formal garden created in the 20C, has an unusually jumbled,
though undoubtedly picturesque, appearance.

When the Industrial Revolution came to Bradford the estate was broken
up for building, and for most of the 19C the house was let out to tenants by
a local iron company, but in 1912 it was presented to the local authority,
which turned it into a museum. A good collection of 16C and 17C wooden
furniture has been introduced into the rooms at the former service end, and
in recent years the hall and the 18C reception rooms have been restored to
something approaching their original appearance; they now contain a
well-chosen (though changing) selection of pictures belonging to the
Bradford Museum Service, with works by Reynolds and other English
artists, and there are several interesting items of furniture, including a
spectacular bed made by Chippendale for Harewood House (qv.) in 1769.

GCT

Bramham Park

5m south of Wetherby on A1, entered from Thorner–Bramham road:
Mr and Mrs George Lane Fox, tel. 0937 844265. Open late June–early
Sept, Sun, Tues, Wed, Thur, Aug BH Mon 1.15–5.30 (grounds only open
other BH weekends). Guided tours.

Bramham boasts the best example in England of a French-inspired garden
of the early 18C—a magical place of long straight 'alleys', clipped hedges,
ponds and unexpected vistas punctuated by buildings and statuary. Both
the gardens and the house, of c 1703–10, were the brainchild of Robert
Benson, MP for York and son of a successful lawyer who acquired the estate.
The younger Benson travelled in Italy, where he 'lived very hand-
somely...without being a drinker though very gallant concerning the
ladies', and later became Chancellor of the Exchequer before being raised
to the peerage as Lord Bingley; his house—which he probably designed
himself, having sought and rejected designs from Thomas Archer—no
doubt played an important part in realising his social and political ambitions. When he died in 1731 the estate passed to his daughter, whose
husband George Fox (later created Lord Bingley) inherited an Irish fortune
from the Lane family and embellished the gardens with temples, one of
which was designed by James Paine, who also may have been involved in
the design of the impressive stable block to the left of the entrance
courtyard. Subsequent owners were less solicitous. Fox's illegitimate
daughter despoiled the house of its fittings and furniture, and in 1828,
during the ownership of George Lane Fox, a particularly dissolute member
of the Prince Regent's set, there was a disastrous fire whose ravages were
not repaired until after 1906. The building was then reinstated as the main
family residence by another George Lane Fox (also Lord Bingley), the
grandfather of the present owner, and the interiors were sensitively remodelled under the direction of the architect, Detmar Blow.

The house, a long, low building of beautifully cut local magnesian
limestone, is carefully sited at the end of an avenue leading west from the
Great North Road. In its dramatic austerity it is quite unlike any other major
house of its date in England. The main block contains two storeys over a
basement, with a 'sloping terras or coach way', as it was called in *Vitruvius
Britannicus*, leading up to the entrance and a balustrade hiding the roof.
Wings project from the ends of the façade, on either side of which Doric
colonnades offer enticing vistas through to the gardens, and the entrance
courtyard is closed by iron gates flanked by sphinxes on pedestals and piers
articulated by heavily rusticated Doric columns.

After the depredations and neglect of the later 18C and 19C, the interior
does not quite live up to this Baroque promise. The most impressive and
unaltered room is the cube-shaped Entrance Hall, its still smoke-blackened
walls embellished with Corinthian pilasters under a richly carved modillion
cornice. The main reception rooms, all remodelled in the neo-Georgian
manner by Detmar Blow, are to the north and west: the Library, hung with
pictures reflecting the family's longstanding interest in field sports, including J.C. Agasse's 'Lord Rivers Coursing' (c 1815); the Dining Room; the
Drawing Room (occupying the site of the original state bedroom); and
finally a spacious Gallery created out of three smaller rooms on the garden
front and now containing the bulk of the family portraits, as well as good
18C French furniture including a Louis XV bureau. Some delicate early-
18C wood carving, reminiscent of that at the slightly later Beningborough

Hall (qv.), survives in the more private rooms to the south of the Hall, along with paintings by Jordaens and others, but the Staircase, hung with sporting pictures, dates from the early 19C, as do the two upstairs bedrooms which are shown to visitors.

GCT

East Riddlesden Hall

1m north east of Keighley to south of Bradford road (A650): National Trust, tel. 0535 607075. Open Apr–Oct Sat–Wed and Thur in July and Aug 12–5.30. Refreshments.

East Riddlesden Hall is a wealthy clothier's house of the 17C built in the distinctive vernacular style of the Pennine parts of the West Riding, with heavy blocks of millstone grit blackened by smoke from the nearby woollen mills and low-pitched roofs of stone slabs. It forms part of a complex of former farm buildings including two barns, a pond and a service wing (now called the Bothy) which carries the date 1642 and the motto VIVE LE ROY. The long, rambling façade of the main house shows three distinct phases of building: a low, single-storeyed structure in the centre which probably represents the rebuilding in stone of a medieval hall; the main house to the left, now called the Murgatroyd Wing and built by the Halifax clothier, James Murgatroyd, soon after he had bought the estate in 1638; and the now-ruinous Starkie Wing, to the right of the Hall, built in 1692 by Edmund Starkie, a Lancashire gentleman who inherited the estate from the extravagant, debauched and litigious Murgatroyds. The Starkies ceased to live in the house in the mid 18C, and it was then let to a succession of tenants before being rescued from the onward march of Keighley's suburbia and presented to the National Trust in 1934.

The house is a good example of the vitality of local building traditions in the English provinces in the 17C. The Murgatroyd Wing is a particularly striking piece of architecture, with its low gables, long mullioned and transomed windows and, above all, its unusual porch, an intriguing synthesis of classical and Gothic motifs (note the rose window over the entrance and the pinnacled roof-line) found in several West Riding manor-houses of the period; the later Starkie Wing, demolished except for the façade in 1905, is more restrained and classical, but still provincial in character.

The outside of the house is more memorable than the interior. The porch gives access to a medieval-style cross-passage, to the right of which is the Hall, with a 20C roof and a staircase of 1668 brought from Guilsborough Grammar School (Northants). It leads to a series of bedrooms redecorated in the 1980s, and containing 17C and 18C furnishings of a high quality. The parlours on the ground floor of the Murgatroyd house (now called the Dining Room and Drawing Room) are panelled in dark wood and contain rich plaster ceilings, furniture and a small number of loaned 17C portraits, of which that of James I's daughter, the 'Winter Queen', by (or attributed to) Gerard Honthorst is the best. The tour concludes in the large farmhouse-like Kitchen, full of cooking implements and solid furniture—a reminder of the earthy quality of the lives of the lesser gentry of the 17C and their dependants.

GCT

Harewood House

8m north of Leeds at junction of A61 Leeds–Harrogate and A659: the Earl
of Harewood, tel. 0532 886331. Open Apr–Oct daily 11–4.30. Refreshments.

The approach to Harewood announces that it is an important house. The
road from the east is lined with estate cottages, and the park is entered
through a formidable stone arch. The creator of this magnificence was
Edwin Lascelles, representative of an old Yorkshire family which had
substantially increased its wealth by investing in the sugar plantations of
Barbados. His father, Henry Lascelles, bought the adjoining estates of
Harewood and Gawthorpe in 1738, and in 1759 Edwin Lascelles called in
John Carr of York, who had already designed a new stable block, to build
a house on a new site overlooking the valley of the Wharf above the old
Gawthorpe manor house, which was later demolished; he also employed
'Capability' Brown to lay out the park. No sooner had work begun than he
began to consult Robert Adam, recently returned from Italy and at the
threshold of his spectacularly successful career as architect. Adam's plans
for redesigning the whole house were set aside, but he was given the
commission to decorate the interiors in 1765–71, and they rank among his
most important works, especially when taken in conjunction with the
furniture made for the rooms by the locally-born Thomas Chippendale,
much of which remains in situ.

When Edwin Lascelles died in 1795 the house went to his cousin, who
was made Earl of Harewood, and it has remained in the family ever since.
Carr's well-proportioned if somewhat stodgy elevations remained unaltered until 1843–50, when the 3rd Earl employed Charles Barry to heighten
the wings and create a new formal garden on the south front; he also
remodelled some of the rooms. Since then the outside has not been
changed, but there have been a number of alterations to the interior, most
recently under the present Earl, who, with the help of the architect Francis
Johnson, has successfully restored much of the original colour and bright-
ness to the main rooms and reinstated some discarded 18C fittings.

The house is made up of a central block with lower wings, hiding internal
courtyards, which terminate in pavilions of the same height as the main
block. Much of the external effect is due to Barry, who added the balustrade
around the central block, thus giving the **north (entrance) front** a disagreeably top-heavy effect, but his **south front**, with its Italianate terraces and
parterres, is a far more successful architectural composition, anticipating
his later work at Cliveden, Bucks (qv.). The tour of the interior proceeds
clockwise from the **Entrance Hall**, and takes in all the ground-floor rooms.
Adam's hand is immediately apparent in the decoration of the Hall, although since the shape of this and other rooms was already fixed by Carr
there was no scope for any flights of fancy in the manipulation of space.
The dominant mood is martial, with engaged Doric columns and military
trophies in plaster against the walls, and the masculine note is intensified
by Jacob Epstein's huge and self-consciously primitive alabaster sculpture
of 'Adam' (1938–39)—a very different kind of man from the suave 18C
architect—brought in by the present Earl. The **Old Library** is also by Adam,
with decorative paintings by Biagio Rebecca, but it has lost its original
colouring. It leads into the **China Room** in which some of the family's
excellent collection of 18C porcelain is displayed, including Sèvres items
acquired after the French Revolution, among them a pink flower pot of 1757

and a blue tea service of 1779 said to have belonged to Marie-Antoinette; there is also a French dinner service of c 1800 decorated with views of English country houses including Harewood.

The next few rooms are in what was originally the more private part of the house. First comes a **Dressing Room**, remodelled by Sir Herbert Baker c 1929 for George V's daughter the Princess Royal, who married the 6th Earl; beyond it, in the west pavilion, is the **bedroom** originally occupied by Edwin Lascelles with its original Chippendale furnishings, some of them in the Chinese style. The present Lord Harewood's Sitting Room (originally a bedroom), at the south end of this block, is hung with pictures by fashionable early-20C artists including Sargent and Munnings (eg, 'The Bramham Moor Hunt', 1928), but there is a change of mood in **Princess Mary's Sitting Room** (originally the state bedroom), which contains several pieces by Chippendale, including the most expensive item of furniture he ever supplied: a commode of 1773 with marquetry decorations in the neo-classical taste, now placed in the original bed alcove. There are also water-colours of the house and estate by most of the well-known English landscape painters of the late 18C and early 19C, including Girtin and Turner, some of them of superb quality, and from the windows there are views over the valley of the Wharfe which figures in some of the pictures.

The next two rooms (originally the state dressing room and saloon) were remodelled as libraries by Barry, though they still retain their Adam ceilings and chimneypieces; the main **Library** contains two early oils of Plompton Rocks by J.M.W. Turner, and four local views by Nicholas Dall originally designed to go over the doors. The remaining rooms constitute a sequence of state rooms wrapped round the main staircase (not shown to the public) and the east courtyard. The first is the **Yellow Drawing Room**, where more Sèvres porcelain is on show, together with portraits by Lawrence of the politicians William Huskisson and George Canning, whose granddaughter married the 4th Earl. The **Cinnamon Drawing Room**, recently redecorated, contains some of the best portraits in the house, with works by Reynolds (eg, Edwin Lascelles, the builder of the house, and Lady Worsley, one of his best female portraits, in riding clothes), Gainsborough (George Canning as a boy in Van Dyck costume), Romney and Lawrence; the gilded mirrors and pier-glasses are by Chippendale, brought from elsewhere in the house, and the cove of the Adam ceiling is enriched with decorative paintings by Alfred Stevens, whose robust colouring is taken up in the new wall hangings. The **Gallery**, which takes up the whole of the east of the house, has also been successfully refurbished, and now houses the bulk of the superb collection of Old Master pictures acquired by the 6th Earl in the 1920s out of a fortune inherited from his great-uncle, the Marquess of Clanricarde. They include works of the highest quality by Bellini ('Madonna and Child with Donor'), Titian (a portrait of Francis I of France), Tintoretto, Veronese, Lorenzo Lotto, Ribera and El Greco ('An Allegory'); there is also a very fine collection of Chinese porcelain of the K'ang Hsi, Yung Cheng and Ch'ien Lung periods, displayed on Chippendale's pier-tables.

The **Dining Room**, largely by Barry, contains some of the best of the furniture Chippendale supplied for the house, including the sideboard, wine cooler and urns on pedestals, of rosewood with ormolu mounts. Last of all comes the **Music Room**, perhaps the most beautiful and certainly the least-altered room in the house. The design of the delicately detailed Adam ceiling is reflected in the carpet, and there is upholstered furniture by

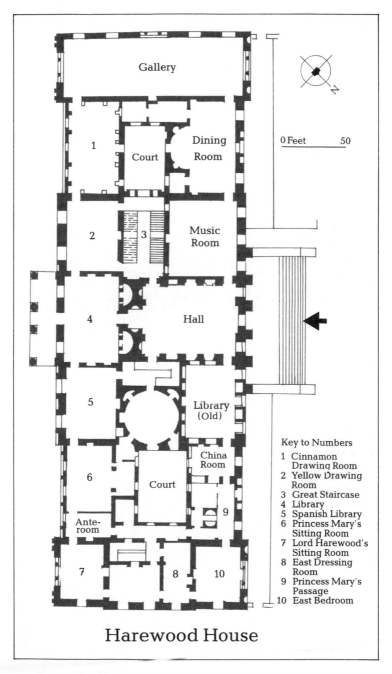

Gallery

1

Court

Dining Room

0 Feet   50

2   3

Music Room

4

Hall

5

Library (Old)

China Room

6

Court

9

Ante-room

7   8   10

Key to Numbers

1 Cinnamon Drawing Room
2 Yellow Drawing Room
3 Great Staircase
4 Library
5 Spanish Library
6 Princess Mary's Sitting Room
7 Lord Harewood's Sitting Room
8 East Dressing Room
9 Princess Mary's Passage
10 East Bedroom

Harewood House

Chippendale, along with pictures of Roman ruins by Antonio Zucchi and, over the fireplace, Reynolds's portrait of Mrs Hale, the 1st Earl's sister-in-law, as Euphrosyne ('Good Cheer'), one of the Three Graces (1764–66)—a fitting focal point for this very attractive room.

GCT

Lotherton Hall

On B1217, 1m east of A1 at Aberford: Leeds City Council, tel. 0532 813259. Open all year daily except Mon (but open BH Mon) 10.30–5.30 (or dusk if earlier). Refreshments.

Lotherton Hall is a largely Edwardian house with a notable collection of furniture and works of art built up by the Gascoignes, an old Yorkshire family, and expertly augmented in recent years by Leeds City Art Galleries. The house originated as a small late-18C building remodelled to the designs of the local architects J.P. Pritchett and Charles Watson shortly after being purchased in 1825 by Richard Oliver Gascoigne. The family had owned land in the area since the 16C, but they lived at Parlington Park (since demolished), on the other side of the Great North Road, and it was not until the time of Richard Gascoigne's grandson, Frederick, that Lotherton became the main family seat. He and his wife carried out a series of enlargements and improvements between 1896 and 1931, creating a new formal garden, and filling the rooms with furnishings and pictures from Parlington. Their house was intended for comfort rather than show, and it displays a taste very different from the glitzy classicism favoured by nouveaux riches like the Wernhers of Luton Hoo, Bedfordshire (qv.) or the Arts and Crafts-inspired neo-vernacular of Lutyens and his early clients. When Frederick Gascoigne's son died in 1970 the house and its contents were left to the City of Leeds, together with an endowment fund which has allowed the already varied collection to grow.

The oldest building at Lotherton is the late-12C Chapel, a low rugged-looking building which stands on its own to the left of the entrance forecourt; it was restored and refitted by Frederick Gascoigne at the time of the First World War and contains a rood screen by Ninian Comper, together with furnishings brought in from churches on the Continent. In front is the west or entrance range added in 1903, probably to the designs of Frederick Gascoigne and his agent. Around the corner is the long garden front, an inchoate composition of no great architectural distinction, with the façade of the original house with its bow window of c 1828 embedded between the 1903 range to the left and an extension of c 1896–1931 to the right (architect J. Osborne Smith). The main reception rooms overlook formal gardens of the kind which appealed to the conventional taste of the early 20C, with placid parkland stretching away to the horizon beyond.

The interiors are more interesting for their well-displayed contents and for the light they throw on early-20C country house life than for any particular felicities of architecture or decoration. The carriage porch on the entrance front of 1903 leads into a vestibule containing a relief carved by Thomas Banks in Rome c 1775, and from here the Main Hall is reached. This is furnished as a living room and is hung with family portraits, including Grand Tour pictures of Sir Edward Gascoigne (Francesco Trevisani c 1724) and Sir Thomas Gascoigne (Pompeo Batoni, c 1779); there are also portrait busts commissioned by Sir Thomas in Rome, and attributed to Christopher Hewetson. The Drawing Room, also of 1903, is decorated in a neo-Adam style and contains some excellent furniture, mostly brought in by the Leeds museum service, including tables and pier-glasses made by Vile and Cobb in 1761 for Adam's new interiors at Croome Court, Worcestershire, and a marble-topped table by William Burges of c 1867; there are also several sculptures, including a bronze of Lord Leighton's 'The Sluggard' (1890). Next comes the Morning Room, part of the original house; over the entrance, framed by Greek Doric columns of c 1828, is a sculpture of 'Cupid and Psyche' by the Leeds-born Joseph Gott, originally at Armley House, near Leeds, and the room also contains furniture by the Gillow firm from Parlington Hall. There is more furniture from Parlington in the Library, built originally as a dining room in the 1890s, and in the present Dining Room, designed in 1908 but not finished until 1931; the Library also contains a pair of chairs designed by the young A.W.N. Pugin for Windsor Castle in 1828.

A service corridor leads back to the main staircase opening out of the Hall, passing en route a display of plate in the former butler's pantry (where it would have originally been kept) and a case in which an unusually good collection of 18C and 19C race cups is shown, one of them, marked 'Doncaster 1828', based on the so-called 'Buckingham Vase' engraved by Piranesi; there is also a picture by Francis Wheatley (1780) of the Irish House of Commons in the building now serving as the Bank of Ireland in Dublin. Upstairs there is a series of bedrooms, furnished with pieces of varying date and quality ranging from an outstandingly ugly suite of papier-mâché furniture of c 1851 (in the Cape Bedroom) to a neo-Georgian suite by Heals (1903; in the Rhodesia Bedroom) and a cabinet by Gimson in Lady Gascoigne's Room; there is also an excellent collection of pictures by early-20C British artists scattered among the rooms, including works by Sickert, Brangwyn, Clausen, Steer, William Nicholson and Matthew Smith. The guest bedrooms over the east (entrance) range have been converted into a series of galleries for the display of 20C costume, and in part of the former service wing to the north of the Hall there is a gallery containing ceramics and porcelain, notably early Chinese pieces, including some from the T'ang dynasty, which were given to the City of Leeds in 1965.

GCT

Nostell Priory

6m south east of Wakefield on A638 Wakefield–Doncaster: National Trust, tel. 0924 863892. Open Apr–June, Sept, Oct Sat, Sun; July, Aug daily except Fri 12–5 (Sun 11–5). Refreshments.

Nostell Priory derives its name from a house of Augustinian canons whose site passed through several hands in the 16C and 17C before being sold in 1650 to George Winn, grandson of a London merchant who had been Draper to Queen Elizabeth I. The present house was begun by his great-grandson Sir Rowland Winn, who went on an unusually lavish Grand Tour soon after inheriting the estate and married an heiress when he returned. In 1731 he obtained plans from the amateur architect Col James Moyser, a member of Lord Burlington's circle, for an ambitious building, loosely based on Palladio's Villa Mocenigo (also one of the sources of Holkham Hall, Norfolk, qv.), in which a porticoed central block would be linked by curved colonnades to four detached pavilions. Construction began c 1736 and proceeded at a stately pace under the direction of James Paine, whose first major work this was, but only two of the wings were ever built and only one (the south west or kitchen wing) survives.

Paine also designed some of the interiors, but in 1765 he was dropped by Sir Rowland's successor, another Sir Rowland Winn, in favour of the younger and more fashionable Robert Adam, who went on to decorate the remaining rooms in his own refined neo-classical style, assisted by the painter Antonio Zucchi, the plasterer Joseph Rose the younger, and the cabinet-maker Thomas Chippendale; this work was finished in 1776, 40 years after the house was begun. Adam also prepared plans to enlarge the house by building a large extension to the north, but Sir Rowland Winn died in 1785 with only part of the work—the present family wing—completed; since then there have been no major structural changes, although Sir Rowland's grandson Charles Winn employed the upholsterer Thomas Ward to embellish some of the interiors in the 1820s. Winn's son, a Tory politician, was raised to the peerage as Lord St Oswald, and in 1953 the house was given to the National Trust, the family staying on as tenants.

The house, of blackened local stone, stands in attractive wooded countryside punctuated by the mines of the Yorkshire coalfield. They are not allowed to impinge on the views from the main building, whose ponderous neo-Palladian **exterior**, dominated by an engaged Ionic portico, forms an instructive contrast to the better-proportioned family wing by Adam to the right. The house is entered through the rusticated ground floor, and a contemporary version of Holbein's 'Sir Thomas More and his family' is displayed in the vaulted **Lower Hall**, while in the passageway beyond there is a meticulously detailed dolls' house of c 1735 attributed to the young Chippendale. The main rooms are on the piano nobile, reached by the **South Staircase**, whose walls are embellished with exuberant plasterwork in the Rococo taste of the 1740s. After this the light and delicate **Upper Hall**, decorated by Adam in 1774, comes as a contrast; the apsidal recess to the left of the entrance, influenced by the architecture of late-Roman baths and palaces, cunningly hides the service stairs. Beyond lie two smaller rooms which are still used by the family and are not always open to the public; one of them, the private **Drawing Room**, contains a self-portrait of Angelica Kauffmann—one of Adam's regular collaborators—flanked by figures representing Art and Music, echoing Reynolds's well-known 'Garrick between Comedy and Tragedy'. Beyond the North Staircase is the large, gloomy **Billiard Room**, now used as an annexe to the Library and housing a relief carving of Paola and Francesca (1838) by the younger Westmacott; this room was originally designed as the main library, but was enlarged by Adam in 1783 as a vestibule leading to the family wing and to a music room which was never built.

The main reception rooms face west over the gardens, their decoration and colouring (despite some modification in the 1820s) beautifully co-ordinated to provide as satisfying a sequence of contrasting visual sensations as can be found in any Adam house. First comes the **Library**, Adam's first room here (1766), with bookcases surmounted by pediments resting on embellished Ionic pilasters, a table by Chippendale (the most costly item of furniture supplied by him), and a portrait showing the younger Sir Rowland Winn and his wife in the newly completed room. The **Tapestry Room** was also decorated by Adam but was adapted in 1822 to house a set of Brussels tapestries of the Four Continents by Van der Borcht (1750); the

The Drawing Room, Nostell Priory, by Robert Adam, 1765–76

furniture is also mostly of the early 19C, as is the group of 'Flora and Zephyr' by R.J. Wyatt, and there are two late-17C cabinets. The less-altered **Saloon** has a coved ceiling decorated with fan-shaped motifs and a representation of Apollo between Evening and Dawn; there are large pictures of classical ruins by Zucchi on three of the walls, and pier-tables and glasses by Adam on the fourth, and Chippendale's furniture is still in situ. The **Dining Room** is in the part of the house decorated by Paine, and the plasterwork (eg, the figure of Ceres on the ceiling) is consequently more robust in style; the arabesque paintings on the walls were an unfortunate addition by Zucchi.

The **State Bedroom** (originally intended as the 'common sitting room') and the adjoining **Dressing Room** were also designed by Paine, but they were furnished and decorated by Chippendale in 1771, without Adam being much involved. Most of the furniture in the Bedroom is in the Chinese taste (note especially the mirror complete with ho-ho birds and the green-painted commode underneath), and the wallpaper and curtains are also Chinese in character, creating a remarkably harmonious and untouched ensemble. The last two rooms to be shown, the **Crimson Bedchamber** and **Breakfast Room** on the east front, were always less richly and expensively decorated, even before being severely damaged by fire in 1980. The fire alas destroyed some of the Old Master paintings acquired by Charles Winn in the early 19C, but some notable works still survive, including a Penitent—though still lascivious-looking—Magdalen by Furini in the Crimson Room, and a 'Procession to Calvary' by Pieter Breughel (1602) and Guercino's 'Persian Sibyl' in the Breakfast Room.

GCT

Oakwell Hall

Near Nutter Lane, Birstall on A652, M62 exit 27: Kirklees Metropolitan Council, tel. 0924 474926. Open all year daily 10–5 (Sun 2–5). Refreshments.

This late-16C manor house of blackened gritstone stands in a rural oasis in the heart of the West Riding conurbation, with only the roar of a nearby motorway to disturb the seclusion. A recarved stone bearing the date 1583 seems to indicate the date of construction, probably by John Batt, whose Halifax-born father, receiver of rents for the powerful Savile family, bought the estate. The house has the usual post-medieval plan of a central hall block flanked by cross-wings, and it is still entered through a porch and screens passage at the 'lower' end. The hall block was originally two-storeyed, but in the mid 17C, in a reversal of the common practice of 'flooring over' medieval halls, the builder's grandson, another John Batt, removed the hall ceiling and inserted a gallery and a large mullioned and transomed window, possibly to emphasise his family's claim to grandeur.

Since then there have been no major structural changes. The estate was split up in 1707, and the house subsequently mouldered away gently, becoming a school in the 19C, when it figured in Charlotte Brontë's *Shirley*. It thus escaped being either Georgianised, like Bolling Hall, Bradford (qv.), or remodelled in the 'Old English' fashion, like Shibden Hall, Halifax (qv.). It finally passed into municipal hands in 1928, and in 1986–88 the interiors were imaginatively restored to their early-17C condition with the help of a 1611 inventory, new furniture in the 17C style being made where no original pieces were available. During the restoration the original painted panelling of the Great Parlour and the Painted Chamber was discovered under layers of later paint and varnish, and today both the house—nearly all of which is open to view—and the expertly re-created formal gardens convey an unusually vivid sense of the past, unobscured by later well-intentioned embellishment.

GCT

Shibden Hall

½m south east of Halifax on A58 Halifax–Leeds: Calderdale Metropolitan Council, tel. 0442 352246/321455. Open Mar–Nov daily 10–5 (Sun 12–5) and Sun in Feb 2–5. Refreshments.

Shibden means 'valley of the sheep' and the timber-framed house which forms the core of the present building seems to have been built by a member of the sheep-farming Otes family in the 15C, when the domestic cloth industry was beginning to develop in the steep Pennine valleys of the Halifax region. The present (restored) façade, with its hall and cross-wings, is a good example of the late-medieval domestic architecture of the Pennine West Riding, before the 'Great Rebuilding' made stone all but ubiquitous. The small estate passed to the Waterhouse family in the 16C and a stone extension was constructed at the rear in 1590, but the most drastic change to the modest original house occurred in 1836–55, during and after the ownership of Anne Lister, descendant of a cloth merchant who had acquired the property in the 17C. She was an enthusiast for the 'Old English' taste, and employed the York architect John Harper, a pupil of Benjamin Dean Wyatt, to restore the 15C façade, reinstate the mullioned windows, remove the ceiling from the hall or 'housebody', and construct a new and grander staircase. The house was also extended by the addition of a tower at the west end and a service wing to the east, and formal gardens were created, so that at Shibden, as at Gawthorpe Hall, Lancashire (qv.), we now see the past through early-Victorian eyes.

Internally the effect is homogeneous and convincing, partly because Harper made a close study of local domestic interiors of the 17C before embarking on the work, and partly because the contents amassed by the Lister family over the years are still intact and in situ. The house was presented to Halifax Corporation by Anne Lister's cousin John, an antiquarian—and pioneer of the Independent Labour Party—in 1933, and it is now displayed in an exemplary way by the local authority. There are no important works of art, but the rooms are full of interesting objects which convey a strong sense of the evolving tastes and life-styles of the minor gentry of the region. At the back of the house there is a splendid late-17C aisled stone barn which has been turned, along with the adjacent farm buildings, into an excellent folk museum.

GCT

Temple Newsam

5m east of Leeds to south of A63 Leeds–Selby: Leeds Metropolitan District Council, tel. 0532 647321 or 641358. Open all year daily except Mon (but open BH Mon) 10.30–5.30. Refreshments.

This massive labyrinthine house is named after the Knights Templar, who acquired the estate in the mid 12C. It passed into private hands after the suppression of the order in the 13C, and at some time in the first two decades of the 16C, Thomas, Lord Darcy, one of Henry VIII's courtiers, built a large courtyard house of brick, parts of which survive in the present building. Darcy was executed after taking part in the Pilgrimage of Grace, and the estate later passed to Henry VIII's niece, the Countess of Lennox, whose son Lord Darnley, the husband of Mary, Queen of Scots (and father of James I) was born in the house. The Earl of Lennox sold it in 1622 to the courtier and financier Sir Arthur Ingram, and he carried out a thorough rebuilding, which was completed by 1637.

The plain exterior has changed relatively little since Jacobean times, but there have been many internal alterations. Sir Arthur Ingram's grandson was raised to the peerage as Viscount Irwin after the Restoration, and in 1738–45 his grandson, the 7th Viscount, employed Daniel Garrett, a protégé of Lord Burlington, to modernise the interior, partly to provide a suitable setting for the works of art collected in Italy by his elder brother, the 4th Viscount. The south range was totally rebuilt in the Jacobean manner in 1796 by the widow of the 9th and last Viscount to the designs of the local architect, Thomas Johnson of Leeds, and several of the rooms inside were redecorated in 1827–28 by her daughter and heiress, the Marchioness of Hertford, one of the Prince Regent's mistresses. The house later passed through the female line, and in the 1890s the Hon. Emily Meynell Ingram brought in the decorator and stained-glass maker C.E. Kempe to make yet more internal changes. By then Leeds had expanded almost to the gates of the park, and in 1922 her nephew, the Hon. Edward Wood (later Lord Halifax), sold the house and park to Leeds Corporation. The contents were dispersed, but several items from the family collection have made their way back to the house, where they have been joined by other objects, some of them of the highest quality. Today Temple Newsam possesses one of the finest accumulations of decorative art in the north of England.

The house consists of a three-storeyed main block, with long wings projecting towards an unspoiled 'Capability' Brown landscape; the east range, which closed the courtyard of the original Tudor house, was demolished by Sir Arthur Ingram and not rebuilt. Close inspection shows that the central (west) range is built of early Tudor brickwork with the usual criss-cross diaper patterning of the period. This is not the hall range, as one might expect from its position, but the great chamber wing; the Hall is in the south range (to the left), with a gallery on the upper floor of the north range opposite. The main visual incident is supplied by the large mullioned and transomed windows and the pious inscription on the balustrade around the courtyard, originally carved in 1628 and replaced in iron in 1796, the date of the cupola over the west range. Otherwise the general effect is surprisingly austere.

Despite later changes, the lopsided arrangement of Sir Arthur Ingram's house has remained to bewilder modern visitors. The entrance is through the **Hall**, embellished in the 'Old English' manner in 1827–28; the side tables of c 1740, attributed to Matthias Lock, were formerly at Ditchley Park, Oxfordshire, and the Italian inlaid tables of c 1820 were until recently at Burton Constable (qv.), to which they will be eventually returned; these are a foretaste of the many objects judiciously bought at country house sales and now intelligently displayed throughout the house. The **Library** to the east of the Hall (on the site of the service end of the Jacobean house) was decorated in the neo-Georgian manner in 1912, and now contains a superb writing table by Chippendale c 1770, formerly at Harewood (qv.), while the furniture and decoration of the adjacent **Drawing Room** (1827–28) is in the bastardised Chinese taste employed by the Prince Regent at the Brighton Pavilion. The **Dining Room**, on the other side of the Hall, occupies the site of the Jacobean parlour, but owes its present Jacobean character to Kempe, who designed the authentic-looking plaster ceiling and chimneypiece (based on one in Hardwick Hall, Derbyshire) c 1888–89. The room has subsequently been furnished with English and Continental pieces of the 16C and 17C.

The spectacular wooden **staircase** of 1894 in the west range, with its intricately carved balusters and newel posts, is also Kempe's; it is hung with pictures including Trevisani's 'Baptism of Christ' (1723) and, on the top landing, Luca Giordano's 'Triumph of David'. The first floor of the west range is taken up by a group of **bedrooms**, some of them with Rococo plasterwork by Richard Wilkinson of York (1741–42), and there are windowless rooms for the servants behind; the main rooms are decorated with carefully researched reproduction wallpapers and silks, and furnished with 18C pieces, including a sophisticated French-style cabinet and commode of c 1745 by John Channon and a set of red japanned chairs made by Giles Grendey (c 1730). From here the route leads to a former bedroom containing mid-18C Gothick furniture made for the Countess of Pomfret's extraordinary (and now vanished) house in Arlington Street, London.

Beyond this is the vast **Picture Gallery**, made out of the long gallery of the Jacobean house in 1738–45 and now the finest and least-altered room in the house. The delicate Rococo plasterwork by Thomas Perritt and Joseph Rose of York incorporates portraits of George II and his family, and there are furnishings in the same taste by the little-known James Pascall, including 20 embroidered chairs and a lively and inventive set of girandoles on the walls. The paintings, mostly collected by the 4th Viscount Irwin and his 18C successors, include works by Antonio Joli (on the overmantels), Giordano, Solimena, Vasari ('The Temptation of St Jerome') and Guardi, along with family portraits by Philip Mercier and others: a good example of an 18C collection, despite the sale of works by some of the more famous masters. At the end of the Gallery is the Georgian **Library**, richly adorned with engaged Corinthian columns along the walls and swirly plasterwork on the ceiling; the room was turned into a chapel in 1877 (the organ designed by G.F. Bodley, architect of Mrs Meynell Ingram's magnificent church at Hoar Cross, Staffordshire, still survives), but it was restored to its original appearance in 1974 and the original library table is now once more in situ.

The tour of the top floor starts in the south range, where there are more bedrooms decorated and furnished in the late 18C and early 19C. Outstanding items here include the Gillow bed of c 1825 in the Prince's Room, and a set of tapestry-covered furniture of 1771 from Moor Park, Hertfordshire (qv.) in the **South Bedroom**, where a portrait by Reynolds of Lady Hertford, the presiding spirit of this part of the house, is displayed; another room contains smaller 18C English paintings, including Morland's seductive 'Fair Nun Unmasked'. The **Darnley Room**, at the junction of the south and west ranges, was redecorated in the neo-Jacobean manner c 1890 (the room did not exist in Lord Darnley's time); the furnishings are of the 16C and 17C and there is a picture attributed to Gheeraerts of a lady who may be Darnley's niece Arabella Stuart, and also a small Ruisdael landscape. An adjoining room contains a very elaborate suite of velvet-covered furniture, probably made by the Huguenot craftsman Philip Guibert c 1700 for the Duke of Leeds and originally housed at the long-vanished Kiveton Park near Sheffield. Next door is the **Tudor Room**, with superb, early-16C linenfold panelling brought from Bretton Hall, near Leeds, and at the north end of the range there are rooms containing silver, by Lamerie and others and ceramics (there is an especially good collection of creamware). Visitors leave by the **Stone Staircase**, in the north-west corner, with Pellegrini's 'Hector and Andromache' from Kimbolton Castle, Cambridgeshire, on one of the walls.

GCT

INDEX OF ARCHITECTS, ARTISTS AND CRAFTSMEN

To keep this index to a reasonable length, only the most prominent architects, artists and craftsmen have been included. Each page number refers to the first mention of an artist within an entry.

INDEX OF HOUSES

Key Map to Atlas Pages

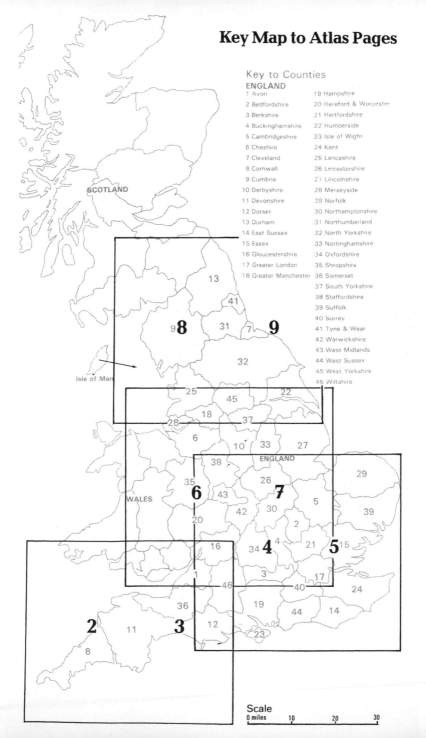

Key to Counties
ENGLAND

1 Avon	19 Hampshire
2 Bedfordshire	20 Hereford & Worcester
3 Berkshire	21 Hertfordshire
4 Buckinghamshire	22 Humberside
5 Cambridgeshire	23 Isle of Wight
6 Cheshire	24 Kent
7 Cleveland	25 Lancashire
8 Cornwall	26 Leicestershire
9 Cumbria	27 Lincolnshire
10 Derbyshire	28 Merseyside
11 Devonshire	29 Norfolk
12 Dorset	30 Northamptonshire
13 Durham	31 Northumberland
14 East Sussex	32 North Yorkshire
15 Essex	33 Nottinghamshire
16 Gloucestershire	34 Oxfordshire
17 Greater London	35 Shropshire
18 Greater Manchester	36 Somerset
	37 South Yorkshire
	38 Staffordshire
	39 Suffolk
	40 Surrey
	41 Tyne & Wear
	42 Warwickshire
	43 West Midlands
	44 West Sussex
	45 West Yorkshire
	46 Wiltshire

SCOTLAND

Isle of Man

WALES

ENGLAND

Scale
0 miles   10   20   30

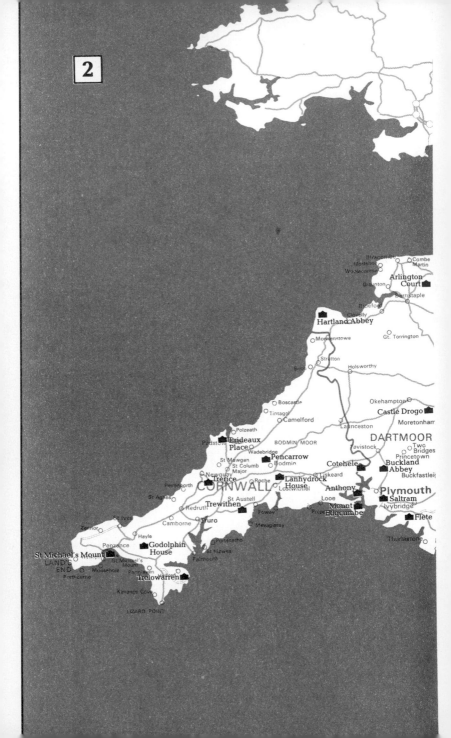

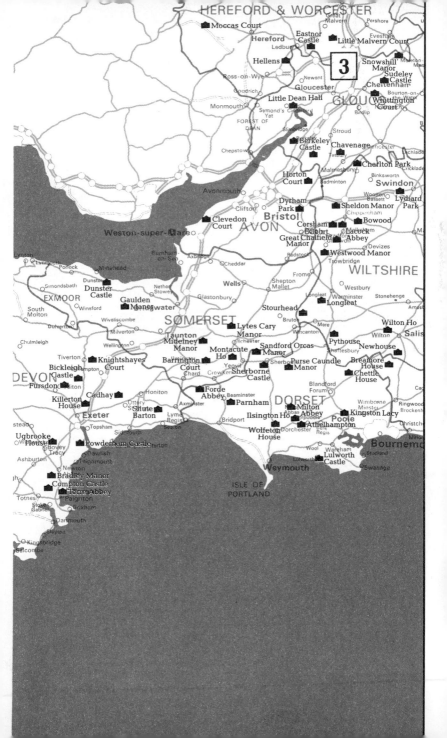

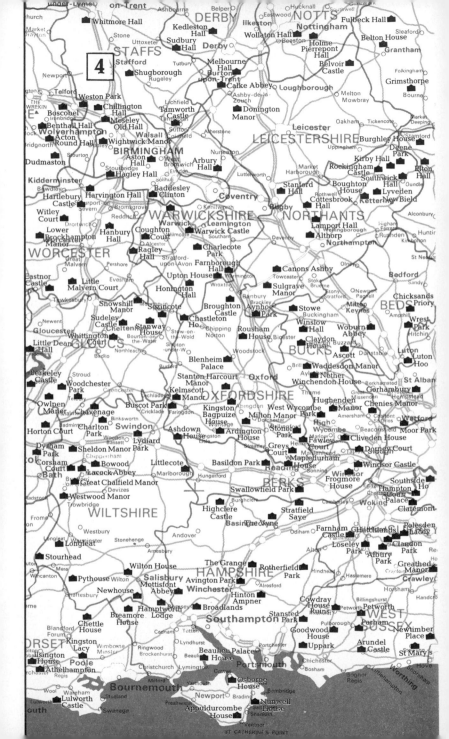

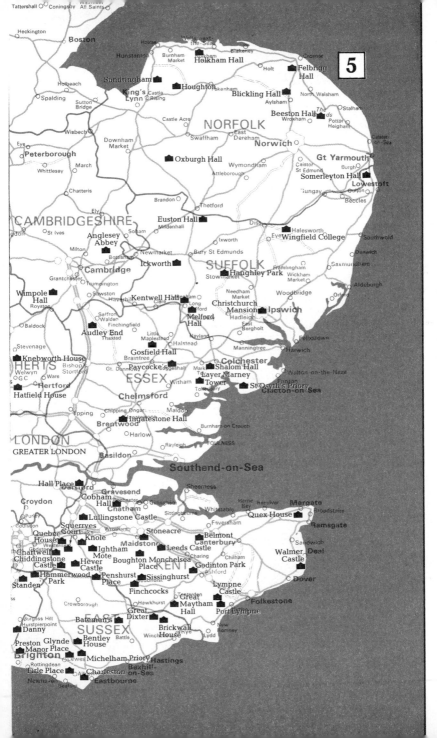

5

Tattershall · Coningsby · Wainfleet All Saints

Heckington

Boston

Holbeach

Spalding · Sutton Bridge

Wisbech

Peterborough

Whittlesey · March

Eye · Chatteris

CAMBRIDGESHIRE

St Ives · Ely

Cambridge · Grantchester · Trumpington

Wimpole Hall · Royston

Baldock

Stevenage

Knebworth House

HERTS

Welwyn GC · Ware

Hertford

Hatfield House

LONDON

GREATER LONDON

Hunstanton · Heacham · Wells-next-the-Sea · Blakeney · Cromer

Burnham Market · Holkham Hall · Holt

Sandringham · King's Lynn · Castle Rising · Houghton · Blickling Hall · Felbrigg Hall · North Walsham

Castle Acre · NORFOLK · East Dereham · Norwich · Beeston Hall · Stalham · The Broads · Potter Heigham

Downham Market · Swaffham

Oxburgh Hall · Wymondham · Attleborough · Caister St Edmund · Burgh · Calster-on-Sea

Gt Yarmouth

Somerleyton Hall

Lowestoft

Brandon · Thetford · Diss · Bungay · Beccles · Oulton

Euston Hall · Mildenhall · Halesworth · Eye · Wingfield College · Southwold

Anglesey Abbey · Newmarket · Ixworth · Dunwich

Milton · Bottisham · Bury St Edmunds · Framlingham · Saxmundham

Ickworth · SUFFOLK · Stowmarket · Haughley Park · Wickham Market · Aldeburgh

Needham Market · Woodbridge · Orford

Saffron Walden · Kentwell Hall · Clare · Long Melford · Christchurch Mansion · Ipswich

Haverhill · Lavenham · Hadleigh · East Bergholt · Felixstowe

Audley End · Thaxted · Melford Hall · Nayland · Manningtree · Harwich

Little Maplestead · Halstead

Gosfield Hall · Braintree · Gt Dunmow · Colchester

Paycocke's · Coggeshall · Mark · Shalom Hall · Walton-on-the-Naze

Finchingfield

ESSEX · Witham · Layer Marney Tower · Tollesbury · Clacton-on-Sea

Bishop's Stortford · St Osyth's Priory

Epping · Chipping Ongar · Chelmsford · Maldon

Ingatestone Hall · Brentwood · Burnham-on-Crouch

Harlow · Rayleigh · FOULNESS

Basildon

Southend-on-Sea

Sheerness

Hall Place · Dartford · Gravesend · Cobham Hall · Rochester · Gillingham · Herne Bay · Reculver · Margate · Broadstairs

Croydon · Purley · Chatham · Sittingbourne · Whitstable · Faversham · Quex House · Ramsgate

Coulsdon · Lullingstone Castle · Wrotham · Stoneacre · Maidstone · Belmont · Canterbury · Sandwich

Squerryes Court · Knole · Leeds Castle · Charing · Chilham · Walmer Castle · Deal

Quebec House · Ightham Mote · Boughton Monchelsea Place · Godinton Park · Ashford

Chartwell · Chiddingstone Castle · Hever Castle · Penshurst Place · Sissinghurst · KENT · Dover

Hammerwood Park · Standen · Finchcocks · Hawkhurst · Tenterden · Great Maytham Hall · Lympne Castle · Folkestone

Crowborough · Great Dixter · Port Lympne

Burgess Hill · Hurstpierpoint · Bateman's · Battle · Brickwall House · Winchelsea · New Romney · Lydd

Danny · EAST SUSSEX · Bentley House

Preston · Glynde · Lewes · Michelham Priory · Hastings

Manor Place · Brighton · Rottingdean · Charleston · Bexhill-on-Sea

Firle Place · Newhaven · Seaford · Eastbourne

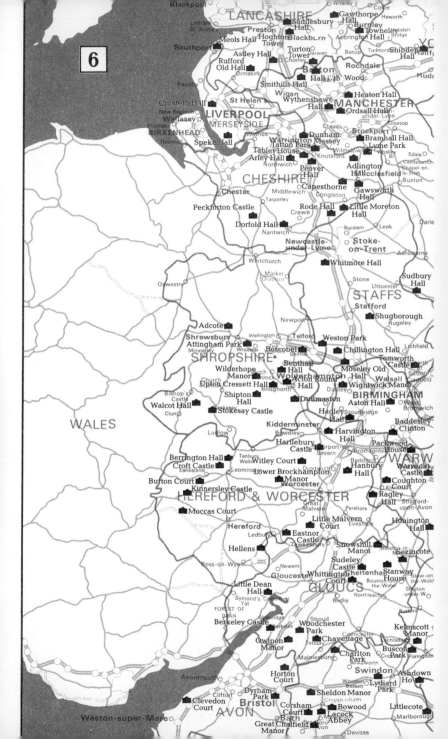

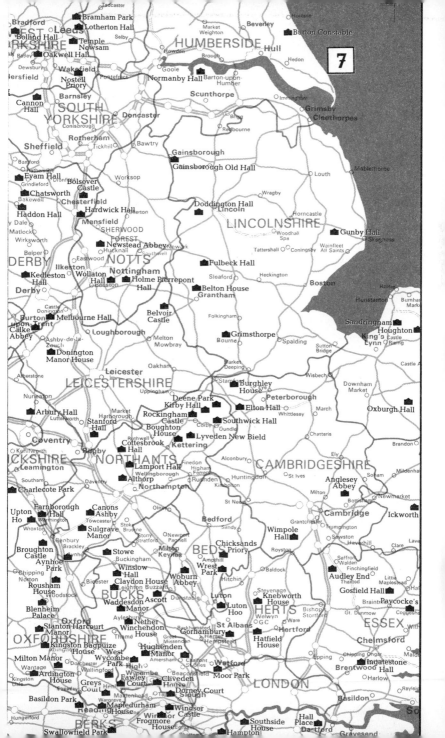

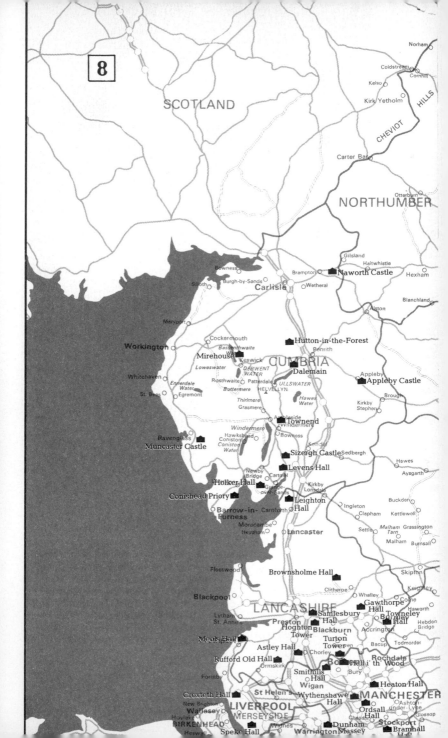

8

SCOTLAND

CHEVIOT HILLS

NORTHUMBER

Norham
Coldstream
Cornhill
Kelso
Kirk Yetholm
Carter Bar
Otterburn

Gilsland
Haltwhistle
Hexham
Bowness
Burgh-by-Sands
Silloth
Brampton
Wetheral
■ Naworth Castle
Carlisle
Blanchland
Alston

Maryport
Cockermouth
■ Hutton-in-the-Forest
Penrith
Workington
Bassenthwaite
■ Mirehouse
Keswick
CUMBRIA
Loweswater
DERWENT WATER
Dalemain
Appleby
■ Appleby Castle
Whitehaven
Enerdale Water
Rosthwaite
Patterdale
ULLSWATER
HELVELLYN ▲
Brough
St. Bees
Egremont
Buttermere
Thirlmere
Hawes Water
Kirkby Stephen
Grasmere
Ambleside
Rydal
Troutbeck
Townend
Windermere
Hawes Water
Ravenglass
Hawkshead
Bowness
Coniston
Coniston Water
Kendal
■ Muncaster Castle
Hawes
■ Sizergh Castle
Sedbergh
Newby Bridge
■ Levens Hall
Aysgarth
Cartmel
Holker Hall ■
Grange-over-Sands
Kirkby Lonsdale
Buckden
■ Conishead Priory
■ Leighton Hall
Ingleton
Clapham
Kettlewell
Barrow-in-Furness
Carnforth
Settle
Malham Tarn
Grassington
Morecambe
Heysham
■ Lancaster
Malham
Burnsall

Fleetwood
Skipton
■ Brownsholme Hall
Keighley
Blackpool
Clitheroe
Whalley
Colne
Haworth
LANCASHIRE
■ Gawthorpe Hall
Lytham St. Annes
■ Samlesbury Hall
■ Towneley Hall
Preston
Hebden Bridge
Hoghton Tower
Blackburn
Accrington
Bacup
Todmorden
■ Meols Hall
■ Astley Hall
Turton Tower
Chorley
Bolton
Hall i' th' Wood
■ Rufford Old Hall
Ormskirk
Rochdale
Smithills Hall
Bury
Formby
Wigan
■ Heaton Hall
Croxteth Hall ■
St. Helen's
Wythenshawe Hall ■
MANCHESTER
New Brighton
Wallasey
LIVERPOOL
Ashton-under-Lyne
BIRKENHEAD
MERSEYSIDE
Ordsall Hall
Stockport
Glossop
Heswall
Speke Hall
Widnes
Warrington
Dunham Massey
Bramhall Hall

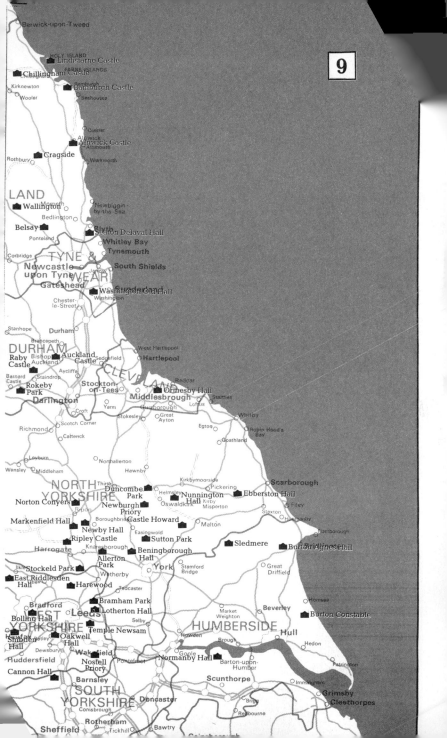

Berwick-upon-Tweed

HOLY ISLAND
Lindisfarne Castle
FARNE ISLANDS
Chillingham Castle

Kirknewton
Wooler
Bamburgh
Bamburgh Castle
Seahouses

Chester

Alnwick
Alnwick Castle
Alnmouth

Rothbury
Cragside
Warkworth

LAND
Morpeth
Wallington
Newbiggin-
by-the-Sea
Bedlington
Belsay
Ponteland
Blyth
Seaton Delaval Hall
Corbridge
Whitley Bay
TYNE &
Tynemouth
Newcastle
upon Tyne
South Shields
WEAR
Gateshead
Jarrow
Washington Old Hall
Chester-
le-Street
Washington
Sunderland

Stanhope
Durham

Brancepeth
DURHAM
West Hartlepool
Raby
Bishop
Auckland
Castle
Auckland
Sedgefield
Hartlepool
Aycliffe
Barnard
Castle
Staindrop
CLEVELAND
Redcar
Rokeby
Stockton-
on-Tees
Ormesby Hall
Park
Darlington
Middlesbrough
Staithes
Croft
Yarm
Guisborough
Loftus
Richmond
Scotch Corner
Stokesley
Great
Ayton
Whitby
Catterick
Egton
Robin Hood's
Bay
Goathland

Leyburn
Northallerton
Wensley
Middleham
Hawnby

NORTH
Thirsk
Kirkbymoorside
Scarborough
YORKSHIRE
Duncombe
Pickering
Park
Helmsley
Nunnington
Ebberston Hall
Norton Conyers
Newburgh
Hall
Filey
Ripon
Priory
Oswaldkirk
Kirby
Misperton
Markenfield Hall
Boroughbridge
Castle Howard
Staxton
Flamborough
Newby Hall
Easingwold
Malton
Ripley Castle
Knaresborough
Sutton Park
Sledmere
Burton Agnes Hall
Harrogate
Allerton
Beningborough
Park
Hall
Great
Ilkley
Wetherby
York
Stamford
Driffield
Stockeld Park
Bridge
East Riddlesden
Otley
Hall
Harewood
Tadcaster
Hornsea
Bradham Park
Market
Beverley
Bradford
Weighton
Burton Constable
WEST
Leeds
Lotherton Hall
Selby
HUMBERSIDE
Bolling Hall
Temple Newsam
Howden
Hull
YORKSHIRE
Brough
Hedon
Shipley
Oakwell
Dewsbury
Hall
Wakefield
Goole
Barton-upon-
Patrington
Huddersfield
Nostell
Pontefract
Normanby Hall
Humber
Cannon Hall
Priory
Scunthorpe
Barnsley
Immingham
SOUTH
Brigg
Grimsby
YORKSHIRE
Doncaster
Cleethorpes
Conisbrough
Rossbourne
Sheffield
Rotherham
Bawtry
Tickhill

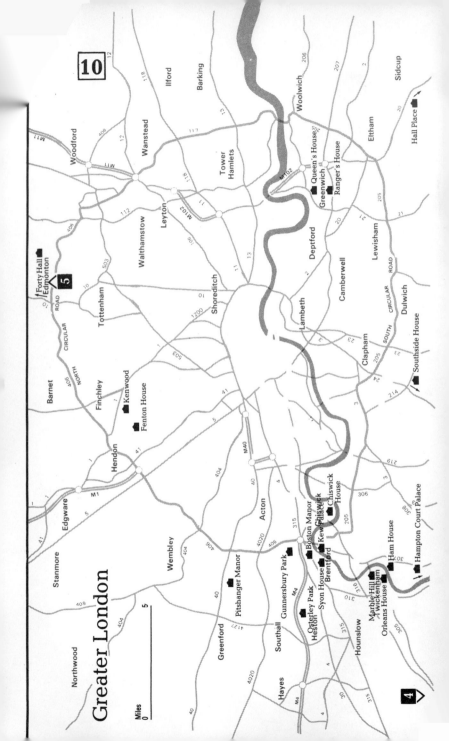

Greater London

10

Miles
0 ___ 5

Northwood
Stanmore
Edgware
Barnet
Finchley
Hendon
Wembley
Greenford
Southall
Hayes
Hounslow
Acton
Woodford
Wanstead
Walthamstow
Tottenham
Leyton
Shoreditch
Tower Hamlets
Ilford
Barking
Deptford
Lambeth
Camberwell
Clapham
Dulwich
Lewisham
Greenwich
Woolwich
Eltham
Sidcup

Forty Hall
Edmonton
5

Kenwood
Fenton House

Pitshanger Manor
Gunnersbury Park
Osterley Park
Heston
Syon House
Brentford
Boston Manor
Kew Palace
Chiswick House
Marble Hill
Twickenham
Orleans House
Ham House
Hampton Court Palace
Southside House
Queen's House
Ranger's House
Hall Place

4

NORTH CIRCULAR ROAD
SOUTH CIRCULAR ROAD